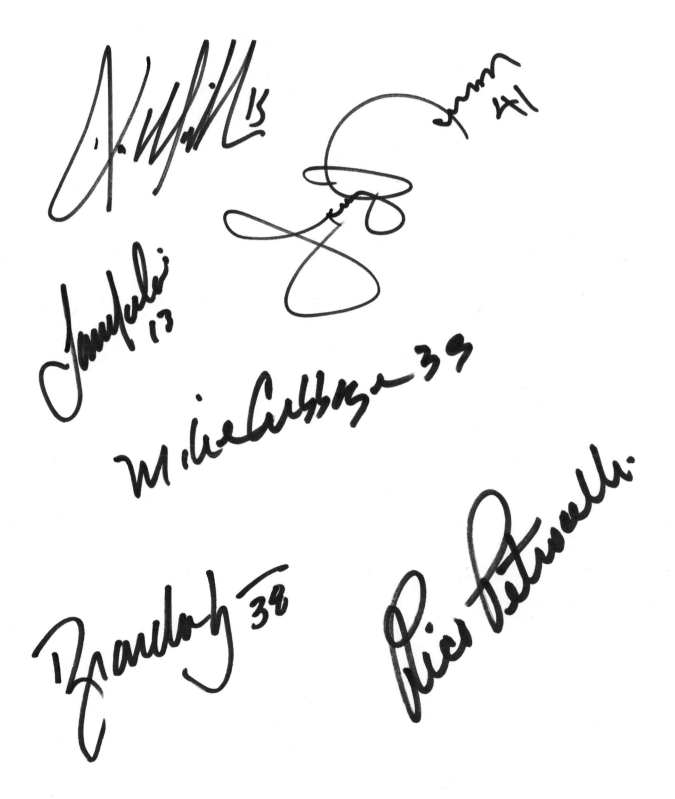

THE RED SOX ENCYCLOPEDIA

By
Robert S. Redmount

SPORTS PUBLISHING, LLC.
www.sportspublishingllc.com

© 2002 Robert S. Redmount
All Rights Reserved.

Book Layout and Design: Julie Dalpiaz Herman, Susan Moyer
Editor: Richard Johnson
Dustjacket Design: Joseph Brumleve

ISBN: 1-58261-244-7

We have made every effort to trace the ownership of copyrighted photos. If we have failed to give adequare credit, we will be pleased to make changes in future printings.

Printed in the United States.

SPORTS PUBLISHING LLC.
http://www. SportsPublishingLLC.com

To my wife, Ellen, who prepared fine meals,
and to my dog, Kipper, who waited patiently for me
to finish my work so we could take our long walks together.

———————————————

CONTENTS

FOREWORD

For the greater part of the last 53 years, I admit that I have had a love affair with the Boston Red Sox. From the time Ernie Johnson signed me as a high school prospect in 1939 out of Lincoln High School in Portland, Oregon, all the way to my continuing role as a special instructor with the Minor League affiliates, my singular objective has been to help the Red Sox win.

During that very first year I discovered a lot about the Red Sox Organization. Mr. Yawkey, Eddie Collins and everyone associated with the ball club truly cared about their players. The Red Sox have always been good to their people and operated their club as a family business.

I've been fortunate to enjoy several different positions with the Boston organization. First as a minor league player then for 10 seasons as a major leaguer. It was a real pleasure and privilege to play alongside such men as Jimmie Foxx, Ted Williams, Bobby Doerr, Dom DiMaggio and Joe Cronin. I was also fortunate to play for two great managers, Joe Cronin and Joe McCarthy. One of my biggest personal thrills came upon my return to the Red Sox in 1946 after three years in the Navy. I hit a home run on Opening Day at Fenway Park. You've got to remember that I was mostly a singles hitter, so all of the home runs stick out in my mind.

In 1961, after five seasons with the Detroit Tigers, the Red Sox hired me as a minor league manager. I was given the opportunity to teach such young stars as Dick Radatz, Earl Wilson, Galen Cisco, Lou Clinton and Don Schwall. Without a doubt, that '61 team was my favorite club. I'm always pleased to say that it was my decision to turn Radatz into a relief pitcher, a role in which he dominated for so many years.

I was thrilled to be chosen by Mr. Yawkey as the Red Sox manager in 1963. Although my stay as manager only lasted two years, I have plenty of memories. I watched Carl Yastrzemski continue to develop into the Hall of Famer he would later become. I brought a young 19-year-old from Swampscott into Fenway Park and on Opening Day 1964 in his first time at bat, he electrified everyone by hitting a home run. I'll always have a fond spot in my heart for Tony Conigliaro.

In 1969 I joined Ken Coleman and Ned Martin in the Red Sox radio booth for a few years. Though I admit that wasn't a totally comfortable role for me, Ken and Ned made me sound as good as I possibly could. We had some great times together.

When I left the broadcast team, I went back down to the field as a coach for Darrell Johnson, Don Zimmer and Ralph Houk. I'm particularly appreciative to The Major for all he taught me. But all of the managers with whom I've worked have had great baseball minds.

Since l986, I've primarily served as an infield and hitting instructor in the Red Sox system. I still get a big kick out of going down to Florida for spring training and trying to teach the young prospects about the world's greatest game. Even though we're in the computer age today, you still have to judge talent with your eyes and your feelings.

I'd be remiss if I didn't mention the jewel of *all* of baseball—Fenway Park. Of all the hundreds of parks I've seen, nothing matches it. The Green Monster in left field remains as baseball's most unique target. Fenway has been the scene for such historical moments as Ted Williams' monstrous blast against the Tigers in 1946, Carlton Fisk's dramatic homer in the 1975 World Series and Roger Clemens' 20 strikeouts against Seattle in 1986. And you can bet your life there will be many more momentous events at the ol' ballpark.

As for Red Sox fans, I love them all. They're probably the most knowledgeable in the game. From generation to generation, they truly appreciate good play and hustle.

I'm flattered to have been asked to write the foreword for *The Red Sox Encyclopedia* and hope that it brings back as many memories for you as it did for me.

Johnny Pesky
Swampscott, Massachusetts

INTRODUCTION AND ACKNOWLEDGMENTS

Red Sox Life and Human Life: No Curses, Just Highs, Mediums and Lows

The Red Sox story, notwithstanding the mythic "Curse of the Bambino," is a matter of pride and achievement, and of pleasure and excitement. It is not all about winning, and there cannot be all about winning. It is not in the nature and character of human experience for there to be only great, good and winning. We should not expect baseball, or the Red Sox, to be different. Those who insist that baseball, and human endeavour generally, is only about winning, that winning is everything or the only thing, have been cheated in their grasp of life. They feed their own despair and disappointment; their resolve is fueled too much by anger and competitiveness. Baseball is a game to be enjoyed, to win with best effort but to play and to see with affection, and it is for this that we want to memorialize it. There is winning and losing but the pride is in good effort, strong intention and credible execution. For this we toast baseball, and the Red Sox, bless 'em.

The literature of baseball is rich and varied. There is the immediacy of newspapers and magazines. There are the chronicles of momentous events and great performances. Encyclopedias record details for memory refresher and history. There are stories to tell of enduring personalities and great careers. There are books on the techniques of play, the rules of the game, the economic issues and the culture impact of baseball. There are stories and accounts that separate wartimes from peacetimes. There is art and music, and artifact and discrete humor, all related to baseball. There are occurrences, observations, judgments and opinions.

This is a rich catalog of the baseball experience, with a lot to fathom and encompass. For those with a special interest in and affinity toward the Red Sox there is much to be said for an encyclopedia that "puts it all in one place" and serves as a dependable reference. This, then, is pretty much the story of Red Sox baseball, for enjoyment and for the record.

The writer, in the production of this book, owes a great deal to forebears and contemporaries who have enriched his baseball experience and knowledge through their writings. It is beyond capacity to cite each and every contributor and contribution. Some sources are indelible in the writer's mind, however, and they are here acknowledged and noted with appreciation.

Total Baseball, beginning with the fifth and the subsequent editions, is a vital resource for both the original and revised editions of the Red Sox Encyclopedia. Total Baseball is the official encyclopedia of Major League Baseball currently edited by John Thorn, Peter Palmer and Michael Gershman. Another major resource for vast information and facts was the Baseball Encyclopedia, Rick Wolff, editorial director, and published by the Macmillan Publishing Company. Another very good fact digest is the Official Major League Baseball Fact Book, published annually by the Sporting News. And, importantly, the Boston Red Sox Media Guide, produced annually by the Boston Red Sox, is an important and reliable source of Red Sox information.

Baseball: A Treasury Of Art And Literature, edited by Michael Ruscoe, is a rich resource, most particularly for its reprint of John Updike's original The New Yorker article, "Hub Fans Bid Kid Adieu." This is one of the great pieces of baseball literature, about Ted Williams' final at bat in his major league career. Baseball's 50 Greatest Games, by Bert Randolph Sugar, has been particularly helpful in the chapter on Games to Remember: Moments of Glory and the Ones That Hurt. The Biographical History of Baseball, by Donald Dewey and Nicholas Acocella is a good resource for information and anecdotes about individual ballplayers and other baseball personnel. The Encyclopedia of Baseball Managers, by Thomas Aylsworth and Benton Minks, is encompassing and inclusive on the subject of big league managers. Boston Red Sox Records, by John A. Mercurio, is a unique and invaluable record of a variety of statistics about the Red Sox. Another useful reference on statistics was The Complete Record of the Boston Red Sox by Henry and Harold Berry. Fred Lieb's The Boston Red Sox, G.P. Putnam's Sons, 1947, is perhaps the best account of early Red Sox baseball through World War II. Inside Sports: World Series Fact Book by George Cantor, is rich in detail about the key plays and players of each and all World Series. Baseball's Greatest Quotations by Paul Dickson and Diamonds Forever, by W. P. Kinsella are distinguished sources for quotable phrases on and about Red Sox and baseball. The Fields of Summer, by James Tackach and Joshua B. Stein, is a splendid resource for events, data and history about ballfields, notably here Fenway Park. Also helpful for its data on Fenway Park and the Huntington Avenue Baseball Grounds was Green Cathedrals by Philip J. Lowry. The chronological and detailed data on uniforms was secured from a standard reference, Baseball Uniforms of the 20th Century, by Marc Okkonen. A helpful source on baseball broadcasters is the book, Voices of the Game by Curt Smith, now in a revised edition. The Boston Red Sox Trivia Book, by David S. Neft, Bob Carroll and Richard M. Cohen, is a rich fund of essential and unessential information about the Red Sox. Finally, and perhaps most succinctly, Encyclopedia of Major League Baseball - American League, edited by Peter C. Bjorkman, has a fine, concise chapter on the Boston Red Sox.

The writer also wishes to give special thanks to Dick Bresciani, Vice President of Public Affairs, and Debbie Matson, Publications Manager, of the Boston Red Sox for their unstinted assistance in making available especially important resources for many facets of the Encyclopedia. Pat Kelly and her staff at the Photo Department in the National Baseball Hall of Fame were most cooperative and responsive to my needs for photos for the book. Thanks also go to Milo Stewart at the Hall of Fame for his creation and photography for the book jacket. Aaron Schmidt of the Print Department at the Boston Public Library was most assiduous and productive in helping me with photo sources from various collections and archives at the Library. Ken Coleman, well-known and long term Red Sox broadcaster, also helped me with the history of Red Sox broadcasters. Lastly, but very importantly, I owe a debt of gratitude to Janice Gibson for her diligent and committed effort and fine result in producing a computer copy of the manuscript from my difficult typewritten and handwritten materials.

Paul Malzone, son of Frank Malzone, popular Red Sox third baseman in the 1950s. (Baseball Hall of Fame Library, Cooperstown, N.Y.).

THE CENTURY HAD EIGHT RED SOX ERAS

1901-1907
The Boston Somerset/Pilgrims – The Pre-Red Sox Era

The Boston entry, a charter team in the new American League, was known for the first two years of existence as the Boston Somersets, after original owner Charles W. Somers. When Somers sold the team after the 1902 season, the team name became the Boston Pilgrims and remained so until permanent conversion to the Boston Red Sox after the 1907 season.

The Boston Somersets/Pilgrims were a pennant-contending team from the very first year of competition in the American League. They successfully raided the older National League, which had placed a lid on player salaries, and fielded a fine team. They acquired a fine hitter and third baseman, Jimmy Collins, who became their player-manager. The great right-handed pitcher, Cy Young, also came over from the National League, followed shortly by his catcher, Lou Criger. Buck Freeman was a star first baseman and outfielder and the Somersets' first slugger. Patsy Dougherty was another stand-out outfielder who joined the Somersets in 1902 and would become famous for his heroics in the 1903 World Series.

The Pilgrims finished in second place in 1901 and in third place in 1902. They were led both years by over-.300 hitting of both Collins and Freeman, the slugging of Freeman and the brilliant third-base play of Collins. Collins was a consistent .300 hitter and later became a Hall of Famer. In the era of the "dead ball" the Somersets had outstanding pitching from Cy Young and Bill Dinneen. Young, who became a Somerset at the age of 33, won 193 games in the eight years he was with the club. He had an earned run average of 2.00 and won 20 or more games six times between 1901 and 1908. Bill Dinneen won 20 or more games three times for the Somerset/Pilgrims.

With the powerful pitching of Young and Dinneen, and the hitting of Buck Freeman, the outfielder-first baseman who led the league with 13 home runs and 104 runs batted in, the Pilgrims won the pennant in 1903. They won by 14½ games over the Philadelphia Athletics and faced the Pittsburgh Pirates of the National League, who won their third straight pennant, in the first World Series. The Pirates had the formidable Honus Wagner, and Fred Clarke, manager and Hall of Fame outfielder, but they had only one healthy pitcher for the World Series, Deacon Phillippe. Phillippe pitched five complete World Series games, winning the first, third and fourth. However, the Pilgrims upset the Pirates and became the first World Series winners as Bill Dinneen won three games and Cy Young won the other two to defeat the Pirates, five games

to three. A highlight in the second game, won by Dinneen, was the two home runs by Patsy Dougherty, the Pilgrim outfielder.

The Pilgrims also won the pennant in 1904. This happened in dramatic fashion. The New York Highlanders, later known as the New York Yankees, still had a chance to win the pennant if they won the final two games of the season in a double header against the Pilgrims at Hilltop Park in New York. Jack Chesbro, who won a nearly unbelievable 41 games for the Hilltoppers in 1904, pitched the first game. He lost the pennant to the Pilgrims when his wild pitch with the bases loaded in the ninth inning won the game for Boston. However, John McGraw, manager of the pennant-winning New York Giants, refused to play a World Series. The older National League did not want to acknowledge again the upstart American League but an agreement was reached after 1904 that a World Series play-off between the two league champions would be held every year.

For the year 1903, the Boston American Leaguers were the world's champions and in 1904 they were again the American League pennant winners.

After 1904, the Pilgrims declined. They finished in last place in 1906, Jimmy Collins was fired as manager, and after 1908 Cy Young was traded to the Cleveland Indians.

DOMINANT YEARS AND DOMINANT PLAYERS

1901

The Boston Somersets, nicknamed after their owner, Charles W. Somers, made an auspicious debut in the fledgling American League. In the very first year for both the league and the team, the Somersets, managed by Jimmy Collins, placed second to the Chicago White Sox, managed by Clark Griffith. They were four games behind the Sox. They were a formidable hitting team, leading the league in home runs with a team total of 37. Their pitching placed second to the White Sox in earned run average at 3.04.

Dominant Players
Five of the Somerset regulars batted over .300. Buck Freeman, first baseman, led with a .345 batting average. He was third in the league behind Nap Lajoie, who batted a remarkable .422. Freeman was also second in the league in home runs, with 12, and second in slugging average.

He was second in runs batted in with 114 and fourth in total bases. The league leader in all of these batting categories, further including most number of hits (229), runs scored and doubles was the fabulous Nap Lajoie, then of the Philadelphia Athletics and later most famed for his Hall of Fame career as a second baseman with the Cleveland Indians.

Jimmy Collins, the Somersets' manager and Hall of Famer, was the league's premier third baseman and he batted .332, second behind Freeman on the Somersets. Collins was third in hits in the league, third in doubles with 42 and tied for third in triples with 16.

Other .300 hitters on the Somersets were centerfielder Chick Stahl, later the team's manager, at .309, shortstop Freddy Parent at .306 and catcher Ossee Schreckengast, who shared catching duties with Lou Criger, at .304. Hobe Ferris distinguished himself at second base by making the most double plays in the league.

Cy Young, who came over to the Somersets after a distinguished 11-year career in the National League, in 1901 led the American League in wins with 33, in earned run average at 1.62, and in strikeouts at 158. He tied for the lead in shut-outs with five, and was second in the league in winning percentage, games pitched, complete games, fewest walks per innings, 0.90, and fewest hits in nine innings, 7.85. The pitcher with the leading winning percentage in the league was Clark Griffith, who had a 24-7 record for a .774 percentage. Griffith was manager of the Chicago White Sox as well as its leading pitcher and led the White Sox to the pennant. He managed for twenty years and later became the Washington Nationals/Senators manager and owner. George Winter was the Somersets second best pitcher in 1901 and he had 16 wins and 12 losses. He had the league's fifth best earned run average at 2.80. Ted Lewis also won 16 games for the Somersets in the only year he played with the team.

Two of the greatest Red Sox pitchers ever, 88-year-old Cy Young (left) and Lefty Grove, spend a moment reminiscing at an Old Timers Day. (Boston Public Library, Print Department).

1902

The Somersets placed third, 6½ games behind the pennant-winning Athletics and 1½ games behind the St. Louis Browns. They still had good pitching as the team's pitchers won the earned run average championship at 3.02.

Dominant Players

Slugger Buck Freeman was tied for second in home runs, with 11, and led the league with 121 runs batted in. He also placed second in the league in triples with 10. Patsy Dougherty, now established in left field, was fourth in the league in batting with an average of .342.

Cy Young had his second consecutive 30-game wins year with a 32-11 record. He tied for third in the league with an E.R.A. of 2.15 and was in third place just behind Rube Waddell of the Philadelphia Athletics, in winning percentage at .744. He pitched the most complete games, 41, followed by teammate Bill Dinneen who had 39 complete games. The two iron horse pitchers were also one-two in games and innings pitched. Young was second in fewest walks given and third in strikeouts in a nine-inning game. He was second to Waddell in total strikeouts.

Bill Dinneen also distinguished himself with 21 wins but he had an unusual 21 wins, 21 losses season, notwithstanding a 2.93 earned run average.

1903

1903 was a banner year for the Boston American League team, now named the Pilgrims. (Owner Somers had sold the team to Henry J. Killilea.)

The Pilgrims won the pennant under Jimmy Collins with a 91-47 record (.659). They led the league in batting with a .272 average and in pitchers' E.R.A. at 2.52.

The Pilgrims played in the first World Series this year, beating the Pittsburgh Pirates five games to three to win the world championship.

Dominant Players

Buck Freeman, right fielder, was still the team's slugger, and he led the league in home runs, 13, and in runs batted in, 104. He was third in doubles with 39 and in triples with 20. Left fielder Patsy Dougherty led the league in hits with 195, runs with 108, and he had 35 stolen bases. Shortstop Freddy Parent was the team's other .300 hitter, at .304.

Cy Young again led all American League pitchers with 28 wins and a 28-9 record that led the league in winning percentage. His earned run average was 2.08, second in the league. He led the league in shutouts and again led the league with fewest walks in nine innings at 0.97. He was tied for most complete games at 34 with Rube Waddell of the Philadelphia Athletics and Wild Bill Donovan of the Detroit Tigers. He also led the league in innings pitched. Big Bill Dinneen was again the Pilgrims' number-two pitcher with 21 wins, 13 losses and a 2.26 E.R.A. He placed second to Young in the league with six shutouts.

The Pilgrims had three 20-game winners in 1903. Besides Young and Dinneen, Long Tom Hughes had 20 wins and 7 losses, placing second in the league in winning percentage after Young with a .741 average.

1904

The Pilgrims won the pennant in a tight race with the New York Hilltoppers. The Hilltoppers were in second place,

1¹/₂ games behind the Pilgrims. The Pilgrims pitching staff was outstanding this year, leading the league with a 2.12 earned run average.

Dominant Players

Buck Freeman was still the team's leading slugger, tying for second in the league with home runs at seven and second in R.B.I. at 84. It was not a hitters' year for the Pilgrims as none of the players batted .300.

Cy Young had another 20-win year with a 26-16 record and he led the league again with fewest walks in nine innings (0.69). He also led in shutouts with 10 and was fourth in strikeouts with 200. (Rube Waddell led the league with 349 strikeouts).

The Pilgrims' number-two pitcher was again Bill Dinneen with 23 wins and 14 losses, and the team again had three 20-game winners, the third being Jesse Tannehill who had a 21-11 record, placing second in the league with a .656 winning percentage.

1904 had three other notable pitching accomplishments. Two Pilgrim pitchers, Cy Young and Jesse Tannehill, pitched no hitters. Cy Young pitched a perfect game against the Philadelphia Athletics, winning 3-0 on May 5. Young also had pitched a no-hitter in 1897 while playing for the National League Cleveland Spiders and he would have another no-hitter in 1908, pitching for the Red Sox against the New York Highlanders. Jesse Tannehill pitched a no-hitter, 6-0, against the White Sox on August 17. In the

The "Royal Rooters," a vocal, combative group of fans who often traveled with the team, were the Boston Pilgrims' secret weapon in 1903.
(Boston Public Library, Print Department).

following year, 1905, Bill Dinneen also pitched a no-hitter for the Pilgrims, beating the White Sox, 2-0, on September 27.

1904 was also the year in which Jack Chesbro of the second place New York Hilltoppers won 41 games, leading the league not only in wins and winning percentage, but also in games pitched, 55, and complete games, 48. Ironically, in the climactic game of the season between the Pilgrims and the Hilltoppers, Chesbro wild-pitched in the winning run, giving the Pilgrims the pennant.

1912-1918

The Great Red Sox Dynasty

The Red Sox assembled some great talent in the years from approximately 1910 through 1918. By 1910, the outfield of Duffy Lewis in left field, Tris Speaker in center field and Harry Hooper in right field, considered by some the best ever, was in place. Speaker and Hooper were later elected to the Hall of Fame. Lewis consistently batted near .300 and was a good fielder. Speaker, the best of the three, hit a lifetime .345, was an excellent fielder with a great arm, and stole more than 25 bases ten times in his career. Hooper was a reliable lead-off man with a great arm and he, too, was an excellent base stealer.

Duffy Lewis (left), Tris Speaker (center) and Harry Hooper, were considered one of the greatest outfields ever when they played together for Boston. (Boston Public Library, Print Department).

home run fame, and was traded to the New York Yankees in 1920.

The Red Sox also had Ernie Shore, Rube Foster, Dutch Leonard and Carl Mays as pitchers. Dutch Leonard threw two no-hitters, in 1916 and 1918, and five times had an earned run average under 2.40, including one record breaking year of 1.01. Later, the Red Sox also acquired Sad Sam Jones and Bullet Joe Bush.

Early in the dynasty, Jake Stahl was the first baseman and he managed the Red Sox to the 1912 world championship. Bill "Rough" Carrigan was the catcher. Later, in 1915 and 1916, Carrigan managed the Sox to two consecutive world championships.

Notably, beside the exceptional outfield, the Red Sox had excellent pitching. Smoky Joe Wood was the best pitcher in baseball in 1912, rivaling the great Walter Johnson and he even beat Johnson in a pitching duel that year, 1-0. Wood had a record of 34 wins and five losses in 1912. Wood won 116 games with the Red Sox in his career and had a 2.03 earned run average but later injured his arm and ended his career as a capable outfielder with the Cleveland Indians. He had a career batting average of .283. Babe Ruth joined the Red Sox as a pitcher in 1914. Ruth won 18 and lost eight for the Red Sox in 1915 and also hit 4 home runs. By 1917 he was considered the best left handed pitcher in the league, averaging more than 20 wins a year, but in 1918 Red Sox manager Ed Barrow decided that Ruth's everyday bat in the line-up was more valuable than his pitching. He became the Babe Ruth of

Larry Gardner was a good-hitting third baseman, Jack Barry, a member of Connie Mack's Philadelphia Athletics "$100,000 infield," was acquired to play second base and Everett "Deacon" Scott was a steady shortstop. Toward the end of the dynasty, Red Sox replacements were Stuffy McInnis, a fine fielding first baseman, and Wally Schang, a capable catcher, both acquired from the Philadelphia Athletics.

The Red Sox won four pennants and four World Series in the period 1912-1918. They were world champions for five of the 16 years from 1903 through 1918 and won an additional pennant in one year (1904) when no World Series was played. The Red Sox did not lose a World Series until their next appearance almost 30 years later in 1946.

In 1912, the Red Sox beat the New York Giants in the World Series, four games to three with one game ending in a tie. The Giants, under John McGraw, had the peerless Christy Mathewson, 23-game winner, and 26-game winner Rube Marquard who set a record by pitching 19 straight wins at the beginning of the season. The Red Sox had won the pennant by 14 games over the Washington Senators and 15 games over the favored Philadelphia Athletics. Smoky Joe Wood won three World Series games. The final game was won by the Red Sox when Fred Snodgrass of the Giants dropped an easy fly ball and Fred Merkle failed to catch a foul pop-up. The error-prone play of the Giants in the final game (they had made five errors in the second game) enabled the Red Sox to win the Series.

In 1915, the Red Sox beat the Philadelphia Phillies in the World Series, four games to one. Coincidentally, this was the second straight year in which a Boston team played a Philadelphia team in the Series. In 1914, the Boston "Miracle Braves" of the National League, who went from last to first place, beat the Philadelphia Athletics of the American League.

In 1915, the Phillies had the great pitcher Grover Cleveland "Pete" Alexander, who won 31 games in the first of three straight 30-win years. "Pete" won the first World Series game, including getting Babe Ruth out as a pinch hitter. Ernie Shore, Rube Foster and Dutch Leonard each won a 2-1 game for the Sox. In the fifth game, Duffy Lewis hit a game-tying two-run home run and Harry Hooper won the game in the ninth inning, 5-4 with his second home run of the contest.

In 1916, the Red Sox beat the Brooklyn Dodgers in the World Series, four games to one. Casey Stengel was the leading batter for the Dodgers in the Series with a batting average of .364. The Red Sox had a formidable pitching staff of Rube Foster, Carl Mays, Ernie Shore, Babe Ruth and Dutch Leonard. In the second game of the Series, Babe Ruth bested Sherry Smith in a pitching duel, 2-1, in 14 innings, both pitchers going all the way. Ernie Shore won two games and Dutch Leonard won one game in which Larry Gardner hit a three-run home run.

In 1918, a year in which the pennant races ended a month early because of World War I, the Red Sox beat the Chicago Cubs in the World Series, four games to two. Babe Ruth pitched and won Game 1, 1-0, and Game 4, 3-2. He set a record performance of pitching 29 and two-thirds straight scoreless innings in the World Series, a record that stood until Ed "Whitey" Ford of the New York Yankees eclipsed it in the 1960s.

Under manager Bill "Rough" Carrigan (left), Tris Speaker led the Red Sox in hitting in from 1913-15. (Boston Public Library, Print Department).

In Game 4 Ruth also hit a crucial two-run triple. Carl Mays won the other two games of the Series for the Red Sox by identical scores of 2-1. Pitching dominated in the Series as the Red Sox batted a cumulative .186 and the Cubs batted .210.

DOMINANT YEARS AND DOMINANT PLAYERS

1912

This is the year Boston's new baseball grounds, Fenway Park, opened. It is also perhaps the best performance year in Red Sox history. The Sox won the American League pennant with a then-record-breaking 105 wins and only 47 losses for a .691 winning percentage. They led the second-place Washington Nationals by 14 games. The manager was Jake Stahl. The Red Sox also won the World Series in 1912, four games to three, over John McGraw's New York Giants.

The Red Sox had powerful hitting, with a league-leading 29 home runs and slugging average of .380. They were second in team batting average. The pitching was also strong, with the pitching staff leading the league in complete games, 108, and in shutouts pitched, 18. The team was second in earned run average at 2.69.

Dominant Players

Tris Speaker, the Hall of Fame center fielder, had a .383 batting average. Remarkably, this was only good enough for third place. Ty Cobb led the league with a .410 batting average and Shoeless Joe Jackson, then playing with the Cleveland Indians, batted .395. Speaker tied for the home run leadership with Frank "Home Run" Baker, then with the Athletics and late in his career with the Red Sox. Each had ten. Speaker was fifth in runs batted in and third in slugging average. He was fourth in stolen bases with 52, third in hits with 222 and second in runs scored with 136. He also led the league in doubles with 53. Speaker, the great fielder, also led the league in outfield assists and in making double plays, and in the number of fielding chances he had per game.

The Chalmers Award, issued for the second year to the M.V.P. in each league, was awarded in 1912 to Tris Speaker.

Just as the offense and regular player positions were dominated by Tris Speaker, so was the pitching dominated by one fireballing right hander, Smoky Joe Wood. Wood won 24 games and lost five for an .872 average and he had an earned run average of 1.91. He led up to this phenomenal year by pitching a no-hitter in 1911 against the St. Louis Browns and winning, 5-0. In 1912, Wood led the league in winning percentage and in wins. He was second in E.R.A. behind Walter Johnson. He led in shutouts with 10, followed by Johnson, and he was second to Johnson in strikeouts. Wood was third in games and innings pitched, behind Ed Walsh of the White Sox and Walter Johnson of the Washington Nationals.

The Red Sox had two other 20-game winners, Buck O'Brien at 20-13 and Hugh Bedient in his first big league year at 20-9. Ray Collins, at 13-8, is also notable for his 2.53 earned run average, fifth best in the league.

1914

The Red Sox placed second in the league in 1914 with 91 wins but nonetheless were 8½ games behind the Philadelphia Athletics. This was their first full season under Bill "Rough" Carrigan. They had a slugging team that led the league in doubles and triples. They led the league with a 2.35 earned run average for the pitching staff.

Dominant Players

Tris Speaker continued to be the dominant player on the team. He batted .338, third in the league behind Ty Cobb and Eddie Collins. Speaker was second behind Cobb in slugging average and fourth in R.B.I. with 90. He stole 42 bases, third in the league. He led the

league in hits with 193 and was fourth in bases on balls. He also led the league with 46 doubles. He continued his spectacular fielding, leading outfielders in putouts, in double plays executed and in number of chances per game. Dick Hoblitzell, in his first year at first base, also batted over .300, at .319.

The Red Sox pitchers were led by Dutch Leonard with 19 wins and five losses, a .792 average, and an unsurpassed earned run average of 1.01. Leonard was second in winning percentage behind Chief Bender of the Philadelphia Athletics who was at 17-3 with an .850 average. He was fourth in the league in wins, third in strikeouts, tied for second in shutouts with seven, and gave the fewest hits in a nine-inning game, 5.70. Ray Collins was another pitching stalwart with 20 wins, 13 losses and a 2.51 E.R.A. Ray Collins was third in the league in wins and fourth in shutouts. Rube Foster, a third pitcher of note in 1914, won 14 and lost eight with a sparkling 1.65 E.R.A. that placed him just behind Dutch Leonard in the league.

1914 was also Babe Ruth's first year in the big leagues. He had only three decisions as a left-handed pitcher with the Red Sox, winning two and losing one in four games with a 3.91 E.R.A.

1915

1915 saw the Red Sox win their third world championship, after the one in 1903 and another in 1912. Under manager Bill Carrigan they won the pennant over Detroit by 2½ games with 101 wins, 50 losses and a .669 winning percentage. They beat the Philadelphia Phillies in the World Series, four games to one. They were second in batting to the Tigers, who had Ty Cobb again leading the league with a .369 average. They were also second in the

Boston's 1915 pitching staff included (from left): Ernie Shore, Dutch Leonard, Rube Foster and Babe Ruth. (Baseball Hall of Fame Library. Cooperstown, N.Y.).

The Century Had Eight Red Sox Eras

league in pitchers' earned run average at 2.31. The Washington Nationals with Walter Johnson leading the league with 27 wins and 337 innings pitched, were first.

Dominant Players.

The Red Sox again had Tris Speaker as their leading hitter with a .322 average. This was to be his last year with the Sox as a salary disagreement with the team's owner, Joe Lannin, resulted in his being traded to the Cleveland Indians just before the 1916 season. Speaker also continued his fielding dominance, leading the league in outfielder putouts and in double plays made. The Sox continued to have the spectacular fielding outfield of Duffy Lewis in

Babe Ruth (left) with Red Sox manager Ed Barrow. It was Barrow who decided that Ruth's everyday bat in the lineup was more important than his pitching. (Baseball Hall of Fame Library. Cooperstown, N.Y.).

left, Speaker in center and Harry Hooper in right, collectively known as "the greatest outfield."

The pitching staff was exceptional with five pitchers winning 15 games or more. Ernie Shore led with 19-8 and a 1.64 E.R.A. Rube Foster was also at 19-8 with a 2.11 E.R.A. Babe Ruth, the only lefthander, was at 18-8 with a 2.44 E.R.A. Dutch Leonard was at 15-7 with a 2.31 E.R.A. He led the league with fewest hits and most strike-outs in nine innings

Smoky Joe Wood, at 15-5, led the league in both winning percentage at .750 and in E.R.A. with a 1.49 average. This was Wood's last pitching year as he injured his arm and then later played outfield for Cleveland.

1916

1916 was the second straight world championship year for the Red Sox. With Bill Carrigan still the manager, the Sox, in a close race, beat the White Sox by two games and the Tigers by four games. They beat the Brooklyn Robins of the National League in the World Series, four games to one.

Dominant Players

Third baseman Larry Gardner was the only Red Sox player to bat over .300, at .308. Everett "Deacon" Scott played his usual steady game at shortstop and led all league shortstops with a .967 fielding average.

The pitching staff was again strong. Babe Ruth went 23-12 with the league's second best winning average of .657. Ruth led the league with an E.R.A. of 1.75. He was third in innings pitched, 324, and he gave the fewest hits per nine-inning game, 6.40. He topped the league with nine shutouts and was third in strikeouts. Ruth had a banner year and was perhaps the league's best pitcher and most certainly the best left-handed pitcher. Strong support came from Dutch Leonard with an 18-12 record, six saves and six shutouts, Carl Mays at 18-13, Ernie Shore whose record was 16-10, and Rube Foster with a 14-7 record. Rube Foster and Dutch Leonard both pitched no-hitters for the Red Sox in 1916, Foster beating the Yankees 2-0 on June 21 and Leonard beating the St. Louis Browns on August 30, 4-0.

1917

The Red Sox, with player-manager Jack Barry, a former member of Connie Mack's "$100,000 infield," playing second base, finished the season in second place, nine games back of the Chicago White Sox. The Red Sox had a good defensive team and again had excellent pitching. They led the league in fielding average and the reliable pitching corps had the most complete games and second best E.R.A..

Dominant Players

Second baseman Barry and shortstop Deacon Scott formed a fine double-play combination. Both led the league in fielding at their respective positions.

Babe Ruth again led all Red Sox pitchers with 24 wins, second in the league, and, with a 24-13 record was fifth in winning percentage at .649. Ruth had 35 complete games, leading the league, and he was fourth giving the fewest hits in nine innings, 6.73. Carl Mays was second in winning percentage at .710, with 22 wins and nine losses. Mays' E.R.A. was the league's second best, 1.74, behind the White Sox Eddie Cicotte's 1.53. Mays was fourth in complete games with 27. Dutch Leonard also had 16 wins and was fourth in complete games with 26. Leonard was third in strikeouts with 144, behind league-leading Walter Johnson and Eddie Cicotte.

This was also the year in which Ernie Shore relieved an ejected Babe Ruth after the first batter was walked in a game on June 23. The runner was thrown out stealing second and Shore then retired the next 26 batters for an unusual no-hitter. The Washington Nationals lost, 4-0.

1918

This was the third championship year in four years for the Red Sox. Under new manager Ed Barrow, later the New York Yankees' general manager and president, they beat the Cleveland Indians in the pennant race by 2½ games, and were four games ahead of the Washington Nationals. They won the World Series from the Chicago Cubs, four games to two.

The baseball year was shortened one month because of World War I, and the Sox went 75-51 for a .595 winning percentage. They again led the league in fielding, and in number of complete games pitched. They had the most pitched shutouts and were second with a 2.31 E.R.A.

Dominant Players

Babe Ruth, now a regular player in left field as well as a pitcher, led the team with a .300 batting average, and led the league in slugging average and in home runs with 11. He also was second behind Tris Speaker, now of Cleveland, in doubles. Harry Hooper, batting .289 was third in the league in bases on balls and runs scored, and he was fourth in doubles and second in triples.

Babe Ruth posted a 13-7 mark as a pitcher in 1918. (Boston Public Library, Print Department).

Leading the league in fielding average at their positions were Stuffy McInnis, another former member of Connie Mack's "100,000 infield", at first base, Deacon Scott again playing solid shortstop and Amos Strunk in center field with only three errors all season.

Sam Jones had the league's best winning average as a pitcher with a 16-5 record. He was fourth with five shutouts. Carl Mays was fourth in winning percentage with a 21-13 record. He and Scott Perry of the Philadelphia Athletics tied for third in both number of wins and complete games. He and Walter Johnson of Washington tied for most shutouts with eight each.

Jones and Mays were the top pitchers, but Joe Bush also won 15 games with a 15-15 record and Babe Ruth, now doing double duty, was 13-7. Bush was fifth in the league with a 2.11 earned run average. He was fourth in complete games and third behind Johnson and Jim Shaw of Washington with 125 strikeouts. Dutch Leonard also pitched his second career no-hitter on June 3, winning for the Red Sox against the Detroit Tigers, 5-0.

1919-1933
Red Sox Downfall—The Harry Frazee Disaster

In early 1917 Harry Frazee bought the Red Sox. The team was riding the crest of two successive world championships. Bill "Rough" Carrigan retired as team manager but Jack Barry, the second baseman, appeared to be a capable replacement and the future looked promising.

Harry Frazee was an entrepreneur and a big investor in Broadway shows. Some thought of him as "a Broadway hustler." He had one notable success on Broadway, "No, No, Nanette," but most of his other shows were risk investments and of more uncertain promise. At first, Frazee kept faith with the Red Sox. In late 1917 he bought pitcher Bullet Joe Bush, catcher Wally Schang and outfielder Amos Strunk from the Philadelphia Athletics. Before the season began in 1918 he also purchased Stuffy McInnis, a fine fielding first baseman, from the Athletics. After a disappointing second-place finish in 1917, the Red Sox won the world championship in 1918.

After 1918, disaster struck, both for the Red Sox and Harry Frazee. Frazee faced financial crisis and continually needed to pump more money into his Broadway shows. His "cash cow" for this purpose was the rich talent on the Red Sox. After the 1918 season, he sold the veteran players Duffy Lewis, Ernie Shore and Dutch Leonard to the Yankees. (Leonard went on to the Detroit Tigers after a salary dispute.)

In 1919, the Red Sox finished in a tie for fifth place, even though Babe Ruth hit an unheard-of 29 home runs that year. Then the sword fell on the Sox. Before the 1920 season, Frazee sold Babe Ruth to the New York Yankees for $125,000 and a $300,000 loan to Frazee from Yankee owner Jacob Ruppert. Ruth obliged with 113 home runs and 308 runs batted in for the Yankees in 1920 and 1921 and followed with perhaps the greatest career in baseball.

After that, the roof fell in. Frazee, seeking the magnet of Yankee money, in a period of four years, sold virtually an entire pitching staff to the New York Yankees, including Carl Mays, Bullet Joe Bush, Sad Sam Jones, Waite Hoyt, Herb Pennock and George Pipgras. He also sold the Sox shortstop fixture, Everett Scott, and catcher Wally Schang to the Yankees. "Jumpin" Joe Dugan, part of a three-way trade, passed through Boston from Washington to the Yankees and became the Yankees' regular third baseman.

Right fielder Harry Hooper, the last remaining member of the fabled Lewis-Speaker-Hooper outfield, was traded to the Chicago White Sox. The Yankees, after all, did not need another right fielder because they had one

year earlier acquired Babe Ruth from the Red Sox.

The catastrophic consequences of selling off such outstanding talent can be appreciated from the subsequent performances of the new Yankees. Mays, Bush and Pennock successively led the American League in winning pitching percentage in 1921, 1922 and 1923, with 27,26 and 19 wins respectively. Jones led the league in saves in 1924. In 1927, Waite Hoyt led the league in winning percentage with 22 wins. Pipgras had the most wins in the American League in 1928, 24 victories. The winning pitchers in 15 of the 18 wins by the Yankees in six World Series from 1921 through 1927, were ex-Red Sox players. As pitcher Ernie Shore said, "The Yankee dynasty was the Red Sox dynasty in Yankee uniforms."

Harry Frazee attended the opening of Yankee Stadium in April 1923. He sat in Yankee owner Jacob Ruppert's box and watched Babe Ruth hit three home runs as the Yankees beat the Red Sox, 4-1. Frazee sold the team before the 1923 season. His fortunes in the theater improved after that, but the legacy he left the Red Sox was dismal.

The Red Sox finished last in the league in 1922, Frazee's last year. They also finished last in 1923 and, after a reprieve in seventh place in 1924, finished last for six straight years, from 1925-1930. They were last again in 1932 with a record of 111 losses and drew 182,150 fans for the entire season, or an average of 2,365 for each game.

Even Charley "Red" Ruffing, who had four straight 20-game win seasons with the Yankees in the 1930s and became a Hall of Famer, could not win with Boston. He led the league in losses in 1928, 25, while pitching for the Sox, and again led the league in losses in 1929 with 22. The only bright spot in the 1920s for the Sox was pitcher Howard Ehmke. He won 20 games for the last-place Sox in 1923, pitching a no-hitter. He then won 19 games in 1924.

1919

. . . .

1919 was the beginning of decline for the Red Sox, as players were sold off and the Red Sox finished tied for fifth with the St. Louis Browns, 20½ games behind the pennant-winning Chicago White Sox. The team again led the league in fielding percentage but otherwise was not outstanding.

Dominant Players
The notable player performance was that of Babe Ruth in

his last year with the Red Sox. He batted .322 and led the league with a record 29 home runs. He also led in runs batted in with 114. He was second in bases on balls and led the league in runs scored. He led his left field position in fielding with a .992 average and made only two errors in 130 games. As a pitcher, he was 9-5 with a 2.97 E.R.A

NEGATIVE YEARS AND NEGATIVE PLAYER PERFORMANCES

1922

The Red Sox finished in last place, 33 games behind the pennant-winning New York Yankees. The team was last in batting average, last in fielding average and sixth in earned run average.

Fair Player Performances
The only pitcher to win more games than he lost was Ray Collins, who was 14-11.

1923

The Red Sox again finished in last place, 37 games behind the New York Yankee pennant winners. They were last in team batting at .261, ten points behind the seventh place St. Louis Browns, and 40 points behind Cleveland's league-leading .301. They were last in team fielding and had the league's worst E.R.A. at 4.20

Mostly Negative Player Performances
No infielder other than first baseman George Burns batted over .254. Burns batted .328. All Sox pitchers except Howard Ehmke had losing records. Ehmke, the ace of the staff, won 20 and lost 17. He also pitched a no-hitter on September 7 and beat the Philadelphia Athletics, 4-0.

1925

The Sox finished last after finishing seventh in 1924. They were 49$^1/_2$ games behind the pennant winners, the Washington Nationals. The team's .266 batting average was 41 points under the league-leading Philadelphia Athletics. They were last in team fielding and in team E.R.A.

Mostly Negative Player Performance
As in the previous year, all pitchers but one lost more games then they won. Again, Howard Ehmke led Red Sox pitchers with more wins than losses with a 19-17 record.

1926

The Red Sox finished last once more, 44$^1/_2$ games behind the pennant-winning Yankees and 15$^1/_2$ games behind the seventh place St. Louis Browns. The Red Sox were last in team batting and team slugging, and last in team E.R.A.

Negative Player Performances
No Red Sox pitchers had a winning record and one, Paul Zahniser, led the league in losses with a 6-18 record.

1927

The Red Sox for the fifth time in the last six years finished last, a memorable 59 games behind the pennant-winning Yankees with a record of 51-103. They were last in batting average at .259, 48 points behind the Yankees and 17 points below the seventh place Browns. They were next to last in fielding and led in errors committed. They were next to last in pitchers' earned run average at 4.68, exceeded only by the Browns 4.95 E.R.A., or nearly five runs a game.

Mostly Negative Player Performances
Only Jack Tobin, right fielder of the Sox, batted over .288 on the team. Tobin batted .310. All the pitchers on the pitching staff had losing records and Slim Harriss lost 21 games.

1928

The Red Sox had another last place team, 43$^1/_2$ games behind the pennant-winning Yankees. They again were last in team batting and in team playing errors. The pitchers' team E.R.A. was 4.39, with only the seventh place Cleveland Indians having a lower E.R.A., 4.47.

Negative Player Performances
None of the pitchers with significant pitching time had a winning record. Red Ruffing, a later Hall of Famer and successful pitcher with the New York Yankees, lost a league-leading 25 games.

1929

The Red Sox, the perennial cellar dwellers, again played at the bottom of the league, 48 games behind the Philadelphia Athletics pennant winners. They were again last in batting and next to last in slugging averages, and were at the bottom of the league with only 28 team home runs. Babe Ruth and Lou Gehrig of the Yankees each had over

35. Jimmie Foxx and Al Simmons of the Philadelphia Athletics had over 33 each in 1929. The Sox were next to last in team fielding average and led in errors committed.

Negative Player Performances
Jack Rothrock, an outfielder, had the most home runs for the Red Sox-six. Red Ruffing again lost over 20 games with a 9-22 record and a 4.86 earned run average. None of the players with substantial playing time had a winning record.

1930

The Red Sox for the sixth consecutive year and eight of the previous nine, finished in last place. They were 50 games behind the pennant-winning Athletics and 10 games behind the seventh place White Sox. They were last in team batting and team slugging and last in team home runs.

Negative Player Performances
This year the Red Sox had *two* 20-game losers, Milt Gaston

at 13-20 and Jack Russell at 9-20. None of the pitching regulars had a winning record.

1932

The Red Sox, after a one-year reprieve in sixth place, again finished last. This time they were 60 games behind the pennant-winning Yankees and had a won-lost record of 43 wins and 111 losses. They were last in batting and slugging. They were next to last in fielding average and in number of errors committed, just ahead of the seventh place Chicago White Sox. Their league-worst pitchers' E.R.A. was over five runs, at 5.02

Mostly Negative Performances
Except for first baseman Dale Alexander, who was traded by the Tigers to the Red Sox early in the year and then won the league batting championship with a .372 average, only one of the entire infield roster batted as much as .260.

1933-1942
Tom Yawkey and the Red Sox Revival

Tom Yawkey was a great baseball fan. His uncle before him, Bill Yawkey, had owned a part of the Detroit Tigers, and Tom Yawkey came to love the game. Though at first reluctant, Yawkey was persuaded to buy the Boston Red Sox. Yawkey was not the kind of owner who viewed a baseball team primarily in terms of its profit-making potential, nor was he the kind of owner who regarded his own baseball "expertise" as essential to running the team. His aim was to develop a respectable team for the Boston franchise and he himself would be the team's number-one fan.

Yawkey's condition for buying the Red Sox was that he have a capable person to oversee baseball operations. To this end, he persuaded Eddie Collins to become general manager. Collins, not to be confused with Jimmy Collins of early Red Sox fame, was somebody Yawkey admired. He was a superb second baseman, later to become a Hall of Famer, and in these years he was "assistant manager" to Connie Mack, the owner-manager of the Philadelphia Athletics who built baseball dynasties.

Eddie Collins set about to rejuvenate the Red Sox. Yawkey was willing to contribute from the lumber fortune he inherited to do this. In late 1933 he acquired Robert Moses "Lefty" Grove, the league's premier left-handed

This plaque, located outside Fenway Park, commemorates long-time Red Sox owner Thomas Yawkey. (Baseball Hall of Fame Library. Cooperstown, N.Y.).

pitcher, from the Philadelphia Athletics for $125,000 and two players. Grove led the league in wins four times for the Philadelphia Athletics dynasty. He led the league in E.R.A. nine times, including four times with the Red Sox.

After the 1934 season, Collins acquired Joe Cronin from the Washington Nationals as a player-manager. Cronin was a consistent .300 hitter, a power hitter and he was the "boy manager" who led the Nationals to the pennant in 1933. The price for Cronin was $225,000 and Lyn Lary, whom Cronin replaced at shortstop.

In late 1935, Collins brought Jimmie Foxx, "Double-X", to the Red Sox from the Athletics for $150,000 and pitcher Gordon Rhodes and minor league catcher George Savino. Foxx was a feared slugger in the Babe Ruth stripe, a home run hitter and a runs batted in leader par excellence. He had twice won the league's Most Valuable Player award playing for the Athletics and hit 58 home runs in 1932. He continued to be a slugger for the Sox.

Grove, Cronin and Foxx were among the elite players of the American League. Collins brought other good players to the Red Sox though their reputations were not as outstanding. Rick Ferrell, a fair hitter and great defensive catcher came over from the St. Louis Browns in 1933. Wes Ferrell, his younger brother, came over from the Cleveland Indians in 1934. Wes was a good-hitting pitcher who won 60 games in three full seasons with the Red Sox (he and Lefty Grove won 45 games for the Sox in 1935) and he still holds the record for home runs by pitchers, 38. In early 1936, "Doc" Cramer, a steady .300 hitter, came over from the Athletics for $75,000 and two players.

In the trade for Lefty Grove, the Red Sox also acquired Eric McNair, a capable shortstop, "Rube" Walberg, a pitcher whose best years were with the Athletics, and Max Bishop, a star second baseman for the A's who was at the end of his career. The Red Sox also purchased Ben Chapman and Joe Vosmik, outfielders who were with the club only briefly. In 1938, Chapman and Vosmik, together with Doc Cramer, were a .300 hitting outfield with the Sox. Chapman hit .340 that year, Vosmik .324 and Cramer .301.

There were other established players who came briefly to the Red Sox "for a cup of coffee." Among these were Bill Werber, a third baseman who led the league in base stealing twice in his three years with the Sox, and "Pinky" Higgins, a third baseman for whom the Sox traded Werber. There were also "Heinie" Manush, outfielder, "Bobo" Newsom, pitcher, and George Pipgras, the pitcher who was traded to the Yankees ten years earlier by the Red Sox and was now with the Sox at the end of his career. Joe Heving, a pitcher, came over briefly from the Cleveland Indians but in two years with the Red Sox managed to

Hall of Fame catcher Rick Ferrell (left) was joined on the Red Sox by his brother, pitcher Wes Ferrell, in 1934. (Boston Public Library, Print Department).

lead the league in relief pitching wins in 1939 and 1940.

The Red Sox also had some home-grown talent, notably Jim Tabor who played a competent third base for the team for six years and Fritz Ostermueller, a journeyman pitcher who pitched seven years for the Sox. However, Eddie Collins' scouting talent was most visible in two exceptional players whom he brought up from the San Diego Padres of the Pacific Coast League. In 1937, he scouted and signed Bobby Doerr who became a Hall of Fame second baseman with the Red Sox. On the same scouting trip to watch Doerr play he discovered Ted Williams, who joined the Red Sox in 1939.

In the 1930s the Red Sox were not distinguished for their pennant-winning successes—they won none—but they were becoming a respectable team. By 1938 and 1939 they placed second to the pennant-winning New York Yankees. In 1940, the Red Sox had a formidable line-up, though they were not yet able to cash in on all the talent. The infield consisted of Jimmie Foxx at first base, Bobby Doerr at second base, Joe Cronin at shortstop and Jim Tabor at third base. The outfield had Ted Williams, Doc Cramer and Dom DiMaggio, a good hitter and slick fielder in his first year with the club. Gene Desautels was the catcher. The pitching staff taken as a whole was not yet at the same level of talent as the rest of the team. The Sox had the venerable Lefty Grove, Joe Heving, Jim Bagby Jr., Jack Wilson, Fritz Ostermueller and Denny Galehouse. However, "Tex" Hughson was beginning his career and the immediate post-World War II years would introduce other star pitchers, notably "Boo" Ferriss, Mel Parnell and Ellis Kinder.

In 1941, Ted Williams hit .406, the last .400 hitter in the big leagues. In 1942, he won the Triple Crown with a

Manager Joe Cronin (left) signs Jimmie Foxx to a contract in 1935. (Boston Public Library, Print Department.)

batting average of .356, 36 home runs and 137 runs batted in. This was a harbinger of better times to come after the hiatus where much talent went off to World War II. Tom Yawkey, the number-one fan, was realizing his ambition. In his 44 years of ownership he had three Red Sox pennant winners, in 1946, 1967 and 1975. Yawkey died in 1976 and his wife, Jean, also a devoted fan, succeeded him as owner for another 16 years, until her death. The Yawkey dynasty lasted for a remarkable 60 years!

Tom Yawkey is one of the few electees to the Hall of Fame as an executive. Among the exceptional Red Sox players of the 1930s and early 1940s, Jimmie Foxx, Lefty Grove, Joe Cronin, Ted Williams, Bobby Doerr and Rick Ferrell are all in the Hall of Fame.

1938

The Red Sox, under the front office management of Tom Yawkey and Eddie Collins, and with Joe Cronin as manager, were making their way back up the American League ladder after the disastrous post-Frazee years. In 1938, they finished in second place, 9½ games behind the New York Yankees pennant winners. They won 88 and lost 61 for a .591 winning average. They led the league in team batting with a .299 average. Their pitchers tied with the Yankee pitchers for the most shutouts, 10.

General manager Eddie Collins discovered Hall of Famers Ted Williams (left) and Bobby Doerr on the same scouting trip in 1937. (Boston Public Library, Print Department).

Dominant Players

Jimmie Foxx was the dominant Red Sox player and the American League's M.V.P. He led the league with a .349 batting average. He also led with 175 R.B.I. and set the Red Sox home run record at 50. In 1938, he was second to Detroit Hank Greenberg's 58 home runs though he beat Greenberg in slugging percentage, .704 to .683.

Three Red Sox Players led the league in most hits, outfielder Joe Vosmik with 201, outfielder Doc Cramer with 198 and first baseman Foxx with 197. Shortstop Joe Cronin led the league in doubles with 51 and outfielder Ben Chapman was third with 40. Jimmie Foxx was second to Greenberg in runs scored with 115. All three Boston outfielders batted over .300, as did infielders Foxx, Cronin, and Pinky Higgins at third base. Bobby Doerr at second base had a respectable .289 average and catcher Gene Desautels batted .291.

Lefty Grove, nearing the end of his career, led the league in earned run average at 3.08. He was 14-4 for a .777 winning percentage. Jim Bagby Jr. had a 15-11 record and was third in the league in games pitched with 43. Jack Wilson had a 15-15 record and was tied for third in shutouts with three. Ironically, former Red Soxer Red Ruffing, pitching for the Yankees, led the league with 21 wins and a winning percentage of .750. This was the third straight year in which he won 20 or more games.

1939

The Red Sox were again a second-place team only, this time they were 17 games behind the Yankees who were experiencing one of their dynasties from 1936 through 1939. The Sox again led the league in batting average at .291, were second to the Yanks in slugging and also second in team home runs and doubles.

Dominant Players

Jimmie Foxx was again a team leader. He batted .360, second to Joe DiMaggio's .381. He led the league in home runs with 35, over the Tigers' Greenberg with 33. He led in slugging percentage at .694, with DiMaggio in second place. Ted Williams in his rookie year in the league, batted .327 and led in total bases. He had 344 total bases and Foxx was second with 324. Williams led the league with 145 runs batted in, and Joe DiMaggio was second. Williams had 31 home runs, third behind Foxx and Greenberg. Williams was second in the league in runs scored with 131, and Foxx was third with 130. Williams was also second in doubles with 44 as third baseman Red Rolfe of the Yankees led the league in both runs scored and doubles.

Lefty Grove won 15 and lost four, and led the league in both winning percentage at .789 and in earned run average at 2.54. Grove was fifth in complete games with 17. Joe Heving, with an 11-3 won-lost record, was third in the league in saves with seven. Fireman Johnny Murphy of the Yankees led in saves with 19. Late in his career, he pitched briefly for the Red Sox.

1940

Dominant Players

The Red Sox finished fourth and the Detroit Tigers won the pennant, but Ted Williams and Jimmie Foxx were both having outstanding years. Williams batted .344, third in the league behind Joe DiMaggio and Luke Appling, the White Sox shortstop. He was third in slugging average and fifth in runs batted in. He led the league in runs scored, with 134, and was fourth in doubles and triples. Foxx batted .297, was second in home runs with 36 to Hank Greenberg's 41 and was fourth in runs batted in with 119. He was third in bases on balls with 101, tied with Charlie Gehringer of the Tigers. Doc Cramer also had a good year, tying for the lead league with 200 base hits and batting .303. Dom DiMaggio, Joe's younger brother, broke into the league playing right field for the Red Sox and batted .301 in his first year. Lou Finney, an outfielder-first baseman, also had a distinguished year with a .320 batting average and tied for second in triples with 15. Bobby Doerr led the league's second basemen in both number of putouts and double plays executed. He batted .291.

1941

The Red Sox again finished second, 17 games behind the Yankees. They led the league in batting at .283 and in slugging at .430. They were second behind the Yankees in home runs and led in doubles.

Dominant Players

This was another great year for Ted Williams. He batted .406, the last player in the big leagues to hit over .400. He was tops in home runs with 37 and also led in slugging percentage at .735. He was fourth in the league in runs batted in and led in runs scored. He also had the most bases on balls and total bases. Williams came in second in the Most Valuable Player poll. Joe DiMaggio, who set a record hitting in 56 consecutive games, won the award. Jimmie Foxx, near the end of his career, batted .300 with 19 homers and 105 runs batted in. Pete Fox, an outfielder, batted .302. Jim Tabor, the Red Sox third baseman, tied for fourth in the league with 17 stolen bases. Joe Cronin batted .311, hit 16 home runs, and batted in 95 runs.

1942

The Red Sox had another fine season with 93 wins and 59 losses for a .612 winning percentage, but they again finished in second place, nine games behind the Yankees. They again led the league in batting average and slugging percentage.

Dominant Players

Ted Williams had another stellar year, leading the league with a Triple Crown. He led in batting at .356, in home runs with 36, and in runs batted in with 137. He led in slugging and total bases. He also had the most bases on balls, 145, and was third in hits with 186. Notwithstanding, Williams placed second to Joe Gordon of the Yankees

in Most Valuable Player balloting. Gordon batted .322 with 18 home runs and 103 runs batted in. The baseball writers who voted the M.V.P. award, did not like an aloof and somewhat disdainful Ted Williams.

Shortstop Johnny Pesky was second in the league with a .331 batting average. Pesky led the league in hits with 205. Dom DiMaggio, who batted .286, was third in runs scored behind Williams and brother Joe DiMaggio. Dom was also fourth in doubles. Bobby Doerr, batting .290., was fifth in runs batted in with 102.

Tex Hughson led the league with 22 wins and was third in winning percentage, .786, with a 22-6 record. Hughson tied with Ernie Bonham of the Yankees for the most complete games pitched with 22. He also tied with Bobo Newsom, then of the Washington Nationals and earlier briefly a Red Sox pitcher, for the most strikeouts with 113. Mace Brown, with a 9-3 record was second in saves, six, behind Johnny Murphy of the Yankees.

1946-1951
Red Sox—Winners and Contenders after World War II

The Red Sox came together as a team in the years immediately after World War II. Their line-up had powerful hitting, including Ted Williams, Bobby Doerr, Vern Stephens and Rudy York. They had good pitching years, notably from Tex Hughson, Boo Ferriss, Mel Parnell and Ellis Kinder.

The Red Sox won the American League pennant in 1946 by 12 games over the Detroit Tigers. It was a remarkable hitting year with Ted Williams batting .342, Johnny Pesky at .335 and Dom DiMaggio, one of three DiMaggio brothers in the big leagues, hitting .316. Bobby Doerr and Rudy York split 233 runs batted in between them. Ted Williams had 38 home runs and Doerr and York had 18 and 17, respectively. Boo Ferris won 25 games, leading the league in winning percentage at .806 and Tex Hughson, the mainstay of the pitching corps, won 20 games. The Red Sox were heavy favorites to win the World Series but they lost, four games to three, to the St. Louis Cardinals. The highlight of the Series was Enos "Country" Slaughter of the Cardinals in the seventh and deciding game, streaking home from first base on a hit in the eighth inning. The Red Sox lost the game, 4 to 3.

Though the Red Sox did not win another pennant in the post World War II years, they remained a dominant and powerhouse team. Epitomizing and leading the performance was Ted Williams who was the league's Most Valuable Player in 1946, won the Triple Crown in batting,

home runs and runs batted in 1947, led the league in hitting in 1948 with a .369 average, and again was named the Most Valuable Player in 1949.

In 1948, the Red Sox tied for the pennant with the Cleveland Indians, this in spite of the fact that three Red Sox players, Stephens at shortstop, Pesky at third base and Birdie Tebbetts, catcher, led the league in errors at their positions. Williams, beside his .369 average, hit 25 home runs, Vern Stephens hit 29 round trippers and Bobby Doerr hit 27. Williams, Doerr and Stephens all drove in more than one hundred runs each. Jack Kramer, Joe Dobson and rookie Mel Parnell won 49 games among them.

It was the year of the transplanted Browns as Kramer, Stephens and Ellis Kinder all came over from the St. Louis club. However, the Sox lost the one game play-off to the Indians, 8-3, with Gene Bearden pitching and Cleveland manager Lou Boudreau having a stellar day at bat with four hits, including two home runs. The Indians went on to beat the Boston entry, the National League Braves, four games to two, in the World Series.

The year 1949 was another powerhouse and banner year for the Red Sox. They had Billy Goodman, a consistent .300 hitter, at first base, the reliable Bobby Doerr with over 100 runs batted in at second base, power-hitting Vern Stephens at shortstop and Johnny Pesky, also a steady .300 hitter, at third base. The outfield consisted of Ted Williams, Dom DiMaggio and Al Zarilla, who was also acquired from the St. Louis Browns. Williams and Stephens shared the league lead for runs driven in with 159 each. Birdie Tebbetts, who had spent most of his playing career with the Detroit Tigers, was the steady catcher. Mel Parnell led the league with 25 pitching victories and he was joined by Ellis Kinder who had 23 victories and led the league with a .793 winning percentage. They were a virtual two-man pitching staff, pitching in relief at times as well as starting.

The Red Sox were one game ahead in the standings down to the end of the season with two games to go against the Yankees. The Yankees won both games, broke the tie in the last game of the season, and won the pennant. The Sox lost the final game, virtually a play-off game, 5-3, as Jerry Coleman of the Yankees had a base-clearing three-run hit.

The years 1948 and 1949 are remembered as years of frustration, as the Red Sox lost the pennant in the final game they played each season. Less noted is the fact that the Sox had powerful, competitive and mostly successful teams in these years. They won 96 games each of the two years with over a .600 winning percentage. Joe McCarthy, one of the great managers in baseball history who had managed the Chicago Cubs to a pennant in 1929 and then managed the New York Yankees to eight pennants and seven world championships during some of their dynasty years, was the eminent manager of good Red Sox baseball teams.

In 1950, two particularly notable events occurred that perhaps were a portent of things to come. Joe McCarthy retired in mid-season, and Ted Williams broke his elbow catching a fly ball in the All-Star game and was unable to play for the rest of the season. The Red Sox finished third and were unable to catch the Yankees, who were winning the first of five consecutive pennants under Casey Stengel, even though the Sox had 94 wins and led the league in batting average at .302.

Billy Goodman won the batting title with a .354 average though he could not crack the starting infield of Walt Dropo at first base. Bobby Doerr and Vern Stephens as the double-play combination at second base and shortstop, and Johnny Pesky as the third baseman. Goodman's role was to show his talents as a versatile player, "filling in" at all infield positions and even in the outfield as needed. Walt Dropo had his one great year with the club. He batted .322, hit 34 home runs and tied teammate Vern Stephens for the league's runs batted in title with 144 each. Dropo was named Rookie of the Year. Stephens, in addition to a share of the runs batted in title, hit 30 home runs. He, Dropo and Doerr together hit 91 homers. Stephens batted .295 as all nine regulars (including

Goodman) batted between Doerr's .294 and Goodman's .354. Mel Parnell, Ellis Kinder and Joe Dobson pitched for a respectable total of forty seven wins among them, though the team's pitching record was not equivalent to the batting and slugging power of the Red Sox.

In the following year, 1951, the Red Sox had dropped 11 games off the pace of the winning New York Yankees. The next several years saw them in gradual decline.

1946

The Red Sox won the American League pennant in 1946 by 12 games over second place Detroit and 17 games over the New York Yankees. They lost to the St. Louis Cardinals in the World Series, four games to three. Under manager Joe Cronin, the Sox won 104 and lost 50 for an impressive .675 winning percentage. They led in team batting average and in slugging average, were second in home runs to the Yankees and led the league in doubles. They were also the best fielding team with a .977 team average.

A young Ted Williams had plenty of reason to smile after being named the league's Most Valuable Player in 1946. (Boston Public Library, Print Department).

Dominant Players

Ted Williams, like many other players, was back from World War II. He batted .342, second in the league, and was also second to Hank Greenberg in home runs with 38 and in runs batted in with 123. He led in slugging percentage with a .667 average. He led in bases on balls and runs scored, and was fourth in hits and doubles. This time, Williams won one of his two Most Valuable Player awards.

Johnny Pesky also had a fine year. He batted .335, third in the league and just behind Williams. He led the league in hits with 208. He was second to Williams in runs scored and third in the league in doubles. Bobby Doerr was one of three Boston players to bat in over 115 runs, the other two being Ted Williams and Rudy York. Dom DiMaggio was fifth in league batting with a .316 average.

Rudy York, coming over from Detroit to play first base, led the league's first basemen in putouts, assists and double-play executions. The reliable Bobby Doerr at second base also led the second basemen in these three categories and, in addition, led in fielding average. Hal Wagner led all catchers with 553 putouts.

The Sox had two 20-game winners, Boo Ferriss who was third in the league with 25 wins and Tex Hughson who was tied for fourth with 20. Ferriss had the league's best winning percentage, at .806 with 25 wins and six losses. Hughson was fifth with 20 wins, 11 losses and a .645 average. Ferriss was third with 26 complete games, behind Bob Feller and Hal Newhouser. Hughson was fifth with 21 complete games. Both Ferriss and Hughson tied for second in the league with six shutouts, behind Bob Feller's ten. Ferriss pitched in 40 games, tied for second in the league behind Feller. Hughson tied for fourth with 39 games. Hughson also gave the fewest average walks per nine-inning game, 1.25. Mickey Harris also had a good year with 17 wins and nine losses and was fourth in the league in winning percentage at .654. Joe Dobson had a 13-7 record and Bob Klinger led the league with nine saves.

1947

Dominant Players
The Red Sox dropped to third place but Ted Williams had yet another outstanding year and once again was a Triple Crown winner. This time he led the league with a .343 batting average, with 32 home runs and 114 runs batted

in. He also led in slugging average and total bases, in bases on balls, runs scored and triples. He was second in doubles. This time he lost the Most Valuable Player award to Joe DiMaggio again. DiMaggio batted .315, had 20 home runs and 97 runs batted in.

Johnny Pesky had another good year, batting .324, third in the league. Pesky again led in hits with 207 and he was fifth in total bases with 250. He was third in runs scored behind Williams and Tommy Henrich of the New York Yankees. He tied for third in stolen bases. Bobby Doerr drove in 95 runs. Catcher Birdie Tebbetts batted .299 and right fielder Sam Mele batted .302.

Doerr was again a fielding leader, placing first among the league's second basemen in assists and double plays executed. Dom DiMaggio, in center field, also led at his position in assists and double plays.

Joe Dobson was the team's leading pitcher with 18 wins and eight losses, and second to Allie Reynolds of the Yankees in winning percentage at .692. Bob Klinger tied for fifth with eight saves and was third in games pitched, 45. Tex Hughson, at 12 wins and 11 losses, was just behind Bob Feller in most strikeouts per nine innings at 5.66.

1948

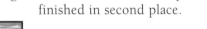

1948 saw the Red Sox lose the pennant to the Cleveland Indians in a play-off game. With Joe McCarthy managing, they won 96 games and lost 59 for a .619 percentage, but finished in second place.

Dominant Players
Ted Williams again led the league in batting with a .369 average. He had 25 home runs and was third in the league with 127 runs batted in. He led in slugging percentage at .615, was third in runs scored and led the league in walks.

The Red Sox had three of the top four players in runs scored, Tommy Henrich of the New York Yankees led with 138, followed by Dom DiMaggio. Williams and Pesky. Dom DiMaggio, who batted .285, was fourth in bases on balls and tied for fourth in doubles. Vern Stephens, in his first year with the Red Sox and playing shortstop while Johnny Pesky moved over to third base, batted .269. He was fourth in the league in home runs with 29 and second to only Joe DiMaggio in runs batted in with 137.

Ted Williams (center) tells Eddie Collins (left) and Joe Cronin a big fish story. (Boston Public Library, Print Department).

He tied Lou Boudreau for fourth place in total bases with 299.

Billy Goodman, batting .310 and playing first base, led the league in most chances per game at his position, as did Dom DiMaggio in center field. Johnny Pesky, new at third base, led at his position in double-play executions but he also led in errors.

Jack Kramer, just over from the St. Louis Browns along with Vern Stephens, led the league's pitchers in winning percentage, at .783, with 18 wins and five losses. Mel Parnell, with 15 wins and eight losses, was fifth in earned run average at 3.14. Joe Dobson, who had a 16-10 record, was fifth in the league in shutouts with five. He was fourth in the league in innings pitched, behind Bob Lemon and Bob Feller of Cleveland and Hal Newhouser of Detroit. Earl Johnson, with a 10-4 record, led the league in relief pitching with nine victories and he also had five saves.

Red Sox manager Joe McCarthy (left) was succeeded as manager of the New York Yankees by Casey Stengel. (Baseball of Fame Library. Cooperstown, N.Y.).

1949

This year again saw the Red Sox lose the pennant in the last days of the season by one game to the New York Yankees. Again under manager Joe McCarthy they won 96 and lost 58 but finished in second place. The Sox were a powerful offensive team. They led the league in batting average and slugging average, in home runs and doubles.

Dominant Players

Ted Williams won his second Most Valuable Player award. He missed winning the batting title and Triple Crown by less than a percentage point to George Kell of the Tigers. Both batted .343. Williams led the league in home runs with 43, with teammate Vern Stephens coming in second at 39. Williams and Stephens tied for the runs batted in title, with 159 each. Williams was first in the league in bases on balls, with 162, in doubles and runs scored. He was second in base hits with 194 and his teammates Dom DiMaggio and Johnny Pesky, placed third and fourth respectively. Dom DiMaggio and Al Zarilla, another St. Louis Browns refugee, placed third and fourth in the league in doubles. Bobby Doerr also had a fine year, batting .309, placing fifth with 109 runs batted in and fifth in total bases.

Vern Stephens at shortstop and Johnny Pesky at third base led the league at their positions in assists and double plays executed. Bobby Doerr at second base, Pesky, and Dom DiMaggio in center field led in their positions with most fielding chances per game. Billy Goodman led all first basemen in fielding with a .992 percentage.

The Red Sox had two 20-game winners, Mel Parnell and Ellis Kinder. Parnell led the league with 25 wins and 295 innings pitched. With a 25-7 record he was second in

winning percentage at .781. Kinder was first in the league in winning percentage at .793, with 22 wins and six losses. Kinder was second in wins with 22. Parnell and Kinder dominated the league, notwithstanding that the Indians had Bob Lemon, Bob Feller, Early Wynn, Mike Garcia and Gene Bearden, and the Yankees had Allie Reynolds, Eddie Lopat, Vic Raschi, Tommy Byrne, and Joe Page in relief.

Parnell was second to Cleveland's Mike Garcia in ERA, at 2.77. Kinder was third in strikeouts with 138, behind Virgil Trucks and Hal Newhouser of Detroit. Parnell had the most complete games in the league with 27, and Kinder tied for the most shut outs with Trucks at six.

1950

The Red Sox, under a retiring Joe McCarthy and then Steve O'Neill, two of the great managers in baseball, won 94 games and lost 60. Still, they were only able to place third behind the pennant-winning Yankees and the Detroit Tigers. The Sox again led the league in batting average and slugging average.

Dominant Players

Billy Goodman won the batting championship with a .354 mark even though he was a position replacement and could not beat out Walt Dropo, Rookie of the Year, at first base, Bobby Doerr at second, Vern Stephens at shortstop and Johnny Pesky at third base. All had good years. Dropo batted .322 and tied for the league lead with Vern Stephens in runs batted in, at 144. Stephens batted .295. Dropo, Doerr and Stephens had 91 home runs among themselves, Dropo with 34, Stephens with 30 and Doerr with 27. Doerr batted .294 and also drove in 120 runs. Dropo was second in the league in home runs, behind Al Rosen of Cleveland, and he was second in slugging behind Joe DiMaggio. Dropo and Stephens led the league, placing first and second, in total bases. Stephens tied for second in runs scored, Pesky was third in bases on balls and Doerr tied for the lead in triples with 11.

The outfield also fared quite well with all three outfielders batting over .300. Al Zarilla in right field batted .325, Dom DiMaggio in center was at .328 and the redoubtable Ted Williams, injured part of the year, still batted .317 in a shortened season for him. Williams also had 28 home runs and 97 runs batted in. Dom DiMaggio was third in the league in hits with 193 and led the league in stolen bases with 15. He also tied for first with Doerr and Hoot Evers of Detroit with 11 triples. Evers not long there-

after was traded to the Red Sox.

Even Birdie Tebbetts, the catcher, batted .310 in a massive season-long offensive display by the Red Sox. Bobby Doerr was his usual steady self out in the field, placing first at his second base position in fielding average. Johnny Pesky had the most chances per game at his third base position.

The pitching was again dominated by Parnell, Kinder and Dobson. Parnell went 18-10, Kinder had a 14-12 record and Dobson was at 15-10. Chuck Stobbs also pitched effectively with 12 wins and seven losses. Parnell tied for fourth in the league in wins. Kinder also pitched in relief and placed fourth in saves with nine. Kinder was also second in games pitched with 48, behind Mickey Harris who was now pitching for the Washington Nationals.

1952-1966
Lowly Red Sox But Some Good Red Sox Players

For most of the 1950s, the Red Sox were in third or fourth place in the American League. However, they were not really in contention for the pennant. From 1951 until they won the pennant in 1967, they never finished closer than 11 games behind the pennant winners. In 1954, though finishing in fourth place, at the end of the season they were 42 games behind the pennant-winning Cleveland Indians.

The 1960s, until they won the pennant, were a reminder of the Red Sox dismal 1920s. The Sox never finished higher than sixth place.

After the league expanded to ten teams in 1961, the Sox were consistently in the second division. In the two years before the reversal year of 1967, they finished ninth, and for four years before the pennant year they never finished better than 26 games behind first place.

The Red Sox did not lack for fine players, however, some of whom gave some exceptional performances. Ted Williams continued to build his record as one of the best players ever, and in the opinion of many earned the reputation he sought as "the greatest hitter who ever lived." Williams played until his retirement in 1960. He served his second tour of duty in the armed forces in 1952-1953, as a Marine pilot in the Korean War. When he returned to full-time baseball play in 1954 he led the league in slugging that year. In 1957 and 1958 he led the league in batting average, hitting .388 in 1957. That year he also had

Red Sox outfielder Jimmy Piersall led the league in doubles with 40 in 1956. (Baseball Hall of Fame Library. Cooperstown, N.Y.).

an exceptional slugging average of .731. From 1954-1958 he batted in more than 115 runs each year and he hit a total of 123 home runs in this five-year period, or nearly 25 home runs per year. In his last year, 1960, at the age of 42, he batted .316 and hit 29 home runs. Williams is as much legend to the Red Sox as Babe Ruth is to baseball.

Billy Goodman, the all-purpose, good-hitting infielder continued his around .300 batting until he was traded to Baltimore in 1957. Mel Parnell had two more good years in the early 1950s, winning 18 in 1951 and 21 in 1953.

There were now, however, new members of the cast. Jimmy Piersall, a fair-hitting but fast, sure-handed out-fielder was with the club from his rookie year in 1952 until his trade to Cleveland after the 1958 season. For five consecutive years, 1953 through 1957, he had at least 20 doubles and led the league in doubles with 40 in 1956.

Frank Malzone was the Red Sox third baseman for ten years, from 1956 through 1965. He won the Gold Glove award for fielding in 1957, 1958 and 1959, or until Brooks Robinson began to develop his reputation as "the human vacuum cleaner" at third base for the Baltimore Orioles.

Jackie Jensen came over to the Red Sox in 1954, hav-ing spent most of his career as a Washington National and New York Yankee outfielder. He led the league three times in runs batted in while with the Sox, and in 1958 he was named the league's Most Valuable Player.

In 1959, Elijah "Pumpsie" Green became the first Afri-can-American player with the Red Sox, 12 years after Jackie Robinson first came up with the Brooklyn Dodg-ers. Green, who spent four of his five major league years with the Red Sox, had a .246 lifetime batting average. Earl Wilson, the second African-American player to come up with the Red Sox, also arrived in 1959. He is best noted not only for his no-hitter in 1962 but also for his home run hitting. Though a pitcher, he hit 35 in his career. Pete Runnels won two batting championships, in 1960 and 1962, while playing with the Red Sox. He played most of the three years with the Sox at second base and most of two subsequent years at first base.

Tony Conigliaro, the "Tony C." of the "Tony C." and younger brother "Billy C." outfield combination, came to the Red Sox in 1954. For five straight years he hit 20 or more home runs and led the league in 1965 with 32 hom-ers. In this league-leading year he was 20 years old, the youngest ever to win the home run championship.

Dick Radatz, the 6-foot-6, 230-pound relief pitcher known as "The Monster", led the league in relief pitching from 1962-64. In all three years he led the league in wins in relief and in two of the three years he also led in saves. Bill Monbouquette, a 20-game winner in 1963, and Dave

Mike "Pinky" Higgins played for and later managed the Red Sox in two tours of duty. (Baseball Hall of Fame Library. Cooperstown, N.Y.).

Morehead were regular members of the staff. Each pitched no-hitters. However, they may be remembered in part for leading the league in losses in 1965. Each lost 18 games.

The most notable new development for the Red Sox was the arrival of Carl Yastrzemski in 1961. Hall of Famer Yastrzemski had one of the longest careers in baseball, twenty three years, all of these were with Boston. Yastrzemski was a stellar outfielder and a constant hitter. He led the league in batting three times, one time before the pennant year in 1967. That year was 1963 and he also led the league in hits then. He led the league in doubles three times, all before the pennant year. His climactic year was 1967 when he won the Most Valuable Player award. Yastrzemski gave the Red Sox continuity in great left fielders from a pe-riod 1939 through 1989. In this period there was first Ted Williams, then Carl Yastrzemski and then Jim Rice.

The Red Sox were not without other notable events in this fallow period for the team, Lou Boudreau and Mike "Pinky" Higgins, both outstanding players who spent a brief period with the Red Sox before the end of their ca-reers, both managed the Sox in the 1950s. Higgins, in fact, was manager of the team in two tours of duty, for a total of more than five years.

Rudy York, also a former Red Sox player for a brief time, could also claim managing experience with the Red Sox. He managed for one game in 1959, taking Higgins' place until a new manager (Billy Jurges) arrived. Johnny Pesky, one of the great Red Sox from his playing years, managed in the 1960s and former player Pete Runnels finished the season as Sox manager in 1966.

The most interesting oddity is that the Red Sox set a record on June 18, 1953, with Ted Williams in military service, by scoring 17 runs in the seventh inning against the Detroit Tigers. Twenty-three batters came to the plate. There were eleven singles, two doubles, a home run and six walks in the inning. Gene Stephens, a reserve outfielder, set a record with three hits in the inning. The Sox, who were leading before the inning, 5-3, won 23-3. The Tigers also had lost on the previous day, 17-1.

1958

The Red Sox, under manager Pinky Higgins, finished third, 13 games behind the Yankees and also behind the Chicago White Sox. However, they had some outstanding player performances.

Dominant Players

Jackie Jensen, Red Sox outfielder, won the league's Most Valuable Player award. He batted .286, was fifth in home runs with 35 and led the league in R.B.I.s. Jensen was second to Mickey Mantle in bases on balls. Ted Williams again led the league in batting average at .328. Pete Runnels, who this year played second base and later won two batting titles playing for the Sox in 1960 and 1962, was second in batting with a .322 average. Jensen, Williams and Runnels were two, three and four in bases on balls, with Mickey Mantle far ahead with 129. Williams was fourth in slugging and Runnels was second in runs scored behind Mantle, fourth in doubles and fourth in base hits.

Frank Malzone at third base had a stellar fielding year. He led the league at his position in assists, double plays executed and number of fielding chances per game. He won the Gold Glove award three years in a row, 1957, 1958 and 1959 for his third-base play. He batted .295 and was second in the league in base hits.

Four Red Sox infielders led the league in the number of fielding chances per game at their positions. Besides Malzone, Dick Gernert led at first base, Don Buddin at shortstop and Pete Runnels at second base. All but Runnels also led in number of errors committed at their position. Jimmy Piersall, center fielder, won the Gold Glove award at his position in the first year the awards were given

separately to players in each league. Jackie Jensen was to win the award in 1959 as a right fielder. The pitchers were not notable in 1958 but by way of retro reference, Mel Parnell in the last year of his career in 1956, pitched a no-hitter for the Red Sox, beating the White Sox, 4-0.

NEGATIVE YEARS AND NEGATIVE PLAYER PERFORMANCES

1965

The Red Sox finished in ninth place in a ten-team league. Managed by Billy Herman they lost 100 games of 162 and were 40 games behind the pennant-winning Minnesota Twins. Notwithstanding, they led the league in slugging average but they were next to last in fielding percentage and tied for last with last-place Kansas City in their pitchers' earned run average.

Mostly Negative Performances

There were no regular pitchers with a winning percentage and Bill Monbouquette and Dave Morehead tied for the league in most losses, each with a 10-18 record. Jim Lonborg also lost 17 games with just nine wins. Dave Morehead had one of the year's few bright moments pitching a no-hitter against the Cleveland Indians on September 16 and winning 2-0. This was the last no-hitter pitched by a Red Sox pitcher through 1998.

The only Red Sox regular to bat over .276 was Carl Yastrzemski at .312. Petrocelli at shortstop and Malzone at third base each batted under .240. Bill Tillman, the catcher, batted .215. Outfielder Tony Conigliaro did lead the league with 32 home runs, and Carl Yastrzemski, both in 1963 and 1965, won the Gold Glove award for his outfield play.

1966

The Red Sox again finished in ninth place in a ten-team league. Led by Billy Herman, who was replaced at the end of the season by Pete Runnels, the Red Sox were 26 games behind first place Baltimore. In an unusual nose-dive, only the New York Yankees placed below the Red Sox, finishing in last place, 26½ games behind the Orioles.

The Red Sox were last in team fielding, whereas they were next to last in the previous year. They were next to last in errors. They had the league's worst E.R.A. at 3.92.

Negative Player Performances

Only Don McMahon, at eight wins and seven losses, had a winning percentage among regular pitchers. The most

The Red Sox Encyclopedia

games won by a pitcher was 12, by Jose Santiago, followed by Jim Lonborg with 10 wins.

No regular position player and none of the subs batted .300. The leading hitter was outfielder Don Demeter at .292. The second base- shortstop combination of George Smith and Rico Petrocelli each batted under .240. First baseman George Scott batted .245 and catcher Mike Ryan batted .214. Even Carl Yastrzemski only batted .278.

1967-1980
Two Pennants, A Near Miss And A World Series To Remember

When the season began in 1967, the Red Sox, ninth-place finishers the previous year, were rated at a dismal 100-to-1 to win the pennant. They had a new manager, Dick Williams, who was in the first of his 21 years as a major league manager with six different teams. Two performances in particular galvanized the Red Sox into winners. Carl Yastrzemski won the Most Valuable Player award, the Triple Crown and one of his seven Gold Glove awards for fielding. He batted .326, hit 44 home runs and drove in 112 runs. Jim Lonborg, who was with the Red Sox for seven years, had his one great year with the team and won the Cy Young award. He led the league with 22 wins, a .710 pitching average and 246 strikeouts. Nobody else on the Red Sox pitching staff won more than 12 games. The supporting cast had George Scott with a .301 batting average and 19 home runs at first base, Rico Petrocelli at shortstop, and Reggie Smith and Tony Conigliaro, who hit 35 home runs between them, in the outfield. The Red Sox won a close pennant race, beating Detroit and Minnesota by one game and the Chicago White Sox by only three games.

The 1967 World Series, in its result, was a repeat of the last World Series the Red Sox were in, in 1946. The St. Louis Cardinals again beat the Red Sox four games to three.

The 1967 Series was a contest between Bob Gibson, a Hall of Fame pitcher for the Cardinals, and the Red Sox ace, Jim Lonborg. Gibson won the first game, 2 to 1. Lonborg won the second game, a 5-1 one-hitter. The Cards won the third game and Gibson came back and won the fourth game for the National Leaguers with a 6-0 shutout. Lonborg, who gave up three hits, one a home run to Roger Maris, won Game 5, 3-1. The Red Sox won Game 6, 8 to 4, getting three home runs in a row from Yastrzemski, Reggie Smith and Petrocelli. It was Petrocelli's second home run of the game.

Entering the seventh game, Gibson had given up one run and 11 hits in 18 innings, and Lonborg had given up one run and four hits also over 18 innings. Lonborg, however, suffered from only two days' rest. Gibson won the seventh game, 7-2, and also hit a home run.

Carlton Fisk was a rookie catcher in 1972, in the first year of his 24-year major league career. He hit .293 and won the Gold Glove award. Luis Tiant, in his second of eight years with the Red Sox, had a 15-6 record and led the league with a 1.91 earned run average in 1972.

However, the Sox were not again a formidable team until 1975. The infield by then consisted of the veteran Carl Yastrzemski now at first base, Doug Griffin in his fifth year at second base, Rick Burleson in his second year at shortstop and Rico Petrocelli as the veteran third baseman. 1975 was the rookie year for both Fred Lynn and Jim Rice and they competed for batting and Most Valuable Player honors. Rice hit .309 with 22 home runs and 102 runs batted in. Lynn hit .331 with 21 home runs and 105 runs batted in, and in addition won a Gold Glove award for his fielding. Lynn was named Rookie of the Year and won the Most Valuable Player award, the only time a player won both honors together. The Red Sox, loaded with talent, also had the superlative fielder and power hitter, Dwight Evans, in the outfield, backed up by the power hitting of Bernie Carbo. Cecil Cooper, with a .311 batting average, was the designated hitter. The pitching staff was equal to the occasion, with Rick Wise winning 19 games, Luis Tiant winning 18 and "Spaceman" Bill Lee winning 17 games.

The 1975 World Series was one to remember. It pitted a good Red Sox team against the Cincinnati Reds of the National League. The Reds team of that year, perhaps one of the best ever, was known as "The Big Red Machine" with an array of powerful hitters, including two Hall of Famers (Joe Morgan and Johnny Bench) and two of Hall of Fame quality (Pete Rose and Tony Perez). Particularly memorable in the Series was Carlton Fisk's home run in the 12th inning of the sixth game to tie the Series for the Red Sox. Fisk wishfully "waved" the ball fair as it went toward the left field foul line while he was running to first base. It stayed fair and the home run won the game for the Sox. The Reds won the seventh and concluding game, and the World Series, four games to three.

1967

This was a great Red Sox year for both team winning and player performance. The Red Sox, under new manager Dick Williams, won the pennant in a close contest with the Detroit Tigers and Minnesota Twins, each one game out, and the Chicago White Sox, three games out. They again lost to the St. Louis Cardinals in the World Series, four games to three. Carl Yastrzemski won the Triple Crown and was named the league's Most Valuable Player. Jim Lonborg won the Cy Young award for pitching.

The Sox led the league in batting average, slugging average, home runs and doubles. They were second in team fielding average behind the New York Yankees who, notwithstanding, finished in ninth place in a ten-team league.

Dominant Players

It was Yastrzemski's career year. He was first in batting with a .336 average, first in runs batted in with 121 and tied for first in home runs with Harmon Killebrew of the Twins, each having 44. Yaz also led the league in slugging and in total bases. He led in hits and runs scored. He was third in doubles and fourth in bases on balls. First baseman George "Boomer" Scott was third in hits. Tony Conigliaro was second on the team behind Yastrzemski in home runs, with 20, and Boomer Scott had 19.

Jim Lonborg led in pitching with 22 wins, the most in the league, along with Earl Wilson's 22 pitching for Detroit. The largest number of wins for any other Red Sox pitcher was 12. Lonborg at 22 wins and nine losses, was second in the league with a .710 winning average. Lonborg led in strikeouts with 246. He also was third in complete games with 15.

1969

Dominant Players

The Red Sox finished in third place in the East Division, in a league that was split into the East and West Divisions. They were 22 games behind the Baltimore Orioles but still managed to lead the league in slugging percentage and home runs.

Reggie Smith, the Red Sox centerfielder, led the league in batting at .309. Rico Petrocelli at shortstop and left fielder Carl Yastrzemski tied for fourth place with 40 home runs each. Petrocelli was third in slugging percentage and, though batting .297, was fifth in batting average. Petrocelli was also fourth in doubles. Yastrzemski tied for fifth in the league in runs batted in with 111. Reggie Smith was tied for second in triples with seven.

Yastrzemski led left fielders with assists, with 17, and won the Gold Glove award for the fifth time. Petrocelli led all shortstops with a .981 fielding percentage.

Sparky Lyle, the Red Sox reliever, was third in games pitched, 71, and he was third in saves with 17.

1975

The Red Sox won the East division under Darrell Johnson, then beat the Oakland A's in the A.L. Division play-offs, three games to none. They lost the World Series to the Cincinnati Reds, four games to three. The Sox led the American League in batting average and slugging average. They were tied for third in the league in home runs and they led in doubles.

Dominant Players

The Red Sox had sensational rookie outfielders Fred Lynn and Jim Rice. Lynn won both the Rookie of the Year and Most Valuable Player awards, a unique accomplishment. Lynn batted .331, had 21 homers and 105 runs batted in. Rice batted .309 with 22 home runs and 102 runs batted in. Lynn was second in the league in batting average and Rice was fourth. Lynn also led in slugging percentage, in doubles and runs scored. He was third in runs batted in. Rice was fifth in runs batted in and fourth in runs scored. Fred Lynn won a Gold Glove for his outfield play.

Carlton Fisk batted .331. Carl Yastrzemski and Cecil Cooper, the designated hitter while Yaz moved over to play first base, each hit 14 home runs.

Rick Wise had 19 pitching wins. Luis Tiant had 18 and Spaceman Bill Lee had 17. Dick Drago led in relief pitching, fifth in the league in saves with 15.

1978

The Red Sox, under Don Zimmer, won 99 games but still finished second in the A.L. East Division to the Yankees. 99 wins and 64 losses resulted in a .607 winning percentage, one game behind the Yankees. The Red Sox actually tied for first place but lost in a one-game play-off with the Yankees when Bucky Dent hit his surprise home run. The Sox had also won 97 games in 1977, again under Don Zimmer, and they lost 64 for a .602 average. This tied them for second place with the Baltimore Orioles, the Yankees again winning the East Division, by 2½ games.

The 1975 Boston Red Sox were American League Eastern Division champions. (Boston Public Library, Print Department).

Dominant Players

Jim Rice won the league's M.V.P. award. He batted .315, third in the league, and led the league in home runs with 46 and R.B.I.s with 139. Rice led the league with a .600 slugging percentage and also had the most total bases with 406, 113 more than the runner up, Eddie Murray of the Orioles. Rice led the league in hits with 213 and in triples with 15. He was second in runs scored. Rice was virtually a one-man wrecking crew and the only regular to bat .300.

Carlton Fisk also had a good year, batting .284 with 20 home runs and 88 runs batted in. Dwight Evans, right fielder, hit 24 home runs, and third baseman Butch Hobson and designated hitter Carl Yastzremski had 17 each. Yaz, Fisk, Lynn and Hobson, in addition to Rice, all drove in 80 or more runs, though Rice drove in 51 more than any other player on the Red Sox.

Dennis Eckersley, at 20 wins and eight losses, was the team's leading starting pitcher. He was fourth in the league with a winning percentage of .714. Eckersley was fifth in games won and fifth in strikeouts. Reliever Bob Stanley of the Red Sox with 10 saves and a 15-2 record was second in winning percentage. He was second to Ron Guidry of the Yankees who had a career year of 25 wins and three losses for an .893 average and a league-leading 1.74 E.R.A.

1979

Don Zimmer led the Red Sox to another 90+ wins but managed only to finish in third place, 3½ games behind Milwaukee in the East Division and 11½ games behind the Division leading Baltimore Orioles. The Red Sox were again a hitting power, leading the league in batting average, slugging average, home runs and doubles.

Dominant Players

Fred Lynn led the league in batting with a .333 average. He and teammate Jim Rice had another competitive year. Rice was fourth in the league at .325. Lynn and Rice tied for second in home runs with 39 each. Lynn was first in slugging percentage and Rice was second. Rice was first in total bases and Lynn was third. Rice was second to Don Baylor of the California Angels in runs batted in, with 130, and Lynn was fourth with 122. Rice was second with 201 hits and Lynn was third in doubles. Rice was third with 117 runs scored and Lynn was fourth with 116.

Lynn won another Gold Glove for his outfield play, having also won in 1975 and 1978, with another Gold Glove to come in 1980. Outfield teammate Dwight "Dewey" Evans also won a Gold Glove for his outfield play in 1978 and 1979, and he won previously in 1976. He would also win Gold Gloves five years in a row from 1981-

1985. Evans was an exceptional out-fielder with a rifle arm.

In 1979, besides Lynn and Rice at 39, Butch Hobson had 28 home runs with 93 runs batted in and Dwight Evans and Carl Yastzremski had 21 home runs each. Bob Watson, the first baseman, batted 337 with 13 home runs.

Rick Burleson, along with the good-fielding outfielders, led all shortstops in fielding with a .980 percentage. Rice, Lynn and Evans fielded .984, .987 and .988 respectively with only ten errors among them.

The Red Sox had three pitchers with more than 15 wins, Dennis Eckersley with 17 and Mike Torrez and Bob Stanley with 16 each. Eckersley was third in the league with a 2.99 E.R.A. and fourth with 17 complete games. Bob Stanley tied for fourth with four shutouts and was fourth in giving up the fewest walks for nine innings, 1.82.

1983

Though the Red Sox finished next to last in the East Division of the American League, 20 games behind league-leading Baltimore, several players made their mark.

Dominant Players

Wade Boggs led the league in batting with a .361 average, the first of five batting championships he was to win within six years. Boggs was second to Cal Ripken of the Orioles in doubles, with 44, and he was third in walks. He was also second to Ripken in hits with 210. Jim Rice had another great year. He batted .305 and led the league in both home runs, 39, and R.B.I.s with 126. He was second in slugging percentage behind George Brett of Kansas City. Tony Armas, who had replaced Fred Lynn in center field, had 31 home runs, second behind Rice in the league, and 107 runs batted in. Bob Stanley, the reliever, had 33 saves, placing second in the league behind Dan Quisenberry's 45.

1986-2001
Good Years, Bad Years, A Pennant and Four Division Playoffs

Red Sox baseball, notably in the past generation, intersperses brilliant individual performance and careers with occasional tense, down-to-the-wire championship competition. In the 1980s and early 1990s the brilliant performances are particularly by Wade Boggs and Roger Clemens. The tense pennant or play-off competition occurred in 1986, 1988, 1990, 1995, 1998, and 1999.

Wade Boggs, a human hitting machine, broke into the big leagues with the Red Sox in 1982. In his first year, though he arrived only in late July, he batted .349. In 1983, he won the first of five batting titles thus far to his credit, batting .361. The exceptional hitter Boggs replaced Carney Lansford at third base. Lansford, ironically, won the batting title in 1981. Jim Rice, in 1983, had another one of his great hitting years, leading the league in home runs with 39 and tying for the runs batted in crown.

The year 1984 marked the appearance of another heavy hitter, Tony Armas, who came over from the Oakland Athletics in a trade for Lansford. Armas led the league with 43 home runs and 123 runs batted in. Rice had yet another superlative year with 28 home runs and contested Armas with 142 runs batted in. Dwight Evans, not to be outdone, had 32 home runs and 104 R.B.I.s. Nineteen eighty-four also marked the first major league appearance of hard-throwing Roger Clemens, who started his exceptional pitching career with nine wins, four losses and a lofty .692 winning percentage. Clemens was to be the bellwether of the Red Sox pitching staff, winning 136 games in seven years, or an average of nearly 20 a season, from 1986 through 1992. He led the league in wins and winning percentages in 1986 and 1987.

In 1986, under manager of the year John McNamara, the Red Sox finally emerged from the middle of the pack in the standings and won the East divisional championship. They were led by batting champion Wade Boggs and Cy Young award winner Roger Clemens. The Sox played the California Angels in the American League Championship Series. With the Angels ahead, three games to one, the Sox were down to their last out. The Angels were leading in the fifth and pennant-clinching game, 5-4. Dave Henderson hit a dramatic two-out, two-run homer to give the Red Sox the lead. The Angels tied the game in the last of the ninth inning but Henderson's sacrifice fly won it for the Sox in the 11th, 7 to 6. The Red Sox easily won Games 6 and 7 to win the pennant from the disappointed Angels, four games to three.

The 1986 World Series between the Red Sox and the New York Mets was another that etched in baseball memory. The Mets won a tough National League Championship Series from the Houston Astros, four games to two. In the sixth game of that series, the Mets rallied from three down to tie the game in the ninth inning, 3-3. Each team scored in the 14th inning. In the 16th inning the Mets scored three runs and Houston two, the Mets finally winning 7-6.

The Red Sox won three of the first five games of the World Series with Bruce Hurst winning two of them. The much ballyhooed competition between pitchers Roger Clemens of the Red Sox and Dwight Gooden of the Mets in Game 2 fell through, as neither survived the fifth inning.

Game 6 was the dramatic moment. The Red Sox were leading in the top of the tenth inning, 5-3, on Dave Henderson's home run, a double by Boggs and a single by Marty Barrett, one of his record-tying 13 hits in the Series. The Red Sox appeared to be the World Series winners for the first time since 1918. Fate and Red Sox bad luck intervened, however. The Mets combined three singles in the last of the tenth, a wild pitch by ace reliever Bob Stanley, and an error on a ground ball to win the game, 6-5. The error, a squibbler between first baseman Bill Buckner's legs allowing in the winning run, made Buckner a World Series goat to remember. The irony is that Buckner was a veteran player in the 18th year of a 23-year playing career in which he batted nearly .290, and three times he established the fielding record for first baseman assists, the latest in 1985.

The Mets won the seventh and final game of the Series, 8-5, and the Red Sox were deprived of a world championship. It was a series in which neither Roger Clemens for the Red Sox nor Dwight Gooden for the Mets won a single game.

The year 1987 was another great individual performance year for Wade Boggs who won another batting championship with a .363 average, and for Roger Clemens, who won the second of his four Cy Young awards with a league-leading 20 wins. Dwight Evans also had another fine year with 34 home runs, 123 runs batted in, a .305 batting average and he exhibited his usual stellar fielding. In 1988, the Red Sox won the East division championship after Joe Morgan replaced John McNamara as manager in mid-season and the team immediately won 19 of its next 20 games. The Red Sox won by one game over the Detroit Tigers and by two games over Milwaukee and Toronto in a tight race. Roger Clemens and Bruce Hurst won 18 games each and Lee Smith had 29 saves. Wade Boggs had another batting championship year at .366. The

outfield of Dwight Evans, Ellis Burks and Mike Greenwell combined had 61 home runs and 322 runs batted in. The 1988 American League Championship Series was a disaster for the Red Sox as they lost to the Oakland A's, a power hitting and good pitching team, four games to none. Dennis Eckersley, the former Red Sox starting pitcher, won the Most Valuable Player award as he saved all four games for the A's in his role as baseball's eminent relief pitcher.

The Red Sox again won the East division title in 1990. Clemens had another banner year with 21 wins and led the league with a 1.93 earned run average. Wade Boggs had his lowest batting average since he entered the league, .302, more than twenty points below his previous low average. Ellis Burks had a good year, however, with a .296 batting average, 21 home runs and 89 runs driven in. The Oakland Athletics again swept the Red Sox in the American League Championship Series, four games to none. The Oakland pitching, led by Dave Stewart's two wins, was sensational. The Red Sox did not score more than one run in any game.

In 1991, another star for the Red Sox appeared in the firmament. He was Mo Vaughn, a slugging first baseman. However, in the 90s the Sox divested themselves of their major stars. Wade Boggs, considered "over the hill", went to the Yankees as a free agent after the 1992 season. Later, the team and Roger Clemens could not agree on salary. The Red Sox would not match other offers to Clemens even though he showed his old brilliance. In 1996, he tied his record of 20 strikeouts in a single game that he had set ten years previously. As the 1997 season approached, Clemens signed with the Toronto Blue Jays. Boggs and Clemens were to have some stellar seasons with their new teams. Boggs, who hit over .300 for the Red Sox ten straight years, hit over .300 four of the five years he was with the Yankees. Clemens returned to his old pitching self for Toronto in 1997 and won the Cy Young award with a record of 21 wins and seven losses. He led the league in earned run average, at 2.06, and in wins, strikeouts, innings pitched and complete games.

Clemens again won the Cy Young award in 1998. Pitching for Toronto, he led the league in wins with 20 and had a 20-6 won-lost record. He led the league with a 2.65 earned run average and 271 strikeouts. In 1999, the Rocket went to the New York Yankees and became one of the team's top starting pitchers He won the Cy Young award for the fifth time in 2001 and had the league's best winning percentage at .870 with a 20-3 won-lost record.

Mo Vaughn became the Red Sox's only star through most of the 1990s and, one may say, carried the team. In 1995, he won the American League's Most Valuable Player Award, batting .300 and leading the league in home runs,

39, and runs batted in, 126. In the eight years Mo played with the Red Sox, he served as a team leader and hit 230 home runs, 213 in his last six years with the team. Unable to agree with management on a new contract, Vaughn signed with the Anaheim Angels where he hit 69 home runs in 1999 and 2000. He was injured, out for the entire season in 2001, and signed to play with the New York Mets in 2002.

During this time the Red Sox as a team had three peaks. They won the Eastern division championship of the American League under manager Kevin Kennedy in 1995. However, in the division play-offs they lost, three games to none, to the Central division champions, the Cleveland Indians.

In 1998, under manager Jimy Williams, the Red Sox earned the American League "wild card" entry into the play-offs with the second-best record in the league, 92-70 (.568). However, they lost to the Cleveland Indians again in the first round of the play-offs, three games to one.

In 1999, the Red Sox again had a good year under manager Jimy Williams. The Red Sox finished second, four games behind the Yankees, but with their 94-68 won-lost record and .580 percentage won the wild-card spot in the American League. Though the Sox had lost 18 of their 19 previous postseason games, they won the American League Division Series from the Cleveland Indians, three games to two. They shellacked the Indians, 23-7, in Game 4 of the Series. The momentum did not carry into the American League Championship Series as the perennial nemesis, the New York Yankees, won the American League pennant from the Sox, four games to one. To add salt to the wound, Roger Clemens was on the Yankee pitching staff, but the Red Sox beat him and the Yankees in Game 3, 13 to 1. It was the high moment of the Series for the Red Sox.

The Red Sox competed well in the first few months in 2000 but then faded, and they dropped further back in 2001, though finishing in second place both times. The year 2001, after a good start, witnessed a good deal of internal dissension. Carl Everett, a slugging outfielder came over from the Houston Astros in 2000, along with some reputation for being a destabilizing influence in the clubhouse. Manager Jimy Williams and General Manger Dan Duquette had some friction, apparently partly over disciplining Everett. Jimy Williams was dismissed after 118 games, or approximately three quarters of the way through the season in 2001 and was replaced by coach Joe Kerrigan. The move was not popular with many Red Sox fans. There was additional ferment over the sale of the team, and a sale was finally approved by the baseball commissioner's office in early 2002. The Jean Yawkey Trust , under chief executive officer John L. Harrington, sold the Red Sox, Fenway Park and a large percentage of the New England Sports Network to a group headed by John Henry, the owner of the Florida Marlins and Tom Werner, former San Diego Padres owner. The announced price was $660 million, a record for a major league baseball team.Larry Lucchino was named president. Immediately assuming control of the club, the new management fired Dan Duquette and made an interior general manager's appointment. A few days later they removed Joe Kerrigan as field manager. Shortly thereafter, Grady Little was appointed Field Manager.

There were some bright spots on the horizon for the Red Sox, most notably two ballplayers who are Hall of Fame prospects. Nomar Garciaparra, the leader of the team, is a permanent fixture at shortstop. After five years, through 2000, he had a batting average of .333 and led the league in batting in 1999 and 2000. He also led the league in hits in 1997 and in his first full four seasons of play never had less than 190 hits a season. He was injured in 2001 and played in only 21 games. He was Rookie of the Year in 1997.

Pedro Martinez is considered by many to be the best pitcher in baseball at the present time. He came over to the Red Sox in 1998 after winning the Cy Young award in Montreal in 1997 with a 19-7 won-lost record. With the Red Sox, Pedro had a 23-4 won-lost record in 1999. He led the league in wins, in winning percentage at .852, in strikeouts with 313 and in earned run average at 2.07. He was an easy Cy Young winner in 1999 and also was named most valuable player in the 1999 All-Star game. He again won the Cy Young award in 2000 with an 18-6 won-lost season. He led the league with a remarkable 1.74 earned run average, giving almost two runs per game less than the second-ranking pitcher in this statistic, who was Roger Clemens of the Yankees. Martinez also led the league with 284 strikeouts in 2000. He was injured in the latter part of the season in 2001 and completed the year with only a 7-3 won-lost record in 18 games.

1986

The Red Sox, under manager John McNamara, finished first in the American League's East Division, 5$\frac{1}{2}$ games ahead of the Yankees. They beat the California Angels, four games to three, in the American League's Division Series. They lost the World Series to the New York Mets in seven games, four games to three.

Dominant Players
Wade Boggs won another one of his batting championships in 1986, with a .357 average. Boggs led the league

The Red Sox Encyclopedia

in bases on balls with Dwight Evans placing second. He was fourth in base hits with 207, Mattingly leading with 238. Boggs placed second in doubles behind Mattingly. Teammates Rice, Marty Barrett and Bill Buckner tied for third in doubles. Jim Rice had another good season, batting .324 with 20 home runs and 110 R.B.I.s. Dwight Evans, though batting only .259, had 26 homers and 97 runs batted in. Bill Buckner at first base batted in 102 runs and designated hitter Don Baylor had 31 home runs and 94 R.B.I.s. Jim Rice was fourth in batting behind Wade Boggs, the leader, Don Mattingly of the Yankees and Kirby Puckett of the Minnesota Twins. Mattingly challenged Boggs with a .352 average. Rice was fourth in runs batted in behind Joe Carter of Cleveland who led with 121, then Jose Canseco who was with Oakland, and then Don Mattingly of the Yankees.

Roger Clemens was the single star player of the team. He won both the Cy Young and Most Valuable Player awards. (He repeated with the Cy Young award again the following year.) He led the league with 24 victories, had a 24-4 record which gave him a league-leading percentage of .857, and he led the league in earned run average at 2.48. A fastball pitcher, he was second in strikeouts to Mark Langston of Seattle with 238. Clemens allowed the fewest hits per nine inning game, averaging 6.34.

Oil Can Boyd was second in Red Sox pitching with 16 wins and 10 losses, and Bruce Hurst was third with 13 wins and eight losses. Hurst tied for second in the league with four shutouts, while Jack Morris of Detroit led with six. Boyd, after Ron Guidry of the Yankees, gave the fewest walks per nine-inning game, 1.89. Hurst beat Clemens for second place in the league in strikeouts per nine-inning game. His average was 8.12 or nearly one an inning.

Both Clemens and Boggs also excelled in 1987. Clemens led the league with 20 wins and again won the Cy Young award. Boggs won another batting crown, batting .363.

1988

After a slow start John McNamara was replaced in mid-season as the Red Sox manager by Joe Morgan. The team immediately won 19 of the next 20 games. The Sox won the East division title in a close race. Detroit was one game behind, both the Milwaukee Brewers and Toronto Blue Jays were two games back and the Yankees were in fourth place, 3½ games off. Boston won with a low .549 average, winning 89 games and losing 73. They lost to the Oakland Athletics in the American League Division Series, four games to none.

The Red Sox led the league in batting average and were second to the Minnesota Twins in slugging. They were also second in fielding behind the Twins. Their pitchers led the league in both shutouts and strikeouts.

Dominant Players

Wade Boggs won another batting title, this time with a mark of .366. He was second behind Kirby Puckett in hits with 214, and he led the league with 125 walks. He also led in runs scored with 128 and in doubles, with 45. Mike Greenwell, who replaced Jim Rice in left field, was third in batting at .325. He hit 22 home runs and batted in 119 runs. He was fifth in the league in slugging and third in total bases. His runs batted in total was third, followed by Dwight Evans who had 111 and was fourth. Greenwell was also third in base hits, and fourth with eight triples. Evans had 21 home runs with his 111 runs batted in and his batting average was .293. Outfielder Ellis Burks was another strong hitter with a .294 batting average, 18 home runs and 92 runs batted in.

Catcher Rick Cerone had an error-free year in 84 games and fielded 1.000. He shared catching duties with Rich Gedman. Wade Boggs, initially erratic in his career at third base, had become a solid third baseman and led the league in putouts at his position.

Both Roger Clemens and Bruce Hurst won 18 games and ace reliever Lee Smith had 29 saves. Hurst was second in the league in winning percentage at 7.50 with an 18-6 record. Both he and Clemens tied for fourth in wins. Clemens, the fireballer, led the league in strikeouts with 291, and he tied for the lead in complete games, 14, with Dave Stewart of the Oakland Athletics. Clemens led the league with eight shutouts and he also had the most strikeouts per nine inning game, 9.92 or more than one an inning. He also was third in innings pitched.

1990

The Red Sox, under manager Joe Morgan, finished first in the American League's East division, two games ahead of the Toronto Blue Jays. They had a winning percentage of only .543 with 88 wins and 74 losses.

The Sox again lost to Oakland, four games to none, in the American League Championship Series. The Sox again led the league in team batting average at .272.

Dominant Players

Wade Boggs was the only .300 hitter among regular Red Sox players. He batted .302. Ellis Burks, who batted .296, had 21 homers and 89 runs batted in.

Tony Pena was a fine defensive catcher, leading the league in putouts and in number of fielding chances per game at 6.6.

Clemens was 21-6 and second in the league in winning percentage at .778. Clemens led in earned run average at 1.93. He was fourth in strikeouts at 209, with Nolan Ryan leading the league with 232. Clemens tied for the lead in shutouts with Dave Stewart of Oakland with four. Clemens was fourth in strikeouts per nine inning game at 8.24 and third in fewest walks per nine inning game at 2.13. Clemens had to wait another year, however, before winning his third Cy Young award. In 1991 he went 18-10 with a league-leading 2.62 E.R.A.

Mike Boddicker also had a fine year in 1990 with 17 wins and eight losses and he was fourth in winning percentage at .680. Jeff Reardon was now the Red Sox prime fireman and he had 21 saves.

1992

The Red Sox, under manager Butch Hobson, finished in last place in the American League's East Division. The team was 23 games behind the East division-leading Toronto Blue Jays. Boston was uncharacteristically next to last in the American League in team batting with a .246 average and was also next to last in team slugging. They tied for next to last place in team fielding in the League.

Negative Player Performances

None of the Sox, including some 16 position players and designated hitters, batted .300. No average was over .276. With the exception of right fielder Tom Brunansky who had 74 R.B.I.s and Mo Vaughn who had 57 R.B.I.s, no player had more than 50. Only Clemens had a good pitching record with 18 wins, 11 losses and a league-leading E.R.A. of 2.41. Jeff Reardon had 27 saves but also a 4.25 E.R.A.

The next year, Wade Boggs, who batted only .259, became a free agent and went to the New York Yankees where he had a rejuvenated career. Ellis Burks, who batted .255, signed on as a free agent with the White Sox and later established his batting power playing for the new National League entry, the Colorado Rockies. Tom Brunansky, who batted .266, signed as a free agent with the Milwaukee Brewers. Jack Clark, the power-packed designated hitter with a .210 batting average, ended his long 18-year career. Ace reliever Jeff Reardon had been traded late in the season to the Atlanta Braves.

The face of the Red Sox was changing, but in 1993 the Red Sox were still under .500 in winning percentage albeit moving up seven games to fifth place in the seven-team East division.

1995

In 1995, the Red Sox, with Kevin Kennedy replacing Butch Hobson as manager, won the East division championship. They won 86 and lost 58 for a .597 average.

The league was now divided into three divisions, the East, Central and West, and a playoff system was developed including the three division winners and the also-ran team in the league with the highest winning percentage. This team was called "the wildcard." The Red Sox won in a five-team East division by seven games over second-place New York. However, they were eliminated in the Division play-offs by the Central Division winner, Cleveland, three games to none.

Dominant Players

Mo Vaughn won the league's M.V.P. award. A slugger and a fine fielding first baseman., he batted .300, tied for fourth place with 39 home runs, and tied with slugger Albert Belle in leading the league in R.B.I.s with 126. John Valentin, then the shortstop, batted .298 and was fourth in the league with doubles. He had 27 home runs and

Knuckleballer Tim Wakefield led the Red Sox in pitching in 1995 with a 16-8 record and a 2.95 ERA. He had a career-high 17 wins in 1998. (Boston Red Sox)

The 1998 Boston Red Sox had the second-best record in the American League, 92-70, and advanced to the play-offs as the league's wild-card entry. (Boston Red Sox).

102 R.B.I.s Tim Naehring at third base batted .307 and right fielder Troy O'Leary batted .308. Jose Canseco, the DH batted .306, had 24 home runs and drove in 81 runs.

Vaughn at first base led the league at his position in double plays executed and in fielding chances per game at 9.9. Luis Alicea, the second baseman who came over from the St. Louis Cardinals this year, also led at his position in double plays executed and in fielding chances per game. John Valentin, the shortstop, led the league in assists at his position but he also led in errors.

Tim Wakefield, a knuckleballer, was the team's leading pitcher with 16 wins and eight losses and a 2.95 E.R.A. Erik Hanson had a 15-5 record and Roger Clemens, soon to leave the Red Sox and join the Toronto Blue Jays, won 10 and lost five. Wakefield was second in the league in earned run average, behind fireballing Randy Johnson of the Seattle Mariners. Hansen was second in winning percentage to Johnson with a .750 average. Tim Wakefield was tied for fourth place in complete games with seven and was third in giving the fewest hits per nine innings, 7.51. Rick Aguilera, who went from the Minnesota Twins to Boston during the season ranked third in number of saves, 32. He had a 2.60 earned run average.

1998

. . . .

The Red Sox, with a consistent winning team, were second only to the Yankees in winning percentage in the American League. However, in the race for the "wild card," things were intense. After the All-Star game, the Baltimore Orioles, who were a season-long disappointment, rallied with a winning streak that cut into the Red Sox' big lead. However, this challenge fizzled as the Orioles had yet another losing streak and did not bounce back enough to be close in the wild card race again. By mid-September there was another rekindling of competition for the wild card. The Toronto Blue Jays went on a winning streak, winning 13 of 15 games, while the Red Sox were losing nine of 11 games. The Red Sox had held a comfortable wild card lead since early in the season, mostly ranging from eight to 12 games ahead of any competition. In the three-week interval from late August to mid-September the Red Sox wild card lead dropped from nine games to three games over the Blue Jays. In the West division, in mid-September, the Rangers were in second place one game behind Anaheim. At that point, they were also in the running for the wild card spot, 4$^1/_2$ games behind the Red Sox. The feeling of deja vu subsided, however, as the Red Sox started to win again and finally clinched the wild card spot three days before the season ended. The Blue Jays never came closer than three games away from the lead and the Angels, who lost the West division to the Rangers, were further back.

The crowds at Fenway Park were large, enthusiastic and loyal, due in part the to the Red Sox being in contention for the play-offs the entire season. It might be noted that on August 30 the large crowd sang "Happy Birthday"

to Ted Williams on his eightieth birthday, televised to his home in Florida. This
was an emotional high moment.

At the end of the season, Mo Vaughn provided the excitement as he challenged the 40-home run mark and
battled Bernie Williams of the Yankees for the American
League batting championship. The most notable low moments had to do with the well-publicized running conflict between team star Mo Vaughn and the Boston front
office. The Red Sox had signed their newest star, Nomar
Garciaparra, to a long-term, multimillion dollar contract
but they did not make an offer acceptable to Vaughn during the season. Vaughn was on schedule to become a free
agent shortly after the season ended. There was much re-
crimination between Vaughn and the Red Sox management, though popular Mo continued to play well and the
matter was ultimately held in abeyance by both parties
until the season was concluded.

Although the Red Sox ended the 1998 season on a
down note, losing in the first round of the playoffs three

*The entire Red Sox starting outfield batted better than .275 in 1998,
including Darren Bragg, who led the group in batting average at .279.
(Boston Red Sox).*

games to one to the Cleveland Indians, they did finish the
season as the second-best team in the American League.
Their 92-70 record was fourteen games better than in
1997, a down year. The promise for the future was their
four superstars, shortstop Nomar Garciaparra, pitcher
Pedro Martinez, reliever Tom Gordon and, if the Red Sox
come to terms with him, team leader Mo Vaughn at first
base. Another jewel in the firmament for 1999 is the
All-Star game, which will be played for the third time in
history at Fenway Park.

Dominant Players

The Red Sox had a number of players with notable achievement in 1998. Pedro Martinez had a fine year, comparable to his Cy Young year at Montreal in 1997, after joining the team as a free agent. He won 19 games and lost
only seven, had an earned run average of 2.89, struck out
251 batters in 234 innings, and was the team's mound
ace. Toward the end of the season he was in competition
for the Cy Young award in the American League with four
other pitchers—David Cohn of the New York Yankees, Rick
Helling of Texas, David "Boomer" Wells of the Yankees
and Roger Clemens again, who was seeking his fifth Cy
Young award, his second with Toronto.

The Red Sox pitching staff offered good support to back
up Martinez. Bret Saberhagen, making it back from the
early 1990s when he had great years with the Kansas City
Royals, won 15 and lost eight for a winning percentage of
.652. Tim Wakefield, the knuckle-ball pitcher, bounced
back from a losing season with a good year. He topped his
previous major league high in wins with a 17-8 record
and a winning percentage of .680. The bullpen had a spectacular closer, Tom "Flash" Gordon. Gordon set the mayjor
league record for consecutive saves at 43. He ended the
season, with 46 saves, a Red Sox record, in 47 attempts.

Of historical note, Dennis Eckersley set a career record
for most games as a pitcher, 1,071.

The Red Sox stars, Vaughn and Garciaparra, had their
hoped for and expected superlative years.

Vaughn, one of the league's leading sluggers and leading first basemen, had a season-ending batting average of
.337 with 40 home runs and 115 runs batted in. Mo played
his usual competent first base and was a team leader, notwithstanding his disaffection with the Red Sox management. He moved up in the Red Sox record book to fifth
place in number of home runs hit by a Red Sox player in
his Red Sox career. Mo earned consideration for Most Valuable Player award again.

Garciaparra, suffering no "sophomore jinx," repeated
his 1997 performance as Rookie of the Year. He batted

.323, had 35 home runs and drove in 122. Vaughn, who batted third in the line-up, and Garciaparra, who batted in the clean-up position, were a potent batting and slugging combination.

Both Vaughn and Garciaparra batted over .320, hit 35 or more home runs and drove in 115 or more runs. They competed for the batting title a good part of the year and into September with Bernie Williams and Derek Jeter of the Yankees. With three games to go in the season Vaughn and Williams were tied for the batting championship at .334. On the last day Mo hit 2 for 4 and Bernie batted 2 for 2. Williams won the batting championship at .339 and Vaughn came in second at .337 The Red Sox outfield, notably the regulars, all batted around .275. Darren Lewis was a fine-fielding centerfielder, supported on either side in the outfield by Troy O'Leary and Darren Bragg.

1999
. . . .

The Red Sox "wild card" team of 1999 was two games better than the 1998 "wild card" team. They won 94 and lost 68 games. They trailed the Yankees, who were in first place most of the season, but this time the New York team did not have the phenomenal won-lost record they had the previous year. The Sox trailed the Yankees by 22 games in 1998. In 1999, they were within two games of the Bronx Bombers in mid-September but then lost some ground and ended the season four games out of first place. The Red Sox were comfortably in the lead for the "wild card" position most of the season. Toronto in the East division and Oakland in the West offered some challenge but were not really close.

The Red Sox season began with some somber notes, and early in the year their line-up suffered some severe setbacks. Mo Vaughn could not come to an understanding with the Red Sox management, and he signed as a free agent with the Anaheim Angels. Red Sox fans were in an angry mood, mostly directed at general manager Dan Duquette. Duquette had let peerless pitcher Roger Clemens sign with Toronto, where he won the Cy Young award in 1997 and 1998. The error ran to insult as Clemens opted to sign with the arch-rival New York Yankees for the 1999 season. Shades of Harry Frazee! The fans' torment and anger at Duquette were all the greater when the Red Sox did not sign their leader and big slugger, Mo Vaughn, and let him move on to Anaheim.

Though the Red Sox had a good start and were in first place briefly at early times in the season, two key players suffered long-term injuries. John Valentin, their steady and good-hitting third baseman, was lost to the team a good part of the season as was the pitching corps' star closer, Tom "Flash" Gordon. Duquette indicated the intention of acquiring another star slugger, but this never happened. Duquette was more confident about the team than were the fans. He felt the farm system would produce good players, and, with adroit acquisitions and especially competent if not exceptional field managing, the Red Sox would do all right.

Dominant Players

Duquette appeared to be prophetic in 1999. Reduced to its most essential terms, the 1999 team was at least superficially like the 1967 champions, with two outstanding stars carrying the team, a good complement of others and some fine field managing. In 1967, Carl Yastrzemski had a Triple Crown year and Jim Longborg was the Cy Young winner. None of the other players approached the exceptional performance. Dick Williams, as the first-year field manager, provided inspired leadership. In 1999, it was Pedro Martinez who had a superlative pitching year, winning 23 and losing four, and winning the Cy Young award for the second time. He had previously won in 1997 while pitching for the Montreal Expos in the National League. Martinez was the dominant pitcher in baseball in 1999. He had 313 strikeouts and Chuck Finley was next highest in the league with 200. He had an earned run average of 2.07, followed by David Cone at 3.44. Martinez's record alone accounted for much of the difference between a good winning season for the Red Sox and a season in which they would be a .500 team.

Nomar Garciaparra, now in his third full season with the Red Sox, had a banner year and solidified a reputation as one of the game's superstars. This year, in contrast to 1998, Garciaparra won the batting championship, beating out his Yankee rivals Derek Jeter and Bernie Williams. Garciaparra batted .357, including 42 doubles.

The Red Sox jelled for most of the 1999 season behind the adroit managing of Jimy Williams, named the "Manager of the Year" in the American League. They performed well in the postseason play, winning the A.L. Division Series against the Cleveland Indians, and then lost a tight A.L.C.S. for the pennant against the New York Yankees.

A jewel in the Red Sox year was the All-Star game, played for the third time at Fenway Park. The American League won, and the star performer and Most Valuable Player was Pedro Martinez of the Sox. He started and won the game, striking out five of the six batters he faced.

2000

The Red Sox competed well in 2000, vying for first place the first three and one half months of the season with the New York Yankees but then ending in second place two and one half games behind with a 85-77 won-lost record and a .512 winning percentage. The result was not good enough to win the wild-card spot in the playoffs, which went to the Seattle Mariners who finished one-half game out of first place, behind Oakland, with a .562 winning percentage. The team lost offensive power, placing next to last in slugging percentage at .423 and next to last in stolen bases at 43. The height of futility occurred on June 29, 2000, when the Red Sox lost to the Yankees, 22-1, in the most lopsided home loss ever. As Boston catcher Jason Varitek said, "It was embarrassing."

Dominant Players

The Red Sox were now well into their two-men tandem of great stars. Nomar Garciaparra led the league in batting at .372 and he also led in doubles with 51. He drove in 96 runs with his 197 hits. Pedro Martinez again won the Cy Young award with an 18-6 won-lost record, a spectacular 1.74 earned run average that led the league, and also a league-leading 284 strikeouts. He led the league in averaging only 5.31 hits per game. Pedro's 1.74 ERA was far ahead of the second best starter in the league, Clemens at 3.70. On August 29, he appeared to be on the way to his first American League no-hitter. The Tampa Bay Devil Rays did not get a hit until the ninth inning as Pedro threw 96 m.p.h. fastballs and sharp off-speed pitches. He struck out 13 in a one-hit, 8-0 win. Martinez had pitched a no-hitter for Montreal in 1997 for nine innings. He gave up a hit in the 10th inning and gave way to a relief pitcher, but the Expos won the game, a one-hitter, 1-0. Derek Lowe also was a high level performer for the Red Sox. He led the league in relief pitching with 42 saves. He had a 2.56 ERA and for the second straight year relieved in 74 games.

2001

The 2001 Red Sox year was not distinguished. The team finished in second place, 13 1/2 games behind the Yankees. They won 82 and lost 79 for a .509 winning percentage. They lost the season series to the Yankees, 13 games to five. The team batting average was .266, approximately the same as in 2000. Seattle led the league at .288. The team earned run average was 4.15, fourth in the league. Nomar Garciaparra was injured and did not play most of the season. Pedro Martinez was also injured late in the season and pitched in only 18 games. Jimy Williams was replaced as manager by coach Joe Kerrigan, after managing for 118 games. The Red Sox were only two games behind in the "wild card" race when Williams left but finished the season 19 1/2 games behind. This was the culmination of a season of some tensions and bickering in the clubhouse that produced a dismal and dispiriting outcome.

Dominant Players

Manny Ramirez, a Cleveland Indians slugging outfielder who had hit 30 or more home runs in a five of the previous six years, joined the Red Sox as a prospective outfield star and one of the Red Sox leading players. In 2001, he batted .306 and had 41 home runs that tied him for fourth in the league. He was also fourth in RBIs with 125, and fourth in slugging percentage at .609. A feared hitter, he was walked intentionally a league leading 25 times. Hideo Nomo, a veteran pitcher who came to the Red Sox in 2001 from the Detroit Tigers, had an inconsistent season. He won 13 and lost 10 with a 4.50 earned run average, but he pitched a no-hitter and a one-hitter for the Red Sox. He led the league in strikeouts with 220, but also led in bases on balls with 96.

The Red Sox Encyclopedia

ROBINSON & CARRIGAN   4D12-4

Managers Wilbert Robinson of Brooklyn (left) and Bill Carrigan of Boston greet each other before a 1916 World Series game. (Baseball Hall of Fame Library. Cooperstown, N.Y.).

WORLD SERIES,
LEAGUE CHAMPIONSHIPS
AND DIVISION PLAY-OFFS

Except for two droughts, from 1919 to 1946 and from 1947 to 1967, the Red Sox have been active in postseason play. They have played in nine World Series. They won the first five Series in the first two decades of their existence, 1901 to 1920. They lost the last four Series, each by four games to three, after World War II.

Since 1969, when the league was divided into two divisions, the East and the West, because of league expansion from ten to twelve teams, the Red Sox have played for the pennant in five American League Championship Series. They won the first two, in 1975 and 1986, and went on to the World Series. They lost the last three ALCS in which they participated, in 1988 and 1990 and 1999. They also won a pennant in 1904, when there was no World Series.

With the advent of three divisions, East, Central and West, because the league now had fourteen teams, the division play-offs were instituted. The three division winners and a "wild card," drawn from the team in the league with the best second-place record, engaged in an elimination to determine who would play for the American League pennant.

The Red Sox played in the division play-offs in the first year, 1995, and lost, as well as lost again in 1998. They won in 1999.

In all, the Sox have won five World Series, ten pennants and they have played in six additional pennant play-off series.

1903

Dinneen And Phillippe Pitching Stars In First World Series

After intense competition between the fledgling American League and the National League for player talent, Pittsburgh Pirate owner Barney Dreyfuss and Red Sox owner Henry Killilea decided to bury the hatchet and conduct a play-off for "the world championship".

The Boston Pilgrims hosted the first World Series in 1903 at the Huntington Avenue Grounds. The Pilgrims beat the Pittsburgh Pirates to win the title. (Baseball Hall of Fame Library, Cooperstown, N.Y.).

Pittsburgh had just won its third straight National League pennant and had an array of fine talent. They had the great Honus Wagner at shortstop who won the league batting championship with a .355 average. Ginger Beaumont, the Pirate center fielder had a great year. He had over 200 hits and led the league in both hits and runs scored. The Pirates had two of the National League's finest pitchers, Sam Leever and Deacon Phillippe. Leever had a 25-7 record and led the league with a 2.06 earned run average. Phillippe was 25-9.

The Pilgrims, in their third year of existence, easily won the pennant, leading the second-place Philadelphia Athletics by 14½ games.

The Pilgrims had two hitting stars, Patsy Dougherty in left field who led the league with 195 hits and 107 runs scored, and slugging right fielder Buck Freeman who led the A.L. in home runs, with 13, in runs batted in with 104, and in total base average, .281.

The Pilgrims had the incomparable Cy Young pitching. Young led the league in wins, with 28, in innings pitched and in complete games. His re-cord was 28-9. The Pilgrims had two other 20-game winners, Bill Dinneen at 21-13 and Long Tom Hughes at 21-7.

The Pirates, though favored to win the best-of-nine series, were handicapped with serious injuries to two of their stars, shortstop Honus Wagner and pitcher Sam Leever. They also lost pitcher Ed Doheny to illness. As a consequence, iron man Deacon Phillippe ended up pitching five complete games for the Pirates, aided only by some travel days and weather postponements. Deacon won all three games captured by the Pirates in the Series. The injured Wagner batted only .222 in the series and had only one hit in the last four games. Manager Fred Clarke, the team's star left fielder and later Hall of Famer, managed to drive in only two runs in 34 at bats.

The Red Sox fared better. Bill Dinneen and Cy Young pitched 69 of the 71 innings in which the Red Sox were in the field. Dinneen, especially, had a successful series. Dinneen started and won three games and lost one. In the first Pilgrim win, in the second game, Dinneen pitched a 3-0 shutout. Dinneen also pitched a shutout in the eighth and decisive game, winning 3-0. Patsy Dougherty was the hitting star of the series with the only two home runs collected by the Pilgrims and he also hit two triples.

The Pirates won the first game, 7-3, starting off with four runs in the first inning off Cy Young. The first home run of the series was hit by the Pirates' outfielder Jimmy Sebring, who drove in a total of four runs.

The second game was the first Pilgrims win with Bill Dinneen pitching his first 3-0 shutout. Patsy Dougherty was the hitting star with three hits and two home runs. Buck Freeman also had two hits and drove in the other run. This was the second game played at Huntington Avenue Grounds in Boston. The Pilgrims drew over 16,000 fans to the first game but, after the loss to the Pirates, they drew only 9,400 in the second game. However, after the Pilgrims' win they bounced back with nearly 19,000 fans in the third game.

Game 3 was a Pirate win as Phillippe pitched a four-hitter, 4-2. The Pirates, with Phillippe pitching, also won Game 4, 5-4, though the Pilgrims came back with three runs in the ninth inning. Honus Wagner led all hitters with three hits in this game. The Pirates now held a 3-to-1 lead in games and the next three games were scheduled to be played in Pittsburgh.

Cy Young won Game 5 easily, 11-2. The Pilgrims had five triples in the game, two of which were hit by Patsy Dougherty.

Bill Dinneen came back and won Game 6 over Sam Leever, 6-3. Game 7 was now the pivotal game, with the Series tied at three games each.

The Record

1903	Red Sox beat the Pittsburgh Pirates in the World Series, five games to three.
1904	Red Sox win pennant but there is no World Series.
1912	Red Sox win World Series from New York Giants, four games to three.
1915	Red Sox beat Philadelphia Phillies in the World Series, four games to one.
1916	Red Sox win World Series, four games to one from Brooklyn Robins.
1918	Red Sox beat Chicago Cubs in World Series, four games to two.
1946	Red Sox win pennant but lose World Series to St. Louis Cardinals, four games to three.
1967	Red Sox pennant winners but St. Louis Cardinals win World Series, four games to three.
1975	Red Sox beat Oakland Athletics, three games to 0, and win American League Championship Series and A.L. pennant.
1975	Cincinnati Reds beat Red Sox in World Series, four games to three.
1986	Red Sox defeat California Angels, four games to win A.L. pennant, but lose World Series to New York Mets, four games to three.
1988	Oakland Athletics win over Boston Red Sox, four games to 0 in American League Championship Series.
1990	Oakland Athletics beat Boston Red Sox, four games to 0, in American League Championship Series.
1995	Cleveland Indians beat Boston Red Sox, three games to 0, in divisional play-offs.
1998	Cleveland Indians beat Boston Red Sox, three games to one, in divisional play-offs.
1999	Red Sox beat Cleveland Indians, three games to two, in divisional play-offs.
1999	Red Sox lose to New York Yankees, four games to one, in American League Championship Series.

The Pirates had men on base in every inning of Game 7 but Cy Young scattered 10 hits to win for the Pilgrims, 7-3. Jimmy Collins, the third baseman/manager for the Pilgrims and Chick Stahl, the centerfielder, each had scoring triples off Phillippe to start the Pilgrims off with a 2-0 lead. The game was marred by the seven errors committed by the two teams.

Game 8 in Boston before only 7,500 fans, was a match-up between Bill Dinneen and a tired Deacon Phillippe. Dinneen pitched a four-hitter to win the championship for the Boston Pilgrims, five games to three. The game was decided in the fourth inning, when the Pilgrims scored two runs and they then added a run in the sixth. The shaky Pirates made three errors. Both Dinneen and Phillippe won three games in the series.

Chick Stahl led the Red Sox hitters with a .303 batting average. Jimmy Sebring was the hitting star for the Pirates. He led both teams with 11 hits and a .367 batting average.

The only home runs in the Series were hit by Patsy Dougherty, who had two in the second game, and Jimmy Sebring who hit the first Series home run ever. The redoubtable but under-the-weather Honus Wagner, who used a fielding glove that barely covered his hand, had six errors in the Series.

Manager Jimmy Collins raises the flag to celebrate the Boston Pilgrims winning the first world championship in 1903. (Boston Public Library, Print Department).

1904

Red Sox Win Pennant But McGraw Refuses To Play A.L. Winner

The Red Sox won the American League pennant by a game and a half over the New York Highlanders (the next year to be renamed the New York Yankees). The Red Sox had three 20-game winners, Cy Young at 26-16, with a 1.97 earned run average, Bill Dinneen at 23-14, and Jesse Tannehill at 21-11. There were no .300 hitters among the regulars but centerfielder Chick Stahl led with a .295 average. Buck Freeman led the team with seven home runs, and they had fine fielding from Candy LaChance, perhaps the best-fielding first baseman in the league.

The New York Giants in the more established National League, still led by the legendary John McGraw, won the pennant by 13 games over the Chicago Cubs. The team won 106 games and lost 47 for a .693 winning percentage. The Giants had Iron Man Joe McGinnity who pitched 408 innings in 51 games. He won 35 games, with a 35-8 record and a 1.61 earned run average. Christy Mathewson, hardly outdone, had a 33-12 record and Dummy Taylor was at 21-15. McGinnity and Mathewson were the pitchers with the best winning record in the National League. In the era of the "dead ball" there were no .300 hitters among the Giants regulars. The team's new shortstop, Bill Dahlen, was the league's leading R.B.I. man with 80 runs driven in. Dan McGann, first baseman, had the team's most homers at six.

McGraw, with a vaunted team and an established league, did not want to repeat the error of 1903 by playing the upstart American League, and worse, running the risk of lost prestige in losing to them again. McGraw, despite entreaties, refused to play the American League winner in a championship series. This was the one and only time this would happen as the owners in the two leagues came together and decided that henceforth, beginning in 1905, the two league winners would get together and play for "the world's championship."

1912

Snodgrass Muff Marks World Series As Red Sox Beat Giants, Four Games To Three

The 1912 World Series is considered by many to be one of the great World Series of all time. The Red Sox won 105 games, setting a record and had a 105-47 season with a .691 winning percentage. They finished 14 games ahead of the Washington Nationals in second place. This was Smoky Joe Wood's career year. He won 34 and lost five for an .872 winning record that included ten shutouts. For this year, at least, he may have been better than the great Walter Johnson, pitching for the Washington Nationals, though Johnson himself had a 33-12 record and led the league with a 1.39 E.R.A. The Red Sox had two other 20-game winners, Buck O'Brien at 20-13 and Hugh Bedient at 20-9. Tris Speaker batted .383, though he lost the league's batting championship to Ty Cobb's .410. Speaker did lead the league with 10 home runs and his sparkling outfield play. Duffy Lewis, the left fielder, led the team with a 109 runs batted in, followed by Speaker with 98. Larry Gardner, the third baseman, batted .315 and Jake Stahl, managing and playing first base, batted .301.

The Giants had another vintage John McGraw team and won the pennant over the second-place Pirates by ten games. The Giants also had a sparkling winning percentage, .682, with 103 wins and 48 losses. Christy Mathewson was the pitching workhorse with 310 innings pitched and a won-lost record of 23-12 with a 2.12 earned run av-

Reporters filed their stories from the Polo Grounds by telegraph during the 1912 World Series between the Red Sox and Giants. (Baseball Hall of Fame Library, Cooperstown, N.Y.).

erage. Rube Marquard had a 26-11 record and at one point won 19 straight games.

First baseman Fred Merkle and second baseman Larry Doyle were at or near the top in batting average or power hitting. Merkle batted .304, had 11 homers and 84 runs batted in. Doyle batted .330 with ten home runs and 90 runs batted in. Chief Meyers, the catcher, led the team in hitting with a .358 average and was second in the league. Fred Snodgrass played left field.

The World Series was actually an eight game affair because Game 2 had to be replayed. After 11 innings in Game 2, the score was tied, 6-6, and the game was called on account of darkness.

Joe Wood of the Red Sox beat the Giants at the Polo Grounds in New York in the first game of the Series, in front of almost 36,000 spectators. Wood won three games in the Series. In Game 1, he gave up six hits but had 11 strikeouts. Game 2, the tie game, would have been a Giant win but for five Giant errors that led to four unearned runs by Boston. The Giants overcame a 4-2 deficit with three runs in the top of the eighth but the Red Sox tied the game. The Giants went ahead again in the tenth in-

ning, 6-5, but Tris Speaker hit a long triple in the bottom of the tenth and scored on the play when the Giants' catcher dropped the ball. Christy Mathewson pitched all the way for the Giants, but it was not one of his better games and was a no-decision.

The Giants, behind Marquard, won Game 3, 2 to 1. Outfielder Hugh Devore saved the game for the Giants in the ninth inning with a two-on, two-out running catch. Buck O'Brien pitched eight good innings for the Red Sox and lost. Game 4 was Smoky Joe Wood's second victory in the Series. He beat the Giants, 3 to 1, giving nine hits but striking out eight. In Game 5, Hugh Bedient out-dueled Christy Mathewson, 2-1, as Mathewson had hard luck throughout the Series and failed to win a game. Mathewson gave back to back triples to outfielder Harry Hooper and second baseman Steve Yerkes, followed by an error, which resulted in the two runs for the Red Sox. After that, Mathewson retired 17 batters in a row but Bedient pitched a 3-hitter for the Sox.

In Game 6, with the Red Sox now leading in the Series three games to one and needing one more win, the Giants took charge quickly. They scored five runs in the first in-

The 1912 Red Sox beat John McGraw's New York Giants to win the World Series. (Boston Public Library, Print Department).

The Red Sox Encyclopedia

ning and blasted Red Sox pitcher Buck O'Brien. The Giants, behind Marquard who was pitching his second victory, won easily, 5-2. The Giants again teed off on Red Sox pitching in Game 7. They scored six runs in the first inning off Joe Wood and won easily 11-4, on 16 hits. The World Series was now tied at three games all.

Game 8, played at Fenway Park in its first season, was the climactic game and 17,600 were in attendance. This was one of the great games in baseball history and is described in greater detail in Chapter Three. The Giants led 1-0 until the Red Sox tied the game in the seventh inning. The Giants scored what appeared to be the winning run in the tenth inning but the Red Sox won the game in the

bottom of the tenth when Snodgrass dropped a pop fly and Merkle let a foul ball drop. The Red Sox won the World Series, four games to three.

The Giants outhit the Red Sox in the Series, .270 to .220, a 50-point margin. Their pitchers had a 1.83 earned run average compared to the Red Sox 2.68. This was the second of three straight years in which the Giants won the National League pennant and lost the World Series. The loss to the Red Sox in 1912 was sandwiched in between two losses to the Philadelphia Athletics. The Athletics were expected to win in 1912 but they finished the pennant race in third place, upset by the Red Sox who had a phenomenal year.

1915
Red Sox Win Series On Three 2-1 Games And Hooper's Homers

The Red Sox had a fine season in 1915, winning the pennant with a 101-50 record and a winning percentage of .669. They won over the Detroit Tigers by 2½ games despite Ty Cobb's heroics. Cobb won his ninth straight batting title and stole a record 96 bases. The Red Sox had outstanding pitching with five pitchers winning 15 or more games. Rube Foster and Ernie Shore led, each with a 19-8 record and Shore with a 1.64 earned run average. Babe Ruth, in his first full season, had an 18-

8 record. Dutch Leonard won 15 and lost seven, and Smoky Joe Wood won 15, lost five and led the league with a 1.49 earned run average. Carl Mays contributed, too, with a league-leading seven saves. It was truly a pitchers' year for Boston. The team E.R.A. was 2.39, second behind the Washington Nationals' league-leading 2.31.

The Red Sox regular players were led by Tris Speaker, who would be traded to Cleveland the following year. Speaker batted .322, fourth in the league. He had his usual

Boston played Philadelphia in the World Series for the second consecutive year in 1915, winning the first of three championships in a four-year period. (Baseball Hall of Fame Library, Cooperstown, N.Y.).

superlative year out in the field and led the league at his position in putouts and double plays executed. Pitcher Babe Ruth batted .315 and, in only 92 at bats, led the team in home runs with four. Duffy Lewis had a good year, batting .291, and so did first baseman Dick Hoblitzell who batted .283.

The Phillies, pennant winners by seven games over the Boston Braves, had the dominant pitcher in baseball in 1915, Grover Cleveland "Pete" Alexander. Alexander won 31 games, the first of three consecutive years in which he won 30 or more games. His record was 31-10 and he led the league with a sparkling 1.22 earned run average. He pitched four one-hitters. Supporting Alexander was Gavvy Cravath, the slugging right fielder. Cravath batted .285 and led the league with a major league-record 24 home runs and 115 runs batted in.

The World Series of 1915 was marked by three unusual occurrences. It was the second straight year in which Boston played Philadelphia for the world championship. However, in 1914 it was Boston's "Miracle Braves" who came from last place in mid-July to first place to easily beat the Giants for the National League pennant. The Braves played Connie Mack's Philadelphia Athletics, who had won three of the previous four World Series, and shut them out four games to none. Ironically, the Red Sox in 1915 played the World Series in Braves Field, which was more spacious than Fenway Park, and drew over 40,000 in each of the games played in Boston. A signal event that began a long tradition of World Series appearances for U.S. presidents was the attendance of President Woodrow Wilson at the second game of the Series in Baker Field, Philadelphia.

The first game of the World Series was won by "Pete" Alexander who scattered eight hits in winning 3-1. Babe

Ruth, in his only appearance in this World Series, came in as a pinch hitter in the ninth inning. Ruth, who led the team with four home runs and could have tied the game with a homer, grounded out, followed by Harry Hooper's pop-up that ended the game.

The Red Sox then proceeded to win the next three games by identical scores of 2 to 1. These pitching masterpieces were pitched consecutively by Rube Foster, who allowed three hits, Dutch Leonard, who also pitched a 3-hitter, and Ernie Shore, who gave up eight hits. Foster, in his game, faced only 30 batters, and Leonard retired the last 20 batters he faced.

Game 5, the concluding game played in Philadelphia, was an exciting affair. The Red Sox were leading, three games to one, and Rube Foster was on the mound again for the Red Sox against Erskine Mayer who for the second straight year had won 21 games for the Phillies. The Phillies scored two runs in the first inning, were leading at 4-2 by the end of the fourth, and carried this lead into the eighth inning. In the eighth, Duffy Lewis, who had doubled in the game winning run in the fourth game, hit a game-tying two-run homer. With the score standing at 4-4, Harry Hooper hit his second home run of the game in the ninth inning, winning both the game and the Series for the Red Sox.

The 1915 World Series was truly a pitchers' series. The pitchers' earned run average for the Red Sox was a collective 1.84, and for the Phillies it was 2.06. Leonard, in his one game, sparkled with a 1.00 E.R.A. For the Phillies, Alexander, who won the first game 3-1, and lost the third to Leonard, 2-1, led his team with a 1.53 E.R.A.

Duffy Lewis batted .444 with eight hits, leading the regulars, and Harry Hooper, at .350 had two home runs. Speaker had a relatively quiet .294 batting average.

1916

Red Sox Beat Robins, Four Games To One, As Babe Ruth Wins 14-Inning Pitching Duel

The Red Sox, in 1916, won a close pennant race over the Chicago White Sox, whom they beat by two games, and the Detroit Tigers, who were four games behind. The Red Sox had a fine pitching staff led by left-hander Babe Ruth who won 23 and lost 12 and led the league with a 2.12 earned run average. Dutch Leonard and Carl Mays each won 18 games, Ernie Shore won 16 and Rube Foster won 14. Third baseman Larry Gardner

was the team's leading hitter at .308. The Red Sox were a fine fielding team, leading the league in fielding, and Everett "Deacon" Scott continued his fielding mastery by leading all league shortstops in fielding average.

The Brooklyn Robins had not won a pennant since 1900, and it would be 25 years, 1941, before the renamed Brooklyn Dodgers won another. The Robins won by two and one-half games over the Phillies and by four over the

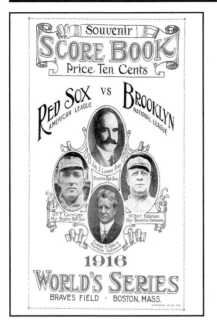

A 1916 World Series program cover. The Red Sox beat the Brooklyn Robins (Dodgers) to win the championship. (Boston Red Sox).

salary dispute—and after the season the infamous Harry Frazee purchased the Red Sox for the sum of $675,000.

The Red Sox again played the Series at Braves Field, drawing nearly 40,000 fans in each of the three games played there. In Game 1, Marquard of the Robins and Ernie Shore of the Red Sox were in a pitching duel for six innings with the Red Sox leading, 2-1. The Red Sox scored three runs in the seventh inning and once in the eighth and then held off the Robins in the ninth to win the game 6-5. Game 2 was a masterpiece. Babe Ruth was hit for an inside-the-park home run in the first inning and then drove in the tying run on a ground out in the third. The score remained at 1-1 until the 14th inning as Ruth and Sherry Smith of the Robins dueled one another. Both pitchers went all the way as the Red Sox won in the 14th inning, 2 to 1. Ruth still holds the record for pitching the longest complete game in World Series history.

Game 3 was won by the Robins, 4-3, as Jack Coombs started and won but was supported by reliever Jeff Pfeffer who retired all eight batters he faced. Dutch Leonard won Game 4 for the Red Sox, 6-2, as Larry Gardner got the Red Sox scoring started with a three-run home run. The Red Sox now led, three games to one.

Ernie Shore won Game 5 handily, beating the Robins, 4-1, on a three-hitter. Shore was the only pitcher in the Series with two wins as he won both the first and last games.

The leading hitter of the Series was right fielder Casey Stengel of the Robins, he of New York Yankees and New York Mets managerial fame. Stengel batted .364. The leading Red Sox hitter was Duffy Lewis at .353. Larry Gardner led with two home runs in the Series. Ernie Shore's two pitching wins were accompanied by a 1.53 earned run average. Ruth, of course, had an 0.64 earned run average because of his 14 inning 2-1 win, the only Series game in which he pitched.

Boston Braves. Jeff Pfeffer won 25 games for the Robins and the pitching staff also included Rube Marquard, who was a star for the New York Giants, and Jack Coombs, who was a pitching ace for the Philadelphia Athletics. Left fielder Zack Wheat hit .312, drove nine home runs and was the league's leading slugger with a .461 average. Jake Daubert, first baseman, was second in the league in batting with a .316 average.

The Dodgers were led by Wilbert Robinson, later called "Uncle Wilbert", and Bill "Rough" Carrigan was trying to win his second straight world championship as manager of the Red Sox. The year was notable in that the Red Sox were without Tris Speaker for the first time since 1909—he had been traded to the Cleveland Indians because of a

1918

Ruth And Mays Pitch All Four Red Sox Wins As Team Beats Cubs In World Series

The 1918 baseball season was shortened to less than 130 games for each team because of World War I. The World Series was played in early September. All teams lost key players to the military. The Red Sox under manager Ed Barrow, who later became general manager and president of the dynastic New York Yankees, bested the Cleveland Indians for the pennant by two and one-half games and won by four over the third-place Washington Nationals. Babe Ruth was the story literally from beginning to end. He won the first game of the season over the Athletics, 7 to 1, and he pitched the Sox pennant-clinching game over the A's, 6-1. In between, Ruth won 11 other games for a 13-7 record in a season in which he was part-time pitcher, and part-time left fielder leading the league with 11 home runs. Because of his part-time status as a pitcher, Ruth was surpassed by Carl Mays who had a 21-13 record, and Sam Jones had 16 wins, Joe Bush 15 and Dutch Leonard eight. All five of this masterful pitching staff had earned run averages between 2.11 and 2.72. As a regular player, Ruth, besides leading the league in home runs, led the Red Sox in batting with a .300 average and in R.B.I.s with 66.

The Chicago Cubs easily won the National League pennant by 10½ games over the New York Giants. Their outstanding player was pitcher Hippo Vaughn who led the league in wins with a 22-10 record. He was a workhorse with 290 innings pitched and he led the league with 148 strikeouts. He was the league's leading pitcher in terms of earned run average, 1.74. The Cubs, like the Red Sox, had a fine pitching staff. In addition to Vaughn, they had two nineteen game winners, Claude Hendrix and Lefty Tyler.

The Red Sox World Series story in 1918 was all Babe Ruth and Carl Mays. Ruth won the first game, 1-0, and the fourth game, 3-2. Mays won both of the games he pitched, including the championship clincher, by scores of 2-1. Hippo Vaughn pitched heroically for the Chicago Cubs, though he only won one and lost two. Vaughn lost the first game to Ruth, 1-0, as both pitchers allowed a total of 11 singles. Vaughn was also the hard luck loser in Game 3, losing to Carl Mays, 2 to 1. Vaughn finally won the fifth game of the Series pitching a shutout against Sam Jones and winning, 3 to 1.

There was little offense in the 1918 World Series. The winning Red Sox had a team batting average of .186. The Cubs, who won two games in the six game Series, had a team batting average of .210. There were no home runs by either team.

The Red Sox pitchers cumulatively had an earned run average of 1.70. The Cubs pitchers were even sharper with an earned run average of 1.04. Both Mays of the Red Sox and Vaughn of the Cubs had 1.00 E.R.A.'s, followed by Ruth at 1.06.

Though no other Red Sox player hit over .250, catcher Wally Schang had four singles in nine at bats and batted .444. For the Cubs, second baseman Charlie Pick led all hitters by more than 100 points and batted .389. Perhaps the most notable enduring mark in the World Series was Babe Ruth's accumulation of 29⅔ consecutive scoreless innings pitched, a record that would stand until Whitey Ford of the Yankees broke it in 1961.

The Red Sox in their 18-year existence now had five world championships and an additional pennant. They had not failed to win in any World Series in which they played, and they had now won the Series in three of the past four years. This, however, was to be their last appearance in a World Series until 28 years later, in 1946.

1918 World Series Composite Score

BOSTON (A.L.)

	AB	H	2B	3B	HR	R	RBI	BA
A. Strunk, of								
S. McInnis, 1b	23	4	1	1	0	1		.174
G. Whiteman, of	20	5	0	0	0	2	0	.250
H. Hooper, of	20	5	0	1	0	2	1	.250
E. Scott, ss	20	4	0	1	0	2	1	.200
D. Shean, 2b	20	2	0	0	0	0		.100
F. Thomas, 3b	19	4	0	0	0	0		.211
W. Schang, c	17	20	0	0	0	2	0	.118
S. Agnew, c	9	4	0	0	0	0		.444
C. Mays, p	9							.000
B. Ruth, of, p	5	1	0	0	0	1		.200
J. Bush, p	5	1	0	0	0	0		.000
J. Dubuc	2	0	0	0	0	2		.200
S. Jones, p	1	0	0	0	0			.000
H. Miller	1	0	0	0	0			.000

Errors: G. Whiteman
Stolen Bases: W. Schang, D. Shean, G. Whiteman

PITCHING

	W	L	ERA	IP	H	BB	SO	SV
C. Hays	2	0	1.00	18	10	3	5	0
B. Ruth	2	0	1.06	17	13	7	4	0
J. Bush	0	1	3.00	9	7	3	0	1
S. Jones	0	1	3.00	9	7	5	5	0

CHICAGO (N.L.)

	AB	H	2B	3B	HR	R	RBI	BA
L. Mann, of	22	5	0	0	0	2		.227
C. Hollocher, ss	21	4	0	0	0	2		.190
D. Paskert, of	21	4	1	0	0	2	0	.190
M. Flack, of	19	5	0	0	0	2		.263
C. Pick, 2b	18	7	1	0	0	2		.389
F. Merkle, 1b	18	5	1	0	0	1		.278
C. Deal, 3b	17	3	0	0	0			.176
B. Killefer, c	17	2	1	0	0	2		.118
H. Vaughn, p	10	0	0	0	0	2		.000
L. Tyler, p	5	1	0	0	0			.200
B. O'Farrell, c	3	0	0	0	0			.000
T. Barber	2	0	0	0	0	2		.000
C. Hendrix, p	1	1	0	0	0			.000
B. McCabe	1	0	0	0	0			1.000
C. Wortman, 2b	1	0	0	0	0			.000
R. Zeider, 3b	1	0	0	0	0			.000

Errors: C. Deal, P. Douglas, M. Flack, C. Hollocher, L. Tyler
Stolen Bases: C. Hollaocher (2), M. Flack

PITCHING

	W	L	ERA	IP	H	BB	SO	SV
H. Vaughn	1	2	1.00	27	17	5	17	0
L. Tyler	1	1	1.17					
P. Douglas	0	1	0.00	23	14	11	4	0
C. Hendrix	0	0	0.00	1	0	0	0	

The Red Sox Encyclopedia

1946

Slaughter's Dash For Home Wins World Series For Cardinals, Four Games to Three

With many key players back from World War II, Joe Cronin's Boston Red Sox easily won the American League pennant in 1946. They were 12 games ahead of the second-place Detroit Tigers. The Red Sox had fine pitching, especially from Boo Ferriss and Tex Hughson, and also from Mickey Harris, Joe Dobson and Bob Klinger. Ferriss, with a 25-6 record, led the league in winning percentage at .806. Hughson was also a 20-game winner, with a record of 20 wins and 11 losses for a .645 winning percentage. Mickey Harris won 17 games with a 17-9 record and a .654 winning percentage. Joe Dobson won 13 games and Bob Klinger led the league in saves with nine. The Red Sox were a winning team with over 100 wins (a 104-50 record) and a winning percentage of .675.

Ted Williams was back and was again one of the league's most potent hitters. He batted second to Mickey Vernon of the Washington Senators with a .342 average. He was second in homers and runs batted in behind Hank Greenberg, with 38 four-baggers and 123 R.B.I.s. He led the league in slugging. He also led in bases on balls and runs scored. Williams was not the only hitting star on the team. Johnny Pesky led the league with 208 hits and batted .335. Dom DiMaggio batted .316. Bobby Doerr was his usual steady self at second base, leading the league at his position in putouts and assists, in double plays executed and in fielding average. Rudy York, traded from the Tigers to the Red Sox, was a superior first baseman, leading at his position in putouts, assists and double plays made. Both Doerr and York had good records at the plate. Doerr hit .271 with 18 home runs, and York hit .276 with 17 home runs.

There were some notable batting moments by Red Sox players in 1946. York hit two grand slam home runs, tying a record and drove in 10 runs in a game against the St. Louis Browns. Williams, in the 1946 All-Star game at Fenway Park hit a mammoth three-run homer in the eighth inning to cap a 12-0 win for the American League. Williams had two home runs in the game, four hits and drove in five runs. He was named the game's Most Valuable Player.

The St. Louis Cardinals had a more exciting pennant race in the National League. They beat the Brooklyn Dodg-

ers in a best-two-of-three play-off to win the pennant. The Cardinals were led by now first baseman Stan Musial who led the league in batting with a .365 average. Like Ted Williams, Musial returned to stardom from the War. He led the National League in slugging and total bases. He had 16 home runs, drove in 103, led in doubles and runs scored, and also led the league with 228 hits.

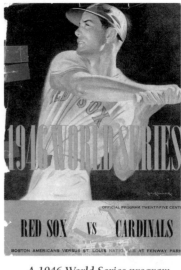

A 1946 World Series program cover. The Cardinals beat the Red Sox for the title in seven games. (Boston Red Sox).

The Cardinals also had another batting star in outfielder Enos "Country" Slaughter. Slaughter batted .300, led the team with 18 home runs and led the league with 130 runs batted in. Whitey Kurowski at third base was a .301 hitter with 14 home runs and 89 runs batted in. The Cardinals had a superlative infield with both Kurowski at third base and Red Schoendienst at second base leading at their respective positions in fielding. And, the Cardinals had the redoubtable Marty Marion, one of baseball's great fielding shortstops.

The Cardinals' leading pitcher was Howie Pollet. He led the league with 21 wins and a 2.10 earned run average, and he had a 21-10 won-lost record. Murry Dickson had the best won-lost record in the league with a .714 average based on 15 wins and six losses. Harry Brecheen also won 15 games and had a fine 2.49 E.R.A.

The 1946 World Series was a close affair. The Red Sox won the first game and then the teams alternated wins until the Cardinals won the seventh and climactic game. In Game 1 the Red Sox were behind, 2-1, in the ninth inning but were able to tie the game with a ground ball that took a bad hop. Rudy York won the game for the Red Sox with a home run in the tenth inning. Game 2 was a 4-hit shutout for Harry Brecheen as he allowed four singles. Brecheen was the pitching hero of the Series with three wins and a 0.45 earned run average.

In Game 3, Boo Ferriss returned the favor and pitched a shutout for the Red Sox, 4-0. Rudy York again won the game for the Sox by hitting a first inning three-run home run. It was his second homer of the Series. Game 4 was a rout for the St. Louis Cardinals as they won, 12-3. Slaughter, Kurowski and catcher Joe Garagiola each had four hits as the St. Louis team had a total of 20 hits and the Red Sox made four errors.

The Red Sox won Game 5 with Joe Dobson the winning pitcher. Harry Brecheen came back for his second win to tie the Series at 3-3 in Game 6. He gave seven hits in a 4-1 win.

Game 7 is one of the great games in baseball history and is described in detail in Chapter 3. The Cardinals won,

4-3, when Enos Slaughter dashed for home on a hit by Harry Walker, catching the Red Sox fielders off guard. Harry Brecheen, in relief, won his third game.

Brecheen was the pitching hero of the Series with his three wins and 0.45 earned run average. Bobby Doerr had nine hits and batted .409. Rudy York had his two home runs to lead both teams in homers. For the Cardinals, Slaughter, the Series hero, batted .320. Kurowski, catcher Garagiola and outfielder Harry Walker all had a good hitting Series. One irony to be noted is that Ted Williams, the Most Valuable Player in the American League, and Stan Musial, the Most Valuable Player in the National League, each batted miserably. Musial batted .222 with six hits in 27 at bats. Williams batted .200 with five hits in 25 at bats and no extra base hits.

1967

Bob Gibson Pitches Cardinals To A Repeat Seven-Game World Series Win Over The Boston Red Sox

The 1967 season was a turnaround year for the Boston Red Sox. After finishing in ninth place in a ten-team league in 1966 and not having won a pennant in 21 years, they finally won one under new manager Dick Williams.

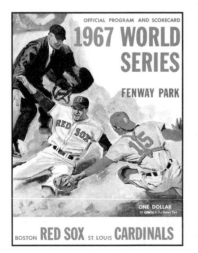

A 1967 World Series program cover. The Cardinals again beat the Red Sox for the title in seven games. (Boston Red Sox).

The Red Sox were in a torrid race, beating both Detroit and Minnesota by one game and the Chicago White Sox by only three games. The Red Sox had two distinct heroes in the 1967 team. Carl Yastrzemski won the Triple Crown and was the league's Most Valuable Player. Jim Lonborg tied for the league lead in wins and won the Cy Young award. The 1967 season, besides the intense pennant race, had a particularly notable

moment. On April 13, Red Sox pitcher Bill Rohr, in his first major league game, had a no-hitter after 8²/₃ innings. Elston Howard of the Yankees singled to break up the no-hitter and Rohr finished the game with a 1-hit, 3-0 triumph.

Yaz's career year was marked by a .336 batting average, 44 home runs and 121 runs driven in. He also led the league in hits and runs scored. The only other Red Sox player to hit over .300 was first baseman George "Boomer" Scott, who batted .303, and had 19 home runs and drove in 82 runs. This was also the third straight year in which Tony Conigliaro hit 20 or more home runs. He hit 20. The pitching was in the capable hands of Jim Lonborg. He led the league with 22 wins and no other Red Sox pitcher had more than 12. Lonborg was also the league's strikeout leader, with 246, and he was the Red Sox work horse pitching 273 innings, second most in the league.

The St. Louis Cardinals had an easier time in 1967. They beat the second place San Francisco Giants for the pennant by nine games. Orlando "Baby Bull" Cepeda, traded by the Giants in 1966, hit a hefty .325 with 25 home runs and led the league with 111 runs batted in. Outfielder Curt Flood also had a good year with a .335 batting average. Outfielder Lou Brock was at .299 with 21

The Red Sox Encyclopedia

home runs and 76 R.B.I.s. Brock, a noted base stealer with a career 938 stolen bases, second all-time only to Ricky Henderson, stole 52 bases. Catcher Tim McCarver batted .295, had 14 home runs and drove in 69 runs.

Star pitcher Bob Gibson broke his leg in July but nonetheless won 13 games, had a 13-7 record, and came back to lead the Cardinals in the World Series. Dick Hughes had 16 wins and led the league with a .727 winning percentage. Steve Carlton and Nelson Briles each won 14 games. Joe Hoerner had 15 saves.

The World Series was a Bob Gibson showcase. He won Game 1, 2-1, scattering six hits and striking out ten. Lou Brock led the Cardinal attack with four singles and two stolen bases. Gibson also won Game 4, 6-0, with a five-hit shutout. Brock again had two hits and stole a base. Tim McCarver and Roger Maris, the home run record holder who had been traded from the New York Yankees, each drove in two runs. The climactic seventh game was all Gibson. Gibson, with three days' rest, beat Lonborg, who had two days' rest, in the final game, 7-2, and the Cardinals won the Series, four games to three. Gibson, as in the first game, struck out ten, and he allowed but three hits. What is more, Gibson himself hit a home run off Lonborg.

Lonborg also had a good World Series but he ran out of gas in the seventh game. He won Game 2, 5-0, pitching a one-hitter. He had retired the first 20 batters. Carl Yastrzemski was the offensive cannon. He hit two home runs, one with two men on base. Lonborg was again sensational in Game 5. After pitching 7 2/3 innings of no-hit ball in Game 2, he held the Cardinals to two hits in 8 2/3

innings in Game 5. Maris collected his second hit in the ninth inning, a home run, but Lonborg completed and won the game, 3-1.

Game 3 was won by the Cardinals' Nelson Briles, 5-2. Game 6 was played at Fenway Park but the Cardinals were leading in the Series 3 games to 2. The Cardinals used eight pitchers, but to no avail, as the Red Sox bombed the St. Louis team, 8 to 4. The Sox set a record with three consecutive home runs in the fourth inning by Yastrzemski, Reggie Smith and Rico Petrocelli. It was Petrocelli's second homer of the game and Yastrzemski's third of the Series.

The World Series of 1967 was marked by the exceptional performances of two pitchers. Bob Gibson started, completed and won three games. He had an E.R.A. of 1.00 and struck out 26 batters. Lonborg also started three games, won two and lost one, and in the first two games he pitched he gave up a total of four hits. Lou Brock was the leading hitter in the Series at .414 and he stole seven bases. Roger Maris batted .385 and led both teams with seven runs driven in. Second baseman Julian Javier batted .360. For the Red Sox, Carl Yastrzemski was the leading regular. He batted .400 with 10 hits, three home runs and five runs batted in. The Red Sox third baseman, Dalton Jones, batted .389 and second baseman Mike Andrews batted .308. Elston Howard, the Red Sox catcher and skilled handler of pitchers, in his next to last season, played in his tenth World Series. With the last game in the 1967 Series, he had played in 54 World Series games, third all time behind Yogi Berra's 75 World Series games and Mickey Mantle's 65.

1969

This was the year in which each league separated into two divisions—an East Division and a West Division. Each league had expanded to 12 teams, six teams to a division. At the end of the season, the league division leaders would play each other to decide who played in the World Series.

1975

Red Sox Sweep Athletics, Three Games to None in American League Championship Series

The Red Sox, led by manager Darrell Johnson, won the East Division by 4 1/2 games over Earl Weaver's Baltimore Orioles, winner the previous two years. 1975 was the year of the fabulous rookie outfielders, Fred Lynn and Jim Rice. Lynn won both the Rookie of the Year award and the league's Most Valuable Player award, the only player ever to do so. Lynn batted .331, second in the league to Minnesota's Rod Carew. He hit 21 home runs, batted in 105 runs and also led the league in doubles and runs scores. He was the league's leader in slugging percentage. Teammate Jim Rice was a worthy competitor. Rice batted .309 with 22 home runs and 102 runs batted in. Carlton Fisk, Rookie of the Year in 1972 and Boston's fine catcher, matched Lynn with a batting average of .331. Cecil Cooper, the designated hitter, batted .311 and he and Yastrzemski had 14 home runs each. Boston, as a team, was the league's batting champion.

The Red Sox had five pitchers with wins in double figures. Bill Lee led in pitching average at .654 with 17 wins and nine losses. Rick Wise won 19 games, Luis Tiant 18, Roger Moret had a 14-3 record in only 145 innings, and Reggie Cleveland won 13 games. Dick Drago had 16 saves.

Oakland, which had won the American League's West Division for four straight years previously, easily beat the Kansas City Royals by seven games. Under the leadership of manager Alvin Dark they continued their dominance. They had the formidable Reggie Jackson in right field who led the league with 36 home runs and drove in 104 runs. They had plenty of home run hitting with catcher Gene Tenace having 29, designated hitter Billy Williams had 23, first baseman Joe Rudi had 21 and third baseman Sal Bando had 15. Outfielder Claudell Washington, a .308 hitter, also had 10. The pitchers were led by Vida Blue with 22 wins and 11 losses. Ken Holtzman had an 18-14 record. Rollie Fingers, relief pitcher extraordinaire, was in a league-leading 75 games, had 24 saves and a 10-6 won-lost record.

Nineteen seventy-five had its notable events. It was the year in which Fred Lynn, in a single game, led a Red Sox 15-1 win over the Detroit Tigers with three home runs, a triple and a single, and a total of 10 runs driven in. The Oakland A's also had a notable game, the last game of the season, when four pitchers combined for a no-hitter. They were first Vita Blue, then Glenn Abbott, then Paul Lindblad and finally mopping up, Rollie Fingers.

The Red Sox, playing the team that had won the last three World Series, won the American League Championship Series in an unexpectedly easy fashion, three games to none. In the first game, the Red Sox Luis Tiant pitched a three-hit, 7-1 victory. The two teams made seven errors, four by Oakland. The Red Sox clinched the game with five runs in the seventh inning as Fred Lynn doubled home two of the runs. In Game 2, Reggie Jackson hit a two-run home run in the first inning but Carl Yastrzemski matched with a homer in the fourth with one on. Dick Drago pitched three innings of scoreless relief as the Red Sox won, 6-3. Game 3 was won by the Sox 5-3, as Boston won in a sweep. Yastzremski was the hero with two hits and two fielding gems.

Luis Tiant was the pitching leader in the championship series with his win. Yastrzemski with five hits in the three games, batted .455. Fisk also had five hits and batted .417. Rick Burleson, the shortstop, batted .444, first baseman Cecil Cooper had a .400 average and Fred Lynn batted .364. For the Oakland A's, third baseman Sal Bando had six hits and batted .500. Reggie Jackson with five hits batted .417.

1975

Fisk Hits Dramatic Home Run But Reds Win World Series

The 1975 World Series, like the 1912 World Series in which the Red Sox beat John McGraw's Giants, will endure in memory. It had many spectacular moments.

The Red Sox came into the Series having just swept the Oakland A's in the A.L. Championship Series. Luis Tiant and Dick Drago were in top pitching form and Rick Wise had pitched well. Roger Moret had pitched only one inning in the ALCS and Bill Lee did not pitch at all but they were coming off good seasons.

Many of the Red Sox regulars had a fine batting series against the A's. Hitting well and in top form were Carl Yastrzemski, Pudge Fisk, Rick Burleson, Cecil Cooper and

Fred Lynn. Jim Rice was out for the remainder of the season because of an injury but the Sox also had Dwight Evans and Rico Petrocelli for a potent lineup.

The Cincinnati Reds of the National League were something special. They were known as "The Big Red Machine" with many outstanding players, including two Hall of Famers and two others whose records gave them Hall eligibility. They had Tony Perez at first base with a .282 batting average, 20 home runs and 109 runs batted in. Joe Morgan, Hall of Fame second baseman, batted .327 with 17 home runs and 94 runs batted in. He also led the league in bases on balls and was second in stolen bases. Davey Concepcion was an outstanding shortstop and the indomi-

The Red Sox Encyclopedia

Carlton Fisk watching the flight of the ball he hit for a home run in the 12th inning to win Game 6 of the 1975 World Series. (Associated Press)

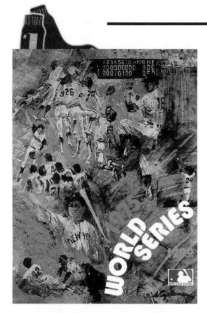

A 1975 World Series program cover. In one of the most dramatic World Series, the Red Sox lost to the Cincinnati Reds in seven games. (Boston Red Sox).

Nolan, Jack Billingham and Don Gullett won 15 games each. Fred Norman won 12, Pat Darcy had 11 wins and Clay Kirby had 10 wins. Rollie Eastwick was a fine relief pitcher who led the league with 22 saves.

The Reds, under manager Sparky Anderson, won the West Division by 20 games over the second-place Los Angeles Dodgers. They won 108 games and lost 54 for a .667 winning percentage. Not only were they a hitting machine but they led the league in fielding percentage as well. In the 1975 National League Division Series, the Reds easily beat the Pittsburgh Pirates, three games to none. Gullett pitched an eight-hitter to win the first game, 8 to 3, and contributed to his win with a home run. Perez hit a home run and had two hits as the Reds won the second game, 6-1. The Reds won the third game in ten innings, 5-3, using five pitchers and with both Rose and Concepcion hitting home runs.

The World Series opened in Boston with the Reds favored to win. Luis Tiant, however, pitched a table Pete Rose, playing third base, batted .317. Ken Griffey and George Foster in the outfield were both .300 hitters, with Foster adding 23 home runs and 78 runs batted in. Hall of Famer Johnny Bench was the Reds' catcher. He batted .283, hit 28 home runs and was second in the league with 110 runs batted in.

The Reds' pitching was capable but not as illustrious. Six pitchers were in double figures with wins. Gary five-hitter in the first game for the Red Sox. He himself singled and scored the first run as the Red Sox won, 6-0. The game was a tight contest, notwithstanding the final score, as Tiant and Don Gullett of the Reds engaged in a 0-0 pitching duel until the Red Sox scored their six runs in the last of the seventh inning.

The Reds evened the score in a thrilling Game 2. Boston led 2-1 going into the ninth inning in this game. In the ninth, Bench doubled to knock out Red Sox starting pitcher Bill Lee. Reliever Dick Drago retired the next two batters and it appeared the Red Sox would win but then Davey Concepcion singled Bench home. He then stole second and scored on Ken Griffey's double, giving the Reds the game, 3-2.

Game 3 was another thriller. The Reds won in ten innings, 6-5. A record total of six home runs were hit, three by each team. The Red Sox, behind 5-3 in the ninth inning, tied the score on Dwight Evans' two-run homer. In the tenth inning, the Reds won when, with the bases loaded, Joe Morgan drove the ball over the center fielder's head for the winning hit.

The Reds now had a two-to-one lead in games, but Luis Tiant won another hard-pitched game for the Red

1975 World Series Composite Score

CINCINNATI (N.L.)

	AB	H	2B	3B	HR	R	RBI	BA
G. Foster, lf	29	8	1	0	0	2		.276
J. Bench, c	29	6	1	0	1	5	2	.207
D. Concepcion, ss	28	5	1	0	1	3	4	.179
T. Perez, 1b	28	5	0	0	3		7	.179
P. Rose, 3b	27	7	0	1	0	3		.370
J. Morgan, 2b	27	10	0	0	3	4		.259
K. Griffey, rf	26	7	3	0	0	4	4	.269
C. Geronimo, cf	25	7	0	1	0	2	3	.280
D. Gullett, p	7	2	0	0	0			.286
M. Rettenmund	3	0	0	0	0			.000
T. Crowley	2	1	0	0	0			.500
J. Billingham, p	2	0	0	0	0			.000
D. Chaney	2	0	0	0	0			.000
D. Driessen	2	0	0	0	0			.000
W. McEnaney, p	1	0	0	0	0			.000
E. Armbrister	1	0	0	0	0			.000
P. Borbon, p	1	0	0	0	0			.000
P. Darcy, p	1	1	0	0	0			1.000
R. Eastwick, p	1	0	0	0	0			.000
G. Nolan, p	1	0	0	0	0			.000
F. Norman, p	1	0	0	0	0			.000

Errors: D. Concepcion, T. Perez
Stolen Bases: D. Concepcion (3), K. Griffey (2), J. Morgan (2), G. Foster, T. Perez

PITCHING

	W	L	ERA	IP	H	BB	SO	SV
D. Gullett	1	1	4.34	18.2	19	10	15	0
J. Billingham	0	0	1.00	9	8	5	7	0
R. Eastwick	2	0	2.25	8	6	3	4	1
W. McEnaney	0	0	2.70	6.2	3	3	4	1
G. Nolan	0	0	6.00	6	6	1	2	0
C. Carroll	1	0	3.18	6	1	2	5	1
P. Darcy	0	0	4.50	5.2	5	2	2	0
F. Norman	0	1	9.00	4	8	3	2	0
P. Borbon	0	0	6.00	3	3	2	1	0

BOSTON (A.L.)

	AB	H	2B	3B	HR	R	RBI	BA
D. Doyle, 2b	30	8	1	1	0	3		.267
C. Yastrzemski, 1b, of	29	9	1	0	0	7	4	.310
R. Petrocelli, 3b	26	8	0	0	0			.308
F. Lynn, cf	25	7	0	0	2	5		.280
C. Fisk, c	25	6	0	1	3	4		.240
R. Burleson, ss	24	7	0	0	2	2		.292
D. Evans, rf	24	7	1	0	2	5		.292
C. Cooper, 1b	19	1	1	1	3			.053
L. Tiant, p	8	2	0	0	0			.250
J. Beniquez, of	8	1	0	0	0			.125
B. Carbo, lf	7	3	1	0	2	3		.429
B. Lee, p	6	1	0	0	0			.167
R. Cleveland, p	2	0	0	0	0			.000
R. Miller, rf	2	0	0	0	0			.000
R. Wise, p	2	0	0	0	0			.000
D. Griffin	1	0	0	0	0			.000
B. Montgomery	1	0	0	0	0			.000

Errors: D. Doyle (3), C. Fisk (2), R. Burleson

PITCHING

	W	L	ERA	IP	H	BB	SO	SV
L. Tiant	2	0	3.60	25	25	8	12	0
B. Lee	0	0	3.14	14.1	12	3	7	0
R. Cleveland	0	1	6.75	6.2	7	3	7	0
J. Willoughby	0	0	0.00	6.1	3	2	5	0
R. Wise	1	0	8.44	5.1	6	2	3	0
D. Moret	0	0	2.25	4	1	6	2	0
J. Burton	0	1	0.00	1.2	2	1	1	0
D. Segui	0	0	9.00	1	1	1	0	0
D. Pole	0	0	0.00	0.0	0	2	0	0

The Red Sox Encyclopedia

Sox, 5-4. He threw 163 pitches and gave four extra base hits but he held on as the Sox scored all five of their runs in the fourth inning. Game 5 put the Reds ahead again as Tony Perez hit two home runs and Don Gullett won his second game of the Series with relief help from Rollie Eastwick.

Game 6 is one of the greatest, if not the greatest, game in World Series history. It is described in more detail in Chapter Three. It is known as the game in which Carlton Fisk, batting in the 12th inning, "directed" his home run inside the foul line in left field to win the game. There was other excitement. The Reds led, 6-3, in the eighth inning but then Bernie Carbo hit a pinch home run with two men on base to tie the game for the Sox. In the eleventh inning Dwight Evans made a spectacular catch to save the game for the Red Sox. And then came Fisk's stay-in-bounds and jump-for-joy home run to give the Sox a 7-6 win. The Reds' Sparky Anderson, also known as "Captain Hook", used eight pitchers in the game.

In Game 7, it appeared that the Red Sox might win the world championship for the first time in 57 years as they took a 3-0 lead in the sixth inning behind " Spaceman"

Bill Lee. Then, Tony Perez, with a man on base, hit his third home run of the Series and in the seventh the Reds tied the game with another run. Joe Morgan hit a two-out single in the ninth inning to win the game for the Reds. 4-3, and the World Series, four games to three. It was the Reds' first championship since 1940.

The 1975 World Series had many heroes. For the Red Sox, Luis Tiant won two complete games. Carl Yastrzemski had nine hits and led the Red Sox regulars with a .310 batting average. Bernie Carbo hit two home runs, one a crucial pinch hit and batted .429 as an off-the-bench player. Rico Petrocelli batted .308 and Carlton Fisk also had two home runs, including the historic one in Game 6.

The Reds also had their star performers. Rollie Eastwick, in relief, won two games and saved another. Pete Rose led both teams with 10 hits and also had the highest batting average among regulars, .370. Cesar Geronimo, the fine-fielding center fielder, had two home runs. Tony Perez had three home runs and batted in seven runs, despite a .179 batting average. Joe Morgan also contributed key hits to win both Games 3 and 7.

It was a Series to remember.

1986
Red Sox Come From Behind To Win ALCS In Seven Games

The Red Sox, after finishing in fifth place in the East division in 1985, 18½ games off the pace, came back to win the division title by 5½ games over the Yankees in 1986. It was the year of Roger Clemens' memorable record-breaking performance with 20 strikeouts in a game against the Seattle Mariners. Clemens led the league with 24 wins, a winning average of .857 with 24 wins and four losses, and a 2.48 earned run average. He was second in the league in strikeouts with 238. Clemens won not only the Cy Young award but also the league's Most Valuable Player award. "Oil Can" Boyd also pitched well with 16 wins and Bruce Hurst had 13 wins.

Wade Boggs won the batting championship for the third time in four years with a .357 batting average. Jim Rice batted .324 with 20 home runs and 110 runs batted in. Don Baylor, traded by the Yankees to the Red Sox in exchange for another designated hitter, Mike Easler, hit 31 home runs and drove in 94 runs. Outfielder Dwight Evans hit 26 home runs and drove in 97, and first baseman Bill Buckner had 18 home runs and drove in 102 runs. Buckner, second baseman Marty Barrett and Boggs had outstanding fielding years, Buckner and Barrett leading at

their positions in assists and Boggs leading in putouts.

The California Angels, West division winners, beat the second place Texas Rangers by five games. California had Wally Joyner at first base with a .290 average, 22 home runs and 100 runs batted in. Doug DeCinces, the third baseman, had 26 home runs and 96 runs batted in. Brian Downing in left field had 20 homers and 95 R.B.I.s. Reggie Jackson, now a designated hitter, had 18 home runs and right fielder Ruppert Jones had 17 homers. Bob Boone was a fine-fielding catcher who led the league at his position in assists and double plays executed.

Mike Witt and Kirk McCaskill were the leading pitchers with 18 and 17 wins respectively. Veteran Don Sutton had 15 wins in a season in which he won his 300th game. Donnie Moore had 21 saves.

The Red Sox won the ALCS in a come-from-behind series after it appeared they would be eliminated in Game 5. Mike Witt won Game 1 for the Angels with a five-hitter, 8-1, after Roger Clemens was cuffed for four runs in the second inning and left the game in the eighth. The Red Sox evened the Series in Game 2 as Bruce Hurst went all the way and won, 9 to 2. The Red Sox scored three runs in the sixth inning and, with three Angel errors, scored three more runs in the seventh inning. Jim Rice hit a homer with a runner on base.

The Angels won Games 3 and 4 to take a three-games-to-one lead. Game 3 was a pitching duel between "Oil Can" Boyd and John Candelaria of the Angels with the score at 1-1 going into the last of the seventh inning. Rick Schofield and Gary Pettis then hit homers for the Angels and they went on to win 5-3. In Game 4, Clemens went into the ninth inning with a 3-0 lead. Calvin Schiraldi, in relief, hit Angels' batter Brian Downing with the bases full to force in the tying run. In the eleventh inning Schiraldi and the Red Sox lost the game as Bobby Grich singled in the winning run for a 4-3 California win.

Game 5 appeared to be the pennant clincher for the Angels as they went into the ninth inning leading 5 to 2 behind the effective pitching of Mike Witt. Then, in the top of the ninth, Dave Henderson came to bat with two out and a runner on base. With two strikes on him, and only one more strike needed to eliminate the Red Sox, Henderson hit a dramatic two-run home run to cap a four run rally and give the Red Sox the lead, 6 to 5. The Angels tied the game in the bottom of the ninth but in the eleventh inning Henderson hit a sacrifice fly to win the game, 7-6.

Now behind, 3 games to 2, and going back to Boston to play Game 6 and possibly Game 7, the Red Sox put on their hitting clothes in earnest. They won Game 6, 10-4, with 16 hits, including four for shortstop Spike Owen and three for second baseman Marty Barrett. "Oil Can" Boyd evened his record with a win to match his earlier loss. The Sox won Game 7, 8 to 1, as Roger Clemens won to even up his record at one win and one loss. Jim Rice had his second home run in the Series, this one also with one man on base, and Dwight Evans also homered. John McNamara led the Red Sox to the pennant but the Angels able manager Gene Mauch, had another year, his 25th, in

1986

Buckner Loses Squibbler As Mets Beat Red Sox In World Series, Four Games to Three

which his team failed to win the pennant.

The Red Sox had just completed a tough, seven-game League Championship Series but they managed to win. Bruce Hurst had won the game he pitched with a fine performance. Clemens and Boyd, the Red Sox's leading pitchers in 1986, had both good and bad outings. The double-play combination of Spike Owen and Marty Barrett were hitting well with 20 hits between them. Owen batted .429 in the ALCS and Barrett batted .367. Rice had hit two home runs with men on base despite the fact that he batted only .161. Gedman, the catcher, batted .357 with 10 hits and Don Baylor, the designated hitter, also hit well with a .346 average. Wade Boggs, Bill Buckner, Dwight Evans and Tony Armas were not up to their season standard but had the World Series in which to redeem themselves.

The New York Mets, led by Davey Johnson, were a solid team. They finished in first place in the East division of the National League by 21½ games over the second place Philadelphia Phillies. They had 108 wins and 54 losses for a .667 winning percentage. They won the National League team batting and slugging championships and their pitchers had the best team earned run average in the

League. Wally Backman, second baseman, led the Mets with a .320 batting average and the exceptional fielding first baseman, Keith Hernandez, batted .310. Darryl Strawberry, the power hitting right fielder, had 27 home runs and 93 runs batted in. Solid catcher Gary Carter had 24 home runs and 105 runs batted in. The Mets were backed by a powerful bench consisting of Kevin Mitchell, George Foster and Howard Johnson. Among them, they hit 35 home runs.

Leading the pitching staff was Bobby Ojeda, ex-Red Sox pitcher, with an 18-5 record, top in the league in winning percentage at .783 and he had a 2.57 E.R.A., second in the League. Immediately behind him and second in winning percentage in the league was Doc Gooden with 17 wins, six losses and a .739 average. He had an E.R.A. of 2.84. Sid Fernandez finished third in the league in winning percentage, .727, with 16 wins and six losses. Ron Darling had 15 wins and six losses, and an E.R.A. of 2.81. The corps of relievers was also outstanding. Roger McDowell had 22 saves and a 14-9 record; Jesse Orosco had 21 saves.

The Mets played Houston in the NLCS, who finished ten games ahead of the second place Cincinnati Reds in the West division. The Mets beat the Astros, four games to two, but not without the league's best pitcher, Mike Scott, winning the two games he pitched against the Mets. He won the first game in a duel with Gooden, 1-0, and he won the fourth game in a three-hitter, 3-1. Bobby Ojeda won the second game for the Mets, 5-1, and the Mets won an exciting Game 3, 6-5. Trailing 4-0, Strawberry unloaded a three-run home run as part of a four-run game-tying rally in the sixth inning and Lenny Dykstra won the game in the last of the ninth with a two-run homer.

The Mets won the last two games. In Game 5, which went 12 innings, Gooden and reliever Orosco pitched well and Strawberry hit another homer as the Mets won 2-1. They beat Nolan Ryan of the Astros who pitched a two-hitter for the first nine innings. Game 6, the clincher for the Mets, was a titanic 16-inning struggle. The Mets were losing, 3-0, in the top of the ninth when they rallied for three runs on R.B.I.s by Mookie Wilson, Keith Hernandez and Ray Knight. The Mets went ahead in the 14th inning on Wally Backman's single but the Astros' Billy Hatcher tied the game in the bottom of the 14th with a home run. The Mets scored three in the bottom of the 16th to lead, 7-4. The Astros almost tied the game again but fell short with only two runs as Orosco struck out the last batter with two men on base. The final score was 7-6.

The League Championship Series in both leagues were exciting and extended, and it appeared the World Series would be anticlimactic. The World Series, however, was equally exciting.

The Mets with their solid hitting and depth of pitching were heavy favorites to win. Notwithstanding, the Series lasted seven games before the Mets finally eked out a triumph, four games to three. In the first game, in Shea Stadium, Bruce Hurst pitched for the Red Sox and allowed just four singles in eight innings. Calvin Schiraldi pitched one inning in relief as the Red Sox won, 1-0. Game 2 was a rout for the Red Sox as they exploded with 18 hits. Dave Henderson and Dwight Evans each had home runs. Neither Roger Clemens for the Red Sox nor Dwight Gooden for the Mets, two of baseball's celebrated pitchers, survived the fifth inning.

Boston fans were hopeful their Red Sox would win their first World Series in nearly 70 years in 1986, but the Mets defeated the Sox in seven games to take the title. (Baseball Hall of Fame Library, Cooperstown, N.Y.).

The Red Sox returned to Boston after two wins in New York and their outlook was bright. Fortunes reversed themselves, however, as the Mets won the first two games in Boston. They won Game 3, 7 to 1, on Bobby Ojeda's fine seven-inning start and Roger McDowell's relief work. Lenny Dykstra hit a home run for the Mets but the Red Sox had a total of only five hits. In Game 4, Ron Darling of the Mets allowed the Red Sox four hits in seven innings and Gary Carter had the heavy lumber with two home runs, one with a man on base. Lenny Dykstra also had his second homer in two games as the Mets won, 6-2.

Bruce Hurst put the Red Sox back in the lead in Game 5. He scattered ten hits for his second win in the Series as the Red Sox won, 4-2.

Game 6 produced one of those unforgettable moments and unforgettable games in baseball history. It is described in more detail in Chapter Three. In Game 6 the Red Sox broke on top, 2-0. They were leading 3-2 with Clemens pitching going into the last half of the eighth inning when Schiraldi relieved him. The Mets scored a run in the bottom of the eighth inning to tie the game. Going into overtime in the tenth inning, Dave Henderson of the Red Sox led off with a home run, and Boggs and Barrett combined for another run. The Red Sox led 5-3 and it appeared they were about to acquire their first victorious World Series in 68 years. Reliever Schiraldi got the first two batters in the tenth inning but then the Mets had three hits producing a run. With men on base, Bob Stanley came in to pitch and he wild pitched in the tying run. Mookie Wilson, after a long at bat, hit a squibbler that inexplicably went through first baseman Bill Buckner's legs and the Mets won the game, 6-5.

Game 6 was a deflating experience for the Red Sox but then they came back to take a 3-0 lead in the seventh and deciding game of the World Series. Rich Gedman and Dwight Evans hit home runs in the three-run second inning. Bruce Hurst pitched steady ball until the last of the sixth inning when the Mets tied the score with four hits and a walk. Ray Knight hit a game-winning home run in the seventh inning and Strawberry also hit a homer as the Mets scored five runs in the seventh and eighth innings and won the game, 8-5, and the Series, four games to three.

It was a memorable Series, most notably for the gyrations in Game 6. Bill Buckner, whose lifetime playing record deserved better, was the goat of the Series. Marty Barrett of the Red Sox had a record-equaling performance with 13 hits and he batted .433. Dwight Evans and Dave

Henderson each had two home runs and Henderson batted .400 while Evans batted .308. Evans had nine runs batted in. Jim Rice batted .333 with a double and a triple but no home runs and Spike Owen batted .300. Bruce Hurst won two games, pitching a total of 17 innings with a 1.96 earned run average.

For the Mets Gary Carter led with two home runs, nine runs batted in and a .276 average. Ray Knight had nine hits and batted .391. Lenny Dykstra had two home runs and batted .296. Wally Backman and Tim Teufel, the two second basemen, had 10 hits between them as Backman batted .333 and Tuefel batted .444. Daryl Strawberry and Mookie Wilson had three stolen bases each. Ron Darling was the best pitcher, winning one game and losing another in three starts, two of which were well-pitched. Darling had an E.R.A. of 1.53. Jesse Orosco had two saves.

The Mets retained the title, "Miracle Mets." The Red Sox were still looking for a winning World Series after losing the last four they were in and not having won since 1918. The promise of outstanding pitching duels between pitching superstars Roger Clemens and Dwight Gooden

1988
Red Sox Change Managers And Come From Behind To Win Close East Division Race, But Oakland Wins ALCS

never happened as neither one pitched well.

The Red Sox, after winning the pennant in 1986 and engaging in an exciting World Series, finished fifth in the East division in 1987, 20 games behind first-place Detroit. They started slowly in 1988 and, just after midseason and 85 games in which the Red Sox won 43 and lost 42, manager John McNamara was replaced by Joe Morgan. The Red Sox immediately won 19 of the next 20 games to place themselves in division championship contention. The Red Sox won a close race by one game over the Detroit Tigers, two games over third-place Toronto and 3¹/₂ games over the Yankees in fourth place. Clemens and Hurst were the leading Red Sox pitchers, with 18 wins each. Hurst had an 18-6 record for a .750 winning percentage that was second in the league. Clemens had a 2.93 earned run average and led the league in shutouts with eight, in strikeouts with 291 and in complete games with 14. He averaged more than a strikeout an inning. Lee Smith, a top-flight relief pitcher now pitching for the Red Sox, had 29 saves.

Wade Boggs won the American League batting cham-

pionship for the fourth straight year and for the fifth time in the last six years. Boggs batted .366 and also led the league in bases on balls, in doubles and in runs scored. Mike Greenwell, in left field, was the only other Red Sox player to bat over .300, at .325. Greenwell also led the team in home runs, with 22. The Red Sox two outfielders, Dwight Evans and Ellis Burks, had 21 and 18 home runs respectively. Jim Rice, now a designated hitter, had 15. The three outfielders, Greenwell, Evans and Burks also led the team in runs batted in. Greenwell had 119, Evans 111 and Burks 92. Rick Cerone, one of two Red Sox catchers, played in 84 games without an error.

The American League West was won by the Oakland A's. Led by Tony LaRussa they won 104 games and lost 58 for a .642 winning average. Oakland had batting power. Right fielder Jose Canseco, who batted .307, led the league with 42 home runs and 124 runs batted in. In this year he also became the first player to hit 40 home runs and have 40 stolen bases in one year. Dave Henderson, former Red Sox star and now with Oakland, batted .304, had 24 home runs and batted in 94. Slugging first baseman Mark

McGwire had 32 home runs and batted in 99 runs.

Dave Stewart was a workhorse pitcher for the Athletics. He pitched 276 innings, more than anyone else in the league, and won 21 games and lost 12. Bob Welch won 17 games and Storm Davis won 16. The Athletics, like the Red Sox, had a gifted reliever. He was Dennis Eckersley, former Red Sox starting pitcher, who led the league with 45 saves. He had a 2.35 earned run average.

The Athletics swept the Red Sox in the American League Championship Series, four games to none. This was the first time that a four-game sweep had occurred in league championship series. In Game 1, Stewart bested Hurst in a pitching duel, 2-1. Hurst pitched all the way but Stewart was relieved by Rick Honeycutt in the seventh inning and Eckersley came in the eighth to gain a save. Canseco hit a home run, one of three he had in the Series. There is irony in the fact that Carney Lansford and Dave Henderson got hits in the eighth inning to provide the winning run and Dennis Eckersley protected the lead with two scoreless innings. All three were former Red Sox players.

Game 2 was also a pitching duel for five innings, with Roger Clemens for the Sox and Storm Davis of the Athletics pitching shutout ball. The Sox got two runs in the sixth inning but this was quickly erased by the A's in the seventh inning with three runs. Canseco hit a two-run home run. After Gedman hit a home run to tie in the last of the

seventh, the A's scored in the ninth inning and won the game, 4 to 3.

The confident Athletics now went back to Oakland, leading the Series two games to none and playing in their home park. In Game 3, the Red Sox jumped ahead in the first two innings, 5-0. The A's, with home runs by Mark McGwire and Carney Lansford, pulled within one run with four runs in the bottom of the second. The following inning, A's catcher Ron Hassey hit a two-run homer to put the A's in the lead, 6 to 5. The A's went on from there, with Dave Henderson adding a two-run homer in the eighth to give Oakland a 10-6 win. The two teams not only scored 16 runs but had 27 hits between them.

The Oakland Athletics now needed only one more win, and that came in the fourth game. Canseco hit a home run in the first inning, his third of the Series. Again it was Stewart, Honeycutt and Eckersley combining to win the game on a four-hitter, 4-1, and the ALCS in a sweep.

Dennis Eckersley more than made his mark as he recorded a save in all four games. He won the series Most Valuable Player award. Gene Nelson, fifth among Oakland pitchers with a 9-6 season record, won two games in relief. The Oakland pitchers had a 2.00 earned run average. Canseco had his three home runs, Dave Henderson batted .375 and McGwire, shortstop Walt Weiss and Canseco batted over .300.

For the Red Sox, there were few heroes. The sure hitter, Wade Boggs, had a .385 average and catcher Rich Gedman batted .357.

1990

Boston Again Swept By Oakland In ALCS, 4 Games to 0

The Red Sox won the East division in 1990 by two games over the previous year's winner, the Toronto Blue Jays. The Sox were again led by Roger Clemens who had 21 wins and six losses, second in the league with a winning percentage of .778. Clemens had the best earned run average in the league, 1.93, the most shutouts at four, and he struck out 209 batters. Mike Boddicker was the number two pitcher on the Red Sox staff with 17 wins and eight losses. Jeff Reardon followed in the Red Sox succession of great relief pitchers with 21 saves.

Wade Boggs did not have his customary superlative hitting year but led the team with a .302 batting average. The two outfield stalwarts in this era, Mike Greenwell and Ellis Burks, batted .297 and .296 respectively. Burks also had 21 home runs and batted in 89 runs.

The Oakland Athletics, the West division opponents of the Red Sox, appeared to have the better team. Oakland had its third straight pennant and were world champions the previous year, 1989. The A's had the league's leading pitcher and Cy Young winner, Bob Welch. He led the league with 27 wins and had the highest winning percentage, .818, with a 27-6 record. Dave Stewart was still the workhorse pitcher. He led the league with 267 innings pitched and had a highly creditable 22-11 record. Stewart also pitched four shutouts. The A's had pitching depth. Scott Sanderson won 17 games and Mike Moore won 13. The incomparable Dennis Eckersley, the acknowledged master of relief pitching, had 48 saves, second in 1990 only to Bobby Thigpen of the Chicago White Sox who had a record 57 saves. Eckersley, in relief, had a remarkable earned run average of 0.61.

Leading the Oakland regulars was Ricky Henderson, the league's Most Valuable Player and lead-off hitter and base stealer par excellence. Henderson batted .325 with 28 home runs and 61 runs batted in. He led in stolen bases, with 65, and in runs scored with 119. The Athletics continued to be a potent hitting team. Jose Canseco had 37 home runs and 101 runs batted in. Mark McGwire had 39 home runs and 108 R.B.I.s Dave Henderson had 20 homers and 63 R.B.I.s.

The Athletics were a clear favorite to win the American League pennant. They had established stars at virtually every position and had won over 100 games to beat second-place Toronto in the West division by nine games. The Athletics, in fact, repeated their 1988 annihilation of the Red Sox with a four-game sweep in the ALCS. They won Game 1, 9 to 1, with Dave Stewart allowing four hits in eight innings and Dennis Eckersley earning the first of three consecutive saves he had in the Series. In actuality, the game was closer than the score suggests. Wade Boggs hit a home run in the fourth inning, the only homer by either team in the Series, and the Red Sox led, 2-1, going into the seventh inning. The A's got single runs in the seventh and eighth innings but then broke the game open with seven runs in the ninth inning.

Game 2 continued Oakland's pitching mastery as they allowed the Red Sox only one run per game in all four Series games. Oakland won Game 2, 4-1, behind Bob Welch with Eckersley again earning a save. Harold Baines, the designated hitter, was the hitting star. He had two hits, including a double, and drove in three of the Athletics' four runs.

In Game 3, Mike Moore was the winning pitcher, 4-1, with another save for Eckersley, and Mike Boddicker went all the way for the Red Sox. Willie Randolph, the ex-Yankee second baseman nearing the end of his career, was in the Oakland line-up because of Walt Weiss' injury and had two R.B.I. singles.

Game 4 was memorable mostly because Red Sox ace Roger Clemens was ejected from the game in the second inning for disputing a walk with the umpire. Oakland scored three runs in the second inning and won the game, 3 to 1. Dave Stewart was again the winning pitcher.

The Red Sox had little to show for the four-game series. Mike Boddicker pitched well, though he lost his only game, and had 2.25 earned run average. Wade Boggs had seven hits and batted an impressive .438. He also had two extra base hits, a double and the Series' only home run.

For the A's, there were many stars. Pitcher Dave Stewart won two games and had a 1.13 earned run average. Welch and Moore also won the games they pitched, each allowing only one run, and Dennis Eckersley had three saves. Carney Lansford, the ex-Red Sox third baseman, had seven hits and batted .438. Catcher Terry Steinbach batted .455. Infielder Mike Gallego batted .400. Harold Baines, the designated hitter batted .357 and Willie Randolph, playing part-time, batted .375. Rickey Henderson, Baines and Randolph each drove in three runs. To add insult to injury, the Athletics had nine stolen bases by six different players while the Red Sox had just one, by Ellis Burks.

The Oakland A's became the first team to win three successive pennants since the New York Yankees of 1976-77-78. They were poised to beat the Cincinnati Reds in the World Series handily but were upset by the Reds, four games to none.

1994

The two leagues now had 14 teams each and both leagues decided to split into three divisions, denominated East, Central and West. Each of the East and Central divisions had five teams, and the West division in each league had four teams. The postseason playoff was to be a three-out-of-five elimination tourney in which the East, Central and West Leaders and a "wild card" team with the best second-place record were to be paired off. The tourney was to be known as the League Division Playoffs. The two winners in each league would then play for the pennant, in the League Championship Series. The pennant winners would then contest the World Series.

Because of the strike that ended the season prematurely in August there were no play-offs in 1994, and the first postseason play under the new arrangement occurred in 1995.

1995

Cleveland Indians Sweep Boston Red Sox In First American League Division Playoffs, Three Games to None

The strike continued into the 1995 season, shortening it from 162 to 144 games for each team. The Red Sox, under new manager Kevin Kennedy, won the East division by seven games over the second-place New York Yankees. First baseman Mo Vaughn was the outstanding player for the Sox, and he won the league's Most Valuable Player award. He batted .300, had 39 home runs and led the league with 126 runs batted in. A huge man at six-feet-one and 225 pounds, he was a very capable fielder. He led all first basemen in the league in putouts, number of double plays executed and number of chances fielded per game. John Valentin was the team's shortstop and he batted .298 with 27 home runs and 102 runs batted in. Tim Naehring, the third baseman, batted .307 and right fielder Troy O'Leary batted .308. Jose Canseco, now a designated hitter with the Sox, batted .306 with 24 home runs and 81 runs driven in. The Red Sox, as a team, had the best power and batting average in the East division but it was a potent Cleveland Indian team that dominated the American League.

In a shortened season there were no 20-game winners in the big leagues. Knuckleballer Tim Wakefield was the Red Sox leading pitcher with 16 wins and eight losses for a .667 winning percentage. He was second in the league to Randy Johnson of Seattle with an earned run average of 2.95. Erik Hanson of the Red Sox was second to Johnson in winning percentage with a 15-5 record. Roger Clemens, not having had a great season since 1992, had a 10-5 record. Rick Aguilera, traded from Minnesota in July, was this year's top reliever for the Red Sox with 20 saves and a 2.67 earned run average.

The Cleveland Indians, the Red Sox opponent in the League Division Series, were just beginning to develop a powerful team and they won their first title of any kind in 41 years. They were playing in Jacobs Field, a new state-of-the-art ballfield in downtown Cleveland. The Indians, under Mike Hargrove, had a spectacular record of 100 wins and 44 losses for a .694 winning percentage. They set a record by beating second place Kansas City by 30 games. The Indians led the league in batting with a team .291 average, and they led in home runs and slugging. Their pitchers were the league leaders with a 3.83 E.R.A.

Outfielder Albert Belle of the Indians had a .323 batting average. He led the major leagues with 50 home runs,

notably in a shortened season, and he was the league leader in runs driven in with 126. The Indians had six regular and two supporting players who batted over .300. Eddie Murray, the designated hitter, led with a .323 average. Both second baseman Carlos Baerga and third baseman Jim Thome batted .314. Center fielder Kenny Lofton batted .310 and also led the league with 13 triples and 54 stolen bases. Manny Ramirez, the right fielder, batted .308. Sandy Alomar, who shared catching duties with the veteran Tony Pena, batted .300. The Indians also had five players who hit 20 or more home runs.

The Indian pitchers were led by Charles Nagy and erst-

John Valentin hit a two-run homer in the first game of the 1998 divisional play-offs (Boston Red Sox).

while former Dodger Ace Orel Hershiser who had matching 16-6 records. Veteran Dennis Martinez, "El Presidente," had a 12-5 record. Reliever Jose Mesa led the league with 46 saves and he had a sparkling 1.13 earned run average.

The Indians, heavy favorites to beat the Red Sox in the first American League Division Play-offs, made short shift of the Sox with three straight wins on the way to winning the A.L. pennant. Game 1 was the closest game of the Play-offs. The Red Sox led with John Valentin's two-run homer in the second inning, and the score remained 2-0 until Roger Clemens gave up three runs in the bottom of the sixth inning. Second baseman Luis Alicea, who had four hits in the game, hit a homer for the Sox in the eighth inning to tie the game. The teams traded home runs in the eleventh inning, Tim Naehring for the Red Sox and Albert Belle for the Indians. Then, in the 13th inning, at 2 a.m. in the morning, after five hours including two rain delays, Tony Pena of the Indians hit a home run to win the game, 5-4.

Game 2 was a 4-0 Indians win as Orel Hershiser and three relievers combined for a three-hit win. Omar Vizquel, Indians' shortstop, drove in two runs with a double and Eddie Murray hit a home run with a man on base. In the

first two games of the playoff neither Red Sox slugger, Mo Vaughn nor Jose Canseco, had a hit.

The Indians sewed up the playoffs in Game 3 with an easy 8-2 victory. Charles Nagy was the starter and winner. Jim Thome had a two-run homer early and the Indians scored five runs in the sixth to put the game away. The Indians went on to beat the Seattle Mariners in the American League Championship Series.

The Red Sox power hitters failed to produce in the playoffs. Mo Vaughn and Jose Canseco went 0 for 27 with nine strikeouts between them. Alicea had a good series with a .600 batting percentage and a home run. Valentin and Naehring had a homer each but Red Sox batters had only two hits in 28 at bats with runners in scoring position. The Red Sox had a team batting average of .184 and the pitchers had a combined 5.16 E.R.A. The Red Sox had now lost 13 postseason games in a row, spread over the last four postseason events in which they participated.

It was a bittersweet experience. The Red Sox were winning their share of East division championships with wins in 1986, 1988, 1990 and 1995 but they were having no success in postseason competition. They were winners and champions nearer the beginning of the twentieth century but, as the end of the century approaches, it has been 84 years since they won a world championship.

1998

Boston Wins First Game, But Cleveland Indians again Defeat Red Sox in Division Play-offs

Play-off season in 1998 began in the American League with the Cleveland Indians, Central division champions, playing the Boston Red Sox, the league's wild card team. In the other division play-off, the New York Yankees, East division champions, played the Texas Rangers, West division champions.

The Red Sox-Indians match-up was a replay of the 1995 division play-offs. In 1995, the Indians were a powerhouse team, finishing 30 games ahead of Kansas City in the Central division. They won 100 games and lost 44 for a .694 winning percentage in the season. The Red Sox were the East division winners with a capable but less spectacular record of 86 wins and 58 losses, a .597 winning percentage, and a seven-game lead over the second-place Yankees. The 1995 Red Sox-Indians play-off resulted in an Indian sweep of three straight games. The Indians went on to win the American League pennant. The Red Sox were

now in the throes of 13 straight losses in the play-offs, including three series sweeps by their opponents.

Nineteen ninety-eight promised a more even match-up. The Indians won their division with an 89-73 record for a .549 winning percentage. The Red Sox, though second to the runaway New York Yankees, won 92 and lost 70 for a .568 winning percentage, the second-best record in the American League. In both batting and earned run average, the Red Sox, as a team, placed ahead of the Indians. In the season competition between them, the Red Sox won 8 of the 11 contests.

Among Red Sox regulars, Mo Vaughn had another slugging year in 1998, comparable to the one in 1995 when he won M.V.P. honors. John Valentin, Troy O'Leary and Reggie Jefferson were also hold-overs from the 1995 squad. Valentin and O'Leary batted about 40 points below their 1995 averages but Jefferson, still a designated hitter, batted about 15 points better. The major difference, and improvement, in the regular lineup of 1998 was the appearance of Nomar Garciaparra, another superstar comparable to Mo Vaughn.

The leading Red Sox pitchers in 1995 were Tim Wakefield, returning in 1998, with 16 wins, and Erik Hanson and Roger Clemens, both no longer with the 1998 team, with 15 and 10 wins, respectively. Rick Aguilera,

Outfielder Troy O'Leary played on both Boston's 1995 and 1998 play-off teams against the Indians. (Boston Red Sox).

the relief specialist, had 20 saves. Nineteen ninety-eight saw the appearance of another Red Sox superstar among the pitchers, Pedro Martinez, who won 19 games. Tim Wakefield had 17 wins and Bret Saberhagen won 15. Their combined record was 51 wins and 22 losses. Tom Gordon had a spectacular record in relief with 46 saves.

The 1998 Indians brought back two regular infielders from their 1995 pennant winners, Omar Vizquel, one of baseball's best shortstops, and Jim Thome, their slugger who moved from third base to first base. Manny Ramirez, their slugging rightfielder, and Kenny Lofton, their fleet centerfielder returned, but such stars as first baseman Paul

Sorrento, second baseman Carlos Baerga, leftfielder Albert Belle, and designated hitter Eddie Murray were gone. In their place were David Justice in centerfield, Travis Fryman in the infield and Sandy Alomar catching. Ramirez had a great year as a slugger in 1998 with 45 home runs and 145 R.B.I.s, improving on a good 1995 season. Vizquel played his usual superb shortstop and Lofton and Thome had good years comparable to 1995.

Among the pitchers, of their three top winners, only Charles Nagy returned from the 1995 team. He won 16 games in 1995 while Orel Hershiser, another 16-game winner, and Dennis Martinez, a 12-game winner, went elsewhere. Their incomparable reliever of 1995, Jose Mesa, who led the league with 46 saves, was also no longer with them. In 1998, no Cleveland pitcher had more than 15 wins, with Nagy and Dave Burba each at 15-10. Bartolo Colon at 14-8 and Jaret Wright at 12-10, led the team. The Indians had a good relief specialist to replace Mesa, Mike Jackson, with 40 saves.

On the face of the team and individual player records, the Red Sox might have been considered slight favorites. They played in a tougher division, had better pitching and in addition had superstars Mo Vaughn, Nomar Garciaparra and Pedro Martinez.

In Game 1 of the play-offs, Mo Vaughn hit two home runs and a double to drive in a postseason record-tying seven runs as the Red Sox won easily at Jacobs Field in Cleveland. The Sox, with three-run homers from Vaughn and Garciaparra, quickly started with a 6-0 lead off Jaret Wright of the Indians. The game saw a total of five home runs, two by Vaughn, one by Garciaparra and one each by the Indians' Kenny Lofton and slugger Jim Thome. The Red Sox scored 11 runs on 12 hits. John Valentin had three hits and a walk. He was on base for each of the Red Sox homers and scored four runs. With the heavy hitting, Pedro Martinez coasted to a win. He pitched seven innings, giving up three runs and seven hits, and Jim Corsi came in to pitch a perfect final two innings. The Red Sox, in winning, broke their 13-game losing streak in postseason play, extending through 1986, 1990 and 1995.

Uncharacteristically, the calls of one umpire may have been a determining factor in the outcome of Game 2. With "Doc" Gooden pitching for Cleveland, plate umpire Joe Brinkman made two highly questionable "ball" calls on two good pitches by Gooden. Three pitches into the game, a protesting manager Mike Hargrove of the Indians came out of the dugout and was promptly thrown out of the game by Brinkman With two Red Sox on base. Nomar Garciaparra hit a double and Darrin Lewis, who had walked, scored easily. John Valentin, who also walked, slid

Scott Hatteberg played catcher for the Red Sox in the 1998 division play-offs. (Boston Red Sox).

home and was called safe in another questionable call by Brinkman. Gooden exploded and was immediately thrown out of the game. Two runs thus scored in the first inning and Dave Burba came in to pitch for Cleveland.

Brinkman's adverse calls may have helped to ignite Cleveland bats. They scored one run in the first inning. In the second inning, they scored five, led by a three-run home run by David Justice. The Indians took the lead, 6-2, after the second inning and were never headed. The final score of the game was 9-5. The Indians had six doubles, two by Sandy Alomar, and the home run by Justice. He drove in four runs in the game. Dave Burba pitched 5⅓ innings, gave up two runs and four hits, and was the winning pitcher. Starter Tim Wakefield of the Red Sox was taken out in the second inning. The game, though fought intensely, was not an artistic masterpiece. The two teams together scored 14 runs on 18 hits. Ten pitchers were utilized, five by either team. Garciaparra had two hits, drove in three and scored once, but the Red Sox, and especially

Mo Vaughn, did not pound the ball as they did in the first game.

Under a clear sky, it started raining home runs in Fenway Park. The third game of the series was a pitchers' duel between Bret Saberhagen and Charles Nagy for 4½ innings. In the bottom of the fifth, Jim Thome broke up Saberhagen's no-hitter with solo homer, his second of the series. Kenny Lofton, hitting his second home run in the playoff, Manny Ramirez and Ramirez again, followed with solo homers in the later innings. That was Cleveland's entire run production. Saberhagen pitched well, giving up only four hits (three of which were solo home runs), with seven strikeouts and a walk in a seven-inning stint. He left with a 3-1 deficit. Ramirez hit his second home run in the ninth inning off reliever Dennis Eckersley to give Cleveland the final total of four runs on five hits.

Meantime, Charles Nagy, a Connecticut native in his ninth year with the Indians, again beat the Red Sox. In his career, he had beaten them four times in Fenway Park without a loss, winning seven of his eight decisions against the Sox overall. Nagy pitched eight innings, gave up four singles, and had three strikeouts with no walks. He left the game with a 4-1 lead. Reliever Mike Jackson pitched the ninth inning and gave up a single to Mo Vaughn, his second of the day. Nomar Garciaparra drove Vaughn in with a home run, his second of the series, and the score was 4-3. The Red Sox scoring ended, too little and too late, and the Sox lost with a total of three runs and six hits.

Game 4 was a well-played pitchers' battle and the game went down to the wire. The Red Sox led after seven innings, 1-0, on Garciaparra's fourth-inning solo home run and starter Pete Schourek's two-hit pitching for 5⅓ innings. The Sox attempted to nail down the victory, bring in star "closer" Tom Gordon to pitch the eighth and ninth innings. Gordon, who had failed only once all season in a closer assignment, and that on April 14, had the misfortune to give up three hits and a walk in the eighth inning. The Indians took the lead, 2-1, and held it through the last two innings for the win.

David Justice, Cleveland leftfielder, was the hero of the day. He hit a double in the eighth inning, his second double of the day, driving in the only runs the Indians scored. He also made two sparkling throws from the outfield, one cutting down a run at home plate in the sixth inning that would have given the Red Sox a 2-0 lead. The game was well-played and well-managed. The Red Sox had six hits, including three doubles, and Garciaparra's home run. Mo Vaughn made some spectacular defensive plays at first base. For Cleveland, Mike Hargrove's managing and manipulation of his pitching was outstanding. With a good

Darren Lewis manned centerfield for the Red Sox in 1998, hitting .268 with 63 R.B.I. (Boston Red Sox).

5²/₃ inning starter performance by Bartolo Colon, Hargrove at one point used five pitchers in less than three innings to hold Boston at bay. He closed with his sixth pitcher, Mike Jackson. The moves were successful and the Red Sox were denied any scoring after the home run in the fourth inning. The Indians had only five hits but Justice's hitting and fielding were the difference in Game 4.

The Red Sox, after winning the first game on a home run barrage, lost the next three. Of the 20 runs scored by the Sox in the four games, Nomar Garciaparra and Mo Vaughn were responsible for driving in 18 of them. Vaughn

had seven hits in 17 at bats, a .412 average, with two home runs and seven R.B.I.s Garciaparra had five hits in 15 at bats, a .333 average, with three home runs and 11 R.B.I.. Valentin with seven hits batted .467. Lewis had five hits and batted .357. The bottom four players in the line up, O'Leary, Hatteberg, Benjamin and Bragg, each had one single in the series. The Red Sox mostly had good pitching performances, notably by starters Martinez, Saberhagen and Schourek. Tom Gordon suffered a rare failure at an inopportune time and Tim Wakefield's knuckleball was not working in his only start. The Indians won the series three games to one, and went on to the American League Championship Series. They met the New York Yankees for the American League pennant.

1999

Red Sox Bombard Cleveland in Come-From-Behind Win in American League Division Play-Offs, Three Games to Two

The Cleveland Indians coasted almost the entire season in winning the A.L. Central Division championship by 21 1/2 games over the second-place Chicago White Sox. They had a powerful team, second only to the Texas Rangers in team batting and home runs, and they had adequate pitching. They scored a season total of 1,009 runs, or more than six runs a game.

The Indians had notable superstars among their regular players. Their double-play combination of Omar Vizquel at shortstop and Roberto Alomar at second base were likely the best in the American League. They had 13 Gold Gloves between them. Their only fielding rivals, the National League, were perhaps Rey Ordonez at shortstop and Edgardo Alfonzo at second base for the New York Mets. Alomar, an M.V.P. candidate, batted .323 with 24 home runs and 120 runs batted in. Teammate Vizquel batted .333 and had 42 stolen bases. Outfielder Manny Ramirez, another M.V.P. candidate, had a phenomenal year with 165 runs batted in, the most since Jimmie Fox batted in 175 for the Red Sox in 1938. Ramirez batted .333 with 44 home runs. Cleveland, in fact, had five players who batted in more than 100 runs each. In addition to Ramirez and Alomar, there were powerful Richie Sexson with 122 and 31 home runs, slugging first baseman Jim Thome with 108 R.B.I.'s and 33 home runs and designated hitter Harold Baines who drove in 103 with a .312 batting average. The pitchers were led by Bartolo Colon

with an 18-5 record, Charles Nagy at 17-11 and Dave Burba with 15 wins and nine losses.

The Red Sox were comfortably in the lead for the league's "wild card" position most of the year. Though Toronto and Oakland surged at different times in the season, the Red Sox ended seven games ahead of the Oakland Athletics in the wild card competition. They also challenged the New York Yankees for the division lead, held by the Yankees for much of the season. In September, they came within two games of first place but ended up four games behind the Yankees.

The Red Sox had a franchise player, Pedro Martinez, who dominated the league with his pitching. He won 23 and lost four, had a 2.07 earned run average and won the Cy Young award. The Red Sox's other superstar was Nomar Garciaparra, who won the league batting title with a .357 average. He also had 27 home runs and 104 R.B.I.'s. Most of the other players were in the nature of a supporting cast. None batted as high as .300. Outfielder Troy O'Leary batted .280 with 28 home runs and 103 runs batted in. There were five other players who hit as many as 20 home runs. Besides O'Leary and Garciaparra, there were nine-year minor leaguer Brian Daubach with 21, Butch Huskey, a late-season acquisition from Seattle with 22 and an improving and now entrenched regular catcher, Jason Varitek, with 20. Third baseman John Valentin, injured part of the season, had a sub-par year. After Martinez, the best record on the pitching staff belonged to Bret Saberhagen with a 10-6 record. Tom "Flash" Gordon, the sensational 1998 "closer" was injured and on the disabled list most of the year.

On paper, the Cleveland Indians appeared to be heavy favorites to take the division series, even if Pedro Martinez were to win two games. The Red Sox, however, were an opportunistic team with careful planning by general manager Dan Duquette and uncanny managing by field manager Jimy Williams.

Game 1 of the division series was exciting, with ace Pedro Martinez pitching against ace Bartolo Colon. Nomar Garciaparra started the scoring with a home run in the second inning, and he scored the second run for the Sox with a double in the fourth inning followed by Mike Stanley's single. Tragedy struck the Sox after the fourth inning when Pedro Martinez had to retire because of a strained back, and it was uncertain whether he would be able to return for the series. Derek Lowe did a creditable job in relief. Jim Thome hit him for a home run with a man on base in the sixth. The game was a tight pitching duel into the ninth inning when Travis Fryman drove in the winning run for Cleveland after a hit batsman, a single and a base on balls loaded the bases. Colon was superb for the Indians, pitching eight innings, allowing five hits and striking out 11.

Game 2 saw Saberhagen starting for the Red Sox and Nagy for the Indians. The Indians blew the game open with six runs in the third inning and five runs in the fourth. The Indians had six walks in the two innings. Baines homered with two on and Jim Thome hit a bases-loaded homer. The Indians won the game, 11 to 1, on only eight hits, and Charles Nagy had an easy victory.

Things looked bleak for the Red Sox. They now had 18 losses in their last 19 postseason games. Martinez continued to have back problems and, as if that catastrophe were not enough, Nomar Garciaparra had a wrist injury and could not play in Game 3. It appeared the Red Sox would be eliminated by the Cleveland Indians in the division play-offs as they were in 1995 and 1998.

The Red Sox pitching staff was in disarray. Ramon Martinez (Pedro's older brother who had been a star pitcher for the Los Angeles Dodgers in the early 1990s and then injured his arm, and who was picked up by the Red Sox late in the 1999 season) started Game 3 for the Red Sox. Ramon pitched a creditable 5 2/3 innings, giving up two runs and five hits, and was succeeded by Derek Lowe who pitched another good relief stint. Dave Burba pitched well for the Indians, and, going into the last of the sixth inning at Fenway Park, the Indians were leading, 3-2. John Valentin then hit a home run over the center field wall,

his first hit in the series, and the Red Sox tied the game. The Sox, quite unexpectedly, broke the game open in the last of the seventh with six runs. After Valentin drove in two with a double, Brian Daubach also hit a home run over the center field wall, with two on base, and this gave the Red Sox an insurmountable lead. They won the game, 9 to 3, on 11 hits.

Game 4 was unbelievable. The Indians started Bartolo Colon with only three days' rest, and the Red Sox dug deep into their pitching staff and started former National Leaguer Kent Mercker. The Red Sox started scoring in the first inning and never stopped. They scored at least two runs in every inning except for a blank in the sixth and ended up with a 23 to 7 win. The scoring was historic: the most runs ever scored by a winning team in a postseason game and the most total runs in a postseason game. Valentin tied a postseason record by driving in seven runs in the game with two home runs and a single (at one point he had six straight hits in the series). Offerman and Varitek also hit home runs as the Red Sox had a total of 24 hits to go with their 23 runs. Despite giving up seven hits and nine bases on balls, the Red Sox staff of Mercker, Garces, Wakefield, Wasdin and Cormier persevered with the enormous lead.

Game 4 was something of an anomaly, and the Red Sox, now going back to Jacobs Field in Cleveland for Game 5, still had pitching problems. There appeared to be no certain starter and it was still uncertain whether Pedro Martinez's strained back had healed sufficiently for him to be able to play in Game 5. Bret Saberhagen started the game and Charles Nagy pitched for the Sox. Saberhagen did not last through the second inning as Thome hit his second home run in the series. Despite Nomar Garciaparra's first-inning home run, the Indians jumped out to a 5-2 lead after two innings. Further scoring in the third inning seemed to indicate another slugfest. Troy O'Leary hit a bases-loaded homer in the third inning, and the Sox scored five runs to lead 7-5. This was the first Red Sox grandslam homer in postseason team history.

In the bottom of the third, Fryman hit a home run and Thome hit his second home run of the game, this with a man on base. He hit four home runs during the series. The Indians again led 8-7, after three innings, notably without much help from slugger Manny Ramirez who went 1 for 18, his only hit coming in the fifth game of the series. The Red Sox scored another run in the fourth inning to tie the game.

Both Saberhagen and Lowe had pitched for the Red Sox, none too effectively. There was some rustling in the Red Sox dugout and bullpen, and out came Pedro Martinez to pitch the fourth inning. Pedro, in typical masterful style, pitched the rest of the game and allowed no runs and no hits. In his six-inning stint, he had eight strikeouts and gave up three bases on balls. Meantime, in the top of the seventh inning, Troy O'Leary hit a home run with two on base. Like Valentin in Game 4 he tied a record with seven R.B.I.'s. Ironically, two other players had driven in seven runs in a postseason game, Mo Vaughn with the Sox in 1998 and previously Edgar Martinez of the Seattle Mariners. All achieved their accomplishments against the Cleveland Indians.

In the final three games of the division play-offs, the Red Sox scored 44 runs and gave up 18. The Red Sox "wild card" team, like their National League counterparts, the New York Mets, won their divisional series. (The Mets upset the Arizona Diamondbacks three games to one.) Now looming ahead was the series all baseball traditionalists hoped for, the Boston Red Sox vs. the archrival New York Yankees for the American League pennant. The Yankees, in their division playoffs, had easily disposed of the Texas Rangers, three games to none.

1999

Renewal of Red Sox-Yanks Classics—Yanks Win Tense ALCS Competition, Four Games to One

The American League play-off for the pennant might have been scripted for a Hollywood production. The Yankees were playing the Red Sox. This was a renewal of one of the richest and most exciting rivalries in sports, and the history is unparalleled. The dramatics began in 1904 when the Pilgrims (Red Sox) beat the Highlanders (Yankees). Jack Chesbro, 41-game winner for the Highlanders, wild pitched in the winning run for the Pilgrims to give the Boston team the pennant. Fenway Park opened in 1912 with the Red Sox beating the Yankees in overtime in the opening game. In 1920, Red Sox owner Harry Frazee sold Babe Ruth to the Yankees and in so doing altered the history of baseball. In 1923, the Red Sox were the competition for the opening of Yankee Stadium and the Yankees won with a three-run home by Babe Ruth. In October 1949, the Red Sox lost the final two games of the season to New York, and the Yankees beat the Red Sox for the pennant by one game. In 1961, Roger Maris hits his record-setting 60th homer against the Red Sox at Yankee Stadium. In 1978, the Yankees, having rallied from 14 games down to tie the Sox for the pennant, beat the Red Sox in a one-game playoff on Bucky Dent's home run.

And so, in 1999, the Red Sox and Yankees, both having won their division series, played each other in the championship series for the American League pennant. The Yankees reached the ALCS in relatively easy fashion. Repeating their 1998 playoff experience, they again beat the Texas Rangers in the division play-offs, three games to none. Similar to the 1998 experience, Yankee pitching allowed the potent Ranger bats just one run in the entire

series. The Yankees now had a 10-game postseason winning streak.

The 1999 Yankees, though similar in personnel to the 1998 Yankees who won 114 games and were 22 games ahead of Boston at season's end, did not fare as well. They won the East Division again but this time with 98 wins and a four-game margin over Boston. They had two bona fide superstars. Derek Jeter was second in batting to his Red Sox shortstop counterpart, Nomar Garciaparra, and had a .349 average. He also led the league in hits with 219, and he hit 27 home runs and drove in 104 runs. He had a superlative year as a fielding shortstop. Bernie Williams, Yankees centerfielder and the league's 1998 batting champion, batted third in the league with a .342 average. He also had over 200 hits, with 25 home runs and 115 runs batted in. He was considered one of the preeminent centerfielders in the game. Tino Martinez led the team with 28 home runs. Four players had over 100 R.B.I.'s. In addition to Jeter and Williams, there were Martinez and Paul O'Neill. The pitchers were led by Orlando (El Duque) Hernandez, with a 17-9 record, and David Cone with a 12-9 record and an E.R.A. of 3.44 that was second in the league to Pedro Martinez of Boston.

The Red Sox had a more difficult time reaching the ALCS. They upset the favored Cleveland Indians three games to two. In the Division series, John Valentin and Troy O'Leary were the heroes, each driving in a record-tying seven runs in a game. Valentin batted .318 and had a slugging average of .818 with two doubles and three home runs. O'Leary batted .200 with a slugging average of .500, including two home runs. Nomar Garciaparra batted .417 with two doubles and two home runs. Mike Stanley led with 10 hits in the series, with a .500 batting average. Five of the Red Sox regulars batted over .315 and the team batting average was .318. The pitching star was ace Pedro Martinez, notably with his six-inning no-hit performance in relief winning the final game of the series.

Game 1 of the ALCS was won by the Yankees at Yankee Stadium in ten innings, 4-3. Bernie Williams opened the tenth inning with a home run into the center field stands to win the game. The Red Sox led 3-0 early in the game but the game was marred by four errors. Garciaparra made two spectacular line-drive catches at shortstop, but he also made two errors. Derek Jeter, the other superstar shortstop, also made a crucial error. The uncommon experience of two great shortstops making critical errors contributed to the scoring in an otherwise tight game.

Game 2 was a real nail-biter. In the eighth inning, Troy O'Leary led off with a double with the Red Sox leading 2-1. Both Dennis Martinez, Pedro's older brother, and David Cone pitched fine games. With O'Leary's hit, managerial strategy dominated the tense inning. Yankees' manager Joe Torre used four pitchers in the inning and Red Sox manager Jimy Williams emptied his bench with three pinch hitters. No runs were scored. The Yankees had scored two runs in the bottom of the seventh and with these won the game, 3-2. The Red Sox left 13 men on base as the Yankees went on to their 12th straight play-off win. The Red Sox were also unlucky enough to have two drives, by Jason Varitek and Troy O'Leary, fall just inches below the top of the wall, resulting in doubles rather than home runs that might have otherwise changed the course of the game.

Game 3 promised to be a classic. Pedro Martinez, the reigning dominant pitcher in baseball was pitching for the Red Sox. He had won a division play-off game and had a 0.00 E.R.A. in the division series. Roger Clemens, the erstwhile Red Sox icon and dominant pitcher in the game, was pitching for the Yankees. He, too, had won a well-pitched division series game and his division series E.R.A. was also 0.00. The game was at Fenway Park and, to indicate the degree of excitement, it was reported that a cardiologist who desperately wanted tickets to the game where there were no tickets available, paid $12,100 to secure four seats. The duel never materialized. In the first two-plus innings, Clemens gave up five runs

on six hits, four of which were for extra bases. He was replaced early in the third inning. Martinez, on the other hand, struck out four in a row in the same two innings and gave up one hit. Martinez had 12 strike outs, and allowed no runs and two hits in his seven-inning stint. The Red Sox in the first seven innings scored nine runs on 14 hits. John Valentin had five R.B.I.'s with three hits, including a home run. Nomar Garciaparra had four hits, including a home run and was on base five times. Both Trot Nixon and Jose Offerman had three hits each, and Brian Daubach had a double and a home run.

"Pay Back" for the Red Sox and Red Sox fans ended with Game 3. The Yankees won Games 4 and 5 and they won the American League pennant, four games to one. They went on to win the World Series, beating the Atlanta Braves, four games to none. In Game 4, Andy Pettitte pitched an excellent game for the Yankees. The Red Sox made four errors, and a close, tense game erupted into an easy victory for New York when they scored six runs in the ninth inning to win 9-2. Bernie Williams had another home run and three hits, and Rickie Ledee hit a home run with the bases loaded in the six-run ninth inning.

Game 5 was another tight game, but "El Duque" Hernandez who pitched and won Game 1 also gave a fine performance in Game 5. He allowed one run and five hits in the seven innings he pitched and the Yankees won, 6-1. The Red Sox rallied from a 4-0 deficit in the eighth inning, scored on Varitek's lead-off home run and then filled the bases. Manager Joe Torre of the Yankees used five pitchers in the eighth inning, the last of whom, Ramiro Mendoza, shut down the Red Sox without any further scoring. It was the second time in the series that he came in in relief with bases loaded and one out, and shut down the Red Sox. Game 5 was closely contested but once again was dominated by Yankee pitching and also Red Sox fielding lapses. The Red Sox made 10 errors in the five-game series, setting a record for ALCS competition. Poor umpiring, especially in the final game, with two obvious and acknowledged bad calls against the Red Sox, incited and angered Boston and its fans, but there is not enough to indicate the outcome would have been different. In brief, Yankee pitching and Red Sox errors established the result. Red Sox futility at crucial times at the plate also helped. In Game 5, despite receiving six bases on balls, the Sox left 11 men on base.

Jose Offerman led both teams in the ALCS with 11 hits and a .458 batting average. Nomar Garciaparra and John Valentin tied for second in number of series hits, eight, and tied for the lead in most R.B.I.'s, at five. Garciaparra had two home runs and batted .400. Valentin had one homer and batted .348. Troy O'Leary batted .350. For the Yankees, Derek Jeter was the leading hitter at .350 and Chuck Knoblauch batted .333. They had 13 hits between them. Scott Brosius had two home runs for the Yanks. Pedro Martinez had an outstanding pitching performance for the Red Sox. The Yankees had surpassing pitching performances from Hernandez, mendoza, Pettitte and the closer, Mariano Rivera, who had a win and two saves.

The Red Sox, for the first time since 1986, won a postseason competition. They beat the Cleveland Indians in the division play-offs. The Sox advanced to the pennant play-off against the New York Yankees and lost in a tense series that was closer than some of the scores indicated. For the entire season, Jimy Williams gave a magnificent managerial performance and the Red Sox unexpectedly fielded a team that proved to be tough, highly competitive, and able to win. This was an outstanding season for the Sox, led by superstars Pedro Martinez and Nomar Garciaparra.

The Red Sox Encyclopedia

Bobby Doerr (left), Ted Williams (center) and Rudy York examine the merchandise at the Louisville Slugger bat factory. (Baseball Hall of Fame Library. Cooperstown, N.Y.).

GAMES TO REMEMBER — MOMENTS OF GLORY AND THE ONES THAT HURT

The Red Sox have played in some of the most memorable games in baseball history. Who can forget "the Snodgrass Muff," Ted Williams' last at bat at Fenway, Carlton Fisk's home run in the 12th inning of the sixth game of the 1975 World Series, Bucky Dent's home run to crush the Red Sox pennant hopes in 1978, and the squibbler through Bill Buckner's legs in the 1986 World Series.

These events create stories worth telling and following are the accounts of famous games.

Great Games—Red Sox Moments of Glory

1. 1912 Red Sox World Series Win—The Snodgrass Muff

2. 1941 All-Star Game—Ted Williams' Dramatic Home Run

3. 1960 Last Home Game—Ted Williams' Last at Bat Home Run

4. 1975 World Series—Carlton Fisk's Game-Winning Home Run

Sad Moments—Red Sox Big Game Losses

1. 1946 World Series—Enos Slaughter Scores From First to Win Series

2. 1948 Play-off Game—Cleveland Beats Red Sox For Pennant

3. 1949 Red Sox Lose Pennant To Yankees In Last Game Of Season

4. 1978 Play-Off Game—Yankees Win Pennant On Bucky Dent's Home Run

Ted Williams hits yet another ball out of Fenway Park. Williams retired in 1960, hitting a home run in the last at-bat of his last game. (Boston Public Library, Print Department).

5. 1986 World Series—Mets Win Crucial Game On Squibbler Through Buckner's Legs

Great Games—Red Sox Moments of Glory

October 16, 1912
Fenway Park, Boston   **#1**

SEVENTH GAME, WORLD SERIES
RED SOX VS. NEW YORK GIANTS
Red Sox Win World Series
Snodgrass Muffs Easy Fly Ball

The year 1912 marked the first pennant year for the Boston Red Sox since 1904. Under manager/first baseman Jake Stahl and with a remarkable 34-win season by Smoky Joe Wood, the Red Sox finished ahead of Clark Griffith's Wash- ington Senators by 14 games. The Sox had a good sup- porting cast of the exceptional Tris Speaker-Harry Hooper -Duffy Lewis outfield. Speaker, showing his offensive and defensive skills, hit .383, led the league with 10 home runs, and led the league with an amazing 35 assists play- ing center field. Third baseman Larry Gardner and first baseman Jake Stahl were two other .300-plus hitters on the team. In addition to Smoky Joe Wood and his phe- nomenal 34-5 year, they had 20-game winners Hugh Bedient and Buck O'Brien.

The New York Giants, led by Manager John McGraw, won the National League pennant, finishing 10 games ahead of the second-place Pittsburgh Pirates. The Giants were repeat pennant winners and in fact won three consecutive pennants in 1911, 1912 and 1913. They were favored to win the 1912 World Series. They had the remarkable rookie pitcher Rube Marquard who started the season with 19 straight wins and had a league-leading 26 victories for the year. They also had the incomparable Christy Mathewson with 23 wins and 17-game winner Jeff Tesreau who led the league with a 1.96 earned run average. Fred Merkle at first base and Larry Doyle at second base were .300-plus hitters and, for that era, hit a respectable 11 and 10 home runs, respectively. Chief Meyers was the Giants' catcher and hit a hefty .358, second in the league. Fred Snodgrass played left field and batted .269. The team had base-running speed, with right fielder Red Murray, Merkle and third baseman Buck Herzog having 112 stolen bases among them.

The World Series opened at the Polo Grounds in New York and the Red Sox won the first game, 4-3, with Smoky Joe Wood outdueling Jeff Tesreau. The second game was called after 11 innings on account of darkness with Christy Mathewson pitching all 11 innings for the Giants. Game 3 went to Marquard of the Giants, 2-1, as 5-foot-6 inch outfielder Josh Devore made a sensational catch in the bottom of the ninth inning to save the victory for the Giants. Smoky Joe Wood put the Sox ahead by winning the fourth game, 3-1, again beating Jeff Tesreau. Boston looked like the likely World Series winner as the Sox then took a three-to-one lead in games on Hugh Bedient's 2-1 win over Mathewson and the Giants, even though Matty allowed only three hits. However, the Giants won the next two games to even the Series at three games all with one tie. Marquard and Tesreau beat the Red Sox.

Game Eight, the deciding game, was played at Fenway Park. Mathewson pitched for the Giants and Bedient started for the homestanding Red Sox. It was a fine pitching duel. The Giants scored one run early and the Red Sox tied the game in the seventh inning when pinch hitter "Swede" Henriksen, batting for Bedient, hit a double to drive in the only Sox run at that point. Smoky Joe Wood came on to pitch for the Red Sox in the eighth inning of the tense game. Neither team scored again in the regulation nine innings and the game went on into the tenth inning. The Giants' Red Murray, with one out, hit a ground rule double off Joe Wood. He was driven in on Fred Merkle's line drive that Tris Speaker, one of baseball history's great fielding center fielders, fumbled. It was one of five Red Sox errors in the game. The Sox now fell behind, 2-1, in the tenth with one last turn at bat.

Into the last of the tenth inning, Christy Mathewson was still pitching a strong game and he had given up only two runs in his last 18 innings. Sox pinch hitter Clyde

Engle started the inning with an easy fly ball to center field that Fred Snodgrass unaccountably "muffed". It was the infamous "Snodgrass muff" of the 1912 World Series that was considered to have opened the flood gates for the Red Sox and allowed them to win the Series. Engle ended up on second base. Snodgrass made a fine catch of a difficult line drive hit by the next batter, Harry Hooper. Mathewson then walked second baseman Steve Yerkes, putting the tying and winning runs on base. Tris Speaker, Boston's great hitter, was the next batter. He hit a pop foul that dropped between first baseman Fred Merkle and catcher Chief Meyers as they could not get together on who would catch the easy out. Speaker then singled to drive in Engle with the tying run and Yerkes took third base. Mathewson then walked Duffy Lewis to fill the bases and set up a double play possibility. Larry Gardner, the good hitting third baseman, next drove a fly ball to right field, sending in Yerkes with the running run. The Red Sox won in ten innings, 3-2.

The Red Sox won the World Series, four games to three with one tie, but Game 8 was a game neither Mathewson nor the Giants should have lost. Prophetically, perhaps, it was the second of three straight years in which the Giants won the pennant and lost the World Series. The Red Sox, on the other hand, were on the threshold of a great dynasty in which they won four pennants and four World Series in seven years.

Line Score

					R	H	E
New York Giants	001	000	000	1	2	9	2
Boston Red Sox	000	000	100	2	3	8	5

July 8, 1941
Briggs Stadium, Detroit   #2

1941 ALL-STAR GAME
Ted Williams' Dramatic Ninth-Inning Home Run
Wins the Game

The All-Star game of 1941, the last before the attrition of great talent before World War II, was a gathering of some of the greatest names in the history of baseball. Twelve future Hall of Famers played in the game. This was the ninth annual All-Star game and the American League had won five of the first eight games.

The American League team had Rudy York and Jimmie Foxx at first base, Bobby Doerr and Joe Gordon at second base, Joe Cronin and Lou Boudreau at shortstop and Cecil

Travis, a transplanted shortstop, at third base. All were outstanding players and all but York, Gordon and Travis became Hall of Famers. The outfield had Jeff Heath and Dom DiMaggio in right field and Hall of Famers Joe DiMaggio and Ted Williams in center and left field, respectively. The catchers were Hall of Famer Bill Dickey and Frankie Hayes.

The pitchers were led by Hall of Famer Bob Feller, who started the game, and lesser lights but solid pitchers Thornton Lee, Sid Hudson and Edgar Smith.

Nineteen forty-one was the year in which Joe DiMaggio set his record of batting safely in 56 straight games and Ted Williams hit .406. Both were young players and already superstars. Williams was the leader in most hitting categories that year, and Joe DiMaggio was not far behind. Jeff Heath of the Indians was a slugger that year and Cecil Travis, the Senators' shortstop hit first behind Williams in season's average, at .359. Bill Dickey, in the 14th year of a magnificent career, led the league in fielding percentage for catchers at .994. Joe Gordon and Lou Boudreau were a fine all-star double play combination. Bob Feller was into a league-leading 25-game winning season and led the league in most pitching categories. Thornton Lee of the Chicago White Sox was also having an exceptional pitching year.

The National League did not have as many great players, but the team consisted of stars of the era. Frank McCormick was at first base, Lonny Frey and Hall of Famer Billy Herman at second base, Hall of Famer Arky Vaughan and Eddie Miller at shortstop, and Stan Hack and Cookie Lavagetto at third base. Bill Nicholson, Bob Elliott and Hall of Famer Enos Slaughter shared right field, Pete Reiser played center field and Terry Moore was in left field. Mickey Owen, Al Lopez and Harry Danning shared the catching. Whitlow Wyatt was the starting pitcher and Paul Derringer, Bucky Walters and Claude Passeau also pitched.

Pete Reiser led the National League in 1941 in both batting and slugging averages, in triples, and in runs scored. Stan Hack of the Chicago Cubs had his usual high on-base percentage, leading the league with 186 hits and receiving 99 walks that year. Bill Nicholson, Frank McCormick and Arky Vaughan were coming off some very strong hitting years in 1940 and Lonnie Frey was a leader in stealing bases.

Frank McCormick led the league in fielding at first base in 1941 with a .995 average and his fellow Cincinnati Red, Lonny Frey, led the second basemen with a .970 average. Eddie Miller of the Boston Braves led the shortstops with a .966 fielding average. Wyatt, with fellow pitcher Kirby Higbe of the Brooklyn Dodgers, led the league in wins in 1941. Bucky Walters and Paul Derringer were coming off

their magnificent 1940 pitching year with the World Champion Cincinnati Reds in which both won 20 or more games, and Walters won 19 games in 1941.

The All-Star game was a pitching duel for six innings with the American League leading 2-1 on runs batted in by Lou Boudreau and Ted Williams. Feller had pitched three scoreless innings and Thornton Lee gave up one run in his three innings. Whitlow Wyatt pitched two scoreless innings for the National League and Paul Derringer and Bucky Walters gave up one run each in their two-inning stints.

In the seventh inning, with Washington's Sid Hudson pitching for the American League, Enos Slaughter singled and Arky Vaughan hit the first of his two home runs in the game, putting the National League in front, 3-2. In the eighth inning the National League added to their lead, batting against the White Sox's Edgar Smith. Johnny Mize had a double and then, with two out, Arky Vaughan hit his second home run, setting an All-Star game record and bidding to become the All-Star game hero. The National League led, 5-2, going into the last of the eighth. In that inning, Joe DiMaggio doubled and brother Dom DiMaggio drove him in with a single. The National League did not score in the ninth inning and going into their last at bat the American League was losing 5-3. Claude Passeau was pitching for the National League.

In the last of the ninth, pinch hitter Ken Keltner got on base with a scratch single. Joe Gordon singled and Cecil Travis drew a walk, filling the bases with one out. Joe DiMaggio came to the plate and hit a hard ground ball to the shortstop that appeared to be a game-ending double play ball. However, after getting an out at second base, the usually reliable Billy Herman threw wide to first base. DiMaggio was safe, with men at first and third, and Keltner had scored to make the game 5-4 in favor of the N.L. The next batter was Ted Williams. He hit a long foul strike on the first pitch. Passeau then pitched two balls, and the count was 2 and 1. Williams on the next pitch hit a powerful line drive that hit the facade on top of the upper stand in right field at Briggs Stadium. It was a tremendous and dramatic blast, a three-run home run that climaxed a four-run ninth-inning rally and gave the win to the American League, 7 to 5. Added to the tremendous cheers of the crowd Williams was greeted and congratulated when he reached home plate by Joe DiMaggio.

Line Score

				R	H	E
National League	000	001	220	5	10	2
American League	000	101	014	7	11	3

September 28, 1960
Fenway Park, Boston #3

LAST HOME GAME OF THE RED SOX SEASON
Ted Williams Hits A Home Run In
His Last At Bat At Fenway

The year 1960 was a dismal year for the Red Sox. They finished in seventh place, 32 games behind the pennant-winning Yankees. Their futility was expressed in the fact that they had three managers that year, Billy Jurges, Del Baker and Pinky Higgins. The last series at Fenway Park, with the Baltimore Orioles, in the last week of the season had no meaning except that Ted Williams had announced he was retiring. These would be his last at bats at home after an incomparable 19 years at Fenway Park with the Red Sox, beginning in 1939.

"The Kid" had his usual more-than-competent year in 1960. In 113 games, at the age of 42, he had a season batting average of .316, hit 29 home runs and drove in 72 runs. With his usual eagle-eye at home plate, he had 75 walks.

On Wednesday, September 28, the last day of the season at Fenway Park, there were only 10,000 fans in the stands. Before the game there was a presentation ceremony for Ted Williams, honoring his career, all of it with Boston. Williams, who generally disdained formality and was not comfortable with ceremonial occasions, acknowledged the awards he received, reminded the press that he did not have friendly feelings toward them, and then expressed his gratitude for a career in Boston, for an owner like Tom Yawkey ("the greatest owner in baseball"), and for the Boston fans ("the greatest fans").

It was announced that Williams' famous number 9 on his uniform would be permanently retired, the first player number to be retired by the Red Sox.

Williams started the game in his usual position in left field, and also as usual batted third in the batting order. The Baltimore Orioles were the opposition and, though not as bad as the Red Sox, they also were out of the pennant chase, albeit in second place. Steve Barber was their starting pitcher. Williams walked in his first at bat on four straight pitches and subsequently scored. Though the Red Sox were staked to a 2-0 lead, they quickly fell behind the Orioles. Barber, however, was replaced by young Jack Fisher before Williams' next at bat. Williams hit a fly ball to center field in his second at bat, in the third inning. In the fifth inning, again against Fisher, he hit a long fly ball to right field but the Orioles' right fielder leaned against the 380-foot mark on the fence and caught it. Ted did not

come to bat again until the eighth inning and at that point he did not have a hit, let alone a home run, in his last game in his career at Fenway Park.

Since "The Thumper's" at bat in the eighth inning seemed likely to be his last one, he was given a standing ovation. Fisher's first pitch to Williams was a ball, and Williams missed the second pitch, so the count was one and one. Williams hit the next ball on a line over the centerfield wall for another dramatic home run. This one, however, had special meaning because it was his last hit and his last home run in his last at bat at the end of his career at Fenway Park. Williams ran the bases on his home run in his customary fashion, with his head down. He did not tip his cap to acknowledge the cheers of the crowd nor did he emerge from the dugout to acknowledge their continuing congratulation, even in this last at bat on the last day. He was typical, vintage Ted Williams, and he was still a Boston hero and a Red Sox legend. He became a more affable, mellower person after his baseball years.

Line Score

		R	H	E
Baltimore Orioles	020 022 000	4	9	1
Boston Red Sox	200 000 012	5	6	1

October 21, 1975
Fenway Park, Boston #4

SIXTH GAME OF THE WORLD SERIES BETWEEN THE RED SOX AND THE REDS
Carlton Fisk's Dramatic 12th-Inning Home Run
Wins The Game

The 1975 World Series between the Boston Red Sox and the Cincinnati Reds is thought by many to have been the best World Series ever played. It matched two strong teams in a dramatic, seesaw set of games.

The Boston Red Sox had won the American League East division by five games over the Baltimore Orioles. They then defeated the Oakland Athletics, three games to none, in the American League Championship Series. The Red Sox were a hard-hitting team, comfortably leading the American League in both hitting and slugging average, by more than ten points in each category. They were a high scoring team, averaging nearly five runs a game. Veteran player and future Hall of Famer Carl Yastrzemski was the first baseman, Doug Griffin and Rick Burleson were the double-play combination and Rico Petrocelli was the third baseman. The Sox had a preeminent outfield consisting of good fielding, hard-hitting Dwight Evans in right field, Fred Lynn who won Rookie of the Year and M.V.P. honors in center field, and rookie Jim Rice, who, like Lynn, batted over .300, hit more than 20 home runs and drove in more than 100 runs in right field. Carlton Fisk with a .331 batting average was the catcher and the hard-hitting reserves were Cecil Cooper, an infielder, and Bernie Carbo, an outfielder. The Sox had three pitchers who averaged 18 wins each, Rick Wise, Luis Tiant and "Spaceman" Bill Lee. Dick Drago was their best reliever.

A powerhouse, the Cincinnati Reds were known as "the Big Red Machine." They beat the L.A. Dodgers by 20 games in the National League West division, and swept the NLCS from Pittsburgh, three games to none. They led the National League West division in batting and slugging by a wide margin and averaged more than five runs a game. They were an all-around team and also led the National League in stolen bases and in fielding average. Their pitching was not exceptional but, nevertheless, they were the favorites to win the World Series. The Reds' line-up had three players who are presently in the Hall of Fame and a fourth, Pete Rose, who many feel should be in the Hall though he has been banned for ethical violations by Major League Baseball. Hard-hitting Tony Perez, who played briefly with the Red Sox, was the Reds' Hall of Fame first baseman. Hall of Famer Joe Morgan was a great all-around player at second base. Johnny Bench was the incomparable Hall of Fame catcher. Dave Concepcion was an exceptional shortstop and hustling Pete Rose, who has more hits in baseball than anybody, was at third base. The outfield consisted of solid-hitting right fielder Ken Griffey, a good centerfielder in Cesar Geronimo, and heavy-hitting George Foster. The pitching staff had three 15-game winners, Don Gullett, Gary Nolan and Jack Billingham. Rollie Eastwick tied for the league lead in saves.

Luis Tiant pitched a shut out in winning Game 1 of the Series for the Red Sox, 6-0. Game 2 was a thriller won by Cincinnati in the ninth inning, 3-2. Trailing 2-1 in their last at bat, Bench came up for the Reds and doubled. Dick Drago replaced starter Bill Lee for the Sox. He retired two batters but then Dave Concepcion singled home Bench, stole second and scored the winning run on Ken Griffey's double. Game 3 was another tight one with the Reds winning, 6-5, in ten innings. A record six home runs were hit, three by each team. The Red Sox trailed in the game, 5-1, and finally tied the score on Dwight Evans' homer in the ninth, but it was not enough. The Red Sox evened the Series in Game 4, another close game, 5-4, a second win

for Tiant. The Reds went ahead in the Series, three games to two, as they won Game 5, 6-2, on Tony Perez's two home runs and four runs batted in.

Game 6, as it always is, was a crucial game. It was played at Fenway Park. Luis Tiant, rested by a three-day rain postponement, pitched for the Red Sox and Gary Nolan pitched for the Reds. In the first inning Fred Lynn hit a three-run home run to put the Sox ahead, 3-0. In the fifth inning, Ken Griffey hit a long triple off the center field wall with two men on base and then scored on Johnny Bench's single, tying the game, 3-3. Fred Lynn, making a desperate effort to catch Griffey's hit, banged against the wall and then crumpled to the ground, a dramatic and hushed moment in which everybody feared injury, but Lynn continued in the game.

In the seventh inning, the Reds scored two more runs on George Foster's double, and in the eighth inning Cesar Geronimo hit a home run to put the Reds ahead, 6-3, with Boston having only two times at bat left. In the last of the eighth, Fred Lynn led off with a single and Rico Petrocelli walked. Ace reliever Rawley Eastwick was brought in by the Reds and he faced pinch hitter Bernie Carbo. In another dramatic moment in the game, Bernie, with the count three balls and two strikes, hit a home run over the center field wall, tying the game, 6 even. It was Bernie's second pinch hit home run of the Series. The Red Sox had a chance to win in the ninth inning, but George Foster, with a rifle arm in left field, threw out Denny Doyle at home plate. The game went into extra innings. In the 11th, Dwight Evans saved the game for Boston with a spectacular catch of Joe Morgan's drive that appeared to be headed for a home run, and then threw out the base runner for a double play. The game was now nearly four hours old as "Pudge" Fisk came to the plate to bat for the Sox in the last half of the 12th inning. He faced Cincinnati's eighth pitcher, Pat Darcy. With the count one ball, Fisk hit a long line drive down the left field foul line. Fisk, starting down the first base line, watched the ball like everyone else. He started waving, both arms overhead, gesturing toward fair territory, as if to compel the ball to stay fair, even as he was running to first base. The ball stayed fair, just barely, and dropped into the stands for a dramatic, game-winning home run. The Boston stands became a bedlam. The Red Sox won in 12 innings, 7-6.

It was anticlimactic and very disappointing that the Red Sox lost the seventh game and the World Series to the Reds. It was another exciting game. The Reds overcame a 3-0 Red Sox lead, Tony Perez hitting another home run with a man on base. The Reds won the game on Joe Morgan's single in the ninth inning with two out, 4-3.

Line Score

		R	H	E
Cincinnati Red	000 030 210 000	6	14	0
Boston Red Sox	300 000 030 001	7	10	1

Sad Games—Red Sox Big Game Losses

October 15, 1946
Sportsmen's Park, St. Louis   #1

SEVENTH GAME, WORLD SERIES RED SOX
VS. ST. LOUIS CARDINALS
Enos Slaughter Scores From First Base
On A Hit To Win The Series

The 1946 season was the year of returning veterans from World War II. The returning stars were back in baseball uniforms, and there were some newer stars as well.

The Boston Red Sox won the American League pennant by 12 games over the Detroit Tigers. They had a powerhouse team that made them clear favorites to win the World Series. They easily led the league in batting and slugging percentage and they were a prolific run-scoring team. Heavy-hitting Rudy York was the first baseman. Hall of Famer Bobby Doerr and good, all-around player Johnny Pesky were the double-play combination. Rip Russell was the third baseman. George Metkovich was the right fielder, dependable Dom DiMaggio was in center field and Ted Williams, who batted .342, hit 38 home runs and drove in 123 runs, was in left field. Williams, York and Doerr each drove in more than 115 runs. Williams, Pesky and Dom DiMaggio all batted over .315. The catcher was Hal Wagner. Pinky Higgins, at third base, and outfielders Leon Culberson and Wally Moses were good substitutes. The pitching was impressive, led by 20-game winners Boo Ferriss and Tex Hughson, 17-game winner Mickey Harris and 13-game winner Joe Dobson.

The St. Louis Cardinals were also a formidable team. However, they had to meet the Brooklyn Dodgers in a playoff for the pennant and won, two games to none. The Cards led the league in most major departments, in batting, slugging and runs scored, in fielding and their pitchers had the league's lowest combined earned run average at 3.01. The Cards had the incomparable Hall of Famer, Stan Musial, at first base. Stan led the major leagues in batting at .365 and he had 16 home runs and 103 runs batted in. Hall of Famer Red Schoendienst was at second base and was joined by a great fielding shortstop, Marty Marion.

Slugger Whitey Kurowski was the third baseman. Hall of Famer Enos "Country" Slaughter who led the league with 130 runs batted in was the right fielder. Harry the Hat Walker was the center fielder and Erv Dusak was the left fielder. The catcher was Joe Garagiola. Terry Moore, a great center fielder who was near the end of his career, and Dick Sisler, son of Hall of Fame first baseman George Sisler who was at the beginning of his career, were capable substitutes. The Cards had 20-game winner Howie Pollet to lead their pitching and they had two other pitchers who won 15 games each and had earned run averages under 3.00, Harry Brecheen and Murry Dickson.

The World Series opened in Sportsmen's Park, St. Louis. The Red Sox won the first game on Rudy York's home run in the tenth inning, 3-2. Howie Pollet pitched all the way and lost for the Cards. Tex Hughson pitched eight innings. Earl Johnson pitched the last two innings in relief and won the game. The Cards evened the Series, winning the second game, 3-0, on Harry Brecheen's four-hitter. Boo Ferriss won the third game, shutting out the Cards as Rudy York hit a three-run home run, his second homer of the Series. Game 4 was a slaughter for the Cards, 12-3 on 20 hits, as Slaughter, Kurowski and Garagiola each had four hits. As the lead in games seesawed, the Red Sox won Game 5, 6-3, as Joe Dobson pitched a fine game. Pinky Higgins' double in the seventh inning drove in Dom DiMaggio with the deciding run. The Cardinals retaliated in Game 6 as Harry Brecheen beat the Red Sox, 4-1. The Series was tied at three games each.

Game 7 saw Boo Ferriss and Murry Dickson starting for their respective teams. It was a well-pitched game with the Cardinals leading going into the top of the eighth inning, 3 to 1. Dickson had gone all the way and Ferriss and Dobson were the Red Sox pitchers. Dobson had replaced Ferriss when the Cards scored two runs in the fifth inning. In the top of the eighth the Red Sox's first two hitters, pinch hitters, got hits. Brecheen then replaced Dickson and immediately got two outs. Matters looked grim for the Red Sox with two on but also two outs. However, Dom DiMaggio doubled to score both runners and tie the game at 3 all. Significantly, DiMaggio twisted his ankle running out the double, and the fleet center fielder

---

Games to Remember – Moments of Glory and the Ones that Hurt

was replaced by Leon Culberson.

Then came the climactic bottom of the eighth inning with Culberson in center field and Bob Klinger, a National Leaguer before 1946, pitching for the Red Sox. Enos Slaughter singled to open the inning, but then Klinger got the next two batters out with Slaughter still at first base. Harry Walker, the next batter, doubled into center field. Slaughter, intending to steal second base before the hit, was streaking around the bases while Culberson, a bit slower than Dom DiMaggio, was chasing after the ball. Culberson fumbled the ball momentarily, quickly retrieved it and fired to cut-off man Johnny Pesky. Pesky, seeing the third base coach's signal to Slaughter to stop at third base, positioned himself for a play on Walker at second base. Slaughter, however, kept streaking around third and, with the whole park shouting, Pesky grasped what was going on too late. Out of position to throw home, Pesky made the throw up line from the plate and Slaughter flew across with the winning run. The Cardinals won the game and the Series before a happily cheering Cardinal crowd, 4-3. Country Slaughter was the hero with his remarkable dash from first to home.

Harry Brecheen, winning the last game in relief, won three games in the Series. Stan Musial and Ted Williams, two super players and super hitters in the big leagues, each had a miserable Series. Stan the Man batted .222. Ted batted .200. Neither had a home run. The Cardinals had played "the Williams shift," inaugurated in that year by Manager Lou Boudreau of the Cleveland Indians against Williams' hitting. Since Williams characteristically drove the ball toward right field, all of the infielders except the third baseman were placed right of second base. The third baseman moved over toward shortstop. Williams had only five hits and none for extra bases in the Series.

Line Score

				R	H	E
Boston Red Sox	100	000	020	3	8	0
St. Louis Cardinals	010	020	01x	4	9	1

October 4, 1948
Fenway Park, Boston   #2

ONE GAME PLAY-OFF FOR THE
AMERICAN LEAGUE PENNANT
Cleveland Indians Beat Red Sox On Lou Boudreau's Hitting

The 1948 American League pennant chase was a tight race between three teams, the Red Sox, the Cleveland Indians

and the New York Yankees. The Red Sox were behind the Yankees and the Indians entering the final scheduled games of the year. The Red Sox had a three-game series with the Yankees. They swept the Yanks and eliminated them from the pennant race. On the season's final day they needed to beat the Yankees, which they did, and Cleveland, with a one-game lead, needed to lose to Detroit, to force a pennant tie. Cleveland ace Bob Feller faced the Tiger's ace Hal Newhouser on

Player/manager Lou Boudreau almost single-handedly beat the Red Sox in the 1948 play-off game for the pennant. Boudreau later played for and then managed the Red Sox. (Baseball Hall of Fame Library. Cooperstown, N.Y.).

the final day in Cleveland, and Newhouser won. There would be a one game play-off for the pennant between the Red Sox and the Indians in Boston.

All three teams, the Red Sox, Indians and Yankees, had a postwar glut of talent. The Red Sox in 1948 had a powerhouse team with a nucleus of veterans Ted Williams, Bobby Doerr, Johnny Pesky and Dom DiMaggio. They had added power with Vern Stephens and good hitting with Billy Goodman. Birdie Tebbetts, the great veteran from the Tigers, was in his second year as Red Sox catcher. On the bench were outfielders Sam Mele and Wally Moses. Williams led the league in batting at .369 and he, Stephens and Doerr each had 25 or more home runs and more than 110 runs batted in. The leading pitchers were Jack Kramer with 18 wins, Joe Dobson with 16 and Mel Parnell with 15.

The Indians led the league in team batting average and home runs, in fielding average and in pitchers' earned run average, shutouts and saves. They were an all-around team who, not having finished higher than fourth place since 1943, appeared to have arrived. Eddie Robinson was a good hitting and fielding first baseman. Joe Gordon and manager Lou Boudreau were an All-Star double play combination and both could hit. Veteran Ken Keltner was a solid power hitter and good fielder at third base. Dale Mitchell and Larry Doby were good hitting outfielders around fine fielding center fielder Thurman Tucker. Jim Hegan, an experienced handler of pitchers, was the catcher. The pitching staff was something special with Hall of Famers Bob Feller and Bob Lemon winning 39 games and rookie Gene Bearden winning 20 and leading the league in earned run average at 2.43. Veteran Russ Christopher led the league with 17 saves.

The Yankees were, as usual, a formidable team. Dependable George McQuinn was the first baseman. Snuffy Stirnweiss and Phil Rizzuto were a good double-play combination. Billy Johnson was the third baseman. Veterans and solid sluggers Tommy Henrich and Joe DiMaggio were in right and center fields, Joe having led the league with 39 home runs and 155 runs batted in. Johnny Lindell, a converted pitcher, was a good-hitting left fielder. Hard-hitting Yogi Berra also played the outfield and shared catching duties with Gus Niarhos. Veteran outfielder Charlie "King Kong" Keller was also still with the club. The pitching staff sparkled with Allie Reynolds, Eddie Lopat and Vic Raschi winning 52 games, backed by reliever Joe Page. The Yankees, not atypically, were between world championships. They won in 1947 and then reeled off five straight championships from 1949 through 1953.

Manager Lou Boudreau nominated Gene Bearden to pitch the play-off game and Red Sox new manager Joe McCarthy, a veteran at winning pennants and world championships with the Yankees, chose Denny Galehouse. Dobson, Kramer and Parnell, after a tough final week chasing the pennant, had tired arms. Boudreau greeted Galehouse with his first home run of the day, in the first inning, giving the Indians a 1-0 lead. In the last of the first inning Pesky doubled and Vern Stephens drove him in with a single, tying the game. In the fourth inning, Boudreau again came to the plate, and singled. Joe Gordon followed and singled. Ken Keltner then drove a three-run homer. Ellis Kinder replaced Galehouse and Larry Doby hit a double, coming around later in the inning for the Indians' fifth run. The Indians led the one game play-off, 5-1. Adding insult to injury Lou Boudreau hit another home run in his next at bat and the Indians led at the end of five innings, 6-1. Bobby Doerr hit a two-run homer in the sixth to close the gap to 6-3 but that was as close as the Red Sox would come. Boudreau had another hit, his fourth, and the Indians scored two more runs. Bearden, except for the pitch to Doerr, pitched a fine five-hit game and the Indians won the game 8-3, and the pennant.

Lou Boudreau led the Indians to the pennant in more ways than one. He not only managed and played a flawless shortstop with eight chances but he had a sensational four hits with two home runs. Ironically, he ended his playing career with Boston, playing in 1951 and very briefly in 1952, and he became the Red Sox manager for three years beginning in 1952.

The Red Sox loss also meant that there would not be for the first time an all-Boston World Series. The Boston Braves finished 6½ games ahead of the St. Louis Cardinals to win the National League pennant. It was their first pennant since the "Miracle Braves" of 1914 went from last place to first place and won the world championship.

Line Score

		R	H	E
Cleveland Indians	100 410 011	8	13	1
Boston Red Sox	100 002 000	3	5	1

October 2, 1949
Yankee Stadium, New York   #3

THE TIGHT PENNANT RACE BETWEEN THE RED SOX AND THE NEW YORK YANKEES
The Red Sox Lose The Pennant
On The Final Day Of The Season

The Red Sox of 1949 were still a postwar powerhouse team and consistent contenders for the pennant. Their potent line-up made them favorites to win the 1949 American League Pennant. The Yankees had put together all the blocks for a dynasty and, prophetically, this was to be the first of many successive championship years under new Manager Casey Stengel.

The Red Sox had almost the same team they had in 1948 that just missed winning the pennant. As a team, they led the league in hitting and slugging and scored nearly six runs a game. Vern Stephens and Ted Williams were still hitting home runs and tied for the league's runs batted in championship with 159 each. Goodman at first base and Pesky at third base were both hitting around .300. Dependable Bobby Doerr had his usual good year with a better than .300 batting average and over 100 runs batted in. Dom DiMaggio in center field had his .300 plus hitting year. Al Zarilla from the St. Louis Browns was now in right field. Birdie Tebbetts was again the catcher. Mel Parnell and Ellis Kinder had great years, each pitching more than 20 wins with Parnell leading the league with 25.

The Yankees' Tommy Henrich played first base and had a good hitting year. Jerry Coleman and Phil Rizzuto were now the double-play combination and both led the league in fielding at their positions. Bobby Brown, later to become the president of the American League, and Billy Johnson platooned at third base. Hank Bauer, Cliff Mapes and Gene Woodling, all good hitters, were the outfielders. Joe DiMaggio was injured and played in only 76 games but he still managed to bat .346, hit 14 home runs and drive in 67 runs. The Yanks still had Johnny Lindell and Snuffy Stirnweiss as reserves. The catcher, now full time at the position, was heavy hitting Yogi Berra. Vic Raschi won 21 games to lead the pitching staff but Allie Reynolds, Eddie Lopat and Tommy Byrne all won 15 or more games. Joe Page was the game's premier relief pitcher, pitching in a league-leading 60 games, winning 13 and placing first with 27 saves.

The 1949 pennant race saw the two teams, the Red Sox and the Yanks, move in opposite directions. The Yankees started off winning and held first place much of the season, despite crippling injuries to many players, including DiMaggio, Henrich, Keller and Berra. The Red Sox in April were in 6th place. By July 4th they were in 5th place, twelve games back of the Yankees. However, in July and August they won two of every three games they played and by the first of September they were only two games out of first place. The Yanks doggedly hung on to first place and a two-game lead, but by the beginning of the last week of the season, the Red Sox surged into first place. By the week's end, with two games left in the pennant race, the Red Sox had a one-game lead over the Yankees. They played the Bombers in Yankee Stadium in these last two games, needing to win only one game to win the pennant. The Sox lost the first game of the series as the Yanks, despite falling behind in the game 4-0, won 5-4 on Johnny Lindell's pinch home run and Joe Page's relief pitching. The two teams were now dead even, atop the American League, and so the last game of the season would determine the pennant winner.

In the final game, two ace pitchers matched up in a pitching duel, 23-game winner Ellis Kinder for the Red Sox and 21-game winner Vic Raschi for the Yankees. In the very first inning, Rizzuto tripled and scored on Henrich's ground ball, giving the Yanks a one-run lead. That was to be the only score in a tense game until the last of the eighth inning. Kinder, having given way to a pinch hitter in the top of the eighth, 25-game winner Mel Parnell was now the pitcher for the Red Sox. With their two 20-game aces pitching, the Red Sox were clearly making a determined effort to win the game and the pennant. Parnell, however, was greeted by a home run from Tommy Henrich, making the score 2-0 in favor of the Yanks. Berra singled and, with that, Tex Hughson replaced Parnell. He faced Joe DiMaggio, weakened by illness, who promptly hit into a double play. The inning wasn't over yet, but it appeared the Red Sox still had a chance to win. However, the next three men got on base for the Yankees and Jerry Coleman drove all three in with a double. The score going

into the ninth inning and the Red Sox's last at bat was 5-0 in favor of the Yankees.

In the top of the ninth, with Raschi pitching a superb game for the Yankees, the Red Sox put their first two men on base and, after one out, Doerr drove them home with a triple. After a second out, Billy Goodman drove Doerr home with a single. The score was now 5-3 and the tying run was at home plate. Birdie Tebbetts was the batter, and he fouled out. Raschi had beaten the Red Sox for the pennant, 5-3, with a five-hitter.

Lightning had struck twice. A powerful and favored Red Sox team had lost the pennant in a play-off game in 1948, and they lost the pennant again in 1949 with a game loss on the final day of the season. Years later, some Red Sox followers given to superstition accounted for these and other critical losses over the years as "the curse of the Bambino." If one believes the superstition, misfortune through the years stemmed from the sale of Babe Ruth to the Yankees in 1920. The myth is that the curse has dogged the Red Sox ever since.

Line Score

				R	H	E
Boston Red Sox	000	000	003	3	5	1
New York Yankees	100	000	04x	5	9	0

October 2, 1978
Fenway Park, Boston   #4

PLAY-OFF GAME FOR THE PENNANT BETWEEN THE RED SOX AND THE YANKEES

Bucky Dent Hits A Dramatic Home Run To Win For The Yankees

The 1978 season was the third time in baseball history that the Yankees and the Red Sox played right down to the last day of the season for the American League pennant. The first time occurred in 1904 when the Yankees' Jack Chesbro, a 41-game winner, wild-pitched in the winning run, giving the Red Sox the pennant. The second occurrence was in 1949 when the Yanks beat the Sox on the final day of the season on Vic Raschi's five-hitter, 5-3. The third Red Sox—Yankees game for the pennant was a play-off game in 1978.

The year 1978, the Red Sox, with a solid team, led the pennant chase most of the season. The Yankees were in turmoil with intra-squad rivalry and tension resulting es-

The Red Sox Encyclopedia

pecially from the big egos and outspoken comments of George Steinbrenner, owner, Billy Martin, manager, and Reggie Jackson, star slugger. The Yankees fell behind the Red Sox by 11½ games at the All-Star game break. On July 17, with the Yankees 14 games behind the Sox, a more mellow Bob Lemon replaced tempestuous Billy Martin as the Yankees manager. The team started to win and, by the beginning of September, was only 6½ games behind the Red Sox.

The Yankees came to Fenway Park for a four game series in early September, now behind by only four games. The four-game series would come to be known as "The Boston Massacre" as the Yankees won all four games, 15-3, 13-2, 7-0, and 7-4. The Yankees continued to win and took the league leadership. The Red Sox fell 3½ games behind. Then, as the season neared its end, Boston won 12 out of 14 games and the last eight in a row to tie the Yankees for the pennant on the last day of the season. The following day the two teams were to have a one-game play-off for the league championship.

The Red Sox in 1978 had quality players at every position. George "Boomer" Scott, a good fielder and a heavy hitter, was the first baseman. Jerry Remy, the league leader in double plays at second base, and Rick Burleson formed the double play combination. Butch Hobson was the heavy hitting third baseman. The team had a class outfield in Dwight Evans in right field, Fred Lynn in center field and Jim Rice in right field. Evans and Lynn were especially talented outfielders and good hitters. Rice, the league's Most Valuable Player, led the league in 1978 in home runs, with 46, and in runs driven in. The veteran catcher was hard-hitting Carlton Fisk. Carl Yastrzemski, nearing the end of his great career, was the designated hitter. The pitching staff was led by 20-game winner Dennis Eckersley, the same "Eck" who was to become dean of major league relief pitchers in the late 1980s and early 1990s. Mike Torrez, who was with the Yankee a year earlier, veteran Luis Tiant and reliever Bob Stanley contributed 44 wins among them.

The Yankees also had a fine team. Chris Chambliss was a hard hitter who led all other American League first basemen in fielding in 1978. Willie Randolph, one of the two best second basemen in the league, and Bucky Dent were the double-play combination. Hard-hitting, good fielding Graig Nettles, with 27 home runs and 93 runs batted in, was at third base. Hall of Famer slugger Reggie Jackson was the right fielder, speedy Mickey Rivers the centerfielder and .314 hitting Lou Piniella was the left fielder. Hall of Famer Thurman Munson, the team captain, was the catcher. Roy White, who platooned in the outfield, and Cliff Johnson, who could slug the ball, were notable substitutes. Ron Guidry had a "career year," lead-

Red Sox nemesis Bucky Dent hit a home run to give the New York Yankees a victory and the pennant over the Red Sox in 1978. (Baseball Hall of Fame Library, Cooperstown, N.Y.).

ing the league in pitching wins with 25 and in earned run average at 1.74. Ed Figueroa also had 20 wins and the Yanks also had an outstanding relief corps led by Goose Gossage, the league leader in saves, and Sparky Lyle. Hall of Famer Catfish Hunter was near the end of his career but still pitched effectively for the Yanks.

Play-off Monday in Fenway Park saw ex-Yankee Mike Torrez pitching for the Red Sox and Cy Young winner Ron Guidry pitching for the Yankees. In a well-pitched game, Torrez was outdueling Guidry into the top of the seventh, 2-0, on Carl Yastrzemski's home run and Jim Rice's run-producing single. At this point, Torrez's game fell apart. He walked Chris Chambliss and Roy White. Bucky Dent, a .243 hitter with four home runs and 37 runs batted in, with no hits in his previous 13 at bats, was the batter. To the immediate shock and amazement of the Boston team and fans, and perhaps all concerned, Dent hit a ball that cleared "The Green Monster" for a three-run home run and a Yankee lead of 3 to 2. It was the dramatic moment of the game and put the Yankees in the lead to stay. Bob Stanley then replaced Mike Torrez, Mickey Rivers then singled and was driven home by Thurman Munson, and the Yankees had a 4-2 lead. Then "Mr. October," Reggie Jackson, hit a homer in the top of the eighth to lengthen the Yankee lead to 5-2.

With Goose Gossage in relief of Ron Guidry, the Red Sox scored two runs in the bottom of the eighth, closing the gap to a 5-4 Yankee lead. In the bottom of the ninth, with one out, Rick Burleson walked and Jerry Remy singled sharply, placing men on first and second base. With the tying and winning runs on base, the Red Sox next two batters were Jim Rice, who had already batted in one run, and Carl Yastrzemski, who had homered. Gossage, with his typical scowl and nearly 100-mile-an-hour fast ball, bore down. Rice hit a fly to right field for the second out, Burleson moving over to third base after the out. Yastzremski then fouled out to end the game.

Bucky Dent was the unlikely hero of the winner-take-all play-off game that gave the Yankees the pennant in 1978. Those with superstition felt warranted that maybe there was a "curse of the Bambino".

Line Score

		R	H	E
New York Yankees	000 000 410	5	8	0
Boston Red Sox	010 001 020	4	11	0

October 26, 1986
Shea Stadium, New York   #5

SIXTH GAME OF WORLD SERIES BETWEEN THE
RED SOX AND THE NEW YORK METS
Mets Win In The Tenth Inning
On Squibbler Between Bill Buckner's Legs

The year 1986 was substantial if not spectacular for the Red Sox. It was highlighted by the record pitcher Roger Clemens set when he struck out 20 Seattle Mariners in a game to set a new major league mark in strikeouts per game. The Red Sox won the American League East division by five games over the Yankees. The Mets, meantime, were experiencing another "you gotta believe" year, as in 1969 when they unexpectedly won the world championship. They started out spectacularly, winning the National League East division by 2$\frac{1}{2}$ games over the second-place Philadelphia Phillies.

It was the League Championship Series, in both leagues, that contributed excitement and suspense as a prelude to an even more exciting World Series. In the American League, the Red Sox faced the California Angels in the best four out of seven series. The first two games were blow outs, the Angels winning the first 8-1, and the Red Sox the second 9-2. The Angels beat "Oil Can" Boyd and the Red Sox, 5-3, in the third game on two seventh-inning home runs. They also won the fourth game 4-3, in 11 innings. Calvin Schiraldi, pitching for the Red Sox, hit a batter with the bases loaded in the ninth inning, tying the game at 3-3. Grich's hit in the 11th inning against Schiraldi won the game. The Red Sox faced elimination in Game 5, and were behind in that game 5-2 in the ninth inning. Don Baylor of the Sox hit a two-run homer to make it 5-4. Rich Gedman was then hit by a pitch and Dave Henderson then came to bat and hit a dramatic two-run homer, putting the Red Sox in the lead 6-5. In the bottom of the ninth inning, the Angels tied the score and had the winning run on third base. Bobby Grich was then retired, the Angels failed to score further, and the game went into extra innings. The Red Sox finally won in the eleventh inning on game hero Dave Henderson's sacrifice fly. The final score was 7-6 in favor of the Red Sox. The Angels, so close yet not a winner, appeared to become demoralized. Oil Can Boyd beat them in Game 6, 10-4, and Roger Clemens won in Game 7, 8-1, with the help of Jim Rice's 2-run homer and Dwight Evans' solo homer. The Red Sox were in the World Series after a four-games-to-three ALCS win.

The Mets also had a spectacular League Championship Series. They played the West division winners in the National League, the Houston Astros. Mike Scott, a former Met, outduelled the Mets' ace, Dwight "Doc" Gooden, in the first game, 1-0. Scott struck out 14 Mets. Bobby Ojeda, late of the Boston Red Sox, pitched and won the second game for the Mets, 5-1. The third game was a thriller. Trailing 4-0 in the sixth inning the Mets rallied for four runs, climaxed by Darryl Strawberry's home run. Houston scored in the top of the seventh but then Lenny Dykstra won the game for the Mets in the last of the ninth 6-5 on a two-run home run. Scott, a tantalizing pitcher and a thorn in the Mets' side, won Game 4 on a three-hitter, 3-1. This time he outduelled Sid Fernandez. Game 5 was another heart stopper. Doc Gooden and the great Nolan Ryan, then pitching for Houston, engaged in a pitching duel for nine innings, with the score 1-1 going into the tenth inning. Charlie Kerfeld replaced Ryan in the tenth. Ryan in his nine-inning stint had given up two hits and, demonstrating why he was the leading strike-out artist in baseball history, struck out 12 Mets. Gooden, after a fine if less spectacular performance, was replaced by Jesse Orosco in the 11th inning. Gary Carter singled in the winning run in the 12th inning, the Mets winning 2-1. The Mets now had a three-games-to-two lead in the series. Game six was the most spectacular of all. Houston, with Bob Knepper pitching, was leading 3-0 in the ninth inning. The Mets rallied for three runs to send the game into extra innings. Both teams had excellent relief pitching. In the 14th in-

The Mets' Mookie Wilson turned out to be the hero in Game 6 of the 1986 World Series when his ground ball went through the legs of Bill Buckner allowing the game-winning run to score for New York. (Baseball Hall of Fame Library, Cooperstown, N.Y.).

Sox again had a solid, slugging outfield with Dwight "Dewey" Evans in right field, Tony Armas in center and Jim Rice in left field. Rich Gedman was a dependable catcher. The Sox also had the new addition of Don Baylor, who in his career played in seven league championship series with five different teams and in three World Series with three teams, as the designated hitter. Oil Can Boyd and Bruce Hurst backed Clemens on the pitching staff with Bob Stanley as the prime reliever.

The Mets had Keith Hernandez, one of baseball's great fielding first basemen and a good hitter, at the first sack. Wally Backman and Rafael Santana were the keystone combination and hard hitting Ray Knight, who spent most of his career with the Cincinnati Reds, was at third base. Darryl Strawberry, left fielder, was the star hitter and home run slugger. Lenny Dykstra, an aggressive player with speed, was the center fielder and popular, quick "Mookie" Wilson was the right fielder. The Mets did considerable platooning with George Foster and Danny Heep in the outfield, and Tim Teufel and Howard Johnson in the infield. The Mets had four top pitchers who gave them a total of 66 wins, Bobby Ojeda, Doc Gooden, Sid Fernandez and Ron Darling. They had two stand-out relief pitchers in Roger McDowell and Jesse Orosco. They were loaded with talent and it was not by accident that they won their regular season competition by 21 1/2 games.

The 1986 World Series opened in Shea Stadium, New York, with Bruce Hurst pitching against Ron Darling. Hurst won the pitchers' duel, 1-0, though both pitchers were relieved in the late innings. The Red Sox took a one-game-to-nothing lead. In the second game, the Red Sox exploded for 18 hits, including home runs by Dave Henderson and Dewey Evans, each with one on. The final score was 9-3 Red Sox, as they started the Series by beating the Mets twice on their home field. The much-heralded duel between Roger Clemens and Doc Gooden never materialized as neither survived beyond the fifth inning in Game Two. Game Three, in Fenway Park, was won by Bobby Ojeda in his first year with the Mets after being traded by the Red Sox. He beat his former teammates, 7 to 1, on a five hitter with notable assistance from Lenny Dykstra's lead-off home run. Ron Darling won the fourth game for the Mets, 6-2, on Gary Carter's two home runs, one with a man on base, and Lenny Dykstra's second home run of the Series with a man on base. The Series now stood at two games even, each team winning in the other's ball park. Pivotal Game 5 was won by the Red Sox as Bruce Hurst outduelled Doc Gooden and Sid Fernandez, 4-2, for his second win.

Game 6, which the Red Sox should have won, was the one that may have broken their spirit, albeit that they

ning, Wally Backman singled off Aurelio Lopez to put the Mets ahead, 4 to 3, but Billy Hatcher homered against Jesse Orosco to tie the score again. The Mets scored three in the 16th inning to lead, 7-4, but the Astros were not through. They scored two runs in the bottom of the 16th but Orosco struck out the last Houston batter with two men on base to win the game and the NLCS for the Mets, four games to two. Both the Mets and the Red Sox had gone through dramatic but draining league championship series before emerging as respective league champions to face each other in the World Series.

The Red Sox of 1986 had, of course, Roger the Rocket Clemens, the league's Most Valuable Player and Cy Young award winner. He led the league with 24 wins, a winning percentage of .857 and a 2.48 earned run average. He finished behind Mark Langston of Seattle in strikeouts, with 238. League batting champion Wade Boggs, the perennial hitting machine, was at third base. Bill Buckner with 18 home runs, 102 runs batted in and the leadership in assists at his position, was at first base. Marty Barrett and Ed Romero were the double play combination. The Red played a competitive Game 7. Game 6, with ace Roger Clemens facing former teammate Bobby Ojeda, saw the Red Sox break on top in the first two innings with a 2-0 lead. The Mets scored two in the fifth to tie the game, each team scored one more run in the regulation nine innings, and by the end of nine the score was tied at 3-3.

Neither Clemens nor Ojeda were still pitching, Calvin Schiraldi having replaced the Rocket in the eighth inning and McDowell, Orosco and now Rick Aguilera had replaced "Bobby O."

The tenth inning was a moment for memory and, though a disappointment to the Red Sox, was one of the great dramatic times in World Series history. The Red Sox led off the tenth inning with a home run by Dave Henderson, his second of the Series, and then they added an insurance run. The Red Sox appeared on their way to their first world championship in 68 years with a 5-3 lead in the tenth in the about-to-be last game of the Series. Calvin Schiraldi retired the first two batters in the last of the tenth inning and the Red Sox had all but sewed up the game and the Series. Then Gary Carter, Kevin Mitchell and Ray Knight all singled with one run scoring and the score standing at 5 to 4. Schiraldi was replaced by Bob Stanley who promptly threw a wild pitch and the runners advanced with the tying run scoring. Mookie Wilson, the next batter, hit a slow roller down toward first base for what appeared to be an easy out that would keep the Red

Sox in the game and bring the 11th inning. This was not to happen as reliable Bill Buckner inexplicably let the ball pass through his legs. The winning run scored, the Mets were saved, and there was bedlam in Shea Stadium.

To the Red Sox credit, they appeared to recover and started off Game 7, now the decisive game, with a 3-0 lead. Evans and Gedman had hit home runs early and Boggs drove in the third run. Bruce Hurst, looking for his third victory, was pitching against Ron Darling. The Mets tied the game in the last of the sixth at 3-3 on Keith Hernandez's bases-loaded single and Gary Carter's run-producing single. Ray Knight's home run in the top of the seventh inning against reliever Schiraldi proved to be the winning run as the Mets won the game 8 to 5, and the championship, four games to three.

This was Boston's fourth World Series since the last of the five world championships the Red Sox won in 1918. The Sox lost all four of these World Series, in 1946, 1967, 1975 and 1986, by four games to three. Neither effort nor talent were lacking but good fortune eluded them. Or, for those who prefer, "the curse of the Bambino" carries on.

Line Score

				R	H	E
Boston Red Sox	110	000	100 2	5	13	3
New York Mets	000	020	010 3	6	8	2

Carney Lansford won the American League batting title for Boston in 1981 with his .335 average. (Baseball Hall of Fame Library. Cooperstown, N.Y.).

SNAPSHOTS OF MEMORABLE EVENTS AND PERFORMANCES IN RED SOX HISTORY

1902

Bill Dinneen, a star pitcher for the Somersets, had 21 wins and 21 losses for a third-place team. Dinneen, after his playing career, had a distinguished career as an American League umpire.

1903

Patsy Dougherty, outfielder for the Pilgrims, became the first player to hit two home runs in a World Series game. The Pilgrims behind Dinneen, won the game 3-0 and the World Series over the Pirates five games to three.

Boston's "secret weapon" was a vocal, combative band of rooters who often traveled with the team. They were a fanatic group known as "The Royal Rooters" and were led by a bar owner named "Nuf Sed" McGreavey. He settled all arguments with the terse phrase, "Nuf Said." Boston mayor John "Honey Fitz" Fitz-gerald, a grandfather of President John F. Kennedy, was a member of "The Royal Rooters."

1904

Cy Young pitched a perfect game for the Pilgrims against Rube Waddell and the Philadelphia Athletics, winning 3-0. Young pitched a second no-hitter in 1908, beating the New York Highlanders 8-0. In 1897, pitching for the Cleveland Spiders of the National League, Young won a no-hitter against the Cincinnati Reds 6-0.

Cy Young, at age 37, had 21 wins and a 1.97 earned run average with the Pilgrims.

Jack Chesbro, who pitched and won 41 games for the New York Highlanders this year, wild pitched in the winning run in a game against the Pilgrims, giving the Pilgrims the pennant. Chesbro pitched briefly for the Red Sox at the end of his career in 1909.

There was no World Series in 1904. The Boston Pilgrims won the pennant but John McGraw, manager of the National League pennant-winning New York Giants, refused to play a team from the upstart American League. The National League was humiliated the previous year, in the first World Series, when the favored Pittsburgh Pirates lost to the Pilgrims.

1906

The Pilgrims, pennant winners in 1904, finished in last place in 1906. At one point, they lost 20 games in a row, and they ended the season with 105 losses. At the end of the year, they were 45^1/$_2$ games out of first place. Four Boston pitchers lost a total of 79 games. Cy Young was at 13-21, Joe Harris a remarkable 2-21, Bill Dinneen at 8-19 and George Winter with six wins and 18 losses.

This was a year in which both Boston teams finished in last place in their respective leagues. The Pilgrims finished last, 45^1/$_2$ games behind the pennant winning Chicago White Sox.

"Nuf Sed" McGreavey, an owner of a local bar, was the leader of a rowdy group of Boston fans in the early 1900s known as the "Royal Rooters." McGreavey also had his own baseball team, pictured above. (Boston Public Library, Print Department).

The Braves finished last in the National League, 66^1/$_2$ games behind the pennant winning Chicago Cubs. The Cubs won 116 games and lost 36 for a .763 winning percentage. In the 1906 all-Chicago World Series, the White Sox beat the Cubs, four games to two.

Smoky Joe Wood, later a Red Sox ace pitcher, began his career playing for a women's barnstorming professional team, the Boston Bloomer Girls.

1907

Chick Stahl, who managed the Pilgrims in 1906, was slated to be the manager in 1907. He took a lethal dose of drugs just before the season began and died. The Pilgrims had four managers that year, Cy Young, George Huff, Bob Unglaub and Deacon McGuire, and finished in seventh place. Chick Stahl and Jake Stahl were both players and managers for the Pilgrims/Red Sox.

The team officially adopted the name " Red Sox" this year. It was not a good year. The Red Sox finished in seventh place, 32½ behind the pennant winning Detroit Tigers. The Red Sox had the league's lowest batting average as a team, .234. Bunk Congalton, who played most of the season with the Red Sox after coming over from the Cleveland Indians, led the team with a .286 batting average. Utility player Freddy Parent batted .286 and then came first baseman Bob Unglaub at .254

1908

At age 41, and still pitching for the Boston Red Sox, Cy Young won 21 games. After 1908, Young pitched another three years with the Cleveland Indians, winning 19 games in 1909. Cy Young set a major league record with 511 wins; he recorded 192 while pitching for Boston.

1912

In the first game ever played in Fenway Park, opening the 1912 season, the Red Sox beat the New York Yankees in 11 innings, 7 to 6. Tris Speaker drove in the winning run. Fenway Park reputedly opened on the day the Titanic sunk. This was not the case, however, as the Red Sox had two postponements on account of the weather and did not open until two days after the Titanic sinking.

Smoky Joe Wood won a pitching duel with Walter Johnson. In that year he challenged Johnson as the best pitcher in baseball. He won 34 and lost five, had 10 shutouts, at one point had 16 straight wins, and also won three World Series games. Wood also batted .290 in 1912. It was the year in which the Red Sox had their season high total of 105 wins, a mark that still stands.

The top five American League batting averages this year were all held by Hall of Fame quality players. All were named to the Hall of Fame except Shoeless Joe Jackson, who was blacklisted because of his involvement in the Black Sox scandal of 1919. Ty Cobb led with a .410 aver-age. Jackson batted .395. The Red Sox's Tris Speaker was at .383. Nap Lajoie of Cleveland batted .368. Eddie Collins, then with the Philadelphia Athletics and later the Red Sox long-time general manager under Tom Yawkey, batted .348. The Chalmers Award for the league's most valuable player was awarded from 1911 through 1914. The Red Sox Tris Speaker won it in 1912. Ty Cobb won in 1911, pitcher Walter Johnson of the Washington Nationals in 1913, and second baseman Eddie Collins of the Philadelphia Athletics won it in 1914.

The year was an exciting one for the Red Sox. The team won the American League pennant with its best ever record, 105 wins and 47 losses. Smoky Joe Wood led pitchers with a remarkable 34-5 year. Tris Speaker batted .383. The World Series that some old-timers consider one of the most exciting ever played was won by the Red Sox over the New York Giants of John McGraw and Christy Mathewson. One of the enduring memories of the Series was "the Snodgrass muff."

Tris Speaker of the Red Sox had 50 doubles and 50 stolen bases, the only player with this accomplishment until the Houston Astros' Craig Biggio repeated the feat in 1998.

1914

Dutch Leonard set a pitching record that still stands. He won 19 games but, more importantly, he had the unsurpassed earned run average of 1.01. Three Red Sox pitchers, two besides Leonard, had earned run averages under 2.00. Rube Foster's E.R.A. was 1.65. Ernie Shore, a rookie pitcher, had an E.R.A. of 1.89. Also of note, Ray Collins, a 20-game winner for the Red Sox, pitched and won two complete games in one day. Red Sox pitchers took three of the top four places in the league in earned run average. The only "outsider" in the top four was Walter Johnson who, like Ernie Shore, had an E.R.A. of 1.72.

1915

In the 1915 World Series, the Red Sox won four consecutive one-run games against the Phillies, three of them by a 2-1 score. This was the first World Series attended by a U.S. president. Woodrow Wilson came to Baker Bowl in Philadelphia and threw out the first pitch in Game 2.

Duffy Lewis, in the World Series, made a game-saving catch in Game 3 and had clutch hits in Games 3, 4 and 5. His World Series batting average was .444. In Game 5 of the Series, Lewis homered to tie the game and Harry Hooper hit his second home run of the game in the ninth inning to win the Series for Boston.

Red Sox pitchers were the top four leading pitchers in the American League in winning percentage. The leader was Smoky Joe Wood with 15 wins and five losses for an average of .750. Second in the league was Ernie Shore with a .704 average based on 19 wins and eight losses. He was tied with Rube Foster who had the identical won-lost record. Babe Ruth, in his first full year, was fourth in pitching percentage at .692, with 18 wins and eight losses. He had an earned run average of 2.44. Of the four, only Babe Ruth was a left hander. Already showing his home run hitting prowess, he tied for the team lead with four home runs.

This was the year of great performance of the entire Red Sox team. The Red Sox fielded one of its greatest teams of all time. The outfield consisted of Duffy Lewis in left field, Tris Speaker in center field and Harry Hooper in right field- the "dream outfield." The infield consisted of Dick Hoblitzell at first base, Jack Barry at second base, Everett "Deacon" Scott at shortstop and Larry Gardner at third base. Pinch Thomas and Hick Cady succeeded manager Bill "Rough" Carrigan as the regular catcher. The formidable pitching staff consisted of Ernie Shore, Rube Foster, Babe Ruth, Smoky Joe Wood (see season records in footnote above), Dutch Leonard at 15-7 with a 2.36 E.R.A., and Carl Mays who led the league in saves. The Red Sox won 101 games and lost 50, beating Hughie Jennings' Detroit Tigers for the pennant by two and a half games. They beat the Philadelphia Phillies in the World Series, four games to one.

1916

Babe Ruth set a record that still stands by pitching a complete 14-inning game in the World Series. He outpitched Sherry Smith of the Brooklyn Dodgers who also went all the way, 2-1. Interestingly, in the 1916 World Series, which the Red Sox won over the Dodgers four games to one, Casey Stengel

of the Dodgers led all regular players with a .364 batting average.

The Red Sox pitchers were again outstanding. Ruth's record was 23-12, Mays 18-13, Dutch Leonard 18-12, Ernie Shore 16-10 and Rube Foster 14-7. The ace of the staff, Ruth led the club with 23 wins and the league with a 1.75 E.R.A. Rube Foster and Dutch Leonard pitched no-hitters. Ruth won three straight shutouts. He pitched 324 innings without giving up a home run while he himself, as a full-time pitcher, hit three homers that year.

Tris Speaker was traded from the Red Sox to the Cleveland Indians after the 1915 season because of a salary disagreement. In his first year with Cleveland, "Spoke" batted .386 and won the league batting title. This broke the streak of nine straight batting titles won by Ty Cobb. Speaker later became the Indians' manager.

1917

Babe Ruth, the Red Sox star left handed pitcher, started a game, walked a batter and then was ejected after arguing with the umpire. Ernie Shore replaced him. The runner was thrown out trying to steal second base. Shore then retired 26 consecutive batters for an unusual no-hit, no-run game.

Babe Ruth had a 24-13 won-lost record for the season with a 2.02 earned run average. He batted .325. In his career with the Red Sox Ruth batted .309 and had 49 home runs, twice leading the league while with the Sox in this category. His career pitching mark with the Sox was 89-46.

1918

Carl Mays pitched and won two complete games in one day. This was also the year in which Mays and Babe Ruth each won two games for the Red Sox in the World Series, the Red Sox defeating the Chicago Cubs, four games to two.

Waite Hoyt pitched nine perfect innings against the Yankees in 1919, but did not pitch a no-hitter or win the game, which went 13 innings. Hoyt later won 227 games for the Yankees, after being traded to New York. (Baseball Hall of Fame Library. Cooperstown, N.Y.).

The Red Sox Encyclopedia

Babe Ruth played in only 95 of 126 games. The season was shortened by one month because of America's participation in the first World War. Ruth tied for the home run lead in the league, hitting 11, and he led the major leagues in slugging percentage.

Babe Ruth pitched twenty nine and two thirds consecutive scoreless innings in the World Series, a record that held up until Whitey Ford of the New York Yankees broke it in 1961.

The house was packed during this game at Fenway Park in 1924. (Boston Public Library, Print Department).

Pennock, who later became a star pitcher for the Yankees.

1921

Stuffy McInnis, who was traded to the Red Sox from the Philadelphia Athletics in 1918, set a record for first basemen with a fielding average of .999. He made one error all season handling 1,549 putouts, 102 assists and participating in 109 double plays. He had 1,700 errorless chances in 1921 and 1922, playing for the Red Sox and the Cleveland Indians.

In the "dead ball" era, the Red Sox batted .186 and scored only nine runs in the World Series. The losing Cubs batted .210 and scored a total of four runs. Ruth and Mays, the winning pitchers, gave up four runs in the four games they pitched.

1922

For the second time both Boston teams finished last. In the American League, the Red Sox were 33 games behind the pennant-winning New York Yankees. In the National League, the Boston Braves were 39½ games behind the New York Giants. In the all-New York World Series, the Giants swept the Yankees, four games to none.

1919

Waite Hoyt, for the Red Sox, pitched nine perfect innings against the Yankees but did not pitch a game no-hitter. He also retired 34 straight batters in the game. The game lasted 13 innings and Hoyt went all the way. He gave up three hits before getting anyone out in the second inning and then did not allow a runner on base until he gave up a hit with one out in the thirteenth. Hoyt lost the game in the 13th inning.

Babe Ruth, still a part-time Red Sox pitcher, hit an astounding 29 home runs, breaking the record and winning the home run championship for the second straight year. Babe broke the record three more times, in 1920 when he hit 54 with the Yankees, in 1921 when he hit 59 with his new club, and in 1927 when he hit the landmark 60 home runs for the Yankees. The Babe's first home run in 1920 for the Yanks was off his former Red Sox teammate, Herb

1923

Howard Ehmke pitched and won 20 games for the Red Sox with a record of 20-17. He also pitched a no-hit, no-run game against the Athletics. What makes this performance unusual is that the Red Sox were a last place team, Ehmke winning one of every three games the team won that year. He also won 19 in 1924, and the Red Sox were a seventh-place team.

1929

Again, the Red Sox and Braves finished in last place. This time the Braves were 43 games behind the pennant winning Chicago Cubs. The Sox were 48 games behind the Philadelphia Athletics, pennant winners.

The Red Sox have had two brother batteries, Milt and Alex Gaston, who played only in 1929, and Wes and Rick Ferrell who were with the team from 1934 through part of 1937.

1930

Babe Ruth, in an effort to help the Red Sox at the gate, agreed to pitch a game again, his first pitching assignment in nine years. Babe beat the Sox for the Yanks, 9-3. He pitched five scoreless innings to start the game and gave up 11 hits in all.

1931

Earl Webb, Red Sox outfielder, hit 67 doubles, a major league record that still stands. In his six-year playing career, aside from 1931, he never hit more than 30 two-baggers in any one season. Webb played two years for the Red Sox, 1930 in which he batted .323. and 1931, in which he hit .333. He then was traded to Detroit for Dale Alexander, who promptly won the batting title in 1932.

1932

Wes and Rick Ferrell, the brother pitching battery for the Red Sox, each hit a home run in the same game. This was no surprise for Wes, the pitcher. He holds the major league record for most career homers by a pitcher, 38. Rick, the catcher had 28 home runs in a career that spanned 18 years. Rick was later elected to the Hall of Fame.

Dale Alexander, first baseman, is the first Red Sox player since Tris Speaker to win the league's batting championship. Traded from Detroit early in the season, he finished with a .367 average. He played one more year with the Red Sox and then was out of major league baseball after a five-year career.

Left fielder Joe Vosmik batted .324 for the Red Sox in 1938. (Baseball Hall of Fame Library. Cooperstown, N.Y.).

1933

Joe Cronin, "boy manager" of the Washington Senators, at the age of 26 led the Senators to the American League pennant. Joe became manager of the Red Sox from 1935 through 1947. When he moved into the Red Sox front office in 1948, Joe McCarthy, ex-manager of the Yankee championship teams, became Red Sox manager.

1934

A crowd of 46,766 came to a game with the Yankees in Fenway Park to bid Babe Ruth farewell after he had announced his forthcoming retirement. The crowd overflowed onto the field.

1935

The Red Sox set an all-time attendance record of 47,607 at Fenway Park when the Sox played the Yankees in a double header. The record is unlikely to be equaled or surpassed as fire regulations now limit attendance at Fenway Park to about 34,000.

1938

Slugger Jimmie Foxx had six bases on balls in one game. This was also the year in which he won his third Most Valuable Player award, his first with the Red Sox. He hit 50 home runs, still the record for a Red Sox player, and he led the league with a .349 batting average and 175 runs batted in. The R.B.I. total is the fourth highest ever, surpassed only by National Leaguer Hack Wilson's 190, Lou Gehrig's 184 and Hank Greenberg's 183.

The entire Red Sox outfield batted over .300. Right fielder Ben Chapman batted .340, centerfielder Doc Cramer batted .301, and left fielder Joe Vosmik batted .324.

Mike "Pinky" Higgins, third baseman for the Red Sox, set a league record with twelve consecutive base hits. Johnny

The Red Sox Encyclopedia

Pesky, who later played third base for the Sox was second in league history with eleven straight hits in 1946.

1939

On July 4, Jim Tabor tied the Major League record of two grand slams in one game, as the Sox beat the A's, 18-12. This was also the day on which Lou Gehrig made his famous farewell speech at Yankee Stadium.

1940

The Red Sox team was notable for having four future Hall of Famers in the regular line-up and an all-.300 hitting outfield. Jimmie Foxx was the first baseman, Bobby Doerr at second base, manager Joe Cronin at shortstop and Ted Williams in his first year, in left field. All later entered the Hall of Fame. The all-.300 hitting outfield consisted of Dom DiMaggio in right field, Doc Cramer in center field and Williams in left. The other regulars were third baseman Jim Tabor and Gene Desautels catching. The team, however, finished fourth, eight games behind the pennant winning Detroit Tigers, because of a mediocre pitching staff on which no one won more than 12 games.

1941

This was an historic baseball year in which Ted Williams hit .406 and Joe DiMaggio of the Yankees set his record hitting in 56 straight games. Joe won the Most Valuable Player award.

On the last day of the season Ted Williams was batting .39955. To protect his .400 average Manager Joe Cronin gave him the option of sitting out the final day doubleheader. Ted opted to play both games, had six hits in eight attempts, and finished with his .406 batting average. This is the last time a player has hit .400 or over in the major leagues.

Ted Williams, in one of the great dramatic performances in baseball history, hit a two-on, two-out mammoth home run in the ninth inning to give the American League All-Stars a come-from-behind victory over the National League All-Stars, 7 to 5, in Detroit's Briggs Stadium.

In midseason, Lefty Grove won his 300th game, beating the Cleveland Indians, 10-6.

1942

Ted Williams won the Triple Crown with a .356 batting average, 36 home runs and 137 runs batted in. Notwithstanding, Joe Gordon of the Yankees won the Most Valuable Player award.

1943

Joe Cronin set a record by hitting a pinch home run in each of two games of a double header. He also set a record with five pinch hit home runs for a year.

1945

David "Boo" Ferriss, a rookie pitcher for the Sox, pitched shutouts in his first two major league starts. He won 21 games in 1945, and 25 in 1946 when he led the league with an .806 winning percentage. After these two great years, his career slipped. He pitched in only four games in 1949, one in 1950, and by 1951 he was out of big league baseball.

1946

The Red Sox, in the first post-war season, had an achieving team. Among pitchers, Boo Ferriss was 25-6, Tex Hughson was 20-11, Mickey Harris at 19-9 and Joe Dobson at 13-7. Ted Williams was second in all Triple Crown categories, batting .342 with 38 home runs and 123 runs batted in. Dom DiMaggio batted .316 and Johnny Pesky was at .335. Rudy York drove in 119 runs and Bobby Doerr 116. The Red Sox won the pennant by 12 games over second-place Detroit and 17 games over the third-place Yankees.

Ted Williams had a field day in the All-Star game played at Fenway Park. He had four hits including two home runs, in the American League's 12-0 win. He had ten total bases and five runs batted in.

In his only World Series appearance, Ted Williams hit only .200. His National League counterpart, Stan Musial, hit only .222. The St. Louis Cardinals won the Series over the Red Sox, four games to three.

Rudy York hit two grand slam home runs in a game, tying the record. He drove in 10 runs in a 13-6 Red Sox win over the Browns.

1948

The Boston Red Sox double-play combination of Bobby Doerr and Vern Stephens had 268 runs batted in between them, the most ever for a second base-shortstop combination. Stephens is one of four players traded by the St. Louis Browns to the Red Sox who played key roles in Red Sox pennant efforts. Stephens, along with pitchers Ellis Kinder and Jack Kramer, came to the Sox in 1948. Outfielder Al Zarilla was traded to the Sox in 1949.

1949

Ted Williams barely lost the league batting crown. He batted .34275. George Kell of the Detroit Tigers won with an average of .34291.

Ted Williams and Vern Stephens shared the runs batted in title with 159 each. Williams also led the league in home runs with 43. Stephens had 39.

1950

The Red Sox had a stellar and memorable regular line-up and good pitching. The team may have been one of the Red Sox best even though they finished in third place, four games behind the pennant-winning Yankees. All eight regulars batted over .290 and six were over .300. Walt Dropo at first base batted .322, Bobby Doerr at second base .294, Vern Stephens at shortstop, .295, Johnny Pesky at third base .312, Al Zarilla in right field, .325, Dom DiMaggio in center field, .328, Ted Williams in left field at .317 and Birdie Tebbetts, catcher, at .310. Mel Parnell and Ellis Kinder, who were both 20-game winners in 1949, won 32 games between them and Joe Dobson won 15 games. More than a footnote to the team was the performance of Billy Goodman, utility infielder, who won the American League batting crown with a .354 average. The Red Sox, notwithstanding, had to compete with a New York Yankee dynasty that won an unprecedented five consecutive World Championships between 1949 and 1953.

Walt Dropo, first baseman, was named Rookie of the Year. He batted .322, hit 34 home runs and led the league with 144 runs batted in. He never again hit .300 or drove in 100 or more runs, and only once did he hit as many as 20 homers. Though Dropo played in the big leagues for 13 years he was traded by the Red Sox to Detroit after two full seasons.

Billy Goodman won the American League batting title with a .354 average yet he couldn't crack the starting line up. Walt Dropo was at first base, Bobby Doerr at second, Vern Stephens at shortstop and Johnny Pesky at third base. Versatile Goodman filled in at various infield positions. Dropo and Stephens shared the league's runs batted in title with 144.

The Red Sox beat the St. Louis Browns in a game, 29 to 4. The Browns, after winning their only pennant in 1944, dropped to third place in 1950 and from then until they moved to Baltimore in 1954 never finished in the first division. They traded away many of their best players, including those sent to the Red Sox.

1951

Charlie Maxwell, an outfielder for the Red Sox, hit three home runs all season. All three were against future Hall of Famers, Bob Feller and Bob Lemon of the Indians and Satchel Paige, then pitching for the St. Louis Browns.

1953

The Red Sox, a perennially good-hitting team, scored 17 runs in the seventh inning in a game against Detroit. They won the game, 23 to 3. Gene Stephens, a reserve outfielder, set a record by getting three hits in three at bats in the inning. At the time, Ted Williams was on military duty in Korea.

1954

Ted Williams had more bases on balls than hits, 136 bases on balls to lead the league and 133 hits. He batted .345. He was known for his keen batting eye and refusal to hit a bad pitch.

Harry Agganis, "The Golden Greek," broke in as the Red Sox first baseman. He was very popular in Boston, having been a great fullback with the Boston University Terriers. One year later, in 1955, Agganis died tragically of a pulmonary embolism.

1957

Ted Williams and Mickey Mantle dueled for batting honors. Williams led the league with a .388 batting average and Mantle was second at .365. Williams was second in home runs, behind Roy Sievers of Washington, with 38.

Mike "Pinky" Higgins played third base for the Red Sox in the 1930s, and then managed the Sox from 1960-62. He is pictured above at Fenway Park with the Goldwyn Girls from the movie, "Guys and Dolls." (Boston Public Library, Print Department).

Mantle was third with 34. Williams led in slugging average at .731 and Mantle was second with .665. Mantle led in bases on balls with 146 and Williams was an unusual second (he was usually first) at 119. In addition, Mantle led in runs scored and was fourth in stolen bases behind Minnie Minoso and Jim Rivera, and the leader, Luis Aparicio, with 28. Mantle won the Most Valuable Player award for the second straight year.

1958

For the second time, Red Sox batters finished one-two in the race for batting honors. Ted Williams won the title both times. He finished at .328 and teammate Pete Runnels finished second at .322. Sixteen years earlier, in 1942, Ted finished first with a .356 average and Johnny Pesky was second at .331. Runnels won two titles in his own right, with averages of .320 in 1960 and .326 in 1962.

1959

Elijah "Pumpsie" Green became the first African-American player on the Red Sox, 12 years after Jackie Robinson broke the color barrier with the Brooklyn Dodgers in 1947. Green, a substitute infielder, batted .233. In a five-year

major league career, four with the Red Sox, Green batted .246. He played regularly one year, in 1960. In 1960, the Red Sox acquired their third African-American player, Willie Tasby, from Baltimore. Tasby was a regular outfielder with the team for the one season he was with Boston. In 1961, he was playing center field for the Washington Senators. Earl Wilson, the Red Sox second African-American player, made brief appearances in 1959 and 1960 and became a regular pitcher with the Red Sox in 1962. He was also a home run hitter who, as a pitcher and pinch hitter, hit 35 home runs in his career. He hit more than 20 of these with the Red Sox. While with Boston in 1962 he also pitched a no-hit, no-run game.

1961

Don Schwall won Rookie of the Year honors pitching for the Red Sox with 15 wins and seven losses. It was his only really successful season in the big leagues and he played for the Red Sox only two years before being traded to Pittsburgh.

Playing in Yankee Stadium, Roger Maris of the New York Yankees hit his record-breaking 61st home run. It was the 162nd and last game of the season. Tracy Stallard was the Red Sox pitcher.

1962

Two Red Sox pitchers pitched no-hitters. On June 26 Earl Wilson no-hit the California Angels, 2-0. On August 1, Bill Monbouquette no-hit the Chicago White Sox, 1-0.

1963

Gene Conley, a pitcher with the Red Sox who had previously played basketball with the Boston Celtics in 1959, 1960 and 1961, started a game against the Chicago White Sox. Ray Herbert started for Chicago but was relieved by Dave DeBusschere in the fourth inning. Debusschere, later in his career, was to play basketball for the New York Knicks, from 1970 through 1973. In their pitching stints on the day they opposed each other in baseball, Conley pitched four plus innings. DeBusschere pitched two-thirds of an inning.

1965

On September 29, the Red Sox had the smallest crowd in

their history. Playing the California Angels in a season in which they finished in ninth place, losing 100 games, they drew 409 spectators. On September 22, 1935, against the Yankees, they drew their largest crowd of 47,607.

Satchel Paige, the famous hurler in black baseball leagues, at the reputed age of 59 had a return stint in the big leagues with the Kansas City Athletics. He started and pitched three consecutive scoreless innings against the Red Sox in a game at the end of the season. He was the oldest player ever to pitch in a big league game. Carl Yastrzemski got the last hit made off Paige in the big leagues.

Tony Conigliaro, at age 20, was the youngest player to win the home run crown. He hit 32.

1967

Dick Williams was a rookie manager with the Red Sox and won the American League pennant in his first season. The Red Sox came from ninth place the previous year and were rated at 100 to 1 to win the pennant. Williams managed three years for the Red Sox, then went on to manage five other teams in a 21-year managerial career. His greatest years were with the Oakland Athletics when he won the American League West Division championship once, and then won two pennants and two World Series in the three years he was with the team.

This was a banner year for the Red Sox. They won the A.L. pennant. Carl Yastrzemski won the Triple Crown and the Most Valuable Player award. Yaz, in addition to the Triple Crown, had six R.B.I.s in the final two must-win games in the regular season (including a three-run homer). The Sox won the pennant on the last day of the season.

Tony Conigliaro, at age 22, became the youngest player to reach the 100-home run mark in his career. From the time he entered the league Tony had six consecutive years in which he hit 20 or more home runs. His effectiveness and his career were foreshortened when he was hit in the head by a pitch and subsequently had vision problems.

Red Sox Rookie Bill Rohr's first big league win, in April, was a one hitter. In fact, he had a no-hitter for eight and two thirds innings. By the All-Star break he was back in the minor leagues.

In Game 2 of the World Series, Jim Lonborg retired the first 20 batters. Julian Javier of the St. Louis Cardinals

doubled for the Cardinals' only hit as Lonborg pitched a one-hit shutout, 5-0. Carl Yastrzemski drove in three runs in the game with two home runs.

In Game 6 of the World Series, three Red Sox players hit home runs in one inning, Carl Yastrzemski, Reggie Smith and Rico Petrocelli.

1968

Carl Yastrzemski won the American League batting championship with the lowest winning average ever recorded, .301. His winning was no fluke, however, as he had previously won the batting title in 1963 with a .326 average.

Pitcher Ray Culp had four straight shutouts in his 16-6 season for the Sox.

1969

Carl Yastrzemski and Rico Petrocelli both hit 40 home runs. Yastrzemski accomplished the same feat in 1970. In his Triple Crown year, 1967, he won the home run title with 44.

1970

Tony and Billy Conigliaro, the brother team of the Red Sox from Revere, Massachusetts, hit 54 home runs between them. Tony hit 36 and Billy hit 18, the most ever hit by a brother combination in one season.

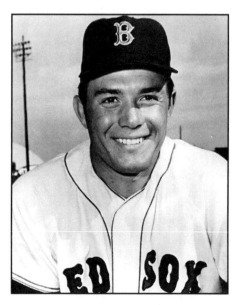

Billy Conigliaro (above) combined with his brother, Tony, to hit 54 home runs for the Red Sox in 1970. (Baseball Hall of Fame Library. Cooperstown, N.Y.).

The Red Sox Encyclopedia

Carl Yastrzemski was named the Most Valuable Player in the All-Star game, won in the 12th inning by the National League, 5-4.

1972

Carlton Fisk made an auspicious full-season entry into the big leagues as the Red Sox catcher and won the Rookie of the Year award. He batted .293 with 22 homers and 61 runs batted in. He was second in the league in slugging percentage with a .538 average. He tied for the lead in triples with nine. Fisk, as a catcher, led the league in putouts and assists. He also had the most chances per game at his position. Fisk was to have a long career, 11 years with the Red Sox and 13 more with the White Sox.

1975

Fred Lynn and Jim Rice, rookies, had a fabulous season. Lynn batted .331, had 21 homers and drove in 105 runs. He led the league in doubles and runs scored. Rice batted .309, had 22 homers and 102 runs batted in. Lynn was named Rookie of the Year and the league's Most Valuable Player, both feats coming in the same year—a record no other player has ever achieved. This was also the year in which the Red Sox won the pennant.

On June 18, Fred Lynn drove in 10 runs with three home runs, a triple and a single, as the Red Sox beat the Tigers, 15-1.

Game 6 of the World Series had a number of Red Sox stars. Bernie Carbo, who hit two pinch hit home runs in the Series to tie a record, tied the game with a three-run homer in the eighth inning, 6 to 6. Dwight Evans made a spectacular catch of Cincinnati Red Joe Morgan's smash toward the seats in the eleventh inning, saving the game for the Red Sox. In the 12th inning, Carlton Fisk hit his dramatic "stay fair" home run down the left field foul line to win the game for the Sox, 7-6.

1977

Carl Yastrzemski fielded 1.000, playing 140 games in left field and seven at first base. He made no errors, had 344 putouts and 22 assists. He won the Gold Glove Award for his play in left field, one of seven such awards he received.

1978

The Red Sox lost a dramatic playoff game for the pennant to the New York Yankees. Bucky Dent, a .243 hitter who had four home runs in the season and had just gone 0 for 13, hit an unexpected three-run home run to win the game for the Yankees. It was the climax to a year of misfortune for the Red Sox. In early September, while they were leading the American League, they played a four game series against the Yankees in Fenway Park. In what has come to be known as "The Boston Massacre" the Yankees won all four games, 15-3, 13-2, 7-0, and 7-4. The sweep enabled the Yankees to tie for the lead.

1979

Jim Rice and Fred Lynn, repeating their 1975 competition, competed for batting honors. Rice batted .325, hit 39 home runs and batted in 130 runs. Lynn led the league in batting at .333, also hit 39 home runs and batted in 122. This time, Jim Rice won the Most Valuable Player award.

1981

Because of a player strike, major league baseball had a split season. Carney Lansford, third baseman for the Red Sox, won the league batting championship with a .336 average. The next year Lansford was traded to the Oakland A's for Tony Armas as Wade Boggs came up to take over third base for the Sox.

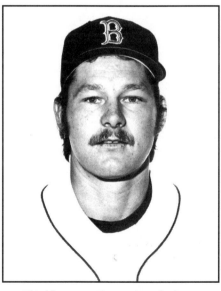

Third baseman Carney Lansford won the American League batting title for the Red Sox in 1981 before being traded to the Oakland A's. (Baseball Hall of Fame Library. Cooperstown, N.Y.).

1983

Jim Rice and Tony Armas competed for the home run championship. Rice led the league with 39 and with 126 runs batted in. Armas hit 36

---

home runs and had 107 R.B.I.s.

1986

Roger Clemens, who led the league with 24 wins and a 2.48 earned run average, struck out 20 in a game against the Seattle Mariners. This broke the single game strikeout record formerly held by Steve Carleton, Nolan Ryan and Tom Seaver. Clemens won the Most Valuable Player and Cy Young awards in 1986. He was also the Most Valuable Player in the All-Star game.

Don Baylor of the Red Sox set an American League record after being hit by the pitcher 35 times in the season.

In the 1986 World Series won dramatically by the New York Mets over the Red Sox, four games to three, neither of the ace pitchers, Roger Clemens of the Red Sox and Doc Gooden of the Mets, won a game. Marty Barrett, however, a second baseman, starred for the Red Sox by getting 13 hits in the Series. He tied the record set by Bobby Richardson of the Yankees.

Dave Henderson was the star of the postseason for the Boston Red Sox. In Game 5 of the American League Championship Series, with the California Angels holding a 3-1 lead in games and about to eliminate the Red Sox, Henderson hit a two-run home run with two strikes and two outs in the ninth inning to tie the game. He drove in the winning run for the Red Sox in the 11th inning, and the Red Sox went on to win the pennant. In the World Series of 1986 he outhit everyone with 10 hits in 15 at bats, including a home run in the tenth inning of Game 6 that the New York Mets ultimately won because of an error in the bottom of the inning (the infamous Buckner squibbler).

1987

The Red Sox finished in fifth place in the East division even though Wade Boggs won the batting championship with a .363 average and Clemens had a 20-9 year and won the Cy Young award for the second year in a row. Dwight Evans had 34 home runs and batted in 123. Ellis Burks had 20 home runs and Mike Greenwell batted .328.

Dave Henderson was a hero for the Red Sox in the 1986 World Series, hitting .667.
(Baseball Hall of Fame Library. Cooperstown, N.Y.).

1988

After Joe Morgan replaced John McNamara, manager of the year in 1986, as Red Sox manager, the Sox won 19 of the next 20 games. They won the East division title.

The Red Sox broke their all-time season attendance record. They had nearly two and one half million fans at Fenway Park.

1991

Jeff Reardon, third all-time in saves to Lee Smith and Dennis Eckersley, saved 40 games for the Red Sox. Despite strong performances from Reardon and Roger Clemens in pitching and Wade Boggs and Jack Clark in hitting, the Red Sox finished second in the East division, seven games behind the Toronto Blue Jays.

1994

On July 8, shortstop John Valentin executed an unassisted triple play as the Red Sox beat Seattle, 4-3.

1995

In a year in which the Red Sox won the American League East Division championship, slugging first baseman Mo Vaughn led the league in home runs, 39, and runs batted in, 126. He incidentally also led the league in strikeouts with 150. Vaughn, who batted .300 for the year, was awarded the league's Most Valuable Player award.

1996

Roger Clemens, for the second time in his Red Sox career, struck out 20 batters in a nine-inning game, tying his own record that he set in 1986.

1997

Nomar Garciaparra, the Red Sox new shortstop, won Rookie of the Year honors. He batted .298, hit 30 home runs and had 98 R.B.I. He led the league with 209 hits. Garciaparra joins a group of superior shortstops now playing in the big leagues.

Two pitchers, one formerly with the Red Sox and the other subsequently to join the team, won the Cy Young awards. Roger Clemens won in the American League pitching for Toronto. Pedro Martinez won in the National League pitching for Montreal.

1998

Bullpen ace Tom "Flash" Gordon set the major league record for consecutive saves with 43 to help the Red Sox to a wild-card entry in the American League play-offs. He led the league with 46 saves in the season.

1999

Pedro Martinez had a career year for the Red Sox, comparable to the great year Roger Clemens had in the pennant-winning year of 1986, Martinez had a 23-4 record with an E.R.A. of 2.08, more than one run better than any pitcher in the league. He was also tops in strikeouts with 313, with only one other league pitcher havng as many as 200. He had 19 games with 10 or more strikeouts. Martinez, previously with Montreal, joined Randy Johnson as the only two pitchers ever to have mor than 300 strikeouts a season with the Cy Young award, his second to add to the one he earned with the Expos in 1997.

The Red Sox, "wild card" winners, were dominated by two players, Martinez, and Nomar Garciaparra, a superstar shortstop who won the batting championship.

TheRed Sox and Fenway Park hosted the All-Star game in July for the third time in baseball history. In July 1946, Ted Williams was the star as the American League won, 12-0. In 1961, the game ended in a 1-1 tie after nine innings, called beause of rain. In 1999, the Red Sox were represented by pitcher Pedro Martinez and shortstop Nomar Garciaparra. Martinez started and struck out five of the six batters he faced. He won the game for the American League and was named the game's Most Valuable Player. The score was 4 to 1.

In the 1999 division play-off series against the Cleveland Indians, John Valentin tied the record for most R.B.I.s in a play-off game in Game 4 with seven. In Game 5, Troy O'Leary also tied the record with seven R.B.I.s in the game.

2000

Team stars shortstop Nomar Garciaparra and pitcher Pedro Martinez are the third pair of teammates to lead their league in batting and earned run average in back-to-back seasons. They did so in 1999 and 2000. Al Simmons, outfielder, and Lefty Grove, pitcher, both of whom played for the Red Sox later in their careers, accomplished the feat playing for the Philadelphia Athletics in 1930 and 1931. Tommy Davis, outfielder, and Sandy Koufax, pitcher, won the awards while with the Los Angeles Dodgers in 1962 and 1963.

Elizabeth Dooley, one of the Red Sox's most loyal fans, died at the age of 87 in 2000. She saw 4,000 consecutive Red Sox games at Fenway Park. Ms. Dooley was a teacher in the Boston school system for 39 years. Before the game following her death, the Red Sox honored her with a moment of silence, and Ted Williams called her "the greatest Red Sox fan there will ever be."

On July 17, 2000, Nomar Garciaparra, batting .400, hit a home run that was the 10,000th home run in Red Sox history.

2001

Hideki Nomo of the Red Sox pitched both a no-hitter and a one-hitter. His no-hitter was on April 4 against Baltimore, 3-0, and he allowed just three walks. His one-hitter was in many respects a better pitched game. Pitching and winning against Toronto on May 25, 4-0, he allowed just one base runner and struck out 14 Blue Jays. At one point he struck out seven straight, just one short of the record.

A Recollection Of Career And Team Performances

The Red Sox won the first five World Series in which they played, in 1903, 1912, 1915, 1916 and 1918. They have since played and lost in four World Series, in 1946, 1967, 1975 and 1986. They lost each of these by four games to three.

The Sox were never out of the second division from 1919 to 1934. From 1922 through 1932, 11 years, they

were in last place nine times. They were in last place six years in a row from 1925 through 1930.

The Red Sox, by contrast, won over 90 games in 1977, 1978 and 1979, yet won no title.

The Red Sox three times have played the New York Yankees in pennant races that went down to the last day of the season. They won the pennant on Jack Chesbro's wild pitch in 1904. They lost to the Yankees on the last day of the season in 1949. And, they lost to the Yanks in a play-off game in 1978 on Bucky Dent's home run.

Boston beat Philadelphia in successive World Series in 1914 and 1915. In 1914 Boston (National League) beat Philadelphia (American League). In 1915 Boston (American League) beat Philadelphia (National League).

From 1921 through 1928, all but three of the New York Yankees World Series victories were pitched by ex-Red Sox pitchers. Hoyt won six games, Pennock won five, Pipgras won three and Mays and Bush won one each. The only victories by pitchers who were not ex-Red Soxers were by Bob Shawkey, Wilcy Moore, and Tom Zachary.

After being traded to the Yanks, Carl Mays at age 28 went on to win 135 games. Waite Hoyt, traded to the Yanks at age 21, went on to win 227 games. Sad Sam Jones, traded to New York at age 29 went on to win 161 games. Bullet Joe Bush, also traded to the Yanks, at age 25 went on to win 87 games. Herb Pennock, yet another pitcher who went to the Yanks, at age 29 went on to win 162 games. George Pipgras was 24 and traded at the start of his career, winning 93 games with the Yanks before being traded back to the Red Sox ten years later.

Babe Ruth, who shared his career essentially between the Red Sox and the Yankees, was a charter member of the Hall of Fame, elected in 1936 along with Honus Wagner, Ty Cobb, Christy Mathewson and Walter Johnson. Tris Speaker, whose career was with the Red Sox and the Cleveland Indians, was elected to the Hall of Fame in the next year, 1937, along with Cy Young, a Red Sox pitcher for part of his career.

Both Ted Williams and Carl Yastrzemski were elected to the Hall of Fame in their first year of eligibility, Williams in 1966 and Yastrzemski in 1989.

The Red Sox have had four players who played 2,000 or more games with the team. Carl Yastrzemski, was second only to Pete Rose in number of games played in the big leagues. Yastrzemski played in 3308 games. Dwight Evans played in 2505, Ted Williams in 2292 and Jim Rice in 2089. All but Evans played their entire career with the Red Sox.

The Red Sox have had two pitchers with 300 or more wins in their careers. Cy Young, who played with five teams, holds the record with 511 wins. Lefty Grove, who played with the Red Sox and the Philadelphia Athletics, won 300.

Ted Williams and Jimmie Foxx each had 17 grand slam home runs in their careers.

Among batting titles won by Red Sox players, Ted Williams has won six times, Wade Boggs five, Carl Yastrzemski three and Pete Runnels twice. Dale Alexander won the first batting title as a Red Sox player, in 1932.

Two pitchers have won 30 or more games while pitching for the Red Sox. Cy Young accomplished this feat twice with 33 wins in 1901 and 32 in 1902. Smoky Joe Wood won 34 in 1912.

The Red Sox from 1939 through 1987, except for the war years—a span of 47 years—have had three left fielders. They were Ted Williams, Carl Yastrzemski and Jim Rice. All three played their entire illustrious careers with the Sox.

Carl Yastrzemski and Dwight Evans have each won seven Gold Glove Awards for their outfield play.

The Red Sox have had three players who hit 400 or more home runs in their careers. Jimmie Foxx, ninth on the all-time list, hit 534 playing for both the Philadelphia Athletics and the Red Sox. Ted Williams, tenth all-time, hit 521. Carl Yastrzemski hit 452. Babe Ruth, of course, with 714 all-time, behind Hank Aaron's major league record of 755, performed primarily as a pitcher for the Boston Red Sox. He hit 49 homers while with the Red Sox.

Among one-two combinations of players who played together, Jim Rice and Dwight Evans had 767 home runs between them. They are behind Babe Ruth and Lou Gehrig who had 1207. Ted Williams and Bobby Doerr had 744.

Red Sox pitchers who have hit grand slam home runs include Babe Ruth in 1919, Lefty Grove in 1935, Wes Ferrell, who leads all pitchers in lifetime home runs with 38, in 1936, and Ellis Kinder in 1950.

Two Red Sox players have had two grand slam home runs in one game, Jim Tabor in 1939 and Rudy York in 1946.

Bobby Doerr and Vern Stephens, individually as second baseman and shortstop, participated in 262 double plays in 1949, 245 in 1950 and 232 in 1948. Doerr and Johnny Pesky, individually as second baseman and shortstop, participated in 225 double plays in 1946 and 208 in 1947.

The Red Sox twice have had four players with more than 100 runs driven in the same season. In 1940, Jimmie Foxx had 119, Ted Williams 113, Joe Cronin 111 and Bobby Doerr had 105. In 1977, Jim Rice had 114, Butch Hobson had 112, and Carl Yastrzemski and Carlton Fisk had 102 each.

Hall of Fame sluggers Bobby Doerr (left) and Jimmie Foxx display their favorite weapons. (Boston Public Library, Print Department).

PLAYERS ROLL CALL —
THE GREATS AND OTHERS
TO BE REMEMBERED

The pantheon of Red Sox players will evoke many memories. There are the unique players, or combination of players, who are legends in Red Sox and even in baseball history. In addition, every epoch in the course of a century had its stars and its durable players with an unquestioned Red Sox identity. There are others who played relatively briefly for the Red Sox but had luminous baseball histories with other teams, or are remembered for some special connection or event, or they for some reason captured the imagination and appreciation of Boston rooters, or their careers are brief but still in progress. Brief baseball biographies follow of the legends, the stars and journeymen, and the short-term players who most readily come to mind.

The First Great Red Sox Pitchers—Cy Young And Smoky Joe Wood

Cy Young and Smoky Joe Wood were dominant pitchers in their contiguous eras, at the beginning of the Pilgrim/Red Sox existence. Young, an original Pilgrim who came over from the Cleveland Spiders of the National League, was the backbone of Boston's first American League teams and he was the preeminent pitcher in baseball. Smoky Joe Wood, who came to the Red Sox shortly afterward, was also a dominant pitcher who, at one point, was considered the equal of or better than the legendary Walter Johnson. He had one unsurpassed year, 1912, and helped to usher in the Red Sox winning dynasty in the Century's second decade.

Cy Young

b. Mar. 29, 1867	Gilmore, Ohio	Pitches right	Bats right
	6'2" 210 lb.	"Red Sox"	1901-1908

"Smoky" Joe Wood

b. Oct. 25, 1889	Kansas City, Mo.	Pitches right	Bats right
	5'11" 180 lb.	Red Sox	1908-1915

Cy Young

Cy Young is baseball's norm for excellence. His lifetime record of 511 victories is unparalleled, and he is the only pitcher to have won 200 victories in the American and National Leagues.

Young's career began with the Cleveland National League team—the Spiders—in 1890 and he remained in the National League with Cleveland and then St. Louis until 1901. In 1901 he joined the Boston Somersets and was with the Boston team for eight of his 22 big league years. He ended his career with the Cleveland Naps, later the Indians.

Young, while with the Somersets/Pilgrims/Red Sox, led the league in wins three times. Five times in his career, he had more than 30 wins in a season, and he had a phenomenal 15 years in which he won 20 or more games. In

Cy Young was Boston's greatest pitcher on the original Somersets team. (Boston Public Library, Print Department).

1903 as a Pilgrim he led the league in winning percentage, .757, one of two times that he led the league in that category. Young has pitched more innings and had more complete games than anyone in baseball history. He pitched 40 or more complete games twice with Boston and seven times earlier in his career with the Cleveland Spiders and St. Louis. While with Boston, Young led the league in shutouts four times, with ten shutouts in 1904. He pitched three no-hit games, in 1897, 1904 and 1908, and he played in one World Series, the first one, against Pittsburgh in 1903, when he won two games for the Boston Pilgrims.

There are some other interesting facts about Denton True Young. He acquired his nickname, "Cy," when an observer saw him warm up before a Canton, Ohio Tri-State league game in 1890. He threw against a wooden fence and shattered the fence, evoking the nickname "Cyclone."

A reporter later shortened this to "Cy." Young not only had the most wins ever—Walter Johnson was second all-time with 417—but having pitched so many games he also holds the record for the most losses, at 316. Young joined the Boston Somersets at the age of 34 and for the eight years he was with the Boston team until he was 42, he won 192 games. When he was 40 and 41 years old he won more than 20 games each season for the Boston team. Young also managed, briefly, in 1907, serving as interim manager for seven games for the Boston Pilgrims.

Smoky Joe Wood (left) shakes hands with rival Walter Johnson. (Hall of Fame Library, Cooperstown, N.Y.).

The highest award for pitching achievement, initiated in 1956, was named for baseball's most winning pitcher, Cy Young. It is the Cy Young award. Young was elected to baseball's Hall of Fame in its second year, 1937.

Smoky Joe Wood

Smoky Joe Wood pitched his first game for the Red Sox at the age of 19. He was with the team from 1908 through 1915, or a total of seven full seasons. He had a phenomenal year in 1912, a year in which the Red Sox won the world championship, with a record of 34-5 and a winning percentage of .872. That year he led the league in complete games and shutouts (10), as well as in wins and winning percentage. He had three of the Red Sox's four wins in the World Series. Wood won a total of 115 games in his seven full years with the Red Sox. His lifetime earned run average was an outstanding 2.03.

Wood, a fireballing right-hander nicknamed for his pitching speed, later had arm trouble. He did not play in 1916. He contacted his old teammate, Tris Speaker, who was then the manager of the Cleveland Indians, and played

for Cleveland for five years as an outfielder, principally from 1918 through 1922. He was with the Indians in their 1920 world championship year. He had a respectable lifetime batting average of .283, including 24 home runs. In 1919, he hit two home runs in a 19-inning game against the New York Yankees. His second home run won the game by a score of 3-2.

Footnotes

Cy Young

In his eight years with the Somersets/Pilgrims/Red Sox, Cy Young led the Boston pitchers in number of wins seven times and was second in the remaining years. He won 20 or more games in this period six times.

In his first five years with the Boston team, the Pilgrims finished in first place twice and in the first division three other times. In his last three years with the team, the team finished in the second division, with one year in seventh place and another in last place.

In his first three years with the Somerset/Pilgrims, 1901, 1902 and 1903, Young led the league each season in wins, with 33, 32 and 28 respectively. He also led the first year in earned run average, 1.62, and in the other two years his ERA's were 2.15 and 2.08 respectively. In 1906, the year of Boston's last-place finish, he led the league in losses with 21.

In his eight years with Boston, Young's earned run average was under 2.15 in all but one season, when it was 3.19. In five of the eight years his ERA was under 2.00. His earned run average in the only World Series he played in was 1.59.

Young was a heavy-duty pitcher. In all eight seasons with the Somersets/Pilgrims/Red Sox, he pitched over 285 innings in each season and in six of the eight years he pitched more than 320 innings a year. In 1902 and 1903 he led the league in innings pitched, with 384.2 and 341.2, respectively. In all but one of these eight years he had 30 or more complete games. He led the league in complete games in 1902, with 41, and in 1903 with 34.

While with Boston, Young led the league three times in shutouts pitched, with five in 1901, seven in 1903 and 10 in 1904.

Cy Young is the all-time leader in the big leagues in wins, 511, in losses, 316, in complete games with 750, and in innings pitched with 7,356. He is fourth all time in shutouts pitched, with 76. In single-season records he is sixth all-time in wins with 35 (1895), tenth in earned run average at 1.26 (1908), seventh in least bases on balls per game, .79 (1906), and seventh in complete games, 44 (1892).

Smoky Joe Wood

In all eight years that he was with the Red Sox, Smoky Joe Wood's earned run average was under 2.62. He led the league in 1915, his last year as a pitcher, with an E.R.A. of 1.49.

In 1915 Joe Wood also led the league in winning percentage, .750, with 15 wins and five losses. This was the second time he led the league in winning percentage. In his phenomenal year of 1912 he won 34 and lost five for a percentage of .872.

Both 1912 and 1915 were world championship years for the Red Sox. Wood performed spectacularly in the 1912 Series but did not play in the 1915 Series because of an arm injury. He pitched and won two complete games of the three he started in the 1912 World Series and he also won one game pitching in relief. He had 11 strike outs in Game 1, which he won.

Smoky Joe, who played in the outfield for Cleveland beginning in 1918, after he injured his pitching arm, also hit well while he played for the Boston Red Sox. He batted over .250 five times in his eight years with the Sox and he batted .286 in the 1912 World Series. He also played four games as an outfielder for the World Champion Cleveland Indians in the 1920 World Series.

After his playing career, Joe Wood became a long-time coach of the Yale University baseball team.

"The Greatest Outfield"—Tris Speaker, Harry Hooper, Duffy Lewis

All three great outfielders, Speaker, Hooper and Lewis, began their careers with the Boston Red Sox. Hooper and Lewis spent most of their careers with the Red Sox. Speaker might have spent most or all of his career with the Red Sox, too, but for a salary disagreement after the 1915 season. He was traded to the Cleveland Indians and had a great career with Cleveland as well as Boston.

Speaker was the first to arrive, in 1907, with seven full-time seasons with the Red Sox from 1909 through 1915. Hooper came to the Red Sox in 1909, playing with the club for 12 years. Lewis arrived in 1910 for eight full seasons with the Sox. In their years together, from 1910 through 1915, Speaker, Hooper and Lewis were known as "the greatest outfield ever," with two of the three, Speaker and Hooper, becoming Hall of Famers.

Speaker, known as "The Grey Eagle," was not only a great hitter but also a spectacular fielder. He played a shallow center field, so shallow that he was virtually a fifth infielder, and he also had the speed to go back and catch long fly balls.

Hooper was also an outstanding hitter, a very good fielder with an exceptional throwing arm, and his speed was notable as well in his base stealing.

Lewis was a reliable if less spectacular hitter, and he patrolled "Duffy's Cliff" in left field in Fenway Park with unrivaled ability and sureness. Duffy Lewis was on three Red Sox world championship teams, in 1912, 1915 and 1916. His World Series batting average was .284 but, interestingly, he batted .444 in 1915 and .353 in 1916. In 1915, he singled home Harry Hooper with the winning run in the bottom of the ninth inning of the third game of the Series, the Sox winning 2-1. Lewis also doubled in the winning run in Game 4 of the Series, the Sox again scoring a 2-1 win. In the decisive fifth game, also won by the Red Sox, Lewis hit a two-run game-tying home run in the eighth inning, to be followed by Hooper's game and Series winning home run in the ninth inning.

Tris Speaker

b. Apr. 4, 1888	Hubbard, Texas	Bats left	throws left
	5'11½" 193 lbs.	Red Sox	1907-1915

Harry Hooper

b. Aug. 24, 1887	Bell Station, Calif.	Bats left	throws right
	5'10" 168 lbs.	Red Sox	1909-1920

Duffy Lewis

b. Apr. 18, 1888	San Francisco, Calif.	Bats right	throws right
	5'10½" 165 lbs.	Red Sox	1910-1917

Tris Speaker

Speaker had seven consecutive .300 plus batting years with the Red Sox, hitting .363 and .383 in two of these years. When he was traded to Cleveland he added three more consecutive .300 plus hitting years. In the first year after being traded by the Red Sox, Speaker led the league with a .386 batting average and he also led in base hits and doubles. Notably, in 18 of 19 years, from 1909 through 1927, he batted better than .300. He ranks fifth in baseball history with a lifetime .345 average. His lifetime records include more doubles (792) than any other player in major league history and he is fifth all-time in hits, sixth in triples and eighth in runs scored. While with the Red Sox, Speaker also tied for the league lead one year (1912) in home runs with ten.

Center fielder Tris Speaker had 200 or more hits in a season four times, ending his career with 3,515 hits. (Baseball Hall of Fame Library. Cooperstown, N.Y.).

Speaker played on three world championship teams, two with Boston in 1912 and 1915 and one with the Cleveland Indians in 1920. There was a short-lived "Chalmers Most Valuable Player" award in the years 1911 through 1914 and "Spoke," as he was also known, won this award in 1912. That year he hit .383, though this placed him only third behind Ty Cobb at .410 and Shoeless Joe Jackson at .395. He tied for the league lead in home runs (10) with Frank "Home Run" Baker, and he led in doubles with 53. He was selected to the Hall of Fame in its second year, 1937, along with Cy Young. The two of them were among the first eight members elected to the Hall of Fame.

Harry Hooper

Harry Hooper had a lifetime batting average of .281. His best batting average years with the Red Sox were in 1911 when he hit .311 and in 1920 when he hit .312. He had 300 stolen bases in his 12 years with the Sox, averaging 25 a year. He averaged 82 runs scored a year.

A speedster and fine defensive outfielder, Harry Hooper had 15 consecutive seasons in which he hit 20 or more doubles. He played on four Boston world championship teams. (Baseball Hall of Fame Library. Cooperstown, N.Y.).

Hooper was on four Boston Red Sox world championship teams, 1912, 1915, 1916 and 1918. His World Series batting average was .293. He scored the winning run in the ninth inning of the third game in 1915, the Red Sox winning 2-1. In the fifth and final game that year, he won the game with his second home run of the day in the top of the ninth inning.

Hooper is a member of the Hall of Fame.

Duffy Lewis

George Edward "Duffy" Lewis is a lifetime .284 hitter. He hit .307 in 1911, one of his two .300 hitting years, and he was fourth in the league that year with seven home runs, behind Home Run Baker, Tris Speaker and Ty Cobb. By fortunate coincidence, both Hooper and Lewis had one of their two .300 hitting years, in 1911. Since Tris Speaker was a perennial .300 hitter and hit .334 in 1911, the Boston Red Sox's "best ever" outfield was also notable because all three outfielders hit over .300 the same year. Speaker batted .334, Hooper .311 and Lewis .307 in 1911.

Footnotes

Tris Speaker

Tris Speaker led the American League in hits twice, in doubles eight times, in home runs and slugging percentage once each. He also led the league one year in pinch hits. This was in an era when he had to compete with, among others, all time great hitters Babe Ruth, Ty Cobb and Shoeless Joe Jackson.

"The Grey Eagle" had 200 or more hits four times and ended his career among the top five all time in hits, with 3,514. Notably, too, he batted .380 or over five times.

Speaker, in three World Series, batted .300, .294 and .320, respectively, with a total of 22 hits. In the 1920 World Series won by Cleveland, Speaker scored six of the team's total of 21 runs, and he scored the only run in Cleveland's Game 6 win.

"Spoke" not only had power but also speed. He stole 433 bases in his career. For ten straight years he stole 25 or more bases a year, eight years with the Red Sox and then two more with the Indians. He stole 52 bases with the Sox in the World Championship year of 1912.

Speaker's style of playing center field, playing in close to the infield and going back on fly balls, enabled him to make unassisted double plays, take pick-off throws from the pitcher or catcher, throw batters out at first base from his position in center field, and even make the pivot at second place on double plays. He had 461 career outfield assists, and led the league's outfielders seven times in fielding chances per game, seven times in putouts, three times in assists, six times in double plays and twice in fielding average. It was for his great soaring and hawking skills that he was known as "The Grey Eagle".

After 1915, Speaker refused a salary cut and was sold just as the 1916 season began to the Cleveland Indians. He became the Indians' playing manager in 1919. He directed the team to its first pennant and World Series championship in 1920 while himself batting .388. The last two years of his playing career "Spoke" played with the Washington Nationals and the Philadelphia Athletics.

Harry Hooper

Harry Hooper had a 17-year big league career from 1909 through 1925. The first 12 years were with the Red Sox and the last five he played with the Chicago White Sox. Hooper was traded to the White Sox just before the 1921 season and was yet another of the Red Sox talent unloaded by owner Harry Frazee.

Hooper had 15 straight years in which he hit 20 or more doubles. In nine of ten years he had 20 or more stolen bases a year. In his first full season, 1910, he had 40 successful steals.

Though mostly a speedster and a fine defensive outfielder, Hooper also had some power. He won the final game of the 1915 World Series with his two homers. He is the only player to have led off both ends of a doubleheader

with home runs, in the year 1911 when his total home run output was four.

Hooper had a fine World Series record. In the four Boston World Championship Series he played in, he had twenty seven hits in 24 games. His cumulative World Series batting average was .293.

Hooper was a brilliant defensive outfielder. He led the league in making double plays twice and in assists once. He is particularly memorable for his bare-handed catch of Larry Doyle's drive for a home run in the final game of the World Series against the New York Giants in 1912.

Though Ed Barrow is properly given credit for having made the move to switch Babe Ruth from pitcher to regular outfielder, Harry Hooper was early and instrumental in recommending the move to Barrow. Ruth, as a regular player, started at first base then moved to left field and finally to right field.

Duffy Lewis

Duffy Lewis was the last of the "greatest outfield" to appear with the Red Sox. Speaker joined the team in 1907, Hooper in 1909 and Lewis in 1910. Lewis had 11 big league years from 1910 through 1921, the first eight years with the Red Sox. He was another of the players bundled off to the New York Yankees, in 1918, by Harry Frazee.

Lewis, though less spectacular than the other two outfielders, was considered the defensive equal of Speaker and Hooper. He mastered "Duffy"s Cliff" at Fenway Park, the left field area where balls would roll uphill to the wall.

In a small footnote, Lewis was also the first player ever to pinch hit for Babe Ruth.

Duffy Lewis played for the Red Sox for eight seasons beginning in 1907. (Baseball Hall of Fame Library. Cooperstown, N.Y.).

The Babe Ruth Era In Red Sox Pitching

Babe Ruth

b. Feb. 6, 1895	Baltimore, Md.	Pitches Left	Bats Left
	6'2" 215 lbs.	Red Sox	1914-1919

Babe Ruth, though better known for his legendary home run exploits with the New York Yankees, is an authentic Red Sox hero. Ruth came to the big leagues, at age 19, as a pitcher for the Boston Red Sox. In his first full season, 1915, at age 20 he won 18 games and also hit four home runs. By 1916 he was acquiring a reputation as the best left handed pitcher in baseball. In that year he won 23 games and led the league with a 1.75 earned run average and nine shutouts. He pitched in the World Series that year, winning the longest complete game in World Series history. It was a 14-inning 2-1 win over the Brooklyn Robins. In 1917 Ruth had 24 victories and led the league with 35 complete games.

In 1918, Ed Barrow, then the manager of the Red Sox, decided that Ruth had more value to the team as an everyday ballplayer. Ruth won 18 of the 19 games he started but he also played the outfield and first base in 95 games. Ruth, in 1918, led the league in home runs with 11, and in slugging percentage at .555. His batting average was .300.

Ironically, though the Babe hit no home runs in Boston's winning 1918 World Series, he pitched and won two of the four games won by the Sox 1-0 and 3-2. He also set a record to last into the 1960s by pitching 29^2/$_3$ scoreless innings in the World Series.

In 1919, though Ruth won nine games as a pitcher he played 130 games primarily as an outfielder. He hit an unheard of 29 home runs, easily breaking the major league record. He also led the league in runs batted in, 114, and batted .322.

Babe Ruth was traded to the New York Yankees after the 1919 season in perhaps the most disastrous and one-sided trade in baseball history, occasioned by owner Harry

Although better known as a New York Yankee hero, Babe Ruth began his Hall of Fame career with the Boston Red Sox at the age of 19 in 1907. (Baseball Hall of Fame Library, Cooperstown, N.Y.)

Frazee's desperate need for money for his non-baseball ventures. After that, Ruth became the legendary "Sultan of Swat," a charismatic figure who made Yankee Stadium into "the house that Ruth built," and led the Yankees in their earliest great dynasty years.

He was also, however, Babe Ruth, the pitcher, the best left-handed pitcher in the game while he was with the Red Sox, and an authentic Boston hero. He was admired and loved by Boston fans. On the occasion when the Babe announced his retirement, in 1934, 46,776 fans came out to a Red Sox-Yankee game to pay tribute to Boston's great left hander and phenomenal pitcher-outfielder.

Footnotes

Babe Ruth

Babe Ruth is perhaps America's most legendary sports figure. He epitomizes grandeur and even excess in everything he was and did. A fine pitcher but ultimately a great home run hitter, he almost single-handedly changed the game from a pitchers' duel to a home-run hitting display, from defense to hitting. His "Ruthian" achievements at bat popularized the game and brought huge crowds to baseball, most notably at Yankee Stadium in New York. To many, Ruth was the greatest player who ever played the game.

Ruth, a charismatic figure in America, was known not only for his unrivaled baseball exploits but also for his bon vivant lifestyle, his gargantuan food and sexual appetites, his free spending and his general good cheer. He was a great favorite and even an inspiration for the youth of America—he was a kid himself. He earned higher baseball salaries than anyone else, rising to $80,000 per year in the 1930s. When told that he was earning a higher salary than the American president, then Herbert Hoover, Ruth was reported to have said, "Why not? I had a better year than he did." He also earned large amounts barn-

---

storming after season with baseball teams made up of major leaguers, played the vaudeville circuit and endorsed various products.

Ruth was at times also baseball's "bad boy". He exasperated and defied baseball's stern commissioner, Judge Kenesaw Mountain Landis, with his extracurricular activities. He was suspended by Landis for his prohibited barnstorming and vaudeville activities, and again for leading the Yankees one year in spring training partying that earned the headline, "Yankees Training on Scotch." His carousing led his roommate, outfielder Ping Bodie, to say that he mainly shared hotel accommodations with Ruth's suitcase. Ruth was also in trouble with his manager, Miller Huggins. He would show up late for games, ignore the manager's batting signals, and generally act like the prima donna (and main man) that he was. Finally Huggins, backed by the team's owners, fined Ruth an unheard of $5,000 and suspended him from the team.

Ruth ended his career playing for the Boston Braves in 1935, 22 years after he started his career with the Boston Red Sox. At the end, he still maintained his slugging prowess by hitting three home runs and a single, and driving in six runs, in a game. The Babe was thwarted in his later ambition to become a major league manager. He coached briefly for the Brooklyn Dodgers but was valued more for his name and reputation in drawing crowds than for his coaching contributions.

Ruth as a player was magnificent. He was a sublime hitter with a .342 lifetime average. His highest single season average was .393 for the Yankees in 1923, remarkably placing him only second that year, behind Harry Heilmann's .403 average. He was a prodigious home run hitter who led the American League 12 times in home runs. He had the single-season home run record, 60 in 1927, until Roger Maris of the Yankees broke the record with 61 in 1961. He held the record for lifetime home runs in major league baseball until this record was broken by Hank Aaron of the Atlanta Braves, who ended up with 755 home runs. Adding insult to the injury of other teams when he was traded from the Red Sox to the Yankees, the first two years after the trade, in 1920 and 1921, the Bambino hit 113 home runs. He hit a home run every eight and one half times at bat during his career, an unmatched record. He established an unparalleled slugging average, .847, in 1920, and followed the next year with an .846 record. He led the American League 13 times in slugging and 11 times in bases on balls. He holds the record for 170 bases on balls in one season and 2,056 in his career.

In the early years of his major league career, from 1914-1919, Ruth was one of the best left-handed pitchers in baseball. Pitching for the Red Sox, he won 65 games in his first three years and led the American League in earned run average in 1916. He pitched and won three World Series games in 1916 and 1918, notably pitching a record 29 2/3 consecutive scoreless innings, a record not broken for 43 years. Traded to the New York Yankees as an everyday player, he later pitched and won five more games with the Yankees

Not surprisingly, Ruth's record in World Series play is phenomenal. As a pitcher in two winning Series with the Red Sox, he is first in history with a winning percentage of 1.000 based on three victories and no defeats. He is third in league history with a career World Series earned run average of 0.87. He pitched and won the World Series record fourteen inning game against Sherry Smith of the Brooklyn Robins, 2-1. In fact, Ruth played in three World Series for the Red Sox. He pitched in the 1916 and 1918 Series but in the 1915 Series did not pitch and had only one at bat.

Babe Ruth played in seven World Series for the New York Yankees, making a total of ten in his career. He played on a World Championship team seven times. He had a .326 lifetime World Series batting average playing in a total of 41 games. In World Series play, he is second all-time in home runs with 15, fourth in runs batted in and second in receiving bases on balls. Given his prodigious swing, not surprisingly he is fourth all-time in the number of times he struck out in World Series games.

In the 1923 World Series, Ruth hit two long home runs in Game 2 against the New York Giants and he hit another long ball to center field in Yankee Stadium that was caught by Giant centerfielder Casey Stengel. Stengel himself had two home runs in the 1923 Series, one an inside-the-parker. In Game 4 of the 1926 World Series, the Babe hit a record three home runs to give the Yankees a 10-5 victory over the St. Louis Cardinals. He hit another home run in the Yanks' losing effort in Game 7. Ruth was the only person to hit any home runs in the Yanks' 1927 sweep of the Pittsburgh Pirates. He hit three of them, two in one game. In the 1932 sweep of the Chicago Cubs Ruth hit two home runs in Game 3. Lou Gehrig also hit two home runs in the game, once back to back with the Babe. 1932 was also the World Series in which Ruth reputedly predicted and then pointed and guided a home run into the center field stand, fulfilling a promise he had made to a little boy whom he had visited in a hospital. This home run, off Charlie Root of the Cubs, has resulted in endless controversy about whether the Babe had in fact pointed his bat to center field with the implied promise of a home run to follow.

Ruth holds a myriad of unexcelled individual batting records. He is first all-time in slugging percentage, at .690, and led the league 13 times. As noted, he is second all-time in home runs at 714 and led the league twelve times in homers. He is first all-time in batting to home run ratio, with a home run every 8.5 at bats. He is second all-time in runs batted in and led the league in R.B.I.s six times. He is first all-time in bases on balls, with 2,056, and led the league 11 times in this category. He also led the league five times in striking out. He is second all-time in runs scored with 2,174, nearly as many as he drove in, and led the league eight times. He is tenth in all-time batting average at .342. It probably would be appropriate to refer to his hitting record as colossal.

A little known fact about the Babe's career is that he stole home ten times.

Great Red Sox Acquisitions—Joe Cronin, Jimmie Foxx, Lefty Grove

The 1930s marked the inauguration of "the Tom Yawkey years." A major part of the Red Sox rehabilitation program involved bringing aboard some established superstars from other teams. Joe Cronin came over to the Red Sox from the Washington Senators in 1934 as playing manager. Jimmie Foxx, a mainstay of one of Connie Mack's great Philadelphia Athletics teams, came over from the A's in 1935. Lefty Grove, a star pitcher with the great Philadelphia teams, came over from the A's two years earlier, in 1933.

Joe Cronin

b. Oct. 12, 1906	San Francisco, Calif.	Bats Right	Throws Right
	5'11½" 180 lbs.	Red Sox	1935-1945

Jimmie Foxx

b. Oct. 22, 1907	Sudlersville, Md.	Bats Right	Throws Right
	6' 195 lbs.	Red Sox	1936-1942

Lefty Grove

b. Mar. 6, 1900	Lonaconing, Md.	Pitches Left	Bats Left
	6'3" 190 lbs.	Red Sox	1934-1941

Joe Cronin

Joe Cronin, who started his 20-year playing career as a second baseman with the Pittsburgh Pirates, played seven years at shortstop for the Washington Senators, and then 11 years at the same position with the Red Sox. He had a lifetime .301 batting average.

Cronin was an outstanding player with the Washington Senators. In a five-year period from 1930 through 1934 he batted over .300 four of those years and had more than 100 runs batted in each of the five years. Traded to the Red Sox, he was a mainstay from 1935-1945 though he played only part time during World War II, near the end of his career. He hit .325 with the Red Sox in 1938 and led the league with 51 doubles that year. In his best years with the Sox, 1937-1940, he averaged nearly 20 home runs per year. For more than ten years he was an outstanding hitting shortstop in the American League.

Cronin, as a 27-year-old player-manager, led the Washington Senators to a pennant in 1933. After the 1934 season he was sent to the Red Sox as a player-manager in a trade that gave the Senators Red Sox shortstop Lyn Lary and $225,000. Cronin was the Red Sox manager for 13 years, from 1935 through 1947. His power-laden Red Sox won the pennant in 1946, losing a close World Series to the St. Louis Cardinals, four games to three. His teams

Hall of Fame shortstop Joe Cronin played for the Red Sox for 11 seasons. He also managed the team for 13 seasons. (Baseball Hall of Fame Library. Cooperstown, N.Y.).

finished four times in second place.

Joe Cronin became general manager of the Red Sox after his tour of duty as manager, and he subsequently became president of the American League. He was elected to the Hall of Fame as a player. An interesting sidelight is that he was one of the five Hall of Fame players (Babe Ruth, Lou Gehrig, Jimmie Foxx, Al Simmons and Joe Cronin) struck out in succession by Carl Hubbell of the New York Giants in the 1934 All-Star game.

Jimmie Foxx

Jimmie Foxx, "Double X," is one of the great power hitters in the history of the game, in a league with Babe Ruth, Lou Gehrig and others. Foxx began his career with the Philadelphia Athletics in 1925 and played with the A's until 1936. He was a key player on Connie Mack's great 1929 and 1930 world champions and 1931 pennant winners with Al Simmons, Mickey Cochrane, Jimmy Dykes, Max Bishop and Lefty Grove as teammates. In 1936, Foxx was traded to the Red Sox, for whom he starred for more than six years.

Foxx had a lifetime batting average of .325, hit more than 500 home runs, including 17 grand slams, and he drove in almost 2,000 runs in his 20-year career. He led the league in home runs four times, in runs batted in three times and in batting average twice. In 1932 he led the league in home runs with his career-high 58, in runs batted in with 169, and in runs scored with 151. The next year, 1933, he led the league in hitting, .356, in homers with 48 and in runs batted in with 163. In his best year with the Red Sox, 1938, Foxx led the league in batting, .349, hit 50 home runs (Hank Greenberg of Detroit hit 58), and he led in runs batted in with 175. He hit over .300 13 times and he batted in over 100 runs 13 years in a row. He also hit 30 or more home runs every year from 1929 through 1940.

Lefty Grove won 300 career games, 105 of them with the Red Sox. (Boston Public Library, Print Department).

Foxx had a lifetime .344 batting average in three World Series with the Athletics. He hit home runs in the first two World Series games in 1929, leading the A's to victories in each of these games. He won a 1929 World Series game with a home run. He also hit a home run in the 1930 Series. Foxx also led the American League to an All-Star game victory in 1935, 4 to 1, driving in three runs with a two-run homer and a single.

Jimmie Foxx was, in addition to his other talents, a versatile fielder. Though a regular first baseman, he also caught on occasion and played third base and the outfield. He came up to the Philadelphia Athletics at the age of 17 as the back-up catcher to the redoubtable Mickey Cochrane. He also pitched in ten games. His awesome talent was recognized with numerous awards. He was named the league's M.V.P. three times, twice with the Athletics and once with the Red Sox. He won the Triple Crown, leading in batting average, home runs and runs batted in, in 1933. He holds the home run record for the two teams with which he played, 58 with the Philadelphia Athletics in 1932, and 50 with the Red Sox in 1938.

Lefty Grove

Robert Moses "Lefty" Grove is one of the great left-handed pitchers in baseball history, and some think the greatest. Like Jimmie Foxx, Lefty Grove spent the first part of his career with the Philadelphia Athletics during some of that team's greatest years. His career began in 1925 and he was the Athletics' star pitcher during most of his nine years with the team. In this period, he won 20 or more games for seven straight years, leading the league four times in both wins and winning percentage, and he scored 31 wins in 1931. While with the Athletics, he was first in earned run average five times. Grove was a fastballer and led the league in strikeouts his first seven years with the team. He led the league three times in complete games. By contrast, he also pitched

The Red Sox Encyclopedia

in relief, saving nine games a season twice, once to lead the league.

Grove was with the Red Sox eight years, from 1934 through 1941. In his second year he won 20 games for the Sox. He led the league in earned run average four times with the Sox, for a total of nine times in his career. He led the league in shutouts, with six, in 1936.

Lefty Grove won a total of 300 games in his career, of which 105 were with the Red Sox. He is fifth in all-time winning percentage, with an average of .680 per season. His lifetime earned run average is 3.06. He pitched in three World Series. In the 1930 World Series he won two complete games and one in relief for the Philadelphia Athletics. He won two games and lost one in the Athletics' losing 1931 World Series. His cumulative World Series earned run average was 1.75. He was the loser in the National League's first All-Star win in 1936, losing to Dizzy Dean of the Cardinals.

Grove won the Most Valuable Player award in the American League in 1931. This was the year in which he won 31 and lost four for an .886 winning percentage. He pitched in the era before Cy Young awards, else he likely would have been a multiple winner. Ironically, great as was "Mose" Grove's pitching career, he never pitched a no-hit game.

Grove, like the other two great Red Sox acquisitions of the 1930s Cronin and Foxx, is a Hall of Famer.

Footnotes

Joe Cronin

Joe Cronin was a consistently good hitter. For the last 17 years of his career, and for all 11 years of his career with Boston, he never hit lower than .280. Eleven years he hit over .300. His highest average for a full season's play was .346 in 1930 playing for the Washington Senators.

Joe was a good doubles hitter. For 11 of 12 years he hit at least 30 a year. He led the league with 51 in 1938 playing for the Red Sox, and he also led the

league with 45 in 1933 playing for the pennant winning Washington Senators. He also led the league in triples one year. In 1943, playing part-time for the Red Sox he led the league in pinch hits.

Cronin had four second-place finishes as a player-manager for the Red Sox in his first 11 years with the club. His player roster included Lefty Grove, Jimmie Foxx, Ted Williams and Bobby Doerr, all future Hall of Famers, but it was not until 1946 that he won a pennant with the Red Sox.

Beginning in 1948 as general manager for the Red Sox, Cronin made a variety of moves to improve the team. Notably, he brought in Lou Boudreau to be player, then manager late in Boudreau's playing career. At various times, he brought in star players—pitchers Sid Hudson and Bob Porterfield and first baseman Mickey Vernon from the Washington Senators—and, from Detroit, pitcher Dizzy Trout, third baseman George Kell, outfielder Hoot Evers and shortstop Johnny Lipon. All were on the downside or near the end of their careers. One notable acquisition was outfielder Jackie Jensen from the Senators who had several good seasons with the Red Sox. The Red Sox did not finish higher than third place in the 1950s.

Cronin presided over the American League 14 years, from 1959 to 1973. It was an era of new franchises and of teams switching city locations. The Senators went to Minnesota, the Athletics moved to Oakland, the Seattle Pilots went to Milwaukee and a second twentieth century Washington team settled in Texas.

Jimmie Foxx holds the Red Sox record for season home runs with 50 in 1938. (National Baseball Library. Cooperstown, N.Y.).

Jimmie Foxx

"Double X" or "The Beast" was one of the all-time great stars in the big leagues. He was considered "the right-handed Babe Ruth." As a Hall of Fame first baseman, he stands tall with the likes of such other great Hall of Fame slugging first basemen as Lou Gehrig, Harmon Killebrew, Johnny Mize, Hank Greenberg, Willie McCovey, Willie Stargell and legendary Buck Leonard of the Homestead Grays in the Negro Baseball Leagues.

Foxx, the slugger, had a lifetime slugging average of .609, placing him fourth all-time behind Babe Ruth, Ted Williams and Lou Gehrig. He led the league in slugging five times. He is also ninth all-time in World Series slugging average, ironically also at .609.

Foxx, like most feared sluggers with prodigious swings, often walked and struck out. He led the league twice in walks, ending up with a career 1,452. He led the league seven times in strike outs, with a career 1,311.

It was Jimmie Foxx who broke the Red Sox record in home runs previously held by Babe Ruth. "The Babe" hit 29 in 1919 for the Sox record. "Double X" hit 50 for the Sox in 1938, a Sox record that still stands. Buck Freeman was the first Red Sox slugger. He hit 12 home runs in 1902 and then beat his own record with 13 in 1903.

Foxx, the pitcher, pitched one inning for the Red Sox in 1939 and 22.2 innings in nine games for the Philadelphia Phillies at the end of his career in 1945. His "lifetime" earned run average was 1.52.

Foxx, after playing different positions in the first four years of his career, became the Athletics' regular first baseman in 1929. The Athletics won three straight pennants and two World Series in 1929, 1930 and 1931. The celebrated team consisted of such baseball greats, in addition to Foxx, as Mickey Cochrane, Al Simmons and pitchers Lefty Grove and George Earnshaw. Also regulars on the team were Max Bishop, Jimmy Dykes, Bing Miller, Mule Haas and pitchers Rube Walberg and Howard Ehmke.

Lefty Grove

Grove, while pitching for the Philadelphia Athletics in their glory years of 1930 and 1931, won the equivalent of the batter's Triple Crown. He led the league both years in wins, with 28 and 31 respectively, in earned run average, at 2.54 and 2.06, and in strike outs with 209 in 1930 and 175 in 1931.

Grove, though a fireballer during his career with the Athletics, became a different kind of pitcher with the Red Sox. He became a finesse pitcher in large part because he could no longer deliver speed. He became a crafty change of pace and curve ball pitcher who was still able to win

Pitching greats Lefty Grove (left) of Boston and Dizzy Dean of the St. Louis Cardinals converse before an exhibition game in 1936. (Boston Public Library, Print Department).

twenty games one year and to top the American League in earned run average four more times.

"Ol' Mose" as he was familiarly known (his full name was Robert Moses Grove), also had a notorious reputation for a violent temper. He was a hard loser, and if the team behind him made egregious errors, he was known to curse the teammates who lapsed. He also did violence to water coolers and destroyed lockers in the clubhouse. As Ted Williams was purported to have observed, for all the explosiveness and destruction he created, he was careful never to subject his left arm to injury.

Lefty Grove gave up a bases-loaded home run to Babe Ruth in 1927, one of the Babe's record 60 that year, and he also gave a hit to Joe DiMaggio in 1941, during the latter's 56 straight games with a hit. Against the Babe, Grove was pitching for the Philadelphia Athletics; against Joe D., he was with the Red Sox.

Ted Williams—"The Splendid Splinter"

Ted Williams			
b. Aug. 30, 1918 San Diego, Calif.	Bats Left	Throws Right	
6'3" 205 lbs.	Red Sox	1939-1960	

Ted Williams is one of the great legends of baseball, and perhaps its greatest all-around hitter. He played all of his 19-year career, from 1939 through 1960, with the Boston Red Sox.

The Red Sox Encyclopedia

Williams' illustrious career began in 1939 when he immediately won the league's runs batted in crown, with 145, and he batted .327. It ended in a dramatic home run in his final at bat in 1960. In between, "The Thumper" (another nickname) won the league batting title six times, and his lifelong batting average of .344 is sixth in baseball history. At age 40, in 1958, he was the oldest ever to win a batting crown. He won the league slugging title nine times, twice slugging over .730, and his lifetime .634 slugging average ranks second all-time, behind only Babe Ruth.

Boston's "Splendid Splinter," Ted Williams is considered by many to be the best hitter of all time. (Baseball Hall of Fame Library. Cooperstown, N.Y.).

slugged at least .650, and he led in bases on balls and runs scored. In 1949, he won two legs of the Triple Crown, home runs and runs batted in, but he lost the batting title to George Kell of Detroit by a fraction of a point. Williams did win the Triple Crown, leading in batting average, home runs and runs batted in, twice, a feat matched only by one other all-time great hitter, Rogers Hornsby. However, in his first Triple Crown year, 1942, Joe Gordon of the New York Yankees was named Most

He won the league's home run and runs batted in titles four times each. He hit a lifetime 521 home runs and had 17 grand slams. He also led the league in scoring six times.

Williams was known for his classic, graceful swing and also for his uncanny batting eye. He made the study of hitting a baseball a science. He would not hit bad pitches. He won the league's bases on balls title eight times and his 2019 lifetime walks places him second in baseball history. Again, only Babe Ruth did better. He leads all other players with an amazing average of just over one walk for every five times at bat.

Ted Williams played in only one World Series, in 1946, but did not distinguish himself. However, he had spectacular All-Star game performances.

In 1941 in Detroit, he hit a two-out, two-men on base home run in the ninth inning to win the game for the American League, 7-5. In the 1946 All-Star game in Boston, Ted had four hits, including two home runs, and drove in five runs as the American League destroyed the National League, 12-0. All told, he played in 18 all-star games with a .304 batting average and an on-base percentage of .438. He singled in his final All-Star at bat in 1960, and he was then nearly 42 years old.

Williams was named the league's Most Valuable Player in 1946 and 1949. In both years he batted over .340 and

Valuable Player, and in 1947, his second Triple Crown year, Joe DiMaggio of the Yankees won Most Valuable Player honors. In 1941, when Williams hit .406, a nearly mythical batting average that no one has matched since, Joe DiMaggio won the Most Valuable Player award. It was the year in which DiMaggio set the remarkable record of hitting safely in 56 straight games. Conceivably, Williams might have won the Most Valuable Player award at least five times. There is some thought that he may have been slighted because he was somewhat aloof and disdainful with baseball writers during his playing career, and the Baseball Writers Association of America names the Most Valuable Player.

Ted Williams' career record is all the more remarkable in that he lost almost all of five years to military service. He was a Marine pilot in World War II and was recalled to service in the Korean War. Williams concluded his career with four years as a manager, three with the Washington Senators and one with the Texas Rangers.

Footnotes

Ted Williams

Ted Williams had a remarkable on-base percentage of .551 in 1941. In more than one out of every two at bats he was on base. He was officially at bat 456 times and had 185 hits for a batting average of .406, the last time any big league player had hit .400 or more. He also led the league in walks in 1941 with 145. This gave him a total of 320 times on base with hits and walks, and to be added are the times he reached base on an error and was hit by a pitch.

Babe Ruth had the most bases on balls in a season, 170 in 1923. Ted Williams holds second, third and fourth places all-time, with 162 in 1947 and 1949, and 156 in 1946. This is testament to his sharp batting eye and refusal to swing at bad pitches. He was one of the most disciplined hitters in baseball.

"The Thumper" is in the top ten lifetime in nine significant batting categories. He is first in bases on balls average at .208, meaning that he walked once every five times at bat. He was second in career bases on balls, and he was second in slugging. He is fourth in home run percentage, with over six in every 100 at bats. He is sixth in batting average, eighth in runs batted in per game, and tenth in home runs, extra base hits and runs batted in.

In career bases on balls, Babe Ruth ranks first with 2,056. Ted Williams of the Red Sox is second with 2,019. Joe Morgan of the Cincinnati Reds in third with 1,865 and Carl Yastrzemski, another Red Soxer, is fourth with 1,845.

Ted Williams played in 18 All-Star games as did Brooks Robinson, third baseman for the Baltimore Orioles. Stan Musial, Hank Aaron and Willie Mays each played in 24 All-Star games.

"The Splinter" twice won the batting title with averages under his career average of .344. In 1947 he won with .343 and in 1948 he won with .328.

Ted Williams hit safely in all the Opening Day games in which he played—14. His Opening Day batting average is .449, 22 hits in 49 at bats.

Ted, as a rookie in 1939, hit a home run off Thornton Lee of the White Sox. In his final year, 1960, he hit a

Ted Williams' career was interrupted for nearly five years while he served as a Marine pilot in World War II and the Korean War. (Boston Public Library, Print Department).

home run off Don Lee of the Washington Senators, Thornton's son.

Ted had three "final" home runs. He hit one in 1952 when a special day was held for him as he was about to return to Marine Corps duty as a pilot in the Korean War. He hit a second "final" home run in 1954 on the last day of the season after he had previously announced that he would retire at the end of the season. His third and final "final" home run was hit in his last game at Fenway Park in 1960, an event memorialized by the author, John Updike, in an article first published in *The New Yorker* magazine, "Hub Fans Bid Kid Adieu." (See Chapter Three.)

Williams three times in his career hit three home runs in one game.

Hugh Duffy's claim to Red Sox fame is that he was a long-time hitting instructor and his most famous pupil was Ted Williams. Duffy was also a Hall of Famer, playing for the Boston National League team in the 1890s. His most illustrious year was 1894 when he won the unofficial Triple Crown with 18 home runs, 145 runs batted in, and a never-rivaled batting average of .438. He also led in doubles and slugging.

Williams, who was fiercely independent, mellowed after his playing days and became a successful batting coach whose advice was constantly being sought. He became a skillful manager and achieved a reputation as a good handler of pitchers. He managed the Washington Senators for four years, beginning in 1969, and stayed with the team as manager when it moved to Texas in 1972.

Great Sox Infielders—Bobby Doerr, Vern Stephens, Johnny Pesky

The linch-pin for some great fielding combinations in the Boston Red Sox infield has been Hall of Fame second baseman Bobby Doerr. In almost every one of his playing years from 1938 through 1950 he was a leader in some fielding category at his position, whether it was most double plays, putouts, assists or chances per game. He was the steady player even when the support around him was not so good. In 1940, for example, Doerr led the league in putouts and double plays, while shortstop Joe Cronin, a better hitter than he was a fielder, and third baseman Jim Tabor led the league in errors at their respective positions.

The keystone sack combinations Doerr formed, first with Johnny Pesky and then with Vern Stephens at shortstop, were exceptional. In 1942, both Doerr and Pesky, at second base and shortstop, respectively, led the league in assists. Doerr also had the top fielding percentage at second base that year, .975. In 1946 Doerr led the league in putouts, assists, double plays and fielding percentage with Pesky again at shortstop, and with strong support from a fine fielding year by Rudy York at first base. Doerr again was the double play leader in 1947, with Pesky at shortstop.

In 1948, Johnny Pesky moved over to third base to make room for new shortstop Vern Stephens

The great Red Sox infield of the early 1950s consisted of (from left): third baseman Johnny Pesky, shortstop Vern Stephens, second baseman Bobby Doerr and first baseman Billy Goodman. (Boston Public Library, Print Department).

who had just come over from the St. Louis Browns. Doerr played his usual steady game at second base with a .993 fielding average while Stephens led the league in assists at shortstop and Johnny Pesky, in his new position at third base, led the league in both double plays and errors. In 1949, Doerr led the league in chances at his position, Stephens led shortstops in double plays and assists, and Pesky led third basemen in putouts, assists and double plays, and Billy Goodman also led at first base with a .992 fielding percentage. In 1950, Doerr again led in fielding at second base, with a percentage of .988, and in putouts, and Pesky led in number of chances per game at third base.

Bobby Doerr

| b. Apr. 7, 1918 | Los Angeles, Calif. | Bats Right | Throws Right |
| | 5'11" 175 lbs. | Red Sox | 1937-1951 |

Vern Stephens

| b. Oct. 23, 1920 | McAlister, N.M. | Bats Right | Throws Right |
| | 5'10" 185 lbs. | Red Sox | 1948-1952 |

Johnny Pesky

| b. Sep. 27, 1919 | Portland, Oregon | Bats Left | Throws Right |
| | 5'9" 168 lbs. | Red Sox | 1942-1952 |

Bobby Doerr

Bobby Doerr, not only a steady second baseman who held the infield together, was also a good hitter. He had a lifetime batting average of .288, led the league in 1944 in slugging percentage and in 1950 in triples. He had 223 lifetime home runs, hitting three home runs in one game in 1950. In 1948, he and Vern Stephens, the keystone combination, had 248 R.B.I.s together and in 1949 they had an exceptional 268 runs batted in as a twosome. In that year, 1949, Stephens and Ted Williams tied for runs batted in league leadership with 159 each and Doerr was fourth with 109. In 1950, Doerr and Stephens combined for 264 R.B.I.

Doerr played in the 1946 World Series and batted .409. He hit a three-run home run to pace the American League to a win in the 1943 All-Star game and he scored the winning run in the American League's 2-1 win in the 1947 All-Star game. Doerr is in the Hall of Fame.

Johnny Pesky

Johnny Pesky was also a fine hitter, with a .307 lifetime batting average. He played seven plus years for the Boston Red Sox, between 1942 and 1952, then moved on to the Detroit Tigers. In his first three years in the big leagues

with the Red Sox, he led the league with more than 200 hits each season. In 1946, he had a streak of 11 consecutive hits and in the same year he scored six runs in one game. It was the year of his highest single-season batting average, .335.

The popular Pesky was a consistent hitter, and in six of the seven full years he played with the Red Sox he batted over .300.

Pesky played in the 1946 World Series. He managed the Boston Red Sox in 1963 and nearly all of 1964, and he again was briefly the Red Sox skipper in 1980.

The preeminent second baseman of his time, Bobby Doerr posted a .299 lifetime batting average and is a member of the Hall of Fame. (Baseball Hall of Fame Library. Cooperstown, N.Y.).

Vern Stephens

Vern Stephens, who played with the Red Sox from 1948 through 1952, was a slugger. In his first three years with the Sox he hit 98 home runs and drove in 440 runs, an average of 33 home runs and 147 runs batted in a season. He led the league in R.B.I.s in 1950 and tied for the league lead with Ted Williams in 1949, each driving in 159.

"Junior," as he was known, also had some strong batting years with the St. Louis Browns, with whom he played from 1941 until 1948. With the Browns he led the league in home runs in 1945 and in R.B.I.s in 1944. His lifetime batting average was .286 and in a 15-year career he batted in 1174 runs. He had 10 grand slam home runs.

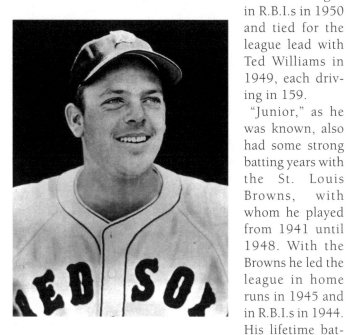

Vern Stephens hit 98 home runs and batted in 440 runs in his first three years with the Red Sox. (Baseball Hall of Fame Library. Cooperstown, N.Y.).

Stephens played in the all-St. Louis 1944 World Series with the Browns.

Footnotes

Bobby Doerr

Bobby Doerr, in his long 14-year career, was the only second baseman never to have played a single game at another position. He was steady, reliable and, but for his stellar play, unnoticeable. Ted Williams said of him that he was the team's most indispensable player.

Doerr batted in over 100 runs in six seasons. For 12 straight years he also hit between 23 and 37 doubles.

Doerr led the American League four times each in fielding average, double plays completed and number of chances per game. Three times he led in putouts and once in assists. He made only six errors all season in 1948 playing 140 games and had his highest seasonal fielding average of .993. In 1943, he led in four defensive categories, putouts, assists, double plays made and fielding percentage.

Johnny Pesky

On Enos "Country" Slaughter's famous dash from first base to home on a double, bringing in the winning run in the seventh and deciding game of the 1946 World Series, Pesky was faulted by some for enabling Slaughter to reach home safely. With Slaughter on first base in the last of the eighth inning for the St. Louis Cardinals, Harry Walker hit a double to left center field. Pesky received the relay throw but then hesitated in throwing home, allowing Slaughter to race around third base and score the game-winning run. The Cardinals won the game, 4-3, and the Series, four games to three.

Infielder Johnny Pesky played for and later managed the Red Sox on two separate occasions. (Baseball Hall of Fame Library. Cooperstown, N.Y.).

Pesky started his career as a shortstop and then switched to third base with the Red Sox when Vern Stephens was traded to the Sox from the St. Louis Browns. Pesky returned to shortstop and second base in the last years of his career. He was a good infielder but it was as a third baseman for the Red Sox in 1949 that he led the league in putouts, assists and double plays, and in number of chances per game.

Pesky did not have great success as a manager for the Red Sox. In 1963 and 1964, in ten team leagues, his team finished seventh the first year and eighth the second year.

The team had below .500 records both years. Pesky managed for only five games at the end of the 1980 season, taking over for Don Zimmer at the Red Sox helm. His team won one and lost four.

Pesky played for the Red Sox for one year, 1942, before he spent three years in military service, and then rejoined the Sox in 1946.

Vern Stephens

Vern Stephens, a star player for the St. Louis Browns, was traded to the Red Sox in the Browns' waning years. The "lowly Browns" had been a perpetual sixth, seventh or eighth place team for nine years from 1933 through 1941. With the redistribution of talent in wartime, the Browns had a spectacular year in 1944 when they won their one and only pennant. The Browns fell back to their losing ways after the war and the franchise was sold in 1953 and moved to Baltimore where the team became the Baltimore Orioles.

After the war, the Browns, always short for money and not drawing well at the gate, began to unload their talent. Stephens and Jack Kramer, a leading pitcher for the Browns, were traded to the Red Sox after the 1947 season. It was a monster deal with six lesser players going

from the Sox to the Browns along with $310,000 in cash. Ellis Kinder, another top Browns' pitcher, and infielder Billy Hitchcock were traded to the Red Sox for three lesser players and $65,000 cash about the same time. Al Zarilla, the Browns' top outfielder, was traded to the Red Sox early in the 1949 season for Stan Spence, an outfielder at the end of his career, and cash.

Stephens, a star with the Browns, was at the height of his career with the Red Sox. In his first three seasons with the Sox, 1948 through 1950, he batted in over 135 runs each season, and tied for the league lead in this category in both 1949 and 1950. In 1949, he and Ted Williams of the Sox tied for the league lead with 159 R.B.I. In 1950, he tied at 144 with Walt Dropo of the Red Sox. He also had won the R.B.I. title with the Browns in their pennant-winning year of 1944.

"Junior," though he played mostly third base at the end of his career, was essentially a shortstop and had his best years at that position. As a shortstop with the Browns he led the league in assists in 1947, and he also led in assists in 1948 while playing shortstop for the Boston Red Sox. He had the league's best fielding average as a shortstop in 1945, playing for the Browns. Notably, too, he led the league in errors at shortstop while with the Browns in 1942 and while with the Red Sox in 1948.

Great Red Sox Outfielders—Carl Yastrzemski And Dwight Evans

The Red Sox in their history have had great outfielders. Notable early in the century was Buck Freeman, followed by the "dream outfield" of Duffy Lewis, Tris Speaker and Harry Hooper. Even Babe Ruth played the outfield for the Sox for a year and a half before joining the New York Yankees. Then came the incomparable Ted Williams. Dom DiMaggio and Jackie Jensen approached greatness. There followed the next superstar, Carl Yastrzemski, and another superior outfielder, Dwight Evans. Later, the Red Sox would also have Fred Lynn and Jim Rice.

Carl Yastrzemski

b. Aug. 22, 1939	Southampton, N.Y.	Bats Left	Throws Right
	5'11" 175 lbs.	Red Sox	1961-1983

Dwight Evans

b. Nov. 3, 1951	Santa Monica, Calif.	Bats Right	Throws Right
	6'2" 180 lbs.	Red Sox	1972-1990

Carl Yastrzemski

"Yaz," along with Ted Williams, is one of the greatest heroes of the Boston Red Sox. He was a durable player who

spent all of his exceptionally long 23-year playing career, from 1961 through 1983, with the Boston Red Sox. Along with Ted Williams and then later Jim Rice, he helped form a tradition of great Red Sox leftfielders.

Yastrzemski played a total of 3,308 big league games in his career and is second all-time to Pete Rose. The combination of his longevity and his talent places him third all-time in at bats, fourth in bases on balls and sixth in hits, sixth in doubles and ninth in runs batted in. He also had 452 home runs. He could hit, and he could hit for power, and parenthetically was also a good-fielding left fielder.

Yastrzemski's lifetime batting average is only .285, but he led the league three times in batting average. In one of these years, 1968, he led with the lowest league-leading batting average ever recorded, .301. To show his versatility as a hitter, in 1967 he led the league in home runs and runs batted in. In 1963 and 1968, he led the league in bases on balls, and in 1967, 1970 and 1974 he led the league in runs scored. His greatest year was 1967 when he won the Triple Crown and the Most Valuable Player award. He batted .326, hit 44 home runs and drove in

ries, hit two home runs in Boston's 5-0 second game win and, with Reggie Smith and Rico Petrocelli, set a World Series record by hitting consecutive home runs in Boston's sixth game win. In the 1975 American League Championship Series against Oakland, Yaz batted .455, his timely hitting and exceptional fielding being a key factor in winning the third and final game. In the World Series that followed, Yaz batted .310 and he played both first base and the outfield. The Red Sox fireworks in this Series were left to Carlton Fisk and Bernie Carbo, and also Dwight Evans and Fred Lynn. Yastrzemski was named an American League All-Star 17 times. He won the award as All-Star game Most Valuable Player in 1970. In the 1975 All-Star game his three-run pinch home run accounted for all of the American League's runs in a losing effort.

Carl Yastrzemski was elected to the Hall of Fame in 1989, the first year he became eligible.

Dwight Evans

Dwight "Dewey" Evans was not Carl Yastrzemski, but he was an exceptional player in his own right. He was a good hitter, could hit for power, was an outstanding fielder and had a rifle-like arm. "Dewey" played 20 years in the big leagues, 1972 through 1991, and the first 19 were with the Boston Red Sox. He had a .272 lifetime batting average and hit 385 lifetime home runs, leading the league in home runs in 1981. For 11 of 12 years, from 1978 through 1989, he had at least twenty home runs a season. He had a keen batting eye and was always somewhere near the scoring action. He led the league in bases on balls three years and in runs scored once. As a nonpareil fielder Evans won the Gold Glove award eight times, and in the period from 1978-85, won the award every year but one.

Evans played in four American League Championship Series but did not distinguish himself. He played in two World Series, in 1975 and 1986, and had a cumulative .300 Series batting average.

Ted Williams' successor in leftfield, Carl Yastrzemski spent his entire 23-year playing career with the Red Sox. (Baseball Hall of Fame Library. Cooperstown, N.Y.).

121 runs. In addition, he led the league that year in slugging percentage, .622, in runs scored with 112 and in hits with 189. He was clearly instrumental, along with pitcher Jim Lonborg, in taking the Red Sox to the World Series in 1967.

Yastrzemski, and more recently Dave Winfield, Eddie Murray, and Cal Ripkin are the only American League players with more than 3,000 hits and 400 home runs. (Only Hank Aaron, Willie Mays and Stan Musial have accomplished the feat in the National League). Ironically, Yastrzemski never had 200 hits in a single season. He had three great home run seasons, once hitting 44 round trippers and twice hitting 40. Yaz also won seven Gold Glove awards in his career and, in 1977, had no errors in the 287 putouts and 16 assists he had in the outfield. His was a record of consistency.

Yastrzemski played in both the 1967 and 1975 Red Sox World Series. He batted .400 in the 1967 World Se-

Dwight Evans could hit for power and in the outfield won eight Gold Glove awards. (Baseball Hall of Fame Library. Cooperstown, N.Y.).

In the third game of the 1975 World Series, Dewey hit a game-tying home run in the ninth inning against Cincinnati, but the Reds won in the tenth inning, 6-5. In the 1986 Series, Evans contributed a home run to the Red Sox scoring spree in Game 2 as the Sox won easily, 9-3. In the final game of the Series, Game 7, Evans hit another home run but the Mets won the game. He tied with Gary Carter of the Mets for the lead in runs batted in in the Series, with nine, but the Mets won the Series.

Footnotes

Carl Yastrzemski

Notwithstanding the great player that he was, Yaz, it might be noted, made the last out in the 1967 and 1975 World Series and in the 1978 play-off game for the pennant against the New York Yankees.

Yastrzemski, like Ted Williams before him, had the experience once of barely missing a league batting championship. Williams missed in 1949 when he hit .34275 against George Kell's .34291. In 1970, Yaz hit .32862 but Alex Johnson of the California Angels won the batting championship with an average of .32899.

Yaz gave his most potent offensive display in the first ten years of his career, and especially in eight years from 1963-70. In that time, he won the batting championship three times, led the league in slugging percentage three times, once each in different years had the most home runs and runs batted in, led the league in hits twice and in doubles three times and he led in bases on balls once

and runs scored twice. In the last 13 years of his career he was a league leader only once, in runs scored in 1974.

As evidence of his durable, rifle-like and accurate throwing arm, Yastrzemski led the league in assists while playing the outfield five times in the 1960s and twice in the 1970s.

Yaz had a superlative hitting record in the 1967 World Series that the Sox lost to the St. Louis Cardinals in seven games. In addition to three home runs, he had two doubles and five singles for a total of ten hits. He drove in five runs and scored four, and he had a batting average of .400.

Dwight Evans

Five times in his career Dewey had a slugging average over .500 and his career slugging average was .470. Of his 2,446 lifetime hits, 483 were doubles and 385 were home runs. More than one third of his hits were extra base hits and he also had a lifetime 1,391 bases on balls. Though in the shadow of Carl Yastrzemski most of his career, he was clearly a slugger to be feared in his own right.

Evans led the league at his position in fielding average in 1976. He had a total of two errors in 339 chances for an average of .994. In four other years in which he had substantial playing time, he made no more than two errors in a season. He was consistently a steady, dependable outfielder.

Evans ended his career playing one year with the Baltimore Orioles in 1991. He was a part-time outfielder and designated hitter, appearing in 100 games. He also became a notable pinch hitter, batting .400 in this capacity with ten hits in 25 at bats.

The Great 1975 Outfield Rookies—Fred Lynn And Jim Rice

The Red Sox pennant in 1975 was due in no small measure to the exceptional performances of outfielders Fred Lynn and Jim Rice. Both batted over .300, each hit more than 20 home runs, and each drove in more than 100 runs. This was the auspicious beginning of two great baseball careers.

Fred Lynn

b. Feb. 3, 1952	Chicago, Ill.	Bats Left	Throws Left
	6'1" 185 lb.	Red Sox	1974-1980

Jim Rice

b. Mar. 8, 1953	Anderson, S.C.	Bats Right	Throws Right
	6'2" 200 lb.	Red Sox	1974-1989

Fred Lynn

Fred Lynn came to the Red Sox briefly in 1974 but as he played in only 15 games his acknowledged rookie year was in 1975. That season was so remarkable that he won both the league's Rookie of the Year and Most Valuable Player awards, the first time this occurred. He played six plus years with the Sox, from 1974-1980. His best years with the team were the rookie year of 1975 and 1979. In his rookie year, in which he batted .331, Lynn led the league in slugging percentage and he had 21 home runs and 105 R.B.I. He also led in doubles and in runs scored. Additionally, he won a Gold Glove award for his play in the outfield, one of three such awards he received in his career. In 1979, Fred led the league with a .333 batting average and a .637 slugging percentage. He hit 39 home

The Red Sox Encyclopedia

runs and drove in 122. He also scored 116 runs. Though his 1979 statistics were better than those in 1975, the Most Valuable Player award was won by Don Baylor, then with the California Angels, who later played with the Red Sox.

Lynn was traded to the California Angels in 1981, played four years with them, and subsequently played with the Baltimore Orioles, Detroit Tigers and San Diego Padres. In all, Lynn had a 17-year career with a lifetime batting average of .283 with 306 home runs.

Fred Lynn played in two American League Championship Series, once with the Red Sox in 1975 and later with the California Angels. He also played in the 1975 World Series with the Sox. In the ALCS of 1975 he hit .364 in three games, but he hit an amazing .611 in five games with the California Angels in 1982. In that series, though California lost, Lynn had 11 hits in 18 at bats. In the dramatic 1975 World Series, the Red Sox vs. the Reds, he batted an undramatic .280. He did hit a three-run home run in the sensational Game 6, won by the Sox with Carlton Fisk's remembered home run in the 12th inning. Lynn was named Most Valuable Player in the All-Star game of 1983, as a representative of the Angels. He hit a grand slam home run and the American League won the game 13 to 3. He also hit home runs in the 1976 and 1979 All-Star games, while representing the Red Sox. His grand slammer was the only one hit in an All-Star game.

Jim Rice

Jim Rice, like Lynn, came up to the Red Sox briefly in 1974 and played 24 games, but his real rookie year was 1975. Rice played his entire career with the Sox, from 1974 through 1989. In these 16 years he accumulated a batting average of .298, hit 382 home runs and drove in almost 1500 runs. Rice batted over .300 seven times in his career. From 1975 through 1986, with the exception of one year, he hit at least 20 home runs and won the league home run championship in 1977, 1978 and 1983. He also batted in more than 100 runs eight times in his career and won the league's runs batted in title in 1978 and 1983.

Jim had his "career year" in 1978. He batted .315 and led the league in slugging with a .600 average. He also led the league in hits, one of four years in which he had at least 200, and he also led in triples. He led in home runs with 46 and in runs batted in with 139. Jim was named the league's Most Valuable Player in 1978.

Rice played in two American League Championship Series in 1986 and 1988. In 1986 he hit a three-run home run in the final game, won by the Red Sox over the California Angels by a score of 8 to 1. In 1988, when Oakland swept Boston in four games, Rice had only two hits in the Series. In the 1986 World Series, Sox vs. Mets, Rice bat-

ted .333 with seven singles, a double and a triple but he had no dramatic hits. In the 1983 All-Star game Rice's home run was overshadowed by Lynn's grand slam performance.

Jim Rice's bat carried on the Ted Williams-Carl Yastrzemski tradition of hard-slugging Boston Red Sox outfielders. (Boston Red Sox).

Footnotes

Fred Lynn

In 1975, Fred Lynn and Jim Rice competed for both Rookie of the Year and Most Valuable Player honors. Lynn hit .331; Rice hit .309.

Lynn had 21 home runs and 105 runs batted in. Rice hit 22 homers with 102 R.B.I.. Lynn's slugging percentage was the league leading .566; Rice's was .491. They had nearly the identical number of hits, Lynn 175 and Rice 174. Lynn led the league with 47 doubles and Rice had 29. Lynn scored 103 runs and Rice scored 92. Rice fielded 1.000 with no errors in 168 chances. Lynn fielded .983 with seven errors in 415 chances. In the matter of fielding it is worth noting that Lynn played center field, the busiest outfield position, and Rice played left field.

The Red Sox outfield in this era was formidable. Along with Rice in left field and Lynn in center field, Dwight Evans played right field. They played together as an outstanding outfield combination from 1975 through 1981, or until Lynn was

Fred Lynn won both Rookie of the Year and Most Valuable Player honors in 1975. (Baseball Hall of Fame Library. Cooperstown, N.Y.).

traded to the California Angels in 1981. Both Fred Lynn and Jim Rice came up to the big leagues and played briefly for the Red Sox in 1974. Lynn's career ended in 1990 and Rice's in 1989. Jim played all 16 years for the Red Sox. Fred played his first seven years for the Sox and then went on to the California Angels and Baltimore Orioles, and briefly at the end to the Detroit Tigers and the San Diego Padres.

Fred, in all but one of his first 15 years in the big leagues, had a slugging percentage over .440. He led the league with a .566 average in 1975 and a .637 average in 1979. He also hit 20 or more home runs ten years, in all but two years in the period 1978 through 1987. His season high in home runs was 39 in 1979.

Jim Rice

Jim Rice led the league three times in home runs, twice in runs batted in, twice in slugging average, and once in hits and once in triples. He led the league in four of these categories in 1978, when he was named the league's Most Valuable Player.

For 11 of 12 years in his Red Sox career, from 1975 through 1986, he had at least 20 doubles. Similarly, for 11 of 12 years in the same period, he hit at least 20 home runs a year.

Rice's total of 406 bases in his "career year" of 1978 was the most since Stan Musial's 429 in 1948 and Joe DiMaggio's American League mark in 1937 of 418.

Rice's career mark in home runs, total hits, total bases and runs batted in places him third in these categories in Red Sox history, behind only his left field predecessors, Ted Williams and Carl Yastrzemski.

For many years, Rice and Lynn were side-by-side sluggers and outfielders with the Red Sox. Subsequently, in 1983, Tony Armas became the center fielder for the Red Sox and replaced Lynn as Rice's power twin. In 1983 Rice led the league with 39 home runs and Armas had 36. Rice also led in R.B.I.s with 126 and Armas had 107. In 1984, Armas led the league with 43 home runs and Rice had 28. Armas also led in R.B.I.s with 123 and Rice had 122.

In the 1986 seven-game American League Championship Series won by Boston over the California Angels, Rice batted only .161 but had two home runs and six runs batted in. His homer in the seventh game with two on base was a key contribution in the 8-1 Sox win. In the 1986 World Series, Rice batted .333 but had no home runs and no runs batted in. Rice did score the winning run in the 1-0 first game of the Series, after getting on base with a walk.

The Peerless Hitter And The Fireballing Pitcher—Wade Boggs and Roger Clemens

The Red Sox have had the good fortune of outstanding players coming up in tandems to start their careers. These players, who came into the big leagues with the Sox within a year or two of each other, provided fine talent for the Sox teams for years at a time. First of note were Tris Speaker, "The Grey Eagle," and Smoky Joe Wood, the great pitcher. Then, within a year of each other, there were Babe Ruth and Carl Mays, the twosome who won all of the games when the Red Sox won the world championship in 1918. Then there were Ted Williams, the Red Sox legend, and Bobby Doerr, the great second baseman, who were discovered together on the San Diego club when San Diego was in the Pacific Coast League. Fred Lynn and Jim Rice were the great "freshman twins" on the pennant-winning 1975 Red Sox team. Add to this list a great-hitting third baseman, Wade Boggs, and a fireballing pitcher, Roger Clemens, who broke in with the Red Sox in the mid-1980s.

Wade Boggs			
b. Jun. 15, 1958 Right	Omaha, Neb.	Bats Left	Throws
	6'2" 190 lbs.	Red Sox	1982-1992

Roger Clemens			
b. Aug 4, 1962	Dayton, Ohio	Pitches Right	Bats Right
	6'4" 205 lbs.	Red Sox	1984-1996

Wade Boggs

Wade Boggs was a hitting phenomenon. In his very first season, 1982, he batted .349. For the next nine years he hit over .300, all but twice over .330. He also averaged nearly 100 walks a season to go along with the over 200 hits he had seven times in this period.

In all but one year from 1983 through 1991, Boggs had at least 40 doubles a season and in seven of these

For 10 consecutive years Wade Boggs hit better than .300 for the Red Sox, including .368 in 1985. (Baseball Hall of Fame Library. Cooperstown, N.Y.).

years he scored more than 100 runs. Wade had a deserved reputation as "a hitting machine."

Boggs won the league batting championship five times, and each time never with an average under .357. In a six year period from 1983 through 1988 he won the batting title five times. His highest average was .368. He also has led the league twice each in bases on balls, doubles and runs scored, and once in number of hits. In 1988 he led the league in batting average, .366, in walks with 125, in doubles with 45 and in runs with 128. In 1987, in something of a switch from his usual style, Wade hit 24 home runs and drove in 89 runs, the only year in his career with Boston in which he hit more than eight home runs. He retained his consistency as a hitter that year, leading the league with a .363 average.

Boggs played in three American League Championship Series with Boston and had a cumulative average of .322. He batted only .233 in the 1986 ALCS but in 1988 he batted .385 and in 1990 an astounding .438 in a losing cause as Oakland swept the Red Sox, four games to none. In the 1986 World Series, the Sox against the New York Mets, Boggs hit .233 and concluded what for him was a generally poor 1986 post season. In the 1989 All-Star game, Wade and "Bo" Jackson hit back to back home runs, leading the American League to a 5-3 win over the National League. Boggs' batting fell off in 1992 and he became a free agent and went to the New York Yankees after 11 seasons with the Red Sox. The Red Sox had some young talent coming up at third base, appearing to make Boggs expendable, but he recovered his hitting stride in his continuing career with the Yankees.

He played five years with the Yankees, batting over .300 four times. Boggs' fielding improved, too, and in two years, 1993 and 1995, he led the league in fielding average at third base. Boggs closed his career with two seasons at Tampa Bay. He had an 18-year career and a lifetime batting average of .328.

Though Boggs played only two years, at the end of his career, at Tampa Bay, the Tampa Bay entry, then only three years in the league, adopted the Tampa resident as their own. They retired Boggs' uniform number, 12, and his is the only honored player plaque on the walls at Tropicana Field in St. Petersburg.

Roger Clemens

Before coming to the big leagues, Roger Clemens pitched the University of Texas baseball team to the collegiate baseball championship in the College World Series. He was a big, strong, fastballing right handed pitcher. He came up to the Red Sox in 1984 and beginning in 1986 has had a series of sensational seasons. He won the Cy Young award a record-breaking six times, with Boston in 1986, 1987 and 1991, with Toronto in 1997 and 1998, and with the New York Yankees in 2001. In 1986 he not only won the Cy Young but also the league's Most Valuable Player award with a 24-4 record, a remarkable .857 winning percentage, an earned run average of 2.48 and 238 strikeouts. He led the league in wins, winning percentage and earned run average and, of

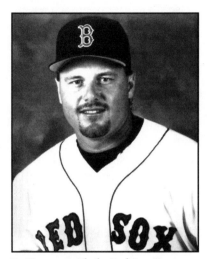

In 13 years with the Red Sox, Roger Clemens posted a 192-111 record and a 2.97 E.R.A. (Baseball Hall of Fame Library. Cooperstown, N.Y.).

course, led the Red Sox to the World Series against the New York Mets. Pitching for the Red Sox in 1986, he broke the record for most strikeouts in a game, with 20 K's and then equaled that record in a game in his final year with the Sox, 1996. Only one other pitcher, Kerry Wood of the Chicago Cubs, equalled this record, in 1998.

Clemens twice won the Cy Young Award two years in a row, first with the Red Sox in 1986 and 1987, and again with the Toronto Maple Leafs in 1997 and 1998. In his second consecutive Cy Young year with the Red Sox, 1987, he again led the league in wins, 20, in winning percentage at .690, in complete games with 18 and in shutouts with seven. He also had 256 strikeouts. Roger had 21 wins in 1990 and led the league in ERA at 1.93. However, Roger's third Cy Young came in 1991, when he won "only" 18 games but led the league with a 2.62 earned run average, 35 complete games, 241 strikeouts and four shutouts. He also led the league in ERA in 1992 at 2.41. His fourth Cy Young award came in 1997 when he was pitching for his new team, the Toronto Blue Jays. He won 21 games and lost seven for a .750 winning percentage. He led the league with a 2.06 earned run average, and also led in strikeouts, innings pitched and complete games. In 1998, Clemens won 20 and lost six for a .769 winning percentage. He led the league with his 20 wins and also led with a 2.65 E.R.A. and 271 strikeouts.

In 2001, another Cy Young year for Clemens, he won 20 and lost three pitching with the Yankees and led the league with an .870 winning percentage.

Through 2001, Clemens has pitched in the big leagues for 18 years. The first 13 were with the Red Sox, then two with the Toronto Blue Jays and three as a mainstay with the New York Yankees. He was 39 at the time that he won the Cy Young Award with the Yankees in 2001. He has won 280 games and lost 145. His lifetime earned run average is 3.10. Clemens led the American League in wins in 1986 and 1987 and in 1997 and 1998. He had the best winning percentage in the league in 1986, 1987, and 2001. He also led the league in earned run average six times, in shut outs six times and in complete games three times. A hard-throwing pitcher and a workhouse, even late into his career, Clemens has accumulated 3,717 strikes outs, leading the league five times. He ranks third all-time in the number of career strikeouts, behind Nolan Ryan with 5,714 and Steve Carleton with 4,136. To many, he was the best pitcher in baseball in the years leading to the mid-1990s. His size, grimness, and concentration on the mound made him a formidable pitching opponent.

Clemens, like Boggs, played in the 1986, 1988, and 1990 American League Championship Series and in the 1986 World Series. Coming to the Yankees in 1999, in all three years, 1999-2001, he played on the pennant-winning team and twice on the World Series champions. Also included in these three years was play in the division play-offs. Clemens played in six different playoff years but, relative to his regular season performances, his postseason record never rose to the same level of excellence.

"The Rocket" was the starting and winning pitcher in the 1986 All-Star game, in one of his Cy Young seasons. He also won the award as All-Star game Most Valuable Player for his performance that year. He pitched in the 1988, 1991 and 1992 All-Star games, all won by the American League.

Footnotes

Wade Boggs

Wade Boggs played 18 years, 1982 through 1999, and his lifetime batting average was .328. His first 11 years, the most productive period in his career, he played third base for the Red Sox. He then played five years for the New York Yankees, including their World Championship year of 1996. There is an enduring photo of him celebrating the World Series win after the last game by jumping on the back of a New York mounted policeman's horse and they trotted around Yankee Stadium. He signed with the American League expansion team Tampa Bay Devil Rays and played with them in 1998 and 1999. He acquired his 3000th hit in 1999.

Boggs had ten straight years in which he hit over .300 for the Red Sox. He hit over .300 four of his five years with the Yankees. In all, Wade has hit over .300 in 14 of the 16 years he has been in the big leagues.

Boggs is considered an exceptional contact hitter, rarely striking out and, often, fouling off pitches he didn't want. He could spray hits to all fields. He is the only left-handed hitter to have had 200 or more hits in seven straight seasons and he had more than 100 bases on balls in four seasons. He was for years the Red Sox lead-off hitter.

Wade was an erratic fielder early in his career. Coming up in 1982, he led the league's third basemen in errors in 1983 and 1984. He improved steadily and became one of the better third basemen in the American League. After his slow fielding start, he has led the league three times at third base in making double plays and three times in putouts. He also led in fielding average twice.

Roger Clemens

Roger, pitching for his second team, the Toronto Blue Jays, won the Cy Young award in 1997 and 1998. The 1998 award was for a record fifth time. In both seasons, Roger had 20 or more wins and was a workhorse pitcher. Pitching for his third team, the New York Yankees, Roger topped his own record, winning the Cy Young Award a sixth time with his 20 won, three lost record in 2001.

In his 13 years with Boston, "the Rocket" won 192 games and lost 111. His lifetime earned run average with Boston was 2.97.

Clemens' record is unparalleled in striking out 20 batters in a game not once but twice. No one has ever struck out more than 19 in a game. Roger broke a strikeout record that had stood for 102 years, before the American League had come into existence. His record of 20 strikeouts was tied in 1998 by rookie Kerry Wood of the Chicago Cubs.

Clemens has led the league six times in earned run

average and six times in pitching shutouts. He had phenomenal years from 1986-1992 and established himself in the eyes of many as baseball's best pitcher at this time.

As Lefty Grove was the modern Red Sox best left-handed pitcher, Roger Clemens was the team's modern top right-handed pitcher.

The Backbone of the Red Sox—Nomar Garciaparra and Pedro Martinez

The Red Sox, at the turn of a new century, were beginning a new tandem of stellar and special players. Boggs and Clemens were gone but in their place as new team luminaries were Nomar Garciaparra at shortstop and pitcher Pedro Martinez. Both are Hall of Fame prospects.

Nomar Garciaparra

b. July 23, 1973	Whittier, Ca.	Bats Right	Throws Right
	6' 165 pounds	Red Sox 1996–	

Pedro Martinez

b. Nov. 29, 1968	Villa Mella, Dominican Republic		Pitches Right
Bats Right	5'11" 170 pounds	Red Sox 1998-	

Nomar Garciaparra

Nomar Garciaparra came up from Pawtucket to the Red Sox in 1996, playing in 24 games in his first season. Almost immediately, he established himself as a superstar. In his first full season, 1997, he batted .306 and led the league with 209 hits. He also led with 11 triples. For the next three full seasons, 1998 through 2000, he batted well over .300 and led the league twice in batting, consecutively in 1999 with a .357 average and in 2000 with a .372 average. He was injured in 2001 and played in only 21 games but he has maintained a .332 lifetime batting average so far in his six-year major-league career. In his four full seasons with the Red Sox, he has 190 or more hits each season. In those four years, 1997-2000, he also had 113 home runs, and he had 174 doubles. On a team not noted for base stealing, he stole 48 bases in the years 1997 through 1999. Nomar is a fine all-around player who can hit for average and for power. He is also a good fielding shortstop with a

Nomar Garciaparra, shortstop for the Red Sox and Rookie of the Year in 1997 is a Hall of Fame prospect. (Baseball Hall of Fame Library, Cooperstown, N.Y.)

good arm. With his personal qualities and record as a star performer he has become a team leader.

Garciaparra was named Rookie of the Year for his first full season in 1997. In 1998, he was second in the voting for the league's Most Valuable Player award. He lost out to Juan Gonzales of the Texas Rangers. He played in 1998 and 1999 Red Sox postseason competition. He batted .333 with three home runs and led both teams with 11 runs batted in in the Red Sox 1998 division playoff loss to the Cleveland Indians, three games to one.

In the 1999 division series against Cleveland, won by the Red Sox, Garciaparra boosted his batting average to .417. He led the regulars on the team. In the American League Championship Series in 1999, playing against the Yankees, Garciaparra hit .400 and had eight hits. He and his teammate, John Valentin, led both teams with each batting in five runs. Notwithstanding, the Yankees won the pennant, four games to one.

Pedro Martinez

Pedro Martinez is considered by many currently to be the best and the most dominant pitcher in baseball. One could say that he succeeds Roger Clemens in this regard. Pedro started his career with the Los Angeles Dodgers in 1992 and was traded to Montreal for infielder Delino DeShields after the 1993 season. He was with the Expos for four years, won 55 games in this time was the National League Cy Young Award winner in 1997. He led the league in 1997 with a most impressive 1.90 earned run average and he also had 305 strikeouts. Coming to the Red Sox in 1998, Pedro has had three notable seasons that established his preeminence as a pitcher. In the years 1998 through 2000, he won 60 games, leading the league with 23 in 1999 and he also had a league-leading .852 won-lost percentage. He led the league in strikeouts in 1999 and 2000. For the years 1997 through 2000, he averaged 288 strikeouts a year. His earned run average was phenomenal for this era. He had ERAs of 1.90, 2.89, 2.07, and 1.74 in the 1997 through 2000 years, and three of these years he led the league in earned run average. Pedro was injured in 2001 and did not pitch a complete season. He was in 18 games and won seven and lost three. He still

averaged more than one strikeout an inning, as he usually did, with 163
strikeouts in 116 2/3 innings pitched.
Martinez, after winning the Cy Young Award with
Montreal in 1997, again won
the award pitching for the
Red Sox in 1999 and 2000.
In the missing year in 1998
he was second in voting to
Roger Clemens, then of the
Toronto Blue Jays. Pedro
pitched for the Red Sox in
the 1998 American League
Division Series and again in
the 1999 ALDS. He gave the
Yankees two hits in seven innings in his only appearance
against the Yankees in the
1999 American League
Championship Series. He
won the game, 13 to 1.
Pedro was named Most Valuable Player in the 1999 All-
Star game while playing on
his home field at Fenway
Park.

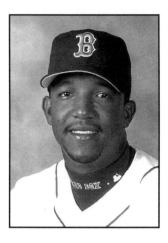

*Pedro Martinez won the Cy
Young award in 1997 and
1999, and he had a sensa-
tional year with the Red Sox
in 1999. (Baseball Hall of
Fame Library, Cooperstown,
N.Y.).*

Footnotes

Nomar Garciaparra became the mainstay of the Red
Sox position players after the departure of Mo Vaughn. In
his first full year, when he won the Rookie of the Year
award he batted .306, led the league with 209 hits and 11
triples, had 30 home runs and drove in 98 runs, and played
excellent shortstop. He has continued to be an all-around
player and strong hitter. In an era of great shortstops, he
is considered one of the top three, all of whom are establishing Hall of Fame credentials. There is much debate as
to who is best among Garciaparra, Alex Rodriguez, formerly of Seattle and now with the Texas Rangers, and
Derek Jeter of the Yankees. Also notable as an amazing
fielding shortstop, often compared to the great Ozzie
Smith, Hall of Famer with the St. Louis Cardinals, is Omar
Vizquel of the Cleveland Indians. Another interesting footnote about Nomar Garciaparra, traveling in the tradition
of other great Red Sox performers, is that he had a 30-
game hitting streak in 1997. This tied with Tris Speaker
who did the same in 1912. The Red Sox record is held by

Don DiMaggio who batted safely in 34 consecutive games
in 1949. The major-league record is held by Dom's brother,
Joe DiMaggio, who riveted baseball's fans' attention with
his safe batting in 56 games in 1941.

Pedro Martinez

Pedro, who has a reputation that now anticipates spectacular feats, produced this effect in both All-Star and
postseason play. In the 1999 All-Star game at Fenway,
which Martinez won and for which he received the Most
Valuable Player award, he pitched two innings. He started
the game, struck out the first four National League batters, and retired all six batters he faced, striking out five.
He left the game with the American League leading, two
to zero, and the A.L. won the game, four runs to one. In
the 1998 American League Division Series, Martinez won
the only game in which he pitched, the opening game, 11
to 3. It was also the only game the Red Sox won as Cleveland took the Series, three games to one. (Jimy Williams,
the Red Sox manager, was criticized for not starting
Martinez in Game 4 of the series, an arguable decision
inasmuch as Pedro had only three days' rest.) In the 1999
American League Division Series, again the Red Sox against
the Indians, Martinez started Game 1 but left with a
strained back muscle. Though the Red Sox were leading
the Indians 2-0 at the time, they lost the game 3-2. It was
uncertain whether Martinez would pitch again in the series.

In the decisive Game 5, with Cleveland winning the
first two games and the Red Sox the next two, the score
was eight to eight going into the Cleveland half of the
fourth inning. Pedro came in to pitch relief and pitched
six innings of no-hit ball. The Red Sox won the game, 12-
8, and the series, three games to two. In the League Championship Series of 1999, Pedro beat the Yankees, 13-1, in
the only game he started and the only game the Red Sox
won in the series.

Pedro Martinez won the pitchers' triple crown in 1999,
and the only other pitcher who accomplished this feat was
Cy Young himself in 1901. Pedro led in won-lost record
with 23 wins and four losses. He also led with 313
strikeouts and with a 2.07 earned run average. Martinez
has had one no-hit game though it was somewhat tar-
nished. Pitching for Montreal against San Diego on June
3, 1995, he pitched nine perfect innings. However, he gave
up a hit in the 10th inning, and was replaced by reliever
Mel Rojas. The Expos won the game, one to nothing, in
the 10th inning and Rojas received credit for the win.

Other Stars and Durable Players

The Pre-Red Sox Era 1901-1907

Jimmy Collins

b. Jan. 16, 1870	Buffalo, N.Y.	Bats Right	Throws Right
	5'9" 178 lbs.	"Red Sox"	1901-1907

Lou Criger

b. Feb. 3, 1872	Elkhart, Ind.	Bats Right	Throws Right
	5'10" 165 lbs.	"Red Sox"	1901-1908

Bill Dinneen

b. Apr. 5, 1876	Syracuse, N.Y.	Pitches Right	Bats Right
	6'1" 190 lbs.	"Red Sox"	1902-1907

Patsy Dougherty

b. Oct. 27, 1876	Andover, N.Y.	Bats Left	Throws Right
	6'2" 190 lbs.	"Red Sox"	1902-1904

Hobe Ferris

b. Dec. 7, 1877	Providence, R.I.	Bats Right	Throws Right
	5'8" 162 lbs.	"Red Sox"	1901-1907

Buck Freeman

b. Oct. 30, 1871	Catasauqua, Pa.	Bats Left	Throws Right
	5'9" 169 lbs.	"Red Sox"	1901-1907

Long Tom Hughes

b. Nov. 29, 1878	Chicago, Ill.	Pitches Right	Bats Right
	6'1" 175 lbs.	"Red Sox"	1902-1903

Freddy Parent

b. Nov. 25, 1875	Biddeford, Maine	Bats Right	Throws Right
	5'7" 154 lbs.	"Red Sox"	1901-1907

Chick Stahl

b. Jan. 10, 1873	Avila, Ind.	Bats Left	Throws Left
	5'10" 160 lbs.	"Red Sox"	1901-1906

Jake Stahl

b. Apr. 13, 1879	Elkhart, Ill.	Bats Right	Throws Right
	6'2" 195 lbs.	"Red Sox"	1903; 1908-13

Jesse Tannehill

b. Jul. 14, 1874	Dayton, Ky.	Pitches Left	Switch Hitter
	5'8" 150 lbs.	"Red Sox"	1904-1908

George Winter

b. Apr. 27, 1878	New Providence, Pa.	Pitches Right	
	5'8" 155 lbs.	"Red Sox"	1901-1908

Jimmy Collins

Collins was the first Red Sox player of distinction. He joined the Somersets/Pilgrims after starring for the Boston Beaneaters of the National League and accepted an offer to become the first manager of the Somersets in 1901. As a player for the Beaneaters and Somersets/Pilgrims he hit over .300 in five seasons and had a lifetime batting average of .294. He led the National League in home runs one year and drove in 100 runs twice. He was a peerless third baseman, considered the best in the league in his era. Collins played for the Somersets/Pilgrims for six-plus years in his 14-year career as a big leaguer. He managed the Pilgrims to the World Championship in 1903 and to the pennant in 1904. When the Pilgrims finished in last place in 1906, Collins was dismissed as manager and then traded to the Philadelphia Athletics where he finished his career in 1908. He was elected to the Hall of Fame in 1945.

Jimmy Collins played third base for the Boston Somersets/Pilgrims for six years and later managed the team to their first World Championship in 1903. (Boston Public Library, Print Department).

Lou Criger

Criger was the catcher for the Somersets in the first year of the franchise. He was known as Cy Young's catcher, both before and after he joined the Somersets.

Coming over from the St. Louis Cardinals of the National League, he played eight years for the Somersets/Pilgrims, from 1901 through 1908. He batted .208 for the Pilgrims and had a lifetime batting average of .221.

He was the Pilgrims' catcher in all eight games of the first World Series in 1903. He had a total of six singles and four runs batted in during the Series.

Criger had a 16-year major league career. He started with

Lou Criger, Cy Young's catcher, came over from the St. Louis Cardinals to join Boston's first American League club in 1901. (Boston Public Library, Print Department).

the Cleveland Spiders of the National League in 1896. After five years in that league he spent the rest of his career in the American League, beginning with the Somersets in their first year. After seeing the Boston entry through three adopted nicknames—Somersets, Pilgrims, Red Sox—he went on to play for the St. Louis Browns, then the Yankees, and ended his career with one game back with the Browns in 1912.

Bill Dinneen

Big Bill Dinneen, who had a 12-year major league playing career, pitched for the Somersets/Pilgrims five plus years,

Bill Dinneen combined with Cy Young to become the mainstays of the Boston pitching rotation from 1902-1904. (Baseball Hall of Fame Library. Cooperstown, N.Y.).

from 1902 through 1907. With Cy Young, he formed the one-two pitching combination for the Somersets/Pilgrims in 1902, 1903 and 1904. Each won 20 or more games each of these seasons, with earned run averages close to 2.00. Dinneen had three of his four 20-win seasons while pitching for the Somersets/Pilgrims. He also pitched a no-hit game for the Pilgrims in 1905, beating the White Sox 2-0 at the end of the season. In the 1903 World Series, when the Pilgrims beat the Pittsburgh Pirates for the championship, Big Bill had half the pitching decisions in the eight-game Series. He won three games and lost one, including two shutout wins, and he had a 2.06 earned run average.

After his playing career, Dinneen became a well-respected, long time American League umpire. He is the only major leaguer to have both pitched and umpired a no-hitter. In his 29 years as an umpire he was one of "the men in blue" in six major league no-hitters.

Patsy Dougherty

Dougherty had a ten-year big league career but spent only the first two and one half years with the Somersets/Pilgrims. He was a good hitting outfielder, and the two years in which he hit over .300 were with the Somersets/Pilgrims (.342 in 1902 and .331 in 1903). He compiled a lifetime average of .284 with the Somerset/ Pilgrims, New York Highlanders (later named the Yankees), and the Chi-

cago White Sox. Dougherty was the first player to hit two home runs in a World Series game. He accomplished this with the Pilgrims in the World Series of 1903, driving in all the runs in the second game, won by the Pilgrims and Bill Dinneen, 3-0.

Dougherty was a good hitter and a speedster. In his first full year with the Pilgrims, 1903, his .331 batting average was third in the league. He led the league in hits, in runs scored and he was third in stolen bases. In 1904, when he played the first third of the season with the Pilgrims and

Patsy Dougherty hit the first two home runs in Boston World Series history, swatting two out of the park in the second game of the 1903 Series. (Baseball Hall of Fame Library. Cooperstown, N.Y.).

the rest of the year with the Highlanders, he again led the league in scoring. Dougherty played his last five and one half years, from mid 1906 through 1911, with the White Sox. He continued to be a speedster on the bases and, in his final five years, stole 157 bases, leading the league with 47 in 1908.

Hobe Ferris

Ferris was the second baseman for the first seven years of the Somersets/Pilgrims franchise, from 1901 through 1907. He was a power hitter for that era with a lifetime 39 home runs and 550 runs batted in. He had a lifetime .239 bat-

Hobe Ferris was Boston's first second baseman, playing with the team from 1901-1907. (Boston Public Library, Print Department).

ting average over a nine-year career, playing his last two years as a third baseman for the St. Louis Browns. He was the Pilgrims' second baseman in the 1903 World Series, batting .290. Ferris had nine hits in the Series, including a triple but no home runs and he drove in seven runs, more than any other Pilgrim.

Buck Freeman

Freeman, one of the Somersets/ Pilgrims originals, also came over to the team from the Boston Beaneaters of the National League. He was a slugging first baseman-outfielder who played six plus years for the Somersets/Pilgrims. He led the National League in home runs in 1899, playing for the Washington Nationals. With the Somersets/Pilgrims he led the league two years in runs batted in and finished with a lifetime batting average of .294. He hit 73 triples in his first four years with the Somersets/Pilgrims and he

Boston's first "slugger," John "Buck" Freeman played six years at first base for the Somersets/ Pilgrims. (Baseball Hall of Fame Library. Cooperstown, N.Y.).

also led the team and the American League in home runs in 1903 with 13. In the 1903 World Series he batted .281, had a total of nine hits, including three triples.

Freeman, for his career batted in 713 runs in eight full seasons, averaging close to 90 a year. He had 131 triples and 82 home runs, and clearly was one of the league's sluggers. He is fourth all-time in triples.

Long Tom Hughes

Long Tom Hughes pitched for the Red Sox in the team's first decade. Long Tom was with the Somersets/ Pilgrims (later Sox) in 1902 and 1903, and won 20 games in 1903. He started and lost one game in the 1903 World Series. Most of his 13-year career was spent with the Washington Nationals.

Long Tom really had only one full year with the Pilgrims, 1903, but he was a key pitcher on the team. He, Cy Young and Bill Dinneen all won 20 or more games in a pennant-winning year. Hughes' record was 20 and seven, and he

Long Tom Hughes won 20 games for Boston in 1903. (Baseball Hall of Fame Library. Cooperstown, N.Y.).

was second to Young in the league in winning percentage. He also pitched 5 shutouts. Hughes started the third game

in the World Series but Phillippe of the Pirates bested him 4-2.

Long Tom also had a younger brother, Ed, who pitched briefly for the Pilgrims in 1905 and 1906.

Freddy Parent

Freddy Parent was the shortstop on the original Somersets/Pilgrim team. He was with the St. Louis Cardinals of the National League in 1899 but really started his career with the Somersets in 1901. He played with the Somersets/ Pilgrims from 1901 through 1907. He then went on to the Chicago White Sox to complete his 12-year career.

Parent was a .262 lifetime hitter but in his first year, 1901, he hit .306 and then in the pennant year of 1903 he hit .304. For four straight years, from 1901 through 1904, he hit more than 20 doubles a year, and in 1903

Freddy Parent, Boston's first shortstop, hit .306 for the team in 1901 and .304 in 1903. (Boston Public Library, Print Department).

he had 17 triples. In the World Series of 1903, he hit three triples, placing first in the league all-time. Parent batted .281 in this, the only World Series he played in. His eight runs led both teams in runs scored.

Chick Stahl

Chick Stahl played four years for the Boston Beaneaters in the National League before he came over to the Somersets in 1901 and played the remainder of his ten-year career, or six years with the Somersets/Pilgrims/Red Sox. He was a lifetime .306 hitter and the regular centerfielder on the team. 1902 was a standout year when he batted .323. He led the league in triples in 1904 with 19. However, his power years were his first four years, with the Boston Beaneaters, from 1897 through 1900.

In the 1903 World Series, Chick Stahl batted .303 and led his team with 10 hits in the eight games played. He had three triples and shares the record for most World Series triples hit with

Outfielder Chick Stahl played six seasons with Boston and managed the club in 1906. (Baseball Hall of Fame Library. Cooperstown, N.Y.).

his teammates, Freddy Parent and Buck Freeman.

Chick Stahl managed the Pilgrims in 1906 to an eighth-place finish, while Jake, later a Red Sox manager, managed the Washington Nationals to a seventh-place finish in the same year, 1906. Chick Stahl was prepared to manage the Pilgrims in 1907 but died tragically the spring before the season began.

Jake Stahl

Jake Stahl started his major league career with the 1901 Somersets, as a catcher, and played in only 40 games. He was then traded to Washington and also played briefly with the New York Highlanders. He came back to the Red Sox in 1908, as a first baseman, and played out his career with the Red Sox through 1913. Jake managed the Red Sox in 1912 and 1913, and managed them to a pennant and World Series Championship in 1912.

Garland "Jake" Stahl played both catcher and first base for Boston and later managed the team to the 1912 World Series title. (Baseball Hall of Fame Library. Cooperstown, N.Y.).

As a player, Jake Stahl had a .260 lifetime batting average. In 1910, he led the Red Sox and the league in home runs with 10, ahead of Ty Cobb and teammate Duffy Lewis with eight. He was tied for fourth in triples with 16. In the 1912 World Series, Jake, the Red Sox manager and first baseman, batted .281. He had nine hits, tying Tris Speaker for the team lead, and he stole two bases. It was to be his only World Series appearance. In 1913, he played in only two games and managed only half the season before being replaced.

Jesse Tannehill

The long history of Red Sox/Yankees trades did not begin in the Harry Frazee era. In the first Red Sox (Pilgrims)-Yankee trade, in late 1903, pitcher Jesse Tannehill was traded to the Pilgrims by the Yankees for pitcher Long Tom Hughes. Tannehill, for the Pilgrims, had a 21-11 record in 1904 and a 22-9 record in 1905 and he also pitched a no-hitter. Tannehill injured his arm and, in

Jesse Tannehill won 43 games for the Pilgrims from 1904-1905. (Baseball Hall of Fame Library. Cooperstown, N.Y.).

1908, was traded to the Washington Nationals.

Tannehill was one of three 20-game winners on the 1904 Pilgrims. Cy Young, Bill Dinneen and Tannehill won 70 games as the Pilgrims won the pennant by 1½ games over the Highlanders. Tannehill was second in the league in winning percentage at .656 with a 21-11 record. The league leader was Jack Chesbro of the New York Highlanders with a phenomenal 41 wins and 12 losses. Tannehill was a control pitcher who gave only 1.05 walks in nine innings. In 1905 Tannehill was the Pilgrims' only twenty game winner, at 22-9 on the fourth-place Pilgrims. He had six shutouts.

Tannehill, in his 15-year career spent mostly with the Pittsburgh Pirates of the National League, had 197 wins and 116 losses for a .629 percentage. He was a 20-game winner six times and led the National League once with a 2.18 earned run average. His lifetime E.R.A. was 2.79.

George Winter

George Winter was a Somersets/ Pilgrims/Red Sox pitcher from 1901 into the 1908 season. He twice won 16 games, in 1901 and 1905. His career record with the Pilgrims was 78-83 until he had a 4-14 record in 1908. Then was traded to Detroit. He did not play for the Pilgrims in the 1903 World Series but joined the Tigers in the last year of his career (1908), long enough to be on Detroit's pennant winners and pitch one inning in the World Series.

George Winter pitched for the Somersets/Red Sox from 1901-1908, striking out 119 in 1905. (Baseball Hall of Fame Library. Cooperstown, N.Y.).

Winter was both a starter and, occasionally, a reliever, in 1905 and 1906. His best strikeout year was 1905, when he had 119, but it is a measure of his skill that he was well behind Cy Young who had 210.

The Great Red Sox Dynasty 1912-1918

Jack Barry

b. Apr. 26, 1887	Meriden, Conn.	Bats Right	Throws Right
	5'9" 158 lbs.	Red Sox	1915-1919

Hugh Bedient

b. Oct. 23, 1889	Gerry, N.Y.	Pitches Right	Bats Right
	6' 185 lbs.	Red Sox	1912-1914

Joe Bush

b. Nov. 27, 1892	Brainerd, Minn.	Pitches Right	Bats Right
	5'9" 173 lbs.	Red Sox	1918-1921

The Red Sox Encyclopedia

Hick Cady

b. Jan 26, 1886	Bishop Hill, Ill.	Bats Right	
Throws Right			
	6'2" 179 lbs.	Red Sox	1912-1917

Bill Carrigan

b. Oct. 22, 1883	Lewiston, Maine	Bats Right	Throws Right
	5'9" 175 lbs.	Red Sox	1906-1916

Ray Collins

b. Feb. 11, 1887	Colchester, Vermont	Pitches Left	Bats Left
	6'1" 185 lbs.	Red Sox	1909-1915

Rube Foster

b. Jan. 5, 1888	Lehigh, Okla.	Pitches Right	Bats Right
	5'7½" 170 lbs.	Red Sox	1913-1917

Larry Gardner

b. May 13, 1886	Enosburg Falls, Vermont	Bats Left	Throws Right
	5'8" 165 lbs.	Red Sox	1908-1917

Dick Hoblitzell

b. Oct. 26, 1888	Waverly, W.V.	Bats Left	Throws Left
	6' 172 lbs.	Red Sox	1914-1918

Sam Jones

b. Jul. 26, 1892	Woodsfield, Ohio	Pitches Right	Bats Right
	6' 170 lbs.	Red Sox	1916-1921

Dutch Leonard

b. Apr. 16, 1892	Birmingham, Ohio	Pitches Left	Bats Left
	5'10½" 185 lbs.	Red Sox	1913-1918

Carl Mays

b. Nov. 12, 1891	Liberty, Ky.	Pitches Right	Bats Left
	5'11½" 195 lbs.	Red Sox	1915-1919

Stuffy McInnis

b. Sep. 19, 1890	Gloucester, Mass.	Bats Right	Throws Right
	5'9½" 162 lbs.	Red Sox	1918-1921

Herb Pennock

b. Feb. 10, 1894	Kennett Square, Pa.	Pitches Left	Switch Hitter
	6' 160 lbs.	Red Sox	1915-1922; 34

Wally Schang

b. Aug. 22, 1889	South Wales, N.Y.	Switch Hitter	Throws Right
	5'10" 180 lbs.	Red Sox	1918-1920

Everett Scott

b. Nov. 19, 1892	Bluffton, Ind.	Bats Right	Throws Right
	5'8" 148 lbs.	Red Sox	1914-1921

Ernie Shore

b. Mar. 24, 1891	East Bend, N.C.	Pitches Right	Bats Right
	6'4" 220 lbs.	Red Sox	1914-1917

Pinch Thomas

b. Jan. 24, 1888	Camp Point, Ill.	Bats Left	Throws Right
	5'9½" 173 lbs.	Red Sox	1912-1917

Heinie Wagner

b. Sept. 23, 1880	New York, N.Y.	Bats Right	Throws Right
	5'9" 183 lbs.	Red Sox	1906-1918

Jack Barry

Barry achieved his reputation as the shortstop in Connie Mack's "$100,000 infield" that played for the Philadelphia Athletics from 1911 through 1914. The Athletics won three pennants in that period. Stuffy McInnis was at first base, Eddie Collins at second base, Barry at shortstop and Frank "Home Run" Baker at third base. Barry was traded to the Red Sox in 1915 and played the rest of his career as the Red Sox second baseman. He was with the Red Sox from 1915 through 1919, excepting 1918. He played on five World Series teams, four for the Athletics in 1910 and 1911, and in 1913 and 1914. He played on the 1915 and 1916 Red Sox world championship teams but he did not play in the 1916 World Series.

Barry had a lifetime .243 batting average. His best batting years were

After playing shortstop for the Philadelphia Athletics, Jack Barry was traded to Boston, where he played second base for the remainder of his career. (Boston Red Sox).

with the Philadelphia Athletics when he batted .275 in 1913 and .265 in 1911. His best year for the Red Sox was in 1919 when he batted .306 in 31 games. Barry in five World Series batted .241 and he is third all-time in number of World Series doubles.

Barry, in his only year as a manager, managed the Red Sox to a second place finish in 1917 with a team that had

90 wins but finished nine games behind the Chicago White Sox.

Hugh Bedient

Hugh Bedient had a three-year pitching career with the Boston Red Sox, 1912-1914, and then he had one more big league year when he jumped to the Buffalo Blues of the upstart Federal League. Bedient in his first year with the Sox won 20 games and lost nine for a .690 winning percentage. On the 1912 world championship team he and Buck O'Brien had 20 wins each but Smoky Joe Wood was the leading pitcher with a 34-5 record and an .872 winning percentage. Six of Bedient's wins in 1912 were in relief as he led the league in relief pitching. In his three years with the Red Sox, Bedient won 43 games and lost 35. In addition to his 20-win season he had a 15-win year in 1913.

In the 1912 World Series, Bedient pitched and won Game 5. He pitched a complete game, a three-hitter, beating Christy Mathewson of the New York Giants, 2 to 1. He started the final game, Game 8, again against Mathewson but was relieved in the eighth inning by Smoky Joe Wood who won the 10-inning contest, 3-2. It was the game of the infamous "Snodgrass muff".

Hugh Bedient pitched three seasons for the Red Sox. He won the fifth game of the 1912 World Series. (Baseball Hall of Fame Library. Cooperstown, N.Y.).

Joe Bush

"Bullet Joe" Bush pitched for the Red Sox from 1918 through 1921, before being traded to the New York Yankees. In his three full seasons with the Sox he won 15 or more games each year. He pitched for the Sox in two games in the 1918 World Series, starting and losing one game. He also was a good hitter and occasion-

Joe Bush pitched three full seasons for the Red Sox, winning a minimum of 15 games each season. (Boston Red Sox).

ally played the outfield. In his four years with the Red Sox he batted .261.

Bush had a 17-year major league career that began with the Philadelphia Athletics in 1912 and ended with the same team in 1928. His best year by far was the year he was traded from the Sox to the New York Yankees. In this year, 1922, he won 26 and lost seven and he led the league with a .788 winning percentage. He also had 19 wins the following year for the Yanks and 17 the year after. In his career he had 195 wins and 183 losses. His best year in terms of earned run average was 1918 when he was with the Red Sox and posted a 2.11 E.R.A.. He pitched seven shutouts that year. Bullet Joe played for three teams in five World Series. Sandwiched around the 1918 World Series with the Red Sox were two with the Athletics and two with the Yankees. His World Series loss for the Sox was by a score of 3 to 1 and he is fifth all-time in number of World Series losses with five.

Forrest "Hick" Cady

Hick Cady played all but the last year of his career with the Boston Red Sox. For six years he was a Red Sox part-time catcher, mostly sharing the catching duties with Bill "Rough" Carrigan. Hick played with the Red Sox from 1912 through 1917. He had a lifetime .240 batting average.

Hick played in 13 World Series games in three World Series with the Red Sox, 1912, 1915 and 1916. He managed six hits. He was the regular catcher in the 1912 Series and in 1915 and 1916 he shared Series catching duties primarily with Pinch Thomas.

A catcher, Hick Cady played in 13 World Series games in three World Series for the Red Sox. (Baseball Hall of Fame Library. Cooperstown, N.Y.)

Bill "Rough" Carrigan

Bill "Rough" Carrigan, a baseball star at Holy Cross, played his entire 10-year big league career as a catcher for the Red Sox and batted .257. He also played in three World Series for the Sox. He was playing manager for the Sox from 1913 through 1916.

Carrigan, as a player, had a .257 lifetime batting average. His best batting year was 1909 when he batted .296. He was an agile

Bill "Rough" Carrigan played his entire 10-year career with Boston and then managed the team. (Baseball Hall of Fame Library. Cooperstown, N.Y.).

catcher and, notably, in 1910 stole ten bases. Bill played in four games in the three World Series in which he participated for the Red Sox, in 1912, 1915 and 1916.

Carrigan managed a total of seven years for the Red Sox. In his first year, 1913, he took over in mid-season from Jake Stahl. Carrigan won two world championships, in 1915 and 1916, but he also finished last in his last three years of managing, 1927-1929.

Ray Collins

Ray Collins, a southpaw, pitched his entire career for the Red Sox, from 1909 through 1915. He won a total of 84 games and lost 62 in this seven-year period. Collins' best years were in 1913 and 1914 when he won 19 and 20 games, respectively. In 1913 he led the team with his 19-8 record and .704 winning percentage. The team finished in fourth place. In 1914, the team moved up to second place and Collins again led in wins on the team with a 20-13 record. He also pitched six shutouts. Walter Johnson of the Washington Senators was the leading pitcher that year with a 28-18 record. This was also the year in which Dutch Leonard of the Red Sox won 19 games, with a 19-5 record, and he set the still existing record for earned run average at 1.01.

Lefty Ray Collins won 84 games in seven seasons for the Red Sox. (Boston Public Library, Print Department).

Collins played only in the 1912 World Series. He started Game 2 and pitched for 7 1/3 innings in a game that was called on account of darkness after 11 innings with the score at 6-6. His mound opponent was Christy Mathewson of the New York Giants. Collins pitched seven innings of relief in Game 6 when Rube Marquard of the Giants beat the Red Sox, 5-2.

George "Rube" Foster

"Rube" Foster was one of the pitching mainstays of the Red Sox World Championship years. His five-year big league career was with the Sox from 1913 through 1917. He won 19 games in 1915 and altogether won 58 games in his short career. In 1914 he had a 14-8 record and a 1.65 earned run average. He started and won two World Series games in 1915. He pitched in one World Series game in 1916, in relief, with no decision.

Foster had a lifetime 58 wins, 34 losses record. In addition to his record as a starter, he relieved in 1916 and four of his 14 wins were in relief. He also had two saves.

Rube Foster pitched five seasons for the Red Sox and won two World Series games in 1915. (Baseball Hall of Fame Library. Cooperstown, N.Y.).

Foster's E.R.A. in 1914 of 1.65 was second in the league behind teammate Dutch Leonard's record 1.01. Leonard, Foster and Ernie Shore had three of the top four earned run averages, the other belonging to Walter Johnson. In 1915, Boston's pitchers led the league with the top four winning percentages. Foster, with Ernie Shore, was right behind Smoky Joe Wood who led with a .750 record. Babe Ruth was fourth with 18 wins and eight losses.

In 1915 Foster pitched and won two complete games in the World Series. Shore and Leonard pitched the other two wins as the Red Sox beat the Philadelphia Phillies, four games to one. Foster won Game 2, 2-1, a three hitter, and he won the final game, 5-4. Foster actually won Game 2 with his single in the ninth inning driving in the winning run.

Larry Gardner

Larry Gardner was with the Red Sox for 10 of his 17 big league years, and he was the team's regular third baseman during three of its world championship years, in 1912, 1915 and 1916. He was both a good hitter and a dependable infielder. His lifetime batting average was .289 and in two of the Red Sox's great years, 1912 and 1916, he batted over .300. In 1914, he led the league in assists as a third baseman. Gardner was in four World Series, three with the Red Sox. He distinguished himself in the 1916 Series when he hit two home runs, the second a three-run homer that was instrumental in winning Game 4 of the five-game Series won by the Sox over the Dodgers.

A third baseman, William "Larry" Gardner played in four World Series, including the 1912, 1915 and 1916 Series with the Red Sox. (Baseball Hall of Fame Library. Cooperstown, N.Y.).

Larry Gardner in 1912 had 18 triples and in 1914 he was second in the league in triples, behind Detroit's Sam

Crawford, with 19. These were two of Gardner's better batting years. He not only batted over .300 and hit many triples, but he also had more than 20 doubles each of the seasons. He had more than 20 doubles per season in eight of his 17 years. He became a top R.B.I. producer later in his career, in 1920 and 1921, when he played with the Cleveland Indians.

In the 1912 World Series Gardner had two doubles, a triple and a home run but it was in the 1916 Series that he distinguished himself with his two home runs in one game. He also led both teams with six R.B.I. in the 1916 World Series.

Dick Hoblitzell

Dick Hoblitzell played 11 years of big league ball, from 1908 through 1918 but he was with the Red Sox only in the last five years of his career. He was the Red Sox first baseman in the 1915 and 1916 World Series.

Dick Hoblitzell played first base for the Red Sox on both the 1915 and 1916 World Series teams. (Baseball Hall of Fame Library. Cooperstown, N.Y.).

Hoblitzell had a lifetime .273 batting average. The only year in which he batted .300 or over came in 1909, before he was with the Red Sox, when he batted .308 for the Cincinnati Reds. This was his other big league team. In the year he was traded to the Red Sox, 1914, he did bat .319 for the Sox, but in only 68 games. Hoblitzell had five singles in the 1915 World Series, Red Sox vs. the Philadelphia Phillies, and he batted .313.

He was not as productive in the 1916 World Series, which the Red Sox won from the Brooklyn Dodgers.

Sam Jones

Sad Sam Jones pitched six years for the Red Sox before being traded to the New York Yankees. He led the league in winning percentage while pitching for the Sox in 1918, winning 16 and losing five for a .762 average. He also started and lost a World Se-

Sad Sam Jones pitched six seasons for Boston. (Baseball Hall of Fame Library. Cooperstown, N.Y.).

ries game in 1918, afterward pitching in three other World Series for the New York Yankees. Pitching for the Sox in his last year with the team, 1921, he won 23 and lost 16.

Jones had a 22-year pitching career with six American League teams, from 1914 through 1935. There were two years in which he won 20 games, in 1921 when his record with the Red Sox was 23-16 and in 1923 when he had a 21-8 year with the Yankees. He also lost 21 games with the Yankees in 1925, with a 15-21 record. He pitched 647 games in his long career, and won 229 and lost 217. His earned run average was 3.84, topped by a sparkling 2.25 with the 1918 champion Red Sox.

In the 1918 World Series, Jones pitched Game 5 and lost to Hippo Vaughn of the Chicago Cubs 3-0.

Hubert "Dutch" Leonard

Leonard, the first of two Dutch Leonards in major league history who had long pitching careers, pitched for the Boston Red Sox from 1913 through 1918. This Leonard was also known as "Hub". The other Dutch Leonard pitched 20 years, from 1933, but did not pitch for the Red Sox.

Dutch or Hub Leonard was one of the Red Sox's leading pitchers during their glory years around the first World War. These were the years of a brilliant staff including first Ray Collins, then Rube Foster, Ernie Shore and Babe Ruth, and later Carl Mays.

Hubert Leonard won 90 games for the Red Sox in six years. He won an average of 16 games per season. In 1914, he had an earned run average of 1.01 which still stands as the lowest ever. He also pitched two no-hit games for the Red Sox, in 1916 and 1918. He played on two Red Sox World Championship teams, in

Hubert "Dutch" Leonard won 90 games in six seasons for the Red Sox, including two World Series contests. (Baseball Hall of Fame Library. Cooperstown, N.Y.)

1915 and 1916. He won one game in each Series. In his 1915 win he pitched a three-hitter against the Philadelphia Phillies, 2-1, and retired the last 20 batters in a row. In his 1916 win, after allowing the Brooklyn Dodgers two runs in the first inning, he pitched a three-hitter the rest of the way and won the game, 6-2.

Leonard was traded to Detroit before the 1919 season, and he ended his career after five years with the Tigers.

Carl Mays

Carl Mays started his career with the Boston Red Sox in 1915, but he had long periods of service with the New York Yankees to whom he was traded in 1920, and then later with the Cincinnati Reds and the New York Giants. Before being traded he was one of the mainstay pitchers of the Red Sox championship years. From 1916 through 1918 he won 61 games. He won more than 20 games each season in 1917 and 1918 and his earned run average was 1.74 the first of these years and 2.21 the second. He also led the league in shutouts in 1918. He pitched in the 1916 and 1918 World Series, starting and winning two complete games for the Red Sox in the '18 Series. He allowed a total of ten hits in the two games and won by identical scores of 2-1. Babe Ruth pitched and won the other two World Series games that gave Boston the championship. Mays was also a good-hitting pitcher with a lifetime .268 average.

Mays was one of the first in Harry Frazee's desperate player-for-cash trades, and in fact brought both players and cash. After he was traded to the Yankees in 1919 he reeled off 80 wins in less than five seasons. In 1920 he won 26 games and in 1921 he led the league with 27 wins. Mays, late in his career with Cincinnati, had 19 and 20 game-winning seasons. He played in two more World Series, with the Yankees, in 1921 and 1922.

Carl Mays combined with Babe Ruth to pitch four victories and win the world championship for Boston in 1918. (Baseball Hall of Fame Library. Cooperstown, N.Y.).

It was while pitching for the Yankees in 1920 that Mays, a right handed submarine baller, beaned Roy Chapman, the Cleveland Indians shortstop. The beaning resulted in Chapman's death, the only player death ever to have occurred from an on-field injury.

John "Stuffy" McInnis

McInnis, the second member of Connie Mack's Philadelphia Athletics' "$100,000 infield" to later play for the Red Sox, was with the Sox four years from 1918 through 1921. He played 19 years in the big leagues, mostly with the

A career .308 hitter, first baseman Stuffy McInnis played in five World Series, including the 1918 series with Boston. (Boston Red Sox).

Philadelphia Athletics. McInnis was the Red Sox first baseman in the 1918 World Series, one of five World Series in which he played. He had a lifetime .308 batting average. After his playing career he managed the Philadelphia Phillies for one year in 1927.

McInnis was a fairly consistent .300 hitter. In six of his first seven years with the Athletics he batted over .300. In four of the five consecutive years, 1919 through 1923, in which he played with the Boston Red Sox and Braves and the Cleveland Indians, he batted over .300. In all, he had 12 years in which he batted over .300 and four more in which he batted over .290. McInnis, early in his career, was a base stealer and he had a lifetime total of 172.

Herb Pennock

Herb Pennock was another of the stable of good Red Sox pitchers traded to the New York Yankees in the Harry Frazee era. He pitched for the Sox for six and one half years, 1915 through 1921, and ended his career with another year with the Sox in 1934. In his Red Sox career he won 61 games and lost 59.

While with the Red Sox Pennock had four productive years, 1919-1922. In these four years he went 54-52. He missed the 1918 Red Sox championship year because of military service but had his best Sox year on his return in 1919—a 16-8 record for the .667 winning percentage.

All told, Pennock had a 22-year career. He became a Hall of Famer with the New York Yankees. He joined Babe Ruth, Joe Bush, Carl Mays and Joe Dugan who had distinguished careers with the Yankees after being traded by the Red Sox. He had two 20-win seasons with the Yankees. He

Herb Pennock pitched for the Red Sox for 6½ years and later became a Hall of Famer with the New York Yankees. (Baseball Hall of Fame Library. Cooperstown, N.Y.).

had the highest winning percentage in the league the year after he was traded, .760 with 19 wins and six losses and he accumulated a 5-0 World Series record with the Yankees. He was in five World Series, one with the Philadelphia Athletics in 1914 before he joined the Red Sox, and four with the Yankees.

After his playing days, Pennock directed the Red Sox farm system and then later served as the general manager for the Philadelphia Phillies. It was in the latter capacity that he was largely responsible for assembling "the Whiz Kids" who won the pennant for the Phillies in 1950.

Wally Schang

Wally Schang, who spent 19 years as a premier catcher in the big leagues from 1913 through 1931, caught for the Red Sox for three years, 1918 through 1920. Schang had a .284 lifetime batting average and played in six World Series with three teams, including the Red Sox in 1918. Most of Schang's career was with strong Philadelphia Athletics and New York Yankees teams.

Catcher Wally Schang batted .306 in 1919 and .309 in 1920 for the Red Sox. (Baseball Hall of Fame Library. Cooperstown, N.Y.).

Schang, an established catcher when he came over from the Philadelphia Athletics, had two good hitting years in his three years with the Red Sox. He batted .306 in 1919 and .305 in 1920. In the World Series of 1918, Schang shared catching duties for the Sox with Sam Agnew. He had four hits in nine at bats for a .444 batting average.

Schang also had a fine World Series with the Philadelphia Athletics in 1913, batting .357 with a triple and a home run. Over his career he played with six American League teams. With the Yankees and the Browns as well as the Red Sox, he batted over .300 two years in a row for each of these teams. Though he was a reasonably good batter, his reputation was as a very skillful catcher and handler of pitchers.

Everett "Deacon" Scott

"Deacon" Scott was a steady shortstop and a mainstay of the infield for both the Boston Red Sox and later the New York Yankees. It was his record of 1307 consecutive games played that Lou Gehrig later broke with 2,130 consecutive games. Scott was the Red Sox shortstop from 1914-1921 and the Yankees' shortstop from 1922-1924. The

last two years of his career, in 1925 and 1926, he played for the Yankees, the Washington Senators, the Chicago White Sox and the Cincinnati Reds. Deacon played on three Red Sox World Series teams and two Yankee World Series teams, with four world championship wins.

Deacon, an excellent fielder, was the anchor of the infield during his tour of duty with the Red Sox, with such notable infield teammates as Dick Hoblitzell and Stuffy McInnis at first base, Jack Barry at second and Larry Gardner at third base. He had a lifetime batting average of only .249 but distinguished himself more for his durability and infield play during a period of time when the Red Sox had great teams. He was another of Harry Frazee's trade-to-the-Yankees players and continued his steady, durable play with the Yankees in some of their great pennant-winning years.

Shortstop Deacon Scott was the anchor of the infield for the Red Sox from 1914-1921. (Baseball Hall of Fame Library. Cooperstown, N.Y.).

Ernie Shore

Ernie Shore was another member of the great Red Sox pitching staffs when they won world championships around World War I. He was with the Red Sox for four years, including the 1915 and 1916 championship years. In those four years, Ernie won 58 games for the Sox, or nearly 15 a year. In the era of the "dead ball" he never had an earned run average over 2.63 while he was with the team and in two years he was under 2.00. He won three World Series games and lost one for the Sox. In the 1916 Series he won the only two games he pitched.

In four seasons with the Red Sox, Ernie Shore never had an E.R.A. higher than 2.63. (Baseball Hall of Fame Library. Cooperstown, N.Y.).

Shore's baseball career was notably intertwined with that of Babe Ruth. He and Ruth were on the same minor league team in Baltimore in 1913 when they were both purchased by the Red Sox for $8,000. They were both star pitchers helping the Sox to the world championship in 1915 and 1916. Perhaps his greatest fame and most notable connection to Ruth came in a game on June 23, 1917. Ruth started that game against the Washington Nationals, walked the first batter and then argued with the umpire and was ejected from the game. Shore replaced Ruth, immediately had a putout when the runner on first base was called out for stealing, and then proceeded to retire the next 26 batters in order for an unusual no-hit, no-run game. Shore was traded to the New York Yankees in December, 1918, and Ruth followed him in January of 1920.

Chester "Pinch" Thomas

Pinch Thomas had a 10-year big league career, the first six years with the Boston Red Sox, from 1912 through 1917, and then the last four years with the Cleveland Indians. Pinch was a part-time catcher throughout his career and had a lifetime batting average of .237.

A back-up catcher for the Red Sox, Pinch Thomas played in nearly 400 games in Boston. (Baseball Hall of Fame Library. Cooperstown, N.Y.).

Pinch was a back-up to Bill Carrigan early in his Red Sox career and later shared catching duties with Hick Cady and then Sam Agnew. He played in close to 400 games with the Red Sox over six years, and he also played on two Red Sox world championship teams in 1915 and 1916. He also played as a substitute catcher with no at bats on the Cleveland world championship team in 1920.

Charles "Heinie" Wagner

Heinie Wagner spent all but one of his 12 big league years with the Red Sox. From 1906 through 1918 he played mostly shortstop but also second and third base. He was the shortstop for the Red Sox in the 1912 World Series. His lifetime batting average was .250. He later managed the Red Sox, in 1930, to a last-place finish.

Wagner in the eight years in which he played a half season or more never batter over .274. He generally hit seven or eight home runs a year and drove in about 40 runs a year. In the 1912 World Series he had only five hits for his 30 at bats but he was the shortstop anchor in the infield with

A utility infielder, "Heinie" Wagner played 11 of his 12 Major League seasons with the Red Sox. (Baseball Hall of Fame Library. Cooperstown, N.Y.).

Steve Yerkes at second base and, on the other side, Larry Gardner at third base. The star quality for the Red Sox was in "the greatest outfield" of Lewis, Speaker and Hooper.

The Harry Frazee Disaster 1919-1933

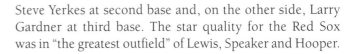

Shano Collins

b. Dec. 4, 1885	Charlestown, Mass.	Bats Right	Throws Right
	6' 185 lbs.	Red Sox	1921-1925

Howard Ehmke

b. Apr. 24, 1894	Silver Creek, N.Y.	Pitches Right	Bats Right
	6'3" 190 lbs.	Red Sox	1923-1926

Danny MacFayden

b. Jun. 10, 1905	North Truro, Mass.	Pitches Right	Bats Right
	5'11" 170 lbs.	Red Sox	1926-1932

Jack Rothrock

b. Mar. 4, 1905	Long Beach, Calif.	Switch Hitter	Throws Right
	5'11½" 165 lbs.	Red Sox	1925-1932

Red Ruffing

b. May 3, 1904	Granville, Ill.	Pitches Right	Bats Right
	6'1½" 205 lbs.	Red Sox	1924-1930

Jack Russell

b. Oct. 24, 1905	Paris, Texas	Pitches Right	Bats Right
	6'1½" 178 lbs.	Red Sox	1926-1932

Jack "Shano" Collins

Shano Collins had a 16-year major league career as an outfielder and at times as a first baseman. Playing from 1910-1925, he was with the White Sox for 11 years and the last five years of his playing career was with the Red Sox. His lifetime batting average was .264 and in only one year in which he played regularly, 1920, when he played with the White Sox, did he bat over .300. In his early career, he was a good doubles hitter and base stealer. In his latter years with the Sox, he played less frequently and was also a pinch hitter.

Shano played in two World Series, both with the White Sox, in 1917 and 1919. He played in four of the eight World Series

Shano Collins both played for and managed the Red Sox. (Baseball Hall of Fame Library. Cooperstown, N.Y.).

games in 1919 with the infamous "Black Sox" and garnered four hits in 16 at bats but he was not one of the tainted players.

Collins managed the Red Sox in 1931 and for half of 1932 but the Sox were a losing team both years.

Howard Ehmke

Howard Ehmke had a 15-year big league career. Starting in the Federal league in 1915, he then played with the Detroit Tigers, Boston Red Sox and Philadelphia Athletics. Ehmke's best years were with the Red Sox and he was a standout pitcher for two of his three plus years with the team.

The best Red Sox pitcher of the 1920s, Howard Ehmke's career in Boston included a no-hitter. (Baseball Hall of Fame Library. Cooperstown, N.Y.).

In 1923 with the Sox he won 20 and lost 17 on a team that was in last place with 61 wins and 91 losses. He pitched 28 complete games. In 1924, he won 19 and lost 17 on a team that finished in seventh place with 67 wins and 87 losses. Though he had nearly 20 wins he led the league in losses with 17, tied with his pitching teammate in this category, Alex Ferguson. A workhorse pitcher, Ehmke pitched 26 complete games and he led the league in innings pitched with 315. He was also second to Walter Johnson in strikeouts with 119 to Johnson's 158.

Ehmke was still a workhorse pitcher for the Red Sox in 1925. While his record was only nine wins and 20 losses he led the league with 22 complete games. Ehmke in his career won 166 games and lost 166 games. He had over 1,000 strikeouts and he pitched 20 shutouts. He did manage to play with some better teams and was with the Philadelphia Athletics in their two world championships and three pennant years from 1929 through 1931. He pitched and won the first game of the 1929 World Series, with a 3-1 win over the Cubs. He broke the World Series strikeout record with 13 in that game.

Ehmke was one of the rare Red Sox stars in the post-Frazee era of Red Sox baseball.

Danny MacFayden

Danny MacFayden began his 17-year career with the Red Sox and was with the team from 1926 into 1932. MacFayden's career carried over into the second World War. He had two stints with the Boston Braves, and ended

his career with the Braves in 1943.

MacFayden was a journeyman pitcher with the Red Sox. His best year with the team was in 1931 when he won 16 and lost 12, the only year in which he had a winning percentage with the Red Sox. This was a good record notably because the Red Sox won 62 and lost 90 in 1931 and finished in sixth place.

In his Red Sox career, MacFayden won 52 games and lost 78. The worst year, other than the year in which he was traded to the Yankees, 1932, with a 1-10 record, was in 1929. MacFayden won 10 and lost 18 but he also led the league in pitching four shutouts, tied with three other pitchers. 1929 was also the year in which four Red Sox pitchers each lost 18 or more games in a last place finish. MacFayden and Jack Russell both lost 18, Milt Gaston lost 19 and Red Ruffing led the league in losing 22 games.

MacFayden in his career won 132 games and lost 159. While his best year with the Red Sox was in 1931 with 16 wins, his best year in baseball was in 1936 when he won 17 games for the Boston Braves.

A journeyman pitcher for the Red Sox, Danny MacFayden won 16 games for Boston in 1931. (Brace Photo.)

Jack Rothrock

Rothrock was a shortstop and then an outfielder for seven plus years with the Red Sox, from 1925 into 1932. His lifetime batting average was .276. He also had a one-inning big league pitching career, pitching in relief for the Red Sox in a game in 1928. Rothrock was a starting outfielder for the St. Louis Cardinals' "Gas House Gang" in the 1934 World Series.

Rothrock was with the Red Sox for most of his 11-year career. In four full seasons with the team he had one year, 1929, in which he

Jack Rothrock played shortstop, outfield and even pitched for the Red Sox in the 1920s and early '30s. (Baseball Hall of Fame Library. Cooperstown, N.Y.).

batted an even .300. In the same year, he was fourth in the league in stolen bases with 23. In 1927 and 1928 Rothrock was an all-purpose player. In 1927 he played all four infield positions. In 1928, he played all four infield positions, the outfield, caught one game and pitched one game. At the end of his career with the Red Sox, in 1930 and 1931, he was also used frequently as a pinch hitter and had nine pinch hits each season.

Charley "Red" Ruffing

"Red" Ruffing was a losing pitcher with losing teams while he was with the Red Sox from 1924 into 1930. In slightly more than six seasons with the team he had a 39-96 pitching record, led the American League in losses in 1928 and 1929, and only once had an earned run average under 3.90. In 1928 he lost 25 games and he had 22 losses in 1929. Traded to the Yankees in 1930 he immediately started to win regularly. He became the team's top right handed pitcher, combining with Lefty Gomez to give the Yankees solid pitching in the Yankee dynasty years. From 1936 through 1939 he had four consecutive years in which he won 20 or more games. At various times, he led the league in victories, winning percentage, strikeouts and shutouts, and he won a total of seven World Series games. Ruffing, originally an outfielder, also was used as a pinch hitter. In his big league career he compiled a .269 batting average and, noted for his power, hit 36 home runs. He was also subsequently elected to the Hall of Fame.

Red Ruffing lost 96 games for the Red Sox in six seasons, but went on to a Hall of Fame career with the New York Yankees. (Baseball Hall of Fame Library. Cooperstown, N.Y.).

Ruffing never had a winning season pitching for the Red Sox from 1924 into 1930. In 14 years pitching for the Yankees, 1931 through 1946, he had only one losing season. Ruffing's lifetime record was 273 wins and 225 losses in a 22-year career. He had ten years with 100 or more strikeouts and led the league in strikeouts in 1932 with 190 while pitching for the World Champion Yankees. He played in seven World Series with the Yankees in the period 1932 through 1942.

Jack Russell

Jack Russell toiled for the Red Sox for six and one half years in the late 1920s and early 1930s. He led the league in losses in 1930 with 20 while pitching for the Sox and he lost 18 games pitching for the team in each of the years

Jack Russell never had a winning season in more than six seasons with Red Sox, but did post winning marks with three other teams. (Baseball Hall of Fame Library. Cooperstown, N.Y.).

1929 and 1931. Between 1926 and 1932 he won 41 games and lost 91. Traded back to the Red Sox briefly in 1936 he lost three more games and won none. Russell had a 15-year big league career pitching for six clubs. He never had a winning year for the Red Sox but had three winning seasons with other teams.

Most of Russell's career was spent with the Red Sox. However, he was with Washington for three years and part of another. He had his best season while with the Washington Nationals in their pennant year of 1933, winning 10 and losing six. He also relieved in one game in the World Series against the New York Giants, losing the last game in the tenth inning, 4-3. Russell had pitched 4 2/3 innings of shutout ball but lost on Mel Ott's homer in the tenth inning as the Giants won the World Series over Joe Cronin's Washington team four games to one.

Russell's lifetime record was 85 wins and 141 losses but he had one other good season, again playing for a pennant winner in 1938, the Chicago Cubs. He won six games and lost one, and he pitched briefly in relief in two World Series games.

Moe Berg

b. Mar. 2, 1902	New York, N.Y.	Bats Right	Throws Right
	6'1" 185 lbs.	Red Sox	1935-1939

Doc Cramer

b. Jul. 22, 1905	Beach Haven, N.J.	Bats Left	Throws Right
	6'2" 185 lbs.	Red Sox	1936-1940

Gene Desautels

b. Jun. 13, 1907	Worcester, Mass.	Bats Right	Throws Right
	5'11" 170 lbs.	Red Sox	1937-1940

Rick Ferrell

b. Oct. 12, 1905	Durham, N.C.	Bats Right	Throws Right
	5'10" 160 lbs.	Red Sox	1933-1937

Wes Ferrell

b. Feb. 2, 1908	Greensboro, N.C.	Pitches Right	Bats Right
	6'2" 195 lbs.	Red Sox	1934-1937

Johnny Lazor

b. Sep. 9, 1912	Taylor, Wash.	Bats Left	Throws Right
	5'9½" 180 lbs.	Red Sox	1943-1946

Fritz Ostermueller

b. Sep. 15, 1907	Quincy, Ill.	Pitches Left	Bats Left
	5'11" 175 lbs.	Red Sox	1934-1940

Jim Tabor

b. Nov. 5, 1916	New Hope, Ala.	Bats Right	Throws Right
	6'2" 175 lbs.	Red Sox	1938-1944

Billy Werber

b. Jun. 20, 1908	Berwyn, Md.	Bats Right	Throws Right
	5'10" 170 lbs.	Red Sox	1933-1936

Jack Wilson

b. Apr. 12, 1912	Portland, Oregon	Pitches Right	Bats Right
	5'11" 210 lbs.	Red Sox	1935-1941

Red Sox catcher Moe Berg (left) converses with New York Times columnist John Kieran. (Baseball Hall of Fame Library. Cooperstown, N.Y.).

Moe Berg

Moe Berg's story is more a matter of human interest than an account of an exceptional baseball career. Moe came to the major leagues as a shortstop with the Brooklyn Dodgers but for 12 of his 15 years in the big leagues he made a career of being second-string catcher with the Cleveland Indians, Washington Nationals, Chicago White Sox and Boston Red Sox. Berg played for the Red Sox in his last five years, from 1935 through 1939. He had a lifetime batting average of .243 and hit only six home runs in his career. He was considered "good field, no hit."

Moe was popular, known for his intelligence, his erudition and his affable and gregarious personality. He had degrees from Princeton University and Columbia Law School. He served with the Office of Strategic Services as an intelligence expert, "a spy," in World War II, and much intrigue attaches to the work he did. Notwithstanding, pitcher Ted Lyons, then a Chicago White Sox teammate, said of Berg, "He can speak 12 languages but he can't hit in any of them."

Roger "Doc" Cramer

"Doc" or "Flit" Cramer had a long 20-year career as an outfielder in the American League in the 1930s and 1940s. He began with the Philadelphia Athletics and then, from 1936 through 1940, had five creditable years with the Red Sox. A .296 lifetime hitter, he hit over .300 for four of his five years with the Red Sox. In his years with Boston he was a steady player and hovered near 200 hits every year, finally hitting that number in 1940. He was not a slugger and in his entire five years with the Red Sox had one home run. Doc averaged scoring over 100 runs a season with the Sox with never under 90 per season in this time. In fact, in his career he had nine straight years in which he scored 90 or more runs. Cramer, after his first seven seasons with the Athletics and then five with the Red Sox, went on to play a year in Washington and then six years with the Detroit Tigers. He played in two World Series, with the pennant-winning Philadelphia Athletics in 1931, and then 14 years later as a regular with the world champion Detroit Tigers.

Outfielder Doc Cramer hit better than .300 in four of his five seasons with the Red Sox. (Baseball Hall of Fame Library. Cooperstown, N.Y.).

Cramer, in his big league lifetime, played over 2,000 games in the outfield. In his total of 2239 games he had 2705 hits and scored 1357 runs. He led the league seven times in number of at bats and, altogether had over 600 at bats a season for nine seasons. He was through most of his big league career a steady, dependable outfielder.

Gene Desautels

Gene Desautels was a journeyman catcher in the big leagues for13 years in the period 1930 through 1946. He played for the Red Sox four years, from 1937 through 1940. His lifetime batting average was .233.

A defensive specialist, catcher Gene Desautels played for the Red Sox from 1937-40. (Baseball Hall of Fame Library. Cooperstown, N.Y.).

While playing with the Red Sox, from 1937 through 1940, he had his best hitting year. This was in 1938 when he batted .291, nearly 50 points higher than his batting average in any other season. 1938 was also the only year in which he played in as many as 100 games. Mostly, he was a defensive specialist and considered a good handler of pitchers.

Rick Ferrell

Rick Ferrell, Wes' older brother by two and one half years, had an 18-year catching career in the big leagues that began with the St. Louis Browns, and he had

Brothers Wes (left) and Rick Ferrell played pitcher and catcher, respectively, for the Red Sox from 1935-37. (Baseball Hall of Fame Library. Cooperstown, N.Y.).

two tours of duty both with the Browns and the Washington Nationals.

Ferrell came to the Red Sox from the Browns in 1933. He was known as a great handler of pitchers and it is primarily because of his superb defensive skills that he was elected to the Hall of Fame. His lifetime batting average was .280 and he batted between .297 and .312 in his years with the Red Sox. His best career batting year was 1936 when he hit .312 for the Sox.

The Ferrell brothers were a pitching-catching battery for the Red Sox from 1934 to 1937. In 1937 they were both traded to the Washington Nationals and continued their careers for several more years. The trade that sent the Ferrell brothers away from Boston was thought to have been precipitated by Wes Ferrell's on-the-mound and club house tantrums. Rick was considered the much more mellow and congenial of the two.

Wes Ferrell

Wes Ferrell, a right-handed pitcher, won 20 or more games each of his first four seasons in the major leagues. These were with the Cleveland Indians. Traded to the Red Sox in 1934 he also won 20 or more games for the Sox in 1935 and 1936, and led the league with 25 wins in 1935. He teamed with Lefty Grove in 1935 to win 45 games between them, and in 1936 together they had 37 wins. They were the stars of the Red Sox pitching staff, not only good pitchers but also tempestuous personalities.

Wes Ferrell was also one of baseball history's great hitting pitchers. He had a lifetime .280 batting average but, more distinctively, had a career high 38 home runs, which is the pitchers' major league record. He led American League pitchers in home runs nine times. He was also a fine pinch hitter, and at one point with the Indians substituted for an injured outfielder and batted .300.

Wes and Rick Ferrell were unusual in that they were a first-line brother battery who pitched and caught for the Red Sox for three-plus years. The Sox also had another less distinguished brother battery for one year in 1929, pitcher Milt and catcher Alex Gaston.

Johnny Lazor

Johnny Lazor, a Red Sox outfielder, lost the batting title in 1945 though he had the highest average of .310 and played in 101 games. American League president Will Harridge ruled that, since Lazor was a pinch hitter in 17 of the 100-game minimum required, the title would go instead to the Yankee infielder, George "Snuffy" Stirnweiss, with an average of .309. Nineteen forty-five was by far Lazor's best year for batting average in his four-year wartime career, all with the Red Sox.

Outfielder John Lazor's career with the Red Sox came as a result of several Red Sox stars, including Ted Williams, serving in the military during World War II. (Baseball Hall of Fame Library. Cooperstown, N.Y.).

Lazor's entire career was with the Red Sox, from 1943-1946. It was during the years of World War II and he had an opportunity to play because such Red Sox stars as Ted Williams, Dom DiMaggio and others were in military service. Other than in his best hitting year of 1945, Lazor saw limited action with the Red Sox and played in fewer than 85 games a season. He was used as a pinch hitter frequently. He had a total of 58 pinch hit at bats in his career with nine hits.

Fritz Ostermueller

Fritz Ostermueller pitched seven years for the Red Sox in the 1930s, in the era when Lefty Grove and Wes Ferrell were with the Sox. He won 59 games and lost 65 with the Sox. He had a 15-year big league career.

Ostermueller never won more than 13 games a season and this he did three times, once with the Red Sox in 1938 and twice with the Pittsburgh Pirates in the 1940s. For nine of his 15 years, his earned run average was over four runs a game and in four other years it was just under four runs. Notwithstanding, Ostermueller was frequently a third or fourth starter with the Red Sox and in his career

Fritz Ostermueller was a third or fourth starter for Boston in the 1930s. (Baseball Hall of Fame Library, Cooperstown, NY)

he was in nearly 400 games and managed to pitch over 2,000 innings.

Jim Tabor

Tabor was with the Red Sox from 1938 through 1944 in a nine-year big league career. He was the team's regular third baseman for six straight years, from 1939 through 1944. Tabor had a lifetime .270 batting average. The only year in which he batted over .300 was his first year, 1938, when he played in only 19 games and batted .316. Tabor had speed. Of his over 1,000 hits in his career, nearly 200 were doubles and he scored nearly 500 times. He also had just short of 70 stolen

Jim Tabor was Boston's starting third baseman from 1939-44. (Baseball Hall of Fame Library. Cooperstown, N.Y.).

bases, mostly concentrated in the years 1939 through 1941 when he was a strong contributor to the Red Sox offense. He also managed at least ten home runs a season for seven straight years, with 21 in 1940. He was a capable third baseman.

In 1946, Tabor was sold to the Philadelphia Phillies for cash. He finished his big league career playing two years for the Phillies.

Billy Werber

Billy Werber was traded by the New York Yankees to the Red Sox in 1933, along with pitcher George Pipgras. A third baseman, Werber played the position for three years with the Sox. He was noted for his speed and led the league in stolen bases in 1934 and 1935 with the Red Sox and in 1937 with the Philadelphia Athletics. Werber had an 11-year career with a lifetime .271 average.

Werber in his 11 big league seasons had fewer than 14 stolen bases a year only in his last and retirement year. He

Third baseman Billy Werber led the American League in stolen bases in 1934 and 1935. (Baseball Hall of Fame Library, Cooperstown, N.Y.)

Jack Wilson was both a starter and a reliever for the Red Sox in the 1930s and '40s. (Baseball Hall of Fame Library. Cooperstown, N.Y.).

generally batted in the .250 to .300 range, and he batted over .300 only one year, .321 in 1934 when he played his first full year with the Red Sox. Werber was traded by the Red Sox after the 1936 season, to the Philadelphia Athletics for another third baseman, Pinky Higgins, who was a regular .300 hitter with the Sox.

Werber played for five big league teams. He was the third baseman on the Cincinnati Reds' pennant-winning teams of 1939 and 1940, batting .370 in the 1940 World Series when the Reds won the world championship.

Jack Wilson

Jack Wilson pitched seven years for the Red Sox from the mid-1930s through the early 1940s. He won 16 games in 1937 and 15 in 1938. In his career with the Red Sox, both starting and in relief, he won 67 games and lost 67 games. Wilson's season with most wins was in 1937 when he won 16, but his best winning percentage was in 1940 when he won 12 and lost· six. He was a steady Red Sox pitching contributor from 1937 through 1940 when he had at least double-digit wins each season. He also suffered more than 10 losses a season in four years and had a lifetime earned run average of 4.59. A journeyman pitcher, he started with the Philadelphia Athletics, played most of his career with

the Red Sox, and ended up with two more teams, Washington and Detroit, in the last year of his career in 1942.

After World War II 1946-1951

Leon Culberson
| b. Aug. 6, 1919 | Halls Station, Ga. | Bats Right | Throws Right |
| | 5'11" 180 lbs | Red Sox | 1943-1947 |

Dom DiMaggio
| b. Feb. 12, 1917 | San Francisco, Calif. | Bats Right | Throws Right |
| | 5'9" 168 lbs. | Red Sox | 1940-1953 |

Joe Dobson
| b. Jan. 20 1917 | Durant, Okla. | Pitches Right | Bats Right |
| | 6'2" 197 lbs. | Red Sox | 1941-1950; 54 |

Walt Dropo
| b. Jan. 30, 1923 | Moosup, Conn. | Bats Right | Throws Right |
| | 6'5" 220 lbs. | Red Sox | 1949-1952 |

Boo Ferriss
| b. Dec. 5, 1921 | Shaw, Miss. | Pitches Right | Bats Left |
| | 6'2" 208 lbs. | Red Sox | 1945-1950 |

Denny Galehouse
| b. Dec. 7, 1911 | Marshallville, Ohio | Pitches Right | Bats Right |
| | 6'1" 195 lbs. | Red Sox | 1939-1940; 1947-1949 |

Billy Goodman
| b. Mar. 22, 1926 | Concord, N.C. | Bats Left | Throws Right |
| | 5'11" 165 lbs. | Red Sox | 1947-1957 |

Tex Hughson
| b. Feb. 9, 1916 | Buda, Texas | Pitches Right | Bats Right |
| | 6'3" 198 lbs. | Red Sox | 1941-1949 |

Ellis Kinder
| b. Jul. 26, 1914 | Atkins, Ark. | Pitches Right | Bats Right |
| | 6' 215 lbs. | Red Sox | 1948-1955 |

Mickey McDermott
| b. Aug. 29, 1927 | Poughkeepsie, N.Y. | Pitches Left | Bats Left |
| | 6'2" 170 lbs. | Red Sox | 1948-1953 |

Mel Parnell
| b. Jun. 13, 1922 | New Orleans, La. | Pitches Left | Bats Left |
| | 6' 180 lbs. | Red Sox | 1947-1956 |

Chuck Stobbs
| b. Jul. 22, 1929 | Wheeling, W.V. | Pitches Left | Bats Left |
| | 6'1" 185 lbs. | Red Sox | 1947-1951 |

The Red Sox Encyclopedia

Birdie Tebbetts

b. Nov. 10, 1912	Burlington, Vermont	Bats Right	Throws Right
	5'11½" 170 lbs.	Red Sox	1947-1950

Al Zarilla

b. May 1, 1919	Los Angeles, Calif.	Bats Left	Throws Right
	5'11" 180 lbs.	Red Sox	1949-1950;
			1952-1953

Leon Culberson

Leon Culberson played in the outfield for the Red Sox for five years, 1943 through 1947, and in all had a six-year career. His lifetime batting average was .266 and he batted over .300 in one year, 1946. Culberson was a substitute outfielder on the Red Sox 1946 pennant winning team. He played in five World Series games that year and hit a home run in Game 5 which the Red Sox won 6-3.

Culberson was used as a pinch hitter in 1947, his last year with the Red Sox. His batting average, after two fairly good years, dropped to .238 and he was traded to the Washington Nationals. 1948 was his last big league season and he had only five hits in 29 at bats.

Dom DiMaggio

Dom DiMaggio, one of three major league baseball playing DiMaggio brothers (the illustrious Joe with the New York Yankees and oldest brother Vince with National League teams), played his entire 11-year major league career from 1940 through 1953 with the Red Sox. In this period, he missed three years while in military service. "The Little Professor," as he was known, was an exceptional centerfielder and a fleet runner. His speed was evidenced in leading the league in triples once, in runs scored twice, and in stolen bases once. For four straight years,

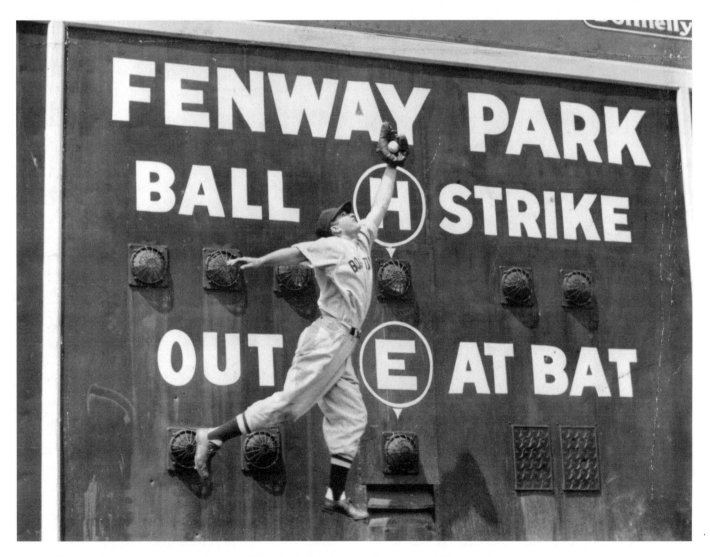

Leon Culberson played five seasons in the outfield for the Red Sox, batting better than .300 in 1946.
(Boston Public Library, Print Department).

Players Roll Call – The Greats and Others to be Remembered

1948 through 1951, he scored more than 110 runs a season. In the same four-year period he drew 352 walks. He had a lifetime batting average of .298 and, in his best hitting year in 1950, his average was .328.

Dom played in the 1946 World Series for the Red Sox. He scored the winning run in Game 5 of a Series the Sox ultimately lost to the St. Louis Cardinals, four games to three.

Bespectacled Dom was a popular player in Boston and some considered him as good or a better centerfielder than his fabled older brother, Joe. He and Ted Williams were standout and steadfast regulars in the Red Sox outfield for many years. Ironically, he also played next to his brother Joe in All-Star games. Another irony, while brother Joe established the major league record with a spectacular 56 straight game hitting streak in 1941, Dom holds the Red Sox record, hitting in 34 consecutive games in 1949.

Fleet centerfielder Dom DiMaggio was considered as good or better an outfielder as his more famous brother, Joe, by many Boston fans. (Baseball Hall of Fame Library, Cooperstown, N.Y.).

Joe Dobson

Joe Dobson pitched nine years for the Red Sox, from 1941 through 1950 and again in 1954. He won 18 games for the Sox in 1947, leading the team in wins and earned run average, and he won 16 games in 1948. He pitched and won a World Series game for the Red Sox against the St. Louis Cardinals in 1946. In his Red Sox career he won 106 games and lost 72.

Dobson was second in the league to Allie Reynolds of the New York Yankees in winning percentage in 1947. He won 18 and lost eight for a .692 winning percentage and he had a 2.95 earned run average. In eight of his 14 years in the big leagues he had double-digit wins, and he won 63 games from 1947 through 1950. In that period he also pitched relief occasionally and had nine saves.

Pitcher Joe Dobson posted double figures in victories for the Red Sox every season from 1941-50. (Baseball Hall of Fame Library, Cooperstown, N.Y.).

Dobson was in three games for the Red Sox in the 1946 World Series, starting in one game and relieving in two. He pitched a complete Game 5, winning over the St. Louis Cardinals, 6-3 in a 4-hitter. None of the Cardinals runs were earned and his earned run average for the Series was 0.00.

Walt Dropo

Dropo, a Connecticut native, is notable for winning league Rookie of the Year honors in 1950. In that year, the first of two full seasons with the Red Sox, Dropo hit .322 with 34 home runs and led the league with 144 runs batted in. He also scored 101 runs. It was by far the best year "Moose" had in his 13-year major league career. He never again batted over .281 and had a lifetime .270 average. A first baseman, he was traded to the Detroit Tigers in 1952 and went on to play with three other teams. While with the

First baseman Walt Dropo won American League Rookie of the Year honors in 1950 after batting .322 with 34 homers and 144 R.B.I. (Baseball Hall of Fame Library. Cooperstown, N.Y.).

Tigers in 1952 he tied Red Sox Pinky Higgins' 1938 record of twelve consecutive hits.

Dropo, in his dominant Red Sox year, 1950, was clearly a new slugger appearing on the scene. Besides leading in home runs and runs batted in, he also led the league in total bases. He was second in the league to Joe DiMaggio in slugging percentage at .583. He had eight triples, the most in any one year in his career, and he had 28 doubles. Dropo had a total of 152 home runs in his career. He hit 29 home runs in the year he was traded to the Tigers in an eight-player deal that brought George Kell and Dizzy Trout to the Red Sox briefly toward the end of their careers and sent Johnny Pesky, near the end of his career, Dropo and two others to the Tigers.

David "Boo" Ferriss

"Boo" Ferriss had a brief big league career of six seasons and in only four of these did he register wins or losses. He was with the Red Sox for his entire career, from 1945 through 1950. His first two years, 1945 and 1946, were sensational. In 1945 Ferriss won 21 games with 26 complete games. In 1946, he had 25 wins, again with 26 complete games. He led the league in winning percentage with an .806 average. His record for the first two years of his pitching career, winning 46 games, is exceptional.

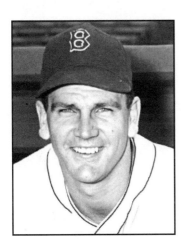

Boo Ferriss posted a 21-win season for the Red Sox in 1945. (Baseball Hall of Fame Library, Cooperstown, NY)

Boo Ferriss in 1945 was the only effective pitcher on the Boston team. As against his 21 wins, no other Sox pitcher won more than eight games. In 1946, Ferriss and a returning-from-war Tex Hughson anchored the pennant winning pitching staff, each with more than 20 wins. Mickey Harris with 17 wins, Joe Dobson with 13 and Bob Klinger in relief gave the Red Sox five formidable pitchers. Ferriss won one game in the 1946 World Series, pitching a six-hit shutout in the third game, 4-0. He also started Game 7 and pitched four innings before being removed in the fifth inning as the St. Louis Cardinals forged ahead, 3 to 1. The Cardinals won the game 4-3, and the Series, four games to three.

Denny Galehouse

Denny Galehouse had a 15-year pitching career stretching from before to after World War II. Most of his career was with the Cleveland Indians and St. Louis Browns but he did have two brief stints with the Red Sox. The second one was at the end of his career and produced his principal claim to special memory. In 1948, in a year the Red Sox finished in a tie with Cleveland for the pennant, Galehouse won eight and lost eight. He was the surprise choice of manager Joe McCarthy to pitch the play-off game even though regular starters Mel Parnell and Ellis Kinder, at 15-8 and 10-7 respectively, were well rested. The Indians battered the Red Sox in the winner-take-all play-off game and won the pennant.

Right-handed hurler Denny Galehouse had two tours of duty with the Red Sox, starting a playoff game for Boston in 1948. (Boston Public Library, Print Department).

Denny first played with the Red Sox in 1939 and 1940 after being with the Cleveland Indians for three full seasons and briefly in two others. He won 15 and lost 16 for the Sox in his first tour of duty with them. Traded back to the Red Sox after playing with the St. Louis Browns in World War II and pitching on their 1944 pennant winning team, he was with the Sox from late in 1947 through 1949. In his second stint with the Red Sox he won 19 games and lost 15. In his big league career he won 109 and lost 118.

Billy Goodman

Billy Goodman had a notable 16-year career as an infielder and sometimes an outfielder. He came to the big leagues with the Red Sox in 1947 and stayed with the team for more than ten years. In his nine years of full-time play with the Sox he never batted under .293. Though he was predominantly a first baseman in his early years, the year 1950 epitomized his versatility. In that year, he played 21 games as a first baseman, five as a second baseman, one as a shortstop, 27 games as a third baseman and 45 in the outfield. Nineteen fifty was also the year in which he led the league with a .354 batting average. It was a career sea-

Although primarily a first baseman, the versatile Billy Goodman played five different positions for the Red Sox in 1950. (Baseball Hall of Fame Library. Cooperstown, N.Y.).

1942 through 1946 he won 72 games, averaging 18 wins a season. He led the league in wins in 1942, in complete games both in 1942 and 1943, and in winning percentage in 1944. His two twenty game win years were in 1942 and 1946. In 1942, 1943 and 1944 no Red Sox pitcher had as many wins as Hughson in any of these years. Hughson was not with the team in 1945. In 1946 and 1947 his record as principal winning pitcher with the team was taken by the sensational performances of Boo Ferriss.

Tex Hughson averaged 18 wins per season for the Red Sox from 1942-46. (Baseball Hall of Fame Library. Cooperstown, N.Y.).

Hughson pitched two games in the 1946 Red Sox-Cardinals World Series. He was the opening game pitcher and pitched eight good innings but the game went into extra innings and was won by the Red Sox by reliever Earl Johnson, 3-2. Hughson lost the fourth game, lasting two innings. Tex was the winning pitcher in the 1944 All-Star game. It was his only appearance in All-Star competition.

Tex Hughson had an eight year major league pitching career, all with the Red Sox, ending in 1949.

son for him since he had a lifetime batting average of .300 and in no other year batted over .313. He will be noted as the player who won the batting championship while a utility player. He filled in at various positions sufficiently to acquire over 400 at bats. He could not land a regular position in the field when Walt Dropo led the league with 144 runs batted in while playing first base, the same R.B.I. number Vern Stephens had playing shortstop. Bobby Doerr was the fixture at second base in a year when he batted .294 and led all second basemen in fielding average, and Johnny Pesky, a fixture at third base, batted .312 and led the league with more fielding chances per game than any other third baseman. All three outfielders, Al Zarilla, Dom DiMaggio and Ted Williams, batted well over .300.

Cecil "Tex" Hughson

Tex Hughson was the bellwether of the Red Sox pitching staff in the years during and just after World War II. From

Ellis Kinder

Ellis Kinder started his career with the St. Louis Browns in 1946 but was traded to the Red Sox before the 1948 season. In his 12-year career he pitched for the Red Sox for eight years, 1948 through 1955. Kinder's best year, like Mel Parnell's, was in 1949. He won 23 games and led the league in winning percentage at .793. He pitched six shutouts that year. Kinder also started the final game of the season against the Yankees for the American League championship. He pitched creditably, with the Red Sox behind only 1-0 after seven innings. He was removed for a pinch hitter and replaced by Mel Parnell, who

Ellis Kinder won 23 games and led the league in winning percentage in 1949. (Baseball Hall of Fame Library. Cooperstown, N.Y.).

gave up another run, the Sox ultimately losing 5-3.

Kinder was also a top relief pitcher from 1950 through 1955 with the Sox. He led the league with relief wins, 10, in both 1951 and 1953. He also led the league those two seasons in saves with 14 in 1951 and 27 in 1953. In his great relief years of 1951 and 1953, he also had scintillating earned run averages. In 1953, pitching in 69 games entirely in relief with a 10-6 record and 27 saves, he had an earned run average of 1.85. In 1951, pitching in 63 games mostly in relief, he had an 11-2 record with 14 saves and an E.R.A. of 2.55.

Maurice "Mickey" McDermott

Mickey McDermott, a Red Sox left handed pitcher for six of his 12 major league years, really had only one good season. He won 18 games and lost 10 for the Sox in 1953, his last year with the team. McDermott was also a fine hitter with a .281 batting average for the Red Sox.

In six years with the Red Sox, 1948 through 1953, he won 48 games and lost 34. In 1951 and 1952 he had over 100 strikeouts each season, a total of 244 in 344 innings pitched or about six per game. McDermott went on to pitch for five other teams and pitched briefly for the New York Yankees in the 1956 World Series. He won a total of 69 games and lost 69 in his big league career.

McDermott was a frequent pinch hitter for five years in his career, from 1953, his last year with the Red Sox, through 1957. Lifetime, he had a total of 25 pinch hits and he also hit nine home runs. In a full season as a pitcher, in 1953, he batted .301 for the Sox.

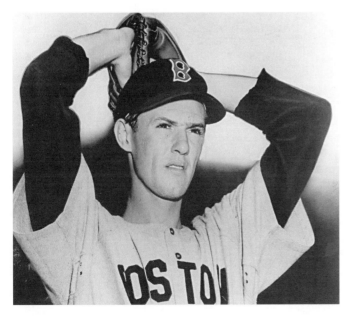

Mickey McDermott was a fine hitter for the Red Sox, as well as a left-handed pitcher. (Baseball Hall of Fame Library. Cooperstown, N.Y.).

Mel Parnell

Mel Parnell, left hander, and Ellis Kinder, right hander, were an outstanding pitching combination for the Red Sox in the late 1940s and 1950s.

Parnell pitched his entire career with the Red Sox, ten years, from 1947 through 1956. He had an exceptional year in 1949 when he led the league with 25 wins, also leading with 27 complete games. He had a 2.77 earned run average. It was a good year for the Red Sox with Parnell and Kinder winning 48 games between them. Nonetheless, the Sox lost the pennant to the New York Yankees in the last two games of the season. From 1948 through 1953, six years, Parnell won 107 games, or nearly 18 games a year. He had his second 20-win season in 1953, pitching five shutouts.

Parnell started the 1949 All-Star game and he also pitched one inning in the 1951 game but did not figure in a decision in either game.

Parnell was the mainstay of the Red Sox pitching staff. For six straight years, 1948 through 1953, he pitched in more than 33 games a season. For those six seasons he was also in double digits in complete games. He had 20

Mel Parnell pitched his entire career with Boston, leading the league in victories in 1949. (Baseball Hall of Fame Library. Cooperstown, N.Y.).

shutouts in his career and also pitched in relief on occasion.

Parnell later became a member of the Red Sox broadcasting team with Ned Martin and Ken Coleman.

Chuck Stobbs

Chuck Stobbs had a 15-year big league pitching career and his first five years were with the Red Sox. In point of fact, he was only in ten games with the Red Sox in his first two seasons, 1947 and 1948. The next three seasons he won 10 or more games each season. His Red Sox record was 33 wins and 23 losses.

Stobbs, was traded to the Chicago White Sox and played for them one year. He pitched seven plus years for Washington in two tours of duty. His best career year was in his second stint with the Senators in 1960 when he won 12 and lost seven with a .632 winning percentage. On the other hand, he also had his worst year with the Senators in his first tour of duty with them. In 1957, he led the league in losses with 20 and had an eight win-20 loss record for the

Chuck Stobbs compiled a 33-23 record for the Red Sox from 1947-51. (Baseball Hall of Fame Library, Cooperstown, N.Y.).

last-place Senators. He was, nonetheless, one of the big three on the pitching staff of the Senators, the other two being Pedro Ramos and Camilo Pascual.

George "Birdie" Tebbetts

"Birdie" Tebbetts, a New Englander, had a 14-year career as a big league catcher, mostly as the stellar backstop for the Detroit Tigers. He was on the Tigers' 1940 pennant winners. He played three and one half years for the Red Sox toward the end of his career from 1947 through 1950. His lifetime batting average was .270. A fine defensive catcher he later managed three teams in the big leagues for a total of 11 years.

Tebbetts batted .310 for the Red Sox in 79 games in 1950. It was his best batting year. In his career he had

After playing most of his career with Detroit, catcher Birdie Tebbetts came to Boston in 1947 and played 3^1/$_2$ seasons, batting .310 in 1950. (Boston Public Library, Print Department).

exactly 1,000 hits and he also stole 29 bases. He was a field leader and understandably later became a manager. Tebbetts managed Cincinnati for nearly all of five years, then Milwaukee for a full season and briefly in another, and finally he managed the Cleveland Indians in two seasons and parts of two others. His teams never finished above third place and were usually at the top of the second division. He was nonetheless considered a smart manager.

Al Zarilla

Al Zarilla, an outfielder, was twice traded to the Red Sox and twice by the same team, the St. Louis Browns, in 1949 and 1952. He had a ten-year career, mostly with the Browns, and was on their 1944 pennant-winning team. Al played almost two full seasons with the Red Sox, in

The original panoramic photo of Fenway Park is available for purchase along with many other panoramic images from LaPayne Photography featuring sporting events, stadiums, arenas, city skylines, and National Parks. Please call LaPayne Photography for questions and ordering information at (800) 280-8994 or visit www.LaPayne.com

This is a panoramic photo of Fenway Park on "Opening Day" 1994, featuring the "Green Monster," the Citgo sign, and many of the buildings in downtown Boston. The photo was taken with a rare, antique, rotating, Cirkut panoramic camera. The original panoramic photograph is 9.5" tall and 66" wide, and approximately 220 degrees angle of view. Please note that this photo has been cropped smaller than the original size for the purpose of this insert.

1949 and 1950, and then two part-time seasons in 1952 and 1953. He batted .325 with the Red Sox in 1950, when the Sox had an outfield of Zarilla, Dom DiMaggio and Ted Williams, all of whom batted over .315. Zarilla had a .276 lifetime batting average.

Zarilla had two seasons in which he batted over .300. In addition to the 1950 season with the Red Sox, he also batted .329 with the Browns in 1948. In that year he also hit 39 doubles and for two successive seasons after that hit more than 30 doubles a season. In his big year with Boston in 1950 he had 10 triples. In the same year, 51 of his 153 hits were extra base hits as he had his best year for slugging percentage, .493. He ended his career mostly as a pinch hitter for the Red Sox in 1953.

Al Zarilla was traded to the Red Sox twice by St. Louis. (Baseball Hall of Fame Library. Cooperstown, N.Y.).

Lowly Red Sox But Some Good Players 1952-1966

Tom Brewer

b. Sep. 3, 1931	Wadesboro, N.C.	Pitches Right	Bats Right
	6'1" 175 lbs.	Red Sox	1954-1961

Tony Conigliaro

b. Jan. 7, 1945	Revere, Mass.	Bats Right	Throws Right
	6'3" 185 lbs.	Red Sox	1964-1970; 75

Ike Delock

b. Nov. 11, 1929	Highland Park, Mich.	Pitches Right	Bats Right
	5'11" 175 lbs.	Red Sox	1952-1963

Mike Fornieles

b. Jan. 18, 1932	Havana, Cuba	Pitches Right	Bats Right
	5'11" 155 lbs.	Red Sox	1957-1963

Dick Gernert

b. Sep. 28, 1928	Reading, Pa.	Bats Right	Throws Right
	6'3" 209 lbs.	Red Sox	1952-1959

Pumpsie Green

b. Oct. 27, 1933	Oakland, Calif.	Switch Hitter	Throws Right
	6' 175 lbs.	Red Sox	1959-1962

Jackie Jensen

b. Mar. 9, 1927	San Francisco, Calif.	Bats Right	Throws Right
	5'11" 190 lbs.	Red Sox	1954-1961

Ted Lepcio

b. Jul. 28, 1930	Utica, N.Y.	Bats Right	Throws Right
	5'10" 177 lbs.	Red Sox	1952-1959

Frank Malzone

b. Feb. 28, 1930	Bronx, N.Y.	Bats Right	Throws Right
	5'10" 180 lbs.	Red Sox	1955-1965

Bill Monbouquette

b. Apr. 11, 1936	Medford, Mass.	Pitches Right	Bats Right
	5'11" 190 lbs.	Red Sox	1958-1965

Dave Morehead

b. Sep. 5, 1942	San Diego, Calif.	Pitches Right	Bats Right
	6'1" 185 lbs.	Red Sox	1963-1968

Russ Nixon

b. Feb. 19, 1935	Cleves, Ohio	Bats Left	Throws Right
	6'1" 195 lbs.	Red Sox	1960-1965; 68

Willard Nixon

b. Jun. 17, 1928	Taylorsville, Ga.	Pitches Right	Bats Left
	6'2" 195 lbs.	Red Sox	1950-1958

Jimmy Piersall

b. Nov. 14, 1929	Waterbury, Conn.	Bats Right	Throws Right
	6' 175 lbs.	Red Sox	1950-1958

Dick Radatz

b. Apr. 2, 1937	Detroit, Mich.	Pitches Right	Bats Right
	6'6" 230 lbs.	Red Sox	1962-1966

Pete Runnels

b. Jan. 28, 1928	Lufkin, Texas	Bats Left	Throws Right
	6' 170 lbs.	Red Sox	1958-1962

Gene Stephens

b. Jan. 20 1933	Gravette, Ark.	Bats Left	Throws Right
	6'3½" 175 lbs.	Red Sox	1952-1960

Frank Sullivan

b. Jan. 23, 1930	Hollywood, Calif.	Pitches Right	Bats Right
	6'6½" 215 lbs.	Red Sox	1953-1960

Sammy White

b. Jul. 7, 1928   Wenatchee,Wash. Bats
Right   Throws Right
6'3" 195 lbs.   Red Sox   1951-1959

Earl Wilson

b. Oct. 2, 1934   Ponchatoula, La.   Pitches Right Bats Right
6'3" 216 lbs.   Red Sox   1959-1966

Tom Brewer

Brewer pitched his eight-year career for the Red Sox from 1954 through 1961. In his best two years, 1956 and 1957, he won 19 and 16 games, respectively. His career record was 91 wins and 82 losses.

Brewer consistently started about 30 games a season for the Red Sox. In his two best years, 1956 and 1957, he completed a career high 15 games each season. He had 13 career shutouts.

Brewer was the Red Sox's leading pitcher in 1956 when he won 19 and lost nine for a .679 winning percentage. It was a year in which the Red Sox finished fourth, 13 games behind the first place Yankees. Brewer still led the Red Sox pitchers in 1957 with a 16-13 record, and the Red Sox finished third, 16 games behind the pennant-winning Yankees.

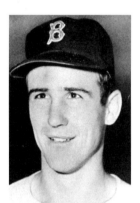

Tom Brewer was the Red Sox's best pitcher in 1956 when he posted a 19-9 record. (Baseball Hall of Fame Library. Cooperstown, N.Y.).

Tony Conigliaro

Tony Conigliaro, the "Tony C" of the Red Sox brother outfield combination either one or both of whom played with the team in the mid-1960s and early 1970s, was both older and better than "Billy C". They were very popular as both grew up in neighboring Revere, Massachusetts.

Tony had a better baseball record and a longer major league career than Billy. Tony first came up with the Red Sox in 1964 and played with them through 1970. In 1967 he suffered a beaning, had vision problems, and did not play in the 1967 postseason or in any of 1968. The beaning affected his great promise and limited his career. He returned and played in 1969 and 1970, then played briefly with the California Angels, and closed out his career playing briefly with the Red Sox again in 1975. Tony suffered

a destructive heart attack in 1982 and died eight years later at age 45.

Tony had six good years with the Red Sox, from 1964 through 1970. Omitting 1968, in these six years he hit 160 home runs, at least 20 each season, and he led the league in homers in 1965 with 32. He generally batted between .250 and .290 and had a lifetime batting average of .264. He was second to league-leading Carl Yastrzemski in 1965 with a .512 slugging average. His 36 home runs with 116 R.B.I. in 1970 were both his career high. He was a feared slugger and three times had more than 110 walks a season.

Tony and Billy Conigliaro were regulars in the Red Sox outfield in 1970, the year Billy came up to the big leagues. They flanked Reggie Smith in the outfield. Tony and Billy hit 54 home runs between them in 1970, 36 for Tony and 18 for Billy. This was a record for one season for a brother combination.

A popular young slugger for the Red Sox in the 1960s, Tony Conigliaro played with his brother, Billy, in the Boston outfield in 1970. (Baseball Hall of Fame Library. Cooperstown, N.Y.).

Ivan "Ike" Delock

Ike Delock was a pitcher with the Red Sox more than 11 years, 1952-1963, and compiled an 84-75 won-lost career record. From 1956 through 1959 he won 47 games, his highest total being in 1958 when he had 14 wins. Ike was a reliever as well as a starter, especially in the early part of his career, and he led the league in relief wins in 1956 with 11. He also had nine saves that year. The

Ike DeLock was both a starter and reliever for the Red Sox . (Baseball Hall of Fame Library. Cooperstown, N.Y.).

following year Ike reversed that record with nine relief wins and 11 saves. Of his 84 wins in his big league career 34 were in relief.

Ike over more than 11 years for the Red Sox started 147 games. While he won 50 games as a starter he was more successful as a reliever. He finished his career pitching briefly for the Baltimore Orioles in 1963.

Mike Fornieles

Mike Fornieles was another of several relief stars for the Red Sox. He pitched for the Sox approximately six years from 1957 through 1963. He led the league in saves with fourteen in 1960 and also had ten relief wins. He also had fifteen saves in 1961. He was a workhorse, pitching in a league leading 70 games in 1960.

Mike Fornieles pitched in 70 games in 1960, leading the league in saves with 14. (Baseball Hall of Fame Library. Cooperstown, N.Y.).

Mike had neither the colorfulness nor the record of a fellow Cuban who came later to the Red Sox, Luis Tiant, but he was an effective pitcher. He won 49 games for the Red Sox in six-plus years and, from 1958 on, pitched almost entirely in relief. His best single-year record was in 1960 when he had 10 wins, five losses and a 2.64 earned run average. It was his career year as he was also the workhorse pitcher in the league. Mike went on to Minnesota in his last year to complete his 12-year career.

Dick Gernert

Dick Gernert played eight years for the Red Sox as a first baseman, from 1952 through 1959. He played very little in 1954 and 1955, when the Sox had first Harry Agganis and then Norm Zauchin at first base, but he was a regular in his other years. He had a lifetime .254 batting average and did not bat as much as .300 in any year. His best year with the Sox was .291 in 1956. It was the year in which he had his best slugging average, .484, and he hit 16 home runs. In his 11-year career he had 103 home runs, starting off well in his first two seasons, 1952 and 1953,

Dick Gernert played eight seasons as a first baseman for the Red Sox. (Baseball Hall of Fame Library, Cooperstown, N.Y.).

Pumpsie Green was the first African-American player to play for the Red Sox. He came up to the team in 1959, 12 years after Jackie Robinson became the first African-American player in the Major Leagues. (Boston Red Sox).

when he had 19 and 21, respectively. He was also used from time to time as a pinch hitter.

Gernert went on to play for the Cubs, Tigers, Reds and Astros. With Cincinnati he played in the 1961 World Series, batting four times without a hit.

Elijah "Pumpsie" Green

"Pumpsie" Green achieved celebrity in being the first African-American player to play for the Red Sox, and the Red Sox were the last team in the big leagues to bring up a black player. This was 1959, 12 years after Jackie Robinson entered the National League. Pumpsie was mostly a reserve infielder with a five-year big league career, the first four of which were with the Red Sox. His lifetime batting average was .246 and, in his best year, 1963 with the New York Mets, he batted .278.

With the Red Sox "Pumpsie" batted .260 in 88 games in 1961. He was used sparingly when he first came up with the Sox and he played in nearly a full schedule of games in 1960. He played both at second base and shortstop. He was used also as a pinch hitter. "Pumpsie" had 13 home runs in his career, six in 1961.

Jackie Jensen

Jackie Jensen was an All-American football player with the University of California before he became a professional baseball player. He started his major league career with the New York Yankees in 1950 but then went on to the Washington Senators and was ultimately traded to the Red Sox before the 1954 season. Jensen played the rest of his career with the Red Sox, a total of seven out of his 11-year major league career. Jensen was a good hitter, a power hitter and he had speed. His career batting average was .279 and his best year for average was in 1956 when he hit .315. In all but his last year with the Red Sox he hit 20 or more home runs and in this time he scored from 80 to 101 runs a season. In 1954, he also led the league in stolen bases. Jensen was a formidable figure with men on base and in five of his seven Boston years he drove in more than 100 runs. He led the league in this category three times, in 1955, 1958 and 1959.

Jackie Jenson earned American League M.V.P. honors for the Red Sox in 1958. (Baseball Hall of Fame Library. Cooperstown, N.Y.).

Jackie had his career year in 1958 when he won the league's Most Valuable Player award. He batted .286 but had 35 home runs and led the league with 122 runs batted in. He also had a Gold Glove award for his fielding in 1959.

Ted Lepcio

Ted Lepcio was a Boston infielder from 1952 until he was traded to the Detroit Tigers early in 1959. He was mostly a utility player at different infield positions and was a regular, at second base, only in 1954. He and Gene Mauch shared the position in 1957. Lepcio's lifetime batting average was .245. His best complete season with the Red Sox was in 1956 when he batted .261. He had as many as 100 hits a season only in 1954, as a regular, when he played in 116 games with nearly 400 at bats. The year 1956 also saw Lepcio in double figures in home runs, 15, the only time in his career.

Primarily a utility infielder, Ted Lepcio was the Red Sox's regular second baseman in 1954. (Baseball Hall of Fame Library. Cooperstown, N.Y.).

In the year Lepcio was traded to the Detroit Tigers he batted .279 for the Tigers in 76 games and ended the season with a .280 batting average. His career ended with Minnesota in 1961.

Frank Malzone

Frank Malzone played all but one of his 12 years in the big leagues with the Red Sox. He was considered a third baseman with few if any peers during his playing years. He won the Gold Glove award in 1957, 1958 and 1959, until the arrival of Brooks Robinson of the Baltimore Orioles, perhaps the greatest fielding third baseman of all time.

Frank Malzone won Gold Gloves for Boston from 1957-59 and was the preeminent third baseman of his time until Brooks Robinson appeared for the Baltimore Orioles. (Baseball Hall of Fame Library. Cooperstown, N.Y.).

Beginning in 1960 Robinson was 16 straight Gold Glove awards at third base but Malzone also continued as a sparkling third baseman.

Malzone's lifetime batting average was .274. He never hit .300 in a full season. For seven straight years, from 1957-1963, he hit 20 or more doubles. In 1962, perhaps his best all-round hitting year, he batted .283, hit 21 home runs and drove in 95 runs. He hit a home run in the 1959 second All-Star game, won by Yogi Berra's two-run homer for the American League, 5 to 3.

Malzone was a popular Boston player. He was a steady and dependable third baseman and also a consistent hitter. In his full Red Sox years he generally hit between .265 and .295. He was in double digits in home runs for eight consecutive years, hitting between 13 and 21 each year in this period. In five years he had a slugging percentage over .400. At the end of his career he was a successful pinch hitter with the California Angels.

Bill Monbouquette pitched a no-hitter for the Red Sox in 1962. (Baseball Hall of Fame Library. Cooperstown, N.Y.).

Bill Monbouquette

Bill Monbouquette played 11 years as a pitcher in the late 1950s and the 1960s. He played his first eight years with Boston and had a 20-game win season in 1963. "Mombo," as he was known, pitched a no-hitter in 1962, the second no-hitter for the Sox that year, coming five weeks after Earl Wilson pitched his.

In his big-league lifetime, Mombo was 114-112. His most productive years were 1960-65 for the Sox, essentially sandwiched around his career year of 1963 with 20 wins. In these six seasons he was 86-80. While he had 10 wins in his last year with the Sox, it was his worst season, as he led the league with 18 losses. The next year he moved to Detroit.

Mombo started 30 or more games six straight seasons with the Sox. He was a durable pitcher and each of these years pitched at least 215 innings. He also struck out more than 110 batters each of these seasons.

Dave Morehead

Dave Morehead was a Red Sox pitcher from 1963, when he started his big league career, through 1968. He went on to Kansas City and ended his career after eight seasons. In his six years with the Red Sox Morehead won 35 games and lost 56. He never won more than 10 games a season and in 1965, won 10 and lost 18, leading the league in number of losses. He was mostly a starting pitcher but he was used sparingly by the Sox after his first three years, 1963 through 1965.

Morehead was a journeyman right hander. He was on the Red Sox roster during the 1967 World Series and pitched three of the last four innings in relief in Game 3, after the St. Louis Cardinals scored their six runs early and won the game, 6-0. He also pitched one third of an inning in the final game, Game 7, which the Cardinals won, 7-2.

The crowning jewel in Morehead's career was the no hitter he pitched against the Cleveland Indians on September 16, 1965. He won the game, 2-0, though, ironically, he led the league in losses that season.

A journeyman right-hander, Dave Morehead was on the Red Sox roster for the 1967 World Series. (Baseball Hall of Fame Library. Cooperstown, N.Y.).

Russ Nixon

Russ Nixon was a catcher with the Red Sox for seven of his 12 major league years. He was with the Sox from 1960 through 1965 and closed his career with the team in 1968.

Russ Nixon was a back-up catcher for the Sox for seven years. (Baseball Hall of Fame Library. Cooperstown, N.Y.).

He had a .268 lifetime batting average. Nixon later managed both the Cincinnati Reds and the Atlanta Braves.

Nixon was typically a back-up catcher first to Jim Pagliaroni and then to Bob Tillman during most of his career with the Red Sox. He was a durable catcher and managed to get into about half the games each season. Russ had a .301 batting year as the regular catcher with the Cleveland Indians before he came to Boston. With the Red Sox his best batting year was his first full year, 1961, when he hit .289. He was a frequent pinch hitter with the Sox. As a pinch hitter in 1961 he had eight hits in 18 tries for a .444 pinch hitting average and, in the next year, 1962, he had 10 hits in 28 attempts for a .357 pinch hitting average.

Jimmy Piersall autographs the first copy of his book, Fear Strikes Out, *for his wife and a publisher's representative.* (*Boston Public Library, Print Department*).

Willard Nixon

Willard Nixon pitched his entire nine-year career with the Boston Red Sox. (Baseball Hall of Fame Library. Cooperstown, N.Y.).

Willard Nixon pitched his entire career for the Red Sox, from 1950 through 1958. His career record was 69 wins and 72 losses. He had 12 wins in both 1955 and 1957, and he had 11 wins in 1954. Except for his last year, 1958, when he had one win and seven losses, he generally had close to an equal number of wins and losses each season. His career earned run average was 4.39. In his best season, 12-10, in 1955, he pitched over 200 innings. He was used almost entirely as a starter, with more than 22 starts a season, and an average of 28 starts between 1954 and 1957. Boston finished in third or fourth place in nearly every year that Nixon pitched.

Jimmy Piersall

Jimmy Piersall, another Connecticut native who played with the Red Sox, broke in with the Sox in 1950. He played his first eight seasons with the Sox in a 17-year career that saw him go to four other major league teams. Piersall was a pesky lead-off man and a fleet center fielder. He was a fair hitter with a lifetime batting average of .272. He topped .300 twice though never while playing with the Sox. His highest average with the Sox was .293 in 1956. In that, his best hitting year with the Red Sox, he led the league in doubles and scored over 90 runs. He also led the league in fielding the same year with a .991 average in center field. This was the year before Gold Glove awards for field-

ing were initiated, an honor Piersall won with the 1961 Cleveland Indians.

Jim Piersall had a long struggle with emotional problems. He suffered an emotional breakdown while with the Red Sox in 1952 that required hospitalization and a lengthy period away from the playing field. He later wrote about his emotional experiences in a best-selling book, *Fear Strikes Out*, that also was adapted for a movie. Piersall, unfortunately, has an enduring reputation for his antics and his pugnacity.

While playing with the Mets in 1963, he celebrated his 100th home run by circling the bases backward. He subsequently became an announcer for Chicago White Sox baseball and was frequently in trouble and in the headlines for his rash and provocative behavior.

Dick Radatz

Dick Radatz was the definitive relief pitcher of his time, leading the league in saves from 1962-64. (Baseball Hall of Fame Library. Cooperstown, N.Y.).

Dick Radatz had a meteoric but phenomenal career, notably focused on the first four years of the seven he spent with the Red Sox. "The Monster," as he was known, was the definitive relief pitcher of the time. In 1962, 1963 and 1964 he led the American League with nine, 15 and 16 wins, respectively, all in relief. He also had another nine relief wins in 1965. At the same time, he led the league in saves in 1962, with 24, and in 1964, with 29. In 1963 and 1965, though he did not lead the league in saves, he had 25 in the first of these years and 22 in the second year. All told, he had 100 saves in four years as relief pitching was more concertedly coming into its own. Radatz, in 1963, struck out 181 batters in 157 innings and, in his major league lifetime, created an unrivalled mark of striking out 9.67 men per nine innings pitched.

Radatz declined quickly in 1966, 1967 and 1969, his last three years in the major leagues, winning a total of only three games.

In his phenomenal career, "The Monster," who was six-feet-six and weighed 230 pounds, was so impressive as a relief pitcher that he was named an All-Star and pitched in the 1963 and 1964 All-Star games. He pitched the last two innings in the American League's losing effort in 1963, 5-3. He was the losing pitcher in the 1964 game. In that game, he pitched two scoreless innings to hold the American League's 4-3 lead. Then, in the ninth inning, Willie Mays walked, stole second and scored the tying run on a single. With two out Johnny Callison hit a two-on home run, making Radatz and the American League the losers, 7-4.

Pete Runnels

Pete Runnels was an all-around infielder for 14 years in the big leagues. His career began with the Washington Senators and he played five years for the Red Sox, from 1958 through 1962. While with the Sox he won two batting championships in 1960 and 1962, and ended with a career batting average of .291. Notably, while with the Red Sox, he batted over .310 every year. He also had 20 or more doubles every year with the team. In the 1962 All-Star game, Pete, representing the Red Sox, hit a home run in the

Infielder Pete Runnels won the American League batting championships for the Red Sox twice in the 1960s. (Baseball Hall of Fame Library. Cooperstown, N.Y.).

American League's 9-4 win over the National League.

Runnels was versatile. He played three years at second base and then two years at first base with the Red Sox. He began his career at shortstop with the Washington Senators and ended at first base with the Houston Astros. He led the league in fielding with a .986 average while playing second base for the Red Sox in 1960. In 1961 with the Red Sox, he led the league in fielding at first base with a .995 average.

In 1966 Runnels was the Red Sox manager for 16 games.

Gene Stephens

Gene Stephens was known principally as Ted Williams' defensive substitute in his eight years with the Red Sox. He had one large hitting moment. In 1953, batting for the Sox in a 17-run seventh inning, he got three hits, a record never paralleled in twentieth century major league baseball.

In all, Stephens played for the Sox from 1952 into a part of 1960. He had a 12-year big league career, playing with three teams after he left the Red Sox and finishing his career in 1964. He had a career batting average of .240.

Stephens, in his career, only once had more than about 240 at bats a season. He was clearly a part-time player and, for a few years, was a regular pinch-hitter as well as a field substitute for Ted Williams. He managed to be in more than 100 games for five of his 12 seasons. He played four of these five seasons with Boston, and the fifth was shared between the Sox and the Baltimore Orioles. It was in this shared season, when he was traded to the Orioles, that he had his most career doubles, 15, career home runs, 7, and scored his career high in runs, 47.

Frank Sullivan

Frank Sullivan pitched the first eight of his 11 years in the "bigs" with the Boston Red Sox, from 1953 through 1960. He led the league in wins with 18 in 1955, starting a league leading 35 games and pitching a league-leading 260 innings. In his Red Sox career Sullivan won 90 games and lost 80.

Sullivan, who was an intimidating 6'6½", 215 lb. pitcher, won 97 and lost 100 in his 11-year career. Clearly, his "career year" was 1955 when he led the Red Sox with an 18-13 record

An eight-year member of the Red Sox, Frank Sullivan led the league in wins in 1955 with 18. (Baseball Hall of Fame Library. Cooperstown, N.Y.).

and a .581 winning percentage. He also had four other seasons in which he had double digit wins in a five-year period from 1954 through 1958. He had a respectable earned run average in each of these seasons, never exceeding 3.57 and twice he was under 3.00. He was a workhorse pitcher in this period with 200 or more innings pitched five times (a bit of a stretch because in 1958 he actually pitched 199 1/3 innings). He struck out more than 100 batters a season from 1953-1959. Sullivan was a prominent pitcher on the Red Sox staff during the 1950s.

Sammy White

Sammy White was the Red Sox catcher from late in 1951 through 1959, a total of nine years. He had a lifetime batting average of .262. He played briefly in the last two years of his career in the National League.

White's best year at bat was 1959 when he batted .284. In his early years, from 1952 through 1955, he showed some power. In each of these four years, he batted over .260, had from 20 to 34 doubles and from 10 to 14 home runs. He had over 100 hits each of these seasons and drove in from nearly 50 to 75 runs. He was a good fielding catcher with a .984 lifetime fielding average.

White was a productive catcher with the Red Sox, though the team never finished above third place when he was with them. He had an 11-year big league career.

Earl Wilson

Earl Wilson was the second black player to play for the Red Sox. He came up with the Sox in 1959, played six-plus years for them, and played the second half of his career predominantly with the Detroit Tigers. Wilson was a fastballer who sometimes had control problems. He led the league in giving bases on balls in 1963 and had walked even more batters the previous year. He did, however, pitch a no-hitter for the Red Sox in 1962. Wilson was also a good power hitter, hitting five home runs or more in a season four times while playing as a pitcher. He ended his

Earl Wilson was not only a pitcher, but also could swing a bat, hitting five or more home runs in a season four times in his career. (Baseball Hall of Fame Library. Cooperstown, N.Y.).

Sammy White was the catcher for the Red Sox for nine years, batting .284 in 1959. (Baseball Hall of Fame Library. Cooperstown, N.Y.).

career with 35 home runs and, as a pitcher, won 121 games and lost 109.

Wilson never won more than 13 games a season for the Red Sox. However, in the year he was traded to Detroit he won 18 games, 14 with the Tigers, and in the following year, 1967, he and Jim Lonborg led the league with 22 wins. It was, coincidentally, the year the Red Sox won the pennant. In fact, though Wilson started and lost the only game he pitched in the 1968 World Series, the Tigers won the world championship and Wilson had his World Series ring.

Pennants, Near Misses and World Series 1967-1980

Mike Andrews

| b. Jul. 9, 1943 | Los Angeles, Calif. | Bats Right | Throws Right |
| | 6'3" 195 lbs. | Red Sox | 1966-1970 |

Juan Beniquez

| b. May 13, 1950 | San Sebastian, P.R. | Bats Right | Throws Right |
| | 5'11" 150 lbs. | Red Sox | 1971-1975 |

Rick Burleson

| b. Apr. 29, 1951 | Lynwood, Calif. | Bats Right | Throws Right |
| | 5'10" 165 lbs. | Red Sox | 1974-1980 |

Bill Campbell

| b. Aug. 9, 1948 | Highland Park, Mich. | Pitches Right | Bats Left |
| | 6'3" 185 lbs. | Red Sox | 1977-1981 |

Bernie Carbo

| b. Aug. 5, 1947 | Detroit, Mich. | Bats Left | Throws Right |
| | 5'11" 173 lbs. | Red Sox | 1974-1976; 1977-1978 |

Reggie Cleveland

| b. May 23, 1948 | Saskatchewan, CAN. | Pitches Right | Bats Right |
| | 6'1" 195 lbs. | Red Sox | 1974-1978 |

Cecil Cooper

| b. Dec. 20, 1949 | Brenham, Texas | Bats Left | Throws Left |
| | 6'2" 165 lbs. | Red Sox | 1971-1976 |

Ray Culp

| b. Aug. 6, 1941 | Elgin, Texas | Bats Right | Throws Right |
| | 6' 200 lbs. | Red Sox | 1968-1973 |

Dick Drago

| b. Jun. 25, 1945 | Toledo, Ohio | Pitches Right | Bats Right |
| | 6'1" 190 lbs. | Red Sox | 1974-1975; 1978-1980 |

Dennis Eckersley

| b. Oct. 3, 1954 | Oakland, Calif. | Pitches Right | Bats Right |
| | 6'2" 190 lbs. | Red Sox | 1978-1984; 98 |

Carlton Fisk

| b. Dec. 26, 1947 | Bellows Falls, Vermont | Bats Right | Throws Right |
| | 6'3" 200 lbs. | Red Sox | 1969-1980 |

Doug Griffin

| b. Jun. 4, 1947 | South Gate, Calif. | Bats Right | Throws Right |
| | 6' 160 lbs. | Red Sox | 1971-1977 |

Butch Hobson

| b. Aug. 7, 1951 | Tuscaloosa, Ala. | Bats Right | Throws Right |
| | 6'1" 193 lbs. | Red Sox | 1975-1980 |

Bill Lee

| b. Dec. 28, 1946 | Burbank, Calif. | Pitches Left | Throws Left |
| | 6'3" 205 lbs. | Red Sox | 1975-1980 |

Jim Lonborg

| b. Apr. 16, 1942 | Santa Maria, Calif. | Pitches Right | Bats Right |
| | 6'5" 200 lbs. | Red Sox | 1965-1971 |

Sparky Lyle

| b. Jul. 22, 1944 | DuBois, Pa. | Pitches Left | Bats Left |
| | 6'1" 182 lbs. | Red Sox | 1967-1971 |

Rick Miller

| b. Apr. 19, 1948 | Grand Rapids, Mich. | Bats Left | Throws Left |
| | 6' 175 lbs. | Red Sox | 1971-1977; 1981-1985 |

Roger Moret

| b. Sep. 16, 1949 | Guayama, P.R. | Pitches Left | Switch Hitter |
| | 6'4" 170 lbs. | Red Sox | 1970-1975 |

Rico Petrocelli

| b. Jun. 27, 1943 | Brooklyn, N.Y. | Bats Right | Throws Right |
| | 6' 175 lbs. | Red Sox | 1963-1976 |

Jose Santiago

| b. Aug. 15, 1940 | Juana Diaz P.R. | Pitches Right | Bats Right |
| | 6'2" 185 lbs. | Red Sox | 1966-1970 |

George Scott

| b. May 23, 1944 | Greenville, Miss. | Bats Right | Throws Right |
| | 6'2" 200 lbs. | Red Sox | 1966-1971; 1977-1979 |

Reggie Smith

| b. Apr. 2, 1945 | Shreveport, La. | Switch Hitter | Throws Right |
| | 6' 180 lbs. | Red Sox | 1966-1973 |

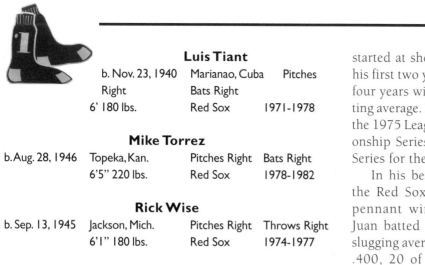

Luis Tiant
b. Nov. 23, 1940   Marianao, Cuba   Pitches
Right   Bats Right
6' 180 lbs.   Red Sox   1971-1978

Mike Torrez
b. Aug. 28, 1946   Topeka, Kan.   Pitches Right   Bats Right
                6'5" 220 lbs.   Red Sox   1978-1982

Rick Wise
b. Sep. 13, 1945   Jackson, Mich.   Pitches Right   Throws Right
                6'1" 180 lbs.   Red Sox   1974-1977

Mike Andrews

Mike Andrews, after starting his major league career with the Red Sox briefly in 1966, became the Red Sox regular second baseman for four years, 1967 through 1970. He was traded to the Chicago White Sox for Luis Aparicio, then late in his long Hall of Fame career.

Mike had a lifetime batting average of .258. In his four regular years with the Red Sox he never had less than 20 doubles a season and, in the last two years, he showed more power with 15 home runs in 1969 and 17 in 1970.

Andrews and Jerry Adair shared second-base duties in the 1967 World Series. Andrews played in five games, pinch hitting in two of them. His Series batting average was .308. He had four singles.

Andrews ended his career in Oakland. He played briefly in the 1973 League Championship Series, and he played in the 1973 World Series with the champion Athletics. He made two critical errors of the nine errors made by the winning Oakland team in the Series. Flamboyant and arrogant owner Charlie Finley scapegoated Andrews for his play and embarrassed him by dropping him from the team.

Second baseman Mike Andrews hugs his boys, Mark (left) and Michael. (Boston Public Library, Print Department).

Juan Beniquez

Juan Beniquez, from Puerto Rico, began his 17-year career with the Red Sox though his stellar years were with the California Angels. In a career beginning in 1971 he started at shortstop for the Sox but played outfield after his first two years in the big leagues. He batted .274 in his four years with the Red Sox, the same as his lifetime batting average. He played in the 1975 League Championship Series and World Series for the Red Sox.

In his best year with the Red Sox, 1975, the pennant winning year, Juan batted .291, had a slugging average just over .400, 20 of his 74 hits were for extra bases, and he was also used as a designated hitter and a pinch hitter. As a pinch hitter, he had five hits in eight at bats.

Beniquez played as a designated hitter in the League Championship Series of 1975 and batted .250. In the World Series that year he played in the outfield in two games and had one hit in eight at bats for the entire Series.

Juan Beniquez played on Boston's 1975 A.L. championship team and in the World Series that year. (Boston Red Sox).

Beniquez was traded seven times in his career, the first time when he went from the Red Sox to the Texas Rangers for Hall of Fame pitcher Ferguson Jenkins who was in his 12th year in his career. In Beniquez' best career years, 1981-1985, with the California Angels, he batted over .300 in three consecutive years.

Rick Burleson

Rick Burleson was the Red Sox shortstop for seven of his 13 big league years, from 1974 through 1980. He was a steady fielder and in 1979 won the Gold Glove award for his play at shortstop. He led the league in putouts as a shortstop in 1977 and in putouts, assists and double plays at the position in 1980. He was the anchor of the double-play combination as his second basemen were Denny Doyle in 1977, Jerry Remy in 1978 and 1979, and Dave Stapleton in 1980.

Burleson batted a lifetime .273, never hit .300 for a season, and his highest average with the Red Sox was .293 in 1977. He played in two American

Shortstop Rick Burleson played seven seasons for Boston, winning a Gold Glove in 1979. (Baseball Hall of Fame Library, Cooperstown, N.Y.).

The Red Sox Encyclopedia

League Championship Series, in 1975 with Boston and in 1986 with the California Angels. He also played in the 1975 World Series with the Red Sox. He batted .444 in the three games ALCS won by the Red Sox over the Oakland Athletics, and .292 in a losing World Series against the Cincinnati Reds the same year.

For the first seven years of his career, all with Boston, Burleson hit over 20 doubles a year. He had good speed and a good batting eye. 67 of his 72 career steals were with the Red Sox, and he averaged 45 walks a year. He was a productive hitter and an even better fielder.

Bill Campbell

Bill Campbell was a relief pitcher for the Red Sox for five years, 1977 through 1981. He made 92 relief appearances and started no games. He led the league in saves in 1977, with 31 for the Red Sox. He had a 15-year career, playing primarily with the Minnesota Twins and the Red Sox. In his last six years he played with five other teams.

Bill's best years were his last with Minnesota, in 1976, and his first with Boston, in 1977. In those two years, he pitched only in relief in 147 games. He had a 17-5 record in 1976, leading the league with a .773 winning percentage. His record in 1977 was 13-9. He had 20 saves in 1976 for the Twins, and he led the league with his 31 saves for the Red Sox in 1977. In remarkably similar years, he walked 62 in 1976, and 60 in 1977. He struck out 115 in 1976 and 114 in 1977. In those years, he was one of the top relief pitchers in the American League along with Sparky Lyle, who had been traded to the Yankees by the Red Sox, and Dave LaRoche of Cleveland and then California.

Reliever Bill Campbell led the American League in saves with 31 in 1977. (Baseball Hall of Fame Library, Cooperstown, N.Y.).

Bernie Carbo

Bernie Carbo had a 12-year career during which he played twice for the Red Sox. He hit one of the most dramatic home runs in World Series history in 1975 when he pinch hit in the eighth inning of the sixth game and slammed a three-run home run to tie the game between the Sox and the Cincinnati Reds. This set the stage for Carlton Fisk's even more dramatic and history-making home run in the 12th inning to win the game for the Red Sox. Carbo also pinch hit a home run in Game 3 of the same Series but the Reds eventually won that game and ultimately the World Championship. Carbo played two full seasons and two 17-game seasons with the Red Sox. He spent much of his early career as an outfielder with the Cincinnati Reds, prior to coming to the Sox. Playing with six teams in all he achieved a .264 lifetime batting average.

Bernie's best career year was in 1971, his first year with the Cincinnati Reds. He played in 125 games, the most he played in any season, batted .310 and hit 21 home runs. His best year for Boston was in 1977 when he batted .289 in 86 games and hit 15 home

Bernie Carbo hit an eighth-inning pinch-hit home run for the Red Sox in the sixth game of the 1975 World Series. (Baseball Hall of Fame Library. Cooperstown, N.Y.).

runs. However, Bernie will be remembered primarily for his heroics in the 1975 World Series with the Red Sox.

Reggie Cleveland

Reggie Cleveland was a pitcher with the Red Sox for four years and the start of another. He was 13-9 for the Red Sox in the pennant winning year, 1975, and his winning percentage of .591 that year was the best in his career. He won a total of 105 games in his career, never more than 14 in any one season, and he lost a total of 106 games. His early success was with the St. Louis Cardinals, his first team for whom he pitched 116 games in four years, winning 40 and losing 41. His next four years, with the Red Sox, he pitched in 150 games, winning 46 and losing 41. Primarily a starting pitcher, he also pitched briefly in relief for the Red Sox.

Reggie started Game 2 of the American League Championship Series in 1975, when Boston swept Oakland in three games. He pitched five innings and left with the score tied, 3-3. Roger Moret won the game in relief, pitching the sixth inning when the Red Sox scored the winning run. Reggie also started Game 5 of the World Series, pitching five innings, and the Red Sox lost the game to the Reds, 6-2. Reggie pitched in relief in two other

Reggie Cleveland posted a 13-9 record in Boston's pennant-winning season of 1975. (Baseball Hall of Fame Library, Cooperstown, N.Y.).

World Series games but ended with a 6.75 earned run average in a total of 6 2/3 innings in the Series.

Cecil Cooper

Cecil Cooper was a first baseman for the Red Sox for six years at the beginning of his 17-year career, from 1971 through 1976. He played the rest of his career as a first baseman with the Milwaukee Braves. Cooper was a slugger who had his best years with the Braves, leading the league twice in runs batted in. His lifetime batting average was .298 and he hit 241 home runs and drove in 1,125. His best season with the Red Sox was the pennant winning year of 1975 and he hit .311. In the League Championship Series that year he batted .400 with four hits in ten at bats. In the World Series he batted .053.

Cecil Cooper was Boston's starting first baseman from 1971-76. (Baseball Hall of Fame Library, Cooperstown, N.Y.).

Beginning in 1975, Cooper hit at least ten home runs a season for 12 consecutive seasons. However, only the first three of these years were with the Red Sox. He had four out of five seasons, 1979 through 1983, when he batted in over 100 runs a season but these were all with Milwaukee. His best R.B.I. year with the Red Sox was in 1976 when he had 78. He had 11 straight seasons in which he hit at least 22 doubles but he was with the Red Sox only in the first year of this streak. Cooper was traded to Milwaukee after 1976 for George "Boomer" Scott, who replaced him at first base, and Bernie Carbo. Both Scott and Carbo were on their second tour of duty with the Red Sox.

Ray Culp

Ray Culp pitched six years for the Red Sox, from 1968 through 1973. In four of those years he won a total of 64 games. He had an 11-year career.

Culp, in his 11 years, won 122 games and lost 101. Seventy-one of these wins were with the Red Sox and twice with the Sox in 1969 and 1970 he won 17 games. In 1968 he was second to Denny McLain of the Tigers, who had a 31-6 record in winning percentage. Culp had 16 wins, six losses and a .727 winning percentage. Culp's earned run average in 1968 was 2.91, leading Red Sox starting pitchers, but well behind five pitchers in the league who were under 2.00. Leading was Luis Tiant of Cleveland with a 1.60 E.R.A. Tiant was later a star with the Red Sox. In

1970 and 1971, especially, Culp was a workhorse pitcher. In 1970 he started 33 games, completed 15, pitched 251 innings and had a career-high 197 strikeouts. In 1971, he started 35 games, completed 12, pitched 242 innings and had 151 strikeouts. In those two years he went 31-30.

Dick Drago

Dick Drago pitched five years for the Red Sox, 1974 through 1975 and again from 1978 through 1980. He saved 15 games in 1975. He won ten

Ray Culp won 71 games for the Red Sox from 1968-73. (Baseball Hall of Fame Library. Cooperstown, N.Y.).

games in relief in 1979 and had 13 saves. He pitched in the 1975 League Championship Series and in the World Series. He lost one World Series game in relief. Drago pitched for 13 years in the American League, mostly with the Kansas City Royals.

Drago started his career with Kansas City and in five years went 61-70. In his five full years with the Sox, Drago won 30 and lost 29, of which 22 were won and 16 lost in relief. He became a reliever during his first year with the Sox.

In the 1975 ALCS, swept in three games by the Red Sox against the Athletics, Drago pitched in both the second and third games and earned a save in each. In the World Series, Drago pitched in two games. Drago pitched three scoreless innings in relief, the ninth, tenth, and eleventh innings, in the dramatic Game 6 won by Carlton Fisk's home run in the twelfth inning. Drago lost Game 2 when he relieved Bill Lee after Cincinnati's Bench doubled to start the ninth inning with the Red Sox leading, 2 to 1. Drago retired the next two batters but then Concepcion of the Reds singled Bench home to tie the game. Concepcion stole second and scored the winning run when Ken Griffey doubled off Drago. The final score in Game 2 was 3-2, Reds.

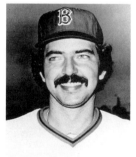

Dick Drago earned two saves in the 1975 American League Championships Series. (Baseball Hall of Fame Library, Cooperstown, N.Y.).

Dennis Eckersley

"The Eck" became the premier relief pitcher in baseball after he left the Red Sox, most notably during his continuing career with the Oakland Athletics. In the unusual odyssey, Eckersley began his career in 1975 as a starting pitcher with the Cleveland Indians, then was traded as a starter to the Boston Red Sox and subsequently went to the Chicago Cubs. He began his spectacular relief career with the Oakland Athletics in 1987, just before Oakland's three-year dynasty, and, after ten years with the A's, signed with the St. Louis Cardinals. For 1998, in his 24th big league year and at age 44, he returned as a relief pitcher with the Boston Red Sox. He won four and lost one for the Sox in 1998 and it was his last big-league year.

Dennis Eckersley played for the Red Sox from 1978-84. He returned to the Red Sox in 1998 for his 24th career season. (Baseball Hall of Fame Library, Cooperstown, N.Y.).

Eckersley was with the Red Sox from 1978 through 1983 and in part of 1984. Prior to coming to the Sox he had pitched a no-hitter for Cleveland, in 1977. In his first year with Boston he won 20 games and had a 2.99 earned run average. He emerged as the team's leading pitcher. He also won the most games as a starting pitcher for the Sox in 1979, with 17 victories. All told, he won 84 games as a Sox starter in his six-plus years with the team.

Eckersley's spectacular relief pitching with Oakland under manager Tony LaRussa is worth noting. In five of his years with the Athletics, from 1988 through 1992, he had 220 saves and generally pitched in 60 or more games each season. He led the league in saves in 1988 with 45 and in 1992 with 51. In the five-year period he never had higher than a 2.96 earned run average and in 1990 his E.R.A. was an exceptional 0.61. He earned saves in each of Oakland's four wins in the American League Championship series in 1988. In 1992, with his monumental 51 saves, he was named both the Cy Young winner and the league's Most Valuable Player. After the year 2001, Eckersley ranks third all-time in saves, behind Lee Smith and John Franco.

Carlton "Pudge" Fisk

"Pudge" Fisk, a native New Englander, was another very popular player with the Red Sox. He probably will be known forever for his dramatic, 12th-inning game-winning home run which he "directed into fair territory" in the sixth game of the 1975 World Series. There is an oft-printed news photo of his waving the ball to stay in fair territory inside the left field pole in Fenway Park as he was running down the first base line with the game-win-

ning blow. Fisk had an estimable 24-year career as a catcher beginning in 1969, his first 11 years with the Red Sox and the last 13 with the Chicago White Sox, ending in 1993. He was elected to the Hall of Fame in 2000. He is one of the great catchers of his era and he played against another great one, Johnny Bench, of Cincinnati in the 1975 World Series. He played 2,499 big league games and, as a power hitter, set the lifetime record for catchers with 351 home runs. He hit 376 home runs over all, some as a designated hitter. He was also a fine defensive catcher and handler of pitchers.

Fisk began his career with the Red Sox in grand fashion. In his first full year, 1972, he was named American League Rookie of the Year. He batted .293, led the league in triples and hit 20 home runs. He was also the Gold Glove award winner coincidentally in a year when Jim Kaat, then pitching for the Minnesota Twins, was winning the award in one of the 14 consecutive seasons in which he was honored for his fielding skills. "Pudge" had a lifetime batting average of .269 but his single best year was

A native New Englander, Carlton Fisk won American League Rookie of the Year honors for Boston in 1972, his first full season in the Majors. He was elected to the Hall of Fame in 2000. (Baseball Hall of Fame Library. Cooperstown, N.Y.).

in 1977 with the Sox when he hit .315 with 26 home runs and 102 runs batted in. He also had a great year for Chicago in 1985 when he hit 37 home runs.

Fisk played in two American League Championship Series, one with the White Sox. He played with the Red Sox in the 1975 ALCS and in the World Series that year. He batted .417 in the three-game ALCS won by the Red Sox. He batted .240 in the World Series but his sixth game home run is unforgettable. He also had a home run in the second game of the Series when a record six home runs were hit. The game was won by the Cincinnati Reds, 6 to 5.

Doug Griffin

Doug Griffin was a Red Sox second baseman for seven of his eight big league years from 1971 through 1977. He had a lifetime .245 batting average and one at bat for the Red Sox in the 1975 World Series. (Denny Doyle was the regular second baseman in that Series.) Griffin's best hitting year was in 1974 when he hit .266.

Doug Griffin was the Red Sox's starting second baseman from 1971-74. (Baseball Hall of Fame Library, Cooperstown, N.Y.).

Griffin was the Red Sox regular second baseman for four years, from 1971 through 1974. He shared the position with Denny Doyle in 1975, who then became the regular second baseman for the following two years. In 1975, when Griffin and Doyle shared second base, Griffin was also used as a pinch hitter and batted .500 with eight pinch hits in 16 at bats.

Clell "Butch" Hobson

"Butch" Hobson played in eight seasons, mostly with the Red Sox and one year each with the California Angels and the New York Yankees. He was a good power hitter with 75 home runs and 85 doubles in a three-year period with the Red Sox, but he also led the league, striking out 162 times in 159 games in 1977. Hobson, a third baseman, made 43 errors and fielded under .900 (.899) in 1978. This was the first time since 1916 that a major league regular player fielded under .900. Hobson, in 1992, became manager of the Red Sox and remained so through 1994. A University of Alabama football player early in his athletic career, playing under the legendary Paul "Bear" Bryant, he was known for his frequent use of football idioms in inspiring and directing his baseball players.

Hobson had a lifetime batting average of .248 and his best year for average was in 1977 for the Red Sox when he batted .265. That year he had his best slugging average, .489, and hit a career-high 33 doubles and 30 home runs. He also batted in a career-high 112 runs. Nineteen seventy-nine was also a good year for him. He hit .261 and had a slugging average of .496 with 26 doubles and 28 home runs. He batted in 93 runs. His production slipped in 1980 and he was traded to the California Angels.

A power-hitting third baseman in the 1970s, Butch Hobson later managed the Red Sox. (Baseball Hall of Fame Library, Cooperstown, N.Y.).

"Spaceman" Bill Lee

Bill Lee was mostly known for his behavior idiosyncrasies though he was also a good pitcher with the Red Sox. His biggest years were with the Sox from 1973 through 1975, when he won 17 games each year. He was with the Red Sox for ten years before going on to the Montreal Expos for four more years. "The Spaceman" was an attention-getting counterculture symbol. He was dedicated to yoga, there were allusions to marijuana and other illegal drug ingestion, and he generally spoke and acted in unconventional ways. His teammate, third baseman John Kennedy, was reported to have given him the name "Spaceman." Lee was something of a provocateur with his statements, at one time claiming to throw spitballs, deprecatingly calling short-statured Red Sox manager Don Zimmer a gerbil, and starting fights with other players. He notably injured his pitching arm and shoulder in such a fight with Yankee third baseman Graig Nettles. Lee, though popular in some quarters, wore out his welcome with the Red Sox and was traded to Montreal, where he had one good year as a starter and one as a reliever.

With the Red Sox, Lee's best season for winning average was 1975 when he won 17 and lost nine for a .654 winning percentage. On the other hand, in 1973 when he won 17 and lost 11, he had a career-best earned run average of 2.74. This was the same earned run average he had in 1971 when he won nine and lost two. Lee, in his career won 119 games and lost 90.

Bill Lee won 17 games each year for the Red Sox from 1973-75. (Baseball Hall of Fame Library, Cooperstown, N.Y.).

The Spaceman started Game 2 of the 1975 World Series and pitched eight good innings, though Cincinnati eventually won the game, 3-2. Lee also started the final game of the Series, Game 7, for the Red Sox and pitched 6⅓ innings. The Red Sox eventually lost this game, 4-3. Lee had no decisions in the World Series but emerged with a 3.14 earned run average for his 14 1/3 innings pitched.

Jim Lonborg

Jim Lonborg pitched the first seven years of his 15-year career with the Red Sox, beginning in 1965. He ended his career in 1979 after pitching his last seven seasons with the Philadelphia Phillies. He was the memorable pitcher in the Red Sox pennant year of 1967 when he won 22 games, ten more than any other Red Sox pitcher that year. He led the league with 39 starts and he also led with 246 strikeouts. Lonborg was named the Cy Young winner in 1967. He, along with Carl Yastrzemski, carried the Red

Jim Lonborg won the Cy Young Award for Boston in 1967. (Baseball Hall of Fame Library, Cooperstown, N.Y.).

Sox to the pennant. It was the year in which Yaz hit for the Triple Crown and was voted M.V.P. Lonborg performed well in the 1967 World Series against the St. Louis Cardinals. He won two games and lost one in his three starts in the seven-game series won by the Cardinals. Only Bob Gibson, the mainstay of the Cardinals' pitching staff and a subsequent Hall of Famer, did better, starting and winning three games in which he gave up a total of only three runs. Lonborg pitched and won a one-hit shutout in the second game of the Series, retiring the first 20 batters he faced. He also won the fifth game with a 3-hitter, 3 to 1. With two days' rest between starts insufficient for him, he lasted only six innings in the seventh and final game, and the Cardinals won 7-2.

Lonborg did not have another year with the Red Sox in which he won more than ten games. He was traded to Milwaukee in 1972, and after one year went on to pitch for the Phillies.

Albert "Sparky" Lyle

"Sparky" Lyle started his career with the Red Sox, but made his reputation as a league premier relief pitcher for the New York Yankees in the 1970s. He pitched five years for the Red Sox, 1967 through 1971, accumulating 69 saves. He is also notable as the writer of *The Bronx Zoo*, a book about the zany New York Yankees and their clubhouse

atmosphere under the volatile managership of Billy Martin, the volatile ownership of George Steinbrenner and the outspoken behavior of Reggie Jackson.

Lyle, with the Red Sox, won 22 and lost 17 in relief from 1967 through 1971. His best year with the Sox was in 1969 when he won eight, lost three, had 17 saves and an earned run average of 2.54. He had 20 saves in 1970 and 16 saves and six wins in 1971. Though he was with the Red Sox in the pennant-winning

Sparky Lyle had 17 saves and a 2.54 E.R.A. for Boston in 1969. (Baseball Hall of Fame Library, Cooperstown, N.Y.).

year of 1967, it was his rookie year and he did not pitch in the World Series.

Lyle's great years as a reliever with the Yankees were in 1972 when he led the league with 35 saves, in 1973 when he had 27, in 1976 when he again led the league with 23 saves, and in 1977 when he had 26. He appeared in two World Series, with the Yankees.

Rick Miller

Rick Miller, an outfielder, played 12 of his 15 big-league years with the Red Sox. He started his career with the Sox in 1971, was traded to the California Angels in 1978, and returned to the Red Sox for his final five years from 1981 through 1985. He had a lifetime .269 batting average and played for the Red Sox in the 1975 World Series.

Rick batted .333 for the Sox in his first year, 1971, when he played in 15 games. He again batted .333 with the Sox in his final season, 1985, when he played in 41 games. In between, in 13 years, his best year for average was in 1981 with the Red Sox when he batted .293. Rick had three straight years with the Angels when he had more than 100 hits. He achieved this twice with the Red Sox, once in his first tour of duty when he had 115 in 1973, and once in his second tour of duty when he had 104 in 1982. Rick was also a base stealer early in his career with the Red Sox, when he stole more than 10 bases a year four times. Rick played in three games in the 1975 World Series for the Red Sox. He was used mostly for defense and had a total of only two at bats.

Outfielder Rick Miller played 12 of his 15 Major League seasons with Boston. (Baseball Hall of Fame Library, Cooperstown, N.Y.).

Roger Moret

Roger Moret was a pitcher for the Red Sox for six of his nine big league years, from 1970 through 1975. In this time he won 41 games for the Sox and lost 18. He had two notably good years, in 1973 when his record was 13 wins and two losses, and

in 1975 when he had 14 wins and three losses. In both seasons he had a winning percentage well over .800. In both seasons while he had the highest winning percentage in the league, he did not qualify for league honors because he had too few appearances. 1975, the Red Sox pennant winning year, was also a year in which Moret pitched in a career-high 36 games and he had four of his 14 victories as a reliever.

Roger Moret won the second game of the 1975 ALCS with one inning of relief work. (Baseball Hall of Fame Library, Cooperstown, N.Y.).

Moret won the second game of the ALCS in 1975 with one inning of relief pitching. This was Game 2 which the Red Sox won, 6-3, in their three-game sweep of Oakland. Moret also pitched a total of $1^2/_3$ innings in two games in the World Series of '75 but had no decisions and gave up a total of two hits and three bases on balls.

Rico Petrocelli

Rico Petrocelli played his entire career at shortstop and third base for the Red Sox, 13 years, from 1963 through 1976. He was a regular for six years first as a shortstop. He then moved on to third base to make room for Luis Aparicio, a future Hall of Famer who played three years with the Red Sox. Rico played third base for six seasons, sharing the last season at that position with Butch Hobson.

He led the league in fielding percentage at shortstop in 1968 and 1969, and led the league in fielding at third base in 1971 with a .976 percentage.

Petrocelli batted a lifetime .251. His best year for average was 1969 when he hit .297. For three years, in the period 1967 through 1971, he hit nearly 100 home runs with a high of 40 in

Rico Petrocelli played his entire 13-year career with Boston, batting .251 as a third baseman and shortstop. (Baseball Hall of Fame Library, Cooperstown, N.Y.).

1969. In these three years he also drove in 289 runs.

Rico played in both the 1967 and 1975 postseason for the Red Sox. In 1967 he hit two home runs in Game 6 of the World Series, helping the Red Sox win the game against the St. Louis Cardinals, 8 to 4. However, Bob Gibson pitched and won Game 7, 7-2, giving St. Louis the World Championship.

Rico also hit a home run in the American League Championship Series in 1975 when the Red Sox swept the Oakland Athletics. In the 1975 World Series Rico batted .308 though the Cincinnati Reds won another close Series lost by the Red Sox, four games to three.

Jose Santiago

Jose Santiago, of Juana Diaz, Puerto Rico, pitched five years for the Boston Red Sox, from 1966 through 1970. Santiago had a notably good year in 1966 when he won nine, lost four and had an earned run average of 2.25. He had also won 12 and lost four in 1967 when his E.R.A. was 3.59. He started and lost two games for the Red Sox in the 1967 World Series against the St. Louis Cardinals.

Santiago, in his eight-year big league career, had 34 wins and 29 losses, mostly all with the Red Sox. He started his career with Kansas City, for whom his record over three seasons was one win and six losses. Santiago started a total of 57 games for the Red Sox, all in three seasons from 1966 through 1968. He was also a key reliever in 1967 when he won eight of his 12 victories in relief and had five saves. In 1966 and 1967, two of his

Jose Santiago started the first game of the 1967 World Series for the Red Sox, losing to Bob Gibson. (Baseball Hall of Fame Library, Cooperstown, N.Y.).

three effective years, he struck out more than 100 batters a year.

In the 1967 World Series, a year and a Series in which Jim Lonborg was the Red Sox star pitcher, Santiago started and lost Game 1 to the Cardinals' Bob Gibson, 2-1, albeit that he pitched seven good innings. He also started and lost Game 4, again against Gibson. This time the score was 6-0 and he lasted only 2/3 of an inning. He also pitched in relief of Lonborg in Game 7 but had no decision as the Cardinals' Gibson beat tired starter Jim Lonborg and won the Series.

George "Boomer" Scott

"Boomer" played his first six years with the Red Sox from 1966 through 1971 and returned to the team for his last three big league years, 1977 through 1979. The last year, 1979, he played over 100 games but split the season among Boston, the Kansas City Royals and the New York Yankees. In between his early and late years, he played five years with the Milwaukee Brewers.

A popular figure in Boston, Boomer Scott won three Gold Gloves for Boston at first base. (Baseball Hall of Fame Library, Cooperstown, N.Y.).

Scott was a power hitter and fine fielder. He was a large, popular figure who played mostly at first base. He was a threat to hit the long ball and his powerful swing could produce a dramatic home run, or a strike out. Boomer had a lifetime .268 batting average. He hit over 150 home runs in his tours of duty with the Red Sox, his best Red Sox year being near the end of his career when he hit 33 "dingers." However, he also had some powerful home run hitting years with the Milwaukee Brewers—he hit 36 with them in 1975 to win the league home run title. His best years in runs batted in were with the Brewers and he led the league in R.B.I.s the year he won the home run title. On the negative side, in his first year with the Red Sox he led the league in strikeouts with 152 and for ten of his 14 years he had over 90 strikeouts a season. For his size, six-feet-two and weighing 200 pounds, George was fast. Interestingly, he stole ten bases in his second Red Sox season and 16 bases in his first Milwaukee season.

Scott was a Gold Glove award first baseman three times with the Red Sox and four times with the Brewers. He played both at first and third base for two years with the Red Sox, in 1969 and 1970.

Scott played in the 1967 World Series for the Sox but hit only .231. He hit a home run with a runner on base in the 1977 All-Star game but the National League won, 7 to 5.

Reggie Smith

Reggie Smith was a powerful switch hitter in his 17-year big league career from 1966 through 1982. He started his career with the Boston Red Sox, played eight years, and then went on to play for the St. Louis Cardinals and for many years with the Los Angeles Dodgers. He ended his 17-year career with one year with the San Francisco Giants. His lifetime batting average was .287 and he hit 314 home runs and 363 doubles. In his third full season with the Red Sox, Reggie won the league batting title with a .309 average. In each of his seven seasons with the Red

Sox he hit twenty three or more doubles, leading the league in doubles in 1968 and 1971. For a six-year period from 1969 through 1974, including five years with the Red Sox and one with the St. Louis Cardinals, Reggie hit more than 20 home runs. He also was a good base runner and in 1968 stole 22 bases.

Smith, along with Carl Yastrzemski, was a Gold Glove award winner in 1968. He played center field and led the league in putouts at that position. He was a durable outfielder and ended up playing in nearly 2,000 games.

Smith made an appearance in a divisional play-off game in three league championship series, all with the Los Angeles Dodgers. He also played in four

In his third full season with the Red Sox, Reggie Smith won the American League batting title with a .309 average. (Baseball Hall of Fame Library. Cooperstown, N.Y.).

World Series, one with the Red Sox in 1967 and three with the Dodgers in 1977, 1978 and 1981. Reggie hit two home runs in Boston's losing effort to the Cardinals in 1967. In the Series he played with the Dodgers in 1977 he hit three home runs and drove in five runs, although the Dodgers lost the Series to the Yankees. In the 1978 Series he hit another home run in the Dodgers' repeat losing performance against the Yankees. Reggie hit a home run in the 1974 All-Star game, representing the St. Louis Cardinals in the National League's defeat of the American League, 7-2

Reggie, a force to be reckoned with on the playing field, also was frequently outspoken in taking positions on issues for himself and other players.

Luis Tiant

"El Tiante" was a very popular Boston player. He was the dominant Red Sox pitcher in the 1970s. In this period he had four 20-game win seasons. He had as his battery mate Carlton Fisk, who had a long and distinguished career as a catcher and contributed some fireworks of his own for the Red Sox in the 1975 World Series. Tiant made a striking appearance as a large Cuban with a Fu Manchu mustache and trimmed beard, and a fierce look on the mound. He had a wind-up style in which he swiveled his body to the rear and raised his head and eyes skyward before he whirled to make his delivery. The style was his signature, as was his large Cuban cigar and affability after games.

"El Tiante" began his major league career with Cleveland and pitched for the Indians for six years. After a year with the Minnesota Twins, he came to the Red Sox in 1971 and pitched for the Sox eight years, until 1979. He subsequently went on to three other teams to complete his 19-year major league career. Tiant had a lifetime 3.30 E.R.A. and led the league twice in this category with marks of 1.60 for the Indians in 1968 and 1.91 for the Red Sox in 1972. He led the league one year in strikeouts and three years in pitching shutouts. A fireballer, he had three years with over 200 strike outs. Tiant ended his career with 229 wins and 172 losses.

Luis Tiant was Boston's dominant hurler in the 1970s, winning 20 games four times during the era. (Baseball Hall of Fame Library, Cooperstown, N.Y.).

With the Red Sox, from 1973-1976 Tiant won 81 games. In his eight-year Red Sox career he won 122 games, having seven productive seasons. While with the Sox he also led the league in shutouts with seven in 1974.

"El Tiante" was a pitching star for the Red Sox in the 1975 World Series against the Cincinnati Reds, winning two games and pitching seven innings in a third game before he tired. He won the first game with a five-hit shutout, 6-0. He won the fourth game, 5 to 4. He pitched the first seven innings of the dramatic 12-inning sixth game in which Carlton Fisk hit his famous home run. Luis also pitched in two American League Championship Series, one with the Minnesota Twins. In the 1975 ALCS, in which the Red Sox swept the Oakland Athletics, Tiant pitched and won the first game with a three-hitter. The Sox won, 7-1, in a game marred by seven errors by the two teams.

Luis started and lost the 1968 All-Star game while with Cleveland. In his two innings he allowed the only run of the game. He was again the loser in the 1974 All-Star game, when he was with the Red Sox. He also pitched in the 1976 game, another American League loss.

Mike Torrez

Mike Torrez won 185 games in his 18-year career. He pitched for seven teams and was with the Red Sox from 1978 through 1982. He probably will be remembered best, at least by Red Sox fans, as the pitcher who threw the home run ball to Bucky Dent of the Yankees at Fenway Park, resulting in the three runs that defeated the Red Sox in the play-off game for the pennant in 1978. Torrez in the previous year had pitched for the Yankees and won 14 games.

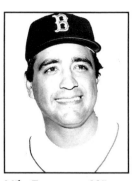

Mike Torrez won 185 games in his career, 60 of them with the Red Sox. (Baseball Hall of Fame Library, Cooperstown, N.Y.).

Torrez won 14 or more games a season for five of the seven teams for which he pitched, including the Montreal Expos, the Baltimore Orioles, the Oakland Athletics, the New York Yankees and the Red Sox. He also had seasons in which he won ten or more games for the other two teams for which he pitched, the St. Louis Cardinals and the New York Mets. Though he had a good career, his pitching was often suspect because of control problems. He gave up 1,371 walks in 3,072 innings and led the league in handing out bases on balls three times, twice for teams in the American League and once for the New York Mets in the National League. On the other hand, he also starred in key games, and won two World Series games pitching for the New York Yankees in 1977.

With the Red Sox for five years, Mike won 16 games twice and had a total of 60 wins against 54 losses. In 1979, when for the second straight year he had a 16-13 record for the Sox, he struck out 125 batters but also led the league with 121 walks.

Rick Wise

Rick Wise, in an 18-year pitching career, pitched four seasons for the Red Sox from 1974 through 1977. In 1975, the Red Sox pennant-winning year, Wise had a record of 19-12 to lead the team in wins. He also won 14 games for the Sox the following year. Rick won one game in the ALCS in 1975 and one game in the World Series that year.

Rick Wise led the Red Sox in victories in their 1975 pennant-winning season, accumulating 19. (Baseball Hall of Fame Library, Cooperstown, N.Y.).

Though Rick played for five big-league teams his career year was in 1975 with Boston, the pennant-winning year, when he, Luis Tiant and Bill Lee combined for 54 wins. He started 35 games, finishing 17, and had 141 strike outs. It was one of five times in his career when he had more than 140 strikeouts.

Over his career Rick posted a 188-181 record. In something of an anomaly, pitching for the Cleveland Indians in 1978, after having been traded by the Red Sox after the 1977 season, he led the league in losses, with 19, and had a 9-19 record for the sixth-place Indians.

In the 1975 ALCS, Wise pitched and won the pennant winning game against the Oakland Athletics, 5-3, with relief help in the eighth inning from Dick Drago, who had a save. In the World Series, Wise won the dramatic Game 6 against the Reds. He pitched one inning in relief, the 12th inning. Wise also started Game 3 but lasted only into the fifth inning as the Cincinnati Reds won the game, 6-5.

A Pennant in Four League Championship Series and Three Divisional Play-Offs, 1986-2001

Tony Armas
b. Jul. 2, 1953 | Anzoatequi, Venezuela | Bats Right | Throws Right
| | 5'11" 182 lbs. | Red Sox | 1983-1986

Marty Barrett
b. Jun. 23, 1958 | Arcadia, Calif. | Bats Right | Throws Right
| | 5'11" 175 lbs. | Red Sox | 1982-1990

Oil Can Boyd
b. Oct. 6, 1959 | Meridian, Miss. | Pitches Right | Bats Right
| | 6'1" 155 lbs. | Red Sox | 1982-1989

Bill Buckner
b. Dec. 14, 1949 | Vallejo, Calif. | Bats Left | Throws Left
| | 6' 185 lbs. | Red Sox | 1984-1987; 90

Ellis Burks
b. Sep. 11, 1964 | Vicksburg, Miss. | Bats Right | Throws Right
| | 6'2" 175 lbs. | Red Sox | 1987-1992

Mark Clear
b. May 27, 1956 | Los Angeles, Calif. | Pitches Right | Bats Right
| | 6'4" 200 lbs. | Red Sox | 1981-1985

Rich Garces
b. May 18, 1971 | Maracay, Venezuela | Pitches Right | Bats Right
| | 6' 215 lbs. | Red Sox | 996—

Rich Gedman
b. Sep. 26, 1959 | Worcester, Mass. | Bats Left | Throws Right
| | 6' 210 lbs. | Red Sox | 1980-1990

Tom Gordon
b. Nov. 18, 1967 | Sebring, Florida | Pitches Right | Bats Right
| | 5'9" 180 lbs. | Red Sox | 1996-1999

Mike Greenwell
b. Jul. 18, 1963 | Louisville, Ky. | Bats Left | Throws Right
| | 6' 170 lbs. | Red Sox | 1986-1996

Bruce Hurst
b. Mar. 24, 1958 | St. George, Utah | Pitches Left | Bats Left
| | 6'4" 200 lbs. | Red Sox | 1980-1988

Reggie Jefferson
b. Sept. 25, 1968 | Tallahassee, Fl. | Bats Left | Throws Left
| | 6'4" 215 lbs. | Red Sox | 1995-1999

Darren Lewis
b. Aug. 28, 1967 | Berkeley, Cal. | Bats Right | Throws Right
| | 6' 189 lbs. | Red Sox | 1998—

Derek Lowe
b. June 1, 1973 | Dearborn, Mich. | Pitches Right | Bats Right
| | 6'6" 170 lbs. | Red Sox | 1997-

Tim Naehring
b. Feb. 1, 1967 | Cincinnati, Ohio | Bats Right | Throws Right
| | 6'2" 190 lbs. | Red Sox | 1990-1998

Trot Nixon
b. April 11, 1974 | Durham, N.C. | Bats Left | Throws Left
| | 6'1" 195 lbs. | Red Sox 1996—

Bobby Ojeda
b. Dec. 17, 1957 | Los Angeles, Calif. | Pitches Left | Bats Left
| | 6' 185 lbs. | Red Sox | 1980-1985

Tony Pena
b. Jun. 4, 1957 | Monte Cristi, D.R. | Bats Right | Throws Right
| | 6'1" 175 lbs. | Red Sox | 1990-1993

Jody Reed
b. Jul. 26, 1962 | Tampa, Fla. | Bats Right | Throws Right
| | 5'9" 170 lbs. | Red Sox | 1987-1992

Jerry Remy
b. Nov. 8, 1952 | Fall River, Mass. | Bats Left | Throws Right
| | 5'9" 165 lbs. | Red Sox | 1978-1984

Bob Stanley
b. Nov. 10, 1954 | Portland, Maine | Pitches Right | Bats Right
| | 6'4" 210 lbs. | Red Sox | 1977-1989

Dave Stapleton
b. Jan. 16, 1954 | Fairhope, Ala. | Bats Right | Throws Right
| | 6'1" 178 lbs. | Red Sox | 1980-1986

John Valentin

b. Feb. 18, 1967   Mineola, N.Y.   Bats Right
Throws Right
6' 170 lbs.   Red Sox   1992-1998

Mo Vaughn

b. Dec. 15, 1967 Norwalk, Conn. Bats Left Throws Right
6'1" 225 lbs. Red Sox 1991-1998

Jason Varitek

b. April 11, 1972 Rochester, Minn. Bats Left, Right Throws Right
6'2" 210 lbs. Red Sox 1997–

Tim Wakefield

b. August 2, 1966 Melbourne, Fl. Pitches Right Bats Right
6'2" 204 lbs. Red Sox 1995–

Tony Armas

Before Tony Armas came to the Red Sox he had played six years for the Oakland Athletics. He established his reputation as an authentic slugger beginning with his last three years in Oakland. In this period, from 1980 through 1982, he hit 85 home runs and drove in 274 runs, or over 90 R.B.I.s a year. He led the league in home runs in 1981, with 22, though he hit 35 the previous year and was only fourth in home runs behind Reggie Jackson, Ben Ogilvie and Gorman Thomas.

In six consecutive years with the Oakland A's and the Red Sox, Tony Armas hit 187 home runs. (Baseball Hall of Fame Library, Cooperstown, N.Y.).

Traded to Boston in 1983, Tony continued his home run hitting and for another three years hit 102, or 34 a year. In six straight years with the A's and Sox he hit 187 home runs. He also kept pace with R.B.I.s in Boston with 294 in the same three Red Sox years, or a total of 568 runs driven in during his spectacular six-year performance with two clubs.

In 1983, Jim Rice beat out his teammate, Tony Armas, for the league's home run championship, 39 to 36, and Rice also won the runs batted in title with 126. Armas had 107. In 1984, Armas won the home run championship with 43. Rice had 28. Armas beat out Rice for R.B.I. honors, 123 to 122. Together they made a potent slugging combination.

Armas, who had a lifetime .252 batting average in 14 years, played six years with the Oakland A's, four years with Boston and his career ended with three years with the California Angels. While with the Red Sox he batted .125 in the 1986 American League Championship Series and he failed in his one at bat in the World Series that year. With Oakland in 1981, he played in the divisional play-offs and the ALCS. He batted .545 in the divisional play-offs, with six hits in the three-game series and drove in the winning run in the second game. He did not distinguish himself in the ALCS which the Athletics lost to the Yankees, three games to none.

Marty Barrett

Marty Barrett played nine years as a second baseman for the Red Sox from 1982 through 1990. He had a lifetime batting average of .278 and played in three League Championship Series and one World Series for the Sox. He batted .433 in the 1986 World Series with 13 hits in the seven games. Marty's younger brother, Tom, played briefly for the Red Sox as a second baseman in 1992.

Second baseman Marty Barrett played in three League Championship Series and one World Series for the Red Sox. (Baseball Hall of Fame Library, Cooperstown, N.Y.).

Marty was the regular second baseman for the Sox for six consecutive years, from 1984 through 1989. In his best year at bat, 1984, he batted .303, the only time in his career he batted over .300. He had over 140 hits for the first five of his six seasons as a regular. He also hit at least 20 doubles in each of those seasons. In two years, 1986 and 1987, he stole 15 bases each season. He was a reliable fielder as well as a good hitter.

Barrett played in three American League Championship Series with the Red Sox in 1986, 1988 and 1990. His 1986 postseason performance was outstanding. He batted .367 with 11 hits in the seven-game ALCS, and his .433 average in the World Series was even better. He had five R.B.I.s in the ALCS and four in the World Series.

Dennis "Oil Can" Boyd

"Oil Can" Boyd was a flamboyant and popular pitcher for the Red Sox from 1982 through 1989, eight years. He had one 16- and one 15-game winning years. He pitched in the 1986 American League Championship Series, winning one and losing one, and he lost one World Series game that year.

Oil Can, in a 10-year big league career, had 78 wins and 77 losses, most of this with the Red Sox. His best year was in the Red Sox pennant-winning year of 1986 when he won 16 and lost 10, second in wins on the team only to Roger Clemens. In his most productive three years, 1984, 1985 and 1986, he had nearly 130 strikeouts or more each year. He also had a total of six shutouts in 1984 and 1985. He gave up a hit or more an inning, on average, in 1984-85-86 but nonetheless did not have a losing season then. In these highlighted three years he won 43 and lost 35.

Boyd started and lost Game 3 in the 1986 ALCS against California but he won Game 6, with help from Bob Stanley, giving up three runs in seven innings for a 10-4 win. In the 1986 World Series, he started Game 3 against the Mets, gave up four runs in the first inning and two more in the seventh as the Mets won 7-1, behind former Red Soxer Bobby Ojeda. Boyd's loss in Game 3 was his only appearance in the Series.

From 1984-86, Oil Can Boyd averaged nearly 130 strikeouts per season. (Baseball Hall of Fame Library, Cooperstown, N.Y.).

Bill Buckner

Bill Buckner had an outstanding 22-year outfielder/first baseman's career, mostly with the Los Angeles Dodgers and Chicago Cubs. He won the batting championship with the Cubs in 1980 and was a fine doubles hitter, leading the National League twice in this category. His lifetime batting average was .289. He also was a very good fielder with a .992 lifetime fielding average. He holds the record for assists by a first baseman and broke this record three times. In 1982 he set a new record with 159 assists, broke this record with 161 in 1983, and again broke the record with 184 in 1985.

"Billy Buck" played with the Red Sox from mid-1984 to mid-1987, playing two full years with the team. In 1985, though he had 201 hits he did not make the .300 batting average mark. He hit .299. He played for the Sox in the 1986 American League

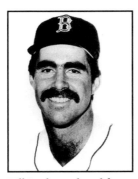

Bill Buckner played first base for the Red Sox from 1984-87, hitting .299 in 1986. (Baseball Hall of Fame Library, Cooperstown, N.Y.).

Championship Series and in the World Series. He likely will be forever known for the dribbler that went between his legs at first base on a play against the New York Mets in the sixth game of the World Series. Apparently being on the way to winning the Series in the sixth game, the Sox not only lost that game because of Buckner's tenth-inning error but also lost the seventh and final game to make the Mets world champions. Buckner had played the Series with bad ankles and sought to protect them by wearing high-top shoes. His fielding was hampered but the error was egregious and, in the eyes of many, inexcusable. Manager John McNamara was criticized after the fact for not substituting defensively a healthy first baseman, Dave Stapleton, then sitting on the bench, for the lame Buckner.

Ellis Burks

Ellis Burks was an outfielder for six years with the Boston Red Sox from 1987 through 1992. He batted .281 with the Sox with 93 home runs and 387 runs batted in. He also played for the Red Sox in 1988 and 1990 League Championship Series, in both of which the Oakland Athletics shut out the Sox, three games to none.

Burks, from 1988 through 1990 with the Sox, batted .294, .303 and .296 respectively. In four of his first five years with the team he had 30 or more doubles a season. He also hit 20 or more homers twice. He scored nearly 90 or more runs three times. In his first three seasons he had

Outfielder Ellis Burks played for Boston from 1987-92, batting .281. (Baseball Hall of Fame Library, Cooperstown, N.Y.).

more than 20 steals a season. He was fast, a good hitter and could hit for power. He played centerfield. Burks, a veteran with 15 years of big-league experience, has played with four teams since leaving the Red Sox in 1992. His reputation is now established as a heavy hitter, a reliable player, and a good clubhouse influence. Beginning in 1996, when he hit 40 home runs for the Colorado Rockies, he has hit over 20 homers a year.

Burks had four hits in each of the 1988 and 1990 ALCS for the Sox.

Mark Clear

Mark Clear was a relief pitcher for the Red Sox, notable for never having started a game in his 220 games with the team from 1981 through 1985. He led the league in relief wins in 1982 with 14.

Clear had an 11-year career and most of it was with the Red Sox, a period of six years. 1982 was the top year in his career. Not only did he lead in relief wins with 14 but he also had 14 saves. He had a 14-9 won-lost record and an E.R.A. of 3.00. Both in 1981 ad 1984 for the Red Sox his record was eight wins and three losses. He had nine saves in the first of these seasons and eight in the second.

Clear went on later in his career to pitch effectively for Milwaukee. He both started and ended his career with stints for the California Angels.

Mark Clear posted a 14-9 record with a 3.00 E.R.A. for the Red Sox in 1982. (Baseball Hall of Fame Library, Cooperstown, N.Y.).

Rich Garces

Rich Garces, whose big-league career began with the Minnesota Twins in 1990, became a right-handed relief pitcher for the Red Sox in 1996. In his six years thus far with the Sox, from 1996 to 2001, he has appeared in a total of 235 games. In 2000 and 2001, he appeared in more the 60 games each season. In 2000, he had eight wins and one loss and in 2001, he won six and lost one. He had one save in each of these years and is mostly a middle reliever. In his 10-year career he has 23 wins and nine loss, and a total of seven saves. His cumulative earned run average in 3.49. He has never started a game. Garces pitched in two games and won one in the 1999 American League Division Series. He pitched twice for a total of three innings in the League Championship Series.

Rich Garces, middle reliever for the Red Sox beginning in the late 1990s. (Boston Red Sox).

Rich Gedman

Rich Gedman was a catcher for the Red Sox for ten-plus years from 1980 into 1990. A lifetime .252 hitter he batted .357 for the Red Sox in both the 1986 and 1988 League Championship Series. He was the catcher for the Sox in the 1986 World Series in which he hit a home run.

Gedman's best hitting year with the Sox was in 1985 when his batting average was .295 and he drove in 80 runs with 30 doubles and 18 home runs. In all but home runs these were career highs for him. He hit 24 home runs in 1984 and also hit 26 doubles with 72 runs batted in and had a .269 batting average.

Gedman played in both the 1986 and 1988 ALCS for the Red Sox. Though he batted .357 both times, he had 10 hits in seven games in 1986, when the Sox won, and five hits in four games in 1988, when the Sox lost. He hit a home run in each ALCS. In the World Series of 1986, against the Mets, he had six hits in seven games and batted .200, including one home run. He was the Red Sox regular catcher in all of these postseason games.

A lifetime .252 hitter, catcher Rich Gedman hit .357 for the Red Sox in the 1986 and 1988 ALCS. (Baseball Hall of Fame Library, Cooperstown, N.Y.).

Tom "Flash" Gordon

Gordon, in his four years with the Red Sox, was a reliever extraordinnaire. This was especially true in 1998 when he was the closer on the ream and led the league with 46 saves. Previously in his career he had been both a starter and a reliever. He pitched for the Kansas City Royals from 1988 through 1995 and came to the Red Sox in 1996. He was out of baseball for a year in 2000 because of injury and came back with the Chicago Cubs in 2001. In his 13-year career thus far he has won 105 games and lost 98 with a total of 71 saves. He pitched in 73 games in his stellar year in 1998, all in relief. His best season record was early in his career, with Kansas City in 1989, when he won 17 and lost nine with 16 starts. He won more than 10 games six times but only in 1989 did he win more than 12 games. He was the closer for the Red Sox while playing in two games in the 1998 American League Division Series and was the loser in the final 2-1 game. He had no decision in the 1999 ALDS but pitched in two games. He was the closer in the Red Sox 23-7 win in Game 4. He pitched in three games in the 1999 American League Championship Series with no decision. He pitched one inning in two

Tom Gordon, Red Sox relief pitcher, led the league in saves in 1998. (Boston Red Sox)

games and less than an inning in a third but only the latter game, Game 2, was close and was won by the Yankees. He also pitched in one inning of the 1998 All-Star game.

Mike Greenwell

Mike Greenwell, though in less impressive fashion, continued the Williams-Yastrzemski-Rice tradition of solid Red

Sox left fielders. He came up in 1985 and, from 1987 through 1996, was a fixture in left field for the Sox over nine years. He had a lifetime .303 batting average. In his first two years as a regular, 1987 and 1988, he batted .328 and .325, respectively. In those two years he batted in 208 runs, 119 alone in 1988. He continued his R.B.I. production with 95 in 1989. He also hit 30 or more doubles five times in his career.

After nine seasons with the Red Sox, during which he batted .303, Mike Greenwell signed a contract to play in Japan in 1996. (Baseball Hall of Fame Library, Cooperstown, N.Y.).

Greenwell played in a division play-off in 1995, in three American League Championship Series in 1986, 1988 and 1990, and he played in the 1986 World Series. His performance was notable only in the 1988 ALCS. Though he batted only .214 in this series that Oakland swept, three games to none, he hit a home run in the third game. Boston led 5-0 early in this game but ultimately lost, 10-6.

Greenwell, after the 1996 season, accepted a contract to play in Japan.

Bruce Hurst

Bruce Hurst was a mainstay for the Boston pitching staff for six of the nine years he played with the Red Sox. He came up to the team in 1980 and from 1983 through 1988 was in double figure wins every year with a total of 81. He also lost 64 in this period. His best year was in 1988 when he won 18 and lost six, a year in which Roger Clemens shared the team lead in wins by also winning 18 games. He figured prominently in the 1986 American League Championship Series and most especially in the World Series. He had two starts in the ALCS, and pitched and won one complete game. He had three starts in the World Series and won two games. He beat Ron Darling and the Mets in a pitching duel in the opening game, 1-0, and he beat Doc Gooden in Game 5, 4-2. Hurst also pitched in the 1988 ALCS for the Sox. He went on to the San Diego

Padres in 1989 and ended with a 15-year playing career.

Hurst in 1988 was second in winning percentage to Frank Viola of the Minnesota Twins. His 18 and 6 record gave him a .750 winning percentage. This was his career year in which he had four shutouts and an earned run average under 3.00 (2.99) for the only time in his 15 years in the big leagues. In 1986 he had 167 strikeouts. For six straight seasons with the Red Sox he also had 115 or more strikeouts a year with 190 in 1987 and 189 in 1985. He pitched four shutouts.

From 1983-88, Bruce Hurst was in double figures in wins every season for Boston. (Baseball Hall of Fame Library, Cooperstown, N.Y.).

Reggie Jefferson

Reggie Jefferson's big-league career began with the Cincinnati Reds in 1991 and ended with the Red Sox in 1999. He played most of his career with the Red Sox, five years from 1995 through 1999. He was an outfielder and a regular in 1996 and 1997. With the Red Sox he batted .347 in 1996, .319 in 1997, and .306 in 1998. His lifetime batting average was .300. Reggie had a .593 slugging average in 1996 with 19 home runs, 30 doubles and 74 runs batted in. In his other really good year in 1997, he had 13 home runs and

Reggie Jefferson lad a lifetime .300 batting average. (Boston Red Sox)

33 doubles. He was frequently a designated hitter, and occasionally played first base, but he was mainly a journeyman outfielder.

Darren Lewis

Darren Lewis, an outfielder, began his career in 1990 in Oakland, came to the Red Sox in 1998 and has been with them four years. He previously played five years with the San Francisco Giants. Lewis was a regular with the Red Sox in 1998 and 1999 and played frequently in 2000 and 2001. He was a fleet outfielder who mostly played center field. Lewis is a lifetime .250 hitter and has never batted .300 or more. Not a power hitter, he was better noted for his speed and his fleetness in the outfield. He led the league with nine triples playing for San Francisco in 1994, and in 1993 he played the entire season without making an error in the field. In fewer games he similarly made no errors the previous four years. He has stolen 246 bases in his career with 29 with the Red Sox in 1998. He had a total of 27 home runs in his 12 major-league years. Darren's best year with the Red Sox was in 1998 when he played in 155 games, had 157 hits and scored 95 runs with a .268 batting average. He also stole 29 bases. He batted .280 in 2001 but played in only 82 games with 164 at-bats. In the 1998 American League Division Series, Lewis played in all four games and batted .357. He had five hits. In the 1999 ALDS he batted .375 with six hits in the four games. In the 1999 American League Championship Series his batting average dropped to .118.

Darren Lewis, a fleet outfielder, never batted .300 but is a good fielder. (Boston Red Sox)

Derek Lowe

Derek Lowe has played almost his entire career with the Red Sox, beginning in 1987 when he came over midyear from the Seattle Mariners. Though initially both a starting and relief pitcher, he has become the predominant closer for the Red Sox. His first saves were in 1998 and, when "Flash" Gordon was injured and was unable to play in 2000, Lowe essentially took over and led the league with 42 saves that year. He had 24 more in 2001 and, in his approximately five years with the team, he has 85 saves. His best ERA year was in 2000 at 2.56. His cumulative won-lost record is 20 wins and 32 losses, with ten losses occurring in 2001 as he backslid from the previous year. He pitched in 74 games, both in 2000 and 2001. Derek pitched in two games in the 1998 American League Division Series, giving three hits in 4 1/3 innings. His earned run average was .208 but he was a mid-game reliever and had no decisions. In the 1999 ALDS Lowe pitched in three of the four games and lost one and won one. He pitched as a set-up man in relief in two games and relieved early in the final game of the series which was a hitters' battle won by the Red Sox, 12–8. In the American League Championship Series Lowe again pitched in three games with

Derek Lowe, a workhorse pitching primarily in relief. (Boston Red Sox)

no decisions. He gave up a total of six hits in 6 1/3 innings with seven strikeouts and he had an earned run average of 1.42. Lowe also pitched one inning in the 2000 All-Star Game.

Tim Naehring

Tim Naehring was an infielder for the Red Sox from the start of his big-league career in 1990. He had an eight-year career, all with the Red Sox. Early in his career, Naehring played mostly shortstop. Then he switched to second base and finally to third base. With Nomar Garciaparra at shortstop, Jose Valentin then took over at third base.

Infielder Tim Naehring played in 126 games for the Red Sox in 1995, batting .307. (Baseball Hall of Fame Library, Cooperstown, N.Y.).

Naehring only in 1995 and 1996 played in as many as 100 games a season. In 1995 when the Red Sox led the East division, Naehring played in 126 games and batted .307. He has had a slugging average consistently over .400. In 1995 his slugging average was a career high .448 and he had 27 doubles and 10 home runs. In 1996, his slugging average was .444 and he had 17 home runs and 16 doubles.

Naehring played in all three games in the 1995 Divisional Play-off Series, which the Red Sox lost to Cleveland, the Central Division winners. He batted .308 with four hits in 13 at bats. He hit a home run in the first game to put the Red Sox ahead in the top of the 11th inning but they eventually lost to the Indians in the 13th inning, 5-4.

Trot Nixon

Trot Nixon, an outfielder, came up to the Red Sox in 1996 but played in only two games and his tour of duty essentially began in 1998. Beginning in 1999, he has played regularly for three seasons with the Sox. He is consistently a .270 to .280 hitter and currently has a lifetime batting average of .277. He is a speedy outfielder and an improving long ball hitter. He has stolen a total of 15 bases in 2000 and 2001. He hit 27 home runs in 2001 and, in the three years, 1999 through 2001, he has had 17 triples. He scored 100 runs in 2001, his best sea-

Trot Nixon, a speedy outfielder, scored 100 runs in 2001. (Boston Red Sox)

son and drove in 88. He has also stuck out 113 times in 535 at-bats in 2001. Nixon played briefly in the 1998 American League Division Series, with three at bats and one hit in the two games in which he played. In the 1999 A.L.D.S., he batted .214 with three hits, all doubles, in the five games. He drove in six runs. In the 1999 American League Championship Series Trot batted .286 with four hits in five games.

Bobby Ojeda

"Bobby O" pitched for the Red Sox at the beginning of his major league career from 1980 through 1985. He won a total of 44 games for the Sox and lost 39. His 12-7 record in 1983 was his best with the team. He had 28 starts and five complete games. In some respects, his 1984 season with the Sox was even better. He won 12 and lost 12, started 32 times and had eight complete games. He struck out 137 batters and led the league by pitching five shutouts. Though he came up with the team in 1980, when the Red Sox won the East division, he did not play in the post season.

Bobby Ojeda started 33 games for Boston in 1984, completing eight of them. (Baseball Hall of Fame Library, Cooperstown, N.Y.).

Ojeda was traded to the Mets in 1986 and led the National League in winning percentage in his very first season, with 18 wins and five losses for a .783 average. His earned run average was 2.57. It was his career year. Ojeda was a thorn to the Red Sox in the 1986 World Series. He beat the Sox in Game 3, 7 to 1. He also started Game 6 and pitched six good innings, leaving with the score tied at two-all. The Mets eventually won the game.

Troy O'Leary

Troy O'Leary, a regular outfielder for the Red Sox from 1995 and well into the 2001 season, started his career with Milwaukee in 1993. He came over to the Red Sox early in the season in 1995 for the waiver price. He has consistently batted between .270 and .309 in his career, though he has begun to slip with a .261 average in 2000 and a .240 average with fewer at bats in 2001. His best year was in 1997 when he batted .309. He has hit more than 28 doubles a year in the period 1995 through 1999 and in only one of these years (1996) did he hit under 30. In 1998 and 1999 he hit 23 and 28 home runs, respectively. He drove in over 100 runs for the first time in 1999.

O'Leary, in his first year with the Red Sox, did not play in the 1995 division play-offs, but he did play for the team in the 1998 and 1999 division play-offs. The Red Sox lost the 1998 series to the Cleveland Indians. They won the 1999 division play-offs in part because of the fireworks provided by O'Leary. He hit a bases-loaded home run, the first by a Red Sox player in postseason play. He also tied a postseason record of seven R.B.I.s in one game with his two home runs, winning Game 5. In the 1999 ALCS, O'Leary batted .350 with seven hits in five games, but O'Leary's and the Red Sox's performance was less spectacular than in the division series.

Tony Pena

Tony Pena from 1980 through 1997 had an 18-year playing career as a big league catcher. Most of his career was with the Pittsburgh Pirates. He played with the Red Sox from 1990 through 1993 and played in the 1990 American League Championship Series for Boston. Never an outstanding hitter he was considered a good fielding catcher and a steadying influence on pitchers.

Pena was the regular catcher for the Red Sox in his

Rightfielder Troy O'Leary batted .309 in 1997 for the Red Sox.

Tony Pena played catcher for the Red Sox from 1990-93, including participating in the 1990 ALCS. (Boston Red Sox).

four years with the team. His best batting year with the team was his first, in 1990, when he batted .263. His worst season for the Sox was his last, in 1993, when he batted .181. Pena, as a catcher with the Sox, fielded an impressive .995 in three seasons, and .993 in the other year.

Pena was the Boston catcher in the 1990 ALCS which the Red Sox lost to Oakland, four games to none. He batted .214 with three hits in the series. He played on two pennant winners, the 1987 St. Louis Cardinals and the 1995 Cleveland Indians.

Jody Reed

Jody was an infielder for the Red Sox for six years from 1987 through 1992. He was the regular second baseman from 1990 through 1992 and played in both the 1988 and 1990 League Championship Series for the Sox.

Second baseman Jody Reed had a lifetime batting average of .280 while with the Red Sox from 1987-92. (Baseball Hall of Fame Library, Cooperstown, N.Y.).

His lifetime Red Sox batting average was .280 and he went on to a ten-year career. He was a good doubles hitter, led the league with 45 doubles in 1990 and for three seasons, 1989 through 1991, hit at least 42 doubles each season.

In the 1988 ALCS, Jody batted .273 for the Sox . He was less successful in the 1990 ALCS when he had two hits in 15 at bats. The Red Sox lost both series.

Jerry Remy

Jerry Remy was a Red Sox second baseman for seven of his ten big league years, from 1978 through 1984. His lifetime batting average was .275. He played the entire season at second base for the Red Sox in three years and hit over .300 twice.

Though Remy started his big-league career with the California

Jerry Remy batted .280 for the Red Sox in 1982 and .295 in 1983. (Baseball Hall of Fame Library, Cooperstown, N.Y.).

Angels, his best years were with the Red Sox. He hit .313 in 63 games in 1980 and .307 in 88 games in 1981. He batted .280 in a full season in 1982 and .275 in another full year in 1983. Remy had speed and quickness, and he stole 208 bases in his career. He was especially successful in his first four years, three with California and one with Boston, when he stole 30 or more bases each season. He had 41 steals in 1977 with the Angels, tying for third place in the league.

Remy in his ten seasons in the big leagues did not play with a team that made it to the postseason.

Bob Stanley

Bob Stanley pitched his entire 13-year career for the Red Sox, from 1977 through 1989. After his first four years, and before he reverted for one year as a starter in 1987, he was another premier relief pitcher. He led the league in relief wins in 1978, with 13, and in 1981 with 10. He had 85 relief wins in his career and 132 saves. He pitched as a reliever in the 1986 and 1988 League Championship Series and in the 1986 World Series with no won-lost record. Stanley's wild pitch helped to advance the winning runner for the Mets in the tenth inning of the sixth game of the World Series, for it was right after that Bill Buckner let the squibbler go through his legs at first base, giving the Mets the winning run and ultimately the Series.

Stanley had a spectacular 15-2 record in 1978, with 13 of his wins in relief. He had an earned run average of 2.60. In 1979, he had a 16-12 record but all but three of his wins were as a starter. He started only three games in 1978 but was essentially converted to a starter in 1979 with 30 starts. In 1980, he had a 10-8 record, starting 17 games and winning six of these. He won four in relief and had 14 saves. He was a reliever in earnest in most of the rest of his career and led the league in 1981 in both relief wins and relief losses. His record was 10-8, with all his wins and seven of his losses in relief. He did better in 1982 with 12 relief wins and 14 saves.

Bob Stanley pitched his entire 13-year career with Boston, primarily as a reliever. (Baseball Hall of Fame Library, Cooperstown, N.Y.).

Stanley pitched in relief in three games in the ALCS, allowing seven hits in 5 2/3 innings. In the 1986 World Series he pitched in relief in five of the seven games, and did not pitch in the two games started and won by Bruce Hurst. He had one save and gave up five hits in a total of 6 1/3 innings in five games. In the 1986 ALCS, he pitched a total of 1 inning in two games, giving up two hits, with the Red Sox winning none of the four games against Oakland.

Dave Stapleton

Dave Stapleton spent his seven-year big league career playing all of the infield positions with the Red Sox. His tenure was from 1980 through 1986, and his best year was his first when he batted over .300. His lifetime batting average was .271. He played as a substitute first baseman both in the League Championship Series and the World Series in 1986, playing behind Bill Buckner.

From 1980-86, Dave Stapleton played every infield position for Boston. (Baseball Hall of Fame Library, Cooperstown, N.Y.).

Stapleton played a full season in 1982 and 1983, mostly as the Red Sox first baseman. From a starting year of .321 his batting average descended each year to the end of his career. In 1982 and 1983, the third and fourth years in his career, he batted .264 and .247 respectively. At the end of his career in 1986, when he played in only 39 games, he batted .128. The first four years he had over 100 hits a season and three years he hit 10 or more home runs. Twice he fielded 1.000 but only with about 100 chances each of the seasons. Stapleton was succeeded at first base by Bill Buckner who came over to the Red Sox in 1984 after 15 years in the National League.

In the 1986 ALCS he had two hits in three at bats and scored two runs. He had one at bat in the World Series.

John Valentin

John Valentin played shortstop for the Red Sox beginning in 1992. When Nomar Garciaparra came to the club for his first full season at shortstop in 1997, Valentin moved over to third base.

John Valentin batted .298 with 27 home runs in 1995. (Boston Red Sox).

Valentin batted over .275 each of his first five big league seasons and he batted .316 in 1994. He had 40 doubles in 1993, third in the American League. He had 27 home runs in 1995 when he batted .298. He had 102 runs batted in that year and scored 108 runs. To climax a great year, he stole 20 bases.

Valentin played in the 1995 Division Playoff Series as one of the team's leading hitters, effectively just behind Mo Vaughn. He had three hits in 12 at bats, including a double and a home run. He drove in two runs with the home run in Game 1 but the Red Sox lost in the 13th inning, 5-4, and proceeded to lose all three games in the series.

Jason Varitek

Jason Varitek came up with the Red Sox in 1997 and was the team's regular catcher for all of 1999 and 2000. He played in fewer games in 2001 because of injury. Jason's best hitting year was in 2001 when he batted .293 in 51 games. In his five-year career with the Red Sox, his lifetime batting average is .263. He hit 20 home runs and 39 doubles in a exceptional power hitting year for him in 1999. He had a .482 slugging average; he also had a .489 slugging average in his shortened 2001 year. Jason played in one game in the 1998 American League Division Series, with Scott Hatteberg doing the bulk of the catching. In the 1999 A.L.D.S., he batted .238 and caught all give games. He and Jim Thome of Cleveland led with each scoring seven runs in the series. His five hits included three

Jason Varitek, Red Sox catcher, had his best power-hitting year in 1999 with 20 home runs and 39 doubles. (Boston Red Sox)

doubles and a home run. In the 1999 American League Championship Series, Jason again caught all five games but he had only four hits in the series and batted .200.

did not play in 2001. He has signed with the New York Mets for the 2002 season. His current lifetime batting average in .298.

Mo Vaughn

Mo Vaughn is a good-natured, very popular, large, long ball hitting first baseman for the Red Sox in the 1990s. His career in the big leagues started in 1991.In eight years with the Red Sox, 1991 through 1998, he hit 230 homers and twice hit 40 or more home runs. In five of the last six years he has played he has driven in more than 108 runs, leading the league with 126 RBIs in 1995. The 1995 season was also the year in which Mo won the American League's Most Valuable Player award with 39 home runs, 126 runs batted in and a .300 batting average. A feared slugger, he can also strike out a lot, and he accumulated 150 strike outs in his M.V.P. year. He is also considered a good fielding first baseman. "Big Mo" is very popular with the fans in Boston for the additional reason that he participates actively in community charities.

Mo Vaughn was the American League M.V.P. in 1995. (Baseball Hall of Fame Library, Cooperstown, N.Y.).

Mo is one of the American League's consistent superstars and long ball hitters in the current era. He was a disappointment in the 1995 Division Playoff Series, however, when he went 0 for 14.

Mo could not agree with Red Sox management on a contract beginning with the year 1999. In an unpopular move that brought a lot of criticism to the management, he signed with Anaheim in 1999. In 1999 and 2000, he hit a total of 69 home runs for the Angels. Mo was injured and

Tim Wakefield

Tim Wakefield in an established knuckle ball pitcher. He came up withe the Pittsburgh Pirates in 1992. He had a remarkable eight-wins and-one-loss year in 1992 and a 2.15 earned run average but he faded in 1993 and was sent back to the minor leagues. Working with the celebrated knuckle ballers, Phil and Joe Neikro, he came back to the big leagues with the Red Sox in 1995 and has been with the club for the past seven years. He is both a starter and a reliever. His first four years with the Red Sox he won 59 games. He also led the league in losses in 1997 with 15. For the period 1995 through 1998 he was almost entirely a starting pitcher. Beginning in 1999 he became predominantly a reliever though he did start 17 games in each of the three seasons, 1999 through 2001. As a knuckle baller prone to hit batsmen,

Wakefield, a knuckleball pitcher, is both a starter and a reliever for the Red Sox. (Boston Red Sox)

Tim led the league in hitting batters in 2001 with 18 nicks. In his career he has won 94 games and lost 89, and he has a cumulative 4.41 earned run average. Wakefield started Game 2 of the 1998 American League Division Series but only lasted one full inning. The Indians scored five runs in the second inning and won the game, nine to five. In the 1999 ALDS Wakefield pitched a total of two innings in two games with an earned run average of 13.50. He did not play in the American League Championship Series that year.

Short Takes On Interesting Red Sox Players and Brief Sox Careers

Harry Agganis

Harry Agganis, "The Golden Greek," was a popular first baseman for the Red Sox in 1954 and 1955. He had been an All-American fullback at Boston University. His career ended abruptly in the 1955 season when he died suddenly and tragically of a pulmonary embolism after developing pneumonia.

Rick Aguilera

Rick Aguilera came to Boston in mid-1995 and pitched a half year for the Red Sox before being traded back to Minnesota. Aguilera started his career with the New York Yankees as a strong starting pitcher and later for a period of six years became one of the American League's premier relief pitchers. In 1996, he reverted back to a starter's role with the Twins. He pitched 55 innings of relief for the Red Sox in 1995 and had a 2-2 record with the team.

Dale Alexander

Dale Alexander had a five-year career as a first baseman, from 1929 through 1933, first with the Detroit Tigers and then with the Boston Red Sox. He was a lifetime .331 hitter and, playing for Detroit, led the league in hits in 1929 with 215. His main claim to fame is that he was the first big leaguer to win a batting championship while playing for two teams. In 1932 he was hitting only .250 for Detroit and, after 23 games, was traded to the Red Sox. He finished the season with a league-leading .367 average.

Luis Alicea

Luis Alicea played second base for one year for the Red Sox in 1995. His principal distinction is that he led the team with a .600 batting average in the Divisional Playoffs against Cleveland. He had four hits in Game 1, including a home run, and a total of six hits in the three-game series. He played five years for the St. Louis Cardinals before coming to the Red Sox and returned to play second base for the Cardinals East division champions in 1996.

Nick Altrock

One of baseball's famous clowns, Altrock had a 16-year pitching career, mostly with the Chicago White Sox and Washington Senators. He pitched three games for the Red Sox in 1902, and one in 1903, losing in three games.

Dale Alexander was the first Red Sox player to win a batting title, doing so in 1932 with a .367 average. (Boston Red Sox).

Fred "Spitball" Anderson

"Spitball" pitched in two years for the Red Sox in 1909 and 1913. He lost six games, winning none.

Luis Aparicio

Luis Aparicio was a Hall of Fame shortstop from Venezuela who played 18 years in the major leagues, mostly with the Chicago White Sox and the Baltimore Orioles. Aparicio ended his career playing three years for the Red Sox from 1971 through 1973. Aparicio batted .253 while playing with the Red Sox and had a lifetime batting average of .262. Aparicio was known primarily for his slick fielding and wide range as a

Luis Aparicio, Hall of Fame shortstop, played briefly with the Red Sox. (Baseball Hall of Fame Library, Cooperstown, N.Y.).

shortstop. He also set a record by leading the American League in stolen bases nine straight years.

Jim Bagby Jr.

Jim Bagby Jr., son of the great Cleveland Indians pitcher Jim Bagby, had a ten-year pitching career of his own. He started out with the Red Sox in 1938, pitched for three years and then was traded to the Cleveland Indians. He came back to the Red Sox for another year in 1946 before ending his career with the Pittsburgh Pirates in 1947. Jim Jr. won 15 games with the Sox in his first year, his best season with the team. He won 37 games and lost 38 with the Red Sox and pitched in the 1946 World Series against the St. Louis Cardinals with no decisions.

The Barretts

The Red Sox had five players with the surname of Barrett, two outfielders, two second basemen and a third baseman. Jimmy Barrett played one plus year in the outfield for the Red Sox in 1907 and briefly in 1908. Bob Barrett played one year as a third baseman for the Red Sox in 1929. Bill Barrett played in 117 games as an outfielder for the Sox in 1929 and briefly in 1930. The best known of the Barretts and the one with a substantial big-league career was Marty Barrett. His brother, Tom, played for the Red Sox in 1992.

Don Baylor

Don Baylor played two years as a designated hitter for the Red Sox in 1986 and 1987. This was near the end of a 19-year outfielder's career with seven teams, primarily with the Baltimore Orioles and the California Angels. Baylor was a "money player" who came through in the clutch. He played in seven league championship series and three World Series, including the league championship and World Series with the Red Sox in 1986. He hit a home run in the 1986 World Series. Baylor had a lifetime batting average of .260 with 338 home runs and 1,276 runs batted in.

Don Baylor was a "money player" and designated hitter with the Red Sox in the 1980s. (Baseball Hall of Fame Library, Cooperstown, N.Y.).

After his playing career, Baylor became manager of the Colorado Rockies.

Max Bishop

Max Bishop was a stellar second baseman for Connie Mack's Philadelphia Athletics during their championship days in the mid-1920s and early 1930s. He ended his career with two years with the Red Sox in 1934 and 1935. He batted .251 for the Red Sox, 20 points below his lifetime average.

Mike Boddicker

Mike Boddicker spent most of his 14-year American League career as a pitcher for the Baltimore Orioles and he led the league in 1984 with 20 wins. He was traded to the Red Sox in midseason 1988, won seven and lost three for the Sox that year, and then played two more years for Boston, compiling 28 wins and 26 losses. After the 1990 season he signed with the Kansas City Royals as a free agent.

Mike Boddicker pitched in three American League Championship Series. (Baseball Hall of Fame Library, Cooperstown, N.Y.).

Mike played in three league championship series, one with Baltimore. In 1983 when he was a 16-8 pitcher for the Orioles, one with the Red Sox in 1988 when his season record first with the Orioles and then with the Sox was a combined 13-15, and a third time with the Sox in 1990 when his season record was 17-8.

Ray Boone and Ike Boone

Ray Boone is the first of three generations of Boones playing in the big leagues.

Ray, also known as Ike, had a 13-year career as a big league infielder, mostly with Cleveland and Detroit, from 1948 through 1960. He finished his career playing 34 games for the Red Sox in 1960 and hit .205.

Ray's son Bob was one of the big league's better catchers for 19 years from 1972 through 1990 and subsequently became a manager.

Bob's son Bret is currently playing in the big leagues. Like his grandfather, he is an infielder.

The Red Sox also had another Boone for three years in the 1920s. This was another Ike Boone who batted over .330 in two full seasons with the Sox and played right field. Ike was not related to the Ray Boone family but his older brother, Danny, pitched for four years in the major leagues.

Lou Boudreau

Lou Boudreau started his career as the "boy" playing manager and shortstop of the Cleveland Indians. He was successful as both player and manager, popular, and became a Hall of Famer.

Coming up in the late 1930s, he was a shortstop in a good double-play combination, notably with Joe Gordon, and he was a good hitter. He won the American League batting championship in 1944 and was named the league's Most Valuable Player in 1948 with a .355 batting average, 18 home runs and 106 runs batted in. This was the same year in which he managed the Indians to the World Championship, beating the Boston Braves in the World Series.

Boudreau ended his career playing for the Red Sox in 1951 and briefly in 1952. He became the Red Sox manager in 1952, managed the Sox for three years out of his 16-year managing career, but the team never rose above fourth place under his stewardship.

Ken Brett

Ken, brother of George Brett, prospective Hall of Fame third baseman for Kansas City, pitched in four years for the Red Sox, 1967-1971. This was at the beginning of his 14-year pitching career. He played in two games as a reliever for the Red Sox in the 1967 World Series, a total of one and one third innings with no decisions.

Mace Brown

Mace Brown was one of the Red Sox's first ace relief pitchers. Most of his career was spent with the Pittsburgh Pirates.

He pitched for the Red Sox in 1942, 1943 and 1946. He led the American League in relief wins in 1942, winning nine games. He also led in games pitched in 1943, 49. His last two years with the Sox he had E.R.A.s of 2.12 and 2.05.

Mace Brown was one of the Red Sox's first outstanding relief pitchers. (Baseball Hall of Fame Library, Cooperstown, N.Y.).

Tom Brunansky

"Bruno" had a 14-year career as a major league outfielder, from 1981 through 1994. He played twice for the Red Sox, from 1990 to 1993 and for most of 1994. He was a power hitter with 271 home runs and 306 doubles in his career. He played two full seasons for the Sox in 1991 and 1992 and hit 31 homers in these two years. He also played on the Red Sox East division champions in 1990 and had one hit and one R.B.I. in the ALCS.

Tom Brunansky "Bruno" was a Red Sox outfielder in the early 1990s. (Baseball Hall of Fame Library, Cooperstown, N.Y.).

Tom Burgmeier

Burgmeier, in a 17-year career in the American League, pitched five years for the Red Sox from 1978-1982. He had a 21-12 record for the Sox as a relief pitcher. His big year with the Sox was in 1980 when he pitched 62 games in relief, won five and lost four with a 2.00 E.R.A. and had a career-high 24 saves. In 1982, he compiled a 7-0 record with a 2.29 E.R.A. in 40 relief appearances. After the 1982 season, at the age of 39, he signed as a free agent with Oakland and played two more years.

George Burns

In 1910 and 1920, there were two George Burns with impressive careers in the big leagues. One George Burns had his entire career of 15 years as an outfielder in the National League and played with the New York Giants in three World Series. The "other" George Burns was strictly an American Leaguer with 16 years as a first baseman and he played in two World Series. First baseman Burns played with the Red Sox in 1922 and 1923 when, in full seasons, he batted .306 and .328 respectively. He was a lifetime .307 hitter and, playing for Cleveland in 1926, led the league with 216 hits and 64 doubles. He also led the league in hits in 1918 playing for the Philadelphia Athletics. He had a career high of 12 home runs

George Burns played first base for the Red Sox in 1922 and 1923, batting .306 and .328, respectively. (Boston Red Sox).

playing for the Sox in 1922 and he hit 79 doubles in his two years with the team. He played with five American League teams.

Dolf Camilli

Dolf Camilli was a star first baseman for the Philadelphia Phillies and later for some of the good Brooklyn Dodger teams in the 1930s and 1940s. He was a power hitter and runs batted in leader. Camilli played the last of his 12 big-league years with the Red Sox in 1945, playing in only 63 games with a .212 batting average and two home runs.

Jose Canseco

Jose Canseco is a slugging outfielder and designated hitter who is a feared home run hitter. For most of his career he has been considered injury prone. He established his slugger's reputation in his first seven-plus years with the Oakland Athletics and he was a leading power hitter through the A's three championship seasons, 1988-1990.

He twice led the league with over 40 home runs and he established a record of 42 home runs and 40 stolen bases in 1988. In four other years he hit over 30 home runs.

Canseco, late in his career, came to the Red Sox as a designated hitter. He hit .306 in 1995 and had 24 home runs. He had 28 homers in 1996 with the team. He has since gone on to become a designated hitter with the Toronto Blue Jays, Tampa Bay, the New York Yankees and the Chicago White Sox. He is a popular and colorful player and an established slugger. He has been in the league 17 years with 462 home runs, 1407 runs batted in and a lifetime .266 batting average.

Jose Canseco (Boston Public Library, Print Department).

Roy and Cleo Carlyle

Brothers Roy and Cleo Carlyle had brief outfield careers with the Red Sox. Roy played 138 games for the Sox in 1925 and 1926. Cleo played 95 games for the Sox in 1927. Roy was a .300 hitter for the Red Sox and brother Cleo batted .234 in his one season. The big-league careers for both players lasted between 1925 and 1927.

Orlando Cepeda

Orlando Cepeda, "the Baby Bull," was another of baseball's top sluggers. (Boston Red Sox).

Orlando Cepeda, the "Baby Bull" from Puerto Rico, starred for the San Francisco Giants and St. Louis Cardinals during a 17-year career as a slugging first baseman. He had a .297 lifetime batting average with 379 home runs and 1,365 runs batted in. He played his next to last year as a designated hitter with the Red Sox in 1973, batting .289 with 20 home runs and 86 R.B.I.s.

Rick Cerone

Rick Cerone had an 18-year big league career as a catcher, mostly starring with the New York Yankees. He played two years with the Red Sox near the end of his career, in 1988 and 1989. A .255 hitter with the Red Sox with a life-

Rick Cerone played most of his 18-year career as a catcher for the Yankees. (Baseball Hall of Fame Library, Cooperstown, N.Y.).

time batting average of .245, his reputation was as a good "glove man" and handler of pitchers.

Esty Chaney

Esty Chaney had a two-game major league pitching career. He pitched one inning in one game for the Red Sox in 1913 and had a 9.00 earned run average. The next year he pitched for four innings for the Brooklyn Tip Tops in the competing Federal League and had an earned run average for his second appearance of 6.75.

Ben Chapman

Ben Chapman had a 15-year career as an outfielder with his best years with the New York Yankees. He was a .302 lifetime hitter. He played for the Red Sox in 1937 and 1938. A good hitter, he was also a good base stealer, leading the league four times in steals. One of those times was in 1937 when he split the season between the Washington Senators and the Red Sox. Chapman achieved notoriety as the manager of the Philadelphia Phillies in the late 1940s when he led the race baiting of Jackie Robinson. When Robinson came to the big leagues in 1947, Chapman led the threat of a players' boycott against Robinson and the Brooklyn Dodgers. The boycott failed on threat of league suspension for all boycotting players. Chapman, a Southerner, was said to have later regretted his attitudes and actions.

Jack Chesbro

Jack Chesbro, the great New York Highlanders' pitcher in the early 1900s, finished his career with the Red Sox in 1909. Ironically, Jack Chesbro won 41 games for the Highlanders in 1903 but then threw a wild pitch in the final game between the Highlanders and the Boston Pilgrims to give the Pilgrims the pennant. The Pilgrims went on to win the first World Series ever played.

Eddie Cicotte

Cicotte was a principal player involved in the Chicago Black Sox scandal of 1919. He pitched for the Red Sox from 1908 into 1912, a total of four-plus years. He won 59 games for the Red Sox, winning 15 games in 1910.

Jack Clark was a feared slugger and designated hitter for the Red Sox late in his career. (Baseball Hall of Fame Library, Cooperstown, N.Y.).

Jack Clark

Jack Clark had an 18-year career, mostly as a feared slugger with the San Francisco Giants and later with the St. Louis Cardinals. He was primarily an outfielder and later a first baseman; he was first baseman on the 1985 St. Louis Cardinals National League pennant winners.

Clark batted .267 in his career in nearly 2,000 games. He hit 340 home runs and had 1180 runs batted in. To indicate the way he was respected for his slugging ability he led the National League three times in bases on balls and had 1,262 walks in his career.

Clark played with the Boston Red Sox the last two years of his career, in 1991 and 1992, and was used almost entirely as a designated hitter. In this capacity he hit 28 home runs and had 87 R.B.I. in 1991. By 1992, his last year, his production had fallen off to five home runs and he batted only .210 in 81 games.

Billy Conigliaro

Billy Conigliaro started with the Red Sox in 1969, played three years, and then played briefly in Milwaukee and Oakland for a five-year career. His lifetime batting average was .264.

In 1970, Tony and Billy together hit 54 home runs, a brother combination record for one season. Tony hit 36 and Billy hit 18. They played together as regulars in the 1970 Boston outfield, flanking Reggie Smith who was in centerfield (Carl Yastrzemski was moved to first base.).

Gene Conley

Gene Conley pitched for the Red Sox from 1961 through 1963. He started his career with the Boston Braves, played with that team when it became the Milwaukee Braves, and also pitched for the Philadelphia Phillies. He had the most wins in his career, 15, while pitching for the Red Sox in 1962. Simultaneously with his baseball career, the six-feet-eight Conley played with the Boston Celtics in the National Basketball Association. He had the unique distinction of playing with championship teams in each sport, with the Celtics who won six championships during his career, and with the Milwaukee Braves who won the World Series in 1957.

Babe Dahlgren

Babe Dahlgren, who dramatically replaced Lou Gehrig at first base for the New York Yankees the day the Iron Horse's consecutive game playing streak came to an end in 1939, started his career with the Red Sox. He played for the Sox in 1935 and 1936 before being traded to the Yankees. Playing in 165 games for the Red Sox he batted .265 and was a lifetime .261 hitter.

Brian Daubach

Brian Daubach, beginning in 1999, has become the first baseman for the Red Sox. He is also utilized as a designated hitter. Daubach has had more than 20 home runs each year from 1999 through 2001 and has driven in an average of 73 runs each of these years. His current lifetime batting average is .266. Daubach played in the 1999 American League Division Series, mostly as a designated hitter, and batted .250. Continuing this role in the AL Championship Series, he batted .176 with one home run.

George "Skeets" Dickey

"Skeets" Dickey, younger brother of the New York Yankees' Hall of Fame catcher Bill Dickey, had a brief playing career that started with the Red Sox in 1935. He was a catcher for the Sox, played in a total of 15 games in 1935 and 1936, and had a six-year playing career in which he batted .204

Denny Doyle

Doyle was a second baseman for the Red Sox from 1975 through 1977, after playing four years with the Philadelphia Phillies and having a brief stint with the California Angels. He succeeded Doug Griffin at second base for the Sox in 1975. In the 1975 World Series he got eight hits, including a double and triple, and batter .267. His lifetime batting average over eight years was .250.

Joe Dugan

Jumpin' Joe Dugan was part of a three-team trade in early 1922 between the Philadelphia Athletics, the Red Sox and the Washington Senators. He was traded from the Athletics, with whom he had played shortstop and third base for five years, to the Washington Nationals. Before the season began he was then traded by the Nationals to the Red Sox and played a half year with the Red Sox in 1922 before being traded to the New York Yankees. In his half year with the Red Sox Dugan batted .287 in 84 games.

Dugan then went on to have a distinguished career with the Yankees for six years and played in five World Series.

Carl Everett

Carl Everett is a slugging, good-hitting outfielder. In his nine years in the big leagues, he has played with four teams. He played two years with the Red Sox, in 2000 and 2001. He batted .300 in 2000 and played in the All-Star game. He then dropped to .257 in 2001. He had 34 home runs and 108 runs batted in in 2000, and 14 home runs and 58 runs batted in 2001. Everett has a history of difficulty with authority and he has a reputation as a disruptive influence in the clubhouse. He was at odds with manager Jimy Williams of the Red Sox, notably in 2001. There was some uncertainty as to whether the general manager backed the manager in disciplining Everett. With the Everett relationship as one factor, Jimy Williams was dismissed as manager in late 2001. Carl Everett was traded to the Texas Rangers and will play for that team in 2002.

Lou Finney

Lou Finney, who played most of his career with the Philadelphia Athletics in the 1930s, was a Red Sox outfielder-first baseman from 1939 through mid 1945. In not quite a full year in 1939 he batted .325 for the Sox. He led the league that year with the most pinch hit at bats, 40. He batted .320 the following year. He had 171 hits and a career high of 31 doubles and 15 triples. Finney was traded to the St. Louis Browns in 1945 and ended his career with the Philadelphia Phillies in 1947. In 15 years, Finney had a lifetime batting average of .287.

Lou Finney played for the Red Sox during WWII. (Baseball Hall of Fame Library, Cooperstown, N.Y.).

Pete Fox

Pete Fox was a regular outfielder for eight years, from 1933 through 1940, with the Detroit Tigers and he played in three World Series with the Tigers. After the 1940 season, he was sold to the Red Sox for cash. Pete played five years for the Red Sox and ended his career in 1945.

Pete had a lifetime .298 batting average and he had a cumulative .327 average in World Series play. His best year with the Red Sox was in 1944 when he hit .315 with 38 doubles. In his career he had 158 stolen bases. He was a reliable outfielder and a steady, dependable player.

Pete Fox was an outfielder for the Tigers and the Red Sox in the 1930s and 1940s. (Baseball Hall of Fame Library, Cooperstown, N.Y.)

Gary Geiger

Gary Geiger was an outfielder with the Red Sox from 1959 through 1965, a period of seven years in a 12-year career. He was a regular outfielder for the Sox

in four seasons. His highest batting average as a regular was .263, in 1963. He had a career .241 batting average and for three years in a row, 1961 through 1963, hit more than 16 home runs each season.

Milt and Alex Gaston

Milt Gaston pitched for the Red Sox from 1929-1931. He led the league in losses in 1930, with 20. He lost 19 in 1929 and 13 in 1931. In his three years with the Red Sox he was 27-52. In his 11 major league seasons he had one winning year, 1925, when he won 15 and lost 14 for the St. Louis Browns. Milt's older brother, Alex, was a catcher for the Red Sox in 1926 and then in 1929, having played four years previously with the New York Giants.

Milt Gaston pitched for the Red Sox from 1929-31, leading the league in losses in 1930. (Baseball Hall of Fame Library. Cooperstown, N.Y.).

Erik Hanson

Erik Hanson pitched one year for the Red Sox, in 1995, a creditable year in which he won 15 and lost five. He pitched most of his career with the Seattle Mariners and, in 1996 he moved to the Toronto Blue Jays.

Hanson started 29 games for the Red Sox and completed one in an era of relief pitching specialists. He started and lost one game for the Red Sox in the 1995 Divisional Playoff Series. He pitched a complete game but the Indians and Orel Hershiser won, 4-0.

Carroll Hardy

Carroll Hardy had a journeyman eight-year major league career, playing as a part-time outfielder for the Red Sox in part of 1960, 1961 and 1962. Though possessed of only a .225 career batting average he may be noted for the fact that, at different times, he pinch hit for Ted Williams, Carl Yastrzemski and Roger Maris.

Carroll Hardy played eight years in the big leagues. (Baseball Hall of Fame Library. Cooperstown, N.Y.).

Tommy Harper

Tommy Harper had a 15-year career as an outfielder, mostly with Cincinnati. He was known as a speedster and had 408 stolen bases in his career, twice leading the league. He led the league with 73 stolen bases in 1969, playing for Seattle. With the Red Sox in 1973 he was the league leader with 54.

Tommy played three seasons for the Red Sox, from 1972-1974. A .257 lifetime hitter, his best year with the Sox was in 1973 when he hit .281 with 159 hits and 17 home runs in addition to his 54 base steals. He went on to play for three other American League teams for a total of eight big-league teams in his career. He played in the 1975 ALCS for Oakland.

Ken "Hawk" Harrelson

Ken Harrelson was an outfielder with the Red Sox for about a year and a half beginning in 1967. He first played with the Kansas City Athletics and Washington Senators and later with the Cleveland Indians. In his full year with the Red Sox he won the league's runs batted in championship. Ken, or "The Hawk," was both an outspoken person and a fashion plate. He was the first to wear batting gloves and off-the-field he wore the popular Nehru jacket. He later became a baseball announcer for the Red Sox and then the White Sox.

Ken Harrelson became known for his fashion statements both on and off the field. He won a R.B.I. title for the Red Sox. (Baseball Hall of Fame Library, Cooperstown, N.Y.).

Greg Harris

Greg Harris, one of two pitchers named Greg Harris in the major leagues in the 1980s and 1990s, pitched for the Red Sox in 1989, four full seasons from 1990 through 1993, and then again in 1994. He had a 15-year career with eight different teams. The "other" Greg Harris pitched most of his career in the National League.

Harris pitched both as a starter and in relief for the Red Sox. As a starter in 1990 he was 13-9. The following year he was 11-12. Switched mostly to relief beginning in 1991, he led the league in relief losses in 1992 and 1993. While with the Red Sox Harris went 39-43. He went on to pitch briefly for the Yankees and the Montreal Expos.

Joe Harris

Harris, a Pilgrims right-handed pitcher, pitched all 24 innings in a game against Jack Coombs and the Philadelphia Athletics. Unfortunately, he lost the game, 4-1, but still shares the record for most innings pitched in an American League game. In 1906, a year in which the Pilgrims finished in last place, Harris won two and lost 21. His career record was three wins and 30 losses.

Joe Harris was one of the early Pilgrim pitchers. (Baseball Hall of Fame Library, Cooperstown, N.Y.).

Mickey Harris

Mickey Harris started his big-league career with the Boston Red Sox in 1940, pitched two seasons, then went into military service in World War II, and returned after the war to pitch three seasons and part of another with the team. His best career year was 1946 when he won 17 and lost nine for the Red Sox. It was the only year in which he won more than eight games. He was traded to Washington in early 1949 and from then on in his career pitched mostly in relief.

Harris, in 1946, was the third starter on the pitching staff, after Boo Ferriss and Tex Hughson. He started and lost two World Series games against the St. Louis Cardinals that year. He did not finish either game and both times he lost to Harry Brecheen, who gave up one run in the two games.

In a career interrupted by service in World War II, Mickey Harris pitched 5 1/2 years for the Red Sox. (Baseball Hall of Fame Library. Cooperstown, N.Y.).

Dave Henderson

Dave Henderson, beginning in 1981, played outfield for 14 years in the big leagues and sandwiched in a brief stint with the Red Sox from late 1986 to late 1987. He played in only 111 games for the Red Sox, but it was in the 1986 postseason that he particularly stood out.

In the American League Championship Series between the Sox and the California Angels, the Angels took a three-games-to-one lead and were about to eliminate the Sox. With two strikes and two outs in the ninth inning of the fifth game, Henderson hit a two-run home run to tie the game. Then in the 11th inning, he drove in the winning run with a sacrifice fly, and the Red Sox went on to win the play-offs, four games to three. Then, in the World Series that year against the New York Mets, Henderson outhit everyone with ten hits in 25 at bats. He hit a home run in the top of the tenth inning of the sixth game, apparently winning the Series for the Red Sox, but the Mets came back to win the game in the bottom of the tenth with the infamous squibbler that went through Bill Buckner's legs.

Dave Henderson excelled in Boston postseason play in 1986 with his timely and dramatic hitting. (Boston Red Sox).

Henderson went on in his career to play for the Oakland Athletics in three American League Championship Series wins and a World Series win.

Olaf Henriksen

Olaf "Swede" Henriksen tied Game 8 of the 1912 World Series for the Red Sox with a single off Christy Mathewson. An early pinch hit specialist, Henriksen stayed with Boston seven years in this capacity. His 1912 single was his only World Series pinch hit. His lifetime batting average was .269. Though "Swede" was his nickname, he was born in Denmark.

Joe Heving

Joe Heving had a 13-year pitching career in the big leagues, spanning from 1930 through 1945. He pitched slightly more than two seasons for the Red Sox, from 1938 through 1940. In his two full seasons with the team, 1939 and 1940, he led the league each year in relief pitching wins with first eleven and then eight wins.

Joe Heving pitched for the Red Sox just before WWII. (Baseball Hall of Fame Library, Cooperstown, N.Y.).

Mike "Pinky" Higgins

"Pinky" Higgins, in his 14-year playing career, played twice for the Red Sox, in 1937 and 1938 and at the end of his career in 1946. He played five outstanding years with the Philadelphia Athletics and six and one half good years with the Detroit Tigers. He played his entire career at third base and, while with the Red Sox, set a record in 1938 with 12 consecutive base hits. (Johnny Pesky, who also played third base for the Red Sox, was second in league history with 11 straight hits in 1946). Higgins' lifetime batting average was .292 and he played in two World Series, one with the Red Sox in 1946. He later managed the Red Sox eight years from 1955 through 1962.

Pinky Higgins set a record with 12 consecutive base hits in 1938. (Baseball Hall of Fame Library, Cooperstown, N.Y.).

Elston Howard

"Ellie" Howard was a great New York Yankee catcher, replacing Yogi Berra. He was a popular Yankee and mainstay from 1955 through 1967. In a startling trade to the Red Sox near the end of his career in 1967, he was considered by many to be "on loan from the Yankees."

Ellie played 42 games for the Sox in 1967, aiding them in their pennant winning year, and he played 71 games in 1968 before retiring and subsequently returning to the Yankees as a coach. His brief tour with the Red Sox included play in the 1967 World Series, having played previously in nine World Series with the Yankees.

A good handler of pitchers, Howard had a lifetime .274 batting average. He also hit for power, with three years in which he hit more than 20 home runs.

Waite Hoyt

Waite Hoyt was a Hall of Fame pitcher who was

Catcher Elston Howard played 42 games for the Red Sox in 1967 and helped them win the pennant, after being traded to Boston from the Yankees. (Baseball Hall of Fame Library. Cooperstown, N.Y.).

The Red Sox Encyclopedia

traded by the Red Sox to the New York Yankees and spent most of his 21-year career with the Yankees. He pitched two years for the Red Sox in 1919 and 1920. Then early in his career, he won 10 and lost 12 while with the Sox. Hoyt later became a well-known baseball broadcaster.

Ed Hughes

Ed Hughes pitched for the Pilgrims in 1905 and 1906 and had a total Pilgrims career record of three wins and two losses. He was the younger brother of Long Tom Hughes.

Ferguson "Fergy" Jenkins

"Fergy" Jenkins has the rare distinction of having pitched 284 victories in a 19-year career and yet he never appeared

Fergie Jenkins was a Canadian-born Hall of Fame pitcher. (Baseball Hall of Fame Library, Cooperstown, N.Y.).

in a postseason game. His early years, 1965-1973, he was with the Philadelphia Phillies and Chicago Cubs. He won 20 or more games for six consecutive years with the Cubs and in 1971 was the National League Cy Young winner. He then pitched for the Texas Rangers and had a 25-win season with them. He pitched for the Red Sox in 1976 and 1977, winning 22 games and losing 21 before being traded back to the Rangers. After four more years with the Rangers he finished his career back with the Chicago Cubs. Jenkins, a Canadian, was a workhorse pitcher who pitched one out less than 5,000 innings in his career. He was also a good hitter and fielder, and was elected to the Hall of Fame.

Earl Johnson

Earl Johnson pitched seven years for the Red Sox, nearly all in the 1940s, with time out for three years of military service. His best years were in 1947 and 1948. He won 12 and lost 11 in 1947, 12 games being the most he won in any one year in the big leagues. He pitched three shutouts and had eight saves. The next year, in 1948, he won 10 and lost four. Nine of these wins were in relief as he led the league in this category. He also had five saves.

Johnson won the first game of the 1946 World Series pitching in relief. Tex Hughson pitched the first eight innings and Johnson the last two as the Red Sox beat the Cardinals in 10 innings, 3-2. He also relieved in the last two games of the Series but had no decisions.

Roy and Bob Johnson

Roy and Bob Johnson were brothers who played outfield briefly for the Red Sox in the 1930s and 1940s.

Roy played for the Sox from 1933 through 1935, hitting over .300 in each of these years. Younger brother Bob played for the Red Sox at the end of his career, in 1944 and 1945. He, too, was a good hitter, batting .324 in 1944 and .280 in 1945.

Smead Jolley

Smead Jolley was an outfielder for the Chicago White Sox and then for the Red Sox in the early 1930s. He had a career .305 batting average but was something of a liability as a fielder.

When the Italian language newspaper, "Notizia," searched for an ethnic baseball hero for the large Italian community in Boston, Jolley achieved his claim to fame. He was "discovered" by Johnny Garro, the newspaper editor, as an Italian and he henceforth referred to Jolley as Smeederino Jolliani.

Eddie Kasko

Eddie Kasko, essentially a Cincinnati Reds infielder, ended his career as a utility infielder for the Red Sox in 1966. He became manager of the Red Sox for four years, 1970 through 1973, with two second-place finishes.

Earl Johnson won the first game of the 1946 World Series for the Red Sox pitching in relief. (Baseball Hall of Fame Library. Cooperstown, N.Y.).

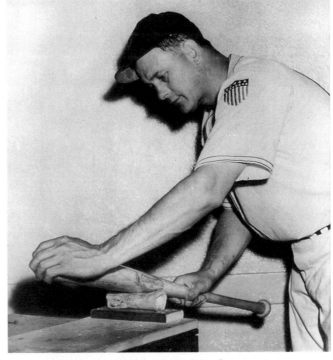

Bob Johnson played outfield for the Red Sox from 1944-45. His older brother, Roy, was in the Boston outfield from 1933-35. Both brothers batted better than .300 for the Red Sox. (Boston Red Sox).

George Kell

George Kell, Hall of Fame third baseman primarily with the Detroit Tigers, played approximately two seasons for the Red Sox over the period 1952 through 1954. He was a lifetime .306 hitter over a 15-year period.

John Kennedy

John Kennedy was a Red Sox part-time infielder for four and one half seasons, beginning in mid 1970 and ending in 1974.

He played 12 years in the big leagues for six teams from 1962 through 1974, and had a .225 lifetime batting average. His best batting year was with Boston in 1971 when he played in 74 games and batted .276. He played with the Los Angeles Dodgers in both the 1965 and 1966 World Series.

Jack Kramer

Jack Kramer, a mainstay pitcher for the St. Louis Browns in the 1940s, including their one and only pennant year in 1944, pitched for the Red Sox in 1948 and 1949. In 1948, he led the league in winning percentage, .783, with

Jack Kramer led the American League in winning percentage in 1948 with his 18-5 (.783) record. (Baseball Hall of Fame Library. Cooperstown, N.Y.)

18 wins and five losses. It was his biggest winning year in the big leagues.

Candy LaChance

Candy LaChance was the Somersets/Pilgrims first baseman from 1902-1904 and briefly in 1905. Buck Freeman played first base and then moved to the outfield.

Candy had a 12-year big league career, beginning with Brooklyn in the National League in 1893. He had a .280 lifetime batting average and never batted more than .279 for Boston. He was known as a good fielding first baseman. He played for the Pilgrims in the 1903 World Series, batting .222 and playing in eight games.

Carney Lansford

Carney Lansford played two years for the Red Sox, in 1981 and 1982, during a long career that was mostly with the Oakland Athletics. His big league career began in the 1970s and ended in the 1990s.

Lansford won the A.L. batting title playing with the Red Sox in 1981 with a .336 average. He also hit over .300 the next season and played a competent third base but, with the appearance of Wade Boggs, was traded to the A's in exchange for Tony Armas.

Tony Lupien

Tony Lupien was the Red Sox first baseman for the first three years of his six-year career before and during World War II. His lifetime batting average was .268, He was notably familiar to Boston fans because he had attended Harvard University and was known as "Harvard Tony."

Danny MacFayden

Danny MacFayden, who had a 17-year career as a big league pitcher, pitched for both the Boston Red Sox and the Boston Braves. He started his career with the Red Sox and was with them for seven years, from 1926 into 1932. He pitched for the Braves from 1935 through 1939 and at the end of his career in 1943. MacFayden with the Red Sox won 52 and lost 78. With the Braves he won 60 and lost 64.

Danny's best year with the Red Sox was his last full year in 1931 when he won 16 and lost 12. In a 10-18 year in 1929 he led the American League with four shutouts. His best season with the Braves was his first full year in 1936 when he won 17 and lost 13. In his career he won 132 and lost 159.

Heinie Manush

Heinie Manush, a Hall of Fame outfielder who spent most of his seventeen year career with the Detroit Tigers and

First baseman Tony Lupien (left) chats with Red Sox all-time great Jimmie Foxx. (Boston Public Library Print Department).

the Washington Senators in the 1920s and 1930s, played one year with the Red Sox in 1936. Manush had a lifetime batting average of .330, more than 2500 hits, and he batted in 1173 runs.

Juan Marichal

Juan Marichal, the Hall of Fame pitcher from the Dominican Republic who spent nearly all of his sixteen year career with the San Francisco Giants, pitched one year for the Red Sox in 1974, winning five games. He ended his career the next season pitching for the Los Angeles Dodgers. Marichal in his career was a blazing fastballer with a big wind-up. He had six 20-game-winning seasons. He won 243 games. His lifetime earned run average was 2.89 and he led the National League in this category with 2.10 in 1969. He also led the league twice each in wins,

Juan Marichal was one of baseball's top pitchers. he is from the Dominican Republic. (Boston Red Sox).

complete games and shutouts. He had 2,303 strikeouts in his career and led the National League with 295 in 1968.

Gene Mauch

Gene Mauch, one of the better managers in baseball history, played the last two years of his playing career with the Red Sox in 1956 and 1957. He was a part-time second baseman then. He played nine years for six teams in the big leagues, including stints with the Boston Braves and then the Red Sox in the 1950s. He was mostly a utility infielder and had a .239 lifetime batting average.

Though Mauch managed four teams in a 26-year managerial career, he never managed the Red Sox. Two of his California Angels teams reached the ALCS but lost, once to the Red Sox.

Tim McCarver

Tim McCarver, one of the better catchers during his era in the big leagues, played 21 years. He spent most of his career with the St. Louis Cardinals, from 1959 through 1969 and again in 1973. He spent the largest part of his remaining career on three Phillies postseason teams and three Cardinal pennant winners, two of whom were World Champions.

Sandwiched in between, McCarver played for the Red Sox. Coming from the Cardinals in the latter part of 1974, Tim was a Bosoxer for 11 games and batted .250. He played for the Sox in 12 more games in 1975, batting .381, before moving on to the Philadelphia Phillies. McCarver had a .271 lifetime batting average.

McCarver, subsequent to his playing career, became a baseball and sports broadcaster.

Eric McNair

Eric McNair, who played most of his career as a shortstop with the Philadelphia Athletics in the early 1930s, played infield for the Red Sox for three years, 1936 through 1938. McNair in his two full playing seasons with the Red Sox, 1936 and 1937, batted a respectable .285 and .292. He stole a career-high 10 bases in 1937. He played in the field in 32 games in 1938 and was a 2-for-14 pinch hitter that season. He was traded to the Chicago White Sox at season's end and played four more years, completing his 14-year career with a .274 batting average.

Sam Mele

Sam Mele started his big-league career with the Red Sox just after World War II and went on to play for five other teams in a ten-year career. In addition, after his first tour of duty with the Red Sox from 1947 to mid-1949, he came back to the team in mid-1954 until he was sold to another team in 1956. In his ten years he was traded four times and sold outright once. He did not play three consecutive, full seasons with any one team.

Sam had a lifetime .267 batting average. He played the outfield his entire career, occasionally substituting at first base. With the Red Sox he batted a career-high .302 his rookie year. He also had eight triples and 12 home runs. He also had a good year with the Washington Nationals in 1951 when he batted .274 and led the league with 36 doubles.

Sam Mele played for the Red Sox first in the 1940s and then in the mid-1950s. (Baseball Hall of Fame Library, Cooperstown, N.Y.)

Sam Mele became the manager of the Minnesota Twins in 1961. In his seven-year managerial career with the Twins he won one pennant.

George Metkovich

George "Catfish" Metkovich played the first four years of his ten-year career with the Red Sox during World War II. His lifetime batting average was .261. His best year was with Pittsburgh in 1951 when he batted .293. With the Red Sox his best year was his first full year, 1944, when he batted .277 with 28 doubles and nine home runs, both career highs. His slugging average was .406 in 1944 and he scored 94 runs, also career highs. Early in his career, the "Catfish" also showed some speed with 13 steals in 1944 and 19 in 1945.

Metkovich batted .500 for the Red Sox in the 1946 World Series, based on one hit in two at bats. These were his last at bats for the Sox as he played the last six years of his career with five other teams.

Bob Montgomery

Bob Montgomery played his entire career, ten seasons, as a catcher for the Red Sox. He was mostly a part-time catcher and caught no more than 79 games in any one season. He averaged 36 games a year catching for the Sox from 1970 through 1979. Montgomery had a lifetime .258 batting average. In his part-time service he had three particularly good seasons at the plate. He batted .349 in 86 at bats in 1979, .320 in 128 at bats in 1973 and .300 with 12 hits in 40 at bats in 1977. He also had one at bat in the 1975 World Series.

After his playing career, Montgomery became a baseball broadcaster for the Red Sox.

Wilcy Moore

Wilcy Moore, mostly a star relief pitcher with the New York Yankees in the late 1920s and early 1930s, also pitched in relief for the Red Sox in 1931 and 1932. In 1931, pitching for the Sox, he led the league in saves with ten. In his first year with the Yankees, 1927, he led the league in relief wins and saves, each with 13, and he led the league with an earned run average of 2.28.

Wally Moses

Wally Moses had a long 17-year career as an outfielder in the American League. His first seven years, from 1935 through 1941, were the best. He played for the Philadelphia Athletics and never batted under .300. For the rest of his career, Moses never batted over .300, including his final three years in 1949-1951 when he came back to play for the Athletics.

Moses played for the Red Sox from mid-1946, when he came over from the White Sox, through 1948. He was mostly a part-time outfielder from the time he was sold to the Red Sox to the end of his career more than six years later.

Moses played in four games for the Red Sox in the 1946 World Series and had five hits in 12 at bats for a .417 average. His lifetime batting average was .291.

Johnny Murphy

Johnny Murphy, the great relief pitcher for the New York Yankees for 12 years in the 1930s and 1940s, and a pitcher on six Yankee World Series teams, pitched the final year of his career for the Red Sox in 1947. He had no decisions and but three saves in his final year, at age 39.

Johnny Murphy was a star relief pitcher, mostly with the New York Yankees and briefly with the Red Sox. (Baseball Hall of Fame Library, Cooperstown, N.Y.)

Bobo Newsom

Bobo Newsom, a loquacious and bombastic pitcher, changed teams 17 times in his 20-year pitching career. He played for the Washington Senators (five times), St. Louis Browns (three times), the Brooklyn Dodgers (twice), the Philadelphia Athletics (twice), and one time each with the New York Yankees, Chicago Cubs, New York Giants, Detroit Tigers, and Boston Red Sox. He had a checkered 20 years, winning at least 20 games three times, but then losing at least 20 games in three other seasons. After pitching more than 3,759 innings in 600 games he ended his career with 211 wins and 222 losses.

Newsom was with the Red Sox for a half season in 1937, winning 13 and losing 10. Newsom was both self-centered and hard to handle. An incident was once reported where player-manager Joe Cronin of the Sox came to the mound for a discussion and pitcher Newsom promptly dismissed him and sent him back to his short-stop position. He pitched well for the St. Louis Browns and the Washington Senators and he was the pitching star for the Detroit Tigers in the 1940 World Series. He started three World Series games, won two and lost one, the latter the seventh game by a score of 2 to 1. He led the Tigers during the 1940 season with 21 wins and five losses. It is said 'Bobo' earned his nickname because this was the way he addressed all his teammates since he seldom stayed around long enough to learn their names.

Al Nipper

Al Nipper, who began his career with Boston in 1983, was a Red Sox starting pitcher from 1984 through 1987. In those four seasons he started at least 24 games a year and compiled a won-lost record of 41 and 42. In his seven-year big league career he never won more than 11 games a season and he did this twice for the Red Sox.

Nipper started and lost one game in the 1986 World Series. He lost Game 4 to Ron Darling and the New York Mets, 6-2. He also pitched a third of an inning in relief in the final game of the Series, one of six pitchers used by manager John McNamara in the Red Sox's 8-5 loss.

Buck O'Brien

Buck had a short three-year big league career from 1911 through 1913. He pitched two years for the Red Sox and half of another before he was sold for cash to the Chicago White Sox and finished his career there. In Buck's one full and productive year, 1912, he contributed to the Red Sox pennant, winning 20 games and losing 13. He was over-shadowed by Smoky Joe Wood who had 34 wins, and Hugh Bedient, who also had 20 wins. It was, nonetheless, Buck's career year. He completed 25 of the 34 games he started and had a 2.58 earned run average. He pitched 275²/₃ innings and had two shutouts.

Buck started and lost the two games he pitched in the 1912 World Series, ultimately won by the Red Sox over John McGraw's New York Giants. Buck lost twice to Rube Marquard, once in Game 3 when the score was 2-1, and again in Game 6 when the final score was 5-2.

Lefty O'Doul

Frank "Lefty" O'Doul, perhaps best known for his out-field career and hitting in the Pacific Coast League, spent 11 years in the big leagues in the 1920s and 1930s. He

Buck O'Brien went 20-14 for the Red Sox in 1912, but was over-shadowed on his own team by Smoky Joe Wood and Hugh Bedient. (Baseball Hall of Fame Library. Cooperstown, N.Y.).

started his career as a pitcher and, in his one year with the Red Sox in 1923, pitched in 23 games with one win and one loss. It was his last year as a big-league pitcher.

Jose Offerman

Jose Offerman is a 12-year major-league veteran who played his first six years with the Los Angeles Dodgers. He is an infielder. In his six years with the Dodgers he was, mostly, the team's regular shortstop. Subsequently, in three years with the Kansas City Royals and then three years with the Red Sox, he has been a second baseman. He also plays at first base and has been a designated hitter. Offerman is speedy and at times hits for power. He led the league in triples in 1998 with the Royals and in 1999 with the Red Sox. During the course of his career, he has stolen 162 bases, with 45 steals in 1998, the year before he came to the Red Sox. His best Red Sox year was in 1999 when he batted .294, scored 107 runs, led the league in triples, also had 37 doubles and stole 18 bases. His current lifetime batting average is .277. Jose batted .389 in the 1999 American League Division Series with seven hits and seven bases on balls. In the ALCS, he batted .458, leading both the Red Sox and Yankees in hits with 11.

Steve O'Neill

Steve O'Neill, one of the more notable managers in baseball history, had a 17-year playing career as a catcher from 1911 through 1928. The first 13 years were with the Cleveland Indians. He was with the Red Sox one year, in 1924, and batted .238. including 2-for-14 as a pinch hitter. He caught in 92 games that year for the Sox in one of their more dismal seasons. O'Neill was a lifetime .263 hitter.

O'Neill managed four teams for 14 years in the big leagues, including the Detroit World Champions in 1945. He managed the Red Sox for two seasons, in 1950 and 1951, finishing third in the league both times.

Mickey Owen

Mickey Owen has his name etched in baseball history because of a miscue in the World Series of 1941. In Game 4, while catching for the Brooklyn Dodgers against the New York Yankees, Mickey allowed a passed ball on a strikeout by pitcher Hugh Casey. As a result the Yankees' Tommy Henrich reached first base safely and the Yanks went on to score four runs in the top of the ninth inning, winning the game 7-4 and ultimately the Series.

Owen, notwithstanding, was a good catcher during his 13 years in the big leagues. He caught regularly for the St. Louis Cardinals and the Dodgers for more than seven years. He finished his career catching 30 games for the Red Sox in 1954, his only year with the team. He had a .255 lifetime batting average.

Spike Owen

Spike Owen, who played 13 years in the big leagues, was a Red Sox shortstop from the latter part of 1986 through 1988. He was a lifetime .246 hitter and only once batted over .270, for California in 1994 near the end of his career. His best fielding years were with the Montreal Expos from 1989 through 1992.

Spike played all seven games at shortstop for the Red Sox in the 1986 ALCS and also in the World Series. He had nine hits in the ALCS and batted .429. He batted in three runs and scored five in the Red Sox win over California. In the World Series he had six hits in 20 at bats for a .300 average. Spike made one appearance for the Red Sox in the 1988 ALCS, but had no official at bat.

Tony Perez

Tony Perez was an important member of Cincinnati's "Big Red Machine." He played 13 years for the Reds, mostly anchored at first base but also as a third baseman. Tony had a 23-year big league career, played in six NLCS (five with the Reds) and in five World Series (four with the Reds). His lifetime batting average was .279 and he hit 379 home runs with 1652 runs batted in.

Tony played against the Red Sox in the 1975 World Series, leading all hitters with three home runs and seven R.B.I.s, although he batted only .179 in the seven games. He joined the Red Sox in 1980 and played three seasons. He played first base in 1980, was both a first baseman and designated hitter in 1981, and he was mostly a designated hitter in 1982. Tony hit 25 home runs and batted in 105 runs with the Sox in 1980, the last time in his career he was in double figures for home runs or drove in more than 45 runs. He batted .275, .252 and .260 in his three seasons with the Sox. He went on to play with the National League champion Philadelphia Phillies in 1983 and then went back to the Reds for three years to complete his career. He was elected to the Hall of Fame in 2000.

Tony managed the Cincinnati Reds for 44 games in 1993 until he was prematurely ousted by notorious Cincinnati owner Marge Schott.

George Pipgras

George Pipgras, who was traded by the Red Sox to the New York Yankees at the outset of his major league career in 1923, pitched eight-plus years for the Yankees. He was traded back to the Red Sox in 1933 and stayed with them through 1934 and 1935. He had a 9-8 record for the Sox in 1933, but then had only one decision, a loss, the rest of his career.

George Pipgras came up with the Boston Red Sox but became a star with the New York Yankees. (Baseball Hall of Fame Library, Cooperstown, N.Y.).

Doc Prothro

Doc Prothro, in most recent memory, was the manager of the last place Philadelphia Phillies for three consecutive years, from 1939 through 1941. His teams won 138 games and lost 320.

Prothro had a five-year playing career as an infielder from 1920 through 1926. In his only full season, 1925, he played third base for the Red Sox and hit .313. His lifetime batting average was .318 in a total of 180 games (119 with the Red Sox).

Jeff Reardon

Jeff Reardon, one of the premier relief pitchers in the big leagues in the 1980s, pitched for the Red Sox in 1990, 1991 and part of 1992. He led the National League in saves in 1985 with 41 while pitching for the Montreal Expos. In his 1991 season with the Red Sox he had 40. In a 16-year career ending in 1994 he set a career record at the time with 367 saves. He is currently third all-time in saves behind Dennis Eckersley, a returning Red Sox pitcher,

Jeff Reardon was one of the premier relief pitchers in baseball in the 1980s. (Baseball Hall of Fame Library, Cooperstown, N.Y.).

and Lee Smith, a former Red Soxer. He played in four league championships series, including one with Boston, and in two World Series.

Win Remmerswaal

Win Remmerswaal was a right-handed pitcher from the Netherlands who spent his two-year big-league career with the Red Sox in 1979 and 1980. His career totals were three wins and one loss. He was a reliever and did not start any games.

Walt and Allen Ripley

Walt Ripley, father, and Allen Ripley, son, both pitched for the Boston Red Sox. Walt pitched one year, in 1935, making two relief appearances. Son Allen pitched two years for the Sox 43 years later, in 1978 and 1979. He had five wins and six losses with the Red Sox.

Billy Rogell

Billy Rogell, who was a fixture as the Detroit Tigers short-stop in the 1930s, started his career as an infielder with the Red Sox. He played with the Sox in 1925, 1927 and 1928. Rogell was a lifetime .267 hitter.

Manny Ramirez

Manny Ramirez, an outstanding slugging outfielder and run producer, signed with the Boston Red Sox beginning with the 2001 season. He had been an American League superstar playing for eight season with the Cleveland Indians. In these years, he hit a total of 236 home runs with 127 in the years 1998 through 2000. He had driven in 804 runs in six full seasons and led the league with 165 R.B.I.s in 1999. He led the league in slugging average in 1999 at .663, and in 2000, he led with a .697 slugging average. His batting average for his eight years with Cleveland was .313.

In his first year with the Red Sox, 2001, Manny batted .306 with 41 home runs and 125 runs batted in. His slugging average was .609 and, not surprisingly, he led the league in

Manny Ramirez, who came over to the Red Sox beginning with the 2001 season, is a premier power hitter and runs batted in leader in the American League. (Boston Red Sox)

intentional base on balls with 25. Thirty years old in 1992, he is prospectively the Red Sox slugging star.

Brian Rose

Brian Rose was a right-handed, mostly starting pitcher with the Red Sox beginning in 1997 and ending in 2000. He pitched his best season with the team in 1999 and pitched substantially one half season in 2000 before going on to the Colorado Rockies, and to the New York Mets and Tampa Bay Devil Rays in 2001. Rose was a journeyman pitcher with the Red Sox. He pitched in a total of 46 games with the Sox and started 39 of them. In his best season, 1999, he won seven and lost six and had a 4.87 earned run average.

Ken Ryan

Ken Ryan pitched for four years for the Red Sox, 1992 through 1995, before going to the Philadelphia Phillies. He won a total of nine games for the Red Sox and also lost nine games. He pitched only in relief and had 13 saves in 1994. Ryan may be mostly notable for the fact that he struck out 21 batters in a high school game the same day that Roger Clemens set the major league record with 20 strikeouts in a game for the Red Sox in 1986.

Ken Ryan struck out 21 batters in a high school baseball game the same day Roger Clemens set a new big league record with 20 strikeouts. (Baseball Hall of Fame Library, Cooperstown, N.Y.).

Bret Saberhagen

Bret Saberhagen was with the Kansas City Royals the first eight years of his career, from 1984 through 1991. He was one of the American League's leading pitchers, most notably in 1989 when he led the league in wins with 23 and in won-lost average at .793 with 23 wins and six losses. He also led in earned run average that year, 2.16, and led in number of complete games pitched. He won the 1989 American League Cy Young Award. He won the 1985 and 1989 American League Cy Young Awards.

Bret injured his arm and his fastball was not nearly as effective subsequently in his career but he did lead the league in winning percentage pitching for the New York Mets in 1994. Saberhagen has been a pitcher for the Red Sox for four years, 1997 through 2001, missing the 2000 season when he was out with an injury. He won 15 games for the Red Sox in 1998 and was the starter in 31 games. He won 10 in 1999 and started in 22 games. His earned run average in 1999 was 2.95. He started a total of four games in Red Sox postseason play in 1998 and 1999 but did not win a game. Now in the twilight of his career, Saberhagen has won 167 games and lost 117 in his 16-year career with a lifetime 3.34 earned run average.

Bret Saberhagen was a Cy Young winner earlier in his career with the Kansas City Royals in the 1980s. (Boston Red Sox)

Bob and Eddie Sadowski

Bob and Eddie were two of three brothers who played in the big leagues, both playing for a time with the Red Sox. Bob closed his four-year career pitching for the Sox in 1966 with a one win, one loss record. Brother Eddie started his career with the Red Sox and caught for one year in 1960 before being traded to the California Angels. Oldest brother Ted pitched three years, one with the Washington Senators and two with the Minnesota Twins in the 60s.

Don Schwall

Don Schwall started with the Red Sox in 1961 and won Rookie of the Year honors by pitching 15 wins against seven losses. It was his most successful season in the big leagues. He had a nine win, 15 loss record the next year and then was traded to the Pittsburgh Pirates. Schwall had a six-year big league career and then played only two-thirds of an inning in 1967. He had 49 wins and 48 losses in his career.

Tom Seaver

Tom Seaver, Hall of Fame pitcher who made his reputation in more than ten seasons with the New York Mets, won 20 games five times and led the league in earned run average three times. He ended his 20-year career pitching for the Boston Red Sox in the last half of 1986. He was 5-7 for the Sox in 16 games. In his career, Seaver won 311 games and lost 205. He is fourth all-time in strikeouts with 3640 and seventh all-time in shutouts with 61.

Calvin Schiraldi

Calvin Schiraldi had an eight-year big-league career in which he pitched for five teams and had a cumulative record of 32-39. Except for 1988 when he was mostly a starting pitcher for the Chicago Cubs, he pitched primarily in relief. He never had more than nine wins or nine losses in a season. Schiraldi was a reliever with the Red

Tom Seaver, Hall of Famer, ended his 20-year pitching career with Boston. (Boston Red Sox).

Sox in 1986 and 1987, going 12-7 with 15 saves in the two years. He was most effective in 1986 when he had a 1.41 E.R.A. but he played more frequently in 1997 and was in 62 games.

Schiraldi lost one game in relief in the 1986 ALCS. He also lost Game 6 of the 1986 World Series pitching in relief. He was removed for Bob Stanley in the tenth inning of Game 6 of the Series, after putting the tying and winning runs on base. The Mets won when Bill Buckner missed the squibbler at first base. Schiraldi also lost Game 7, pitching one-third of an inning, as the Mets won, 8-5.

Al Simmons

Al Simmons, the Hall of Fame outfielder, who was one of the stars of the Philadelphia Athletics dynasty teams in the 1920s and early 1930s, played one year near the end of his career with the Red Sox. This was in 1943 when he

The Red Sox Encyclopedia

was 41 years old and he still managed nine home runs in 40 games.

Simmons, who played for seven teams in his 20-year career, played in four World Series and had a lifetime batting average of .334. He drove in 1,827 runs in his career.

Lee Smith

Lee Smith was one of the premier relief pitchers in baseball history. (Baseball Hall of Fame Library. Cooperstown, N.Y.).

Lee Smith was a reliever par excellence in an era of good relief pitchers. He pitched 17 years in a career from 1980-1996. A formidable fastballer, he had 478 lifetime career saves, a major league record. He led the National League in 1983 with 29 saves while pitching for the Chicago Cubs, and he led the same league in 1991 and 1992 with 47 and 43 saves, respectively, while pitching for the St. Louis Cardinals. He pitched for the Red Sox two plus years, in 1988 and 1989, and briefly in 1990, until he was traded to the Cardinals. While with the Sox in his two full seasons of 1988 and 1989 he had 50 saves. Smith was a workhorse pitcher who, as a reliever, regularly pitched in more than 60 games each year. He pitched in league Championship series twice, once with the Cubs and once with the Red Sox. Toward the end of his career he pitched for the New York Yankees, the Baltimore Orioles and the California Angels.

Mike Stanley

Mike Stanley had a 15-year big-league career from 1986 through 2000, mostly as a catcher the first years and then as first baseman and a designated hitter. His first 10 years, as a catcher, were with the Texas Rangers and New York Yankees. Stanley had two brief tours of duty with the Red Sox from 1996 until he was traded back to the New York Yankees in 1997, and from 1998, having started and played most of that season with the Toronto Blue Jays, until mid-2000, when he went in late season to the Oakland Athletics. He played a total of 459 games with the Red Sox over a period of four years. In his first full season with the Sox in 1996, he caught 105 games and hit 24 home runs. In his second full season wiht the Red Sox, 1999, he played 111 games at first base. Over a period of four years with the Red Sox, he was used as a designated hitter 137 times. Nearly an all-purpose player, he was popular in Boston. He had some "pop" in his bat with a lifetime total of 187 homers and 702 runs batted in. He batted .270 lifetime. He was also an excellent catcher and good handler of pitch-

ers, exhibited mostly in his earlier career. Mike played in the postseason four years, twice with the Yankees and twice with the Red Sox. In a Red Sox 23-7 win in the American League Division Series in 1999, Stanley had five hits. He also played in an All-Star game.

Dick Stuart

Dick Stuart, "Dr. Strangeglove," was a power hitter and a poor fielder. (Baseball Hall of Fame Library. Cooperstown, N.Y.).

Dick Stuart was a slugging first baseman but a notoriously poor fielder. He played for the Red Sox in two years of his 10-year major league career, in 1963 and 1964. He hit more than 20 home runs six times in his career, and hit 42 home runs one year with the Red Sox. While he was known as "Dr. Strangelove" for his inept play at first base, he led American League first basemen in assists and putouts while playing for the Red Sox in 1963. He also led the league in errors that season.

Frank Tanana

Frank Tanana had a 21-year pitching career in the big leagues, mostly with the California Angels and the Detroit Tigers. He was a fireballer in his early years, until he lost his fastball, led the league in strikeouts once, and for a period of four seasons won at least 15 games a year for the Angels. He pitched for the Red Sox only one year, in 1981, and had an uncharacteristic four wins, 10 losses season. In his long career he won 240 games and lost 236.

Bobby Thomson

Bobby Thomson, the "Staten Island Scot" hit "the shot heard round the world" in 1951 to win the pennant for the New York Giants over the Brooklyn Dodgers that year. Entering the ninth inning with the Giants behind, 4-1, in the decisive game Thomson hit a three-run homer off Ralph Bronca to win the game and the pennant. His "shot" is one of the great memories in baseball history.

Thomson, in a 15-year career, played most of his final season with the Red Sox, in 1960. He was in 40 games for the Sox and had a .263 batting average. His lifetime batting average was .270 and he hit 264 home runs, though none as famous as his 1951 blast.

Faye Throneberry

Faye Throneberry started his big-league career as an outfielder with the Boston Red Sox in 1952. He played with the Red Sox in 1952, 1955 and 1956 and then was traded to the Washington Senators early in 1957. Throneberry had speed and in his first season with the Red Sox stole 16 bases. He was a journeyman player, both in the outfield and at bat. He had a lifetime .236 batting average over eight seasons, his best years being with the Sox when he batted .258 in 1952 and .257 in 1955.

Mickey Vernon

Mickey Vernon had a 20-year career in the big leagues as a first baseman, mostly in two tours of duty with the Washington Nationals. He was a lifetime .286 hitter and twice led the American League in batting. He batted .353 to lead the league in 1946 and he led in 1953 with a .337 average in his second tour of duty with the Nationals. He also led the American League three times in doubles, in 1946 and in the 1953 and 1954 seasons, playing for Washington. Vernon had 2495 hits in his career and twice had more than 200 a season. He also stole 137 bases in his career.

Vernon played for the Red Sox in 1956 and 1957, near the end of his career, a career that spanned four decades from 1939 through 1960 with two years off for military service. With the Sox in his first year he played first base and batted .310. He had 28 doubles and 15 home runs. He played first base in only 70 games the next season, though he pinch hit 22 times for six hits, and he had a batting average of .241. He was waived to the Cleveland Indians after the 1957 season and spent the last three years of his career with three different teams.

Frank Viola

"Frankie V" or "Sweet Music" had a 14-year pitching career, with his first, longest and most successful tour of duty with the Minnesota Twins. He was the leading pitcher on the Twins' 1987 World Championship team, winning two games and losing one in the World Series that year. He won 20 games twice, once when he led the league with 24 wins pitching for the Twins in 1988 and once when he won 20 games for the New York Mets in 1990.

"Frankie V" pitched for the Red Sox three years, in 1992, 1993 and 1994. He won a total of 25 games with the Sox and lost 21. He had his most wins with the team, 13, in 1992 when he also had 121 strikeouts in the 35 games he started. His best winning percentage with the team was in 1993 when he was 11-8 for a .579 average.

Joe Vosmik

Joe Vosmik was the Red Sox left fielder in 1938 and 1939 when they also had as regulars Jimmie Foxx at first base, Bobby Doerr at second, Joe Cronin at shortstop and first Pinky Higgins and then Jim Tabor at third base. In 1938, the outfield consisted of Vosmik, Ben Chapman and Doc Cramer, all of whom hit over .300, with Vosmik at .324. In 1939, the outfield had Vosmik, Doc Cramer and Ted Williams, with only Vosmik batting under .300, at .276. The Red Sox finished second to the Yankees both years. Vosmik played only two of his 13 years with the Red Sox.

He played most of his career with the Cleveland Indians and had a lifetime .307 batting average.

Catcher Hal Wagner batted .332 in 66 games for the Red Sox before being traded to the Oakland Athletics. (Baseball Hall of Fame Library. Cooperstown, N.Y.).

Hal Wagner

Hal Wagner had a 12-year career as a catcher in the big leagues from 1937 through 1949, mostly with the Philadelphia Athletics. He was mostly part-time and played only one season in which he caught as many as 100 games. This was in 1946, his only full year with the Red Sox, when he caught 116 games. He also caught most of the World Series for the Red Sox in 1946, with no hits in 13 at bats in five games. Wagner's lifetime batting average was .248. He batted .332 in 66 games for the Red Sox when he was traded by the Athletics to the Sox in 1944. He did not play in 1945. In 1947, he batted .231 in 21 games and was traded to Detroit for Birdie Tebbetts.

George "Rube" Walberg

"Rube" Walberg, who pitched on the great Philadelphia Athletics teams of the 1920s and early 1930s, and who pitched in three World Series with the Athletics, pitched late in his career for the Red Sox. He was with the Sox from 1934 through 1937 and ended his 15-year career with them. He won 21 games and lost 27 in his years with the Boston Red Sox.

Bucky Walters

Bucky Walters, before he became a great pitcher for the Cincinnati Reds in the late 1930s and 1940s, was a third

Rube Walberg pitched for the Red Sox from 1934-37, ending his 15-year career with the team. (Baseball Hall of Fame Library. Cooperstown, N.Y.).

baseman for three teams, the Boston Braves, the Philadelphia Phillies and the Boston Red Sox. He played with the Red Sox in 1933 and part of 1934. He was converted to a pitcher by the Phillies in 1935 and became one of the top pitchers in baseball with the Cincinnati Reds beginning in 1939. Walters later managed the Reds in 1948 and 1949.

Bill Wambsganss

Bill Wamsganss will go down in baseball history for the unassisted triple play he executed while playing second base for the Cleveland Indians in the fifth game of the 1920 World Series, the Indians winning the Series over the Robins, five games to two. Wambsganss had a 13-year big league career, mostly as a shortstop and then as a second baseman with the Indians. His lifetime batting average was .259 but his reputation was as a fielder.

Wambsganss played second base for the Red Sox in 1924 and 1925, toward the end of his career. He batted .274 and then .231 but the Red Sox were a seventh-place team in 1924 and a last-place team in 1925.

John Wasdin

John Wasdin, in a career beginning in 1995, pitched for the Red Sox from 1997 until he went to the Colorado Rockies for the latter part of the 2000 year. Though he had 16 starts with the Red Sox in 170 games, he was mostly a relief pitcher. He won 19 games in his career with Boston and lost 16. He was essentially a journeyman pitcher who played in close to 50 games a season with the Sox from 1997 through 1999. He pitched briefly in the 1998 and 1999 American League Division Series.

Bob Watson

Bob Watson was a slugging first baseman in his 19-year playing career, beginning in 1966 mostly with the Houston Astros. He also played on the 1980 East division winners, the New York Yankees, batting .500 with six hits in the three-game American League Championship Series,

and he was the first baseman on the New York Yankees pennant winning team of 1981, batting .318 in the World Series. He had a .295 lifetime batting average, a .447 slugging average and hit 184 home runs. He drove in more than 100 runs twice, playing for the Astros in 1976 and 1977.

Watson was traded to the Red Sox by the Astros in June of 1979. He played 84 games with the Red Sox, primarily as the team's first baseman and batted .337. The next year he played for the New York Yankees and subsequently ended his career with the Atlanta Braves in 1984.

Watson became a general manager and was the G.M. of the New York Yankees World Champions in 1996.

Vic Wertz

Vic Wertz spent 17 years as a big league outfielder and later as a first baseman, from 1947-1963. Most of his distinguished career was spent with the Detroit Tigers and the Cleveland Indians. He played first base for the Red Sox from 1959 into 1961, a total of two and one half years. Wertz had a lifetime .277 average and was considered a power hitter. Perhaps his biggest claim to memory is the tremendous drive he hit to spacious center field in the Polo Grounds in New York while playing for Cleveland against the New York Giants in the 1954 World Series. Willie Mays made one of the great catches in baseball history on that drive, catching the ball over his shoulder while running back to the wall, then wheeling to throw the ball back to the infield about 400 feet away.

Dick Williams

Dick Williams, the fiery manager who led the Red Sox from next to last place to first place in one year and won the American League pennant in 1967, was also a player for the Sox at the end of his career. He was a utility infielder and outfielder for the Sox in 1963 and 1964, batting .257 in 79 games in 1963 and .159 in 61 games in 1964.

Williams had a 13-year playing career with five teams, all but one in the American League. He started his career with the Brooklyn Dodgers in 1951 and was a substitute outfielder on the Dodgers' pennant-winning team of 1953.

Bob Watson was another of the Red Sox's slugging first basemen. (Baseball Hall of Fame Library. Cooperstown, N.Y.).

Dick Williams was mostly a utility infielder but later distinguished himself as a Red Sox manager. (Boston Red Sox).

Joe Wood Jr.

Joe Wood Jr., son of the great Red Sox pitcher Smoky Joe Wood, had a three-game big league career pitching for the Red Sox in 1944. His career record is 0-1.

Rudy York

Rudy York spent most of his career as a star for the Detroit Tigers, playing catcher and first baseman from 1934-1945. He hit 277 career home runs and had more than 1,000 R.B.I.s York played for Boston in 1946 and part of 1947, closing his career in 1948. He was the Red Sox first baseman in the 1946 World Series against the St. Louis Cardinals, batting .261 with two home runs. He was an interim manager for the Red Sox for one game in 1959.

Rudy York was a slugging catcher/ first baseman for the Red Sox after WWII. (Baseball Hall of Fame Library. Cooperstown, N.Y.).

Ed Barrow, manager of the 1918 Red Sox world champions, is credited with converting Babe Ruth from a pitcher to an everyday player. (Baseball Hall of Fame. Cooperstown, N.Y.).

THE ROSTER OF
NOTABLE
RED SOX MANAGERS

Managers of Red Sox Pennant and World Series Winners

The Red Sox have won a total of ten pennants and five World Series. Only two Sox managers repeated their pennant success. Jimmy Collins won two pennants and the first World Series ever played. There was no World Series in the year of his second pennant win. Bill "Rough" Carrigan won both two pennants and two world championships in 1915 and 1916.

Jimmy Collins

Jimmy Collins was the manager of the Boston Pilgrims in 1903 when they won the pennant by 14½ games over Connie Mack's Philadelphia Athletics. His team also upset the favored Pittsburgh Pirates, with Honus Wagner and Fred Clarke, in the first World Series ever played. The Sox won, five games to three, in what was then the best-of-nine series. Collins was not only the manager. He was also the star third baseman, a later Hall of Famer, a good hitter and considered peerless in the field. He was joined by heavy-hitting Buck Freeman and three 20-game winners, Cy Young, Bill Dinneen and Long Tom Hughes.

In 1904, the Red Sox with Collins managing won the pennant by only a game and a half over Clark Griffith's New York Highlanders (whose name later changed to the Yankees). Boston hitting dropped off in 1904, the team going from a league-leading average of .272 in 1903 to .247 in 1904. The team still had, however, three 20-game winners, Cy Young and Bill Dinneen again and Jesse Tannehill. There was no World

Series in 1904 as John McGraw refused to let his National League pennant-winning New York Giants play a team from the upstart American League.

Thereafter, Collins' Red Sox teams went downhill during his leadership. They finished fourth in 1905 and last in 1906. Collins was dismissed as manager before the end of the season. Collins managed a total of five years as the first manager of the Red Sox, the first pennant winner (he won two) and the first manager of a World Series winner.

Jake Stahl

Jake Stahl managed the Washington Nationals without success in 1905 and 1906. Stahl came to the Red Sox from the New York Yankees in 1908 as their first baseman and he played three years. He did not play in 1911 but in 1912 he became the Red Sox playing manager. He inherited a Red Sox team that finished in fifth place the previous year. In their first year in Fenway Park, 1912, Stahl's Red Sox won the pennant and the world championship. They won 105 games, more than any other Red Sox team, and beat the second-place Washington Nationals by 14 games. The Nationals were managed by Clark Griffith, the New York Highlanders' manager in the last pennant-winning year of the Red Sox. After managing the Highlanders and the Cincinnati Reds he became the Senators' manager in 1912 and later became the team's owner.

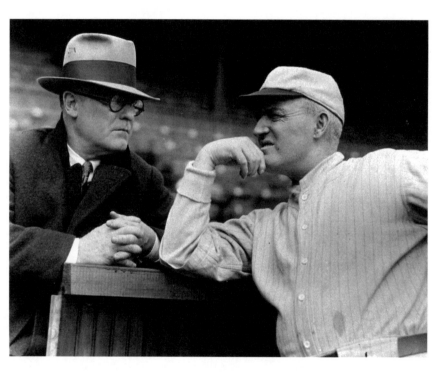

Boston owner Bob Quinn (left) chats with manager Bill Carrigan. Carrigan, who directed the team to two world titles in 1915 and 1916, managed the Red Sox to three last-place finishes in 1927, 1928 and 1929. (Baseball Hall of Fame Library. Cooperstown, N.Y.).

Boston Managers

Jimmy Collins	1901-1906
Chick Stahl	1906
Cy Young	1907
George Huff	1907
Bob Unglaub	1907
Deacon McGuire	1907-1908
Fred Lake	1908-1909
Patsy Donovan	1910-1911
Jake Stahl	1912-1913
Bill "Rough" Carrigan	1913-1916
Jack Barry	1917
Ed Barrow	1918-1920
Hugh Duffy	1921-1922
Frank Chance	1923
Lee Fohl	1924-26
Bill "Rough" Carrigan	1927-1929
Heinie Wagner	1930
Shano Collins	1931-1932
Marty McManus	1932-1933
Bucky Harris	1934
Joe Cronin	1935-1947
Joe McCarthy	1948-1950
Steve O'Neill	1950-1951
Lou Boudreau	1952-1954
Pinky Higgins	1955-1959
Rudy York	1959
Billy Jurges	1959-1960
Del Baker	1960
Pinky Higgins	1960-1962
Johnny Pesky	1963-1964
Billy Herman	1964-1966
Pete Runnels	1966
Dick Williams	1967-1969
Eddie Popowski	1969
Eddie Kasko	1970-1973
Eddie Popowski	1973
Darrell Johnson	1974-1976
Don Zimmer	1976-1980
Johnny Pesky	1980
Ralph Houk	1981-1984
John McNamara	1985-1988
Joe Morgan	1988-1991
Butch Hobson	1992-1994
Kevin Kennedy	1995-1996
Jimy Williams	1997-2001
Joe Kerrigan	2001
Grady Little	2002-

Stahl's 1912 Red Sox team had hard-hitting, all-around player Tris Speaker and a fabled outfield of Duffy Lewis, Tris Speaker and Harry Hooper. They also had 34-game winner Smoky Joe Wood, the league's leader in wins, and two 20-game winners in Hugh Bedient and Buck O'Brien. The Sox beat the New York Giants in the World Series, four games to three, on Wood's three winning games and famous lapses by the Giants' Fred Snodgrass and Fred Merkle.

Stahl stayed only one full year as manager of the Red Sox, being dismissed the next season after disagreement with the owner.

Bill "Rough" Carrigan

Rough Carrigan, whose more proper name was Bill Carrigan, led the Red Sox to pennant and World Series wins in 1915 and 1916. After Jake Stahl was fired, Rough took over the Red Sox, adding the manager's duties to his playing duties as the team's steady, dependable catcher. Under Carrigan the Red Sox finished fourth, then second and finally won the pennant in 1915. Rough was considered a fine field leader and, in fact, Babe Ruth regarded him as the best manager he ever had.

In 1915, Rough was no longer playing regularly, still had the fabulous Lewis-Speaker-Hooper outfield, and he had five pitchers who won 15 or more games, Rube Foster and Ernie Shore with 19 wins each, Babe Ruth in his first full season with 18, and Dutch Leonard and Smoky Joe Wood with 15 each. The Red Sox won a tight race by one game over Hughie Jennings' Detroit Tigers. Rube Foster won two games, including a three-hitter as the Red Sox beat the Phillies in the World Series, four games to one.

In 1916, Tris Speaker had been traded to the Cleveland Indians but the Red Sox won the pennant by two games over the Chicago White Sox. Larry Gardner at third base had a good year but the pitching staff made the difference. Dutch Leonard and Carl Mays each had 18 wins. Ernie Shore had 16 and Rube Foster had 14. In the World Series, Babe Ruth and Sherry Smith of the Dodgers duelled for 14 innings, Babe and the Sox winning, 2 to 1. It was the highlight of the Series as the Red Sox beat the Dodgers, four games to one.

Rough Carrigan was not invited back to manage the Red Sox, in spite of his fine reputation and excellent winning record. He was brought back to manage the team in 1927, after the team had experienced last place finishes two years in a row. They were in the throes of their dismal post-Frazee years. Carrigan's talents did not make a difference as his team finished in last place in the three years of his second tour of duty.

Ed Barrow

Ed Barrow, who had never played in the big leagues, managed Detroit in 1903 and 1904. He was named Red Sox manager in 1918. Nineteen eighteen was a baseball year shortened by World War I and the regular season ended on September 2, about one month earlier than usual. The Red Sox won the pennant by 2½ games over the Cleveland Indians. Babe Ruth was now playing regularly in the outfield for the Red Sox and still doing some pitching. He batted .300 and led the league with 11 home runs and he managed to win 13 games as a pitcher. Carl Mays was a 20-game winner and Sad Sam Jones and Bullet Joe Bush between them won 31 games. Two Red Sox pitchers in the World Series won two games each to give the Sox a four-games-to-two-win over the Chicago Cubs. The pitchers were Babe Ruth and Carl Mays. It was clearly a pitching Series as the Cubs scored a total of 10 runs and the Red Sox scored only nine. The winner in all five games never scored more than three runs.

Ed Barrow, "Cousin Ed," also managed the Red Sox in 1919 and 1920 but with the loss of key players to the Yankees the Sox were beginning to descend in the American League. They finished sixth in 1919 and fifth in 1920. Babe Ruth was traded to the Yankees before the 1920 season and Ed Barrow followed him as general manager and later president in a long front office career with the New York club.

Ed Barrow was known as a smart baseball man. Likely, his smartest move was converting Babe Ruth from a pitcher to a full time player. This opened up the home run era and, to the chagrin of the Red Sox, helped to create great dynasties in Yankee baseball.

Joe Cronin

Joe Cronin, at age 26, was the "boy manager" of the Washington Senators in 1933 and led them to the pennant. He was also the team's shortstop and became a member of the Hall of Fame after a 20-year playing career. Cronin, the manager, managed two clubs for a total of 15 years. He managed the Senators for one more year in 1934, when his team dropped to seventh place. He was then traded by his father-in-law, Washington owner Clark Griffith, to the Red Sox for their shortstop, Lyn Lary, and $225,000.

Cronin became the player-manager for the Red Sox for 11 years and went on to manage two more non-playing years, all told from 1935 through 1947. Most of Cronin's years as manager were rebuilding years and, as the Red Sox began to move more consistently into the first division, attrition of players because of the second World War had its effect. Cronin's early years were known for the acquisition of stars from other teams, most notably Lefty Grove and Jimmie Foxx from the Philadelphia Athletics' dynasty teams at the end of the 1920s. The Red Sox in the 30s and early 40s finished second four times but did not win a pennant.

After managing the Red Sox, Joe Cronin (left) went on to become the team's general manger. He and his successor as manager, Joe McCarthy (pictured above), light up their cigars at a Boston Baseball Writers' dinner. (Boston Public Library Print Department).

Finally, in 1946, there was a clamor in Boston for a pennant. The Sox had a powerful team. The incomparable Ted Williams was back from military service, along with other returning veterans. The Red Sox had hard-hitting Rudy York at first base and an outstanding second base-shortstop combination in Bobby Doerr and Johnny Pesky. Dom DiMaggio was in center field. The pitching staff was led by 25-game winner Boo Ferriss and 20-game winner Tex Hughson. The Red Sox won the pennant by 12 games over Detroit and were favorites to win the World Series over the St. Louis Cardinals. However, the Cardinals won the Series on Enos Slaughter's "run for home", scoring from first base on a hit, late in the seventh and deciding game.

Joe Cronin managed one more year, in 1947, and the Red Sox finished third. He then went on to the front office as Red Sox general manager and ultimately became president of the American League.

Dick Williams

Dick Williams was the manager of the next Red Sox pennant winner, 21 years after the last pennant in 1946. Dick Williams was a rookie manager when he took over the Red Sox in 1967. He had had an unspectacular 13-year playing career that ended in 1964.

Williams, a smart, aggressive, determined manager and a good tactician, took the Red Sox from ninth place in 1966 to the pennant in 1967, his first year. It was a near miracle performance as the Red Sox were rated at no better than 100 to 1 to win the pennant when the season started. The Red Sox had a superlative year from Carl Yastrzemski who was a Triple Crown winner and the league's Most Valuable Player. They also had the Cy Young winner, Jim Lonborg, who had 22 wins. There were also some other powerful hitters on the team, George "Boomer" Scott, Rico Petrocelli, Tony Conigliaro and Reggie Smith. Joey Foy also had a good year. The Red Sox won a close race, beating the Detroit Tigers and Minnesota Twins by one game and the Chicago White Sox, "the hitless wonders," by two games. The Red Sox once again played the St. Louis Cardinals in the World Series and again lost, four games to three. This time they were beaten by Hall of Fame pitcher Bob Gibson who pitched and won three complete games, allowing a total of three runs.

Williams managed the Red Sox for two more years but the team finished fourth in 1968 and third in 1969. He was dismissed in 1969. He went on to what became a 21-year career as manager. He managed five other teams besides the Red Sox, the Oakland Athletics, the California Angels, the Montreal Expos, the San Diego Padres and the Seattle Mariners. His "golden years" were in

Dick Williams took the Red Sox from ninth place in 1966 to an American League pennant in 1967. (Baseball Hall of Fame Library. Cooperstown, N.Y.).

1971-1973 at Oakland when he built a dynasty that won three pennants and two World Series. He won a pennant with San Diego in 1984 but lost the World Series to Detroit. He managed 3,023 career games, winning 1,571.

Williams, as a player, was mostly a utility infielder-outfielder for several teams between 1951 and 1964. He played with the Red Sox the last two years of his career and had a lifetime batting average of .260.

Darrell Johnson

Darrell Johnson was also a rookie big-league manager when he first managed the Red Sox in 1974. He had a six-year playing career as a catcher that ended in the early 1960s. After a third-place finish in 1974, the Red Sox won the pennant in 1975, winning the East division by four and one half games over the Baltimore Orioles. They swept the Oakland Athletics, three games to none, in the American League Championship Series. They lost an exciting World Series to the Cincinnati Reds, four games to three.

The 1975 Red Sox had the veteran Carl Yastrzemski at first base. They had an exceptional outfield in Dwight Evans, Fred Lynn and Jim Rice. Rice and Lynn had sensational rookie years, and Lynn was named both Rookie of the Year and Most Valuable Player in the league. They had Rico Petrocelli and Rick Burleson

Darrell Johnson's 1975 Red Sox won the American League pennant and battled the Cincinnati Reds in the World Series. (Boston Red Sox).

in the infield. Carlton "Pudge" Fisk was a solid catcher who would distinguish himself in the World Series by hitting a dramatic home run in the 12th inning of Game 6 to win it for the Red Sox. Bernie Carbo, who was to etch himself in memory with timely pinch hit home runs in the postseason, and Denny Doyle were capable support players. Luis Tiant, Spaceman Bill Lee and Rick Wise gave the Sox 54 victories during the regular season. They provided solid competition for a powerful Cincinnati Reds team in the World Series. The Reds had established a reputation as "The Big Red Machine."

The Red Sox loss in the 1975 World Series was again a disappointment for Boston. Darrell Johnson's Red Sox team was disappointing in 1976 and in midseason he was replaced by Don Zimmer. The team finished third. Johnson went on to manage Seattle and then the Texas Rangers but his teams were not successful. He ended his eight-year major league managerial career with Texas in 1982.

John McNamara

John McNamara had an 18-year managing career in the major leagues. He had 13 years of experience managing four teams, the Oakland Athletics, the San Diego Padres, the Cincinnati Reds and the California Angels when he took over the Red Sox in 1985.

He won the National League West division with Cincinnati in 1979 but lost to the Pittsburgh Pirates in the National League Championship Series.

In 1984 the Red Sox finished fourth in the East Division and were not especially promising. In McNamara's first year with the Sox, in 1985, they finished fifth, 18½ games out of first place, and there was no indication 1986 would be a great year. In 1986, however, McNamara piloted the Red Sox to the East division championship by 5½ games over the Yankees. For this achievement, he was named Manager of the Year. Boston defeated the California Angels, four games to three, in an exciting American League Championship Series. The World Series was unexpectedly lost to the New York Mets, four games to three, because of an error on a simple ground ball in the sixth game, when it appeared the Red Sox had the Series won.

Boston had a Cy Young and Most Valuable Player Award year from Roger Clemens in 1986. Dwight Evans, Tony Armas and Jim Rice were a powerful outfield and Wade Boggs was a steady hitter and league batting champion at third base. Rich Gedman was a dependable catcher and Don Baylor was the designated hitter.

John McNamara earned Manager of the Year honors when his Red Sox won the 1986 American League pennant. (Baseball Hall of Fame Library. Cooperstown, N.Y.).

With a good team and a disappointing end result in 1986 Boston fans and team management were expecting to win in 1987. They were frustrated by the Red Sox slow start and a fifth place finish in the A.L. East division in which they won 78 games but lost 84. When the Red Sox played only .500 ball in 1988 McNamara was replaced in midseason by Joe Morgan. The Red Sox immediately won 19 of 20 games and went on to win the American League East division championship.

John McNamara went on to manage Cleveland in 1990 and 1991 but without much success. He was replaced in 1991, having served with six teams for 18 years as a big league manager.

Red Sox Managers Who Just Missed

Some managers have experienced "near misses" in their service with Boston, coming close to winning pennants for the Sox. These managers are Joe McCarthy, Don Zimmer, Joe Morgan and Kevin Kennedy. Pinky Higgins is notable for two tours of duty and six full years and two part years managing the Sox.

Joe McCarthy

Joe McCarthy had one of the most illustrious managing careers in baseball history. He managed three teams for a total of 24 years and had success with each of them. He managed the Chicago Cubs for five years, winning the National League pennant once and never finishing out of the first division.

His greatest achievement was with the New York Yankees whom he managed for 16 years, 1931-1946, to eight pennants and seven World Series victories. His 1936-1939

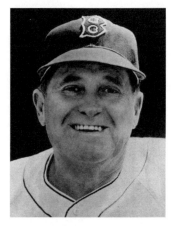

Joe McCarthy managed the Red Sox to within one game of the pennant in 1948 and 1949. (Baseball Hall of Fame Library. Cooperstown, N.Y.)

Yankees were one of the great dynasty teams, reeling off four world championships in a row. Four times his Yankee teams finished second and his teams never finished out of the first division.

McCarthy retired after the 1946 season because of ill health. He was persuaded in 1948 to take over the reins of the Boston Red Sox, a good-hitting team with a lot of talent who had won the pennant in 1946 and finished third in 1947. The

Red Sox had an infield of Billy Goodman, Bobby Doerr, Vern Stephens and Johnny Pesky. Their outfield had Ted Williams and Dom DiMaggio. Birdie Tebbetts was the catcher and Mel Parnell, Ellis Kinder and Joe Dobson were the leading pitchers. McCarthy's 1948 and 1949 Red Sox teams won 96 games each of these seasons, and the team finished with a winning percentage over .615 each time. Notwithstanding, Boston lost the pennant to the Cleveland Indians in 1948 in a play-off game and again lost the pennant in 1949 to the Yankees on the last day of the season.

McCarthy's retired near midseason in 1950 with a combined record of teams having nine pennants and seven World Series. None of McCarthy's teams in his 24-year service ever finished out of the first division. This record is unparalleled in baseball history and he joins the ranks of such winning managers as John McGraw and Miller Huggins and two others with periods of spectacular success, notably Connie Mack and Casey Stengel.

As a footnote, McCarthy never played in the big leagues. He managed 15 years in the minor leagues and won two championships with Louisville of the American Association.

Don Zimmer

Don Zimmer had a 13-year managing career in both the American and National Leagues. He was the manager of the Red Sox for five years, from 1976 through 1980. His Red Sox teams never finished out of the first division and in three years, 1977, 1978 and 1979, his teams scored over 90 wins each season. Zimmer's near miss occurred with the 1978 Red Sox team. With such talent as Carl Yastrzemski at first base, Dwight Evans, Fred Lynn and Jim Rice in the outfield, Carlton Fisk catching and pitcher Dennis Eckersley producing 20 wins, the Red Sox finished the season with 99 wins, one game off first place. The Yankees won 100 games that year, the climax being the play-off game in which the Yanks beat the Red Sox on Bucky Dent's three-run home run.

Zimmer has spent well over 40 years in the big leagues as player, coach and manager. He also managed San Diego, Texas and the Chicago Cubs. In 1996 he

Don Zimmer's teams won more than 90 games each season from 1977-79. (Baseball Hall of Fame Library. Cooperstown, N.Y.).

became chief lieutenant and bench coach for manager Joe Torre and the New York Yankees. Zimmer was an infielder for 12 years, mostly in the National League. He played for the World Champion Brooklyn Dodgers of 1955 and Los Angeles Dodgers of 1959. His lifetime batting average was .235.

Joe Morgan

Joe Morgan's only major league managerial experience has been with the Boston Red Sox. He took over the managerial reins from John McNamara in midseason 1988 when the Red Sox were in fourth place. The team immediately reeled off 19 wins in the next 20 games and went on to win the American League East division title. They lost the pennant to the Oakland Athletics, four games to none, in the American League Championship Series. The Red Sox again won the East division title under Morgan in 1990, and again lost the pennant to the Athletics, four games to none in the 1990 ALCS.

Morgan managed the Red Sox a total of four years, his other two teams finishing in second and third place. He had great talent in regular batting champion Wade Boggs and in Cy Young award-winning pitcher Roger Clemens. Ellis Burks and Mike Greenwell were capable replacements in the outfield for such illustrious predecessors as Dwight Evans and Jim Rice. However, the Red Sox did not win a pennant and the fans and team management were hurting for a championship team. Butch Hobson replaced Joe Morgan as manager for the 1992 season.

Joe Morgan won the American League East Division in 1988 when the Red Sox won 19 of 20 games immediately following his being named manager in midseason. (Baseball Hall of Fame Library. Cooperstown, N.Y.).

Kevin Kennedy

Kevin Kennedy managed the Red Sox for two years, 1995 and 1996. In 1995, his Red Sox won the American League East division title but lost in the division play-offs to the Central division winners, the Cleveland Indians.

Kevin Kennedy's first major league experience was as a coach with the Montreal Expos. After a brief experience here he went on to manage the Texas Rangers. In his first year with the Rangers the team finished in second place in the West division. In 1994, the Rangers were in first place in the Central division, one game ahead of Cleveland, until player-owner conflict both shortened and ended the season prematurely. There were no play-offs in this first year of divisional reorganization that moved Texas from the West division in a two-division system to the Central division in a three-division system.

In 1995, Kennedy moved on to manage the Red Sox to an 86-58 season in the East division. The .597 percentage, Kennedy's best year, was enough to place the Red Sox in first place, seven games ahead of the second-place Yankees.

Kevin Kennedy managed the Red Sox to an East Division title in 1995. Boston won by seven games over the New York Yankees. (Baseball Hall of Fame Library. Cooperstown, N.Y.).

Cleveland, which had won the Central division by 30 games over the second place Kansas City Royals, had a superior team with an accumulation of stars such as Albert Belle, Eddie Murray, Kenny Lofton, Jim Thome, Carlos Baerga, Orel Hershiser, Charles Nagy and Dennis Martinez. They whitewashed the Red Sox in the playoffs.

In 1996, the Red Sox finished in third place, seven games behind the East division winning Yankees. Kennedy was replaced for the 1997 season by Jimy Williams, one-time manager of the Toronto Blue Jays.

Jimy Williams

Jimy Williams is the 41st person to manage the Red Sox in the team's history. His Red Sox managerial tour of duty began in 1997. His team finished fourth in the East division in 1997 and then was the second-place "wild card" team in the American League in both 1998 and 1999. In the latter two years, his teams won 186 games and lost 138. The Sox were swept by Cleveland in the 1998 Division play-offs but then upset the Indians in the 1999 Division play-offs, three games to two. The Red Sox went on to play their archrivals, the New York Yankees, for the American League pennant, updating a rich history of season-ending competitions between the Red Sox and the Yankees. The Yankees again won the pennant in 1999.

Prior to becoming the Red Sox manager, Williams was the Toronto Blue Jays' manager from 1986 into the 1989 season. His 1987 and 1988 Toronto team finished two

games behind the East division leader each year. He was a Blue Jays coach from 1980 through the 1985 season. He coached the Atlanta Braves from 1990 through the Braves' 1996 pennant-winning season. He started with the Braves as a minor-league instructor. Prior to 1980, Williams was a minor-league manager for six years.

Jimy Williams played in two seasons

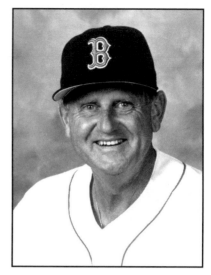

Jimy Williams was named A.L. Manager of the Year in 1999. (Boston Red Sox)

with the St. Louis Cardinals. In 1966 and 1967 he played in 14 games with the Cardinals as an infielder. Perhaps most memorable in his major-league playing career is that he was struck out by Sandy Koufax in his first major league at bat but then got the first of his three major-league hits of Juan Marichal. Both pitchers became Hall of Famers.

Jimy Williams has a reputation as a smart and sometimes wily, common-sense manager. His intuitive moves as a manager often worked out well. Notably, for his work in 1999, he was named the A.L.'s "Manager of the Year."

The Red Sox failed to make the postseason competition in 2000-2001 and, with some turmoil in the dugout, Williams was dismissed as manager the latter part of 2001. This was not a popular decision with the Red Sox fans and there was some feeling that Red Sox management did not adequately back the field manager. Joe Kerrigan,the pitching coach and briefly a pitcher in the big leagues from 1976 through 1980, took over as amanger for the final 43 games of the season.

Pinky Higgins

Mike "Pinky" Higgins managed the Red Sox from 1955 until he was dismissed in 1959, and then he was rehired in midseason 1960 and managed the Red Sox through the 1962 season. From 1953 through 1956, four straight years, the Red Sox finished in fourth place. Higgins was the manager in two of these years and in the next two years under his tutelage they moved up to third place. These were his best years as a big league manager, and the Red Sox were the only major league team he managed. He was replaced

Pinky Higgins was one of 21 Boston managers who at some time in their playing careers played with the team. (Baseball Hall of Fame Library. Cooperstown, N.Y.).

for the 1963 season by another former Red Sox third baseman, Johnny Pesky.

Higgins, in his best managing years, had such outstanding players as Frank Malzone at third base and Ted Williams, Jimmy Piersall and Jackie Jensen in the outfield. However, the Red Sox did not have the talent to compete with the New York Yankees who, from 1955 through 1958, won four pennants in a row.

Red Sox Managers Who Were Also Red Sox Players

Of their 41 field managers the Red Sox have had 21 who at some time in their playing careers played with the team.

Notable as both players and managers for the Red Sox were Joe Cronin, Jimmy Collins, Jake Stahl and Bill "Rough" Carrigan. Mike "Pinky" Higgins and Dick Williams also were both Sox players and managers. Higgins was perhaps a better player and Williams a better manager. Lou Boudreau, though at one time a Red Sox player and manager, had his most distinguished playing and managing careers previously, with the Cleveland Indians.

More notable for their playing than their brief managing were Jack Barry, Johnny Pesky and Butch Hobson. Barry's best playing years were with the Philadelphia Athletics as a member of the "$100,000 infield." He played three years with the Red Sox and managed one year, 1917. Johnny Pesky had a 24-year career as an infielder, mostly after World War II. He had a distinguished seven and one half year career with the Red Sox as a popular shortstop and third baseman. He managed the Red Sox in 1963 and 1964, and briefly in 1980. "Butch" Hobson was a Red Sox slugger and third baseman in the 1970s, though not a good

fielder. He managed the Sox for three years, from 1992-1994. Eddie Kasko was a journey man who played briefly for and managed the Red Sox. In his playing days he was primarily an infielder with the Cincinnati. He managed the Red Sox four years, from 1970-1973, with two second place finishes.

There were some Red Sox managers who did not play for the Sox but were distinguished players for other teams. Hugh Duffy was a Hall of Fame outfielder with the Boston Braves of the National League. He managed four teams in an eight-year managing career, managing the Red Sox two years in 1921 and 1922. Billy Herman was a Hall of Fame second baseman, mostly with the Chicago Cubs and also with the Brooklyn Dodgers. He managed the Red Sox for two-plus years, 1964- 1966, finishing in eighth and ninth place. Billy Jurges was a great shortstop for the New York Giants and the Chicago Cubs in the 1930s and 1940s. He had a seventeen year playing career. He managed the Red Sox for parts of two seasons, in 1959 and 1960.

There were some notable "cup of coffee" managers for the Red Sox, managers who were primarily in interim appointments and managed the Sox for less than 30 days.

games in 1960; Rudy York, a star catcher-first baseman for the Detroit Tigers in the 1930s and 1940s and later briefly with the Red Sox, managed the Sox for one game in 1959; and Pete Runnels, who won a batting title while playing infield for the Red Sox from 1958-1962 and managed the Red Sox for 16 games in 1996.

A particular oddity is the careers of the Stahls, who shared only the same name. Both Jake and Chick played for and managed the Red Sox. Chick was one of the original Boston Somersets players who came over from the Boston Beaneaters National League team along with team manager and star player Jimmy Collins. He was a Somerset/Pilgrim outfielder for six years and became the team manager in 1906. Though the team finished last he was re-hired for the 1907 season but then died suddenly from a drug overdose shortly before the season began. Stahl's death, if intentional, appeared related not to a last place finish but to his love entanglements.

Jake Stahl was briefly a catcher with the Red Sox in 1903 and then the team's regular first baseman from 1908-1910 and then in 1912. He managed the Red Sox two years, in 1912 and 1913, winning the World Championship in 1912.

Long Managing Careers, Brief Managing Stints With The Red Sox

The Red Sox, in addition to Joe McCarthy and Joe Cronin, have had other managers who have had long and distinguished careers as managers.

Frank Chance

Chance was the "The Peerless Leader" and Hall of Fame first baseman who had most of his success with the Chicago Cubs. His Cubs finished first four times and won two world titles. He managed the Red Sox in the last year of his 11-year managerial career to a last-place finish.

Bucky Harris

Harris managed for a remarkable 29 years. He managed five teams, the Washington Senators three times and the Detroit Tigers twice. He won two pennants and a world championship with the Washington Senators in 1924 and 1925, and a world championship with the Yankees in 1947. He managed from 1924 through 1956 and was the Red Sox manager for one year, in 1934.

Steve O'Neill

O'Neill managed for 14 years in the big leagues. He managed four teams, the Indians, Tigers and Phillies as well as the Red Sox. He won the World Series with the Detroit Tigers in 1945. He was a Red Sox manager in 1950 and 1951, finishing in the first division as he did with most of his teams.

Ralph Houk

Houk managed for 20 years in the big leagues, principally with the New York Yankees and the Detroit Tigers. Succeeding Casey Stengel as manager, he won three pennants and two World Series with the Yankees. "The Major" managed Boston for four years, 1981 through 1984, with one second-place finish. During his playing career with the Yankees, Houk was a second-string catcher behind Yogi Berra.

Lee Fohl

Fohl was a big league manager for 11 years, mostly with the Cleveland Indians and also the St. Louis Browns. He managed the Red Sox three years, in 1924, 1925 and 1926, and the team finished in last place twice and next to last once.

Lou Boudreau

Boudreau started his career as the "boy" playing manager and shortstop of the Cleveland Indians. He was successful as both player and manager and became a Hall of Famer. He managed for 16 years, nine with the Indians. As manager, he designed "The Williams shift," placing extra players on the right side of the field when the Sox formidable pull hitter, Ted Williams, was batting. Boudreau's Cleveland team won the world championship in 1948 with the redoubtable pitching combination of Bob Feller, Bob Lemon and Gene Bearden. Two years later he would also have pitchers Early Wynn, Mike Garcia and Satchel Paige but the team finished fourth. Traded to the Red Sox as a player in 1951, Boudreau became bench manager for the team from 1952-1954. He had mediocre years managing the Sox, went on to manage two other teams and ultimately became an announcer for the Chicago Cubs.

A long-time baseball executive, Red Sox owner Bob Quinn donned the team uniform to inspire his players one day. After some lean years with the Boston franchise, Quinn sold the team to Thomas Yawkey. (Boston Public Library Print Department).

THE BOSTON
FRONT OFFICE

Charles W. Somers

Charles W. Somers, a coal, lumber and shipping millionaire, was a good friend of Ban Johnson, president of the American League who was intent on establishing this new league against the competition of the dominant and more entrenched National League. Somers helped Johnson in his purpose and helped the American League through his ownership of the Cleveland franchise, his seed money for both the Philadelphia Athletics and the St. Louis Browns, his capital for the new Chicago White Sox ballpark (Comiskey Park) and his bill-paying for the Boston Red Sox. In the early days of the American League such multiple funding was acceptable, even necessary, and no conflict of interest was seen. In time, such arrangements became untenable because of questions about loyalty and commitments.

At the behest of Johnson, Somers became the owner of the Boston American League entry and, among the many early names associated with the team, it became known as the Somersets.

Somers, in this early tenure, was critical in influencing acceptance of the American League by the National League owners.

Somers sold the Boston franchise to Henry J. Killilea in 1903. The team promptly changed its name to the Pilgrims. Somers stayed in baseball, however, with his continued ownership of the Cleveland Indians. He was the Indians owner from 1901 to 1915.

Henry J. Killilea

Henry J. Killilea was a Milwaukee lawyer who had helped to negotiate the end of the war between the upstart American League and the established National League. He was instrumental in developing a "National Agreement" that would govern organized baseball.

Killilea purchased controlling interest in the Pilgrims from Somers. Among his early accomplishments was the agreement he negotiated with Barney Dreyfuss, owner of the National League Pittsburgh Pirates, to have a best-of-nine series between the Pilgrims, the American League winners, and the Pirates, the National League winners, in 1903. This was to be the first "World Series."

Killilea lost favor, however, with some of his skinflint practices. While Dreyfuss shared his World Series money with his players, Killilea kept all the money and gave the players none. He also charged the press for their World Series seats.

Killilea sold the Boston club to General Charles H. Taylor.

Boston Owners

Charles W. Somers	1901-1902
Henry J. Killilea	1903-1904
John I. Taylor	1904-1911
James R. McAleer	1912-1913
Joseph J. Lannin	1913-1916
Harry H. Frazee	1917-1923
J.A. Robert Quinn	1923-1933
Thomas A. Yawkey	1933-1976
Jean R. Yawkey	1976-1977
J. R. Y. Corporation	1978-1986
Jean R. Yawkey	
Haywood C. Sullivan	
Edward G. (Buddy) LeRoux, Jr.	
J. R. Y. Corporation	1987-1992
Jean R. Yawkey	
Haywood C. Sullivan	
J. R. Y. Corporation	1992-1993
Haywood C. Sullivan	
Jean R. Yawkey Trust	1994-2002
John L. Harrington, C.E.O.	
John Henry, Tom Werner et al.	2002-
Larry Lucchino, President and C.E.O.	

Charles H. Taylor and John I. Taylor

General Taylor, a retired Army officer, was the owner and publisher of *The Boston Globe*. General Taylor turned the club over to his son, John I. Taylor, as something of a toy. John Taylor had a reputation as a playboy with no focused interest in life.

After the National League's Boston Braves had abandoned the color red in their stockings following the 1907 season, Taylor appropiated the red color for the stockings of the Boston American League entry. He changed the team name from the Pilgrims to the Red Sox, beginning in 1908.

Taylor lost favor when he made the unpopular decision to sell Boston's star pitcher, Cy Young, to the Cleveland Indians before the 1909 season. He also interfered with field management, contributing to numerous managerial changes in the first decade of the team's existence. He caused Tris Speaker into threatening to leave the team.

Ban Johnson, taking note of the disaffection in Boston, influenced the sale of the team to James McAleer and his partner, Bob McRoy.

John Taylor changed the named of the Boston American League franchise from the Pilgrims to the Red Sox. (Boston Public Library Print Department).

James R. McAleer

James McAleer was at one time a centerfielder with the Cleveland Spiders of the National League, in the 1890s. McAleer was reputedly a Ban Johnson favorite and Ban Johnson had tremendous power in running the American League. With Johnson's secret financial backing, McAleer formed a partnership with Bob McRoy to buy a half-interest in the Red Sox in 1912. This enabled him to run the team.

McAleer alienated the team and fans alike. He interfered with manager Jake Stahl's choice of pitchers in the 1912 World Series. He angered the Royal Rooters, Boston's loyal fans, by selling seats for the World Series in their special section to outsiders. At one point, the Royal Root-

ers, who counted among their leaders James "Honey Fitz" Fitzsimmons, Boston's mayor, boycotted the Red Sox. McAleer subsequently replaced Jake Stahl as manager, after he had won the pennant and World Series in 1912.

Ban Johnson, in his careful "behind the scenes" manipulative manner, arranged for the McAleer/McRoy interests to be sold to Joseph J. Lannin.

Joseph J. Lannin

Joseph J. Lannin was a Canadian-born real estate tycoon. He purchased a half-interest in the Red Sox in 1914 and subsequently ran the club.

Lannin led the battle against the insurgent Federal League in 1914 who were pirating players from the established major leagues. Lannin had a good relationship with Jack Dunn, owner of the Baltimore Orioles in the International League. For the sum of $8,000, Lannin managed to buy both Babe Ruth and Ernie Shore from Baltimore for the Red Sox team.

Lannin, after the Red Sox won the world championship in 1915, could not agree with Tris Speaker on Speaker's salary for 1916. Just before Opening Day of 1916, Lannin traded Speaker to the Cleveland Indians. This created a complete shock in Boston. Speaker was to the Red Sox what Ty Cobb was to Detroit and Christy Mathewson was to the New York Giants. These were three of the most illustrious stars in baseball.

Lannin, by trading Speaker, broke up "the greatest outfield" of Speaker, Henry Hooper and Duffy Lewis. Speaker continued his Hall of Fame career, playing 11 years for Cleveland and the last two with the Washington Nationals and the Philadelphia Athletics. He later became playing-manager of the Cleveland Indians' 1920 World Championship team.

Lannin, again with the quiet, "behind the

Owner Joe Lannin brought Babe Ruth to the Red Sox, but also traded away Tris Speaker over a salary dispute. (Baseball Hall of Fame Library. Cooperstown, N.Y.).

scenes" manipulation of Ban Johnson, and also being in failing health, sold the majority interest in the Red Sox to Harry Frazee and Hugh Ward.

Harry Frazee

Harry Frazee bought the Red Sox from Joe Lannin in 1917, partly with cash and partly on credit. He was a Broadway producer whose subsequent losses in his stage ventures necessitated his selling many of the best Red Sox star players to the money-rich New York Yankees in the period 1918 through 1921. The money received from the baseball transactions helped to float the Broadway musical, "No! No! Nanette." The Red Sox lost the heart of their team, including pitchers Carl Mays, Ernie Shore, Dutch Leonard, Joe Bush, Sam Jones, Waite Hoyt, Herb Pennock, George Pipgras, pitcher-turned-outfielder Babe Ruth, shortstop Everett Scott, outfielder Duffy Lewis and catcher Wally Schang. The Red Sox-Yankee connection came under suspicion in 1922 when it was revealed Yankee owner Colonel Jacob Ruppert had insisted on being "consulted" by Red Sox owner Frazee before Frezee made any player deal with another club. Ruppert had given Frazee a money loan of $350,000 as part of the payment for Babe Ruth. Frazee had contemplated the sale of another player to the Detroit Tigers and Ruppert, though unable to stop the deal, unavailingly protested it. Frazee alienated the other American League owners who banded together under American League president Ban Johnson to force the sale of the Red Sox. The Red Sox were sold by Frazee to a consortium headed by Bob Quinn in early 1923.

Theatrical producer and speculator Harry Frazee bought the Red Sox in 1917 and then brought the team to ruin by selling off many of its key players to raise capital for his other enterprises. (Baseball Hall of Fame Library. Cooperstown, N.Y.).

Bob Quinn

Bob Quinn was a career baseball executive. Between the years 1917 and 1944 he was a part of management for the St. Louis Browns, then the Boston Red Sox, subsequently the Brooklyn Dodgers and finally the Boston Braves. Quinn, a member of a consortium, became the presiding owner of the Red Sox from 1923 to 1933 after purchasing the team from Harry Frazee.

These were among the worst years in Red Sox baseball history. Bereft of team stars by Frazee, Quinn continued some ill-advised deals with the Yankees, who received future Hall of Fame pitcher Charley "Red" Ruffing from the

Boston General Managers	
Edward Y. (Eddie) Collins	1933-1947
Joseph E. (Joe) Cronin	1948-1958
Stanley R. (Bucky) Harris	1959-1960
Richard H. (Dick) O'Connell	1961-1962
Exec. VP for Baseball & Finance	
Michael F. (Mike) Higgins	1963-1965
Exec. VP for Baseball	
Richard H. (Dick) O'Connell	1965-1977
Haywood C. Sullivan	1978-1983
James (Lou) Gorman	1984-1993
Daniel F. (Dan) Duquette	1994-2002

Red Sox in 1930. Quinn hired a procession of managers for a team that regularly finished last or next to last in the league. He was also the victim of bad luck when a principal backer died in 1926 and a fire destroyed a substantial part of Fenway Park. Attendance was generally poor and, ultimately, the crash of the stock market reduced Quinn's fortunes further.

When Tom Yawkey offered to buy the club in 1933 for little more than the $350,000 value of debts owed, Quinn accepted. Quinn then went on to become general manager of the Brooklyn Dodgers who because of their ineptness were known at the time as "the Daffiness Boys." He hired Casey Stengel as manager during Stengel's losing years as a big league manager and before he became skipper of the perennial world champion New York Yankees.

Tom Yawkey

Tom Yawkey was the owner of the Boston Red Sox for more than four decades, from 1934 through 1976. He was the nephew of one-time Detroit Tigers owner, William Yawkey. Considered a benevolent owner, a person who enjoyed the company of his star players, and a true fan, Yawkey resolved to turn the perpetually losing Boston franchise around. His ownership was in the pattern of rich sportsmen who enjoyed the challenge to win and cared less about the financial outcome in their baseball investments.

Among such owners at the time were Jacob Ruppert of the New York Yankees, William Wrigley Jr. of the Chicago Cubs and Walter Briggs Sr. of the Detroit Tigers.

Yawkey hired Eddie Collins as his general manager and then opened up his checkbook to secure by trade the likes of Lefty Grove, Jimmie Foxx, Joe Cronin, Rick Ferrell, Heinie Manush and, from the Yankees, pitcher George

Tom and Jean Yawkey, long-time owners of the Red Sox, invested large sums of money in the team in the 1930s to help make the team competitive again. (Boston Public Library Print Department).

Pipgras and third baseman Billy Werber. The Red Sox became respectable, a pennant contender, but did not win a pennant until 1946. By then, players such as Bobby Doerr and Ted Williams had come up from the minor leagues. Yawkey brought the fans back to Fenway Park and won three pennants (1946, 1967 and 1975) but never a World Series.

Though known for his generosity, Yawkey was also resistant to bringing blacks into major league baseball. The Red Sox, though they had a chance to have Willie Mays and Jackie Robinson earlier, were the last major league team to acquire a black player, Pumpsie Green in 1959.

Eddie Collins
Eddie Collins was one of baseball's great second basemen, playing for 20 years with the Philadelphia Athletics and the Chicago White Sox, with a lifetime batting average of .333. He was the keystone player in Connie Mack's "$100,000 infield" composed of Collins, first baseman Stuffy McInnis, short-stop Jack Barry and third baseman Frank "Home Run" Baker. He played on five pennant winners and four World Championship teams. He was elected as a player to the Hall of Fame. Tom Yawkey, when he bought the Red Sox,

Eddie Collins was instrumental in bringing such players as Lefty Grove, Jimmie Foxx, Ted Williams and Bobby Doerr to Boston. (Baseball Hall of Fame Library. Cooperstown, N.Y.).

insisted upon Eddie Collins as the general manager. Collins held the position for nineteen years, from 1933-1950. He died in Boston before the 1951 season began. It was Collins who arranged for trades that brought Lefty Grove, Jimmie Foxx and Joe Cronin to Boston, and he brought Ted Williams and Bobby Doerr up from the minor leagues. He also had an opportunity to acquire Jackie Robinson in the 1940s but deferred to Yawkey's objection.

Dick O'Connell
Dick O'Connell was the embattled G.M. of the Red Sox between the mid-1960s and the mid-1970s, and he later served briefly in the same embattled position in the 1980s.

O'Connell became head of baseball operations in 1965 and one of his earlier moves was to hire Dick Williams, who at the time had no previous major league managing experience, as manager in 1967. Williams turned the Red Sox around and they went from ninth place in 1966 to pennant winners in 1967. However, O'Connell had to fire Williams after the 1969 season because Williams' brusque methods alienated team star Carl Yastrzemski, a favorite of Yawkey's, and some of the players rebelled. For a long time thereafter, the Red Sox were known as "twenty-five players who took twenty-five cabs" after games.

As head of baseball operations, Dick O'Connell brought in Dick Williams to manage the Red Sox in 1967. (Baseball Hall of Fame Library. Cooperstown, N.Y.).

General manager Dick O'Connell (left) helps celebrate Haywood Sullivan's 35th birthday at Fenway Park. (Boston Public Library Print Department).

The Boston Front Office

O'Connell, in the mid 1970s, was in a struggle with then scouting director Haywood Sullivan, who criticized the general manager for his laxity in signing up key veteran players, for his extravagance in some player salaries he granted, and for the trade he proposed. Sullivan accused O'Connell of failing to negotiate re-hire contracts with Fred Lynn, Rick Burleson and Carlton Fisk yet he was willing to pay millions to Oakland for star relief pitcher Rollie Fingers and dependable outfielder Joe Rudi. This was the time when Oakland owner Charlie Finley was selling off all his good players.

Baseball Commissioner Bowie Kuhn stepped in and prevented the sale of Fingers and Rudi to the Red Sox. Sullivan kept up the critical drumbeat by accusing O'Connell of over paying free agent pitcher Bill Campbell. He succeeded in persuading Jean Yawkey to limit O'Connell's financial control.

When Sullivan soon afterward bought the club with Buddy Leroux and Jean Yawkey, O'Connell was dismissed in 1978.

Haywood Sullivan

Haywood Sullivan had a seven-year playing career as a catcher. He started his career with the Red Sox, though he played in only eight games over alternating years after he came up, as he shuffled between the parent team and the minor leagues. Finally, in 1960, he played in 52 games and had a season batting average of .161 before being traded the next year to Kansas City.

Haywood Sullivan went from mediocre catcher to scouting director and ultimately to owner of the Red Sox. (Baseball Hall of Fame Library. Cooperstown, N.Y.).

Red Sox manager Joe Cronin (left), owner Tom Yawkey (second from left) and Yankees manager Joe McCarthy (far right) look on as Governor Hurley throws out the first ball at Fenway Park. (Boston Public Library Print Department).

Sullivan, the former Red Sox player, and subsequent scouting director, and Buddy LeRoux, the former team trainer had sought to purchase the Red Sox from the Tom Yawkey estate upon Yawkey's death. However, they lacked sufficient capitalization and only could consummate the deal by including Jean Yawkey, Tom Yawkey's widow, as a part of the new ownership. Jean Yawkey provided the necessary financial capital. When Sullivan finally purchased the Red Sox with Buddy LeRoux and Jean Yawkey in 1977, he became Director of Baseball operations. He and Jean Yawkey became good allies in the struggle that subsequently developed with LeRoux over how to run the Red Sox.

Buddy Leroux

Buddy Leroux, the former Red Sox trainer, had become a real estate speculator and became active in an effort to buy the Red Sox after Tom Yawkey died. He allied himself with Haywood Sullivan in a bid for the team. When he and Sullivan became successful in getting Jean Yawkey to join them, Leroux became a co-owner.

Initially a partner with Haywood Sullivan in purchasing the Red Sox, Buddy LeRoux later fell out of favor with Sullivan and was forced to sell his interest. (Baseball Hall of Fame Library. Cooperstown, N.Y.).

Disagreement soon developed between Leroux and Sullivan about management of the franchise. Leroux became increasingly alienated as Sullivan and Yawkey mostly joined forces. Finally, in 1983, Leroux sought to engineer a coup in order to acquire managerial control of the Red Sox organization. He brought Dick O'Connell back as nominal general manager and had a rump group of his own executives. The struggle for control, with two competing slates of management, ended up in the courts. The courts ruled in favor of Sullivan and Yawkey. O'Connell again left the organization soon afterwards. Leroux was forced by the courts to sell his interest in the club.

Dan Duquette

Dan Duquette is the current general manager of the Red Sox, succeeding James (Lou) Gorman after the latter's 10-year rein in the position. Duquette came over from the Montreal Expos in 1994, after three years as general manager with the Expos. He acquired a reputation first as director of player development, by helping Montreal to develop an excellent farm system that produced a number of major league stars. Among these were Larry Walker, John Wetteland, Marquis Grissom, Ken Hill and Mel Rojas. The Expos were successful in the field and also had a low player payroll.

With the Red Sox, Duquette assumed active control as general manager. He was initially criticized, particularly for failing to re-sign one of Boston's favorite stars, pitcher Roger Clemens. Clemens signed as a free agent with the Toronto Blue Jays. He was also criticized for not being able to come to an agreement with popular first baseman Mo Vaughn after the 1998 season and allowing him to sign with Anaheim instead.

In 1998, however, the Red Sox fortunes were looking up. Duquette outbid other teams for the services of Pedro Martinez, the Cy Young youthful pitcher who came over from the impoverished Montreal Expos in the National League. Martinez developed into the dominant pitcher in baseball. He also brought up Nomar Garciaparra who became Rookie of the Year for his play as the Red Sox shortstop. Duquette also arranged to contract with pitching retreads Bret Saberhagen and Steve Avery who had good comeback years in 1998. And, he brought heavy hitters Carl Everett and Manny Ramirez to the Red Sox.

As the 2002 season approached, however, Duquette's status was uncertain. He incurred additional animosity from the fans for his handling and dismissal of Manager Jimy Williams in 2001. When new owners John Henry, Tom Werner, et al, took over the Red Sox in early 2002, and appointed Larry Lucchino as President and CEO, Duquette was immediately fired. A few days later, Joe Kerrigan was also dismissed as field manager. Grady Little was appointed the new field manager.

Red Sox broadcasters (from left) Ned Martin, Mel Parnell and Curt Gowdy broadcast a game from the outfield at Fenway Park. (Boston Public Library Print Department).

RED SOX
SPORTSCASTERS

An important component of baseball experience is the contribution made by experts in mass media, notably sportswriters and sportscasters. Their words and comments provide visual images so that large audiences not in immediate attendance at the game can be aware of what is happening. Some provide "color," which is to say they denote and elaborate important bits and pieces of information about the game and its people.

Some are baseball experts who provide analysis and insight for a better understanding of the game. And, most importantly, their reporting and comments provide continuity for those who are not in constant or daily attendance on what is happening in the world of baseball.

Reportage has long been an associated characteristic of the game. Sportscasting began as the technical facilities of radio and television developed.

The Earliest Radio Accounts of Red Sox Baseball

The first radio accounts of baseball in Boston, according to newspaper sources, were the broadcasts of some Boston Braves home games by announcer Ben Alexander and Charles Donelan over station WNAC in 1925. Commissioner Kenesaw Mountain Landis approved play-by-play broadcast of the 1925 World Series anywhere in the country. Boston's WEEI broadcast the Series and this historic event was handled by, among others, the first celebrated sportscaster, Graham McNamee.

American League owners, however, were mostly opposed to the broadcasting of baseball. They denied permission to station WMAQ of Chicago to broadcast from Comiskey Park. Their logic was that radio accounts of the game would discourage personal attendance at the game. It was a pocketbook issue.

Attitudes slowly changed. In 1926, Bob Quinn, then the owner of the Red Sox, announced that New England radio fans would hear the play-by-play of the opening day game at Fenway Park. The Red Sox were playing the Yankees. Though it is not clear if this indeed occurred it is certain that the Yankees beat the Red Sox on opening day, 12-11.

Fred Hoey—Boston's Broadcasting Pioneer

The year 1927 is notable as the year in which some Red Sox games were broadcast from Fenway Park. The radio station was WNAC and the first announcer was Gerry Harrison. In that year, Fred Hoey, a newspaperman who wrote for the *Journal*, *Post*, and *American*, Boston dailies, appeared upon the radio scene and began broadcasting Red Sox games. Fred Hoey was the first established broadcaster of Red Sox baseball. He broadcast mostly on WNAC from 1927 through 1938. He broadcast on both the Yankee and Colonial networks. Notable commercial sponsors at the time were Kentucky Club pipe tobacco and Mobil's Flying Red Horse gasoline. Hoey broadcast the Boston Braves games in 1930 and John Shepard broadcast the Red Sox games. In 1931 Hoey started broadcasting both the Braves and Red Sox home games. Hoey became a fixture for sports fans in Boston radio broadcasting. Notably, on his "watch," Hoey broadcast the first sabbath game permitted to be played in Boston. This was in 1929, an exhibition game between the Red Sox and the Braves at Braves Field which the Braves won, 4-0.

The Celebrated Radio Broadcasters

Jim Britt

Jim Britt and his sidekick Tom Hussey, broadcast Red Sox baseball over radio from 1940 through 1950. Theirs was the voice of Red Sox baseball. It was in this period that recreations of "away" games were broadcast to Red Sox fans, most notably by Tom Hussey and Leo Egan. They would receive telegraphed signals and then broadcast the information in a way that dramatized the game as if it were done live. This was also the period when commercial sponsorship of broadcast baseball became prevalent. A chief sponsor in those early years was Narragansett beer.

Jim Britt's approach to baseball broadcasting set a professional model. Among much else, he was precise in his use of English and enunciated clearly. He also was the first broadcaster associated with a young, struggling charity enterprise, Boston's own Jimmy Fund. He did both Red Sox and Braves games but then, in 1950, he became exclusively the Braves' broadcaster for a rival beer sponsor, Ballantine beer.

In 1950, Hall of Famer Frankie Frisch, "the Fordham Flash," took over as Red Sox radio broadcaster for one year, in between stints as manager of the St. Louis Cardinals and the Pittsburgh Pirates.

Curt Gowdy

Tom Yawkey invited Curt Gowdy to become the sportscaster of Boston Red Sox baseball beginning in 1951. Gowdy had been a sidekick of the celebrated Mel Allen, "Voice of the Yankees," in New York. Gowdy, "the Wyoming cowboy," broadcast the games over radio station WHOH and its 50-station network from 1961 through 1965. Among his sidekicks over those years were Tom Hussey and Bob Delaney and, for a five-year period, Bob Murphy. Murphy is particularly notable because he and Ralph Kiner became the original broadcasters for the New York Mets who became an expansion team in 1962. They teamed for more than 30 years. Kiner became strictly a TV caster and Bob Murphy became the chief radio broadcaster. Thirty-seven years later in 1998, Murphy is still broadcasting for the Mets.

After Murphy, Gowdy had as his broadcast partners in Boston, Bill Crowley and Art Gleeson. And, finally in the Gowdy period, Ned Martin and Mel Parnell made up the broadcasting team with Curt. It was typical for the broad-casters, performing as a team, to switch off and take turns on both radio and television broadcasting.

Gowdy subsequently left Boston baseball to become a celebrated sportscaster on the NBC network. This began in 1966 when he became the broadcaster for NBC's "Game of the Week" and chief broadcaster for ten years for both the annual All-Star game and the World Series. Gowdy is one of America's distinguished broadcasters. In 1970 he was the first sportscaster to receive the George Foster Peabody award for excellence in broadcasting. The citation praised him for "versatility . . . and blend of reporting accuracy, knowledge, good humor, infectious honesty and enthusiasm." He was elected to Baseball's Hall of Fame as a broadcaster in 1984.

Ned Martin

Ned Martin began radio broadcasting with Curt Gowdy in 1961. Martin was initially part of the team of Gowdy, Martin and Gleeson, with Mel Parnell substituting for Gleeson in 1965. When Gowdy departed, Martin then

As voices of the Red Sox, Ned Martin (left), Ken Coleman (center) and Mel Parnell became popular media figures in Boston. (Boston Red Sox).

became associated with Ken Coleman in the broadcast of Red Sox baseball. He broadcast in most of the years from 1961 through 1988, a 28-year period. Among his broadcasting colleagues in this period were Gowdy and Parnell in the early period, then Ken Coleman, John McLean, Dave Martin and Johnny Pesky and still later Jim Woods. Most of the radio broadcasts while Martin was on the air were on WHOH.

Ned Martin and Jim Woods were a particularly popular broadcast team, known for their candor and even-handed approach to the game. Woods, "the Possum," was "second banana" to some of baseball's top broadcasters. His broadcast career began in the 1930s when he took over from "Dutch" Reagan broadcasting University of Iowa football games. (Dutch Reagan went on to Hollywood and became even more famous as President Ronald Reagan.) Woods then joined Mel Allen and Red Barber as a New York Yankee broadcaster. He later broadcast with Russ Hodges of the Giants, Bob Prince of the Pirates and Jack Buck of the Cardinals before joining Martin in Boston.

Ken Coleman

Ken Coleman first broadcast Red Sox baseball in 1966, coming on the scene after Curt Gowdy left. He came over from broadcast duties with the successful Cleveland Browns football team and he was the broadcaster for a number of years for Cleveland Indians baseball. In Bos-

ton, he teamed with Ned Martin and Mel Parnell. They were the team on the Red Sox airwaves until 1972. Coleman became the radio "Voice of the Red Sox." In 1975, Coleman went to Cincinnati and broadcast the Cincinnati Reds games for four years, from 1975 through 1978. He returned to the Red Sox broadcasting booth in 1979, doing radiocasts with Rico Petrocelli, Johnny Pesky, Jon Miller and finally with Joe Castiglione in Boston. Coleman did the radio broadcasts for the Red Sox through 1985. He, like Fred Hoey, Jim Britt, Curt Gowdy and Ned Martin, had a long tour of duty, roughly 20 years with the exception of his four-year stint with Cincinnati. A native of the Boston area, he was a devoted Red Sox fan and broadcast in some of the Red Sox most successful years.

Joe Castiglione

Joe Castiglione, who has become the "voice" of the Red Sox radio baseball, began Red Sox broadcasting with Ken Coleman in 1983. Through the year 2001, Joe was the radio broadcaster for 19 years with the Red Sox. His sidekick in recent years, Jerry Trupiano, was in his ninth season in 2001, broadcasting for the Red Sox. Jerry took over from Bob Star in 1993. The flagship station for the seventh season in 2001 was Red Sox Radio 850, WEEI-AM. Castiglione, it might be noted, had brief stinsts in TV baseball in Cleveland with Ken Coleman and in Milwaukee before becoming a regular radio braodcaster for Boston baseball.

The Celebrated Television Broadcasters

The 1948 season was the first year of television broadcasts of Red Sox baseball. Some of the Red Sox games were on TV with Jim Britt and Tom Hussey as the principal broadcasters. They were joined by Bump Hadley on Channel 4 and by Leo Smith on Channel 7. The Britt et al TV cast of Red Sox games lasted through 1950 when Britt became a broadcaster for the Boston Braves.

Curt Gowdy

A new team took over TV casting for the Red Sox in 1951. The team first consisted of Curt Gowdy, Tom Hussey and Bob Delaney, and they did their telecasts on Channel 4 or Channel 7. Gowdy was the "main man" on TV from 1951 through 1965, and he then left to become a featured sportscaster on the NBC network. Gowdy's TV associates were the same as those on radio, namely, after Delaney, Bob Murphy, then Bill Crowley and Art Gleeson, and finally Ned Martin and Mel Parnell.

Ned Martin

Ned Martin paralleled his radio broadcasting career on Red Sox TV. He was first a telecaster with Gurt Gowdy in 1961 and, upon Gowdy's departure, teamed with Ken Coleman and Mel Parnell. Their TV casts were on Channel 5. Martin, in his tour on Red Sox TV, had as his colleagues

The dean of Red Sox sportscasters, Curt Gowdy went on to network television after doing Red Sox TV broadcasts for several years. (Baseball Hall of Fame Library. Cooperstown, N.Y.).

first Ken Coleman, and Mel Parnell, and then Johnny Pesky. Subsequently, Martin telecast Red Sox games on TV 38 with Ken Harrelson and then Bob Montgomery. In 1985, he began his TV casts on cable and the New England Sports Network (NESN). His colleagues were Bob Montgomery and then Jerry Remy. Bob Kurtz, in recent years, has also emerged as a play-by-play announcer on NESN.

Ken Coleman

Coleman, like his principal predecessors, broadcast both radio and TV baseball for the Red Sox. His TV casts began in 1966 with his colleagues, Ned Martin and Mel Parnell. Subsequently, he and Johnny Pesky became the TV broadcasting team on Channel 4 until 1975. Coleman subsequently did mostly radio baseball when he returned from the Cincinnati Reds in 1979.

Sean McDonough

Sean McDonough first began TV casting for the Red Sox in 1988. He was on TV 38 with Bob Montgomery. At about that time Jerry Remy went on cable TV (NESN) with Ned Martin. The team subsequently became Sean McDonough and Jerry Remy on NESN (Channel 68) and, later, McDonough, Bob Kurtz, and Remy on NESN. McDonough, in 2001, was in his 14th season with the Red Sox, currently doing play-by-play for Fox 25–WFXT-TV. Fox 25 in 2001 was in its second season with the Red Sox. Color commentary for Red Sox TV continued to be provided by former Sox player Jerry Remy, who through 2001 provided six seasons of commentary for the Red Sox Television Network. Sean McDonough is also a leading sportscaster for CBS. He calls the All-Star Game, League Championships, and the World Series. He is also a Winter Olympics broadcaster for CBS.

The New England Sports Network (NESN) in its 18th season with the Red Sox in 2001, now utilizes Don Orsillo for play-by-play. Jerry Remy, for the 14th year in 2001, provides Red Sox color commentary for NESN, in addition to his assignment at Fox.

Ex-Ball Players As Color Broadcasters

A trend has developed in baseball broadcasting for ex-ball players to join the broadcast team and, with their expertise in the game, become commentators or provide "color." In some baseball locations, the broadcast assignments have been taken over entirely by ex-ballplayers, many of whom have become very skilled sportscasters after their playing careers.

For the Red Sox, the earliest experience with ex-ballplayer broadcasts was Frankie Frisch's broadcast with Tom Hussey in 1939 on radio station WAAB. Frisch, "the Fordham Flash," was a Hall of Fame second baseman with the New York Giants and St. Louis Cardinals, and also a big league manager.

In 1948, the first year of television broadcasts, Irving "Bump" Hadley, who had pitched for six big-league teams, most notably for the Washington Nationals and then some championship New York Yankee teams in the 1930s, became a Boston broadcaster. He joined the TV team of Jim Britt and Tom Hussey televising Red Sox games on Channel 7 in 1949 and 1950.

Subsequently, and beginning with Mel Parnell, the ex-ballplayer broadcasters were ex-Red Sox players. These included Parnell, a Red Sox pitching star in the late 1940s and 1950s, Johnny Pesky, a popular Red Sox infielder and former manager, Ken "Hawk" Harrelson, a stylish and outspoken former Red Sox outfielder who teamed briefly with sportscaster Dick Stockton as well as Ned Martin, catcher Bob Montgomery, briefly former infielder Mike Andrews and ex-second baseman Jerry Remy.

Broadcasts in Spanish

The Carter Radio Network, with the flagship station WROL, was the radio broadcaster for Red Sox games in Spanish. Bobby Serrano and his colleague Hector Martinez were commentators. In its fourth year in 2001, Caliente 1330 AM became the Boston flagship station for the Spanish Beisbol Network. Serrano continues as commentator and in 2001, was in his 12th season in Spanish broadcasts. J.P. Villaman joined Bobby for their third year together in 2001 as the broadcaster on the Spanish network.

The Style of Red Sox Broadcasters

Red Sox broadcasters mostly have a reputation as straightforward baseball announcers and commentators. As distinguished baseball broadcaster Ernie Harwell said of the early broadcasters Fred Hoey and Curt Gowdy, they were "low key . . . play it down the middle." There is relatively little of the sensational or idiosyncratic styles associated with some baseball broadcasters in other cities. They do not lead in the singing of "Take Me Out To The Ball Game" as the late Harry Carey did in Chicago. They do not imitate Phil Rizzuto in his folksy baseball broadcasting for the New York Yankees, with perhaps as much attention to announcing the birthdays of friends as to the baseball game. They do not mash the English language as did the celebrated baseball player and announcer Dizzy Dean, for whom "the runner slud into third base." The Red Sox broadcasters, like most team broadcasters, support the team but not in a manner that suggests rampant favoritism. They are, from time to time, critical of plays and players, and perhaps even of team management, but not to the extent of constant carping and biting.

*Built in 1912, Fenway Park, including the "Green Monster,"
is one of Major League baseball's great old stadiums.
(Baseball Hall of Fame Library. Cooperstown, N.Y.).*

THE HISTORY OF
TEAM NAMES,
UNIFORMS
AND RED SOX BALL FIELDS

Team Names: Puritans, Plymouth Rocks, Americans, Somersets, Red Sox

When the Boston entry in the American League was established in 1901, it became known by several different names but none were official. Writers and other referred to the team as the Puritans, the Plymouth Rocks, the Americans and the Somersets. The team seemed to have adopted the name Americans because, in 1902, the jerseys worn by the players had a distinctive "B" on one side and "A" on the other side on the front.

Notwithstanding, however, it appeared as official, and is so noted in baseball encyclopedia, that the team name was the Somersets. The name derived from the team's first owner, Charles W. Somers. The Boston Somersets of the American League.

By 1903, Somers had sold his interest in the team and moved from being a principal financial angel of various American League teams to a concentrated interest and control in the Cleveland American League entry. Forthwith, the name of the Boston team changed to an official "Pilgrims," The Boston Pilgrims. The team on the other side of town in the National League maintained its name at the time as the Boston Beaneaters.

At the end of the 1906 baseball year, the Boston Beaneaters divested themselves of the distinctive solid red socks in their uniforms. The team uniforms changed to white with maroon lettering, though the team returned to red stockings and red lettering in 1908 and used red from then on and from time to time in the team's history.

The Boston American League entry seized upon the color red in its uniforms and wore red stockings beginning in 1907. Almost immediately the team became known as the Red Stockings or the Red Sox. In 1908, with the issuance of new uniforms and the abundant use of red it became clear that the Boston team was henceforth the Red Stockings or Red Sox. It became a settled matter that the team was the Red Sox—The Boston Red Sox. To create shortened monikers, the team also became known as the Bosox, or simply, the Sox, not to be confused with the Chicago White Sox. "The Boston Red Sox" has remained the name of the team for nearly the entire century, notwithstanding that the Red Sox uniform designers have dropped the color red in the uniforms from time to time.

The Team Uniforms

The Earliest Uniforms

The earliest uniforms for the Boston American League entry were picked out by manager Jimmy Collins. The uniforms were a standard white. In a carry over from the 1890s and until 1910, the jerseys had regulation turned down collars with lacing partway down the front. Baseball trousers uniformly had built-in quilted padding for protection in sliding. The caps were pill-box shaped with two stripes around the crown. The socks were solid blue.

In 1902, the lettering on the jersey front was changed to an Old English "B" and "A" on the right and left breast of the uniform, respectively. Notable early photos of Cy Young and Jimmy Collins at this time show this. The lettering replaced the earliest BOSTON in black across the front of the uniform. The "B" and "A" uniform lasted for only one year. The decorative Old English letters were used on many other uniforms but the only team to survive with this distinctive lettering is the Detroit Tigers with their traditional Old English "D."

The Boston Red Sox And The Uniforms Of 1908

With the National League Boston Beaneaters abandonment of red in their uniforms in 1907, the Boston Pilgrims quickly moved in. The Red Sox name and uniform became established with the element of the color red most notably in the new uniforms of 1908. The jersey used the abbreviated Sox in red. Centered on the chest was a slanted red stocking. The socks were a solid red. In 1909, the lettering on the uniform reverted to a standard BOSTON, but in red and no longer blue or black. The pill box caps were a plain white. In 1910, the solid red stockings were changed to a single wide band of red. Laced, turned-down collars were replaced with a button front with a stand-up, cadet style collar. In 1912, the uniform displayed RED SOX across the front instead of BOSTON and for awhile the uniforms, like most in the league, had pin stripes. The uniforms remained this way, with minimal changes, for about twenty years. The Red Sox dress was uniform and, some would say, plain. Some would say dreary, as was the Red Sox team for most of the twenties and early '30s.

The New Red Sox Uniforms Of The 1930s

Beginning in the 1930s, the Red Sox no longer used basic block letters on their uniforms but a fancier lettering style. Both the Red Sox and the National League Boston Braves had a patch on the left sleeve, a large Pilgrim hat design, to symbolize and celebrate the city's tri-centennial. There also appeared at this time a pair of red socks on the sleeve and a small red sock on the cap front. The lettering on uniforms began to use a navy blue trim. The wide red stripe on the stockings was extended to the entire sock except for white stripes. In time, blue and white stripes were added to the upper half of the stockings. For the first time in 1933 and 1934 a solid navy blue cap appeared and the letter "B" in red color was introduced on the cap front. A white outline was added to the B on the caps in 1946. The uniform of the mid-1930s became substantially the Red Sox standard uniform for the next thirty years.

The Uniform Revolution of the 1970s

Beginning in the 1970s, the Red Sox, like other teams in baseball, started to wear more comfortable double knits instead of wool uniforms. The double knits featured a pull-over jersey and a built-in sash belt. The uniform collar became a V-neck with red and navy striping for trim. Caps changed to a solid red crown with a navy blue bill. On the cap was a "B" in navy blue with a white trim. There were variations in cap colors. Red shoes were also introduced to complement the double units. A new fad developed of stretching stirrups full up and under the trousers, effectively concealing navy and white stripes on the upper part of the stocking.

Earl Webb (left) and Smead Jolley display the Boston uniforms of the early 1930s. (Boston Red Sox).

Outfielder Lou Finney displays a Boston uniform of the 1940s, which by this time included the solid navy cap with a red "B", which remains essentially the same today. (Boston Red Sox).

Uniform Fashions of the 1980s and 1990s

Though the familiar button front jerseys and belt loop trousers returned in 1979, the more comfortable double knits remained. What notably changed was the manner in which the players wore their uniforms. For most of the century baggy knickers were characteristic of baseball uniforms. In most recent decades this style has changed for most players to tight skin-fitting uniforms, most notable in the trousers. Some of the players became conscious of being fashion plates. In the first half of the century, socks with stripes were uniformly worn and showing with the trouser length extending to at or just below the knee. Gradually, the players began to wear the trousers to a longer length. Currently and in recent years, most players wear their trousers to ankle length or below with little showing of the stockings. In the past few years, some players, perhaps as a mark of their speedster identification began exposing their solid socks to knee height again. Currently, some players no longer wear stirrups but wear mostly solid color, plain socks to knee length.

The Boston Red Sox uniform has, for the most part, been conservative and consistent. This is certainly so when compared to the uniforms of some teams. The Red Sox have not adopted striking and revolutionary colors such as owner Charles Finley adopted for the Oakland Athletics. The Oakland team has become familiar in variations of Kelly green and Tulane gold with white shoes. Neither have the Red Sox come close in their choice of jersey color and design to the Houston Astros of 1975 with their horizontal rainbow design of several hues of orange. And, they did not revolutionize uniform design as owner Bill Veeck did briefly with his White Sox in 1976, who wore an approximation of Bermuda shorts with exposed knees and long knee-length socks.

The Red Sox Ball Parks—The Huntington Avenue Baseball Grounds And Then Fenway Park

Huntington Avenue Baseball Grounds

When a franchise was granted for Boston to have a charter team in the American League a place to play was needed. A baseball field was built at the Huntington Avenue Grounds, a location presently occupied by a sports building in Northeastern University. The Huntington Avenue Baseball Grounds, an all-wooden structure later thought by many to be a fire trap, had a seating capacity of 9,000. It was used by the Boston American League team as its field of play from 1901 through 1911. The Boston games in the first World Series in 1903 were played here. The first game at the Huntington Grounds was played on May 8, 1901 with an overflow crowd of 11,500 fans and Cy Young pitched the Boston team to a 12-4 win over the Philadelphia Athletics.

The Huntington field, for the most part, did not have unusual dimensions. The distance from home plate to a left field barrier was 350 feet. It was 440 in left center and first 530 feet and later 635 feet in center field. The distance in right field was 280 feet and later 320. There was a tool shed in deep center field that was considered to be in fair territory. There were large patches of sand in the outfield where grass would not grow. Nonetheless, the crowds at Somerset/Pilgrim/Red Sox games were sometimes overflowing.

Fenway Park

Owner John I. Taylor of the Boston Red Sox decided that a new field with more seating capacity was required and it was built in 1912. It was built in an area of the city known

The Huntington Avenue Baseball Grounds were the home of the Boston American League entry from 1901-1912. (Boston Public Library Print Department).

Carl Yastrzemski raps out a hit at Fenway Park in the final 1967 regular-season game. Fenway hosted the World Series that year. (Boston Public Library Print Department).

as the Fens and naturally enough came to be known as Fenway Park.

Fenway Park was built in the then-newer tradition of steel-and-concrete stadia. It was built in the same year of similar new stadiums at Navin Field in Detroit and Crosley Field in Cincinnati. It opened on the same day as Navin Field (now Tiger Stadium) though this was largely a coincidence. Fenway Park was due to open two days earlier, on April 18, 1912, but there were two postponements on account of rain. A momentous event did occur, however, on April 18; the luxury liner Titanic sunk in the North Atlantic. Opening day for Fenway Park was on April 20, 1912 and before 27,000 fans, Boston beat the New York Highlanders (later named the Yankees) by a score of 7-6 in 11 innings. Tris Speaker drove in the winning run.

The contours of Fenway Park were irregular and reflected the street patterns just outside the outfield wall. It was 302 feet from home plate to the right field pole and the wall was six feet high. The wall then sloped to 380 feet at the bullpens in front of the right field bleachers.

The distance here was originally 405 feet but was reduced when the bullpens were built. This was at a time when the great Ted Williams was here and he was, among other things, a long-distance hitter. It was thought that the change was made to favor Williams' hitting and the area came to be known as "Williamsburg."

It was 420 feet from home plate to straight away center field though at one time, in the early 1930s, it was 593 feet. At that time this was the distance to the deepest corner of the wall virtually behind the right center field bleachers. It was considered fair territory.

Left field, from Fenway Park's earliest days, was destined to be a conversational gem and a players' nightmare for those who did not learn how to play an idiosyncratic left field position. Originally, there was a ten-foot incline running to the wall, and the left fielder had to play the territory running uphill. This was so well mastered by Boston's first star left fielder, Duffy Lewis, that the area became known as "Duffy's Cliff." Smead Jolly, a .350 career hitter and a notoriously poor fielder for the Red Sox said, "They taught me how to run up the cliff, but they never taught me how to run down it."

The Green Monster

The "Green Monster" is an important part of the lore of Fenway Park. In 1917, the ten-foot-high wall in left field was raised to 37 feet. The lower part of the wall was concrete and the upper part was tin-covered wood. It remained that way until 1976 when the wall was converted to hard plastic. In 1936, a 23-foot screen was placed on top of the 37-foot wall so that outgoing baseballs wouldn't hit windows on Lansdowne Street. In 1947, the wall was coated with green paint and became, and remains, "the Green Monster."

In 1934, Tom Yawkey arranged to flatten the ground in left field so that "Duffy's Cliff" no longer existed, but "the Green Monster" remained. From 1912 to 1934, the outfielder in left field had to contend with either/and Duffy's Cliff and the 37-foot-high left-field wall. The wall is officially said to be 315 feet from home plate at the foul line.

Fenway Park had other interesting characteristics. In the left field wall, the Park had one of the last hand-operated scoreboards in the major leagues. Green and red lights are used to signal balls, strikes and outs. There is also a large electronic scoreboard, installed in 1976. A ladder was also built into the wall in left field so that a groundskeeper could retrieve balls that were hit over the 37-foot wall but into the screen above it that served as a net. The initials TAY and JRY, for Tom Yawkey and Jean Yawkey, appear in Morse code in two vertical stripes on the scoreboard in left field.

The grandstands of Fenway Park hung closely around the field, providing a feeling of intimacy for the fans with the players and the field. One notable change occurred in 1982 when luxury boxes were built behind the home plate area. This not only generated more revenue but, because of the height and massiveness of the new structure, swirling winds were not uncharacteristic in this section of the ball park. Catching a pop fly became an adventure for the infielders and the catcher in this area.

Fenway Park, to most, remains a dramatic site for baseball. Reportedly, no ball was ever hit over the right field roof. Six balls are reported to have been hit out of the park to the right of the flagpole in fair territory. These were by Hank Greenberg, Jimmie Foxx, Bill (Moose)

Skowron, Carl Yastrzemski, Bobby Mitchell and Jim Rice. "Yaz," who was the closest thing to a permanent resident on the field at Fenway Park —he played for the Sox for 23 seasons—with permission from Tom Yawkey took the bluegrass sod off the field after the World Series of 1967 and placed it on the lawn of his suburban Lynnfield home.

Historic Events At Fenway Park

Fenway Park has produced many great memories. Firstly, the largest crowd ever to attend a game at Fenway Park was 47,627 on September 22, 1935. This was for a double-header with the New York Yankees. On August 12, 1934 a then-record crowd of 46,776 came to Fenway Park to say good-bye to Babe Ruth. He announced that this was to be his last season and the Boston fans love for Ruth remained notwithstanding that he had become an established New York Yankee. The Babe actually did not retire at the end of the season but played in one more year with the Boston Braves. No sooner did the Babe Ruth finale set the attendance record at Fenway Park then the record was broken the following week, with 46,995 attending a double-header with the pennant-bound Detroit Tigers.

The current capacity of Fenway Park is about 34,000.

Ted Williams (right) jogs past "The Green Monster" while warming up prior

"Wally the Green Monster" is the official mascot of the Boston Red Sox and Fenway Park. (Boston Red Sox).

Shortly after World War II it was decreed that Fenway could no longer hold larger crowds because of new fire regulations.

The smallest crowd recorded for a game at Fenway Park was 409 for a game with the Kansas City Royals on September 29, 1965. It was the end of the season and, in a ten team American League, the ninth-place Red Sox were playing the tenth-place Royals.

Fenway Park was the scene of the World Series in 1912, 1914 and 1918, and then not again until 1946, 1967, 1975 and 1986. This was a total of seven of the ten World Series in which the Red Sox participated. The 1914 World Series was something of an anomaly because it was the "miracle" Boston Braves playing the Philadelphia Athletics in the Series. The location of Fenway Park was agreed upon because it could hold more fans than Braves Field which was only then being enlarged.

Ironically, with the enlarged Braves Field, the Red Sox played their 1915 and 1916 World Series game at the Boston National League site. The first World Series, in 1903, of course found the Boston Pilgrims at their Huntington Avenue Grounds home field.

There were many memorable World Series moments but perhaps the most notable were (1) the exciting 1912 World Series against the New York Giants and the game with "the Snodgrass muff" and (2) the equally exciting 1975 World Series against the Cincinnati Reds and the game with Carlton Fisk's "pointed" home run in the 12th inning.

Two All-Star games were played at Fenway Park. The first, in 1946, was the occasion for Ted Williams' batting assault. He had four hits, two home runs, and five runs batted in the game. This is a performance such as has not been equalled in All-Star competition. The second All-Star game at Fenway Park was in 1961. This occasion was also unusual because the game ended in a tie after nine innings and was called by rain.

Fenway was also witness to two of the first three play-off games in American League history, in 1948 and 1978. In 1948, the Red Sox lost to the Cleveland Indians and the hitting onslaught of manager Lou Boudreau. In 1978, the Red Sox lost to the New York Yankees and the unexpected and dramatic homer of Bucky Dent.

There have been some other particularly notable games at Fenway Park. On June 23, 1917, Babe Ruth, who pitched to one batter and was ejected, and Ernie Shore who pitched to the next 26 batters, "combined" for an unusual no-hit, no-run game.

In 1929 Sunday baseball was approved but the Red Sox played all of their Sunday games at Braves Field in both 1930 and 1931. This was said to be because Fenway Park was near a church. The first Sunday game at Fenway was on July 3, 1932 when the Red Sox lost to the Yankees, 13-2

In 1947 night lights and night ball games came to Fenway Park. The first night game was on June 13, 1947 when the Red Sox beat the White Sox, 5-3. The first night game in major league baseball was played in Cincinnati in 1935.

On September 28, 1960, Ted Williams closed his career at Fenway Park with his 521st and last home run.

On April 29, 1986, Roger Clemens broke the record by striking out 20 players in a game against the visiting Seattle Mariners.

Fenway Park also had its misfortunes. Fire destroyed the bleachers along the left field foul line in 1926, and there was subsequently another, smaller fire in the left field area. With the advent of Tom Yawkey, repairs were made and the Park was restored "like new." Fenway Park, quaint though it is today, is a matter of much affection for Boston fans. It, like Wrigley Field in Chicago and Tiger Stadium in Detroit, currently remain, as an enduring marker of the past, replete with a handsome history of baseball. Visually, a landmark attracts those in Boston's Back Bay to Fenway. It is noticeable both outside and inside the ball park. It is the long-standing Citgo sign, built in 1965, atop a building on Beacon Street near Kenmore Square. It is a reminder for Red Sox fans that one is close to or near hallowed ground.

Bibliography

Books

Barrow, Edward Grant with James M. Kahn, *My Fifty Years In Baseball.* Coward-McCann, 1951.

Baylor, Don with Claire Smith, *Don Baylor - Nothing But The Truth: A Baseball Life.* St. Martins, 1989.

Berry, Henry, *Boston Red Sox.* Collier Books, 1975.

Berry, Henry and Berry, Harold, *Boston Red Sox; The Complete Record Of Red Sox Baseball.* MacMillan, 1984.

Boggs, Wade, *Boggs!* Contemporary Books, 1986.

Boston Red Sox, *Media Guide.* Boston Red Sox Official Yearbook.

Boswell, John, *Fenway Park: Legendary Home of the Boston Red Sox,* 1992.

Bresciani, Dick, Ed., *Boston Red Sox 1984 Official Yearbook.* Sports Productions, Inc. 1984.

Bresciani, Dick, *Boston Red Sox 1984 Scorebook Magazine.* Public Relations Department, Boston Red Sox, 1984.

Chadwick, Bruce, *The Boston Red Sox: Memories and Mementoes of New England's Team.* Abbeville Press, 1991.

Clark, Ellery Harding, *Boston Red Sox: 75th Anniversary History, 1901-1975.* Exposition Press, 1975.

Clark, Ellery Harding, *Red Sox Forever.* Exposition Press. 1977.

Clemens, Roger with Peter Gammons, *Rocket Man: The Roger Clemens Story.* Stephen Greene, 1987.

Cole, Milton, *Baseballs Greatest Dynasties: The Red Sox.* Gallery Books, 1990.

Coleman, Ken and Valenti, Dan, *The Impossible Dream Remembered: The 1967 Red Sox.* Stephen Greene, 1987.

Conigliaro, Tony with Jack Zanger, *Seeing It Through.* MacMillan, 1970.

Cramer, Richard Ben, *Ted Williams: The Seasons Of The Kid.* Prentiss Hall Press, 1991.

Crehan, Herbert F., *Lightning In A Bottle: The Sox of '67.* Branden Publishing Co. 1992.

Davidoff, Nicholas, *The Catcher Was A Spy: The Mysterious Life Of Moe Berg.* Pantheon Books, 1994.

Frommer, Harvey, *Baseball's Greatest Rivalry: The New York Yankees And Boston Red Sox.* Rev. Ed. Atheneum, 1984.

Gammons, Peter, *Beyond The Sixth Game.* Houghton Mifflin, 1985.

Germano, Eddie, *Red Sox Drawing Board: 25 Years Of Cartoons.* Stephen Greene, 1989.

Golenbock, Peter, *Fenway: An Unexpurgated History of the Boston Red Sox.* G. P. Putnam, 1992.

Halberstam, David, *Summer of '49.* W. Morrow, 1989.

Higgins, George V., *The Progress Of The Seasons: 40 Years of Baseball In Our Town.* Henry Holt & Co., 1989

Hirschberg, Al, *Red Sox, The Bean And The Cod,* 2nd Ed. Waverly Press, 1948.

Hirschberg, Al, *What's The Matter With The Red Sox?* Dodd, Mead, 1973.

Honig, Donald, *The Boston Red Sox: An Illustrated Tribute.* St. Martin's Press, 1984.

Hough, John Jr., *A Player For A Moment: Notes From Fenway Park.* Harcourt, Brace, Jovanovich, 1988.

Italia, Bob, *Boston Red Sox.* Abdo & Daughters, 1997.

Kaese, Harold, *A Rooter's Guide To The Red Sox: Facts, Fun and Figures,* 1974.

Keene, Kerry, Sinibaldi, Raymond and Hickey, David, *The Babe In Red Stockings.* Sagamore Publishing, 1997.

Lautier, Jack, *Fenway Voices.* Yankee Books, 1990.

Lieb, Fred, *The Boston Red Sox.* G. P. Putnam's Sons, 1947.

Linn, Edward, *The Great Rivalry: The Yankees And The Red Sox.* Ticknor & Fields, 1991.

Linn, Edward, *Hitter: The Life And Turmoil Of Ted Williams.* Harcourt, Brace, Jovanovich, 1993.

Liss, Howard, *The Boston Red Sox.* Simon and Schuster, 1982.

Martin, Mollie, *Boston Red Sox.* Creative Education, 1982.

McSweeny, Bill, *The Impossible Dream: The Story of the Miracle Boston Red Sox.* Coward-McCann, 1968.

Meany, Thomas, *The Boston Red Sox.* A. S. Barnes, 1956.

Mercurio, John A., *A Chronology Of Red Sox Records.* Perennial-Harper & Row, 1989.

Neft, David S., Carroll, Bob,Cohen, Richard M., *The Red Sox Trivia Book*. St. Martin' s Press, 1993.

Piersall, James and Hirschberg, AL., *Fear Strikes Out: The Jim Piersall Story*. Atlantic-Little, Brown, 1955.

Prime, James and Nowlin, William, *Ted Williams: A Tribute*. Masters Press, 1997.

Rambeck, Richard, *Boston Red Sox: A L East*. Creative Education, 1992.

Reynolds, William, *Lost Summer: The '67 Red Sox And The Impossible Dream*. Warner Books, 1992.

Riley, Dan, Ed., *The Red Sox Reader*. Ventura Arts, 1987.

Rothaus, James R., *Boston Red Sox*. Creative Education, 1987.

Ruth, Babe, As Told To Bob Considine, *The Babe Ruth Story*. Dutton, 1948.

Seidel, Michael, *Ted Williams: A Baseball Life*. Contemporary Books, 1991.

Shaughnessy, Dan, *One Strike Away: The Story of the 1986 Red Sox*. Beaufort Books, 1987.

Shaughnessy, Dan, *The Curse Of The Bambino*. E. P. Dutton, 1990.

Shaughnessy, Dan, *At Fenway: Dispatches from Red Sox Nation*. Crown Publishers, Inc. 1996

Smith, Curt, *The Red Sox Fan's Little Book Of Wisdom: A Fine Sense Of The Ridiculous*. Diamond Communications, 1994.

Sullivan, George, *The Picture History Of The Boston Red Sox*. Bobbs-Merrill, 1979

Tsiotos, Nick, Harry Agganis, *The Golden Greek: An All-American Story*. Hellenic College Press. 1995

Valenti, Dan, *From Florida To Fenway*. Literation, 1982.

Walton, Edward H., *This Date in Boston Red Sox History*. Scarborough-Stein and Day, 1978.

Walton, Edward H., *Red Sox Triumphs And Tragedies*. Scarborough-Stein and Day, 1980.

Williams, Red, with John Underwood, *My Turn At Bat: The Story of My Life*. Simon and Schuster, 1969.

Wolff, Rick, *Ted Williams*. Chelsea House, 1993.

Yastrzemski, Carl, *Yaz: Baseball, The Wall, And Me*. Doubleday. 1990.

Zingg, Paul J., *Harry Hooper: An American Baseball Life*. University Of Illinois Press.

Articles

1990s

Ivor-Campbell, Frederick, "Boston Red Sox-Their Foot Shall Slide – Baseball' s Most Potent Myth," in *Encyclopedia of Major League Baseball, American League (1993)*. Peter C. Bjarkman, Ed. Carroll & Graf Publishers, 1993 Edition.

Kurkjian, Tim, "Bombs Away In Beantown," *Sports Illustrated* LXXIV (April 15, 1991), 90-93.

Kurkjian, Tim, "Pennant Pains," *Sports Illustrated* LXIII (October 1, 1990), 18-21.

Kurkjian, Tim "A Run On Hose" *Sports Illustrated* LXIII (July 16, 1990), 40-43.

Montcille, Leigh, "Boston' s Wildest Weekend," *Sports Illustrated* LXII (May 7, 1990), 13-23.

Montville, Leigh, "Long Gone," *Sports Illustrated* (July 2, 1990), 18-23.

Rushin, Steve, "The Home Stretch," *Sports Illustrated* LXXV (Sept 30, 1991), 18-23.

Shalin, Mike, "The Sox Are Locks," *Beckett Baseball Card Monthly VIII* (June 1991), 96-97.

Wendel, Tim, "Battle On To Erase The Past," *USA Today Baseball Weekly I* (September 27, 1991), 36-38.

Williams, Pete, "Team That Loves To Tease Renews Annual Flirtation," *USA Today Baseball Weekly I* (August 23, 1991), 37-39.

Wulf, Steve "A Boost From The Rocket," *Sports Illustrated* LXXIII (August 8, 1990). 26-31

Wulf, Steve, "Zip! Zip! Zip! *Sports Illustrated* LXXIII (September 3, 1990), 20-23.

1980s

Breslau, Maurice, "Mother And The Boston Red Sox," *Reader's Digest* CXXIV (May 1984), 103-106.

Brown, Gary, "Fans Face Shock Of Red Sox Without Yaz." in *Best Sport Stories of 1984*, Editors of *The Sporting News*, Ch. 28.

DiMauro, Thomas M., "Cheer Up! You May Still Live To See The Red Sox Win It All," *Baseball Research Journal* XVI (1987), 17-18.

Downey, Mike "Unite Fans Of Boston Strugglers," in *Best Sports Stories of 1987*, Ed. Tom Barnidge of *The Sporting News*, 183-185.

Ducovny, Amram, "Blessed Are The Bums," *Boston* LXXIX (April 1987), 114-115.

Gabriel, Daniel, "A Brief and Biased History Of The Boston Red Sox," *The Minneapolis Review Of Baseball* IV (Spring 1984), 28-31.

Gammons. Peter, "And The Beat Goes On," *Sports Illustrated* LXIX (August 8, 1988), 18-20.

Gammons, Peter, "Living And Dying With the Red Sox, *Sports Illustrated* LXV (November 3, 1986), 22-23.

Gammons, Peter, "A New Year For The Sox," *Sports Illustrated* LXII (June 24, 1985), 30.

Gammons, Peter, "1978: The Boston Massacre," in *The Fireside Book of Baseball*, Ed. Charles Einstein. 4th Ed. 1987. 126-130.

Gammons, Peter, "Off To The Races," *Sports Illustrated* LXIX (Sept 19, 1988), 30-35.

Gammons, Peter, "Poised For Another El Foldo," *Sports Illustrated* LXV (August 4, 1986), 33.

Gammons, Peter, "Red Hot," *Sports Illustrated* LXIX (August 1, 1988), 24, 29.

Gammons, Peter, "Word From The Sox: No 'Clemensy!'" *Sports Illustrated* LXIV (June 30, 1986), 12-15.

Jacobson, Steve, "Red Sox History Filled With Frustrated Hopes," *Baseball Digest* XLVIII (October 1989), 64-68.

Kuenster, John, "With Decent Pitching, The Boston Red Sox Can Be Fearsome," *Baseball Digest* XLV (August 1986), 15-17.

Lavin, Thomas S., "Red Sox of 1950 Scored 1,027 Runs, But Still Finished Third," *Baseball Digest* XLIV (September 1985), 79-84.

Lonborg, Jim, "The Impossible Dread," *Boston* LXXVIII (July 1986), 94-97.

Patton, Phil and Dennard, Jack, "The Wall And Other Bizarre Afflictions Pertaining To Boston's Crypto-Mythical Red Sox," *Connoisseur*, CCXVI (September 1986), 77-83.

Ross, Philip, "Those Darned Red Sox," *Sport* LXXIV (June 1983), 76-77.

Sanoff, Alvin P., "Up Against The Wall In Beantown," *U.S. News And World Report* CIII (July 27, 1987), 54-55.

Stout, Glenn, "Diamonds Aren't Forever," *Boston* LXXVIII (Sept. 1986), 92.

Stout, Glenn, "The Manager's End Game," *Boston* LXXVIII (May 1986), 134.

Swift, E.M., "Pow! Pow! Pow!." *Sports Illustrated* LXVI June 1,1987), 42-44.

Teitell, Beth, "Two Minutes With A Red Sox Trivia Expert," *Boston* LXXXI (April 1989), 24.

Wulf, Steve, "The Darned Red Sox Haven't Any Holes." *Sports Illustrated* LVI (May 24, 1982), 62.

Wulf, Steve, "The Fight Is Over The Red Sox, Not In Them," *Sports Illustrated* LVIII (June 20, 1983), 24-28.

1970s

Blount, Roy Hr., "Kid Whiz Hefts Hub Halo: Boston Red Sox," *Sports Illustrated* XLII (May 5, 1975), 73-75.

Devaney, John, "Zen And The Art Of Baseball Maintenance," *Sport* LXV (October 1977), 42-47.

Dexter, Charles, "The Red Sox – After the Miracle," *Baseball Digest* XXVII (July 1968) 83-87.

Donnelly, Joe, "Dissension On The Red Sox," *Sport* XXXVII (April 1964), 14-17.

Elderkin, Phil, "Why the Red Sox Fell From Pennant Contention," *Baseball Digest* XXXV (November 1976), 36-38.

Falls, Joe, "When The Red Sox Scored 17 Runs In One Inning," *Baseball Digest* XXXI (April 1972), 64-69.

Fimrite, Ron, "Time To Shout For The Sox: Playoff Victory." *Sports Illustrated* XLIII (October 13, 1975), 37-38.

Fitzgerald, Roy, "Why The Red Sox Hate The Yankees," *Baseball Digest* XXXVI (July 1977), 76-85.

Hannon, Kent, "Boom!: Boston Red Sox," *Sports Illustrated* XLVII (July 4, 1977), 10-15.

Kaese, Harold, "The Red Sox-So Close, But So Far," *Baseball Digest* XXXII (February 1973), 66-69.

Kaufman, Daniel, "Hot Shots," *Boston* LXIX (October 1977), 121-123.

Keith, Larry, "Hoping For The Best, Expecting The Worst," *Sports Illustrated* LI (July 30, 1979), 20-22.

Keith, Larry, "Suddenly, They're Up In Arms In Boston," *Sports* Illustrated XLIX (July 3, 1978), 14-17.

Keith, Larry, "What' s The Pox On The Sox?," *Sports Illustrated* XLV (August 23, 1976), 40-41.

Keith, Larry, "Yankee Doodle Series Was A Dandy: New York Yankees vs.Boston Red Sox," *Sports Illustrated* XLIV (May31, 1976), 18-21.

Keith, Larry and Gammons, Peter, "Home Free At Last: Yankee-Red Sox Pennant Race," *Sports Illustrated* XLIX (Oct. 9. 1978), 30-35.

Kram, Mark, "Rising To The Grand Old Occasion: Baltimore Orioles vs.Boston Red Sox," *Sports Illustrated* XLI (July 15, 1974), 24-25.

Leggett, William, "Tightening Up At The Fens," *Sports Illustrated* XXXIV (May 24, 1971), 26-28.

Linn, Edward, "Want To Buy A Pennant?" *Sport* LXIV (April 1977), 87-96.

Lupica, Mike, "Darning The BoSox," *Boston* LXVIII (April 1975), 34-37.

Mulvoy, Mark, "Strangers In Paradise," *Sports Illustrated* XLI (August 26, 1974). 14-17.

Mulvoy, Mark, "The Team That Eats Managers," *Sports Illustrated* XXXII (March 16, 1970), 20-21.

Murray, Tom, "Listen My Children And You Shall Hear Why The Red Sox Fell In The Bicentennial Year," *Sport* LXIV (January 1977), 56-62.

Quirk, Kevin, "A Tale Of Two Cities: The Yankees vs. The Red Sox," *Baseball Quarterly* II (Summer 1978), 28-37.

Schwartz, John, "Day Of Light And Shadows:1978 Yankees-Red Sox Playoffs," *Sports Illustrated* L (Feb, 26, 1979), 56-63.

1960s

Angell, Roger, "1967: The Flowering and Subsequent Deflowering of New England," in *The Third Fireside Book Of Baseball, Charles* Einstein, Ed. Simon and Schuster (1968).

Clary, Jack "Are The Red Sox The Next Super Team?," *in Baseball Sports Stars of 1968*, Stan Fischler and Larry Borstein, Eds. Hewford Publications (1968).

Donnelly, Joe, "Dissention On The Red Sox," *Sport* XXXVII (April 1964), 14-17.

Hirschberg, Al, "The Sad Case Of The Red Sox," *Saturday Evening Post* CCXXXII (May 21, 1960), 38-39.

Leggett, William, "Wild Finale And It's Boston," *Sports Illustrated* XXVII (Oct. 9, 1967), 32-34.

Linn, Edward, "The Day The Red Sox Won The Pennant," *Sport* XLIV (December 1967), 14-15.

Mulvoy, Mark, "Virtue Is Rewarded: The Boston Red Sox In The Pennant Race*," Sports Illustrated* XXVII (August 21, 1967), 12-17.

Schecter, Leonard, "Baseball-Great American Myth: Boston Red Sox," *Life* LXV (August 9, 1968), 48-50.

Updike, John, "Hub Fans Bid Kid Adieu," Reprinted in Updike, John, *Assorted Prose*. Albert A. Knopf, Inc. (1960). Originally published in *The New Yorker*.

1950s

Clark, Ellery H., "A Red Sox Fan Remembers," *Baseball Magazine* XLVIII (June 1956), 8-10.

Cunningham, William, "The Boston Red Sox" in *The American League*, Ed. Fitzgerald, Ed. A. S. Barnes (1952).

Moore, Gerry, "The Boston Story Today," *Baseball Magazine* XLVIII (June 1956), 6-7.

Povich, Shirley, "Stengel Sizes Up The Red Sox," *Baseball Digest* XIV (September 1955), 43-45.

Sheldon, Harold, "Red Sox Eye The Golden Age." Baseball Digest XV (January-February 1956), 5-8.

Smith, Lyall, "The Trouble With The Red Sox," *Baseball Digest* X (August 1951), 57-59.

Terrell, Roy, "The Boston Red Sox Have Ideas," *Sports Illustrated* III (August 22, 1955), 24-27

Terrell, Roy, "The Red Sox Are No Longer The Dead Sox," *Sports Illustrated* III (July 4, 1955), 52-53.

1940s

Kaese, Harold, "What' s The Matter With The Red Sox?," *Saturday Evening Post* CCXVIII (March 23, 1946), 24-25.

Rumill, Ed., "This May Be Tom Yawkey's Year," *Baseball Magazine* LXXVI (January 1946), 275-277.

Smith, Walter "Red", "Red Sox Sound Their A's," *Baseball Digest* V (October 1946), 15-17.

1930s

Bloodgood, Clifford, "The Red Sox Situation," *Baseball Magazine* LX (February 1938), 389-390.

Cunningham, William, "Starch For The Red Sox," *Colliers* XCII (August 5, 1933), 23.

Appendix A

RED SOX CAREER STATISTICS

1,403 players had appeared in at least one game for the Red Sox through the 2001 season. The following are those players' career statistics.

BATTERS

BA -	Batting Average	3B -	Triples	BB -	Bases On Balls
SA -	Slugging Average	HR -	Home Runs	SO -	Strike Outs
AB -	At Bats	R -	Runs Scored	SB -	Stolen Bases
H -	Hits	RBI -	Runs Batted In	NA-	Not Available
2B -	Doubles				

A

NAME	YRS	BA	SA	AB	H	2B	3B	HR	R	RBI	BB	SO	SB
Jerry Adair	1958-1970	.254	.347	4019	1022	163	19	52	378	366	208	499	29
Harry Agganis	1954-1955	.261	.404	517	135	23	9	11	65	67	57	67	8
Sam Agnew	1913-1919	.204	.253	1537	314	41	14	2	105	98	102	216	29
Israel Alcantara	2000-Cont.	.277	.446	83	23	2	0	4	12	10	6	20	1
Dale Alexander	1929-1933	.331	.497	2450	811	164	30	61	369	459	248	197	20
Manny Alexander	1992-2000	.234	.328	1198	280	46	11	15	161	108	81	259	37
Luis Alicea	1988-Cont.	.255	.367	2384	608	115	36	27	310	254	321	387	64
Gary Allenson	1979-1985	.221	.325	1061	235	49	2	19	114	131	130	192	3
Mel Almeda	1933-1939	.284	.367	2483	706	107	27	15	363	197	214	150	56
Luis Alvarado	1968-1977	.214	.271	1160	248	43	4	5	116	84	49	160	11
Brady Anderson	1988-Cont.	.257	.427	6419	1648	334	67	209	1058	756	942	1167	311
Ernie Andres	1946	.098	.146	41	4	2	0	0	0	1	3	5	0
Kim Andrew	1975	.500	.500	2	1	0	0	0	0	0	0	0	0
Mike Andrews	1966-1973	.258	.369	3116	803	140	4	66	441	316	458	390	18
Luis Aparicio	1956-1973	.262	.343	10230	2677	394	92	83	1335	791	736	742	506
Tony Armas	1976-1989	.252	.453	5164	1302	204	39	251	614	815	260	1201	18
Charlie Armbruster	1905-1907	.149	.186	355	53	11	1	0	24	12	52	0	6
Asby Asbjornson	1928-1932	.235	.303	221	52	10	1	1	19	27	9	45	0
Billy Ashley	1992-1998	.233	.409	618	144	23	1	28	56	84	63	236	0
Ken Aspromonte	1957-1963	.249	.338	1483	369	69	3	19	171	124	179	150	7
Doyle Aulds	1947	.250	.250	4	1	0	0	0	0	0	0	1	0
Bobby Avila	1949-1959	.281	.388	4620	1296	185	25	80	725	465	562	399	78
Ramon Aviles	1977-1981	.268	.347	190	51	9	0	2	21	24	21	22	0
Joe Azcue	1960-1972	.252	.344	2828	712	94	9	50	201	304	207	344	5

B

NAME	YRS	BA	SA	AB	H	2B	3B	HR	R	RBI	BB	SO	SB
Bob Bailey	1962-1978	.257	.403	6082	1564	234	43	189	772	773	852	1126	85
Gene Bailey	1917-1924	.246	.303	634	156	16	7	2	95	52	63	61	13
Floyd Baker	1943-1955	.251	.297	2280	573	76	13	1	285	196	382	165	23
Jack Baker	1976-1977	.115	.231	26	3	0	0	1	1	2	1	6	0
Tracy Baker	1911	.00000	.000	0	0	0	0	0	0	0	0	0	0
Neal Ball	1907-1913	.251	.314	1609	404	56	17	4	161	151	99	13	92
Walter Barbare	1914-1922	.260	.315	1777	462	52	21	1	173	156	88	121	37
Babe Barna	1937-1943	.237	.346	664	154	22	9	12	88	96	76	98	9
Bill Barrett	1921-1930	.288	.405	2395	690	151	30	23	318	328	211	239	80

Name	Years	AVG	SLG	AB	H	2B	3B	HR	R	RBI	BB	SO	SB
Bob Barrett	1923-1929	.260	.357	650	169	23	5	10	57	86	37	61	6
Jimmy Barrett	1899-1908	.291	.359	3306	962	83	67	16	580	255	410	NA	143
Marty Barrett	1982-1991	.278	.347	3378	938	163	9	18	418	314	304	209	56
Tom Barred	1988-1992	.202	.214	45	12	1	0	0	6	5	10	15	0
Jack Barry	1908-1919	.243	.303	4146	1009	142	38	10	533	429	396	142	153
Matt Batts	1947-1956	.269	.391	1605	432	95	11	26	163	219	143	163	6
Don Baylor	1970-1988	.260	.436	8198	2135	366	28	338	1236	1276	806	1068	285
Juan Bell	1989-1995	.212	.298	836	177	30	6	10	107	71	84	189	16
Esteban Beltre	1991-1996	.237	.287	401	95	153	10	81	310	369	206	438	47
Juan Beniquez	1971-1988	.274	.379	4651	1274	190	30	79	610	476	349	552	104
Mike Benjamin	1989-Cont.	.204	.373	856	175	40	5	17	104	71	52	190	26
Todd Benzinger	1987-1995	.257	.386	2856	733	135	18	66	316	376	181	552	21
Lou Berberet	1954-1960	.230	.350	1224	281	34	10	31	118	153	200	195	2
Moe Berg	1923-1939	.243	.299	1812	441	71	6	6	150	206	78	117	11
Boze Berger	1932-1939	.236	.329	1144	270	51	8	13	146	97	94	226	12
Charlie Berry	1925-1938	.267	.374	2018	539	88	29	23	196	256	160	196	13
Sean Berry	1990-2000	.272	.445	2413	657	153	10	81	310	369	206	438	47
Damon Berryhill	1987-1995	.239	.369	1863	445	98	6	44	158	234	119	380	3
Hal Bevan	1952-1961	.292	.417	24	7	0	0	1	2	5	0	3	2
Dante Bichette	1988-Cont.	.299	.499	6381	1906	401	27	274	934	1141	355	1078	152
Elliott Bigelow	1929	.284	.374	211	60	16	0	1	23	26	23	18	1
John Bischoff	1925-1926	.262	.369	271	71	20	3	1	20	35	22	32	2
Max Bishop	1924-1935	.271	.366	4494	1216	236	35	41	966	379	1153	452	43
Tim Blackwell	1974-1983	.228	.305	1044	238	40	11	6	91	80	154	183	3
Greg Blosser	1993-1994	.077	.103	39	3	1	0	0	3	2	6	11	1
Red Bluhm	1918	.000	.000	1	0	0	0	0	0	0	0	0	0
Wade Boggs	1982-1999	.328	.443	9180	3010	578	61	118	1513	1014	1412	745	24
Milt Bolling	1952-1958	.241	.345	1161	280	50	7	19	127	94	115	88	5
Ike Boone	1922-1932	.319	.470	1159	370	77	10	26	176	192	140	68	3
Ray Boone	1948-1960	.275	.429	4589	1260	162	46	151	645	737	608	463	21
Lou Boudreau	1938-1952	.295	.415	6030	1779	385	66	68	861	789	796	309	51
Sam Bowen	1977-1980	.136	.273	22	3	0	0	1	3	1	3	7	1
Hugh Bradley	1910-1915	.261	.344	913	238	46	12	2	84	117	59	NA	23
Ciiff Brady	1920	.228	.267	180	41	5	1	0	16	12	13	12	0
Darren Bragg	1994-Cont.	.258	.388	1986	512	122	10	39	273	227	257	449	48
Fritz Bratchi	1921-1927	.276	.342	196	54	11	1	0	12	22	14	17	0
Ed Bressoud	1956-1967	.252	.401	3672	925	184	40	94	443	365	359	723	9
Rico Brogna	1992-Cont.	.269	.445	2958	795	176	13	106	379	458	227	655	32
Jack Brohamer	1972-1980	.245	.327	2500	613	91	12	30	262	227	222	178	9
Mike Brumley	1987-1995	.206	.272	635	131	17	8	3	78	38	46	136	20
Tom Brunansky	1981-1994	.245	.434	6289	1542	306	33	271	804	919	770	1187	69
Jim Bucher	1934-1945	.266	.351	1792	474	66	19	17	242	193	91	113	19
Bill Buckner	1969-1990	.289	.408	9397	2715	498	49	174	1077	1208	450	453	183
Don Buddin	1955 1932	.241	.359	2289	551	123	12	41	342	225	410	404	15
Damon Buford	1993-Cont.	.242	.385	1853	448	86	9	54	280	218	173	430	56
Bob Burda	1962-1972	.224	.319	634	142	21	0	13	53	78	70	65	2
Jesse Burkett	1890-1905	.339	.448	8413	2853	322	183	75	1718	952	1029	230	389
Morgan Burkhart	2000-Cont.	.255	.434	106	27	4	0	5	19	22	18	36	0
Ellis Burks	1987-Cont.	.292	.512	6483	1893	363	62	313	1128	1086	719	1178	176
Rick Burleson	1974-1987	.273	.361	5139	1401	256	23	50	656	449	420	477	72
George Bums	1914-1929	.307	.429	6573	2018	444	72	72	901	948	363	433	153
Jim Busby	1950-1962	.262	.350	4250	1113	162	35	48	541	438	310	439	97
Jim Byrd	1993	.000	.00	0	0	0	0	0	0	0	0	0	0

NAME	YRS	BA	SA	AB	H	2B	3B	HR	R	RBI	BB	SO	SB
Hick Cady	1912-1919	.240	.320	901	216	47	11	1	83	74	66	91	4
Ray Caldwell	1910-1921	.248	.322	1164	289	46	8	8	138	114	78	158	23
Ivan Calderon	1984-1993	.272	.442	3312	901	200	25	104	470	440	306	556	97
Dolf Camilli	1933-1945	.277	.492	5353	1482	261	86	239	936	950	947	961	60
Paul Campbell	1941-1950	.255	.358	380	97	17	5	4	61	41	28	54	4
Jose Canseco	1985-Cont.	.266	.515	7057	1877	340	14	462	1186	1407	906	1942	200
Bernie Carbo	1969-1980	.264	.427	2733	722	140	9	96	372	358	538	611	26
Tom Carey	1935-1946	.275	.348	1520	418	79	13	2	169	169	66	75	3
Walter Carlisle	1908	.100	.100	10	1	0	0	0	0	0	1	NA	1
Swede Carlstrom	1911	.167	.167	6	1	0	0	0	0	0	0	NA	0
Cleo Carlyle	1927	.234	.345	278	65	12	8	1	31	28	36	40	4
Roy Carlyle	1925-1926	.318	.460	494	157	31	6	9	61	76	24	57	1
Bill Carrigan	1906-1916	.257	.314	1970	506	67	14	6	196	235	206	59	37
Danny Cater	1964-1975	.276	.377	4451	1229	191	29	66	491	519	254	406	26
Orlando Cepeda	1958-1974	.297	.499	7927	2351	417	27	379	1131	1365	588	1169	142
Rick Cerone	1975-1992	.245	.343	4069	998	190	15	59	393	436	320	450	6
Chet Chadbourne	1906-1918	.255	.316	1353	345	41	18	2	183	82	146	5	78
Wes Chamberlain	1990-1995	.255	.424	1263	322	72	6	43	144	167	77	249	20
Ed Chaplin	1920-1922	.184	.237	76	14	2	1	0	10	7	13	11	2
Ben Chapman	1930-1946	.302	.440	6478	1958	407	107	90	1144	977	824	556	287
Joe Christopher	1959-1966	.260	.374	1667	434	68	17	29	224	173	157	277	29
Lloyd Christopher	1945-1947	.243	.297	37	9	0	1	0	5	4	5	6	0
Joe Cicero	1929-1945	.222	.358	81	18	3	4	0	14	8	2	13	0
Bill Cisseil	1928-1938	.267	.360	3707	990	173	43	29	516	423	212	250	114
Danny Clark	1922-1927	.277	.392	582	161	36	8	5	75	93	73	36	5
Jack Clark	1975-1992	.267	.476	6847	1826	332	39	340	1118	1180	1262	1441	77
Phil Clark	1992-1933	.276	.425	543	150	30	0	17	62	65	27	76	4
Lu Clinton	1960-1997	.247	.418	2153	532	112	31	65	270	269	188	418	12
George Cochran	1918	.127	.127	63	8	0	0	0	8	3	11	7	3
Jack Coffey	1909-1918	.188	.242	368	69	5	6	1	33	26	22	8	6
Alex Cole, Jr.	1990-1996	.280	.351	1760	493	58	26	5	286	117	217	296	148
Dave Coleman	1977	.000	.000	12	0	0	0	0	1	0	1	3	0
Michael Coleman	1997-Cont.	.194	.254	67	13	1	0	1	8	9	1	26	1
Jimmy Collins	1895-1908	.294	.408	6796	1997	352	116	65	1055	983	426	32	194
Shano Collins	1910-1925	.264	.365	6386	1687	309	133	22	746	705	331	391	225
Merrill Combs	1947-1952	.202	.241	361	73	6	1	2	45	25	57	43	0
Bunk Congalton	1902-1907	.290	.348	1163	337	27	13	5	115	128	57	NA	31
Billy Conigliaro	1969-1973	.256	.429	1130	289	56	10	40	142	128	86	244	9
Tony Conigliaro	1964-1975	.264	.476	3221	849	139	23	166	464	516	287	629	20
Bud Connally	1925	.262	.346	107	28	7	1	0	12	21	23	9	0
Ed Connolly	1929-1932	.178	.229	371	66	11	4	0	13	31	29	50	0
Joe Connolly	1921-1924	.268	.417	168	45	12	2	3	32	32	21	18	2
Bill Conroy	1935-1944	.199	.274	452	90	13	3	5	45	33	77	85	3
Billy Consolo	1953-1962	.221	.289	1178	260	31	11	9	158	83	161	297	9
Dusty Cooke	1930-1938	.280	.415	1745	488	109	28	24	324	229	290	276	32
Jimmy Cooney	1917-1928	.262	.327	1575	413	64	16	2	181	150	76	58	30
Cecil Cooper	1971-1987	.298	.466	7349	2192	415	47	241	1012	1125	448	911	89
Scott Cooper	1990-1995	.272	.393	1642	446	88	11	30	185	196	176	267	6
Wil Cordero	1992-Cont	.279	.426	2298	642	141	11	58	313	287	162	394	40
Vic Correll	1972-1980	.229	.366	1132	259	60	4	29	124	125	128	220	2
Marlan Coughtry	1960-1962	.185	.185	54	10	0	0	0	5	4	10	18	0
Ted Cox	1977-1981	.245	.324	771	189	29	1	10	65	79	59	98	3
Doc Cramer	1929-1948	.296	.375	9140	2705	396	109	37	1357	842	571	345	62
Gavvy Cravath	1908-1920	.287	.478	3950	1134	232	83	119	575	719	561	514	89
Pat Creeden	1931	.000	.000	8	0	0	0	0	0	0	1	3	0
Lou Criger	1896-1912	.221	.290	3202	709	86	50	11	336	342	309	NA	58
Joe Cronin	1926-1945	.301	.468	7579	2285	515	118	170	1233	1424	1059	700	87
Leon Culberson	1943-1948	.266	.379	1217	324	59	18	14	148	131	107	126	28
Midre Cummings	1993-Cont.	.256	.381	1057	271	56	8	20	126	117	89	187	8
Milt Cuyler	1990-1996	.236	.322	1350	323	45	23	9	224	116	120	273	77

D

NAME	YRS	BA	SA	AB	H	2B	3B	HR	R	RBI	BB	SO	SB
Babe Dahlgren	1935-1946	.261	.383	4045	1056	174	37	82	470	569	390	401	18
Pete Daley	1955-1961	.239	.349	1084	259	49	8	18	93	120	87	187	2
Dom Dallesandro	1937-1947	.267	.381	1945	520	110	23	22	242	303	310	150	16
Babe Danzig	1909	.244	.304	135	33	6	1	0	12	12	11	7	3
Bobby Darwin	1962-1977	.251	.412	2224	559	76	16	83	250	328	160	577	15
Brian Daubach	1998-Cont.	.266	.498	1298	345	94	8	64	170	223	134	335	2
Bob Daughters	1937	.000	.000	0	0	0	0	0	1	0	0	0	0
Andre Dawson	1976-1996	.279	.482	9927	2774	503	98	438	1373	1591	589	1509	314
Rob Deer	1984-1993	.220	.442	3831	844	145	13	226	569	591	561	1379	43
Pep Deininger	1902-1909	.263	.331	175	46	10	1	0	22	16	11	0	5
Alex Delgado	1996	.250	.250	20	2	0	0	0	5	1	3	3	0
Don Demeter	1956-1967	.265	.459	3443	912	147	17	163	467	563	180	658	22
Sam Dente	1947-1955	.252	.305	2320	585	78	16	4	205	214	167	96	9
Jim Derrick	1970	.212	.242	33	7	1	0	0	3	5	0	11	0
Gene Desautels	1930-1946	.233	.285	2012	469	73	11	3	211	186	233	168	12
Mickey Devine	1918-1925	.226	.302	53	12	4	0	0	7	4	3	6	1
Al DeVormer	1918-1927	.258	.333	477	123	20	5	2	50	57	20	46	7
Bo Diaz	1977-1989	.255	.387	3274	834	162	5	87	327	452	198	429	9
George Dickey	1935-1947	.204	.253	494	101	12	0	4	36	54	63	62	4
Bob Didier	1969-1974	.229	.273	751	172	25	4	0	56	51	59	72	2
Steve Dillard	1975-1982	.243	.343	1013	246	50	6	13	148	102	76	147	15
Dom DiMaggio	1940-1953	.298	.419	5640	1680	308	57	87	1046	618	750	571	100
Bob DiPietro	1951	.091	.091	11	1	0	0	0	0	0	1	1	0
Pat Dodson	1986-1988	.202	.424	99	20	8	1	4	12	10	17	33	0
Bobby Doerr	1937-1951	.288	.461	7093	2042	381	89	223	1094	1247	809	608	54
John Donahue	1923	.278	.389	36	10	4	0	0	5	1	4	5	0
Pat Donahue	1908-1910	.212	.267	307	65	6	1	3	24	35	29	NA	3
Chris Donnels	1991-1995	.238	.332	596	142	27	4	7	62	53	75	119	5
Tom Doran	1904-1906	.145	.183	131	19	3	1	0	10	4	12	NA	3
Patsy Dougherty	1902-1911	.284	.360	4558	1294	138	78	17	679	413	378		261
Tommy Dowd	1891-1901	.271	.345	5511	1492	163	88	23	903	501	369	NA	366
Danny Doyle	1943	.209	.233	43	9	1	0	0	2	6	7	9	0
Denny Doyle	1970-1977	.250	.316	3290	823	113	28	16	357	237	205	310	38
Walt Dropo	1949-1961	.270	.432	4124	1113	168	22	152	478	704	328	582	5
Jean Dubuc	1908-1919	.230	.314	652	150	23	10	4	57	56	30	63	2
Frank Duffy	1970-1979	.232	.311	2665	619	104	14	26	248	240	171	342	49
Joe Dugan	1917-1931	.280	.372	5405	1515	277	46	42	664	571	250	418	37
Cedric Durst	1922-1930	.244	.351	1103	269	39	17	15	146	122	75	100	7
Jim Dwyer	1973-1990	.260	.398	2761	719	115	17	77	409	349	401	402	26

E

NAME	YRS	BA	SA	AB	H	2B	3B	HR	R	RBI	BB	SO	SB
Mike Easler	1973-1987	.293	.454	3677	1078	189	25	118	465	522	321	696	20
Elmer Eggert	1927	.000	.000	3	0	0	0	0	0	0	1	1	0
Clyde Engle	1909-1916	.265	.341	2822	748	101	39	12	373	318	271	58	128
Nick Esasky	1983-1990	.250	.446	2703	677	120	21	122	336	427	314	712	18
Al Evans	1939-1951	.250	.326	2053	514	70	23	13	188	211	243	206	13
Dwight Evans	1972-1991	.272	.470	8996	2446	483	73	385	1470	1384	1391	1697	78
Hoot Evers	1941-1956	.278	.426	3801	1055	187	41	98	556	565	415	420	45
Homer Ezzell	1923-1925	.266	.314	738	196	20	8	0	105	61	47	58	25

F

NAME	YRS	BA	SA	AB	H	2B	3B	HR	R	RBI	BB	SO	SB
Carmen Fanzone	1970-1974	.224	.372	588	132	27	0	20	66	94	74	119	3
Doc Farrell	1925-1935	.260	.320	1799	467	63	8	10	181	213	109	120	14
Duke Farrell	1888-1905	.275	.383	5679	1563	211	123	51	826	912	477	246	150
Rick Ferrell	1929-1947	.281	.363	6028	1692	324	45	28	687	734	931	277	29

Name	YRS	BA	SA	AB	H	2B	3B	HR	R	RBI	BB	SO	SB
Hobe Ferris	1904-1909	.239	.340	4800	1146	192	89	39	473	550	161	NA	89
Chick Fewster	1917-1927	.258	.326	1963	506	91	12	6	282	167	240	264	57
Lou Finney	1931-1947	.287	.388	4631	1329	203	85	31	643	494	329	186	39
Mike Fiore	1968-1972	.227	.333	556	126	18	1	13	75	50	124	115	5
Carlton Fisk	1969-1993	.269	.457	8756	2356	421	47	376	1276	1330	849	1386	128
Howie Fitzgerald	1922-1926	.257	.279	140	36	3	0	0	15	14	8	11	2
Ira Flagstead	1917-1930	.290	.406	4139	1201	261	49	40	644	450	465	288	71
John Flaherty	1992-Cont.	.254	.376	2732	695	134	3	64	255	321	145	394	8
Al Flair	1941	.200	.333	30	6	2	1	0	3	2	1	1	1
Scott Fletcher	1981-1995	.262	.342	5258	1376	243	38	34	688	510	514	541	99
Chad Fonville	1995-1999	.244	.269	546	133	10	2	0	80	31	45	77	30
Eddie Foster	1910-1923	.264	.326	5652	1490	191	71	6	732	446	528	255	195
Bob Fothergill	1922-1933	.325	.459	3269	1064	225	52	36	453	582	202	177	40
Boob Fowler	1923-1926	.326	.406	175	57	7	2	1	30	18	6	19	3
Pete Fox	1933-1945	.298	.415	5636	1678	315	75	65	895	694	392	471	158
Jimmie Foxx	1925-1945	.325	.609	8134	2646	458	125	534	1751	1921	1452	1311	88
Joe Foy	1966-1971	.248	.372	2484	615	102	16	58	355	291	390	405	99
Buck Freeman	1891-1907	.294	.462	4207	1238	199	131	82	586	713	272	NA	92
John Freeman	1927	.000	.000	2	0	0	0	0	0	0	0	0	0
Charlie French	1909-1910	.207	.231	377	78	5	2	0	34	20	26	NA	13
Barney Friberg	1919-1933	.281	.373	4169	1170	181	44	38	544	471	471	498	51
Owen Friend	1949-1956	.227	.339	598	136	24	2	13	69	76	55	109	2
Jeff Frye	1992-Cont.	.293	.399	1540	451	107	10	12	229	151	150	196	47
Frank Fuller	1915-1923	.175	.175	63	11	0	0	0	11	3	11	12	6

G

NAME	YRS	BA	SA	AB	H	2B	3B	HR	R	RBI	BB	SO	SB
Fabian Gaffke	1936-1942	.227	.361	321	73	14	4	7	43	42	30	47	2
Phil Gagliano	1963-1974	.238	.313	1411	336	50	7	14	150	159	163	184	5
Del Gainer	1909-1922	.272	.390	1608	438	75	36	14	218	185	149	156	54
Gary Gaetti	1981-2000	.255	.434	8951	2280	443	39	360	1130	1341	634	1602	96
Bob Gallagher	1972-1975	.220	.275	255	56	6	1	2	34	13	16	56	1
Jim Galvin	1930	.000	.000	2	0	0	0	0	0	0	0	0	0
Bob Garbark	1934-1945	.248	.275	327	81	9	0	0	31	28	26	17	0
Nomar Garciaparra	1996-Cont.	.333	.573	2436	812	176	29	117	451	436	184	257	58
Billy Gardner	1954-1963	.237	.327	3544	841	159	18	41	356	271	246	439	19
Larry Gardner	1908-1924	.289	.385	6684	1931	300	129	27	867	929	654	282	165
Ford Garrison	1943-1946	.262	.329	687	180	22	3	6	80	56	37	67	11
Alex Gaston	1920-1929	.218	.284	514	112	13	6	3	58	40	29	56	5
Rich Gedman	1980-1992	.252	.399	3159	795	176	12	88	331	382	236	509	3
Gary Geiger	1958-1970	.246	.394	2569	633	91	29	77	388	283	341	466	62
Charlie Gelbert	1929-1940	.267	.374	2869	766	169	43	17	398	350	290	245	34
Wally Gerber	1914-1929	.257	.313	5099	1309	172	46	7	558	476	465	357	41
Dick Gernert	1952-1962	.254	.426	2493	632	104	8	103	357	402	363	462	10
Doc Gessier	1903-1911	.281	.371	2959	831	127	49	14	369	363	333	142	
Chappie Geygan	1924-1926	.252	.340	103	26	5	2	0	7	4	5	19	0
Joe Giannini	1911	.500	1.000	2	1	1	0	0	0	0	0	0	
Ross Gibson	1967-1972	.228	.311	794	181	34	4	8	49	78	44	123	2
Andy Gilbert	1942-1946	.083	.083	12	1	0	0	0	1	1	1	3	0
Don Gile	1959-1962	.150	.258	120	18	2	1	3	12	9	5	35	0
Frank Gilhooley	1911-1919	.271	.323	1068	289	30	10	2	142	58	140	37	
Bernard Gilkey	1990-Cont.	.275	.434	4061	1115	244	24	118	606	546	466	708	115
Grant Gillis	1927-1929	.245	.327	196	48	12	2	0	26	23	12	13	0
Joe Ginsberg	1948-1962	.241	.320	1716	414	59	8	20	168	182	226	125	7
Harry Gleason	1901-1905	.218	.276	944	206	24	11	3	88	90	48	NA	31
Joe Glenn	1932-1940	.252	.334	718	181	34	5	5	76	89	81	91	6
John Godwin	1905-1906	.213	.235	230	49	3	1	0	15	25	9	NA	9
Chuck Goggin	1972-1974	.293	.343	99	29	5	0	0	19	7	10	21	0
Eusebio Gonzalez	1918	.500	1.500	2	1	0	1	0	1	0	0	0	0
Johnny Gooch	1921-1933	.280	.355	2363	662	98	29	7	227	293	206	141	11
Billy Goodman	1947-1962	.300	.378	5644	1691	299	44	19	807	591	669	329	37
Jim Gosger	1963-1974	.226	.331	1815	411	67	16	30	197	177	217	316	25

Name	YRS	BA	SA	AB	H	2B	3B	HR	R	RBI	BB	SO	SB
Charlie Graham	1906	.233	.278	90	21	1	0	1	10	12	10	NA	1
Lee Graham	1983	.000	.000	6	0	0	0	0	2	1	0	0	0
Skinny Graham	1934-1935	.246	.316	57	14	2	1	0	8	4	7	16	3
Craig Grebek	1990-Cont.	.261	.356	1988	518	116	8	19	239	187	228	274	4
Lenny Green	1957-1968	.267	.379	2956	788	138	27	47	461	253	368	260	78
Pumsie Green	1959-1963	.246	.364	796	196	31	12	13	119	74	138	132	12
Mike Greenwell	1985-1996	.303	.463	4623	1400	275	38	130	657	726	460	364	80
Doug Griffin	1970-1977	.245	.299	2136	524	70	12	7	209	165	158	204	33
Ray Grimes	1920-1926	.329	.480	1537	505	101	25	27	269	263	204	133	21
Moose Grimshaw	1905-1907	.256	.340	894	229	31	16	4	104	116	60	NA	15
Turkey Gross	1925	.094	.156	32	3	0	1	0	2	2	2	2	0
Creighton Gubanich	1999	.277	.426	47	13	2	1	1	4	11	3	13	0
Mike Guerra	1937-1951	.242	.303	1581	382	42	14	9	168	168	131	123	24
Mario Guerrero	1973-1980	.257	.312	2251	578	79	12	7	166	170	84	152	8
Bob Guindon	1964	.125	.250	8	1	1	0	0	0	0	1	4	0
Hy Gunning	1911	.111	.111	9	1	0	0	0	0	2	2	NA	0
Jackie Gutierrez	1983-1988	.237	.285	957	227	24	5	4	106	63	33	123	25
Don Gutteridge	1936-1948	.256	.362	4202	1075	200	64	39	586	391	309	444	95

H

NAME	YRS	BA	SA	AB	H	2B	3B	HR	R	RBI	BB	SO	SB
Odell Hale	1931-1940	.289	.441	3701	1071	240	51	73	551	573	353	315	57
Ray Haley	1915-1917	.248	.294	214	53	8	1	0	17	15	11	32	2
Charley Hall	1906-1918	.197	.288	371	73	10	9	2	32	40	17	16	1
Garry Hancock	1978-1984	.247	.358	570	141	21	3	12	5764	12	42	2	
Fred Haney	1922-1929	.275	.342	1977	544	88	21	8	338	228	282	123	80
Carroll Hardy	1958-1967	.225	.330	1117	251	47	10	17	172	113	120	222	13
Tommy Harper	1962-1976	.257	.379	6269	1609	256	36	146	972	567	753	1080	408
Billy Harrell	1955-1961	.231	.237	342	79	7	1	8	54	26	23	54	17
Ken Harrelson	1963-1971	.239	.414	2941	703	94	14	131	374	421	382	577	53
Joe Harris	1914-1928	.317	.472	3035	963	201	64	47	461	517	413	188	35
Grover Hartley	1911-1934	.268	.337	1319	353	60	11	3	135	144	135	50	29
Bill Haselman	1990-Cont.	.261	.419	1424	372	87	3	44	169	192	103	274	9
Billy Hatcher	1984-1995	.264	.364	4339	1146	210	30	54	586	399	267	476	218
Fred Hatfield	1950-1958	.242	.321	2039	493	67	10	25	259	165	248	247	15
Scott Hatteberg	1995-Cont.	.276	.438	722	199	47	2	22	96	87	86	130	0
Grady Hatton	1946-1960	.254	.374	4206	1068	166	31	91	562	533	646	430	42
Jack Hayden	1901-1908	.268	.325	578	155	14	8	1	60	32	36	NA	11
Frankie Hayes	1933-1947	.259	.400	4493	1164	213	32	119	545	628	564	627	30
Ed Hearn	1910	.000	.000	2	0	0	0	0	0	0	0	NA	0
Danny Heep	1979-1991	.257	.357	1961	503	96	6	30	208	229	220	242	12
Bob Heise	1967-1977	.247	.293	1144	283	43	3	1	104	86	47	77	3
Tommy Helms	1964-1977	.269	.342	4997	1342	223	21	34	414	477	231	301	33
Charlie Hemphill	1899-1911	.271	.341	4541	1230	117	68	22	580	421	435	NA	207
Dave Henderson	1981-1994	.258	.436	5130	1324	286	17	197	710	708	465	1105	50
Tim Hendryx	1911-1921	.276	.377	1288	355	68	22	6	152	191	185	128	26
Olaf Henriksen	1911-1917	.269	.329	487	131	12	7	1	84	48	97	43	15
Mike Herrerra	1925-1926	.275	.333	276	76	14	1	0	22	27	17	15	1
Johnnie Heving	1920-1932	.265	.330	984	261	37	12	1	103	89	65	59	4
Piano Legs Hickman	1897-1908	.301	.447	3968	1194	218	92	59	484	614	153	NA	72
Pinky Higgins	1930-1946	.292	.428	6636	1941	374	50	141	930	1075	800	590	61
Shea Hillenbrand	2001-Cont.	.263	.391	468	123	20	2	12	52	49	13	61	3
Hob Hiller	1920-1921	.167	.267	30	5	1	1	0	4	2	2	5	0
Gordie Hinkle	1934	.173	.280	75	13	6	1	0	7	9	7	23	0
Paul Hinson	1928	.000	.000	0	0	0	0	0	1	0	0	0	0
Billy Hitchcock	1942-1953	.243	.299	2249	547	67	22	5	231	257	264	230	15
Dick Hoblitzell	1908-1918	.278	.374	4706	1310	194	88	27	591	619	407	256	173
Butch Hobson	1975-1982	.248	.423	2556	634	107	23	98	314	397	183	569	11
Johnny Hodapp	1925-1933	.311	.425	2826	880	169	34	28	378	429	163	136	18
Mel Hoderlein	1951-1954	.252	.306	294	74	10	3	0	22	24	31	37	2
John Hoey	1906-1908	.232	.272	500	116	10	5	0	39	35	15	NA	13
Glenn Hoffman	1980-1989	.242	.331	2163	524	106	9	23	247	210	136	309	5

Fred Hofman	1919-1928	.247	.339	1000	247	49	11	7	98	93	77	120	6
Dave Hollins	1990-Cont.	.261	.422	3329	868	166	17	112	577	482	464	684	47
Billy Holm	1943-1945	.156	.177	282	44	4	1	0	22	15	41	40	2
Harry Hooper	1909-1925	.281	.387	8785	2466	389	160	75	1429	817	1136	412	375
Sam Horn	1987-1995	.240	.468	1040	250	49	1	62	132	179	132	323	0
Tony Horton	1964-1970	.268	.430	2228	597	102	15	76	251	297	140	319	12
Dwayne Hosey	1995-1996	.274	.466	146	40	10	3	4	33	10	15	33	12
Wayne Housie	1991-1993	.208	.292	24	5	2	0	0	4	1	2	4	1
Elston Howard	1955-1968	.274	.427	5363	1471	218	50	167	619	762	373	786	9
Paul Howard	1909	.200	.267	15	3	1	0	0	2	2	3	NA	0
Terry Hughes	1970-1974	.209	.279	86	18	3	0	1	6	7	7	22	0
Buddy Hunter	1971-1975	.294	.412	17	5	2	0	0	5	2	5	2	0
Herb Hunter	1916-1921	.163	.224	49	8	0	0	1	8	4	2	6	0
Butch Huskey	1993-2000	.267	.442	2078	555	98	4	86	259	336	164	384	21

J
. . . .

NAME	YRS	BA	SA	AB	H	2B	3B	HR	R	RBI	BB	SO	SB
Ron Jackson	1954-1960	.245	.395	474	116	18	1	17	54	52	45	119	6
Baby Doll Jacobson	1915-1927	.311	.451	5507	1714	328	94	84	787	819	355	410	86
Chris James	1986-1995	.261	.413	3040	794	145	24	90	343	386	193	490	27
Hal Janvrin	1911-1922	.232	.287	2221	515	68	18	6	250	210	171	197	79
Reggie Jefferson	1991-1999	.300	.474	2123	637	131	11	72	285	300	146	451	2
Tom Jenkins	1925-1932	.259	.336	459	119	14	6	3	42	44	28	53	1
Jackie Jensen	1950-1961	.279	.460	5236	1463	259	45	199	810	929	750	546	143
Marcus Jensen	1996-Cont.	.192	.299	308	59	16	1	5	31	25	46	95	0
Keith Johns	1998			0	0	0	0	0	0	0	1	0	0
Bob Johnson	1933-1945	.296	.506	6920	2051	396	95	288	1239	1283	1073	851	96
Deron Johnson	1960-1976	.244	.420	5941	1447	247	33	245	706	923	585	1318	11
Roy Johnson	1929-1938	.296	.438	4358	1292	275	83	58	717	556	489	380	135
Smead Jolley	1930-1933	.305	.475	1710	521	111	21	46	188	313	89	105	5
Charlie Jones	1901-1908	.233	.304	1782	416	56	27	5	215	143	92	NA	100
Dalton Jones	1964-1972	.235	.343	2329	548	91	19	41	268	237	191	309	20
Jake Jones	1941-1948	.229	.368	790	181	31	5	23	80	117	69	130	8
Eddie Joost	1936-1955	.239	.366	5606	1339	238	35	134	874	601	1041	827	61
Duane Josephson	1965-1972	.258	.358	1505	388	58	12	23	147	164	92	174	5
Joe Judge	1915-1934	.298	.420	7898	2352	433	159	71	1184	1037	965	478	213
Ed Jurak	1982-1989	.265	.344	302	80	11	5	1	35	33	38	49	1

K
. . . .

NAME	YRS	BA	SA	AB	H	2B	3B	HR	R	RBI	BB	SO	SB
Marty Karow	1927	.200	.300	10	2	1	0	0	0	0	0	2	0
Benn Karr	1920-1927	.245	.311	392	96	20	0	2	43	49	27	59	3
Eddie Kasko	1957-1966	.264	.331	3546	935	146	13	22	411	261	265	353	31
George Kell	1943-1957	.306	.414	6702	2054	385	50	78	881	870	620	287	51
Red Kellett	1934	.000	.000	9	0	0	0	0	0	0	1	5	0
Ken Keltner	1937-1950	.276	.441	5683	1570	308	69	163	737	852	514	480	39
Fred Kendall	1969-1980	.234	.312	2576	603	86	11	31	170	244	189	240	5
John Kennedy	1962-1974	.225	.323	2110	475	77	17	32	237	185	142	461	14
Marty Keough	1956-1966	.242	.379	1796	434	71	23	43	256	176	164	318	26
Billy Klaus	1952-1963	.249	.351	2513	626	106	15	40	357	250	331	285	14
Red Kleinow	1904-1911	.213	.269	1665	354	45	20	3	146	135	153	NA	42
John Knight	1905-1913	.239	.309	2664	636	96	24	14	301	270	211	NA	86
Andy Kosco	1965-1974	.236	.394	1963	464	75	8	73	204	267	99	350	5
John Kroner	1935-1938	.262	.385	702	184	47	9	7	83	105	68	56	3
Marty Krug	1912-1922	.278	.374	489	136	25	5	4	73	67	48	43	9
Randy Kutcher	1986-1990	.228	.377	448	102	25	6	10	83	40	36	112	13

The Red Sox Encyclopedia

L

NAME	YRS	BA	SA	AB	H	2B	3B	HR	R	RBI	BB	SO	SB
Candy LaChance	1893-1905	.280	.379	4919	1377	197	86	39	678	690	219	NA	192
Ty LaForest	1945	.250	.353	204	51	7	4	2	25	16	10	35	4
Roger La Francois	1982	.400	.500	10	4	1	0	0	1	1	0	0	0
Joe Lahoud	1968-1978	.223	.372	1925	429	68	12	65	239	218	309	339	20
Eddie Lake	1939-1949	.231	.323	2595	599	105	9	39	442	193	546	312	52
Bill Lamar	1917-1927	.310	.417	2040	633	114	23	19	303	245	86	78	25
Rick Lancellotti	1982-1990	.169	.292	65	11	2	0	2	4	11	2	18	0
Jim Landis	1957-1967	.247	.375	4288	1061	169	50	93	625	46	588	767	139
Sam Langford	1926-1928	.275	.382	495	136	22	8	5	61	57	26	42	3
Carney Lansford	1978-1992	.290	.411	7158	2074	332	40	151	1007	874	553	719	224
Mike Lansing	1993-Cont.	.271	.401	4150	1124	254	17	84	554	440	299	570	119
Frank La Porte	1905-1915	.281	.376	4212	1185	198	80	14	501	560	288	NA	101
Lyn Lary	1929-1940	.269	.372	4604	1239	247	56	38	805	526	705	470	162
Johnny Lazor	1943-1946	.263	.357	596	157	30	4	6	57	62	40	53	8
Dud Lee	1920-1926	.223	.275	732	163	20	9	0	80	60	88	70	12
Lou Legett	1929-1935	.202	.226	124	25	3	0	0	13	8	5	22	2
Paul Lehner	1946-1952	.257	.364	1768	455	80	21	22	175	197	127	118	6
Nemo Leibold	1913-1925	.266	.327	4167	1109	145	48	4	638	283	571	335	133
Mark Lemke	1988-1998	.246	.324	3230	795	125	15	32	349	270	348	341	11
Don Lenhardt	1950-1954	.271	.450	1481	401	64	9	61	192	239	214	235	6
Ted Lepcio	1952-1961	.245	.398	2092	512	91	11	69	233	251	210	471	11
Dutch Lerchen	1910	.000	.000	15	0	0	0	0	1	0	1	NA	0
Darren Lewis	1990-Cont.	.250	.322	4002	1002	134	36	27	600	335	396	503	246
Duffy Lewis	1910-1921	.284	.384	5351	1518	289	68	38	612	793	352	353	113
Jack Lewis	1911-1915	.247	.310	684	169	20	10	1	63	80	32	NA	13
Jim Leyritz	1990-2000	.264	.415	2527	667	107	2	90	325	387	337	581	7
John Lickert	1981	.000	.000	0	0	0	0	0	0	0	0	0	0
Johnny Lipon	1942-1954	.259	.324	2661	690	95	24	10	351	266	347	152	28
Greg Litton	1989-1994	.241	.355	809	195	43	5	13	78	97	58	167	1
Don Lock	1962-1969	.238	.417	2695	642	92	12	122	359	373	373	776	30
George Loepp	1928-1930	.249	.324	185	46	10	2	0	29	17	25	21	0
Steve Lomasney	1999	.000	.000	2	0	0	0	0	0	0	0	2	0
Walt Lonergan	1911	.269	.269	26	7	0	0	0	2	1	1	NA	1
Harry Lord	1907-1915	.278	.356	3689	1024	107	70	14	505	294	226	NA	206
Derek Lowe	1997-Cont.	.000	.000	1	0	0	0	0	1	0	0	1	0
Johnny Lucas	1931-1932	.000	.000	3	0	0	0	0	0	0	0	1	0
Tony Lupien	1940-1948	.268	.355	2358	632	92	30	18	285	230	241	111	57
Walt Lynch	1922	.500	.500	2	1	0	0	0	1	0	0	0	0
Fred Lynn	1974-1990	.283	.484	6925	1960	388	43	306	1063	1111	857	1117	72
Steve Lyons	1985-1993	.252	.340	2162	545	100	17	19	264	196	156	364	42

M

NAME	YRS	BA	SA	AB	H	2B	3B	HR	R	RBI	BB	SO	SB
Mike MacFarlane	1987-1999	.252	.430	3602	906	221	17	129	458	514	295	700	12
Shane Mack	1987-1994	.299	.458	2518	754	133	27	71	392	352	232	449	80
Tom Madden	1909-1911	.287	.329	143	41	4	1	0	10	11	5	13	0
Jim Mahoney	1959-1965	.229	.314	210	48	4	1	4	32	15	11	47	1
Jose Malave	1996-1997	.226	.368	106	24	3	0	4	12	17	2	27	0
Jerry Mallett	1959	.267	.267	15	4	0	0	0	1	1	1	3	0
Frank Malzone	1955-1966	.274	.399	5428	1486	239	21	133	647	728	337	434	14
Felix Mantilla	1956-1966	.261	.403	2707	707	97	10	89	360	330	256	332	27
Jeff Manto	1990-2000	.230	.415	713	164	35	2	31	97	97	97	182	3
Heinie Manush	1923-1939	.330	.479	7653	2524	491	160	110	1287	1173	506	345	114
Ollie Marquardt	1931	.179	.205	39	7	1	0	0	4	2	3	4	0
Bill Marshall	1931-1934	.125	.125	8	1	0	0	0	1	0	0	2	0
Mike Marshall	1981-1991	.270	.446	3593	971	173	8	148	434	530	247	810	26
Babe Martin	1944-1953	.214	.291	206	44	6	2	2	13	18	13	27	0
John Marzano	1987-Cont.	.242	.334	661	160	38	1	7	66	60	30	114	0

Name	Years	AVG	SLG	AB	H	2B	3B	HR	R	RBI	BB	SO	SB
Tom Matchik	1967-1972	.215	.270	826	178	21	6	4	63	64	39	148	6
Gene Mauch	1944-1957	.239	.312	737	176	25	7	5	93	62	104	82	6
Charlie Maxwell	1950-1964	.264	.451	3245	856	110	26	148	478	532	484	545	18
Wally Mayer	1911-1919	.193	.266	274	53	14	3	0	22	20	42	51	1
Chick Maynard	1922	.125	.125	24	3	0	0	0	1	0	3	2	0
Dick McAuliffe	1960-1975	.247	.403	6185	1530	231	71	197	888	697	882	974	63
Tom McBride	1943-1948	.275	.340	1186	326	39	16	2	140	141	93	63	13
Emmett McCann	1920-1926	.227	.268	194	44	6	1	0	19	18	8	8	2
Tim McCarver	1959-1980	.271	.388	5529	1501	242	57	97	590	645	548	422	61
Amby McConnell	1908-1911	.264	.319	1506	398	30	22	3	200	119	107	NA	72
Ed McFarland	1893-1908	.275	.369	3004	825	146	50	12	398	383	254	NA	65
Ed McGah	1946-1947	.157	.216	51	8	1	1	0	3	3	10	7	0
Willie McGee	1982-1999	.295	.396	7649	2254	350	94	79	1010	856	448	1238	352
Art McGovern	1905	.114	.136	44	5	1	0	0	1	1	4	NA	0
Deacon McGuire	1884-1912	.278	.372	6290	1749	300	79	45	770	787	515	NA	115
Jim McHale	1908	.224	.313	67	15	2	2	0	9	7	4	NA	4
Stuffy McInnis	1909-1927	.308	.381	7822	2406	312	101	20	872	1060	380	189	172
Walt McKeel	1996-1997	.000	.000	3	0	0	0	0	0	0	0	1	0
Larry McLean	1901-1915	.262	.323	2647	694	90	26	6	183	298	136	79	20
Marty McManus	1920-1934	.289	.430	6660	1926	401	88	120	1008	996	674	558	127
Norm McMillan	1922-1929	.260	.352	1356	353	74	16	6	157	147	95	133	36
Eric McNair	1929-1942	.274	.392	4519	1240	229	29	82	592	633	261	328	59
Mike McNally	1915-1925	.238	.267	1078	257	16	6	1	169	85	92	97	39
Jeff McNeely	1993	.297	.378	37	11	1	1	0	10	1	7	9	6
Norm McNeil	1919	.333	.333	9	3	0	0	0	0	1	1	0	0
Bill McWilliarns	1931	.000	.000	2	0	0	0	0	0	0	1	0	0
Roman Mejias	1955-1964	.254	.391	1768	449	57	12	54	212	202	89	238	20
Sam Mele	1947-1956	.267	.408	3437	916	168	39	80	406	544	311	342	15
Oscar Melillo	1926-1937	.260	.340	5063	1316	210	64	22	591	548	327	306	69
Bob Melvin	1985-1994	.233	.337	1955	456	85	6	35	174	212	98	396	4
Mike Menosky	1914-1923	.278	.370	2465	685	98	38	18	382	250	295	260	90
Orlando Merced	1990-2001	.279	.428	3535	987	199	23	94	509	529	446	578	50
Andy Merchant	1975-1976	.333	.333	6	2	0	0	0	1	0	1	2	0
Lou Merloni	1998-Cont.	.280	.387	496	139	34	2	5	59	59	25	89	4
Jack Merson	1951-1953	.257	.363	452	116	22	4	6	47	52	23	45	1
George Metkovich	1943-1954	.261	.367	3585	934	167	36	47	476	373	307	359	61
Dee Miles	1935-1943	.280	.353	1468	411	53	24	2	175	143	50	74	15
Bing Miller	1921-1936	.312	.462	6212	1937	389	95	117	947	990	383	340	128
Elmer Miller	1912-1922	.243	.335	1414	343	43	20	16	170	151	113	140	29
Hack Miller	1916-1925	.322	.490	1200	387	65	11	38	164	205	64	103	10
Otto Miller	1927-1932	.274	.335	837	229	39	6	0	95	91	49	46	3
Rick Miller	1971-1985	.269	.350	3887	1046	161	35	28	552	369	454	583	78
Buster Mills	1934-1946	.287	.390	1379	396	62	19	14	200	163	131	137	24
Doug Mirabelli	1996-Cont.	.231	.395	549	127	29	2	19	57	72	78	152	1
Johnny Mitchell	1921-1925	.245	.296	1175	288	38	8	2	152	63	119	81	14
Keith Mitchell	1991-1998	.260	.380	242	63	5	0	8	38	29	34	42	4
Kevin Mitchell	1984-1998	.284	.520	4134	1173	224	25	234	630	760	491	719	30
Freddie Moncewicz	1928	.000	.000	1	0	0	0	0	0	0	0	1	0
Bob Montgomery	1970-1979	.258	.372	1185	306	50	8	23	125	156	64	268	6
Bill Moore	1926-1927	.207	.230	87	18	2	0	0	9	4	13	12	0
Ed Morgan	1928-1934	.313	.467	2810	879	186	45	52	512	473	385	251	36
Red Morgan	1906	.215	.264	307	66	6	3	1	20	21	16	NA	7
Guy Morton	1954	.000	.000	1	0	0	0	0	0	0	0	1	0
Gerry Moses	1965-1975	.251	.381	1072	269	48	8	25	89	109	63	184	1
Wally Moses	1935-1951	.291	.416	7356	2138	435	110	89	1124	679	821	457	174
Doc Moskiman	1910	.111	.111	9	1	0	0	0	1	1	2	NA	0
Les Moss	1946-1958	.247	.369	2234	552	75	4	63	210	276	282	316	2
Greg Mulleavy	1930-1933	.260	.342	292	76	14	5	0	28	28	20	23	5
Freddie Muller	1933-1934	.184	.245	49	9	1	1	0	7	3	6	5	1
Bill Mundy	1913	.255	.255	47	12	0	0	0	4	4	4	12	0
Tony Muser	1969-1978	.259	.323	1268	329	41	9	7	123	117	95	138	14
Buddy Myer	1925-1941	.303	.406	7038	2131	353	130	38	1174	850	965	428	156
Hap Myers	1910-1915	.268	.322	1251	335	42	7	4	203	116	119	NA	132

N

NAME	YRS	BA	SA	AB	H	2B	3B	HR	R	RBI	BB	SO	SB
Tim Naehring	1990-1997	.282	.420	1872	527	104	4	49	254	250	236	312	5
Bill Narkeski	1929-1930	.265	.341	358	95	25	1	0	42	32	28	27	4
Ernie Nietzke	1921	.240	.240	25	6	0	0	0	3	1	4	4	0
Jeff Newman	1976-1984	.224	.357	2123	475	85	4	63	189	233	116	369	7
Skeeter Newsome	1935-1947	.245	.304	3716	910	164	15	9	381	292	246	194	67
Gus Niarhos	1946-1955	.252	.308	691	174	26	5	1	114	59	153	56	6
Reid Nichols	1980-1987	.266	.391	1160	308	63	8	22	156	131	99	149	27
Al Niemiec	1934-1936	.200	.243	235	47	3	2	1	24	23	29	20	2
Harry Niles	1906-1910	.248	.310	2270	562	58	24	12	278	152	163	NA	107
Otis Nixon	1983-1999	.270	.314	5115	1379	142	27	11	878	318	585	694	620
Russ Nixon	1957-1968	.268	.361	2504	670	115	19	27	215	266	154	279	0
Trot Nixon	1996	.000	.000	4	2	1	0	0	2	0	0	NA	1
Red Nonnenkamp	1933-1940	.262	.300	263	69	6	2	0	49	24	34	24	6
Les Nunamaker	1911-1922	.268	.339	1990	533	75	30	2	194	215	175	150	36
Jon Nunnally	1995-2000	.246	.469	885	218	47	12	42	162	125	146	239	19

O

NAME	YRS	BA	SA	AB	H	2B	3B	HR	R	RBI	BB	SO	SB
Mike O'Berry	1979-1985	.191	.247	376	72	10	1	3	38	27	43	77	1
Jack O'Brien	1899-1903	.259	.335	1226	317	39	14	9	171	133	27		42
Syd O'Brien	1969-1972	.230	.347	1052	242	35	8	24	135	100	60	155	5
Tommy O'Brien	1943-1950	.277	.392	714	198	30	14	8	110	78	70	66	2
Lefty O'Doul	1919-1934	.349	.532	3264	1140	175	41	113	624	542	333	122	36
Jose Offerman	1990-Cont.	.277	.375	5120	1417	223	68	48	759	471	695	828	162
Ben Ogilvie	1971-1986	.273	.450	5913	1615	277	33	235	784	901	560	852	87
Len Okrie	1948-1952	.218	.256	78	17	1	1	0	3	3	9	16	0
Troy O'Leary	1993-Cont.	.276	.457	3563	984	213	38	119	502	526	286	583	13
Gene Oliver	1959-1969	.246	.427	2216	546	111	5	93	268	320	215	420	24
Joe Oliver	1989-Cont.	.247	.391	3367	831	174	3	102	320	476	248	637	13
Tom Oliver	1930-1933	.277	.340	1931	534	101	11	0	202	176	105	61	12
Karl Olson	1951-1957	.235	.316	681	160	25	6	6	74	50	43	94	3
Marv Olson	1931-1933	.241	.300	457	110	15	6	0	67	30	70	30	1
Bill O'Neill	1904-1906	.243	.276	746	181	15	2	2	77	42	46	NA	41
Steve O'Neill	1911-1928	.263	.337	4795	1259	248	34	13	448	537	592	383	30
George Orme	1920	.333	.333	6	2	0	0	0	4	1	3	0	0
Frank O'Rourke	1912-1931	.254	.333	4069	1032	196	42	15	547	430	314	377	101
Luis Ortiz	1993-1996	.228	.359	145	33	7	3	2	14	26	7	26	0
Harry Ostdiek	1904-1908	.143	.238	21	3	0	1	0	1	3	3	NA	1
John Ostrowski	1943-1950	.232	.373	557	129	19	9	14	72	74	67	125	7
Marv Owen	1931-1940	.275	.367	3782	1040	167	44	31	473	497	338	283	30
Mickey Owen	1937-1954	.255	.322	3649	929	163	21	14	338	378	326	181	36
Spike Owen	1983-1995	.246	.341	4930	1211	215	59	46	587	439	569	519	82
Frank Owens	1905-1915	.245	.334	694	170	25	11	5	59	65	34	NA	9

P-Q

NAME	YRS	BA	SA	AB	H	2B	3B	HR	R	RBI	BB	SO	SB
Jim Pagliaroni	1955-1969	.252	.407	2465	622	98	7	90	269	326	330	494	4
Jim Pankovits	1984-1990	.250	.349	567	142	25	2	9	62	55	44	115	8
Stan Papi	1974-1981	.218	.331	523	114	26	6	7	49	51	24	99	2
Freddy Parent	1899-1911	.262	.340	4984	1306	180	74	20	633	471	333	NA	184
Larry Parrish	1974-1988	.263	.439	6792	1789	360	33	256	851	992	529	1359	30
Roy Partee	1943-1948	.250	.303	1090	273	41	5	2	89	114	132	120	2
Ben Paschal	1920-1929	.309	.488	787	243	47	11	24	143	139	72	93	24
Hank Patterson	1932	.000	.000	1	0	0	0	0	0	0	0	0	0
Don Pavletich	1957-1971	.254	.420	1373	349	73	8	46	163	193	148	237	5
Johnny Peacock	1937-1945	.262	.325	1734	455	74	16	1	175	194	183	63	14

Name	Years	BA	SA	AB	H	2B	3B	HR	R	RBI	BB	SO	SB
Eddie Pellagrini	1946-1954	.226	.316	1423	321	42	13	20	167	133	128	201	13
Rudy Pemberton	1995-1997	.336	.515	134	45	13	1	3	22	23	7	22	3
Tony Pena	1980-1997	.260	.364	6489	1687	298	27	107	667	708	455	846	80
Tony Perez	1964-1986	.279	.463	9778	2732	505	79	379	1272	1652	925	1867	49
Jack Perrin	1921	.231	.231	13	3	0	0	0	3	1	0	3	0
Johnny Pesky	1942-1954	.307	.386	4745	1455	226	50	17	867	404	663	218	53
Bob Peterson	1906-1907	.191	.237	131	25	1	1	1	11	9	11	NA	1
Rico Petrocelli	1963-1976	.251	.420	5390	1352	237	22	210	653	773	661	926	10
Dave Philley	1941-1962	.270	.377	6296	1700	276	72	84	789	729	596	551	102
Val Picinich	1916-1933	.258	.361	2874	741	165	25	27	297	298	313	382	31
Calvin Pickering	1995-Cont.	.217	.391	115	25	2	0	6	12	16	22	35	1
Urbane Pickering	1931-1932	.257	.372	798	205	41	9	11	95	92	72	124	6
Jimmy Piersall	1950-1967	.272	.386	5890	1604	256	52	104	811	591	523	583	115
Greg Pirkl	1993-1996	.224	.466	116	26	4	0	8	12	16	2	27	0
Pinky Pittenger	1921-1929	.263	.306	959	252	32	3	1	118	83	37	50	27
Phil Plantier	1990-1997	.243	.439	1883	457	90	3	91	260	292	237	476	13
Herb Plews	1956-1959	.262	.348	1017	266	42	17	4	125	82	74	133	3
Nick Polly	1937-1945	.200	.200	25	5	0	0	0	2	3	0	2	0
Ralph Pond	1910	.250	.250	4	1	0	0	0	0	0	0	NA	1
Tom Poquette	1973-1982	.268	.373	1226	329	62	18	10	127	136	81	82	13
Dick Porter	1929-1934	.308	.414	2515	774	159	37	11	427	284	268	186	23
Ken Poulsen	1967	.200	.400	5	1	1	0	0	0	0	0	2	0
Arquimedez Pozo	1995-1997	.189	.311	74	14	4	1	1	4	14	2	15	1
Del Pratt	1912-1924	.292	.403	6826	1996	392	117	43	856	966	513	360	246
Larry Pratt	1914-1915	.193	.298	57	11	3	0	1	7	2	5	4	4
Curtis Pride	1993-Cont.	.256	.414	706	181	33	12	18	118	76	79	186	28
Doc Protho	1920-1926	.318	.408	600	191	34	10	0	66	81	69	40	13
Billy Purtell	1908-1914	.230	.278	1124	259	26	11	2	82	104	63	7	24
Frankie Pytlak	1932-1946	.282	.363	2399	677	100	36	7	316	272	247	97	56
Ray Quinones	1986-1989	.243	.357	1533	373	75	6	29	173	159	89	240	5
Carlos Quintana	1988-1993	.276	.362	1376	380	59	1	19	163	165	153	207	3

R

NAME	YRS	BA	SA	AB	H	2B	3B	HR	R	RBI	BB	SO	SB
Dave Rader	1971-1980	.257	.349	2405	619	107	12	30	254	235	245	180	10
Manny Ramirez	1993-Cont.	.312	.594	3999	1248	270	13	277	758	929	622	927	28
Johnny Reder	1932	.135	.162	37	5	1	0	4	3	6	6	0	0
Jody Reed	1987-1997	.270	.350	4554	1231	263	10	27	566	392	542	407	40
Bobby Reeves	1926-1931	.252	.329	1598	402	55	22	8	203	135	175	218	21
Bill Regan	1926-1931	.267	.387	2364	632	158	36	18	236	292	122	245	38
Wally Rehg	1912-1919	.250	.319	752	188	24	11	2	86	66	52	66	26
Dick Reichle	1922-1923	.257	.327	385	99	18	3	1	43	39	22	36	3
Jerry Remy	1975-1984	.275	.328	4455	1226	140	38	7	605	329	356	404	208
Bill Renna	1953-1959	.239	.391	918	219	36	10	28	123	119	99	166	2
Rip Repulski	1953-1961	.269	.436	3088	830	153	23	106	407	416	207	433	25
Carl Reynolds	1927-1939	.302	.458	4497	1357	247	107	80	672	695	262	308	112
Karl Rhodes	1990-1995	.224	.349	590	132	29	3	13	74	44	74	121	14
Hal Rhyne	1926-1933	.250	.323	2031	508	98	22	2	252	192	127	13	
Jim Rice	1974-1989	.298	.502	8225	2452	373	79	382	1249	1451	670	1423	58
Jeff Richardson	1989-1993	.176	.255	153	27	6	0	2	13	13	11	29	1
Al Richter	1951-1953	.091	.091	11	1	0	0	0	1	0	3	0	0
Joe Riggert	1911-1919	.240	.366	558	134	18	14	8	68	44	46	64	20
Topper Rigney	1922-1927	.288	.387	2326	669	113	39	13	324	314	377	176	44
Ernest Riles	1985-1993	.254	.365	2504	637	92	20	48	309	284	244	409	20
Pop Rising	1905	.111	.278	18	2	1	1	0	2	2	2		0
Luis Rivera	1986-1994	.232	.335	2113	491	110	11	28	233	199	163	420	19
Billy Jo Robidoux	1985-1990	.209	.286	468	98	21	0	5	43	43	71	106	1
Aaron Robinson	1943-1951	.260	.412	1839	478	74	11	61	208	272	337	194	0
Floyd Robinson	1960-1968	.283	.409	3284	929	140	36	67	458	426	408	282	42
Bill Rodgers	1915-1916	.243	.328	268	65	15	4	0	30	19	22	40	11
Carlos Rodriguez	1991-1995	.278	.365	241	67	16	1	1	21	20	14	17	1
Steve Rodriguez	1995	.179	.205	39	7	1	0	0	5	0	6	10	2

The Red Sox Encyclopedia

Name	Years	BA	SA	AB	H	2B	3B	HR	R	RBI	BB	SO	SB
Tony Rodriguez	1996	.239	.299	67	16	1	0	1	7	9	4	8	0
Billy Rogell	1925-1940	.267	.370	5149	1375	256	75	42	755	609	649	416	82
Red Rollings	1927-1930	.251	.299	355	89	13	2	0	36	28	27	23	5
Ed Romero	1977-1990	.247	.302	1912	473	79	1	8	218	155	140	159	9
Mandy Romero	1997-1998	.186	.286	70	13	1	0	2	10	5	6	24	1
Kevin Romine	1985-1991	.251	.325	630	158	30	1	5	89	55	49	124	11
Buddy Rosar	1939-1951	.261	.334	3198	836	147	15	18	325	367	315	161	17
Si Rosenthal	1925-1926	.266	.375	357	95	17	5	4	40	42	26	21	5
Braggo Roth	1914-1921	.284	.416	2831	804	138	73	30	427	422	335	389	189
Jack Rothrock	1925-1937	.276	.370	3350	924	162	35	28	498	327	299	312	75
Rich Rowland	1990-1995	.213	.365	230	49	8	0	9	22	26	22	71	0
Stan Royer	1991-1994	.250	.384	164	41	10	0	4	14	21	4	41	0
Joe Rudi	1967-1982	.264	.427	5556	1468	287	39	179	684	810	369	870	25
Muddy Ruel	1915-1934	.275	.332	4514	1242	187	29	4	494	532	606	238	61
Pete Runnels	1951-1964	.291	.378	6373	1854	283	64	49	876	630	844	627	37
Rip Russell	1939-1947	.245	.356	1402	344	52	8	29	133	192	83	142	4
Babe Ruth	1914-1933	.342	.690	8399	2873	506	136	714	2174	2211	2056	1330	123
Jack Ryan	1929	.000	.000	3	0	0	0	0	0	0	0	0	0
Mike Ryan	1964-1974	.193	.280	1920	370	60	12	28	146	161	152	370	4
Gene Rye	1931	.179	.179	39	7	0	0	0	3	1	2	5	0

S

NAME	YRS	BA	SA	AB	H	2B	3B	HR	R	RBI	BB	SO	SB
Donnie Sadler	1998-Cont.	.214	.301	515	110	20	5	5	81	34	34	103	16
Eddie Sadowski	1960-1966	.202	.319	495	100	20	1	12	55	39	39	94	5
Tom Satriano	1961-1970	.225	.303	1623	365	53	5	21	130	157	214	225	7
Dave Sax	1982-1987	.267	.383	60	16	4	0	1	3	3	3	5	0
Russ Scarritt	1929-1932	.285	.385	1037	296	44	25	3	119	120	49	91	17
Wally Schang	1913-1931	.284	.401	5306	1506	264	90	59	769	710	849	573	122
Bob Scherbarth	1950	.000	.000	0	0	0	0	0	0	0	0	0	0
Chuck Schilling	1961-1965	.239	.317	1969	470	76	5	23	230	146	176	236	11
Rudy Schlesinger	1965	.000	.000	1	0	0	0	0	0	0	0	0	0
Dave Schmidt	1981	.238	.405	42	10	1	0	2	6	3	7	17	0
Dick Schofield	1953-1971	.227	.297	3083	699	113	20	21	394	211	390	526	12
Ossee Schreckengost	1897-1908	.271	.345	3053	828	136	31	9	304	338	102	NA	52
Everett Scott	1914-1926	.249	.315	5837	1455	208	58	20	552	549	243	282	69
George Scott	1966-1979	.268	.435	7433	1992	306	60	271	957	1051	699	1418	69
Bob Seeds	1930-1940	.277	.382	1937	537	27	21	28	268	233	160	190	14
Kip Selbach	1894-1906	.293	.411	6161	1803	299	149	44	1064	779	783	NA	334
Bill Selby	1996	.274	.411	95	26	4	0	3	12	6	9	11	1
Wally Shaner	1923-1929	.278	.394	629	175	45	8	4	80	74	43	54	13
Howard Shanks	1912-1925	.253	.337	5699	1440	212	97	25	604	619	414	442	185
Red Shannon	1915-1926	.259	.336	1070	277	38	22	0	124	91	109	178	21
Al Shaw	1901-1909	.200	.240	459	92	9	3	1	31	32	35	NA	6
Merv Shea	1927-1944	.220	.277	1197	263	39	7	5	105	115	189	145	8
Danny Sheaffer	1987-1997	.232	.323	946	219	38	5	13	87	110	60	122	6
Dave Shean	1906-1919	.228	.285	2167	495	59	23	6	225	166	155	133	66
Andy Sheets	1996-Cont.	.210	.314	811	170	34	3	15	100	91	64	234	14s
Neil Sheridan	1948	.000	.000	1	0	0	0	0	0	0	0	1	0
Strick Shofner	1947	.154	.308	13	2	0	1	0	1	0	0	3	0
Chick Shorten	1915-1924	.275	.349	1345	370	51	20	3	161	134	110	68	12
Terry Shumpert	1990-Cont.	.223	.365	858	191	52	11	16	101	92	59	178	44
Norm Siebern	1956-1968	.272	.423	4481	1217	206	38	132	662	636	708	749	18
Al Simmons	1924-1944	.334	.535	8761	2927	539	149	307	1507	1827	615	737	87
Ted Sizemore	1969-1980	.262	.321	5011	1311	188	21	23	577	430	469	350	59
Camp Skinner	1922-1923	.196	.239	46	9	2	0	0	2	3	0	4	1
Jack Slattery	1901-1909	.212	.243	288	61	5	2	0	14	27	6	NA	3
Charlie Small	1930	.167	.222	18	3	1	0	0	2	0	0	1	0
Al Smith	1953-1964	.272	.429	5357	1458	258	46	164	843	676	674	768	67
Broadway Aleck Smith	1897-1906	.264	.324	955	252	30	12	1	107	130	26	NA	38
Elmer Smith	1914-1925	.276	.437	3195	881	181	62	70	469	540	319	359	54
George Smith	1963-1966	.205	.309	634	130	27	6	9	64	57	59	142	9

NAME	YRS	BA	SA	AB	H	2B	3B	HR	R	RBI	BB	SO	SB
John Smith	1931	.133	.133	15	2	0	0	0	2	1	2	1	1
Paddy Smith	1920	.000	.000	2	0	0	0	0	0	0	0	1	0
Reggie Smith	1966-1982	.287	.489	7033	2020	363	57	314	1123	1092	890	1030	137
Wally Snell	1913	.375	.375	8	3	0	0	0	1	0	0	0	1
Chris Snopek	1995-1998	.234	.346	607	142	27	1	13	76	66	49	108	7
Moose Solters	1934-1943	.289	.449	3421	990	213	42	83	503	599	221	377	42
Tris Speaker	1907-1926	.345	.500	10197	3514	792	223	117	1882	1559	1381	220	433
Stan Spence	1940-1949	.282	.437	3871	1090	196	60	95	541	575	520	248	21
Tubby Spencer	1905-1918	.225	.277	1326	298	43	10	2	106	132	87	46	13
Andy Spognardi	1932	.294	.324	34	10	1	0	0	9	1	6	6	0
Ed Sprague	1991-Cont.	.247	.419	4095	1010	225	12	152	506	558	358	833	6
Chick Stahl	1897-1906	.306	.417	5069	1552	219	117	37	858	623	470	NA	189
Jake Stahl	1903-1913	.260	.382	3421	891	149	87	31	405	437	221	NA	178
Matt Stairs	1992-Cont.	.265	.495	2485	658	140	6	140	398	470	358	520	21
Jerry Standaert	1925-1929	.318	.424	132	42	10	2	0	14	18	8	10	0
Mike Stanley	1986-2000	.270	.458	4222	1138	220	7	187	625	702	652	929	13
John Stansbury	1918	.128	.149	47	6	1	0	0	3	2	6	3	0
Dave Stapleton	1980-1986	.271	.398	2028	550	118	8	41	238	224	114	162	6
Jigger Statz	1919-1928	.285	.373	2585	737	114	31	17	376	215	194	211	77
Ben Steiner	1945-1947	.256	.331	308	79	8	3	3	41	20	31	29	10
Red Steiner	1945	.190	.203	79	15	1	0	0	6	6	15	6	0
Mike Stenhouse	1982-1986	.190	.291	416	79	15	0	9	40	40	71	66	1
Gene Stephens	1952-1964	.240	.355	1913	460	78	15	37	283	207	233	322	27
Vern Stephens	1941-1955	.286	.460	6497	1859	307	42	247	1001	174	692	685	25
Al Stokes	1925-1926	.181	.261	138	25	3	4	0	14	7	12	36	0
George Stone	1903-1910	.301	.396	3271	984	106	68	23	426	268	282	NA	132
Jeff Stone	1983-1990	.277	.375	941	261	23	18	11	129	72	60	186	75
Howie Storie	1931-1932	.200	.200	25	5	0	0	0	2	0	3	2	0
Lou Stringer	1941-1950	.242	.348	1196	290	49	10	19	148	122	121	192	7
Amos Strunk	1908-1924	.283	.373	4994	1415	212	96	15	695	528	573	331	185
Dick Stuart	1958-1969	.264	.489	3997	1055	157	30	228	506	743	301	957	2
George Stumpf	1931-1936	.235	.296	260	61	7	3	1	31	32	25	26	5
Chris Stynes	1995-Cont.	.292	.410	1526	445	68	5	34	239	150	113	180	45
Denny Sullivan	1905-1909	.239	.285	923	221	25	7	1	106	51	59	NA	31
Haywood Sullivan	1955-1963	.226	.318	851	192	30	5	13	94	87	109	140	2
Marc Sullivan	1982-1987	.186	.258	360	67	11	0	5	37	28	18	92	0
Carl Sumner	1928	.276	.379	29	8	1	1	0	6	3	5	6	0
Bill Swanson	1914	.200	.300	20	4	2	0	0	0	1	3	4	0
Bill Sweeney	1928-1931	.286	.370	1050	300	58	8	5	127	107	44	73	22

T-U

NAME	YRS	BA	SA	AB	H	2B	3B	HR	R	RBI	BB	SO	SB
Jim Tabor	1938-1947	.270	.418	3788	1021	191	29	104	473	598	286	377	69
Doug Taitt	1928-1932	.263	.369	824	217	43	16	4	81	95	58	64	13
Arlie Tarbert	1927-1928	.186	.209	86	16	2	0	0	6	7	4	13	1
Jose Tartabull	1962-1970	.261	.320	1857	484	56	24	2	247	107	115	136	81
LaSchelle Tarver	1986	.120	.120	25	3	0	0	0	3	1	1	4	0
Willie Tasby	1958-1963	.250	.367	1868	467	61	10	46	246	174	201	327	12
Bennie Tate	1924-1934	.279	.351	1560	435	68	16	4	144	173	118	51	5
Jim Tatum	1992-1996	.199	.272	151	30	6	1	1	12	16	7	39	0
Jesus Tavarez	1994-1998	.239	.303	423	101	12	3	3	63	33	30	62	13
Birdie Tebbetts	1936-1952	.270	.358	3705	1000	169	22	38	357	469	389	261	29
Fred Thomas	1918-1920	.225	.293	859	193	19	14	4	88	45	84	90	24
George Thomas	1957-1971	.255	.389	1688	430	71	9	46	203	202	138	343	13
Lee Thomas	1961-1968	.255	.397	3324	847	111	22	106	405	428	332	397	25
Pinch Thomas	1912-1921	.237	.284	1035	245	27	8	2	88	102	118	82	12
Bobby Thomson	1946-1960	.270	.462	6305	1705	267	74	264	903	1026	559	804	38
Jack Thoney	1902-1911	.237	.298	912	216	23	12	3	112	73	36	NA	42
Faye Throneberry	1952-1961	.236	.358	1302	307	48	12	29	152	137	127	284	23
Bob Tillman	1962-1970	.232	.371	2329	540	68	10	79	189	282	228	510	1
Lee Tinsley	1993-1997	.241	.234	870	210	334	4	13	131	79	88	231	41
Jack Tobin	1914-1927	.309	.420	6174	1906	294	99	64	936	581	498	172	147

Name	Yrs	BA	SA	AB	H	2B	3B	HR	R	RBI	BB	SO	SB
Johnny Tobin	1945	.252	.289	278	70	6	2	0	25	21	25	24	2
Phil Todt	1924-1931	.258	.395	3415	880	182	58	57	372	453	207	229	29
Andy Tomberlin	1993-1998	.233	.374	305	71	6	2	11	40	38	26	103	6
Tony Tonneman	1911	.200	.400	5	1	1	0	0	0	3	1	NA	0
Frank Truesdale	1910-1918	.220	.249	668	147	12	2	1	69	40	91	40	41
Tommy Umphlett	1953-1955	.246	.314	1160	285	45	8	6	108	111	75	107	7
Bob Unglaub	1904-1910	.258	.328	2150	554	67	35	5	188	216	88		66

V

NAME	YRS	BA	SA	AB	H	2B	3B	HR	R	RBI	BB	SO	SB
Tex Vache	1925	.313	.464	252	79	15	7	3	41	48	21	33	2
Julio Valdez	1980-1983	.207	.264	87	18	2	0	1	11	8	1	18	3
John Valentin	1992-Cont.	.281	.460	3709	1043	266	17	121	596	528	441	487	47
Dave Valle	1984-1996	.237	.373	2775	658	121	12	77	314	350	258	413	5
Al VanCamp	1928-1932	.261	.333	444	116	20	6	0	44	41	24	42	4
Jason Varitek	1997-Cont.	.263	.439	1327	349	94	4	44	175	199	144	249	4
Mo Vaughn	1991-Cont.	.298	.533	4966	1479	250	10	299	784	977	652	1262	30
Bobby Veach	1912-1925	.310	.442	6659	2064	393	147	64	953	1166	571	367	195
Wilton Veras	1999-2000	.262	.340	282	74	12	2	2	35	27	12	34	0
Mickey Vernon	1939-1960	.286	.428	8731	2495	490	120	172	1196	1311	934	869	137
Sammy Vick	1917-1921	.248	.335	641	159	28	11	2	90	50	51	91	12
Ossie Vitt	1912-1921	.238	.295	3760	894	106	48	4	560	294	455	131	114
Clyde Vollmer	1942-1954	.251	.402	2021	508	77	10	69	283	339	243	330	7
Joe Vosmik	1930-1944	.307	.438	5472	1682	335	92	65	818	874	514	272	23

W

NAME	YRS	BA	SA	AB	H	2B	3B	HR	R	RBI	BB	SO	SB
Hal Wagner	1937-1949	.248	.334	1849	458	90	12	15	179	228	253	152	10
Heinie Wagner	1902-1918	.250	.326	3333	834	128	47	10	400	343	310	63 1	44
Chico Walker	1980-1993	.246	.329	1217	299	37	7	17	150	116	109	212	67
Tilly Walker	1911-1923	.281	.427	5067	1423	244	71	118	696	679	415	501	130
Jimmy Walsh	1912-1917	.231	.316	1770	409	70	31	6	235	150	249	204	92
Bucky Walters	1931-1950	.243	.344	1966	477	99	16	23	227	234	114	303	12
Fred Walters	1945	.172	.194	93	16	2	0	0	2	5	10	9	1
Roxy Walters	1915-1925	.222	.259	1426	317	41	6	0	119	115	97	151	13
Bill Wambsganss	1914-1926	.259	.327	5241	1359	215	59	7	710	519	490	356	142
Pee Wee Wanninger	1917-1925	.234	.295	556	130	15	8	1	53	31	23	43	5
Jack Warner	1895-1908	.249	.297	3494	870	81	35	6	348	303	181	NA	83
Rabbit Warstler	1930-1940	.229	.287	4088	935	133	36	11	431	332	405	414	42
Bob Watson	1966 1984	.295	.447	6185	1826	307	41	184	802	989	653	796	27
Cliff Watwood	1929-1939	.283	.363	1423	403	66	16	5	192	148	154	103	27
Earl Webb	1925-1933	.306	.478	2161	661	155	25	56	326	333	260	202	8
Ray Webster	1959-1960	.195	.325	77	15	2	1	2	11	11	6	7	1
Eric Wedge	1991-1994	.233	.430	86	20	2	0	5	13	12	14	25	0
Frank Welch	1919-1927	.274	.398	2310	634	100	31	41	310	295	250	225	18
Herb Welch	1925	.289	.342	38	11	0	1	0	2	2	0	6	0
Bill Werber	1930-1942	.271	.392	5024	1363	271	50	78	875	539	701	363	215
Vic Wertz	1947-1963	.277	.469	6099	1692	289	42	266	867	1178	828	841	9
Sammy White	1951-1962	.262	.377	3502	916	167	20	66	324	421	218	381	14
George Whiteman	1907-1918	.272	.358	257	70	17	1	1	32	31	27	11	11
Mark Whiten	1990-2000	.259	.415	3104	804	129	20	105	465	423	378	712	78
Ernie Whitt	1976-1991	.249	.410	3774	938	176	15	134	447	534	436	491	22
Del Wilber	1946-1954	.242	.389	720	174	35	7	19	67	115	44	96	1
Joe Wilhoit	1916-1919	.257	.321	782	201	23	9	3	93	73	75	82	28
Buff Williams	1911-1918	.265	.352	1186	314	51	23	2	111	145	95	80	27
Dana Williams	1989	.200	.400	5	1	1	0	0	2	1	3	6	0
Denny Williams	1921-1928	.259	.290	328	85	4	3	0	46	18	28	19	5
Dib Williams	1930-1935	.267	.385	1574	421	74	12	29	198	201	133	140	7
Dick Williams	1951-1964	.260	.392	2959	768	157	12	70	358	331	227	392	12
Ken Williams	1915-1929	.319	.531	4860	1552	285	77	196	860	913	566	287	154

NAME	YRS	BA	SA	AB	H	2B	3B	HR	R	RBI	BB	SO	SB
Ted Williams	1939-1960	.344	.634	7706	2654	525	71	521	1798	1839	2019	709	24
Archie Wilson	1951-1952	.221	.300	140	31	5	3	0	9	17	7	14	0
Gary Wilson	1902	.125	.125	8	1	0	0	0	0	1	0	0	0
Les Wilson	1911	.000	.000	7	0	0	0	0	0	0	2	0	0
Squanto Wilson	1911-1914	.188	.188	16	3	0	0	0	2	0	2	0	0
Herm Winningham	1984-1992	.239	.334	1888	452	69	26	19	212	147	157	417	105
Tom Winsett	1930-1938	.237	.341	566	134	25	5	8	60	76	69	113	3
Larry Wolfe	1977-1980	.230	.338	361	83	16	1	7	43	50	54	53	0
Harry Wolter	1907-1917	.270	.369	1905	514	69	42	12	286	167	268	90	95
Smoky Joe Wood	1908-1922	.283	.411	1952	553	118	30	24	267	325	208	189	23
Ken Wood	1948-1953	.224	.393	995	223	52	7	34	110	143	102	141	1
Tom Wright	1948-1956	.255	.355	685	175	28	11	6	75	99	76	123	2

Y-Z

NAME	YRS	BA	SA	AB	H	2B	3B	HR	R	RBI	BB	SO	SB
Carl Yastrzemski	1961-1983	.285	.462	11988	3419	646	59	452	1816	1844	1845	1393	168
Steve Yerkes	1909-1916	.268	.350	2520	676	125	32	6	307	254	207	62	54
Rudy York	1934-1948	.275	.483	5891	1621	291	52	277	876	1152	791	867	38
Al Zarilla	1943-1953	.276	.405	3535	975	186	43	61	507	456	415	382	33
Norm Zauchin	1951-1959	.233	.408	1038	242	28	2	50	134	159	137	226	5
Bob Zupcic	1991-1994	.250	.346	795	199	47	4	7	99	80	57	137	7

PITCHERS

W-	Wins	SO -	Strike Outs
H -	Hits Allowed	ERA-	Earned Run Average
L-	Losses	ShO -	Shut Outs
BB -	Bases On Balls Allowed	SAVES-	Games Saved in Relief
PCT-	Winning Average	G-	Game Appearances
IP	Innings Pitched		

A

NAME	YRS	W	L	PCT	ERA	G	IP	H	BB	SO	ShO	SAVES
Don Aase	1977-1990	66	60	.524	3.80	448	1109	1085	457	641	5	82
Bob Adams	1925	0	0	.000	7.94	2	5	10	3	1	0	0
Doc Adkins	1902-1903	1	1	.500	5.00	6	27	40	12	3	0	1
Rick Aguilera	1985-2000	86	81	.515	3.57	732	1291	1233	351	1030	0	318
Nick Altrock	1898-1924	83	75	.525	2.67	218	1515	1455	272	425	16	7
Larry Anderson	1975-1994	40	39	.506	3.15	699	996	932	311	758	4	49
Fred Anderson	1909-1918	53	58	.477	2.86	178	986	912	247	514	11	8
Ivy Andrews	1931-1938	50	59	.459	4.14	249	1041	1151	342	257	2	8
Luis Aponte	1980-1984	9	6	.600	3.27	110	220	222	68	113	0	7
Frank Arellanes	1908-1910	24	22	.522	2.28	74	410	358	85	148	2	8
Rolando Arrojo	1988-Cont.	36	39	.480	4.50	129	619	632	228	461	2	5
Jim Atkins	1950-1952	0	1	.000	3.60	4	15	15	11	2	0	0
Eldon Auker	1933-1942	130	101	.563	4.42	333	1963	2230	706	594	14	2
Steve Avery	1990-1999	94	83	.531	4.17	278	1539	1510	562	974	6	0

B

NAME	YRS	W	L	PCT	ERA	G	IP	H	BB	SO	ShO	SAVES
Lore Bader	1912-1918	5	3	.625	2.51	22	75	83	36	27	1	1
Jim Bagby Jr.	1938-1947	97	96	.503	3.96	303	1666	1815	608	431	13	9
Cory Bailey	1933-1995	0	2	.000	5.70	19	24	24	17	20	0	0
Al Baker	1938	0	0		9.39	3	8	13	2	2	0	0

The Red Sox Encyclopedia

Scott Bankhead	1986-1995	57	48	.543	4.18	267	901	876	289	614	3	1
Willie Banks	1991	31	38	.449	4.85	152	571	600	288	402	1	1
Frank Barberich	1907-1910	1	1	.500	6.23	4	17	26	7	1	0	0
Brian Bark	1995	0	0		0.00	3	3	2	1	0	0	0
Brian Barkley	1998	0	0		9.82	6	11	16	9	2	0	0
Steve Barr	1974-1976	3	7	.300	5.14	24	84	88	57	32	0	0
Frank Barrett	1939-1950	15	17	.469	3.51	104	218	211	90	90	0	12
Ed Barry	1905-1907	1	6	.143	3.53	12	79	74	25	34	0	0
Frank Baumann	1955-1965	45	38	.542	4.11	241	797	856	300	384	4	13
Bill Bayne	1919-1930	31	32	.492	4.82	198	661	710	296	259	2	8
Rod Beck	1991-Cont.	35	41	.461	3.28	642	709	651	171	597	0	266
Hugh Bedient	1912-1915	58	53	.523	3.08	179	937	930	236	420	4	19
Stan Belinda	1989-2000	41	37	.526	4.15	585	685	590	285	622	0	79
Gary Bell	1958-1969	121	117	.508	3.68	519	2015	1794	842	1378	9	51
Dennis Bennett	1962-1968	43	47	.478	3.69	182	863	850	281	572	6	6
Frank Bennett	1927-1928	0	1	.000	2.70	5	13	16	6	1	0	0
Al Benton	1934-1952	98	88	.527	3.66	455	1689	1672	733	697	10	66
Charlie Beville	1901	0	2	.000	4.00	2	9	8	11	2	0	0
Jack Billingham	1968-1980	145	113	.562	3.83	476	2231	2272	750	1141	27	15
Doug Bird	1973-1983	73	60	.549	3.99	432	1213	1273	296	680	3	60
Dave Black	1914-1923	8	10	.444	3.18	43	181	166	52	72	0	0
Clarence Blethen	1923-1929	0	0	.000	7.32	7	20	33	10	2	0	0
Mike Boddicker	1980-1993	134	116	.536	3.80	342	2124	2082	721	1330	16	3
Larry Boemer	1932	0	4	.000	5.02	21	61	71	37	19	0	0
Bobby Bolin	1961-1973	88	75	.540	3.40	495	1576	1364	597	1175	10	50
Tom Bolton	1987-1994	31	34	.477	4.56	209	540	614	244	336	0	1
Toby Borland	1994-1998	9	6	.600	3.81	146	55	201	30	33	0	7
Tom Borland	1960-1961	0	4	.000	6.75	27	52	70	23	32	0	3
Stew Bowers	1935-1936	2	1	.667	4.60	15	29	36	19	5	0	0
Joe Bowman	1932-1945	77	96	.445	4.40	298	1466	1656	484	502	5	11
Ted Bowsfield	1958-1964	37	39	.487	4.35	215	662	699	259	326	4	6
Oil Can Boyd	1982-1991	78	77	.503	4.04	214	1390	1427	368	799	10	0
Herb Bradley	1927-1929	1	4	.200	5.93	24	74	87	25	20	1	0
King Brady	1905-1912	3	2	.600	3.08	8	50	64	10	20	1	0
Mark Brandenburg	1995-1997	5	8	.385	4.49	97	144	161	56	121	0	0
Darrell Brandon	1966-1973	28	37	.431	4.04	228	590	556	275	354	2	13
Ken Brett	1967-1981	83	85	.494	3.93	349	1526	1490	562	807	9	11
Tom Brewer	1954-1961	91	82	.526	4.00	241	1509	1478	669	733	13	3
Ralph Brickner	1952	3	1	.750	2.18	14	33	32	11	9	0	1
Jim Brillheart	1922-1931	8	9	.471	4.19	86	286	314	137	98	0	1
Dick Brodowski	1952-1959	9	11	.450	4.76	72	216	212	124	85	0	5
Hal Brown	1951-1964	85	92	.480	3.81	358	1680	1677	389	710	13	11
Lloyd Brown	1925-1940	91	105	.464	4.20	44	1693	1899	590	510	10	21
Mace Brown	1935-1946	76	57	.571	3.47	387	1075	1125	388	435	3	48
Mike Brown	1982-1987	12	20	.375	5.75	61	254	324	102	115	1	0
Kirk Bullinger	1998-2000	1	0	1.000	7.30	15	12	20	2	6	0	0
Fred Burchell	1903-1909	13	15	.464	2.93	49	286	268	92	124	0	0
Tom Burgmeier	1968-1984	79	55	.590	3.23	745	1258	1231	384	584	0	102
Jim Burton	1975-1977	0	1	.000	9.00	30	56	60	20	42	0	1
Joe Bush	1912-1928	195	183	.516	3.51	489	3092	3001	1263	1319	35	20
Jack Bushelman	1909-1912	1	2	.333	3.38	7	27	24	19	13	0	0
Frank Bushey	1927-1930	0	1	.000	6.32	12	33	36	17	4	0	0
Bill Butland	1940-1947	9	3	.750	3.88	32	151	138	56	62	2	1
Bud Byerly	1943-1960	22	22	.500	3.70	237	492	519	167	209	0	14

C

NAME	YRS	W	L	PCT	ERA	G	IP	H	BB	SO	ShO	SAVES
Ray Caldwell	1910-1921	133	120	.526	3.21	343	2242	2085	737	1005	20	9
Bill Campbell	1973-1987	83	68	.550	3.55	700	1229	1139	495	864	1	126
Hector Carrasco	1994-2000	24	33	.421	4.10	402	493	479	249	385	0	14
Ed Carroll	1929	1	0	1.000	5.61	24	67	77	20	13	0	0
Jerry Casale	1958-1962	17	24	.415	5.08	96	370	376	204	207	3	1

Name	YRS	W	L	PCT	ERA	G	IP	H	BB	SO	ShO	SAVES
Joe Cascarella	1934-1938	27	48	.360	4.84	143	541	602	267	192	3	8
Carlos Castillo	1997-Cont.	10	7	.588	5.04	111	211	210	82	130	0	1
Frank Castillo	1991-Cont.	76	88	.463	4.49	258	1427	1481	442	985	3	1
Rex Cecil	1944-1945	6	10	.375	5.18	18	106	118	60	63	0	0
Bob Chakales	1951-1957	15	25	.375	4.54	171	420	445	225	187	1	10
Esty Chaney	1913-1914	0	0	.000	7.20	2	5	8	4	1	1	0
Pete Charton	1964	0	2	.000	5.26	25	65	67	24	37	0	0
Ken Chase	1936-1943	53	84	.387	4.27	188	1165	1188	694	582	4	1
Charlie Chech	1905-1909	33	31	.516	2.52	94	606	602	162	187	6	3
Robinson Checo	1997	1	1	.500	3.38	5	13	12	3	14	0	0
Jack Chesbro	1899-1909	198	132	.600	2.68	392	2897	2642	690	1265	35	5
Nels Chittum	1958-1960	3	1	.750	3.84	40	68	68	24	30	0	0
Jin Ho Cho	1998-1999	2	6	.250	6.52	13	58	73	11	31	0	0
Eddie Cicotte	1905-1920	208	149	.583	2.37	502	3224	2897	827	1374	35	25
Galen Cisco	1961-1969	25	56	.309	4.56	192	659	681	281	325	3	2
Otie Clark	1945	4	4	.500	3.06	12	82	86	19	20	1	0
Mark Clear	1979-1990	71	49	.592	3.85	481	804	674	554	804	0	0
Roger Clemens	1984-Cont.	213	118	.644	2.89	417	3040	2563	924	2882	42	0
Lance Clemons	1971-1974	2	1	.667	6.11	19	35	42	21	23	0	0
Reggie Cleveland	1969-1981	105	106	.498	4.02	428	1809	1843	543	930	12	25
Tex Clevenger	1954-1962	36	37	.493	4.18	307	695	706	298	361	2	30
Bill Clowers	1926	0	0		0.00	2	2	2	0	0	0	0
Ray Collins	1909-1915	84	62	.575	2.51	199	1345	1251	271	513	19	4
Rip Collins	1920-1931	108	82	.568	3.99	311	1712	1795	684	569	16	5
Ralph Comstock	1913-1918	11	14	.440	3.72	40	203	222	39	100	0	4
David Cone	1986-Cont.	193	123	.611	3.44	445	2881	2484	1124	2655	22	1
Gene Conley	1952-1963	91	96	.487	3.82	276	1589	1606	511	888	13	9
Ed Connolly	1964-1967	6	12	.333	5.88	42	130	143	98	118	1	0
Guy Cooper	1914-1915	1	0	1.000	5.33	11	27	26	13	8	0	0
Rheal Cormier	1991-Cont.	48	48	.500	4.18	353	898	955	200	544	1	1
Jim Corsi	1988-1999	22	24	.478	3.25	368	481	450	191	290	0	7
Fritz Coumbe	1914-1921	38	38	.500	2.79	193	761	773	217	212	4	13
Paxton Crawford	2000	2	1	.667	3.41	7	29	25	13	17	0	0
Steve Crawford	1980-1991	30	23	.566	4.17	277	563	643	186	320	0	19
Bob Cremins	1927	0	0	.000	5.06	4	5	5	3	0	0	0
Zach Crouch	1988	0	0	.000	6.75	3	1	4	2	0	0	0
Rick Croushore	1998-2000	5	11	.313	4.88	111	142	131	83	149	0	11
Ray Culp	1963-1973	122	101	.547	3.58	322	1897	1677	752	1411	22	1
Nig Cuppy	1892-1901	162	98	.623	3.48	302	2284	2520	609	504	9	5
Steve Curry	1988	0	0	.000	8.18	3	11	15	14	4	0	0
John Curtis	1970-1984	89	97	.478	3.96	438	1641	1695	669	825	14	11

D

NAME	YRS	W	L	PCT	ERA	G	IP	H	BB	SO	ShO	SAVES
Danny Darwin	1978-1998	171	182	.484	3.84	716	3017	2951	874	1942	9	32
Cot Deal	1947-1954	3	4	.429	6.55	45	89	111	48	34	0	1
Ike Delock	1952-1963	84	75	.528	4.03	329	1238	1236	530	672	6	31
Brian Denman	1982	3	4	.429	4.78	9	49	55	9	9	1	0
Mel Deutsch	1946	0	0	.000	5.68	3	6	7	3	2	0	0
Hal Deviney	1920	0	0	.000	15.00	1	3	7	2	0	0	0
Emerson Dickman	1936-1941	22	15	.595	5.33	125	350	403	153	126	1	8
Bill Dinneen	1898-1909	170	177	.490	3.01	391	3075	2957	829	1127	24	7
Ray Dobens	1929	0	0	.000	3.81	11	28	32	9	4	0	0
Joe Dobson	1939-1954	137	103	.571	3.62	414	2170	2048	851	992	22	18
Sam Dodge	1921-1922	0	0	.000	5.14	4	7	12	4	3	0	0
John Doherty	1992-1996	32	31	.508	4.87	148	521	613	140	177	2	9
Pete Donohue	1921-1932	134	118	.532	3.87	348	2112	2439	422	571	16	12
John Dopson	1985-1994	30	47	.390	4.27	144	725	752	264	386	1	1
Harry Dorish	1947-1956	45	43	.511	3.83	323	834	850	301	332	2	44
Jim Dorsey	1980-1985	1	3	.250	11.63	8	24	43	20	14	0	0
Dick Drago	1969-1981	108	117	.480	3.62	519	1876	1901	558	987	10	58
Clem Driesewerd	1944-1948	6	8	.429	4.54	46	141	160	39	39	0	2
Bob Duliba	1959-1967	17	12	.586	3.47	176	257	257	96	129	0	14
George Dumont	1915-1919	10	23	.303	2.85	77	347	294	130	128	4	3

| Ed Durham | 1929-1933 | 29 | 44 | .397 | 4.45 | 143 | 642 | 677 | 202 | 204 | 3 | I |

E

NAME	YRS	W	L	PCT	ERA	G	IP	H	BB	SO	ShO	SAVES
Amold Earley	1960-1067	12	20	.375	4.48	223	381	400	184	310	0	14
Dennis Eckersley	1975-1998	197	171	.535	3.50	1071	3286	3076	738	2401	20	390
Howard Ehmke	1915-1930	166	166	.500	3.75	427	2821	2373	1042	1030	20	14
Hack Eibel	1920	0	0		3.48	3	10	10	3	5	0	0
Dick Ellsworth	1958-1971	115	137	.456	3.72	407	2156	2274	595	1140	9	5
Steve Ellsworth	1988	I	6	.143	6.75	8	36	47	16	16	0	0
Todd Erdos	1997-Cont.	2	0	1.000	5.57	63	94	105	45	58	0	2
Vaughn Eshelman	1995-1997	15	9	.625	6.07	83	212	256	111	118	0	0
Bill Evans	1949-1951	0	I	.000	4.98	13	22	21	16	4	0	0

F

NAME	YRS	W	L	PCT	ERA	G	IP	H	BB	SO	ShO	SAVES
Steve Farr	1984-1994	48	45	.516	3.25	509	824	751	334	668	I	132
Jeff Fassero	1991-Cont.	104	95	.523	3.87	486	1669	1658	580	1405	2	22
Alex Ferguson	1918-1929	61	85	.418	4.93	256	1239	1453	481	397	2	10
Wes Ferrell	1927-1941	193	128	.601	4.04	374	2623	2849	1040	985	17	13
Boo Ferriss	1945-1950	65	30	.684	3.64	144	880	914	314	296	12	8
Joel Finch	1979	0	3	.000	4.89	15	57	65	25	25	0	0
Tom Fine	1947-1950	I	3	.250	6.81	23	73	94	44	16	0	0
Gar Finnvold	1994	0	4	.000	5.94	8	36	45	15	17	0	0
Hank Fischer	1962-1967	30	39	.435	4.23	168	547	587	174	369	5	7
Bill Fleming	1940-1946	16	21	.432	3.79	123	442	442	193	167	3	3
Bryce Florie	1994-Cont.	20	24	.455	4.47	261	494	500	243	395	0	2
Ben Flowers	1951-1956	3	7	.300	4.49	76	168	190	54	86	I	3
Frank Foreman	1884-1901	97	92	.513	3.94	229	1727	1859	659	591	8	4
Happy Foreman	1924-1926	0	0	.000	3.18	6	11	10	9	4	0	0
Mike Fornieles	1952-1963	63	64	.496	3.96	432	1157	1165	421	576	4	55
Gary Fortune	1916-1920	0	5	.000	6.61	20	78	89	46	23	0	0
Tony Fossas	1988-1999	17	24	.415	3.90	567	416	434	180	324	0	7
Rube Foster	1913-1917	58	34	.630	2.35	138	843	724	305	297	15	3
Ray Francis	1922-1925	12	28	.300	4.65	82	337	409	110	96	2	3
Hersh Freeman	1952-1958	30	16	.652	3.74	204	359	387	109	158	0	37
Todd Frohwirth	1987-1996	20	19	.513	3.60	284	417	389	172	259	0	11
Oscar Fuhr	1921-1925	3	12	.200	6.35	63	176	249	69	59	I	0
Curt Fullerton	1921-1933	10	37	.213	5.11	115	423	483	211	104	0	3

G

NAME	YRS	W	L	PCT	ERA	G	IP	H	BB	SO	ShO	SAVES
Rich Gale	1978-1984	55	56	.495	4.53	195	971	997	457	518	5	2
Denny Galehouse	1934-1949	109	118	.480	3.98	375	2003	2148	735	851	17	13
Ed Gallagher	1932	0	3	.000	12.55	9	24	30	28	6	0	0
Rich Garces	1990-Cont.	23	9	.719	3.49	261	320	269	152	280	0	7
Mike Gardiner	1990-1995	17	27	.386	5.21	136	394	420	161	239	0	5
Wes Gardner	1984-1991	18	30	.375	4.90	189	466	476	218	358	0	14
Mike Garman	1969-1978	22	27	.449	3.63	303	434	411	202	213	0	42
Cliff Garrison	1928	0	0	.000	7.88	6	16	22	6	0	0	0
Milt Gaston	1924-1934	97	164	.372	4.55	355	2105	2338	836	615	10	8
Norwood Gibson	1903-1906	34	32	.515	2.93	85	609	525	208	258	3	0
Bob Giliespie	1944-1950	5	13	.278	5.07	58	202	223	102	59	0	0
Ralph Glaze	1906-1908	15	21	.417	2.89	61	340	303	85	137	I	0
Joe Gonzales	1937	I	2	.333	4.35	8	31	37	11	11	0	0
Tom Gordon	1988-Cont.	105	98	.517	4.13	491	1690	1548	823	1498	4	98
Dave Gray	1964	0	0	.000	9.00	9	13	18	20	17	0	0
Jeff Gray	1988-1991	4	7	.364	3.33	96	122	104	29	96	0	10

NAME	YRS	W	L	PCT	ERA	G	IP	H	BB	SO	ShO	SAVES
Vean Gregg	1911-1925	92	63	.594	2.70	239	1392	1240	552	720	14	12
Marty Griffin	1928	0	3	.000	5.02	11	38	42	17	9	0	0
Guido Grilli	1966	0	2	.000	7.08	22	20	24	20	12	0	1
Marv Grissom	1946-1959	47	45	.511	3.41	356	810	771	343	459	3	58
Kip Gross	1990-2000	7	8	.467	3.90	73	148	168	66	81	0	0
Lefty Grove	1925-1941	300	141	.680	3.06	616	3941	3849	1187	2266	35	55
Ken Grundt	1996-1997	0	0		10.80	3	3	6	0	0	0	0
Randy Gumpert	1936-1952	51	59	.464	4.17	261	1053	1099	346	352	6	7
Eric Gunderson	1990-2000	8	11	.421	4.95	254	229	274	84	137	0	2
Mark Guthrie	1989-Cont.	44	48	.478	4.20	632	888	914	340	710	1	13

H

NAME	YRS	W	L	PCT	ERA	G	IP	H	BB	SO	ShO	SAVES
Casey Hageman	1911-1914	3	7	.300	3.07	32	120	108	40	47	0	1
Chris Hammond	1990-1998	46	55	.455	4.54	191	844	902	313	513	3	1
Erik Hanson	1988-1998	89	84	.514	4.15	245	1555	1604	504	1175	5	0
Tim Harikkala	1995-1999	1	2	.333	9.15	9	21	26	9	9	0	0
Harry Harper	1913-1923	57	76	.429	2.87	219	1256	1100	582	623	12	5
Bill Harris	1923-1938	24	22	.522	3.92	121	433	467	109	149	2	8
Greg Harris	1986-1995	45	64	.413	3 98	243	909	883	303	605	2	16
Joe Harris	1905-1907	3	30	.091	3.35	45	317	284	88	137	1	2
Mickey Harris	1940-1952	59	71	.454	4.18	271	1050	1097	455	534	2	21
Reggie Harris	1990-1999	2	3	.400	4.91	86	121	106	81	95	0	0
Slim Harriss	1920-1928	95	135	.413	4.25	349	1750	1963	630	644	6	16
Jack Harshman	1952-1960	69	65	.515	3.50	217	1169	1025	539	741	12	7
Chuck Hartenstein	1966-1972	17	19	.472	4.52	187	297	317	89	135	0	23
Mike Hartley	1989-1995	19	13	.594	3.70	202	319	287	139	259	1	4
Charlie Hartman	1908	0	0	.000	4.50	1	2	1	2	1	0	0
Herb Hash	1940-1941	8	7	.533	4.98	38	128	130	91	39	1	4
Andy Hassler	1971-1985	44	71	.383	3.83	387	1123	1125	520	630	5	29
Clem Hausmann	1944-1949	9	14	.391	4.21	64	263	270	131	73	2	4
Bob Heffner	1963-1968	11	21	.344	4.51	114	353	360	107	241	2	6
Randy Heflin	1945-1946	4	11	.267	3.86	25	117	118	73	45	2	0
Fred Heimach	1920-1933	62	69	.473	4.46	296	1289	1510	360	334	5	7
Bill Henry	1952-1969	46	50	.479	3.26	527	913	842	296	621	2	90
Butch Henry	1992-1999	33	33	.500	3.83	148	621	677	149	345	2	7
Jim Henry	1936-1939	6	2	.750	4.77	33	115	114	59	51	0	1
Ramon Hernandez	1967-1977	23	15	.605	3.03	337	431	399	135	255	0	46
Tom Herrin	1954	1	2	.333	7.31	14	28	34	22	8	0	0
Joe Hesketh	1984-1994	60	47	.561	3.78	339	962	947	378	726	2	21
Eric Hetzel	1989-1990	3	7	.300	6.12	21	85	100	49	53	0	0
Joe Heving	1930-1945	76	48	.613	3.90	430	1038	1136	380	429	3	63
Dave Hillman	1955-1962	21	37	.362	3.87	188	624	639	185	296	1	3
Paul Hinrichs	1951	0	0	.000	21.60	4	3	7	4	1	0	0
Harley Hisner	1951	0	1	.000	4.50	1	6	7	4	3	0	0
George Hockett	1934-1935	4	4	.500	4.08	26	88	105	18	25	2	0
Billy Hoeft	1952-1966	97	101	.490	3.94	505	1847	1820	685	1140	17	33
Ken Holcombe	1945-1953	18	32	.360	3.98	99	375	377	170	118	2	2
Tom House	1971-1978	29	23	.558	3.79	289	536	516	182	261	0	33
Chris Howard	1993-1995	2	0	1.000	3.13	44	46	40	16	25	0	1
Les Howe	1923-1924	2	0	1.000	23.38	16	37	34	9	10	0	0
Peter Hoy	1992	0	0	.000	7.36	5	4	8	2	2	0	0
Waite Hoyt	1918-1938	237	182	.566	3.59	674	3763	4037	1003	1206	26	52
Joe Hudson	1995-1998	6	7	.462	4.82	102	127	151	73	62	0	2
Sid Hudson	1940-1954	104	152	.406	4.28	380	2151	2384	835	734	11	13
Ed Hughes	1905-1906	3	2	.600	4.78	8	43	53	12	11	0	0
Long Tom Hughes	1900-1913	132	173	.433	3.09	399	2644	2610	853	1368	25	17
Tex Hughson	1941-1949	96	54	.640	2.94	225	1376	1270	372	693	19	17
Bill Humphrey	1938	0	0	.000	9.00	2	2	5	1	0	0	0
Ben Hunt	1910-1913	2	4	.333	3.95	9	55	51	29	25	0	0
Tom Hurd	1954-1956	13	10	.565	3.96	99	186	177	97	96	0	11
Bruce Hurst	1980-1994	145	113	.562	3.92	379	2417	2463	740	1689	23	0

Bert Husting	1900-1902	24	21	.533	4.16	69	437	499	199	122	I	I

I-J

NAME	YRS	W	L	PCT	ERA	G	IP	H	BB	SO	ShO	SAVES
Daryl Irvine	1990-1992	4	5	.444	5.68	41	63	71	33	27	0	0
Pete Jablonski	1927-1945	57	66	.463	4.30	341	1141	1187	486	420	6	26
(Later played as Pete Appleton)												
Beany Jacobson	1904-1907	23	46	.333	3.19	88	612	618	148	195	I	0
Charlie Jamerson	1924	0	0	.000	18.00	I	I	I	3	0	0	0
Bill James	1911-1919	65	71	.478	3.20	203	1180	1114	576	408	9	5
Ray Jarvis	1969-1970	5	7	.417	4.64	44	116	122	57	44	0	I
Ferguson Jenkins	1965-1983	284	226	.557	3.34	664	4500	4142	997	3192	49	7
Adam Johnson	1914-1918	23	30	.434	2.92	72	450	401	151	169	6	2
Earl Johnson	1940-1951	40	32	.556	4.30	179	546	556	272	250	4	17
Hank Johnson	1925-1939	63	56	.529	4.75	249	1066	1107	567	568	4	II
John Henry Johnson	1978-1987	26	33	.441	3.89	214	603	585	250	407	2	9
Vic Johnson	1944-1946	6	8	.429	5.06	42	126	152	69	31	I	2
Joel Johnston	1991-1995	3	5	.375	4.31	59	86	66	37	61	0	2
Rick Jones	1976-1978	6	9	.400	4.04	37	158	197	70	72	0	0
Sad Sam Jones	1914-1935	229	217	.513	3.84	647	3883	4084	1396	1223	36	31
Oscar Judd	1941-1948	40	51	440	3.90	161	772	744	397	304	4	7

K

NAME	YRS	W	L	PCT	ERA	G	IP	H	BB	SO	ShO	SAVES
Rudy Kallio	1918-1925	9	18	.333	4.17	49	222	234	93	75	2	I
Ed Karger	1906-1911	48	67	.417	2.79	164	1089	1006	313	410	9	3
Andy Karl	1943-1947	19	23	.452	3.51	191	423	451	130	107	0	26
Al Kellett	1923-1924	0	I	.000	8.10	6	10	II	10	I	0	0
Win Kellum	1901-1905	20	16	.556	3.19	48	347	337	63	97	2	2
Ed Kelly	1914	0	0	.000	0.00	3	2	I	I	4	0	0
Russ Kemmerer	1954-1963	43	59	.422	4.46	302	1067	1144	389	505	2	8
Bill Kennedy	1948-1957	15	28	.349	4.71	172	465	497	289	256	0	II
Dana Kiecker	1990-1991	10	12	.455	4.68	50	192	201	77	114	0	0
Joe Kiefer	1920-1926	0	5	.000	6.16	15	50	56	30	9	0	0
Leo Kiely	1951-1960	26	27	.491	3.37	209	523	562	189	212	I	29
Jack Killilay	1911	4	2	.667	3.54	14	61	65	36	28	0	0
Sun-Woo Kim	2001-Cont.	0	2	.000	5.83	20	42	54	21	27	0	0
Ellis Kinder	1946-1957	102	71	.590	3.43	484	1480	1421	529	749	10	102
Walt Kinney	1918-1923	II	20	.355	3.59	63	291	274	136	129	I	2
Bruce Kison	1971-1985	115	88	.567	3.66	380	1809	1693	662	1073	7	12
Bob Kline	1930-1934	0	0	.000	27.00	I	I	4	I	0	0	0
Ron Kline	1952-1970	114	144	.442	3.75	736	2078	2113	731	989	8	108
Bob Klinger	1938-1947	66	61	.520	3.68	265	1090	1153	358	357	7	23
Brent Knackert	1990-1996	I	2	.333	7.Q4	32	47	66	28	33	0	0
Hal Kolstad	1962-1963	0	4	.000	6.59	34	72	81	41	42	0	2
Cal Koonce	1962-1971	47	49	.490	3.78	334	971	972	368	504	3	24
Jack Kramer	1939-1951	95	103	.480	4.24	322	1637	1761	682	613	14	7
Len Krausse	1961-1974	68	91	.428	4.00	321	1284	1205	493	721	5	21
Rick Kreuger	1975-1978	2	2	.500	4.47	17	44	42	20	20	0	0
Rube Kroh	1906-1912	14	9	.609	2.29	36	216	182	67	92	3	0

L

NAME	YRS	W	L	PCT	ERA	G	IP	H	BB	SO	ShO	SAVES
Kerry Lacy	1996-1997	3	I	.750	5.59	44	56	75	30	27	0	3
Jack LaMabe	1962-1968	33	41	.446	4.24	285	711	753	238	434	8	5
Dennis Lamp	1977-1992	96	96	.500	3.93	639	1831	1975	549	857	7	35
Bill Landis	1963-1969	9	8	.529	4.46	102	170	154	91	135	0	4
John LaRose	1978	0	0	.000	22.50	I	2	3	3	0	0	0

Bill Lee	1989-1982	119	90	.569	3.62	416	1945	2122	531	713	10	19
Sang-Hoon Lee	2000	0	0		3.09	9	12	11	5	6	0	0
Bill Lefebvre	1938-1944	5	5	.500	5.03	36	132	162	51	36	0	3
Regis Leheny	1932	0	0	.000	16.88	2	3	5	3	1	0	0
John Leister	1987-1990	0	2	.000	8.50	10	36	56	16	19	0	0
Dutch Leonard	1913-1925	139	112	.554	2.77	331	2190	2025	663	1158	33	13
Louis LeRoy	1905-1910	3	1	.750	3.22	15	73	66	15	39	0	1
Ted Lewis	1896-1901	94	64	.595	3.53	183	1405	1379	511	378	7	4
Derek Lilliquist	1989-1996	25	34	.424	4.13	262	483	532	134	261	1	17
Hod Lisenbee	1927-1945	37	58	.389	4.81	207	969	1076	314	253	4	1
Dick Littlefield	1950-1958	33	54	.379	4.71	243	761	750	413	495	2	9
Skip Lockwood	1969-1980	57	97	.370	3.55	420	1236	1130	490	829	5	68
Tim Lollar	1980-1986	47	52	.475	4.27	199	906	841	480	600	4	4
Jim Lonborg	1965-1979	157	137	.534	3.86	425	2465	2400	823	1475	15	4
Brian Looney	1993-1995	0	1	.000	11.37	7	13	24	6	11	0	0
Joe Lucey	1925	0	1	.000	9.00	7	11	18	14	2	0	0
Lou Lucier	1943-1945	3	5	.375	3.81	33	102	118	47	31	0	1
Del Lundgren	1924-1927	5	15	.250	6.58	55	182	220	114	53	2	0
Sparky Lyle	1967-1982	99	76	.566	2.88	899	1391	1292	481	873	0	238

M

NAME	YRS	W	L	PCT	ERA	G	IP	H	BB	SO	ShO	SAVES
Danny MacFayden	1926-1943	132	159	.454	3.96	465	2706	2984	872	797	18	9
Bill MacLeod	1962	0	1	.000	5.40	2	2	4	1	2	0	0
Keith MacWhorter	1980	0	3	.000	5.57	14	42	46	18	21	0	0
Mike Maddux	1986-2000	39	37	.513	4.05	472	862	873	284	564	1	20
Pete Magrini	1966	0	1	.000	9.82	3	7	8	8	3	0	0
Ron Mahay	1997-Cont.	7	2	.778	4.08	103	132	124	69	107	0	2
Pat Mahomes	1992-Cont.	41	37	.526	5.57	283	654	683	363	416	0	5
Chris Mahoney	1910	0	1	.000	3.27	2	11	16	5	6	0	1
Paul Maloy	1913	0	0	.000	27.00	2	2	2	1	0	0	0
Josias Manzanillo	1991-1995	5	5	.500	4.55	77	111	103	50	95	0	3
Phil Marchildon	1940-1950	68	75	.476	3.93	185	1214	1084	684	481	6	2
Johnny Marcum	1933-1939	65	63	.508	4.66	195	1099	1269	344	392	8	7
Juan Marichal	1960-1975	243	142	.631	2.89	471	3509	3153	709	2303	52	2
Pedro Martinez	1992-Cont.	132	59	.691	2.66	296	1693	1262	467	1981	15	3
Ramon Martinez	1988-Cont.	135	88	.605	3.67	301	1896	1691	795	1427	20	0
Walt Masterson	1939-1956	78	100	.438	4.15	399	1650	1613	886	815	15	20
Bill Matthews	1909	0	0	.000	3.24	5	17	16	10	3	0	0
Carl Mays	1915-1929	207	126	.622	2.92	490	3020	2912	734	862	29	31
Dick McCabe	1918-1922	1	1	.500	3.46	6	13	17	2	4	0	0
Windy McCall	1948-1957	11	15	.423	4.22	134	254	249	103	144	0	12
Tom McCarthy	1985-1989	3	2	.600	3.61	40	85	88	26	34	0	1
Mickey McDermott	1948-1961	69	69	.500	3.91	291	1317	1161	840	757	11	14
Allen McDill	1997-Cont.	0	0		7.79	38	35	38	18	28	0	0
Jim McDonald	1950-1958	24	27	.471	4.27	136	468	489	231	158	3	1
Lynn McGlothen	1972-1982	86	93	.480	3.98	318	1498	1553	572	939	13	2
Bob McGraw	1917-1929	26	38	.406	4.89	168	591	677	265	164	1	6
Marty McHale	1910-1916	11	30	.286	3.57	64	358	381	81	131	1	1
Archie McKain	1937-1943	26	21	.553	4.26	165	486	529	208	188	1	16
Jud McLaughlin	1931-1933	0	0	.000	10.27	16	24	42	17	4	0	0
Doc McMahon	1908	1	0	1.000	3.00	1	9	14	0	3	0	0
Don McMahon	1957-1974	90	68	.570	2.96	874	1311	1054	579	1003	0	153
Gordon McNaughton	1932	0	1	.000	6.43	6	21	21	22	6	0	0
Jose Melendez	1990-1994	16	14	.533	3.47	109	221	197	60	172	0	3
Mike Meola	1933-1936	0	3	.000	8.16	18	43	63	25	15	0	1
Kent Mercker	1989-2000	63	61	.508	4.31	301	1896	1691	795	1427	20	0
Spike Merena	1934	1	2	.333	2.92	4	25	20	16	7	1	0
Russ Meyer	1946-1959	94	73	.563	3.99	319	1531	1606	541	672	13	5
John Michaels	1932	1	6	.143	5.13	28	81	101	27	16	0	0
Dick Midkiff	1938	1	1	.500	5.09	13	35	43	21	10	0	0
Dick Mills	1970	0	0	.000	2.25	2	4	6	3	3	0	0

The Red Sox Encyclopedia

NAME	YRS	W	L	PCT	ERA	G	IP	H	BB	SO	ShO	SAVES
Rudy Minarcin	1955-1957	6	9	.400	4.66	70	170	169	89	70	1	3
Nate Minchey	1993-1994	3	5	.375	5.63	11	56	79	22	33	0	0
Charlie Mitchell	1984-1985	0	0	.000	4.00	12	18	19	6	9	0	0
Fred Mitchell	1901-1905	31	48	.392	4.10	97	718	806	303	216	2	1
Herb Moford	1955-1962	5	13	.278	5.03	50	157	143	64	78	0	3
Vince Molyneaux	1917-1918	1	0	1.000	4.41	13	33	21	28	5	0	0
Bill Monbouquette	1958-1968	114	112	.504	3.68	343	1961	1995	462	1122	18	3
Wilcy Moore	1927-1933	51	44	.537	3.69	261	692	732	232	204	2	49
Dave Morehead	1963-1970	40	64	.385	4.15	177	820	730	463	627	6	1
Roger Moret	1970-1978	47	27	.635	3.67	168	722	656	339	408	5	12
Cy Morgan	1903-1913	78	78	.500	2.51	210	1445	1180	578	667	15	3
Ed Morris	1922-1931	42	45	.483	4.19	140	674	702	293	256	2	6
Deacon Morrisey	1901-1902	1	3	.250	2.23	6	44	45	14		0	0
Kevin Morton	1991	6	5	.545	459	16	55	93	40	45	0	0
Earl Moseley	1913-1916	50	49	.505	3.01	136	856	775	340	469	12	2
Walter Moser	1906-1911	0	7	.000	4.58	14	71	97	30	30	0	0
Jamie Moyer	1986-Cont.	151	117	.563	4.22	405	2292	2388	664	1381	6	0
Gordy Mueller	1950	0	0	.000	10.29	8	7	11	13	1	0	0
Billy Muffett	1957-1962	16	23	.410	4.33	125	376	407	132	188	1	15
Joe Mulligan	1934	1	0	1.000	3.63	14	45	46	27	13	0	0
Frank Mulroney	1930	0	1	.000	3.00	2	3	3	0	2	0	0
Johnny Murphy	1932-1947	93	53	.637	3.50	415	1045	985	444	378	0	107
Rob Murphy	1985-1995	32	38	.457	3.64	597	623	598	247	520	0	30
Tom Murphy	1968-1979	68	101	.402	3.78	439	1443	1425	493	621	3	59
Walter Murphy	1931	0	0	.000	9.00	2	2	4	1	0	0	0
George Murray	1922-1933	20	26	.435	5.38	110	416	450	199	114	0	0
Matt Murray	1995	0	3	.000	9.64	6	14	21	8	4	0	0
Paul Musser	1912-1919	1	2	.333	3.35	12	40	42	24	24	0	1
Alex Mustaikis	1940	0	1	.000	9.00	6	15	15	15	6	0	0
Elmer Myers	1915-1922	55	72	.433	4.06	185	1101	1148	440	428	8	7

N

NAME	YRS	W	L	PCT	ERA	G	IP	H	BB	SO	ShO	SAVES
Chris Nabholz	1990-1995	37	35	.514	3.94	141	612	542	278	405	2	0
Judge Nagle	1911	5	3	.625	3.48	13	54	60	12	23	0	1
Mike Nagy	1969-1974	20	13	.606	4.15	87	419	431	210	170	1	0
Hal Neubauer	1925	1	0	1.000	12.19	7	10	17	11	4	0	0
Don Newhauser	1972-1974	4	3	.571	2.38	42	53	44	42	37	0	5
Bobo Newsom	1929-1953	211	222	.487	3.98	600	3759	3771	1732	2082	31	21
Dick Newsome	1941-1943	35	33	.515	4.50	85	526	575	214	138	4	0
Chet Nichols	1951-1964	34	36	.486	3.64	189	603	600	280	266	4	10
Al Nipper	1983-1990	46	50	.479	4.52	144	798	846	303	381	0	1
Merlin Nippert	1962	0	0	.000	4.50	4	6	4	4	3	0	0
Willard Nixon	1950-1958	69	72	.489	4.39	225	1234	1277	530	616	9	3
Hideo Nomo	1995-Cont.	82	71	.536	4.05	216	1349	1162	612	1432	7	0
Chet Nourse	1909	0	0	.000	720	3	S	5	5	3	0	0

O

NAME	YRS	W	L	PCT	ERA	G	IP	H	BB	SO	ShO	SAVES
Frank Oberlin	1906-1910	5	24	.172	3.77	44	227	236	88	80	0	0
Buck O'Brien	1911-1913	29	25	.537	2.63	64	432	391	159	204	4	0
Tomokazu Ohka	1999-Cont.	7	17	.292	4.66	43	189	225	61	116	0	0
Bobby Ojeda	1980-1994	115	98	.540	3.65	351	1884	1833	676	1128	16	1
Hank Olmstead	1905	1	2	.333	3.24	3	25	18	12	6	0	0
Ted Olson	1936-1938	1	1	.500	7.18	18	58	75	25	18	0	0
Emmett O'Neil	1943-1946	15	26	.366	4.76	66	356	348	260	144	2	0
Steve Ontiveros	1985-2000	34	31	.523	3.67	207	662	622	207	382	2	19
Dan Osinski	1962-1970	29	28	.509	3.34	324	590	556	264	400	2	18
Fritz Ostermueller	1934-1948	114	115	.498	3.99	390	2067	2170	835	774	11	15

P

NAME	YRS	W	L	PCT	ERA	G	IP	H	BB	SO	ShO	SAVES
Mike Palm	1948	0	0	.000	6.00	3	3	6	5	1	0	0
Al Papai	1948-1955	9	14	.391	5.37	88	240	281	138	70	0	4
Larry Pape	1909-1912	13	9	.591	2.80	51	283	287	91	84	2	3
Mel Parnell	1947-1956	123	75	.621	3.50	289	1753	1715	758	732	20	10
Stan Partenheimer	1944-1945	0	0	.000	6.91	9	14	15	18	6	0	0
Casey Patten	1901-1908	105	128	.451	3.36	270	2062	2154	557	757	17	5
Marty Pattin	1968-1980	114	109	.511	3.62	475	2038	1933	603	1179	14	25
Mike Paxton	1977-1980	30	24	.556	4.70	99	467	536	146	230	3	1
Alejandro Pena	1981-1996	56	52	.519	3.11	503	1057	959	331	839	7	74
Jesus Pena	1999-2000	2	1	.667	5.21	48	47	49	42	40	0	1
Juan Pena	1999	2	0	1.000	0.69	2	13	9	3	15	0	0
Brad Pennington	1993-1996	3	6	.333	6.90	78	75	66	86	83	0	4
Herb Pennock	1912-1934	240	162	.597	3.61	617	3558	3900	916	1227	35	33
Bill Pertica	1918-1923	22	18	.550	4.27	74	331	370	138	98	2	2
Gary Peters	1959-1972	124	103	.546	3.25	359	2081	1894	706	1420	23	5
Dan Petry	1979-1991	125	104	.546	3.94	370	2081	1984	852	1063	11	1
Ed Phillips	1970	0	2	.000	5.25	18	24	29	10	23	0	0
Hipolito Pichardo	1992-Cont.	50	43	.538	4.41	349	769	835	285	394	1	20
Jeff Pierce	1995	0	3	.000	6.60	12	15	16	14	12	0	0
Bill Piercy	1917-1926	27	43	.386	4.29	115	604	667	266	165	2	0
George Pipgras	1923-1935	102	73	.583	4.09	276	1488	1529	598	714	15	12
Juan Pizarro	1957-1974	131	105	.555	3.43	488	2034	1807	888	1522	17	28
Jeff Plympton	1991	0	0	.000	0.00	4	5	5	4	2	0	0
Jennings Poindexter	1936-1939	0	2	.000	4.83	14	41	42	31	14	0	0
Dick Pole	1973-1978	25	37	.403	5.05	122	531	607	209	239	1	1
Bob Porterfield	1948-1959	87	97	.473	3.79	318	1568	1571	553	572	23	8
Mark Portugal	1985-1999	109	95	.534	4.03	346	1826	1813	607	1134	4	5
Nels Potter	1936-1949	92	97	.487	3.99	349	1686	1721	582	747	6	22
George Prentiss	1901-1902	3	3	.500	5.31	11	58	76	21	10	0	0
Joe Price	1980-1990	45	49	.479	3.65	372	906	839	337	657	1	13
Tex Pruiett	1907-1908	4	18	.182	2.83	48	232	221	80	82	3	5
Bill Pulsipher	1995-Cont.	13	19	.406	5.13	101	323	356	139	201	0	0

Q

NAME	YRS	W	L	PCT	ERA	G	IP	H	BB	SO	ShO	SAVES
Paul Quantrill	1992-Cont.	52	64	.448	3.89	530	937	1084	262	555	1	18
Frank Quinn	1949-1950	0	0	.000	3.38	9	24	20	10	4	0	0
Jack Quinn	1909-1933	247	217	.532	3.27	755	3935	4234	860	1329	28	57

R

NAME	YRS	W	L	PCT	ERA	G	IP	H	BB	SO	ShO	SAVES
Dick Radatz	1962-1969	52	43	.547	3.13	381	694	532	296	745	0	122
Chuck Rainey	1979-1984	43	35	.551	4.50	141	670	738	287	300	6	2
Pat Rapp	1992-Cont.	70	91	.435	4.68	259	1387	1468	683	825	5	0
Jeff Reardon	1979-1994	73	77	.487	3.16	880	1132	1000	358	877	0	367
Jerry Reed	1981-1990	20	19	.513	3.94	238	480	477	172	248	0	18
Win Remmerswaal	1979-1980	3	1	.750	5.56	22	55	65	21	36	0	0
Steve Renko	1969-1983	134	146	.479	4.00	451	2493	2438	1010	1455	8	6
Carlos Reyes	1994-2000	20	33	.377	4.62	283	518	536	215	347	0	4
Gordon Rhodes	1929-1936	43	74	.368	4.85	200	1049	1196	477	356	1	5
Woody Rich	1939-1944	6	4	.600	5.06	33	117	127	50	42	0	1
Allen Ripley	1978-1982	23	27	.460	4.51	101	465	521	148	229	0	1
Walt Ripley	1935	0	0	.000	9.00	2	4	7	3	0	0	0
Jay Ritchie	1964-1968	8	13	.381	3.49	167	291	301	94	212	0	8
Jack Robinson	1949	0	0	.000	2.25	3	4	4	1	1	0	0
Mike Rochford	1988-1990	0	1	.000	9.58	8	10	18	9	2	0	0

Frank Rodriguez	1995-Cont.	29	39	.426	5.53	184	654	737	282	371	0	5
Lee Rogers	1938	1	3	.250	6.14	26	51	55	28	18	0	0
Gary Roggenburk	1963-1969	6	9	.400	3.64	79	126	132	64	56	0	7
Billy Rohr	1967-1968	3	3	.500	5.64	27	61	61	32	21	1	1
Vicente Romo	1968-1982	32	33	.492	3.36	335	646	569	280	416	1	52
Brian Rose	1997-Cont.	15	23	.395	5.86	68	284	331	110	151	0	0
Buster Ross	1924-1926	7	12	.368	5.01	64	190	233	74	31	1	1
Red Ruffing	1924-1947	273	225	.548	3.80	624	4344	4294	1541	1987	48	16
Allan Russell	1915-1925	71	77	.480	3.52	345	1393	1382	610	603	5	42
Jack Russell	1926-1940	85	141	.376	4.47	557	2050	2454	571	418	3	38
Jeff Russell	1983-1996	56	73	.434	3.75	589	1099	1065	415	693	2	186
Babe Ruth	1914-1933	94	46	.671	2.28	163	1221	974	441	488	17	4
Jack Ryan	1908-1911	5	5	.500	2.88	24	103	101	26	32	0	1
Ken Ryan	1992-1999	14	16	.467	3.91	240	286	266	164	225	0	30
Mike Ryba	1935-1946	52	34	.605	3.66	240	784	817	247	307	2	16

S

NAME	YRS	W	L	PCT	ERA	G	IP	H	BB	SO	ShO	SAVES
Bret Saberhagen	1984-Cont.	167	117	.588	3.34	399	2563	2452	471	1715	16	1
Bob Sadowski	1963-1966	20	27	.426	3.87	115	440	416	130	257	1	8
Joe Sambito	1976-1987	37	38	.493	3.04	461	628	562	195	489	1	84
Ken Sanders	1964-1976	29	45	.392	2.98	408	656	564	258	360	0	86
Marino Santana	1998-1999	0	0		7.94	10	11	17	11	14	0	0
Jose Santiago	1963-1970	34	29	.540	3.74	163	556	518	200	404	3	8
Bill Sayles	1939-1943	1	3	.250	5.61	28	79	87	46	52	0	0
Ray Scarborough	1942-1953	80	85	.485	4.13	318	1429	1487	611	564	9	14
Charley Schanz	1944-1950	28	43	.394	4.34	155	627	658	332	243	3	14
Calvin Schiraldi	1984-1991	32	39	.451	4.28	235	553	522	267	471	1	21
Biff Schliter	1908-1914	10	15	.400	3.51	44	223	211	73	88	2	1
George Schmees	1952	0	0	.000	3.00	2	6	9	2	2	0	0
Johnny Schmitz	1941-1956	93	114	.449	3.55	366	1813	1766	757	746	17	19
Pete Schourek	1991-Cont.	66	77	.462	4.59	288	1149	1198	420	813	1	2
Al Schroll	1958-1961	6	9	.400	5.34	35	118	121	64	63	0	0
Don Schwall	1961-1967	49	48	.505	3.72	172	743	710	391	408	5	4
Tom Seaver	1967-1986	311	205	.603	2.86	656	4783	3971	1390	3640	61	1
Diego Segui	1962-1977	92	111	.453	3.81	639	1808	1656	786	1298	7	71
Aaron Sele	1993-Cont.	107	68	.611	4.33	242	1466	1580	548	1082	7	0
Jeff Sellers	1985-1988	13	22	.371	4.97	61	330	364	164	226	2	0
Merle Settlemire	1928	0	6	.000	5.47	30	82	116	34	12	0	0
John Shea	1928	0	0	.000	18.00	1	1	1	1	0	0	0
Rollie Sheldon	1961-1966	38	36	.514	4.08	160	725	741	207	371	4	2
Keith Shepherd	1992-1996	2	5	.286	6.71	41	63	80	30	34	0	3
Ben Shields	1924-1931	4	0	1.000	8.27	13	41	55	27	9	0	0
Ernie Shore	1912-1920	65	43	.602	2.45	160	987	914	274	311	9	5
Bill Short	1960-1969	5	11	.313	4.73	73	131	130	64	71	1	2
Brian Shouse	1993-1998	0	1	.000	6.75	13	12	16	6	8	0	0
Sonny Siebert	1954-1975	140	114	551	3 21	399	2153	1919	692	1512	21	16
Pat Simmons	1928-1929	0	2	.000	3.67	76	75	41	41	18	0	2
Dave Sisler	1956-1962	38	44	.463	4.33	247	656	622	368	355	1	29
Craig Skok	1973-1979	4	7	.364	4.86	107	150	170	68	85	0	5
Steve Slayton	1928	0	0	.000	3.86	3	7	6	3	2	0	0
Heathcliff Slocumb	1991-2000	28	37	.431	4.08	548	631	636	358	513	0	98
Bobo Smith	1955-1959	4	9	.308	4.05	91	167	174	83	93	0	2
Charlie Smith	1902-1914	66	87	.431	2.81	213	1360	1309	353	570	10	3
Dan Smith	1999-2000	4	9	.308	6.10	22	93	106	42	73	0	0
Doug Smith	1912	0	0	.000	3.00	1	3	4	0	1	0	0
Eddie Smith	1936-1947	73	113	.392	3.82	282	1596	1554	739	694	8	12
Frank Smith	1904-1915	139	111	.556	2.59	354	2273	1975	676	1051	27	6
George Smith	1926-1930	10	8	.556	5.33	132	331	354	218	135	0	3
Lee Smith	1980-1997	71	92	.436	3.03	1022	1289	1133	486	1251	0	478
Pete Smith	1962-1963	0	1	.000	6.75	7	19	18	8	7	0	0
Riverboat Smith	1958-1959	4	4	.500	4.75	30	97	97	59	60	0	0
Zane Smith	1984-1996	100	115	.465	3.74	360	1919	1980	583	1011	16	3

Mike Smithson	1982-1989	76	86	.469	4.58	240	1356	1473	383	731	6	2
Rudy Sommers	1912-1927	4	8	.333	4.81	33	101	113	53	44	0	0
Allen Sothoron	1914-1926	91	100	.476	3.31	264	1582	1583	596	576	17	9
Bill Spanswick	1964	2	3	.400	6.89	29	65	75	44	55	0	0
Tully Sparks	1897-1910	121	138	.467	2.79	313	2336	2231	629	778	19	8
Jack Spring	1955-1965	12	5	.706	4.26	155	186	195	78	86	0	8
Bobby Sprowl	1978-1981	0	3	.000	5.40	22	47	54	27	34	0	0
Tracy Stallard	1960-1966	30	57	.345	4.17	183	765	716	343	477	3	4
Lee Stange	1961-1970	62	61	.504	3.56	359	1216	1172	344	718	8	21
Rob Stanifer	1997-2000	3	6	.333	5.43	82	106	119	42	61	0	2
Bob Stanley	1977-1989	115	97	.542	3.64	637	1708	1858	471	693	7	132
Mike Stanton	1989-Cont.	46	36	.561	3.85	756	746	712	280	644	0	65
Elmer Steele	1907-1911	18	24	.429	2.41	75	418	367	68	147	3	3
Jerry Stephenson	1963-1970	8	19	.296	5.69	67	239	265	145	184	0	1
Sammy Stewart	1978-1987	59	48	.551	3.59	359	957	863	502	686	1	45
Dick Stigman	1960-1966	46	54	.460	4.03	235	923	819	406	755	5	16
Carl Stimson	1923	0	0	.000	22.50	2	4	12	5	1	0	0
Chuck Stobbs	1947-1961	107	130	.451	4.29	459	1920	2003	735	897	7	19
Dean Stone	1953-1963	29	39	.426	4.47	215	686	705	373	380	5	12
Tom Sturdivant	1955-1964	59	51	.636	3.74	335	1137	1029	449	704	7	17
Jim Suchecki	1950-1952	0	6	.000	5.38	38	104	130	50	53	0	0
Frank Sullivan	1955-1963	97	100	.492	3.60	351	1732	1702	559	959	15	18
Jeff Suppan	1995-Cont.	40	48	.455	4.96	157	880	978	296	501	2	0
George Susce	1955-1959	22	17	.564	4.42	117	410	407	170	177	1	3
Greg Swindell	1986-Cont.	123	120	.506	3.82	630	2200	2275	496	1519	12	7
Len Swormstedt	1901-1906	3	4	.429	2.22	8	65	58	10	22	0	0

T

. . . .

NAME	YRS	W	L	PCT	ERA	G	IP	H	BB	SO	ShO	SAVES
Frank Tanana	1973-1993	240	236	.504	3.66	638	4188	4063	1255	2773	34	1
Jesse Tannehill	1894-1911	197	116	.629	2.79	359	2750	2787	477	943	34	7
Ken Tatum	1969-1974	16	12	.571	2.92	176	283	230	117	156	0	52
Harry Taylor	1946-1952	19	21	.475	4.10	90	358	344	201	127	3	4
Scott Taylor	1992-1993	1	2	.333	9.39	3	15	25	5	10	0	0
Yank Terry	1940-1945	20	28	.417	4.09	93	457	463	196	167	0	2
Jake Theilman	1905-1908	30	28	.517	3.16	65	475	483	107	158	3	0
Blaine Thomas	1911	0	0	.000	0.00	2	5	3	7	0	0	0
Tommy Thomas	1926-1937	117	128	.478	4.12	397	2173	2339	712	735	15	12
Hank Thormahlen	1917-1925	29	30	.492	3.33	104	565	550	203	148	4	2
Luis Tiant	1964-1982	229	172	.571	3.30	573	3486	3075	1104	2416	49	15
Mike Torrez	1967-1984	185	160	.536	3.96	494	3044	3043	1371	1404	15	0
John Trautwein	1988	0	1	.000	9.00	9	16	26	9	8	0	0
Joe Trimble	1955-1957	0	2	.000	7.48	7	22	23	16	10	0	0
Rick Trlicek	1992-1994	2	3	.400	5.22	55	88	93	39	49	0	1
Dizy Trout	1939-1957	170	161	.514	3.23	521	2726	2641	1046	1256	28	35
Mike Trujuillo	1985-1989	12	12	.500	5.02	83	235	267	88	96	1	3
John Tudor	1979-1990	117	72	.619	3.12	281	1797	1677	475	988	16	1
Bob Turley	1951-1963	101	85	.543	3.64	310	1713	1366	1068	1265	24	12

V

. . . .

NAME	YRS	W	L	PCT	ERA	G	IP	H	BB	SO	ShO	SAVES
Carlos Valdez	1995-1998	1	1	.500	5.00	15	18	20	13	11	0	0
Sergio Valdez	1986-1995	12	20	.375	5.06	116	303	332	109	190	0	0
Hy Vandenburg	1935-1945	14	10	.583	4.32	90	292	304	128	120	1	5
Ben Van Dyke	1909-1912	0	0	.000	3.32	5	22	20	11	13	0	0
Tim Van Egmond	1994-1996	5	9	.357	5.96	23	99	105	50	60	0	0
Bob Veale	1962-1974	120	95	.558	3.08	397	1926	1684	858	1703	20	21
Dario Veras	1996-1998	5	3	.625	4.67	53	61	64	29	46	0	0
Frank Viola	1982-1996	176	150	.540	3.73	421	2836	2827	864	1844	16	0
Jake Volz	1901-1908	2	4	.333	6.10	11	38	34	29	12	0	0

W

NAME	YRS	W	L	PCT	ERA	G	IP	H	BB	SO	ShO	SAVES
Jake Wade	1936-1946	27	40	.403	5.00	171	668	690	440	291	3	3
Charlie Wagner	1938-1946	32	23	.582	3.91	100	528	532	245	157	5	0
Gary Wagner	1965-1970	15	19	.441	3.71	162	267	250	126	174	0	22
Tim Wakefield	1992-Cont.	94	89	.514	4.41	312	1513	1498	644	1020	6	18
Rube Walberg	1923-1937	155	141	.524	4.17	544	2644	2795	1031	1085	15	32
Murray Wail	1950-1959	13	14	.481	4.20	91	193	196	63	82	0	14
Bucky Walters	1934-1950	198	160	.553	3.30	428	3105	2990	1121	1107	42	4
John Wasdin	1995-Cont.	31	29	.517	5.07	258	598	633	184	416	0	3
Gary Waslewski	1967-1972	11	26	.297	3.44	152	411	368	197	229	1	5
Monte Weaver	1931-1939	71	50	.587	4.36	201	1052	1137	435	297	2	4
Bob Weiland	1928-1940	62	94	.397	4.24	277	1388	1463	611	614	7	7
Johnny Welch	1926-1936	35	41	.461	4.66	172	648	735	262	257	3	6
Tony Weizer	1926-1927	10	14	.417	4.60	77	323	381	128	86	1	1
Fred Wenz	1968-1970	3	0	1.000	4.71	31	42	36	25	38	0	1
Bill Werle	1949-1954	29	39	.426	4.69	185	665	770	194	285	2	15
David West	1988-1998	31	38	.449	4.66	204	569	525	311	437	0	3
Al Widmar	1947-1952	13	30	.302	5.21	114	388	461	176	143	1	5
Bill Wight	1946-1958	77	99	.438	3.95	347	1563	1656	714	574	15	8
Dave Williams	1902	0	0	.000	5.30	3	19	22	11	7	0	0
Stan Williams	1958-1972	109	94	.537	3.48	482	1764	1527	748	1305	11	43
Jim Willoughby	1971-1978	26	36	.419	3.79	238	551	558	145	250	1	34
Ted Wills	1959-1965	8	11	.421	5.51	83	186	210	97	133	0	5
Duane Wilson	1958	0	0	.000	5.68	2	6	10	7	3	0	0
Earl Wilson	1959-1970	121	109	.526	3.69	338	2052	1863	796	1452	13	0
Jack Wilson	1934-1942	68	72	.486	4.59	281	1132	1233	601	590	5	20
Jim Wilson	1945-1958	86	89	.491	4.01	257	1539	1479	608	692	19	2
John Wilson	1927-1928	0	2	.000	4.45	7	30	37	19	9	0	0
Hal Wiltse	1926-1931	20	40	.333	4.87	102	500	589	211	134	2	1
Ted Wingfield	1923-1927	24	44	.353	4.18	113	553	624	181	68	3	5
George Winn	1919-1923	1	2	.333	4.69	12	40	50	7	7	0	0
George Winter	1901-1908	83	102	.449	2.87	220	1656	1552	379	568	9	4
Clarence Winters	1924	0	1	.000	20.57	4	7	22	4	3	0	0
Rick Wise	1964-1982	188	181	.509	3.69	506	3127	3227	804	1647	30	0
Johnnie Wittig	1938-1949	10	25	.286	4.89	84	307	343	163	121	1	4
Bob Wolcott	1995-1999	16	21	.432	5.86	66	326	391	113	178	0	0
Smoky Joe Wood	1908-1920	116	57	.671	2.03	225	1434	1138	421	989	28	11
Joe Wood	1944	0	1	.000	6.52	3	9	13	3	5	0	0
Wilbur Wood	1961-1978	164	156	.512	3.24	651	2684	2582	724	1411	24	57
John Woods	1924	0	0	.000	0.00	1	1	0	3	0	0	0
Pinky Woods	1943-1945	13	21	.382	3.97	85	379	388	206	124	1	3
Rob Woodward	1985-1988	4	4	.500	5.04	24	100	118	36	45	0	0
Hoge Workman	1924	0	0		8.50	11	18	25	11	7	0	0
Al Worthington	1953-1969	75	82	.478	3.39	602	1247	1130	527	834	3	110
Jim Wright	1978-1979	9	4	.692	3.82	35	139	141	31	71	3	0
John Wyatt	1961-1969	42	44	.488	3.47	435	687	600	346	540	0	103
John Wyckoff	1913-1918	23	34	.404	3.55	109	574	494	357	299	1	3

Y-Z

NAME	YRS	W	L	PCT	ERA	G	IP	H	BB	SO	ShO	SAVES
Cy Young	1890-1911	511	316	.618	2.63	906	7356	7092	1217	2803	76	17
Matt Young	1983-1993	55	95	.367	4.40	333	1190	1207	565	857	5	25
Tim Young	1998-2000	0	0		6.23	18	13	13	°6	13	0	0
Paul Zahniser	1923-1929	25	47	.347	4.66	125	619	746	284	145	4	1
Matt Zeiser	1914	0	0	.000	1.80	2	10	9	8	0	0	0
Bill Zuber	1936-1947	43	42	.506	4.28	224	786	767	468	383	3	6

Appendix B

RED SOX TEAM AND INDIVIDUAL RECORDS AND HONORS

All-Time Career Leaders

All-Time Career Batting Records

Batting Average
(Minimum 500 Games)
1. Ted Williams .344
2. Wade Boggs .338
3. Tris Speaker .337
4. Nomar Garciaparra .332
5. Jimmie Foxx .320
   Pete Runnels .320
7. Roy Johnson .313
   Johnny Pesky .313
9. Fred Lynn .308
10. Billy Goodman .306

At Bats
1. Carl Yastrzemski 11,988
2. Dwight Evans 8,726
3. Jim Rice 8,225
4. Ted Williams 7,706
5. Bobby Doerr 7,093
6. Harry Hooper 6,270
7. Wade Boggs 6,213
8. Dom Dimaggio 5,640
9. Rico Petrocelli 5,390
10. Frank Malzone 5,273

Hits
1. Carl Yastrzemski 3,419
2. Ted Williams 2,654
3. Jim Rice 2,452
4. Dwight Evans 2,373
5. Wade Boggs 2,098
6. Bobby Doerr 2,042
7. Harry Hooper 1,707
8. Dom DiMaggio 1,680
9. Frank Malzone 1,454
10. Mike Greenwell 1,400

Extra Base Hits
1. Carl Yastrzemski 1,157
2. Ted Williams 1,117
3. Dwight Evans 925
4. Jim Rice 834
5. Bobby Doerr 693

6. Wade Boggs 554
7. Rico Petrocelli 469
8. Dom DiMaggio 452
9. Jimmie Foxx 448
10. Mike Greenwell 443

Home Runs
1. Ted Williams 521
2. Carl Yastrzemski 452
3. Jim Rice 382
4. Dwight Evans 379
5. Mo Vaughn 230
6. Bobby Doerr 223
7. Jimmie Foxx 222
8. Rico Petrocelli 210
9. Jackie Jensen 170
10. Tony Conigliaro 162
    Carlton Fisk 162

Doubles
1. Carl Yastrzemski 646
2. Ted Williams 525
3. Dwight Evans 474
4. Wade Boggs 422
5. Bobby Doerr 381
6. Jim Rice 373
7. Dom DiMaggio 308
8. Mike Greenwell 275
9. Joe Cronin 270
10. John Valentin 266

Triples
1. Harry Hooper 130
2. Tris Speaker 106
3. Buck Freeman 90
4. Bobby Doerr 89
5. Larry Gardner 87
6. Jim Rice 79
7. Hobe Ferris 77
8. Dwight Evans 73
9. Ted Williams 71
10. Jimmy Collins 65

Slugging Average
1. Ted Williams .634
2. Jimmie Foxx .605

3. Nomar Garciaparra .570
4. Mo Vaughn .542
5. Fred Lynn .520
6. Jim Rice .502
7. Vern Stephens .492
8. Tony Conigliaro .488
9. Joe Cronin .484
10. Tris Speaker .482

Total Bases
1. Carl Yastrzemski 5,539
2. Ted Williams 4,884
3. Jim Rice 4,129
4. Dwight Evans 4,128
5. Bobby Doerr 3,270
6. Wade Boggs 2,869
7. Dom DiMaggio 2,363
8. Harry Hooper 2,303
9. Rico Petrocelli 2,263
10. Mike Greenwell 2,141

Runs Batted In
1. Carl Yastrzemski 1,844
2. Ted Williams 1,839
3. Jim Rice 1,451
4. Dwight Evans 1,346
5. Bobby Doerr 1,247
6. Jimmie Foxx 788
7. Rico Petrocelli 773
8. Mo Vaughn 752
9. Joe Cronin 737
10. Jackie Jensen 733

Runs
1. Carl Yastrzemski 1,816
2. Ted Williams 1,798
3. Dwight Evans 1,435
4. Jim Rice 1,249
5. Bobby Doerr 1,094
6. Wade Boggs 1,067
7. Dom DiMaggio 1,046
8. Harry Hooper 983
9. Johnny Pesky 776
10. Jimmie Foxx 771

Stolen Bases

I.	Harry Hooper	300
2.	Tris Speaker	267
3.	Carl Yastrzemski	168
4.	Heinie Wagner	141
5.	Larry Gardner	134
6.	Fred Parent	129
7.	Tommy Harper	107
8.	Billy Werber	107
9.	Chick Stahl	105
10.	Jimmy Collins	102
	Duffy Lewis	102

Bases on Balls

I.	Ted Williams	2,019
2.	Carl Yastrzemski	1,845
3.	Dwight Evans	1,337
4.	Wade Boggs	1,004
5.	Harry Hooper	826
6.	Bobby Doerr	809
7.	Dom DiMaggio	750
8.	Jim Rice	670
9.	Rico Petrocelli	661
10.	Jimmie Foxx	606

Pinch Hits

I.	Dalton Jones	55
2.	Rick Miller	49
3.	Russ Nixon	43
4.	Ted Williams	33
5.	Joe Cronin	29
	Olaf Henriksen	29
7.	Jack Rothrock	27
8.	Gene Stephens	24
9.	Lou Finney	23
	Rich Gedman	23
	Pumpsie Green	23

All-Time Career Pitching Records

Most Wins

I.	Cy Young	192
	Roger Clemens	192
3.	Mel Parnell	123
4.	Luis Tiant	122
5.	Smoky Joe Wood	117
6.	Bob Stanley	115
7.	Joe Dobson	106
8.	Lefty Grove	105
9.	Tex Hughson	96
	Bill Monbouquette	96

Most Losses

I.	Cy Young	112
2.	Roger Clemens	111
3.	Bob Stanley	97
4.	George Winter	97
5.	Red Ruffing	96
6.	Jack Russell	94
7.	Bill Monbouquette	91
8.	Bill Dinneen	85
9.	Tom Brewer	82
10.	Luis Tiant	81

Winning Percentage
(Minimum 100 decisions)

I.	Smoky Joe Wood	.676
2.	Babe Ruth	.659
3.	Tex Hughson	.640
4.	Roger Clemens	.634
5.	Cy Young	.633
6.	Lefty Grove	.629
7.	Ellis Kinder	.623
8.	Mel Parnell	.621
9.	Jesse Tannehill	.620
10.	Wes Ferrell	.608

Earned Run Average
(Minimum 1,000 Innings)

I.	Smoky Joe Wood	1.99
2.	Cy Young	2.00
3.	Dutch Leonard	2.13
4.	Babe Ruth	2.19
5.	Carl Mays	2.21
6.	Ray Collins	2.51
7.	Bill Dinneen	2.81
8.	George Winter	2.91
9.	Tex Hughson	2.94
10.	Roger Clemens	3.06

Games

I.	Bob Stanley	637
2.	Roger Clemens	383
3.	Ellis Kinder	365
4.	Cy Young	327
5.	Ike Delock	322
6.	Bill Lee	321
7.	Mel Parnell	289
8.	Greg Harris	287
9.	Mike Fornieles	286
	Dick Radatz	286

Complete Games

I.	Cy Young	275
2.	Bill Dinneen	156

3.	George Winter	141
4.	Smoky Joe Wood	121
5.	Lefty Grove	119
6.	Mel Parnell	113
	Luis Tiant	113
8.	Babe Ruth	105
9.	Roger Clemens	100
10.	Tex Hughson	99

Innings Pitched

I.	Roger Clemens	2,776
2.	Cy Young	2,728
3.	Luis Tiant	1,774
4.	Mel Parnell	1,753
5.	Bob Stanley	1,707
6.	Bill Monbouquette	1,622
7.	George Winter	1,600
8.	Joe Dobson	1,544
9.	Lefty Grove	1,540
10.	Tom Brewer	1,509

Strike Outs

I.	Roger Clemens	2,590
2.	Cy Young	1,341
3.	Luis Tiant	1,075
4.	Bruce Hurst	1,043
5.	Pedro Martinez	1,011
6.	Smoky Joe Wood	986
7.	Bill Monbouquette	969
8.	Tim Wakefield	910
9.	Frank Sullivan	821
10.	Ray Culp	794

Bases On Balls

I.	Roger Clemens	856
2.	Mel Parnell	758
3.	Tom Brewer	669
4.	Joe Dobson	604
5.	Jack Wilson	564
6.	Tim Wakefield	534
7.	Willard Nixon	530
8.	Ike Delock	514
9.	Mickey McDermott	504
10.	Luis Tiant	501

Shut Outs

I.	Cy Young	38
	Roger Clemens	38
3.	Smoky Joe Wood	28
4.	Luis Tiant	26
5.	Dutch Leonard	25
6.	Mel Parnell	20
7.	Ray Collins	19
	Tex Hughson	19

9.	Sad Sam Jones	18	
10.	Babe Ruth	17	
	Joe Dobson	17	

Saves

1.	Bob Stanley	132
2.	Dick Radatz	104
3.	Ellis Kinder	91
4.	Jeff Reardon	88
5.	Derek Lowe	85
6.	Sparkey Lyle	69
7.	Tom Gordon	68
8.	Lee Smith	58
9.	Bill Campbell	51
10.	Mike Fornieles	48
	Heathcliff Slocum	48

Relief Wins

1.	Bob Stanley	85
2.	Dick Radatz	49
3.	Ellis Kinder	39
4.	Mark Clear	35
5.	Ike Delock	34
6.	Mike Fornieles	31
7.	Bill Campbell	28
8.	Jack Wilson	26
	Mike Ryba	26
10.	Charlie Hall	24
	Earl Johnson	24

All-Time Single-Season Batting Records

Batting Average

1.	Ted Williams	.406	1941
2.	Ted Williams	.388	1957
3.	Tris Speaker	.383	1912
4.	Dale Alexander	.372	1932
	Nomar Garciaparra	.372	2000
6.	Ted Williams	.369	1948
7.	Wade Boggs	.368	1985
8.	Wade Boggs	.366	1988
9.	Tris Speaker	.363	1913
	Wade Boggs	.363	1987

At Bats

1.	Nomar Garciaparra	684	1997
2.	Jim Rice	677	1978
3.	Bill Buckner	673	1985
4.	Rick Burleson	663	1977
5.	Doc Cramer	661	1940
6.	Doc Cramer	658	1938
7.	Jim Rice	657	1984
8.	Wade Boggs	653	1985

9.	Dom DiMaggio	648	1948
10.	Tom Oliver	646	1930
	Chuck Schilling	646	1961
	Carl Yastrzemski	646	1962

Hits

1.	Wade Boggs	240	1985
2.	Tris Speaker	222	1912
3.	Wade Boggs	214	1988
4.	Jim Rice	213	1978
5.	Wade Boggs	210	1983
6.	Nomar Garciaparra	209	1997
7.	Johnny Pesky	208	1946
8.	Johnny Pesky	207	1947
	Wade Boggs	207	1986
	Mo Vaughn	207	1996

Extra Base Hits

1.	Jimmie Foxx	92	1938
2.	Ted Williams	86	1939
	Jim Rice	86	1978
4.	Ted Williams	85	1949
	Nomar Garciaparra	85	1997
6.	Earl Webb	84	1931
	Jim Rice	84	1979
8.	Ted Williams	83	1946
	Jim Rice	83	1977
10.	Fred Lynn	82	1979

Home Runs

1.	Jimmie Foxx	50	1938
2.	Jim Rice	46	1978
3.	Carl Yastrzemski	44	1967
	Mo Vaughn	44	1996
5.	Ted Williams	43	1949
	Tony Armas	43	1984
7.	Dick Stuart	42	1963
8.	Jimmie Foxx	41	1936
9.	Mo Vaughn	40	1998
10.	Carl Yastrzemski	40	1969
	Rico Petrocelli	40	1969
	Carl Yastrzemski	40	1970

Doubles

1.	Earl Webb	67	1931
2.	Tris Speaker	53	1912
3.	Nomar Garciaparra	51	2000
	Joe Cronin	51	1938
	Wade Boggs	51	1989
6.	John Valentin	47	1997
	Wade Boggs	47	1986
	George Burns	47	1923
	Fred Lynn	47	1975
10.	Tris Speaker	46	1914
	Bill Buckner	46	1985

Triples

1.	Tris Speaker	22	1913
2.	Buck Freeman	20	1903
3.	Chick Stahl	19	1904
	Buck Freeman	19	1902
	Larry Gardner	19	1914
	Buck Freeman	19	1904
7.	Tris Speaker	18	1914
	Larry Gardner	18	1912
9.	Harry Hooper	17	1920
	Jimmy Collins	17	1903
	Russ Scarritt	17	1929
	Freddie Parent	17	1903

Slugging Average

1.	Ted Williams	.735	1941
2.	Ted Williams	.731	1957
3.	Jimmie Foxx	.704	1938
4.	Jimmie Foxx	.694	1939
5.	Ted Williams	.667	1946
6.	Babe Ruth	.657	1919
7.	Ted Williams	.648	1942
8.	Fred Lynn	.637	1979
9.	Ted Williams	.635	1954
10.	Ted Williams	.634	1947

Total Bases

1.	Jim Rice	406	1978
2.	Jimmie Foxx	398	1938
3.	Jim Rice	382	1977
4.	Mo Vaughn	370	1996
5.	Jimmie Foxx	369	1936
	Jim Rice	369	1978
7.	Ted Williams	368	1949
8.	Nomar Garciaparra	365	1997
9.	Carl Yastrzemski	360	1967
	Mo Vaughn	360	1998

Runs Batted In

1.	Jimmie Foxx*	175	1938
2.	Ted Williams	159	1949
	Vern Stephens	159	1949
4.	Ted Williams	145	1939
5.	Walt Dropo	144	1950
	Vern Stephens	144	1950
7.	Jimmie Foxx	143	1936
	Mo Vaughn	143	1996
9.	Jim Rice	139	1978
10.	Ted Williams	137	1942
	Vern Stephens	137	1948

* — 4th All-time (Tied with Lou Gehrig)

The Red Sox Encyclopedia

Runs

1.	Ted Williams	150	1949
2.	Ted Williams	142	1946
3.	Ted Williams	141	1942
4.	Jimmie Foxx	139	1938
5.	Tris Speaker	136	1912
6.	Ted Williams	135	1941
7.	Ted Williams	134	1940
8.	Ted Williams	131	1939
	Dom DiMaggio	131	1950
10.	Jimmie Foxx	130	1939
	Jimmie Foxx	130	1936

Stolen Bases

1.	Tommy Harper	54	1973
2.	Tris Speaker	52	1912
3.	Tris Speaker	46	1913
4.	Tris Speaker	42	1914
	Otis Nixon	42	1994
6.	Harry Hooper	40	1910
	Billy Werber	40	1934
8.	Harry Hooper	38	1911
9.	Harry Lord	36	1909
10.	Patsy Dougherty	35	1903
	Tris Speaker	35	1909
	Tris Speaker	35	1910

Bases On Balls

1.	Ted Williams*	162	1947
	Ted Williams*	162	1949
3.	Ted Williams**	156	1946
4.	Ted Williams	145	1941
	Ted Williams	145	1942
6.	Ted Williams	144	1951
7.	Ted Williams	136	1954
8.	Carl Yastrzemski	128	1970
9.	Ted Williams	126	1948
10.	Wade Boggs	125	1988

* – 2nd all-time
** – 5th all-time

Pinch Hits

1.	Joe Cronin	18	1943
2.	Rick Miller	16	1983
	Dick Williams	16	1963
4.	Rick Miller	14	1984
	Lenny Green	14	1966
6.	Dalton Jones	13	1967
	Dalton Jones	13	1966
	Bing Miller	13	1935
	Lou Finney	13	1939
10.	Herm Winningham	12	1992
	Charley Maxwell	12	1954

All-Time Single-Season Pitching Records

Most Wins

1.	Smoky Joe Wood*	34	1912
2.	Cy Young**	33	1901
3.	Cy Young	32	1902
4.	Cy Young	28	1903
5.	Cy Young	26	1904
6.	Wes Ferrell	25	1935
	Boo Ferriss	25	1946
	Mel Parnell	25	1949
9.	Babe Ruth	24	1917
	Roger Clemens	24	1986

* – 4th all-time, A.L.
** – 5th all-time, A.L.

Most Losses

1.	Red Ruffing	25	1928
2.	Red Ruffing	22	1929
3.	Bill Dinneen	21	1902
	Joe Harris	21	1906
	Cy Young	21	1906
	Slim Harriss	21	1927
7.	Sad Sam Jones	20	1919
	Howard Ehmke	20	1925
	Milt Gaston	20	1930
	Jack Russell	20	1930

Winning Percentage

1.	Bob Stanley	.822	1978*
2.	Smoky Joe Wood	.872	1912
3.	Roger Moret	.867	1973
4.	Roger Clemens	.857	1986
5.	Pedro Martinez	.852	1999
6.	Roger Moret	.824	1975
7.	Boo Ferriss	.806	1946
8.	Ellis Kinder	.793	1949
9.	Dutch Leonard	.792	1914
10.	Lefty Grove	.789	1939

*–8th all-time

Earned Run Average

1.	Dutch Leonard	0.96*	1914
2.	Cy Young	1.26	1908
3.	Smoky Joe Wood	1.49	1915
4.	Ray Collins	1.62	1910
	Cy Young	1.62	1901
6.	Ernie Shore	1.64	1915
7.	Rube Foster	1.65	1914
8.	Smoky Joe Wood	1.69	1910
9.	Carl Mays	1.74	1917
	Pedro Martinez	1.74	2000

*–2nd all-time

Games

1.	Greg Harris	80	1993
2.	Dick Radatz	79	1964
3.	Heathcliff Slocomb	75	1996
4.	Rob Murphy	74	1989
	Derek Lowe	74	2000
	Derek Lowe	74	1999
7.	Tom Gordon	73	1998
8.	Sparky Lyle	71	1969
	Tony Fossas	71	1993
10.	Mike Fornieles	70	1960
	Greg Harris	70	1992

Complete Games

1.	Cy Young	41	1902
2.	Cy Young	40	1904
3.	Bill Dinneen	39	1902
4.	Cy Young	38	1901
5.	Bill Dinneen	37	1904
6.	Smoky Joe Wood	35	1912
	Babe Ruth	35	1917
8.	Cy Young	34	1903
9.	Cy Young	33	1907
10.	Bill Dinneen	32	1903
	Cy Young	32	1905

Innings Pitched

1.	Cy Young	385	1902
2.	Cy Young	380	1904
3.	Cy Young	371	1901
	Bill Dinneen	371	1902
5.	Smoky Joe Wood	344	1912
6.	Cy Young	343	1907
7.	Cy Young	342	1903
8.	Bill Dinneen	336	1904
9.	Babe Ruth	326	1917
10.	Babe Ruth	324	1916

Strike Outs

1.	Pedro Martinez	313	1999
2.	Roger Clemens	291	1988
3.	Pedro Martinez	284	2000
4.	Smoky Joe Wood	258	1912
5.	Roger Clemens	257	1996
6.	Roger Clemens	256	1987
7.	Pedro Martinez	251	1998
8.	Jim Lonborg	246	1967
9.	Roger Clemens	241	1991
10.	Roger Clemens	238	1986

Bases On Balls

1.	Mel Parnell	134	1949
2	Maury McDermott	124	1950

Red Sox Team and Individual Records and Honors

3.	Don Schwall	121	1962
	Mike Torrez	121	1979
5.	Howard Ehmke	119	1923
	Wes Ferrell	119	1936
	Bobo Newsom	119	1937
	Jack Wilson	119	1937
9.	Babe Ruth	118	1916
	Red Ruffing	118	1929

Shut Outs

1.	Cy Young	10	1904
2.	Smoky Joe Wood	10	1912
3.	Babe Ruth	9	1916
4.	Carl Mays	8	1918
	Roger Clemens	8	1988
6.	Cy Young	7	1903
	Dutch Leonard	7	1914
	Ray Collins	7	1914
	Bullett Joe Bush	7	1918
	Roger Clemens	7	1987
	Luis Tiant	7	1987

Saves

1.	Tom Gordon	46	1998
2.	Derek Lowe	42	2000
3.	Jeff Reardon	40	1991
4.	Jeff Russell	33	1993
	Bob Stanley	33	1983
6.	Heathcliff Slocumb	31	1996
	Bill Campbell	31	1977
8.	Dick Radatz	29	1964
	Lee Smith	29	1988
10.	Ellis Kinder	27	1953
	Jeff Reardon	27	1992

Relief Wins

1.	Dick Radatz	16	1964
2.	Dick Radatz	15	1963
3.	Mark Clear	14	1982
4.	Bill Campbell	13	1977
	Bob Stanley	13	1978
6.	Bob Stanley	12	1982
7.	Ike Delock	11	1956
	Joe Heving	11	1939
9.	Dick Drago	10	1979
	John Wyatt	10	1967
	Mike Fornieles	10	1960
	Ellis Kinder	10	1953
	Ellis Kinder	10	1951
	Bob Stanley	10	1981

All-Time Single-Season Fielding Records

Fielding Average

1st Base

1.	Stuffy McInnis	.999	1921
2.	Phil Todt	.997	1928
3.	Carl Yastrzemski	.996	1975
	Stuffy McInnis	.996	1920
	Nick Esasky	.996	1989

2nd Base

1.	Bobby Doerr	.993	1948
2.	Chuck Schilling	.991	1961
3.	Bobby Doerr	.990	1943
	Doug Griffin	.990	1973
	Jerry Remy	.990	1983
	Marty Barrett	.990	1988
	Jody Reed	.990	1990

3rd Base

1.	Rico Petrocelli	.976	1971
	Grady Hatton	.976	1955
3.	Johnny Pesky	.974	1950
4.	George Kell	.972	1953
5.	Wade Boggs	.971	1988

Shortstop

1.	Vern Stephens	.981	1950
	Rico Petrocelli	.981	1969
	Rick Burleson	.981	1978
4.	Rick Burleson	.980	1979
5.	John Valentin	.979	1994

Outfield

1.	Carl Yastrzemski	1.000	1977
	Ken Harrelson	1.000	1968
3.	Darren Bragg	.996	1998
	Babe Ruth	.996	1919
5.	Ted Williams	.995	1957
	Dwight Evans	.995	1973

Catcher

1.	Pete Daley	1.000	1957
	Rick Cerone	1.000	1988
3.	Tony Pena	.995	1990
	Tony Pena	.995	1991
	Tony Pena	.995	1993
	Damon Berryhill	.995	1994

Put Outs

1st Base

1.	Phil Todt	1,755	1926
2.	Candy LaChance	1,691	1904
3.	Stuffy McInnis	1,586	1920
4.	Stuffy McInnis	1,549	1921
5.	Candy LaChance	1544	1902

2nd base

1.	Bill Wambsganss	463	1924
2.	Bobby Doerr	443	1950
3.	Hobe Ferris	424	1907
4.	Bobby Doerr	420	1946
5.	Bobby doerr	415	1943

3rd Base

1.	Jimmy Collins	203	1901
2.	Jimmy Collins	191	1904
3.	Larry Gardner	187	1914
4.	Johnny Pesky	184	1949
5.	Harry Lord	181	1908

Shortstop

1.	Everett Scott	380	1921
2.	Heinie Wagner	373	1908
3.	Heinie Wagner	332	1912
4.	Everett Scott	330	1920
5.	Freddie Parent	327	1904

Outfield

1.	Dom DiMaggio	503	1948
2.	Tom Oliver	477	1930
3.	Jimmy Piersall	455	1956
4.	Doc Cramer	443*	1936
5.	Dom DiMaggio	439*	1942

Catcher

1.	Jason Varitek	972	1999
2.	Bob Tillman	897	1964
3.	Jason Varitek	867	2000
4.	Rich Gedman	866	1986
5.	Tony Pena	864	1991
	Tony Pena	864	1990

Pitcher

1.	Oil Can Boyd	42	1985
2.	Smoky Joe Wood	41	1912
3.	Bill Monbouquette	31	1963
	Roger Clemens	31	1991
5.	Mike Boddicker	29	1990

ASSISTS

1st Base

1.	Bill Buckner	184	1985
2.	Bill Buckner	157	1986
3.	Carlos Quintana	137	1990
4.	Dick Stuart	134	1963
5.	Phil Todt	126	1926

2nd Base

1.	Bill Wambsganss	494	1924
2.	Bobby Doerr	490	1943
3.	Del Pratt	484	1922
4.	Bobby Doerr	483	1946
5.	Bobby Doerr	480	1940

3rd Base

1.	Frank Malzone	378	1958
2.	Frank Malzone	370	1957
3.	Wade Boggs	368	1983
4.	Frank Malzone	357	1959
5.	Jim Tabor	338	1939

Shortstop

1.	Heinie Wagner	569	1908
2.	Vern Stephens	540	1948
3.	Everett Scott	528	1980
	Rick Burleson	528	1980
5.	Rick Burleson	523	1979

Outfield

1.	Tris Speaker	35	1909
	Tris Speaker	35	1912
3.	Ira Flagstead	31	1923
4.	Tris Speaker	30	1913
	Harry Hooper	30	1910

Catcher

1.	Lou Criger	156	1903
2.	Lou Criger	147	1905
3.	Bill Carrigan	134	1910
4.	Wally Schang	131	1919
5.	Bill Carrigan	127	1913

Pitcher

1.	Carl Mays	122	1918
2.	Carl Mays	118	1917
3.	Carl Mays	117	1916
4.	Smoky Joe Wood	110	1912
5.	Jesse Tannehill	107	1904

Double Plays

1st Base

1.	Rudy York	154	1946
2.	Jimmie Foxx	153	1938

3.	Tony Perez	150	1980
	George Scott	150	1977
5.	Tony Lupien	149	1943

2nd Base

1.	Bobby Doerr	134	1949
2	Bobby Doerr	132	1943
3.	Bobby Doerr	130	1950
4.	Bobby Doerr	129	1946
5.	Chuck Schilling	121	1961

3rd Base

1.	Johnny Pesky	48	1949
2.	Frank Malzone	45	1961
3.	Wade Boggs	40	1983
	Frank Malzone	40	1959
5.	Rico Petrocelli	38	1972

Shortstop

1.	Rick Burleson	147	1980
2	Vern Stephens	128	1949
3.	Vern Stephens	115	1950
4.	Vern Stephens	113	1948
	Nomar Garciaparra	113	1997

Outfield

1.	Tris Speaker	12	1909
	Tris Speaker	12	1914
3.	Chick Stahl	9	1906
	Duffy Lewis	9	1910
	Tris Speaker	9	1912
	Nemo Leibold	9	1921

Catcher

1.	Muddy Ruel	17	1922
2	Wally Schang	15	1919
	Roxy Walters	15	1920
	Tony Pena	15	1991

Pitcher

1.	Boo Ferriss	10	1945
2.	Howard Ehmke	8	1923
	Bob Stanley	8	1980
4.	Tom Brewer	7	1958
	Tex Hughson	7	1942
	Bob Weiland	7	1932
	Joe Bush	7	1920

Total Chances Per Game

1st Base

1.	Phil Todt	12.4	1926
2.	Stuffy McInnis	12.2	1918
3.	Candy LaChance	11.7	1902
4.	Bob Unglaub	11.6	1907
5.	Stuffy McInnis	11.4	1920

2nd Base

1.	Oscar Melillo	6.4	1935
	Bill Regan	6.4	1926
	Bill Wambsganss	6.4	1924
4.	Hobe Ferris	6.3	1901
	Johnny Hodapp	6.3	1933

3rd Base

1.	Jimmie Collins	4.2	1901
2.	Jimmie Collins	3.9	1902
3.	John Knight	3.8	1907
	Billy Werber	3.8	1934
	Billy Werber	3.8	1935

Shortstop

1.	Heinie Wagner	6.6	1907
	Heinie Wagner	6.6	1908
3.	Rabbit Warstler	6.2	1932
4.	Freddie Parent	6.1	1902
	Everett Scott	6.1	1921

Outfield

1.	Dom DiMaggio	3.4	1948
2.	Dom DiMaggio	3.3	1947
3.	Ira Flagstead	3.2	1925
	Tom Oliver	3.2	1930
5.	Tris Speaker	3.1	1913

Catcher

1.	Bob Tillman	7.3	1964
2.	Gerry Moses	7.1	1970
	Carlton Fisk	7.1	1972
4.	Rich Gedman	7.0	1986
5.	Lou Criger	6.9	1903
	Bob Tillman	6.9	1965

Pitcher

1.	Carl Mays	4.2	1918
	Babe Ruth	4.2	1918
3.	Joe Harris	4.1	1906
4.	Carl Mays	4.0	1917
5.	Smoky Joe Wood	3.6	1912

Red Sox American League Standings Year-By-Year

Year	Place	Won-Lost	Average	Games Behind	Manager(s)	
1901	2	79-57	.581	4	Jimmy Collins	
1902	3	77-60	.562	6	Jimmy Collins	
1903	1	91-47	.659	+14½	Jimmy Collins	
1904	1	95-59	.617	+12½	Jimmy Collins	
1905	4	78-74	.513	16	Jimmy Collins	
1906	8	49-105	.318	45½	Jimmy Collins	W. 44-L. 92
					Chick Stahl	W. 5-L. 13
1907	7	59-90	.396	32½	Cy Young	W. 3-L. 4
					George Huff	W. 3-L. 5
					Bob Unglaub	W. 8-L. 20
					Deacon McGuire	W. 45-L. 61
1908	5	75-79	.487	15	Deacon McGuire	W. 53-L. 62
				½	Fred Lake	W. 22-L.17
1909	5	88-63	.583	9½	Fred Lake	
1910	4	81-72	.529	22½	Patsy Donovan	
1911	5	78-75	.510	24	Patsy Donovan	
1912	1	105-47	.691	+14	Jake Stahl	
1913	4	79-71	.527	15½	Jake Stahl	W. 39-L. 41
					Bill Carrigan	W.40-L. 30
1914	2	91-62	.595	8½	Bill Carrigan	
1915	1	101-50	.669	+2½	Bill Carrigan	
1916	1	91-63	.591	+2	Bill Carrigan	
1917	2	90-62	.592	9	Jack Barry	
1918	1	75-51	.595	+2½	Ed Barrow	
1919	6	66-71	.482	20½	Ed Barrow	
1920	5	72-81	.471	25½	Ed Barrow	
1921	5	75-79	.487	23½	Hugh Duffy	
1922	8	61-93	.396	33	Hugh Duffy	
1923	8	61-91	.401	37	Frank Chance	
1924	7	67-87	.435	25	Lee Fohl	
1925	8	47-105	.309	49½	Lee Fohl	
1926	8	46-107	.301	44½	Lee Fohl	
1927	8	51-103	.331	59	Bill Carrigan	
1928	8	57-96	.373	43½	Bill Carrigan	
1929	8	58-96	.377	48	Bill Carrigan	
1930	8	52-102	.338	50	Heinie Wagner	
1931	6	62-90	.408	45	Shano Collins	
1932	8	43-111	.279	64	Shano Collins	W. ll-L. 46
					Marty McManus	W. 32-L. 65
1933	7	63-86	.423	34½	Marty McManus	
1934	4	76-76	.500	24	Bucky Harris	
1935	4	78-75	.510	16	Joe Cronin	
1936	6	74-80	.481	28½	Joe Cronin	
1937	5	80-72	.526	21	Joe Cronin	
1938	2	88-61	.591	9½	Joe Cronin	
1939	2	89-62	.589	17	Joe Cronin	
1940	4 (tie)	82-72	.532	8	Joe Cronin	
1941	2	84-70	.545	17	Joe Cronin	
1942	2	93-59	.612	9	Joe Cronin	
1943	7	68-84	.447	29	Joe Cronin	

The Red Sox Encyclopedia

1944	4	77-77	.500	12	Joe Cronin	
1945	7	71-83	.461	17½	Joe Cronin	
1946	1	104-50	.675	+12	Joe Cronin	
1947	3	83-71	.539	14	Joe Cronin	
1948	2*	96-59	.619	1	Joe McCarthy	
1949	2	95-58	.623	1	Joe McCarthy	
1950	3	94-60	.610	4	Joe McCarthy	W. 31-L. 28
					Steve O'Neill	W. 63-L. 32
1951	3	87-67	.565	11	Steve O'Neill	
1952	6	76-78	.494	19	Lou Boudreau	
1953	4	84-69	.549	16	Lou Boudreau	
1954	4	69-85	.448	42	Lou Boudreau	
1955	4	84-70	.545	12	Pinky Higgins	
1956	4	84-70	.545	13	Pinky Higgins	
1957	3	82-72	.532	16	Pinky Higgins	
1958	3	79-75	.513	13	Pinky Higgins	
1959	5	75-79	.487	19	Pinky Higgins	W. 31-L. 41
					Rudy York	W. 0-L. 1
					Billy Jurges	W. 44-L. 38
1960	7	65-89	.422	32	Billy Jurges	W. 34-L. 47
					Pinky Higgins	W. 31-L. 42
1961	6	76-86	.469	33	Pinky Higgins	
1962	8	76-84	.475	19	Pinky Higgins	
1963	7	76-85	.472	28	Johnny Pesky	
1964	8	72-90	.444	27	Johnny Pesky	W. 70-L. 90
					Billy Herman	W. 2-L. 0
1965	9	62-100	.383	40	Billy Herman	
1966	9	72-90	.444	26	Billy Herman	W. 64-L. 82
					Pete Runnels	W. 8-L. 8
1967	1	92-70	.568	+1	Dick Williams	
1968	4	86-76	.531	17	Dick Williams	
1969	3**	87-75	.537	22	Dick Williams	W. 82-L. 71
					Eddie Popowski	W. 5-L. 4
1970	3	87-75	.537	21	Eddie Kasko	
1971	3	85-77	.525	18	Eddie Kasko	
1972	2	85-70	.548	½	Eddie Kasko	
1973	2	89-73	.549	8	Eddie Kasko	
1974	3	84-78	.519	7	Darrell Johnson	
1975	1	95-65	.594	+4½	Darrell Johnson	
1976	3	83-79	.512	15½	Darrell Johnson	W. 41-L. 45
					Don Zimmer	W. 42-L. 34
1977	2 (tie)	97-64	.602	2½	Don Zimmer	
1978	2	99-64	.607	1	Don Zimmer	
1979	3	91-69	.589	11½	Don Zimmer	
1980	4	83-77	.519	19	Don Zimmer	W. 82-L. 73
					Johnny Pesky	W. 1- L. 4
1981 (1st Half)	5***	30-26	.536	4	Ralph Houk	
(2nd Half)	2	29-23	.558	½		
1982	3	89-73	.549	6	Ralph Houk	
1983	6	78-84	.481	20	Ralph Houk	
1984	4	86-76	.531	18	Ralph Houk	
1985	5	81-81	.500	18½	John McNamara	
1986	1	95-66	.590	+5½	John McNamara	

Year	Pos	Record	Pct	GB	Manager	W-L
1987	5	78-84	.481	20	John McNamara	
1988	1	89-73	.549	1	John McNamara	W. 43-L. 42
					Joe Morgan	W.46-L. 31
1989	3	83-79	.512	6	Joe Morgan	
1990	1	88-74	.543	2	Joe Morgan	
1991	2 (tie)	84-78	.519	7	Joe Morgan	
1992	7	73-89	.451	23	Butch Hobson	
1993	5	80-82	.494	15	Butch Hobson	
1994	4****	54-61	.470	17	Butch Hobson	
1995	1	86-58	.597	+7	Kevin Kennedy	
1996	3	85-77	.525	7	Kevin Kennedy	
1997	4	78-84	.481	20	Jimy Williams	
1998	2	92-70	.568	22	Jimy Williams	
1999	2	94-68	.580	4	Jimy Williams	
2000	2	85-77	.525	2	Jimy Williams	
2001	2	82-79	.509	13 1/2	Jimy Williams	W.65-L.53
				1/2	Joe Kerrigan	W.17-L.26
				1/2		

* – Tied for first place but play-off game lost to Cleveland
** – American League Split into two divisions. Red Sox in Eastern Division
*** – Split season. Winners of first half and second half play each other for American League pennant
**** – American League Split into three divisions. Red Sox remain in Eastern Division

Red Sox Managers' Records

Most Wins-Manager

1912	105	Jake Stahl
1946	104	Joe Cronin
1915	101	Rough Carrigan
1978	99	Don Zimmer
1977	97	Don Zimmer
1948	96	Joe McCarthy
1949	96	Joe McCarthy
1904	95	Jimmy Collins
1975	95	Darrell Johnson
1986	95	John McNamara

Most Losses-Manager

1932	111	Shano Collins; Marty McManus
1926	107	Lee Fohl
1906	105	Jimmy Collins; Chick Stahl
1925	105	Lee Fohl
1927	103	Rough Carrigan
1965	100	Billy Herman
1928	96	Rough Carrigan
1929	95	Rough Carrigan
1922	93	Hugh Duffy
1923	91	Frank Chance

Highest Winning Percentage-Manager

1912	.691	Jake Stahl
1946	.675	Joe Cronin
1915	.669	Rough Carrigan
1903	.659	Jimmie Collins
1949	.623	Joe McCarthy
1948	.619	Joe McCarthy
1904	.617	Jimmy Collins
1942	.612	Joe Cronin
1950	.610	Joe McCarthy
1978	.608	Don Zimmer

Lowest Winning Percentage-Manager

1932	.279	Shano Collins; Marty McManus
1926	.301	Lee Fohl
1925	.309	Lee Fohl
1906	.318	Jimmy Collins; Chick Stahl
1927	.331	Rough Carrigan
1930	.338	Heinie Wagner
1928	.373	Rough Carrigan
1929	.377	Rough Carrigan
1965	.383	Billy Herman

1907	.396	Cy Young; George Huff; Bob Unglaub; Deacon McGuire
1922	.396	Hugh Duffy

Red Sox Coaches since 1921

Beginning 1920s
Jimmy Burke
John Ryan
Lefty Leifield
Heinie Wagner
Bob Coleman

Beginning 1930s
Jack McCallister
Hugh Duffy
Rudy Hulswitt
Tom Daly
Bib Falk
Jack Onslow
Al Schacht
Herb Pennock
Bing Miller
Moe Berg

The Red Sox Encyclopedia

Beginning 1940s
Frank Shellenback
Larry Woodal
Bill Burwell
Dell Baker
Tom Carey
Paul Schreiber
Earl Combs
Kiki Cuyler
John Shulte

Beginning 1950s
Steve O'Neill
George Susce
Eddie Mayo
Bill McKechnie
Oscar Melillo
Buster Mills
Jack Burns
Dave Ferriss
Mickey Owen
Rudy York

Beginning 1960s
Billy Herman
Sal Maglie
Len Okrie
Harry Dorish
Al Lakeman
Harry Malmberg
Bob Turley
Billy Gardner

Pete Runnels
Mace Brown
Bobby Doerr
Eddie Popowski
Darrell Johnson

Beginning 1970s
Charlie Wagner
George Thomas
Doug Camilli
Don Lenhardt
Harvey Haddix
Lee Strange
Don Bryant
Don Zimmer
Johnny Pesky
Stan Williams
Eddie Yost
Walt Hriniak
Al Jackson

Beginning 1980s
Tommy Harper
Johnny Padres
Bill Fischer
Rene Lachman
Joe Morgan
Tony Torchia
Rac Slider
Jerry McNertney
Al Bumbry
Richie Hebner
Dick Berardino

Beginning 1990s
John McLaren
Al Nipper
Rick Burleson
Dave Oliver
Gary Allenson
Jim Rice
Mike Easler
Sammy Ellis
Rich Gale
Dave Carlucci
Mike Roarke
Dave Jauss
Herm Starrette
Joe Kerrigan
Frank White
Wendell Kim
John Wathan
Grady Little
John Cumberland
Tim Johnson
Dick Pole
Dana Levangie

Beginning 2000
Rick Down
Tommy Harper
Gene Lamont
Norman Nelson
Buddy Bailey

Red Sox Team Records

Highest Batting Average

		Team Finish
1950	.302	3
1938	.299	2
1939	.291	2
1940	.286	4 (Tie)
1944	.286	4
1991	.283	2
1979	.283	3
1980	.283	4
1984	.283	4
1988	.283	1
1996	.283	3

Highest Fielding Average

		Team Finish
1988	.984	1
2000	.982	2
1987	.982	5
2001	.981	2
1948	.981	2 (Play-off)
1950	.981	3
1971	.981	3
1982	.981	3
1991	.981	2 (Tie)
1949	.980	2
1989	.980	3
1990	.980	1
1993	.980	5

Highest Earned Run Average

		Team Finish
1904	2.12	1
1917	2.20	2
1908	2.27	5
1918	2.31	1
1914	2.35	2
1915	2.39	1
1907	2.45	7
1910	2.46	4
1916	2.48	1
1903	2.57	1

Lowest Batting Average

		Team Finish
1905	.234	4
1907	.234	7
1968	.236	4
1906	.239	8
1966	.240	9
1943	.244	7
1908	.246	5
1917	.246	2
1992	.246	7
1904	.247	1

Lowest Fielding Average

		Team Finish
1901	.941	2
1906	.949	8

1911	.949	5
1905	.953	4
1910	.954	4
1902	.955	3
1908	.955	5
1909	.955	4
1912	.957	1
1925	.957	1

Lowest Earned Run Average

		Team Finish
1932	5.02	8
1925	4.97	8
1940	4.89	4 (tie)
1950	4.88	3
1986	4.77	1
1926	4.72	8
1930	4.70	8
1927	4.68	8
1960	4.62	7
1931	4.60	6

World Series, Pennant, League Championship Series and Division Playoff Records

World Series Winners - 5 Times

1903	Red Sox over Pittsburgh Pirates	5 Games to 3
1912	Red Sox over New York Giants	4 Games to 3
1915	Red Sox over Philadelphia Athletics	4 Games to 1
1916	Red Sox over Brooklyn Robins	4 Games to 1
1918	Red Sox over Chicago Cubs	4 Games to 2

Pennant Winners - 10 Times

1903	Red Sox by 14^1/$_2$ Games over Athletics	Red Sox Win
1904	Red Sox by 1^1/$_2$ Games over Highlanders	No World Series
1912	Red Sox by 14 Games over Senators	Red Sox Win
1915	Red Sox by 2^1/$_2$ Games over Tigers	Red Sox Win
1916	Red Sox by 2 Games over White Sox	Red Sox Win
1918	Red Sox by 2^1/$_2$ Games over Indians	Red Sox Win
1946	Red Sox by 12 Games over Tigers	Cardinals Win, 4 Games to 3
1967	Red Sox by 1 Game over Tigers and Twins	Cardinals Win, 4 Games to 3
1975	Red Sox by 4^1/$_2$ Games over Orioles	Reds Win, 4 Games to 3
1986	Red Sox by 5^1/$_2$ Games over Yankees	Mets Win, 4 Games to 3

American League Championship Series East vs. West Division Winners - 2 Sox Wins

		League Championship Series
1975	Red Sox by 4 1/2 Games over Orioles	Sox Beat A's 3 Games to 0
1986	Red Sox by 5 1/2 Games over Yankees	Sox Beat Angels 4 Games to 3
1988	Red Sox by 1 Game over Tigers	A's Beat Sox 4 Games to 0
1990	Red Sox by 2 Games over Blue Jays	A's Beat Sox 4 Games to 0
1999	Red Sox Finish Second-Wild Card	Yankees Beat Sox 4 Games to 1

The Red Sox Encyclopedia

American League 3 - Division Play-offs

1995 Red Sox by 7 Games over Yankees
1998 Red Sox Wild Card Team
1999 Red Sox Wild Card Team

Division Play-off

Indians beat Sox 3 Games to 0
Indians beat Sox 3 Games to 1
Sox beat Indians 3 Games to 2

Career World Series Batting Records

Batting Average

(Minimum 10 at Bats)

1.	Marty Barrett	.433
2.	Wally Moses	.417
3.	Carlton Fisk	.417
4.	Carl Yastrzemski	.400
	Cecil Cooper	.400
	Dave Henderson	.400

Home Runs

1.	Carl Yastrzemski	3
	Larry Gardner	3
	Dwight Evans	3
4.	Harry Hooper	2
	Patsy Dougherty	2
	Rudy York	2
	Dave Henderson	2
	Rico Petrocelli	2

At Bats

1.	Harry Hooper	92
2.	Duffy Lewis	67
3.	Larry Gardner	62
4.	Everett Scott	54
5.	Dwight Evans	50

Hits

1.	Harry Hooper	27
2.	Duffy Lewis	19
	Carl Yastrzemski	19
4.	Dwight Evans	15
5.	Tris Speaker	14

Doubles

1.	Duffy Lewis	6
2.	Hal Janvrin	3
	Harry Hooper	3
	Dom DiMaggio	3
	Dwight Evans	3
	Wade Boggs	3

Triples

1.	Tris Speaker	3
	Buck Freeman	3
	Freddie Parent	3
	Chick Stahl	3

5.	Harry Hooper	2
	Larry Gardner	2
	Steve Yerkes	2
	Jimmy Collins	2
	Patsy Dougherty	2

Runs

1.	Harry Hooper	13
2.	Carl Yastrzemski	11
3.	Freddie Parent	8
	Larry Gardner	8
	Duffy Lewis	8

Runs Batted In

1.	Dwight Evans	14
2.	Larry Gardner	10
3.	Carl Yastrzemski	9
4.	Duffy Lewis	8
5.	Hobe Ferris	7
	Rico Petrocelli	7

Stolen Bases

1.	Jimmy Collins	3
	Harry Hooper	3
3.	Chick Stahl	2
	Jake Stahl	2

Career World Series Pitching Records

Most Wins

Babe Ruth	3
Ernie Shore	3
Bill Dinneen	3

Most Losses

Buck O'Brien	2
Mickey Harris	2
Smoky Joe Wood	3
Calvin Schiraldi	2
Jose Santiago	2

Most Innings Pitched

1.	Bill Dinneen	34
2.	Ernie Shore	34.2
3.	Cy Young	34

4.	Babe Ruth	31
5.	Luis Tiant	25

Fewest Hits Per Innings Pitched

(Minimum 10 Innings)

		Innings Pitched	Hits
1.	Joe Dobson	12.2	4
2.	Dutch Leonard	18	8
3.	Jim Lonborg	24	14
4.	Hugh Bedient	18	10
5.	Babe Ruth	20	19

Most Strike Outs Per Innings Pitched

(Minimum 10 Innings)

		Innings Pitched	Ks
1.	Roger Clemens	11.1	11
2.	Smoky Joe Wood	22	21
3.	Joe Dobson	12.2	10
4.	Bill Dinneen	35	*28
5.	Bruce Hurst	23	17

* – Most World Series Strikeouts by Red Sox Pitcher

Fewest Walks Per Innings Pitched

(Minimum 10 Innings)

		Innings Pitched	BB
1.	Ray Collins	14.1	0
2.	Jim Lonborg	24	2
3.	Rube Foster	21	2
4.	Cy Young	34	4
5.	Smoky Joe Wood	22	3

Earned Run Average

(Minimum 10 Innings)

			Innings Pitched
1.	Joe Dobson	0.00	12.2
2.	Hugh Bedient	0.50	18
3.	Babe Ruth	0.87	31
4.	Dutch Leonard	1.00	18
5.	Cy Young	1.59	34

League Championship and Division Play-Off Batting Records (through 1998)

Batting Average
(Minimum 10 At Bats)

1.	Luis Alicea	.600
2.	Carl Yastrzemski	.455
3.	Jose Offerman	.429
4.	Carlton Fisk	.417
5.	Cecil Cooper	.400

Home Runs

1.	Nomar Garciaparra	7
2.	John Valentin	5
3.	Mo Vaughn	2
	Jim Rice	2
	Rich Gedman	2

At Bats

1.	John Valentin	72
2.	Dwight Evans	63
3.	Wade Boggs	59
4.	Troy O'Leary	56
5.	Mike Stanley	53

Hits

1.	John Valentin	25
2.	Wade Boggs	19
3.	Nomar Garciaparra	18
	Mike Stanley	18
	Jose Offerman	18

Doubles

1.	John Valentin	6
2.	Nomar Garciaparra	5
	Otis Nixon	5
4.	Jason Varitek	4
5.	Dwight Evans	3
	Don Baylor	3
	Ellis Burks	3

Triples

1.	Wade Boggs	1
	Spike Owen	1
	John Valentin	1
	Jason Varitek	1

Runs

1.	John Valentin	15
2.	Nomar Garciaparra	12
3.	Jim Rice	8
	Jose Offerman	8
5.	Jason Varitek	7

Runs Batted In

1.	Nomar Garciaparra	20
2.	John Valentin	19
3.	Jose Offerman	8
	Troy O'Leary	8
5.	Jim Rice	7

Stolen Bases

1.	Darren Lewis	3
2.	Juan Beniquez	2
3.	Spike Owen	1
	Ellis Burks	1
	Luis Alicea	1
	Duane Hosey	1
	Carlton Fisk	1
	Don Buford	1

League Championship and Division Play-Off Pitching Records (through 1999)

Most Wins

1.	Pedro Martinez	2

(9 pitchers won 1 game)

Most Losses

1.	Bret Saberhagen	3
2.	Roger Clemens	2
	Bruce Hurst	2
	Tim Wakefield	2
	Lee Smith	2
	Mike Boddicker	2

Most Innings Pitched

1.	Roger Clemens	44.1
2.	Bruce Hurst	28
3.	Pedro Martinez	24
4.	Derek Lowe	19
5.	Bret Saberhagen	16.2

Earned Run Average
(Minimum 10 Innings)

1.	Pedro Martinez	1.12
2.	Bruce Hurst	2.25
3.	Derek Lowe	3.79
4.	Roger Clemens	4.06
5.	Oil Can Boyd	4.61

Most Strikeouts

1.	Roger Clemens	34
2.	Pedro Martinez	31
3.	Bruce Hurst	20
4.	Derek Lowe	16
5.	Bret Saberhagen	14

Saves

1.	Dick Drago	2
2.	Calvin Schiraldi	1

Games Started

1.	Roger Clemens	8
2.	Bruce Hurst	4
	Bret Saberhagen	4
4.	Pedro Martinez	3
	Kent Mercker	3
	Luis Tiant	3

Individual Player/Manager Honors

Players with Ten or More Seasons with the Red Sox

*Carl Yastrzemski	23 years	Outfielder	1961-1983
*Ted Williams	19 years	Outfielder	1939-1960
*Jim Rice	16 years	Outfielder	1974-1989
*Bobby Doerr	14 years	2nd Baseman	1937-1951
*Rico Petrocelli	13 years	Infielder	1963-1976
Roger Clemens	13 years	Pitcher	1984-1996
*Bob Stanley	13 years	Pitcher	1977-1989
Harry Hooper	12 years	Outfielder	1909-1920
Rick Miller	12 years	Outfielder	1971-1978;
			1981-1985
Joe Cronin	11 years	Shortstop	1935-1945
*Dom DiMaggio	11 years	Outfielder	1940-1953
Frank Malzone	11 years	3rd Baseman	1955-1965
Carlton Fisk	11 years	Catcher	1969-1980
Wade Boggs	11 years	3rd Baseman	1982-1992
*Mike Greenwell	11 years	Outfielder	1985-1996
Heinie Wagner	11 years	Infielder	1906-1918
Billy Goodman	10½ years	Infielder	1947-1957
*Mel Parnell	10 years	Pitcher	1947-1956
"Spaceman" Bill Lee	10 years	Pitcher	1969-1978
Rich Gedman	10 years	Catcher	1980-1990
Larry Garadner	10 years	3rd Baseman	1908-1917
*Rough Carrigan	10 years	Catcher	1906;
			1908-1916
*Bob Montgomery	10 years	Catcher	1970-1979
John Valentin	10 years	Infielder	1992-2001

*entire career with Red Sox

Retired Numbers

#4	Joe Cronin	SS
#1	Bobby Doerr	2B
#9	Ted Williams	OF
#8	Carl Yastrzemski	OF
#27	Carlton Fisk	C

Red Sox League Most Valuable Players

(Chalmers Award 1911-1914)

			Avg.	HR	R.B.I.
1912	OF	Tris Speaker	.383	10	90

(Award Voted By Baseball Writers Association of America, Beginning in 1931)

			Avg.	HR	R.B.I.
1938	IB	Jimmie Foxx	.349	50	175
1946	OF	Ted Williams	.342	38	123
1949	OF	Ted Williams	.343	43	159
1958	OF	Jackie Jensen	.286	35	122
1967	OF	Carl Yastrzemski	.326	44	121
1975	OF	Fred Lynn	.331	21	105
1978	OF	Jim Rice	.315	46	139
1995	IB	Mo Vaughn	.300	39	126

			Pct.	W-L	E.R.A.
1986	P	Roger Clemens	.857	24-4	2.48

Red Sox Cy Young Award Winners

			Pct.	W-L	E.R.A.

(Award Voted By Baseball Writers Assoc. of America, beginning in 1956)

1967	P	Jim Lonborg	.710	22-9	2.46
1986	P	Roger Clemens	.857	24-4	2.38
1987	P	Roger Clemens	.690	10-9	3.56
1991	P	Roger Clemens	.643	18-10	2.41
1999	P	Pedro Martinez	.852	23-4	2.07
2000	P	Pedro Martinez	.750	18-6	1.74

Red Sox Most Valuable Player – League Championship Series

(Award Beginning in the American League in 1980)

Marty Barrett	2nd Base	1986

Red Sox Most Valuable Player – World Series

(Award Begun by Sport Magazine in 1955)

None

(Babe Ruth Award Begun in 1949)

Luis Tiant	P	1975

Red Sox Rookie of the Year Awards

(Award Voted By Baseball Writers Association of America, Beginning in 1947)

			Avg.	HR	R.B.I.
1950	IB	Walt Dropo	.322	34	144
1972	C	Carlton Fisk	.293	22	83
1975	OF	Fred Lynn	.331	21	105
1997	SS	Nomar Garciaparra	.306	30	98

			Pct.	W-L	E.R.A.
1961	P	Don Schwall	.682	15-7	3.22

Red Sox All-Star Game Most Valuable Player Award

(Arch Ward Memorial Award, Beginning 1962; Known as Commissioner's Trophy 1970-1984)

1970	OF	Carl Yastrzemski
1986	P	Roger Clemens
1999	p	Pedro Martinez

Red Sox Manager of the Year Awards

(Award Voted By Baseball Writers Association of America, Beginning in 1980)

1986	John McNamara	Red Sox Pennant Winners
1999	Jimy Williams	Red Sox "Wild Card" Winners

Red Sox American League Batting Champions

1932	Dale Alexander*	.372
1938	Jimmie Foxx	.349
1941	Ted Williams	.406
1942	Ted Williams	.356
1947	Ted Williams	.343
1948	Ted Williams	.369
1950	Billy Goodman	.354
1957	Ted Williams	.388
1958	Ted Williams	.328
1960	Pete Runnels	.320
1962	Pete Runnels	.326
1963	Carl Yastrzemski	.321
1967	Carl Yastrzemski	.326
1968	Carl Yastrzemski	.301
1979	Fred Lynn	.333
1981	Carney Lansford	.336
1983	Wade Boggs	.361
1985	Wade Boggs	.368
1986	Wade Boggs	.357
1987	Wade Boggs	.363
1988	Wade Boggs	.366
1999	Nomar Garciaparra	.357
2000	Nomar Garciaparra	.372

* – 23 Games with Detroit; 101 Games with Red Sox

Red Sox Triple Crown Winners

			Avg.	HR	R.B.I.
1942	OF	Ted Williams	.356	36	137
1947	OF	Ted Williams	.343	32	114
1967	OF	Carl Yastrzemski	.326	44	121

Red Sox Gold Glove Award Winners

(Award Voted By League's Managers and Coaches, Beginning in 1957)

OF	Dwight Evans	8 Times
OF	Carl Yastrzemski	7 Times
OF	Fred Lynn	4 Times
33	Frank Malzone	3 Times
IB	George Scott	3 Times
OF	Jimmy Piersall	1 Time
OF	Jackie Jensen	1 Time
OF	Reggie Smith	1 Time
C	Carlton Fisk	1 Time
2B	Doug Griffin	1 Time
SS	Rick Burleson	1 Time
P	Mike Boddicker	1 Time
OF	Ellis Burks	1 Time
C	Tony Pena	1 Time

No-Hit Games

1904	Cy Young vs. Philadelphia Athletics *(Perfect Game)*	3-0
1904	Jesse Tannehill vs. Chicago White Sox	6-0
1905	Bill Dinneen vs. Chicago White Sox	2-0
1908	Cy Young vs. New York Highlanders	8-0
1911	Smoky Joe Wood vs. St. Louis Browns	5-0
1916	Rube Foster vs. New York Yankees	2-0
1916	Dutch Leonard vs. St. Louis Browns	4-0
1917	Ernie Shore vs. Washington Senators *(Babe Ruth walked first batter-then was ejected)*	4-0
1918	Dutch Leonard vs. Detroit Tigers	5-0
1923	Howard Ehmke vs. Philadelphia Athletics	4-0
1956	Mel Parnell vs. Chicago White Sox	4-0
1962	Earl Wilson vs. Los Angeles Angels	2-0
1962	Bill Monbouquette vs. Chicago White Sox	1-0
1965	Dave Morehead vs Cleveland Indians	2-0
1992	Matt Young vs Cleveland Indians (8 innings)	1-2
2001	Hideo Nomo vs Baltimore Orioles	3-0

Grand Slams

Ted Williams	17
Rico Petrocelli	9
Bobby Doerr	8
Jim Rice	7
Jimmie Foxx	7
Jackie Jensen	7
Carl Yastrzemski	7
Jim Tabor	6
Mo Vaughn	6
Ellis Burks	5
Tony Conigliaro	5
Dom DiMaggio	5
Dwight Evans	5
Joe Foy	5
Vern Stephens	5
Vic Wertz	5

Single-Season Grand Slams

Babe Ruth	4
Jimmie Foxx	3
Jimmie Foxx	3
Ted Williams	3
Vic Wertz	3
Dick Stuart	3
Carl Yastrzemski	3
Mo Vaughn	3
Rico Petrocelli	3

All-Star Game Selections
(All-Star Games Begun in 1933; 2 Games Played in 1959-1962)

1.	Carl Yastrzemski	19 Times	OF
2.	Ted Williams	17	OF
3.	Bobby Doerr	10	2B
4.	Joe Cronin	10	SS
5.	Frank Malzone	8	3B
	Jim Rice	8	OF
	Wade Boggs	8	3B
8.	Dom DiMaggio	7	OF
	Carlton Fisk	7	C
10.	Jimmie Foxx	6	1B
	Fred Lynn	6	OF
12.	Roger Clemens	5	P
	Lefty Grove	5	P
12.	Pete Runnels	5	1B-2B
15.	Doc Cramer	4	OF
	Rick Ferrell	4	C
	Bill Monbouquette	4	P
	Vern Stephens	4	SS
19.	Rick Burleson	3	SS
	Dwight Evans	3	OF
	Tex Hughson	3	P
	Mo Vaughn	3	1B
	Nomar Garciaparra	3	SS

58 Other Red Sox Players Selected Once Or Twice For The All-Star Game; 16 Red Sox Managers and Coaches Selected For The All-Star Game

All-Star Games At Fenway Park

1946	American League 12, National League 0
1961	American League 1, National League 1 (Tie) *(2nd Game)*
1999	American League 4, National League 1

Red Sox All-Star Game Home Runs

1.	Ted Williams	4	(2 in 1946 All-Star Game)
2.	Fred Lynn	3	
3.	Bobby Doerr	1	
	Frank Malzone	1	
	Pete Runnels	1	
	Carl Yastrzemski	1	
	George Scott	1	
	Jim Rice	1	
	Wade Boggs	1	

Red Sox All-Star Game Winning and Losing Pitchers

Winners

1986	Roger Clemens
1999	Pedro Martinez

Losers

1982	Dennis Eckersley
1974	Luis Tiant
1964	Dick Radatz
1960	Bill Monbouquette
1955	Frank Sullivan
1944	Tex Hughson
1936	Lefty Grove

Red Sox and the Hall of Fame

Red Sox Hall of Fame Members
(Five Or More Seasons Playing With The Red Sox)

Babe Ruth (Elected 1936)
22-Year Career. First Six Years a Pitcher For The Red Sox . . . Led American League Once In Shut Outs and Once In Complete Games . . . 2.28 Lifetime Earned Run Average . . . Won 3 Lost 0 In World Series . . . 0.87 World Series Earned Run Average - 3rd All-Time . . . 15 of Last 16 Years In Career, A New York Yankees Outfielder . . . 1st All-Time In Slugging Percentage at .690; 2nd All-Time In Home Runs at 714; 1st All-Time In Bases On Balls at 2056; 2nd All-Time In Runs Batted In And Runs Scored . . . Led League in Slugging Percentage 13 Times, In Home Runs 2 Times, In Runs Batted In 6 Times and In Runs Scored 8 Times, In Bases On Balls 11 Times . . . Lifetime Batting Average of .342 . . . Won American League Batting Title Once . . . Played In 10 World Series . . . In World Series, 2nd All-Time In Home Runs With 15; 2nd All-Time In Slugging Percentage at .744; 4th All-Time In Runs Batted In and 3rd All-Time In Runs Scored.

Cy Young (Elected 1937)
511 Wins-1st All-Time. More Than Thirty Wins A Season 5 Times . . . More Than Twenty Wins a Season 15 Times . . . Lifetime Earned Run Average of 2.63 . . . 750 Complete Games Pitched - 1st All-Time . . . 40 Or More Complete Games A Season - 9 Times . . . 76 Shut Outs-4th All-Time. Three No-Hitters.

Tris Speaker (Elected 1937)
.345 Lifetime Batting Average - 5th All-Time . . . Batted Over .380 5 Times . . . 1st All-time in Doubles . . . Led League 8 Times In Doubles . . . 3,514 Lifetime Hits . . . Led League At Position In Fielding Chances 7 times, In Putouts 7 Times, In Double Plays Executed 6 Times . . . Chalmers Most Valuable Player Award in 1912.

Jimmy Collins (Elected 1945)
The Red Sox First Third Baseman, Considered A Fine Defensive Player And A Good Hitter With Occasional Power . . .

Lifetime Batting Average of .294 ... Batted Over .300 5 years .
..Won National League Home Run Championship In 1898.

Lefty Grove   **(Elected 1947)**
.680 Lifetime Winning Percentage - 5th All-Time ... 300 Wins .
.. 20 or More Wins – 7 Consecutive Seasons ... Led League In
Most Wins 4 Times ... Led League In Earned Run Average 9
Times ... Led League In Strike Outs 7 Consecutive Years ...
League's Most Valuable Player - 1931.

Herb Pennock   **(Elected 1948)**
22-Year American League Career ... Best Years With New
York Yankees ... 240 Career Wins, 162 With Yankees ... Led
League 1 Year In Winning Percentage at .760, And One Year In
Shut Outs with 5 ... Won 5 World Series Games and Lost
None.

Jimmie Foxx   **(Elected 1951)**
.534 Lifetime Home Runs ... 30 Or More Home Runs 12
Straight Years ... 17 Grand Slam Home Runs ... American
League Batting Champion-2 Times ... Led League in Home
Runs 4 Times And In Runs Batted In 3 Times ... Won Triple
Crown Once. Named League's Most Valuable Player 3 Times.

Joe Cronin   **(Elected 1956)**
20-Year Playing Career ... Hit Over .300 11 Years ... Lifetime
Batting Average of .301 ... Led League In Doubles Twice And
In Triples Once ... Led League In Pinch Hits Once.

Ted Williams   **(Elected 1966)**
19-Year Career, All With Red Sox ... American League Batting
Champion 6 Times ... Batted .406 In 1941 ... Named An
All-Star 16 Times ... League's Most Valuable Player 2 Times ...
Triple Crown Winner Once ... Lifetime Batting Average of
.344 ... 521 Home Runs ... Home Runs And Runs Batted In
Leader 4 Times Each ... Led League In Bases On Balls 8 Times,
2nd All-time Behind Babe Ruth.

Red Ruffing   **(Elected 1967)**
22-Year Pitching Career ... Best Years With New York Yankees
... 273 Wins ... 4 Twenty Win Seasons ... Led League In Wins
And In Winning Percentage 1 Year, In Strike Outs 1 year and In
Shut Outs Twice ... Won 7 World Series Games and Has
Cumulative 2.63 World Series Earned Run Average ... Lifetime
Batting Average of .269 ... 36 Lifetime Home Runs.

Harry Hooper   **(Elected 1971)**
17-Year Career ... 281 Lifetime Batting Average of .281 ... Hit
Over .300 5 Years ... 20 Or More Doubles 15 Straight Years ..
. 20 Or More Stolen Bases 9 Out Of 10 Years ... 375 Lifetime
Stolen Bases ... 293 Batting Average In 4 World Series ... A
Fine Defensive Outfielder.

Rick Ferrell   **(Elected 1984)**
18-Year American League Career ... Lifetime Batting Average
of .281 ... Fine Defensive Catcher And Handler Of Pitchers.

Bobby Doerr   **(Elected 1986)**
14 Year Career - All With Red Sox ... Lifetime Batting Average
of .288 ... 223 Home Runs ... Over 100 Runs Batted In - 6
Times ... 23 Or More Doubles 12 Straight Years ... Leader In
Fielding Average At Second Base 4 Times ... Leader In Double
Plays Executed 4 Times, In Put Outs 3 Times, And In Assists 1
Time ... 409 Batting Average In 1946 World Series

Carl Yastrzemski   **(Elected 1989)**
23 Year Career - All With Red Sox ... American League
Batting Champion 3 Times ... Triple Crown Winner Once ...
League Most Valuable Player Once ... 17 All-Star Games ...
All-Star Game Most Valuable Player Once ... 3,419 Hits - 6th
All Time ... 452 Home Runs ... 352 World Series Batting
Average For Two Series ... Eight Gold Glove Awards ... Led
League In Assists 7 Times.

Carlton Fisk   **(Elected 2000)**
24-Year Career ... Lifetime Batting Average of .270 ... Rookie
Of The Year In 1972 ... Most Home Runs By Catcher, 351 ...
376 Total Career Home Runs ... Led League In Triples Once ..
. Batted .417 In 1975 American League Championship Series.

An All-Red Sox Hall of Fame Team
(Five or More Seasons Playing With The Red Sox)

Jimmie Foxx	First Base
Bobby Doerr	Second Base
Joe Cronin	Shortstop
Jimmy Collins	Third Base
Ted Williams	Outfield
Tris Speaker	Outfield
Carl Yastrzemski	Outfield
Harry Hooper	Outfield
Rick Ferrell	Catcher
Carlton Fisk	Catcher
Cy Young	Right-Handed Pitcher
Herb Pennock	Right-Handed Pitcher
Red Ruffing	Right-Handed Pitcher
Lefty Grove	Left-Handed Pitcher
Babe Ruth	Left-Handed Pitcher

Current Red Sox Hall of Fame Prospects

Jim Rice
16 -Year Career, All With Red Sox ... League's Most Valuable
Player Once ... 382 Home Runs ... Led League In Home Runs
3 Times, In Triples 1 Time and In Hits 1 Time ... Led League In
Slugging 2 Times And in Runs Batted in 2 Times ... 200 or
More Hits a Season 4 Times ... 20 or More Home Runs Per
Season 11 Of 12 Years ... More Than 100 Runs Batted In 8
Times ... Batting Average Over .300 7 Times ... Lifetime
Batting Average of .298.

Wade Boggs

American League Batting Champion 5 Times . . . Batted Over .300 10 Straight Years . . . 200 or More Hits 7 Consecutive Years . . . More Than 100 Bases On Balls 8 Of 9 Years . . . More Than 40 Doubles 7 Straight Years . . . More Than One Hundred Runs Scored 7 Straight Years . . . Led League Twice In Doubles, Runs And Bases On Balls . . . Led Once In Hits . . . Batted .322 In 3 American League Championship Series and .290 In World Series . . . Reached 3,000-hit plateau in 1999.

Roger Clemens

Cy Young Award Winner 6 Times . . . Led League In Earned Run Average 5 Times With Lifetime ERA of 2.80 . . . Led League In Shut Outs 5 Times, In Strike Outs And In Complete Games Twice . . . Led League in Wins Twice And In Winning Percentage Three Times . . . Career Winning Percentage .659 - 10th All-Time . . . .857 Winning Percentage 1 Year . . . Set Record with 20 Strike Outs Per Game Twice . . . Most Valuable Player In League Once . . . Most Valuable Player - 1986 All-Star Game . . . Still Active Entering 2002 Season.

Hall of Famers – Fewer Than Five Years with Red Sox

Name	Position	Years of Play	Primary Team(s)	Yrs W/Sox	Elected
Luis Aparicio	SS	1956-1973	Orioles-White Sox	1971-1973	1984
Lou Boudreau	SS	1938-1952	Cleveland Indians	1951-1952	1970
Jesse Burkett	OF	1890-1905	Cleveland Spiders	1905	1946
Jack Chesbro	P	1899-1909	Pirates-Highlanders	1909	1969
Waite Hoyt	P	1918-1938	New York Yankees	1919	1969
Ferguson Jenkins	P	1965-1983	Cubs-Rangers	1976-1977	1991
George Kell	3B	1943-1957	Detroit Tigers	1953-1954	1983
Heinie Manush	OF	1923-1939	Tigers-Nationals	1936	1964
Juan Marichal	P	1960-1975	San Francisco Giants	1974	1983
Tom Seaver	P	1967-1986	Mets-Reds	1986	1992
Al Simmons	OF	1924-1944	Philadelphia Athletics	1943	1953
Tony Perez	1B	1964-1986	Cincinnati Reds	1980-82	2000
Orlando Cepeda	1B	1958-1974	San Francisco Giants	1973	1999

Non-Playing Hall of Famers with Red Sox Affiliations

Managers
Bucky Harris	Manager 29 Years; Managed Red Sox 1934	Elected 1975
Joe McCarthy	Manager 24 Years; Managed Red Sox 1948-1950	Elected 1957

Executives
Tom Yawkey	Owner And President Of Red Sox, 1933-1976	Elected 1980
Eddie Collins	General Manager, Red Sox 1933-1951	Elected 1939 (as a player)

Manager And Executive
Ed Barrow   Manager 5 years; Managed Red Sox 1918-1920   Elected 1953
             Executive-General Manager, President of New York Yankees, 1921-1944

Chris Nixon, son of Russ Nixon who was a catcher for the Red Sox in the 1960s. *(Baseball Hall of Fame Library, Cooperstown, N.Y.)*

Appendix C

QUOTES WORTH REPEATING ABOUT THE

BOSTON RED SOX AND BASEBALL

About Ted Williams

"All I want out of life is that when I walk down the street folks will say 'There goes the greatest hitter who ever lived!' "

Ted Williams, as a rookie

"I don't like the way he stands at the plate. He bends his front knee inward and moves his foot just before he takes a swing. That's exactly what I do before I drive a golf ball, and knowing what happens to the golf ball I drive, I don't believe this kid will ever hit a midget's weight in a bathing suit."

Bill Cunningham, a Boston writer, on seeing Ted Williams in spring training in 1938

"If he'd just tip his cap once, he could be elected mayor of Boston in five minutes."

Eddie Collins, Hall of Fame player and once Red Sox general manager

Joe McCarthy became manager of the Red Sox in 1948. McCarthy had a reputation as a strict disciplinarian with a dress code that required players to wear ties. Ted Williams was just as notable for the open sport shirts he wore, and no ties. McCarthy backed off, saying, *"If I don't get along with a .400 hitter, it'll be my fault."* In the first formal sit-down meal in the spring, McCarthy showed up wearing a brightly colored sport shirt.

"Did they tell me how to pitch to Williams? Sure they did. It was great advice, very encouraging. They said he had no weakness, won't swing at a bad ball, has the best eyes in the business, and can kill you with one swing; he won't hit at anything bad, but don't give him anything good."

Bobby Shantz, Philadelphia Athletics pitcher, in discussing how to pitch to Ted Williams

Ted Williams walked 2,019 times in his major league career, the equivalent of four full seasons of walking every time at bat. Of this accomplishment Williams said, *"It's my proudest record."*

"He is a big clog in their (the Red Sox) machine."

Yogi Berra

"Baseball is the only field of endeavour where a man can succeed three times out of ten and be considered a good performer."

Ted Williams

"I remember in 1961 when I was a scared rookie, batting .220 after the first three months of my baseball season, doubting my ability. A man was fishing up in New Brunswick. I said, "Can we get hold of him? I need help. I don't think I can play in the big leagues.' He flew into Boston, worked with me for three days, helped me mentally and gave me confidence that I could play in the big leagues. I hit .300 for the rest of the season. I'd like to thank Ted Williams."

Carl Yastrzemski, in his acknowledgment speech when he was entered into the Hall of Fame

General manager Eddie Collins (left) signs Ted Williams to one of his many contracts with the Boston Red Sox. (Boston Public Library).

About Babe Ruth

"You know, I saw it all happen, from beginning to end. But sometimes I can't believe what I saw: this 19-year-old kid, crude, poorly educated, only lightly brushed by the social veneer we call civilization, gradually transformed into the idol of American youth and the symbol of baseball the world over—a man loved by more people and with an intensity of feeling that perhaps has never been equalled before or since."

    Harry Hooper, Hall of Fame Red Sox player who played with
    Babe Ruth on the Red Sox

"Ruth made a grave mistake when he gave up pitching. Working once a week, he might have lasted a long time and become a great star."

    Tris Speaker, commenting on Babe Ruth's future
    in 1921

"As soon as I got out there I felt a strange relationship with the pitcher's mound. It was as if I'd been born out there. Pitching felt like the most natural thing in the world. Striking out batters was easy."

    Babe Ruth, commenting on pitching at the age of 14 or 15

Babe Ruth pitched a 14-inning game for the Red Sox against the Dodgers in the 1916 World Series. *Casey Stengel* was an outfielder for the Dodgers but did not play in that game. Casey later said, *"That game was so famous they never used me."*

"The more I see of Babe, the more he seems a figure out of mythology."

    Burt Whitman, a writer, said in 1918

"Ruth was not an enemy player as much as a "blood relation" whom the gypsies had stolen away . . . He was always first-page news in Boston."

    Ed Linn, writer

"The Ruth is mighty and shall prevail."

    Heywood Broun, writer

About Jimmie Foxx

Lefty Gomez, a famous Yankee pitcher, raconteur and banquet speaker, often used Jimmie Foxx as the object of his humor. Foxx was a large, hulking man and a powerful hitter. Gomez said of him, *"He wasn't scouted—he was trapped."*

"I gave up wearing glasses because of Foxx. I had been having trouble with my eyes. One day my glasses fogged up while I was pitching. When I cleaned them I looked toward the plate and saw Foxx coming to bat very clearly. It frightened me so much I never wore glasses again."

    Lefty Gomez

Gomez was pitching to Foxx with two men on base in a game between the Yankees and the Red Sox. Gomez kept shaking off catcher **Bill Dickey**'s signs. Dickey called time, went out to the mound, and asked, *"What do you want to throw?"* El Senor replied, *"I don't want to throw anything to that brute."* *"Well,"* Dickey said, *"Let's try to buzz the fast one past him."* "The fast one" went straight out to a seat high and fair in the left field grandstand.

In another version of Bill Dickey coming to the mound to discuss with **Lefty Gomez** what he wanted to pitch to Jimmie Foxx, Gomez said, *"I don't want to throw him nothin'. Maybe he'll just get tired of waitin' and leave."*

When astronaut Neil Armstrong first set foot on the moon he and all the space scientists were puzzled by an unidentifiable white object. *Lefty Gomez* said, *"I knew immediately what it was. That was a home run hit off me in 1933 by Jimmie Foxx."*

"He had muscles in his hair."

    Lefty Gomez

Johnny Broaca, pitching for the Yankees, was beating the Red Sox 1-0 with two outs in the ninth inning, and the tying run on first base. Joe Cronin came to bat, followed by the dangerous Jimmie Foxx. Broaca walked Cronin, in spite of Yankee manager Joe McCarthy's admonition to pitch to Cronin and avoid Foxx. Foxx came to bat and hit the ball to the deepest part of center field in Yankee Stadium. DiMaggio, after a long chase after the ball made a spectacular catch for the third out. Broaca said afterward, *"I was afraid of Cronin, but I knew I could get Foxx."*

About Lefty Grove

Lefty Grove was a notorious tantrum thrower who would wreck a locker room when he lost. **Ted Williams** once said of teammate Grove, *"He was a moody guy, a tantrum thrower like me, but when he punched a locker or something he always did it with his right hand. He was a careful tantrum thrower."*

"He could throw a lamb chop past a wolf."
Westbrook Pegler, newspaper columnist

About Wade Boggs

"When I was six years old."
Wade Boggs, when asked when he knew he would play in the major leagues

"A woman will be elected president before Wade Boggs is called out on strikes. I guarantee that."
George Brett, Hall of Fame third baseman

About Others

Walter Johnson, Hall of Fame pitcher known as "The Big Train," responded to a question about him and Red Sox pitcher Smoky Joe Wood. *"Can I throw harder than Joe Wood? Listen, Mister, no man alive can throw any harder than Smoky Joe Wood."*
Said after the 1912 season when Wood's record was 34-5

"He is one of the very few who played the game hard and retired with no enemies."
Tommy Henrich, former Yankee, of Bobby Doerr

"It has to be physical. That's why I'm soakin' my arm now. If it was mental I'd be soaking my head."
Jim Lonborg, Red Sox pitcher, when asked if the difficulty in pitching after just two days' rest was physical or mental

"What do you expect from a northpaw world?"
Red Sox pitcher Spaceman Bill Lee, when asked why southpaws are always depicted as flakes

"He's even-tempered. He comes to the ballpark mad and stays that way."
Joe Garagiola, baseball player and commentator, of Red Sox shortstop Rick Burleson

"I feel like I'm turning my back on an old friend."
Carlton Fisk, in a White Sox uniform after playing ten years with the Red Sox, upon coming to Fenway Park and gazing at "The Green Monster."

"The guy's got a fault? Dandruff, maybe."
Leo Durocher, big league manager, commenting on Red Sox third baseman Frank Malzone

"I had such a good year that I didn't want to forget it."
Dick Stuart, Red Sox player, explaining to a policeman why his car still had 1963 plates in 1964

About the Red Sox

"The Red Sox are a religion. Every year we reenact the agony and the temptation in the Garden. Baseball, child's play? Hell, up here in Boston it's a passion play."
George Higgins, a writer

"I think if you're Red Sox, well, it's something you're born with, and affection you have."
Johnny Pesky, former Red Sox player

"All the King's horses and all the King's men couldn't put Boston baseball together again."
Tom Meany, a sportswriter, commenting on the sale of Babe Ruth to the Yankees and the break-up of "the greatest ever" 1915 outfield

"Baseball isn't a life-and-death matter, but the Red Sox are."
Unknown

"The Red Sox truly are the boys of summer; it's always been the fall that's given them trouble."
Dan Shaughnessy, writer

"I finally came to understand the unique nature of the Red Sox pain—not like Cubs pain (never to get there at all), or Phillies pain (lousy teams, though they did win the Series in 1980) but the deepest possible anguish of running a long and hard course, again and again, to the very end, and then self-destructing one inch from the finish line."
Stephen Jay Gould, university professor and a Yankee fan

About Baseball

"In the big inning, God created heaven and earth."
Anonymous

There is an apocryphal story about **Abraham Lincoln** on his deathbed. He is said to have summoned Major General Abner Doubleday, who was in attendance. Mr. Lincoln, whispering to Doubleday, said, *"Abner, don't let baseball die,"* and then he expired.

"Baseball has the largest library of law and love, and custom and ritual, and therefore, in a nation that fundamentally believes it is a nation under law, baseball is America's most privileged version of the level field."
Bart Giamatti, former Commissioner of Baseball

"All I ever wanted to be was president of the American League." (This was before his career as a baseball executive, which included being president of the National League.).

> Bart Giamatti on being named president of
> Yale University

"It's just got everything."

> George Bush, former president, of his fascination with baseball

"I never look back. I love baseball and you have to be patient and take the good with the bad. After all, it's only a game."

> Tom Yawkey

"Baseball. It's just a game – as simple as a ball and a bat, yet, as complex as the American spirit it symbolizes. It's a sport, business, and sometimes even religion."

> Ernie Harwell, baseball broadcaster

"The other sports are just sports. Baseball is a love."

> Bryant Gumbel, newscaster

"In football the object is to march into enemy territory and cross his goal. In baseball the object is to go home."

> George Carlin, comedian

"Every boy likes baseball and if he doesn't, he's not a boy."

> Zane Grey, author

"Surely, it is no mere happenstance that the last two words of the Star Spangled Banner are, 'Play Ball.'"

> Frank DeFord, writer

"All baseball fans can be divided into two groups; those who come to batting practice, and others. Only those in the first category have much chance of amounting to something."

> Thomas Boswell, writer

"Any person claiming to be a baseball fan who does not also claim to have invented the quickest, simplest and most complete method of keeping score probably is a fraud."

> Thomas Boswell, writer

"Nothing flatters me more than to have it assumed that I could write prose – unless it be to have it assumed that I once pitched baseball with distinction."

> Robert Frost, distinguished poet

"Well, this year I'm told the team did well because one

pitcher had a fine curve ball. I understand that a curve ball is thrown with deliberate attempt to deceive. Surely, that is not an ability we should want to foster at Harvard."

> President Charles Eliot of Harvard, explaining why he wished to
> drop baseball as a college sport

"Any baseball team could use a man who plays every position superbly, never strikes out and never makes an error, but there is no way to make him lay down his hot dog and come out of the grandstand."

> Unknown

"I do not know if it will take a constitutional amendment to keep baseball traditions alive, but if we forsake the great Americana of broken bat singles and pine tar, we will certainly have lost our way as a nation."

> Representative Richard Durban, on the cutting of trees in order
> to have wooden rather than aluminum bats in baseball

"Baseball fans are junkies, and their heroin is the statistic."

> Robert Winter, writer

"I watch a lot of baseball on the radio."

> Gerald Ford, former president

"To a pitcher, a base hit is the perfect example of negative feedback."

> Steve Hurley, pitcher

"It ain't nothin' till I call it."

> Umpire Bill Klem

"I take a national view of the American League and an American view of the National League."

> Hubert Humphrey, former vice president, when asked to pick a
> World Series choice

"When I was a small boy in Kansas, a friend of mine and I went fishing and as we sat there in the warmth of a summer afternoon on a river bank we talked about what we wanted to do when we grew up. I told him that I wanted to be a real major league player, a genuine professional like Honus Wagner. My friend said that he'd like to be president of the United States. Neither one of us got our wish."

> Dwight Eisenhower, when he was President of the United States

"The Baseball Hall of Fame in Cooperstown, N. Y., sends a questionnaire to every ex-major leaguer it can find. One of the questions is "If you had to do it over, would you play professional baseball?" In all the years the questionnaire has been in existence no one ever said 'No.'"

> W.P. Kinsella, author of Field of Dreams

"With those who don't give a damn about baseball, I can only sympathize. I do not resent them. I am even willing to consider that many of them are physically clean, good to their mothers and in favor of world peace. But while the game is on, I can't think of anything to say to them."

Art Hill, a writer

A British visitor, unable to understand the game, left as the scoreboard read:

100 000 000
100 000 000

When asked by a kid outside the gate, *"What's the score?,"* he shrugged and said, *"Oh, it's up in the millions."*

"Scratch an intellectual and you'll find a baseball fan."

Anonymous

"I enjoy the game because it's a beautifully designed game. It's a beautiful game to watch, but, principally because it makes me feel American. It makes me feel connected with this culture. And I think there are only three things that America will be known for 2,000 years from now when they study this civilization: the Constitution, jazz music, and baseball. They're the three most beautifully designed things this culture's ever produced.

Gerald Early, author